Printing for Profit
The Commercial Publishers of
Jianyang, Fujian (11th–17th Centuries)

Harvard-Yenching Institute Monograph Series 56

Printing for Profit

The Commercial Publishers of
Jianyang, Fujian (11th–17th Centuries)

Lucille Chia

Published by the Harvard University Asia Center
for the Harvard-Yenching Institute
Distributed by Harvard University Press
Cambridge (Massachusetts) and London, 2002

Printed in the United States of America

The Harvard-Yenching Institute, founded in 1928 and headquartered at Harvard University, is a foundation dedicated to the advancement of higher education in the humanities and social sciences in East and Southeast Asia. The Institute supports advanced research at Harvard by faculty members of certain Asian universities and doctoral studies at Harvard and other universities by junior faculty at the same universities. It also supports East Asian studies at Harvard through contributions to the Harvard-Yenching Library and publication of the *Harvard Journal of Asiatic Studies* and books on premodern East Asian history and literature.

Library of Congress Cataloging-in-Publication Data

Chia, Lucille.
    Printing for profit : the commercial publishers of Jianyang, Fujian (11th-17th centuries) / Lucille Chia.
        p. cm. -- (Harvard-Yenching Institute monograph series ; 56)
    Includes bibliographic references and index.
    ISBN 0-674-00955-X (alk. paper)
    1. Printing industry--China--Jianyang Xian (Fujian Sheng)--History. 2. Book industries and trade--China--Jianyang Xian (Fujian Sheng)--History. 3. China--History--960-1644.
    I. Title: Commercial publishers of Jianyang, Fujian, 11th-17th centuries. II. Title. III. Series.

Z244.6.C6 C438 2002
338.4'76862'0951245--dc21   2002027348

Index by the author

☉ Printed on acid-free paper

Last number below indicates year of this printing

12 10 09 08 07 06 05 04 03 02

To my Mother and Father
and to the memory of
Piet van der Loon

Acknowledgments

Like everyone entranced by the history of Chinese books, I have found studying it an immensely satisfying but challenging endeavor because these books can be frustratingly reticent about themselves. In the past fifteen years, however, the study of Chinese books and printing has increasingly engaged the efforts of scholars working on Chinese history, art history, literature, religion, and science. Thanks to their persistence and imaginative approaches in coaxing data out of Chinese manuscripts and imprints, we now understand more about Chinese book culture and have devised new ways to learn even more.

In the course of my own work on the commercial publishers of Jianyang, I had the chance to learn from and be inspired by many of these scholars. A number of them also provided useful suggestions on this manuscript or the earlier dissertation. The book's imperfections arise from my obduracy in not heeding sufficiently the advice offered and from my own limited knowledge about so many of the topics I discuss.

First, I wish to thank my Ph.D. adviser, Robert Hymes, who helped teach me the craft of a social historian and who provided comments on the dissertation that still proved useful as I recast it into a book.

Cynthia Brokaw, who thoroughly critiqued both my dissertation and my book manuscript, has surely earned an astronomical number of points in her ledger of merits. Her continuing support and encouragement, as well as her own work on and deep interest in Chinese books and publishing, have helped to sustain my conviction about the value and fascination of learning about the history of the Chinese book.

I thank Piet van der Loon for the trenchant comments and tips he gave me out of his immense knowledge of Chinese literature in general and of Jianyang publishing in particular. I dedicate this book to his memory and hope that it does not fall too short of his expectations.

A number of scholars gave detailed and honest comments about my work. To Kathryn Lowry and Karin Myhre, who generously took time out from writing their own dissertations to offer suggestions about mine and to send a variety of useful materials, I happily acknowledge my debt. In reading my dissertation, Joseph McDermott came up with many stimulating remarks and posed some hard questions that cannot be easily answered, but the challenge of addressing those issues have helped me rethink important aspects of the history of the Chinese book, and of Chinese history in general. Thanks to Joe, I expect to continue thinking about them for a long time to come. Mark Halperin offered a very detailed reading of several chapters of the manuscript. In addition to thoughtful challenges to some of my arguments, he also took the time and effort to catch a few howlers and to insist that I present my arguments more stylishly. Beverly Bossler read the chapters on the Song and Yuan with great care and reminded me to not to lose sight of the broader historical issues to which books and printing were related. My colleague in the Department of History at UC Riverside, Piotr Gorecki, a historian of medieval Europe, generously and valiantly read through much of the manuscript, and provided me with many penetrating comments. I learned to pay close attention to all his remarks, including those solitary and eloquent exclamation points.

I also want to thank the scholars who have contributed greatly to my continuing education in Chinese studies. To Sören Edgren with his vast knowledge of Chinese rare books I am deeply grateful for taking the time from his very busy schedule to read the entire dissertation and offer many valuable insights on the traditional Chinese imprint. My many citations of Anne McLaren's works merely hint at how much I have learned from her about Ming literature. Each time I visit the Harvard-Yenching Rare Book Collection, I enjoy the added benefit of learning more from its curator, Shen Jin 沈津, one of the leading experts on Chinese rare books. I am grateful to Martin Heijdra not only because of his help as the guardian of the Gest Library Rare Book Collection at Princeton, but because of his amazing knowledge of Chinese history, which he generously shares with anyone with the good sense to listen. If my discussion on bamboo paper-making in Fujian in this work sounds well-informed and interesting, it is due in large part to what

I have learned from Christian Daniels. I also thank Pan Jixing 潘吉星 for sharing his expertise on traditional Chinese paper-making and wish that I had asked him many more questions; I will do so the next time I see him.

During my research work in China, a number of scholars were particularly generous with their help. Fang Yanshou 方彥壽, of the Zhu Xi Research Institute in Jianyang, shared with me his knowledge and experience in finding and examining the genealogies of the publisher families described in this work. I also wish to thank Di Chongde 狄寵德, my adviser at the History Institute of the Fujian Academy of Social Science, from whom I learned much of both Chinese rare books and the history of the Minbei area. To Professor Di I also owe my rudimentary skills in repairing and binding Chinese books and in seal-carving. Hou Zhenping 侯眞平, of the History Department of Xiamen University, unhesitatingly supplied me with enough information on Fujian blockcarvers of the Ming for another study.

Whatever clarity and smoothness of writing this book enjoys result in large part from the efforts of my editor, John Ziemer. Like his other authors, I count it my good fortune that my manuscript came under his attentive and understanding care. Because of John, this book will not be known as the last *Mashaben*.

I also wish to thank the Committee for Scholarly Communication with China, which supported my dissertation research in China (1992–93), and the Fulbright-Hays DDRA Program, which supported my work in Taiwan and Japan (1993–94). In Tokyo, I was made welcome by the Tōyō bunko, of whom I was a Foreign Research Fellow. I thank Shiba Yoshinobu 斯波義信 for making this possible. In continuing my research after completing the dissertation in 1997, I received a Harvard-Yenching Library Travel Grant and a Short-term Visiting Fellowship for the Princeton University Library, both of which I gratefully acknowledge.

Finally, I thank the various libraries that gave permission for reproductions of pages from Chinese rare books in their holdings: the Naikaku bunko, the National Central Library in Taipei, the Seikadō bunko, the National Diet Library of Japan, the Hōsa bunko, the Tenri Central Library, the British Library, and the Württembergische Landesbibliothek in Stuttgart.

L.C.

Contents

Tables, Maps, and Figures

Tables

Maps

Figures

Abbreviations

BMTZ	*Ba Min tongzhi* 八閩通志
CSJC	*Congshu jicheng* 叢書集成
CZFJTZ	*Chongzuan Fujian Tongzhi* 重纂福建通志
DMB	*Dictionary of Ming Biography*
FJTJ	*Fujian Tongji* 福建通紀
JNFZ	*Jianning fuzhi* 建寧府志
JYXZ	*Jianyang xianzhi* 建陽縣志
SHY	*Song Huiyao* 宋會要
SKQS	*Siku quanshu* 四庫全書
SRZJ	*Song ren zhuanji ziliao suoyin* 宋人傳記資料索引
SS	*Song shi* 宋史
TJSY	*Guji banben tiji suoyin* 古籍版本題記索引
ZBK	*Zhongguo banke tulu* 中國版刻圖錄

Note on page citations for primary Chinese sources: *juan* and page numbers for the original imprint, as well as any page number for a modern reprint are given, wherever applicable. Full publication information is given in the Works Cited.

On Chinese terms and titles: translations are given at the first instance they appear in the text and again in the Glossary-Index or in the Works Cited.

Dynasties and Reign Periods

Northern Song

Emperor (temple name)	Reign dates
Taizu 太祖	960–75
Taizong 太宗	976–97
Zhenzong 眞宗	998–1022
Renzong 仁宗	1023–63
Yingzong 英宗	1064–67
Shenzong 神宗	1068–85
Zhezong 哲宗	1086–1100
Huizong 徽宗	1101–1025
Qinzong 欽宗	1126

Southern Song

Emperor (temple name)	Accession	Reign period	Dates
Gaozong 高宗	1127	Jianyan 建炎	1127–30
		Shaoxing 紹興	1131–62
Xiaozong 孝宗	1163	Longxing 隆興	1163–64
		Qiandao 乾道	1165–73
		Chunxi 淳熙	1174–89
Guangzong 光宗	1190	Shaoxi 紹熙	1190–94

Southern Song, *cont.*

Emperor (temple name)	Accession	Reign period	Dates
Ningzong 寧宗	1195	Qingyuan 慶元	1195–1200
		Jiatai 嘉泰	1201–4
		Kaoxi 開禧	1205–7
		Jiading 嘉定	1208–24
Lizong 理宗	1225	Baoqing 寶慶	1225–27
		Shaoding 紹定	1228–33
		Duanping 端平	1234–36
		Jiaxi 嘉熙	1237–40
		Chunyou 淳祐	1241–52
		Baoyou 寶祐	1253–58
		Kaiqing 開慶	1259
		Jingding 景定	1260–64
Duzong 度宗	1265	Xianchun 咸淳	1265–74
Gongdi 恭帝	1275	Deyou 德祐	1275
Duanzong 端宗	1276	Jingyan 景炎	1276–77
Dibing 帝昺	1278	Xiangxing 祥興	1278

Yuan

Emperor (temple name)	Accession	Reign period	Dates
Taizu 太祖	1206		
Taizong 太宗	1229		
Dingzong 定宗	1246		
Xianzong 憲宗	1251		
Shizu 世祖	1260	Zhongtong 中統	1260–63
		Zhiyuan 至元	1264–94
Chengzong 成宗	1295	Yuanzhen 元貞	1295–96
		Dade 大德	1297–1307
Wuzong 武宗	1308	Zhida 至大	1308–11
Renzong 仁宗	1312	Huangqing 皇慶	1312–13
		Yanyou 延祐	1314–20
Yingzong 英宗	1321	Zhizhi 至治	1321–23
Taiding di 太定帝	1324	Taiding 太定	1324–27
		Zhihe 致和	1328

Yuan, *cont.*

Emperor (temple name)	Accession	Reign period	Dates
Mingzong 明宗	1329	Tianli 天曆	1329
Wendi 文帝	1330	Tianli 天曆	1330
		Zhishun 至順	1330–32
Shundi 順帝	1333	Yuantong 元統	1333–34
		Zhiyuan 至元	1335–40
		Zhizheng 至正	1341–67

Ming

Emperor (temple name)	Accession	Reign period	Dates
Taizu 太祖	1368	Hongwu 洪武	1368–98
Huidi 惠帝	1399	Jianwen 建文	1399–1402
Chengzu 成祖	1403	Yongle 永樂	1403–24
Renzong 仁宗	1425	Hongxi 洪熙	1425
Xuanzong 宣宗	1426	Xuande 宣德	1426–35
Yingzong 英宗	1436	Zhengtong 正統	1436–49
Daizong Jingdi 代宗景帝	1450	Jingtai 景泰	1450–56
Yingzong 英宗	1457	Tianshun 天順	1457–64
Xianzong 憲宗	1465	Chenghua 成化	1465–87
Xiaozong 孝宗	1488	Hongzhi 弘治	1488–1505
Wuzong 武宗	1506	Zhengde 正德	1506–21
Shizong 世宗	1522	Jiajing 嘉靖	1522–66
Muzong 穆宗	1567	Longqing 隆慶	1567–72
Shenzong 神宗	1573	Wanli 萬曆	1573–1619
Guangzong 光宗	1620	Taichang 泰昌	1620
Xizong 熹宗	1621	Tianqi 天啓	1621–27
Zhuanglie di 莊烈帝	1628	Chongzhen 崇禎	1628–43

Printing for Profit
The Commercial Publishers of
Jianyang, Fujian (11th–17th Centuries)

Part I

1

Introduction

Purpose and Scope of Study

The Chinese have printed their books for over eleven centuries, but little is known about the people involved in the book trade. Most of our knowledge comes from detailed examination of extant imprints and from annotated bibliographies compiled by generations of scholars. This information, however, relates mainly to the bibliographical aspects of the book[1] and concerns publications by various government offices, high-quality private editions, and religious works such as the Buddhist Tripitaka and the Daoist Canon, which do not adequately reflect the broad and varied tastes and needs of the many different kinds of readers in Chinese society. To understand the reading habits, literary tastes, and literacy of different social groups, we must consider the activities and products of profit-minded commercial publishers who had to respond to and even anticipate quickly the many demands of their customers.

In this study, I focus on three families of publishers (Liu 劉, Yu 余, and Xiong 熊) of Jianyang 建陽 in northern Fujian (Minbei 閩北—see Map 1), who wrote, edited, printed, and sold books for over six hundred years, from the late Northern Song through the beginning of the Qing dynasties (mid-eleventh through late seventeenth centuries). The commercial printers of Jianyang[2] occupy a conspicuous if not highly respectable position in the history of Chinese books. The area, already noted for its flourishing paper industry, rapidly became one of the most important centers of the book trade in the country as printing burgeoned during the Song. From the start, Jianyang

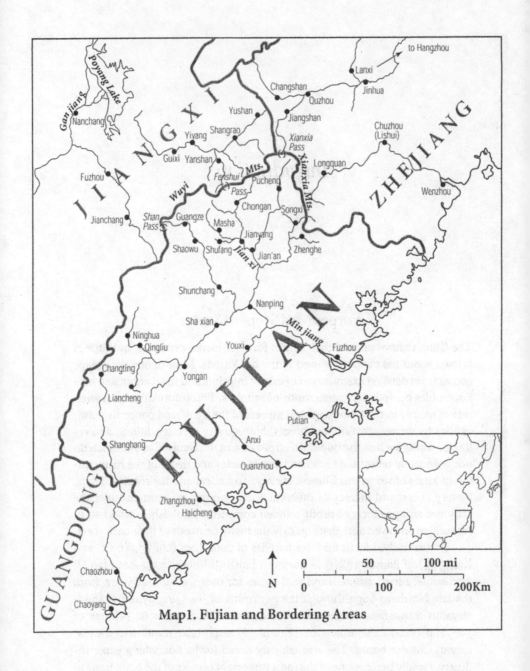

Map1. Fujian and Bordering Areas

publishers had the reputation (not fully deserved) of producing shoddy editions on cheap paper with blurred impressions, which nevertheless sold throughout China, as well as Japan and Korea. These works ranged from the Classics to dictionaries, histories, geographies, medical texts, encyclopedias, collections of anecdotes, school primers, poetry anthologies, plays and ballads, and historical novels. Because of the broad cultural, historical, and geographical scope of the Jianyang book trade, findings from this study should help us understand the history of the book in traditional China in general.

There are other good reasons for choosing to study the Jianyang printing industry. First, because of the great productivity of the Jianyang printers, their books represent a significant portion of the Chinese rare books extant in public and private collections and those described in the annotated catalogues of past collections.[3] Second, Fujian is benefiting from the current upsurge of interest in local histories, genealogies, and related materials. Much of what has been unearthed still awaits detailed examination by scholars, and indications are that other uncatalogued materials in libraries and archives do exist and may have significant historical value. Although Minbei has not captured the attention of scholars to the extent that coastal Fujian has, it has been the subject of several modern studies, including one on Minbei dialects, another comparing the agricultural economies of the Minbei and southern coastal regions of Fujian during the Ming, and a third on the tea trade in northern Fujian in the Qing and Republican periods.[4] In addition, because the Jianyang area was one of the strongholds of Neo-Confucianism during the Southern Song, many studies dealing with Neo-Confucian scholars, including Zhu Xi 朱熹 (1130–1200), who lived and taught there for over forty years, have touched on the history of the region. Most important for this study, the genealogies of several descent groups of Jianyang printers have recently been discovered and described. By correlating the information in all these sources, we can begin to understand how a remote mountainous area traditionally regarded as hard to govern and frequently ignored by the central government developed into one of the most important and long-lived printing centers of imperial China. Having done so, we may then be able to understand better why other rural areas (e.g., Sibao Changting 四堡長汀 in western Fujian, and Huizhou 徽州 in Anhui) also became printing centers in late imperial China.[5]

This study consists of seven chapters in three parts. Part I discusses why and how we can study the social history of the book in China. The present chapter explains the purpose and scope of the work, briefly considers some of the issues to be examined, describes the chief kinds of primary sources used, and gives a brief geographical description of Minbei. Chapter 2 deals with the visual appearance of Jianyang commercial imprints. In order to understand

how Chinese read and looked at books in the past and how commercial publishers developed their technical and business practices, we must first examine these works and consider how the paper, ink, calligraphy, page layout,
and illustrations affected readers' perception and reception of the printed
book. In the past, such knowledge has largely been limited to experts in the
field of Chinese bibliographic studies (*banben xue* 版本學), but as Chapter 2
shows, it is essential for understanding the cultural uses of print. Part II examines publishing in Jianyang during the Song and Yuan. Chapter 3 traces
the rapid rise and development of the Jianyang printing industry during these
dynasties. It begins with a brief discussion of the historical background of the
region in this period and then focuses on the publishers of Minbei. Chapter 4
discusses the imprints themselves, first examining their physical appearance,
then looking at the low-quality *Mashaben* 麻沙本 for which Jianyang was
notorious, and finally offering a general survey of printed works from the
area. The history of Jianyang books and printing during the Ming is examined in Part III. Chapter 5 looks at conditions in Minbei in relation to the
Jianyang book trade, which revived in the mid-Ming in the early sixteenth
century, after a long lull of over a hundred years, and the publisher families
most active during the Ming. Chapter 6 considers the wealth of Jianyang imprints from the Ming, as compared to earlier periods, which allows us to
speculate on more certain grounds about issues such as the authorial and
editorial contributions of the publishers, the different kinds of audiences for
commercial imprints, and the links among the printers in the major book
trade centers of central and south China. The final chapter offers general conclusions and suggestions for future research. Because this study concentrates
on the commercial printing industry of Jianyang, works published in the region by private individuals, religious organizations, or government offices
(county, prefectural, or regional) are mentioned but not analyzed in detail,
since these imprints do not necessarily reflect the trends in scholarly and
popular reading of the time, as do the output of the commercial publishers.[6]

In fact, however, the distinctions, traditionally made by scholars of Chinese rare books, among official (*guanke* 官刻), private (*sike* 私刻), and
commercial (*fangke* 坊刻) publishing, turn out to be deceptively clear-cut
and often of little use. For example, in imperial China, printing books was a
means of earning money for central, regional, and local government offices
and schools, religious organizations, and private individuals, as well as establishments whose main business was printing. By "commercial publishers," I
refer to the last category—nonofficial publishers not known to be printing
works under official auspices or those of a religious organization, such as a
temple or monastery, and whose imprints often have some indication that

they were meant to be sold on the open market (e.g., a printer's colophon advertising the merits of the book). These descriptive guidelines are generally adequate for distinguishing commercial publishers from government and religious organizations. It is more difficult to differentiate between a private individual and a commercial printshop. One possible way is to consider the motive(s) for printing a book, as expressed in a preface or postface, if available. Often the reason given is quite specific—an act of filial piety in publishing the works of one's ancestor to preserve and broadcast them, or to do a public service by making available to other scholars a rare edition in one's family library (though this second reason is sometimes used by commercial publishers as well). Although such intentions do not preclude the person from profiting by the sale of the imprint, he is not in the business of routinely printing a variety of works for sale. Unfortunately, because so many Chinese books that were printed have been lost, we cannot determine with any certainty whether a publisher was "commercial" by the number of titles associated with a person or the name of the printshop (*tangming* 堂名).[7] For example, a survey of Jianyang imprints of the Ming reveals that often there is only one known work associated with a particular publisher, even though such imprints are clearly commercial editions, to judge by their physical appearance, contents, printer's notes, and other marks. A more difficult problem arises in deciding whether the family schools (*jiashu* 家塾) that figured so importantly among Jianyang printers in the Song should be considered commercial printers. I have included them in my discussion in Chapters 3 and 4 because they printed much the same kinds of works as other printers that can clearly be classified as commercial.[8] In short, there is no absolutely unambiguous method of differentiating between a commercial and a private publisher. I have used the criteria mentioned above to make a reasonable decision for some uncertain cases among the Jianyang printers studied here.

Jianyang and the History of Chinese Publishing

In any given period, printing's potential as "an agent of change," in Elizabeth Eisenstein's words, depends on the development of written culture in that society, the variety and extent of literacies, the interactions between recorded and oral cultures, the specific printing technology, and the identity of those participating in and controlling the production and dissemination of printed materials. Thus, the impact of printing has been as momentous in China as in Europe, but its story is quite different.[9]

To begin with, printing using woodblocks (xylography) rather than movable type was the dominant method in China from the early eighth century at the latest and continued to be the preferred method until movable type and lithography became popular in the late nineteenth century. Xylography owed its long ascendance in China not only to technical reasons, such as its greater suitability for Chinese characters, but also to the continued importance of commercial printing, in which economy and efficiency were vital. Indeed, religious and commercial uses of printing began long before the Chinese state started exploiting the potential of print in the Song. Block printing was first utilized for replicating Buddhist texts and images.[10] In addition, in some areas, such as Sichuan and the lower Yangzi River valley, where the natural resources for block-printing materials (paper, ink, brushes, and woodblocks) were easily available, printing was already fairly advanced in this earliest period, as revealed by the private calendars, dictionaries, simple school primers, and works on astrology, divination, and geomancy produced.[11] The rise of Jianyang's book industry in the eleventh century and its subsequent rapid growth can be understood in terms of these factors. Not only did the mountainous Minbei area offer an abundance of raw materials for woodblock printing, but for centuries the publishers there could produce their books more cheaply than any of the major urban printing centers in the country, partly because of the cheaper labor costs as well.

A second difference between the development of printing in China and in the West is the sequence in which different groups in society began using printing routinely, often for different purposes. For example, the profound effect of printing on the social formation of the scholar-official elite and on various intellectual and philosophical movements began only in the Northern Song, over two centuries after the invention of printing, and was rather longer in coming than comparable changes in Western Europe. But when this phenomenon occurred, changes in the ways of learning, remembering, reading and writing and in the ways that texts could be collated and conveyed in a stabilized and easily replicable form began to affect all areas of learning, as they did in Western Europe during the Renaissance. In contrast, for less educated groups, such as peddlers, shopkeepers, certain artisans, some peasants, and most women, the impact of the printed word is a more complicated story. Although the printed materials of the Tang and Five Dynasties noted above argue an earlier start than for scholarly works, other kinds of materials, such as illustrated fiction and household encyclopedias apparently appeared much later, probably no earlier than the Southern Song. Again, the long history of commercial printing in Jianyang affords us an opportunity to survey these different sequences of the shift from script to print.

The early part of this history, the rise of Jianyang publishing in the Song, illustrates in detail the complex interactions between the state and commercial publishing. The active role played by the Chinese state in printing ensured far greater official influence over the printed word than censorship measures alone by any government. This is especially clear in the Northern Song, when the emphasis on book learning was such a fundamental part of the emperors' and the officials' approach to governing. The monumental government projects to compile and publish the Classics, Histories, lexicographical works, medical works, and certain encyclopedic works resulted in their somewhat greater availability to scholars. Commercial and private publishers also benefited from these official editions, which provided them with exemplars of new or previously rare works. Indeed, the Jianyang book printing industry probably would not have developed to any significant extent without the Song state's publishing efforts.

The dissemination of these imprints in turn helped spur the literati's enthusiasm for re-examining and re-collating the received texts.[12] Such activities were further encouraged by the rapid growth of commercial printing, which allowed scholars increasing opportunities to see one another's efforts in print—and to continue correcting them. We see in this an example of the continuing conflict between certain official and private uses of print in imperial China. Specifically, the government's efforts to preserve standardized texts without any deliberate effort to disseminate them widely often clashed with the efforts of scholars and commercial printers to transform the texts, for a variety of motives, for better or for worse, which were then meant to be published widely. Song official editions, especially of central government organizations like the Directorate of Education, are generally highly esteemed, and it is an ironic tribute to them that the many commercial editions descended from them, directly or indirectly, succeeded in subverting official efforts to preserve a standardized text and ultimately effected many more of the text-shifting changes facilitated by printing. Among the worst offenders, as the Song government discovered, were the Jianyang publishers, particularly with their notorious *Mashaben*, which offered cheaper, bowdlerized versions of well-collated full-length editions.

The low esteem generally accorded commercial publishers by the educated elite is another important difference between China and Western Europe. During the European Renaissance, for example, a number of the humanist printers, such as the Amerbachs, Aldus Manutius, and Joost Baade,[13] were friends of the most celebrated thinkers of the day as well as recognized scholars in their own right. In contrast, commercial printing in China was not considered an honorable activity mainly because the printers were in it for profit. It was also seen as demeaning work, whose technical aspects were best left to artisans and unskilled workers. A notable exception was Zhu Xi, who closely supervised the printing of some of the Classics and his own works. It is rather telling that he felt defensive about these activities when a friend remarked that such things were unworthy of a scholar's notice.[14] And even centuries later, in the late Ming and early Qing, we can only speculate about the possible involvement in commercial publishing of literati such as Feng Menglong 馮夢龍 (1574–1646), Chen Jiru 陳繼儒 (1558–1639), and Li Yu 李漁 (1611–ca. 1680), men who were hardly reticent about their literary activities.

This contempt for commercial printing in traditional China has meant a dearth of sources on the subject compared to those for Europe. We know little about the publishers themselves. We do not have, for example, the equivalents of the account books and business records that permit the re-creation, almost on a daily basis, of the activities of Christopher Plantin's Antwerp printing establishment, or the wealth of notarial documents relating to the Crombergers' printing activities in Seville, or the abundance of correspondence to and from Aldus Manutius in Venice, or the collected letters of the Amerbach family.[15] For Liu Hongyi 劉洪毅, a contemporary of Manutius and one of the foremost Jianyang printers of the late fifteenth and early sixteenth centuries, we have, other than some 45 known imprints, just a few slivers of information in his family's genealogy: an imagined portrait by a much later artist accompanied by a brief eulogy (*xiangzan* 像贊) and his name incorrectly recorded in the genealogical table. Yu Xiangdou 余象斗, a contemporary of Plantin and the most famous (or infamous) Jianyang printer in the late sixteenth–early seventeenth centuries, was hardly modest about praising his own publications in his printer's notes and prefaces. He listed his publications in at least two of his imprints and even inserted his portrait in a few of his publications.[16] Otherwise, however, we have only an extremely terse entry for him in the genealogy, which gives nothing more than the names of his father and his son. Apparently, even the publishers themselves, as well as their families and associates, subscribed to the general disregard for their work by remaining resoundingly silent about it. Information about a printer in his genealogy, a eulogy, or a local history almost never mentions his publishing activities.[17]

This silence extends to the business of printing, publishing, and book selling. We have almost no data on print runs and the prices of books. For the entire history of Chinese block-printed books, such information can be summarized in a few pages, and little of it pertains to the commercial imprints from Jianyang.[18] Even in advertisements in their own imprints, the commercial publishers said so little about themselves that we know next to nothing of their motives, the reasons behind their choices of what to publish, or their business practices. Rarely do we have specific clues about their relationships with their authors, editors, booksellers, and readers. Nevertheless, these obscure figures played such an important role in the writing, compiling, printing, and disseminating of information for both elite scholarly and non-scholarly "popular" cultures—often assuming all these functions in several segments along Darnton's "communications circuit".[19]—that studying them is essential to understanding the history of the Chinese book. In the case of the Jianyang publishers, we luckily have over two thousand extant imprints from which we can glean information.

The story of how the visual appearance and format of the printed book diverged from those of the manuscript is also quite different in China and Europe. Although a number of early European books slavishly imitated the written text, the impulse to exploit the capabilities of movable type soon resulted in imprints that looked very different from manuscripts. In contrast, most woodblock carving is facsimile carving—the surface of the wood is cut away by faithfully following the handwritten or hand-drawn original inked onto the block. Thus the connection between the original hand copy and the final printed copy is inevitable and explicit. This accounts for the common aesthetic criteria for judging both manuscripts and imprints in China; beautiful calligraphy rendered on superior paper is highly valued in both. One reason why many commercial imprints were held in such contempt was that the text was badly written and badly printed on poor paper. Physical shoddiness and bad editing were common complaints about Jianyang books.

Nevertheless, some of the changes in the appearance of the book introduced or popularized by commercial publishers ultimately gained wide if reluctant acceptance. For instance, as we will see, the use of the character styles known as *jiangti* 匠體 became common in the late Ming, especially among commercial imprints such as those from Jianyang, although it was generally regarded as ugly. This craftsman style, however, not only facilitated the carving of the characters but also improved their legibility, and we can interpret its growing use as an example of technological innovation in xylography driven by a rapidly growing book market.

The enduring interaction of manuscript and print in China has also meant that written and printed texts were easily and routinely transformed into each other, a process that persisted even after the use of printing became widespread. Thus a reader might copy the contents of a hard-to-acquire book by hand or hire one of the numerous copyists available—quite possibly the same ones employed by local printing establishments. Sometimes a manuscript or printed copy's worth would be significantly enhanced by marginalia added by a renowned scholar, and a new printed edition incorporating the handwritten notes and possibly elevating them to minor canonical status would quickly appear on the book market. Fully aware of this phenomenon, many Jianyang printers would tout their publications as newly compiled editions of works that incorporated the heretofore private notes of well-known scholars, a claim that often turned out to be specious. In any case, these newest editions might well in turn become another segment in the cycle as they were copied by readers.

Another significant difference between Chinese woodblock and European movable type imprints is the method of illustration. By the late sixteenth century in Europe, woodblock illustrations had been replaced for the most part by copper engravings and etchings, which were capable of much finer detail and expression of light and shade.[20] In contrast, woodblock image and text were inseparable on the printed leaf of a Chinese book for the simple reason that they were often carved on one block.[21] Consequently, illustrations in Chinese books were subject to the technical limitations of wood carving. This does not mean that woodblock pictures of high artistic merit were not produced, but fairly simple line drawings could easily be copied from an older work and cut by a carver of average skill. In other words, illustrations in a mediocre commercial imprint could be produced easily, efficiently, and cheaply with little originality and little skill and perpetuated for a very long time. Images that appeared in a calendar from the ninth century (and which probably originated even earlier) can be seen in near identical form over seven hundred years later, a continuity unmatched in European books. Moreover, these drawings, diagrams, and maps appeared in all kinds of books, including the Classics, Histories, medical works, encyclopedias, and fictional works, which meant that readers from a wide cross-section of Chinese society were exposed to them for many generations. These points will be graphically demonstrated as we look at Jianyang imprints and their near-duplicate pictures (and text).

The complex relationship between handwritten and printed materials has also led to questions of when print culture truly became "dominant" in China. Although both official and commercial publishing had undeniably burgeoned by the early twelfth century of the Song and probably earlier, a number of scholars have argued that the uses of print became widespread among both the literati and the less learned only sometime during the Ming in the mid- to late sixteenth century. They base this assertion on the persistent and overwhelming dominance until that time of manuscripts over imprints in private and public collections, some evidence on the lowering of book production costs and book prices, and observations of various writers about the scarcity of books until the late Ming.[22] Although we lack sufficient information to prove or disprove this argument, the examination of the Jianyang publishing industry from the Song through the end of the Ming presented in this work suggests that the issue is far too complex and rich to justify a simple yes or no answer. Certainly we have many more extant Jianyang imprints from the Ming than from earlier periods, even after trying to correct for the variation in survival rates with time. But when we consider that the variety of imprints in the Song and Yuan was not significantly less than in the late Ming, that the impact of printed materials does not correlate in any simple direct fashion with their numbers, and that lists of titles in collections may not reflect the actual reading habits of their owners and certainly do not reflect those of other readers, then fixing a date for the ascendance of print may not be very useful.

Since this study focuses on the commercial publishers of Jianyang, it will offer only limited speculations concerning readership and reading practices, based mostly on clues from the imprints examined. As many scholars have pointed out, the fascinating topic of readership and readers' responses is fraught with questionable assumptions, including those that lead one to postulate some "implied reader."[23] When we confront the wealth of Jianyang commercial imprints, it is highly tempting to imagine who their audiences might have been and how they read, looked at, or listened to the books. Of course we cannot know for certain the actual response to a given work of any one reader or even of readers within a narrowly defined socioeconomic group with shared knowledge and at least some shared cultural values. But we can and should at least offer some judicious conjectures that enrich our understanding of the publishers' role.

For example, there were at least six different editions of collections of Su Shi's verses from Jianyang alone in the late twelfth century, and we can arrive at the safe and not particularly stunning conclusion that he was an immensely popular poet, however different readers might have responded specifically to his writings. Furthermore, since Su's verse and prose collections continued to be published in the Yuan and Ming dynasties, we may chart his long-lasting popularity for several centuries after his death. Even more interesting, however, is the presence of Su's works in a variety of writing manuals and literary anthologies from the Song onward, suggesting that Su appealed not just to poetry lovers in general but also to aspiring authors, who looked to his writing style as a model.

In examining commercial imprints for information about possible readers and their reading practices, we should exercise extra care in not taking the publishers at their word about their intended readers. For example, by the mid-sixteenth century at the latest, terms such as *tongsu yanyi* 通俗演義 (common or popular elaboration), *yufu yufu* 愚夫愚婦 (unlearned men and women), *tianxia zhi ren* 天下之人 (all the people in the world), *simin* 四民 (the four classes of people) appeared in the titles, publishers' notices, and prefaces of commercial imprints. It would seem obvious that the publishers of such works were targeting the broad audience of "common people" rather than the highly educated literati elite. But as we will see in Part III, even a casual survey of these imprints reveals a wide variety of styles, commentaries, and necessary reading levels; we must read the texts and look at the illustrations and the page layouts closely and consider other evidence outside the imprints to determine just who might have constituted the actual audiences.

This brief discussion of some issues that need to be examined in order to assess the impact of woodblock printing on Chinese society, and the comparisons with early modern Western Europe show that while we can be inspired by the huge amount of work being done for the history of the book in the West,[24] we are also exploring a different territory that has remained uncharted for much longer. The neglect does not mean that the topic has not deeply interested scholars in Chinese studies, but that the sources have appeared particularly disparate and recalcitrant. Recently, however, scholars have begun to tackle these issues.[25] As their work and this study show, some of the questions we ask differ from those asked in Western studies, and the answers grow out of a different assortment of sources beset with their own particular limitations.

A Note on the Main Sources

Ironically, because the printing of books began in China about seven centuries before it did in Europe, the earlier part of the story for China is harder to study. This is not only because many relevant materials no longer exist, but also because by the Song, when commercial printing took off, the tremendous changes generated by the printed text did not catch the attention of contemporaries in the same ways as they did in Europe for the two centuries or so after Gutenberg. Thus although Song literati were quite aware of the power of print to replicate, disseminate, and transform texts, they were most likely to comment on the last phenomenon and to complain about the abuses of print, if they mentioned the subject at all. In addition, as we have noted, most scholars thought the technology and economics of printing to be beneath their notice. This silence by those most likely to leave written records of their thoughts has deprived us, in large measure (though not entirely), of one potentially valuable source. As a result, finding extant contemporary sources and extracting from them information for studying the social history of the Chinese book pose quite different challenges from those encountered by researchers of early modern Europe. What we have is an assortment of local histories, genealogies, the writings of the publishers' contemporaries, a few government documents, the imprints themselves (which occasionally recorded details such as the names of calligraphers and blockcarvers), and annotated library catalogues and bibliographies compiled throughout the centuries by scholars and book collectors that describe these imprints.

The most important source for this work is the imprints themselves. In the course of this study, I have compiled a bibliography of over two thousand Jianyang imprints.[26] Aside from counting how many different titles and different editions were printed when by which publisher, we can also obtain much useful information by thoroughly examining the physical features of each work, the occasional recording of the names of calligraphers and blockcarvers, and the paratexts, including advertising features (printer's colophon, printer's note), prefaces and postfaces, editorial notes, page layout, and calligraphic styles (for more on these subjects, see Chapter 2). Indeed, even lacking all the other sources just mentioned, we could still wrest from the imprints nearly everything we can know about the history of the Jianyang publishing industry.

The annotated catalogues used in compiling this bibliography served as a necessary substitute for imprints not easily accessible or no longer extant by providing information such as the contents of the printer's note or colophon, passages from prefaces and postfaces, occasional comparisons with other editions, and sometimes the history of a particular copy as derived from the owners' seals and handwritten notes. The authors of these catalogues come from a long tradition of Chinese bibliographic studies and show the limitations of this discipline as well as its virtues. For example, an author may repeat an unsubstantiated value judgment by another bibliographer or decide that a book is a "Jianben" without giving his reasons in detail. This assessment is usually based on many years of connoisseurship on the part of the writer, but without a satisfactory explanation, I have been cautious about accepting such pronouncements.

Another set of sources for this study is eighteen genealogies[27] of descent groups in the Jianyang area.[28] Four of these genealogies (two for branches of the Liu family, and one each for the Xiong and Yu) are particularly relevant for this research, since they are for the families of the publishers studied here—a number of men with these surnames were involved in the printing industry during the Song and Yuan, and many Ming publishers can be identified in the genealogical tables (*shixi* 世系).[29] In addition, clues such as the generational names that they share with other men *not* recorded in the genealogies but listed as publishers, editors, or collators in Jianyang imprints show that printing was often a family business. Moreover, although some printers' names as they appear in the imprints (in colophons, prefaces) cannot be found in the genealogies, recent investigators have managed to equate a printer with a name in the genealogy by a bit of detective work usually involving the names of the printshop, the father's or grandfather's name, relevant dates, and references in prefaces and contemporary writings.[30] As already noted, these genealogies can be frustrating because they contain virtually no information on the printing activities of these men. All too often, if one of them has merited a biographical sketch, it notes his filial piety, his love of scholarship, his academic successes and government service (if any), his leadership in the local community, and any other virtues associated with a member of the educated elite. Almost the only time printing is mentioned is when the man was involved in compiling and printing a new edition of the genealogy itself.[31]

Although few publishers can be identified in the other fourteen genealogies examined, most are for Minbei families that were nationally or locally prominent in the Song, Yuan, or Ming.[32] For example, several branches of the Zhu family descended from Zhu Shu, Zhu Xi's eldest son, can be traced through the late Qing in their genealogy. Another genealogy is that of the Cai descent group, among whose members were prominent *Daoxue* scholars of the Song and Yuan, such as Cai Yuanding 蔡元定 (1135–98) and his sons, Yuan, Hang, and Chen. Also useful is the genealogy of the family of the Song scholar and publisher of some highly esteemed editions of the Classics, Liao Yingzhong 寥瑩中 (?–1275).[33] Information collated from all eighteen genealogies examined reveals that intermarriage among these families was fairly frequent, and such marriage ties are useful in providing supporting evidence for the social and intellectual networks to which the publishers belonged.

In addition, these genealogies do give information on the social, political, and economic conditions of the descent groups. If sufficiently complete, this information allows comparisons of wealth and academic and official success to be made among various *fang* 房 of a *zu* 族, and among the various *pai* 派 of a *fang*. Furthermore, the prefaces to the genealogies, commemorative essays, and biographies of family members often contain information not (easily) available in other sources. For example, starting in the Northern Song, family schools (variously termed *jiashu* or *shuyuan*) were established in increasing numbers in the Jianyang area. These schools, which played an important role in the rise of the printing industry in Jianyang (see Chapter 3), are rarely mentioned in other sources. The commemorative essays found in the genealogies are valuable for the information on the schools' founding, records of land endowments, and activities. Thus, as frustratingly uninformative as the genealogies can be, in other ways, they give us a much closer glimpse of the Jianyang publishers and their families and associates than any other source.

The local histories used in this study include provincial gazetteers for Fujian, prefectural gazetteers for Jianning and neighboring regions, and county gazetteers, especially for the counties in Jianning prefecture (Jianyang, Jian'an

建安, Ouning 歐寧, Pucheng 浦城, Songxi 松溪, Zhenghe 政和, and Shou-ning 壽寧).[34] Most of the information in these works does not relate directly to printing, but instead provides a general picture of the geography and history of the region. Diverse facts on county and prefectural schools, private academies (*shuyuan*) and the books they owned, the lists of degree holders, and the biographies of men related to, or who had social and business dealings with, publishers can be found in the local gazetteers. As for the commercial printers themselves, none from the Song or Yuan and very few from the Ming appear in any gazetteer. One of the latter, Xiong Zongli 熊宗立 (1409–82), is described as the author and editor, but not printer, of some twenty medical books. And Liu Longtian 劉龍田, one of the most prolific of all Jianyang printers during the late sixteenth century, very likely earned his brief biography among the "Virtuous and able" (*xianliang* 賢良) because his eldest son was a *jinshi* and official who had his father posthumously ennobled.[35] Nevertheless, the compilers of the various editions of the Jianyang county gazetteer were aware of the area's lively printing industry, even if they were reluctant to admit their own possible use of its products. They noted which books in school collections were Jianyang imprints, mentioned with some pride how merchants from all over visited the book market held every month in Chonghua 崇化 (Shufang), and listed books as a native product.[36]

The collected writings (*wenji* 文集) of the publishers' contemporaries and of later men who commented on Jianyang books or on the book trade in general or on the Minbei area constitute the most diverse sources. On practical details of the book trade, such as book prices, print runs, and how the books were sold, these texts are all too silent. Although numerous Jianyang imprints recorded as editors and collators men who lived or served as officials in the area, such activities are almost never mentioned in the men's own writings, other than those of Zhu Xi, whose description of his own printing activities to supplement his meager income and to promote his ideas has already been noted. Much more often, one finds a writer deploring the low quality of Jianyang books even as he notes their ubiquity. Typical is the well-known remark of Ye Mengde in the late Northern Song about the low quality of Fujian books printed from blocks of soft wood. Ye's opinion was echoed by other observers in the Song and later in the Yuan and Ming, and defective Jianyang imprints, or *Mashaben*, were the target of various sarcastic anecdotes. From other *wenji*, however, it is possible to learn about the literati's changing attitudes toward the printed text through different periods. For example, the litany of complaints by Song scholars that the greater availability of books because of printing has led to superficial reading and less understanding of texts is gradually replaced in the Yuan and the Ming by a more favorable assessment of the benefits of the printed text. Thus, there are bits of information available, but these are serendipitous finds that must be gleaned from examining a huge number of *wenji*.

Very few government documents specifically mention the Jianyang book trade. For the Song, aside from general laws on publishing, there are occasional memorials and decrees pertaining to the illegal activities of the Jianyang printers that contributed to the general negative view of *Mashaben* of the time. There is practically nothing for the Yuan, except in the *Yuan dianzhang* 元典章 (Institutions of the Yuan). The situation is much the same for the Ming; discussions of government attitudes toward commercial imprints and official measures dealing with them are more likely to be found in *wenji*.[37] The overall dearth of official documents probably reflects in part the state's tacit and reluctant acknowledgment of its inability to control the book trade, a task whose difficulty grew with the spread of commercial and private publishing.

The Geography of Minbei

Minbei refers to the northwest portion of Fujian province (Map 1); most of it lies in the 27,288 sq km (10,533 sq mi) now designated as the Nanping district (南平地區). This includes areas that were part of Jianning, Shaowu 邵武, and Yanping 延平 prefectures in the late imperial period.[38] The relatively low but rugged Wuyi Mountains 武夷山 extend along the border between Minbei and Jiangxi to the west, and to the north the Xianxia Mountains (仙霞嶺) straddle part of the boundary with Zhejiang.

The weather in the region, like that of the rest of Fujian, is subtropical. The average temperature ranges from 13°C in December–January to 28°C in July in the valleys. The area is also the wettest in the province, receiving an average annual rainfall of 1,700 mm, about 60 percent of which occurs from March to July.[39] Because of variations in temperature and precipitation, the number of frost-free days differs from place to place; the valleys have about 290 such days.

About 90 percent of the Minbei area is either hilly or mountainous, with narrow river valleys. The predominant soils are red and yellow podzolic types formed from the chemical and mechanical degradation of the original rocks under humid, subtropical conditions. Many inorganic materials have been leached out and turned into insoluble alkaline metal hydroxides, which give the soils their characteristic colors. Many of the organic constituents have also been leached out. Consequently, the soils are acidic, low in humus content, and not very fertile. Nevertheless, they are used for cultivation of rice, wheat, fruits, vegetables, tea, and tong trees. The soils also support an evergreen broadleaf forest (mainly fir, pine, and bamboo)[40] that covers over half the region, making it one of the most important timber preserves in China.[41]

Minbei is criss-crossed with a dense network of waterways. The main river in the region, the Jian Stream 建溪, although a tributary of Minjiang 閩江, is as broad as the latter. Except during spring thaw, the Minbei waterways are relatively shallow. A heavy downpour can, however, turn a placid stream into an impassable torrent. Moreover, the swift currents, the multitude of large, semi-submerged rocks, and the many sandbars make navigation hazardous. According to Hu Sanxing (1230–87), "Following the current from the Jianxi and descending eastward to Fu prefecture, the river takes a winding course for several hundred *li*, and the current is very swift. A light boat starting at dawn will arrive in the evening."[42] Presumably, only a shallow-draft vessel such as Hu's "light boat" or a raft can make the journey successfully. In the seventeenth-century work *Tiangong kaiwu* 天工開物 (The exploitation of the works of nature; original preface dated 1637), Song Yingxing 宋應星 described two kinds of boats, the "clear-stream" (*qingliu* 清流) and the "mizzen-sail" (*shaopeng* 稍篷), which plied between the small streams from Guangze 光澤 and Chongan in the Minbei area down to the Hongtang 洪塘 seawall of Fuzhou. The clear-stream boats were used for transporting merchants and their goods; the larger mizzen-sail boats had sleeping quarters for traveling officials and their families.[43] The bottoms of both kinds of boats were made from fir and suffered frequent damage from rocks and shoals. Because of such natural hazards and bandits on the water or on the shore, boatmen were reluctant to travel at night and preferred to put up at the nearest town. Thus a journey downstream often took longer than Hu Sanxing's optimistic estimate. Travel upstream, against the most rapid flow of any major river in China, was an entirely different experience and far slower, even in stretches where rowing or sailing was feasible. Until the advent of motor launches, rapids were negotiated by having men on shore tow the boats, which made them an even easier target for bandits. In any case, the going was very slow: some six days from Fuzhou to Yanping.[44] All the rivers of the Minbei region eventually flow into the Minjiang. In the imperial period, Minbei produce, such as rice, tea, paper, timber, and bamboo (the last two floated down the river), and goods from Jiangnan were shipped to the coast in exchange for salt, fish, textiles, ironware, fruits, and such products from overseas as spices and aromatic woods.

The Minbei waterways functioned as the main transport routes in the region well into the twentieth century. All the prefectural and county seats in Minbei, as well as many of the larger towns and villages, are situated on a river or at the junction of two or more waterways. Thus, Masha is on the Mayang

Stream 麻陽溪 (a tributary of the Jian Stream), about 52 km west and up-stream of the Jianyang county seat. Further southwest, Shufang is on a smaller tributary about the same distance from Jianyang. By following the Jian Stream north from Nanping municipality, one reaches in succession Jian'an (now Jian'ou 建歐), Jianyang, and Chongan (now Wuyi municipality). Branching off the Jian Stream at Jian'an is the Song Stream 松溪, which leads in a northeast direction to the seat of Songxi county, or along a different stream to Zhenghe 政和. Pucheng 浦城 can be reached along the Pucheng Stream 浦城溪, which enters Jian Stream between Jian'an and Jianyang. To this day, the most important roads in the region faithfully follow the twists and turns of these waterways.

The most important route from northern Fujian into Zhejiang, used ex-tensively since at least the Northern Song, proceeds from Pucheng north, first by water and then by land, through Xianxia Pass 仙霞關 and into Zhejiang. There, again by a combination of water and land transportation, one passes through Jiangshan 江山 and Quzhou 衢州 and eventually reaches Hang-zhou.[45] This route was the shortest and most direct way to Jiangnan, but it was a quite narrow and tortuous path over several mountains. Moreover, unlike the other routes north from the Minbei area, there was no government postal courier station along it until the Ming.

Another route, largely by water, also proceeded from Pucheng into Chu-zhou 處州 in Zhejiang and eventually reached Wenzhou 溫州 on the coast. In fact, throughout the imperial period, Wenzhou may have been the port of choice for many Minbei imports and exports. One modern scholar has sug-gested that many of the Jianyang imprints that eventually reached Japan and Korea may have been shipped from Wenzhou.[46] Another scholar has argued convincingly that pottery from Minbei and Jiangxi kilns active in the Song and Yuan was transported over this route to Wenzhou (or a northern Fujian port) rather than to Quanzhou on the southern Fujian coast.[47] Finally, a nineteenth-century English traveler noted that salt from coastal Fujian was shipped to Wenzhou and then transported to Pucheng.[48] All this evidence be-speaks the difficulties of land travel in northern Fujian and of shipping bulk commodities up the Minjiang.

A third route, known since the Han dynasty, went from Guangze in Shao-wu through Shan Pass 杉關 in the Wuyi Mountains into Jiangxi, first by land to Jianchang 建昌, then by water to Fuzhou 撫州 and beyond to Nanchang 南昌 and down the Gan River 贛江 to Guangdong, or to Poyang Lake and eventually on to Nanjing via the Yangzi. This route from Guangze was relatively easy: the land roads were fairly level, and the waterways were not too difficult to navigate. It was not, however, as important a commercial route as the others, probably because it was longer and more circuitous and went from Shaowu rather than the commercial centers in the more populous Jianning area.

The fourth and most important route was through Chongan, past Fenshui Pass 分水關 in the Wuyi Mountains into Jiangxi, where the first important stop was at Hekou 河口 (modern Yanshan 鉛山).[49] Westward from Hekou, a water route went through Guixi 貴溪 into Poyang Lake and then south on the Gan River to Nanchang and eventually to Guangdong. An easterly route from Hekou via the Xin River 信江 led to Shangrao 上饒 and Yushan 玉山, then overland to Changshan 常山 in Zhejiang, and from there on easily navigable rivers and canals to Hangzhou or Ningbo. The courier service, toll stations, and government patrol posts on this route attest to its importance. Wang Shimao 王世懋 (1536–88), who was generally unimpressed with the roads in Fujian during his travels there in the 1580s, noted the busy commercial traffic through two of the mountain passes in the Minbei area.

Not one day passes but the silks of Fuzhou, the gauzes of Zhangzhou, the indigo of Quanzhou, the ironware of Fuzhou and Yanping, the oranges of Zhangzhou, the lichees of Fuzhou and Xinghua, the sugar of Quanzhou, and the paper [products] of Shunchang go through the Fenshui mountain pass and the pass at Pucheng and down to Zhejiang (Wu 吳) and Jiangsu (Yue 越) like flowing water.[50]

These routes reveal several important characteristics of the Minbei area. First, its orientation was inland across the mountains toward Jiangnan and beyond at least as much as, or more than, toward the sea. Minbei was the first area of Fujian to be settled by Han immigrants from the north; as far back as the end of the second century CE during the Eastern Han, settlers came across the mountains following the routes described above.[51] Before the rise of the Fujian maritime trade, Minbei's overland and water routes were the main conduits of trade between the Fujian coast and the inland; they remained important even after the economic development of coastal Fujian.[52] Second, these trade networks stayed active even when the region was in many other ways an economic, cultural, and political backwater. Merchants from outside would come to buy its tea, timber, paper, and books. Since books are relatively small items, the book trade probably followed the same routes as bulk exports. Third, social unrest moved as easily as merchandise over the borders between Fujian and Jiangxi or Zhejiang.[53] The routes were frequented by rebels, bandits, tea and salt smugglers, and migrant workers, such as tea pickers and miners, as well as by the shack people (*pengmin* 棚民), whose numbers began to grow noticeably in the late Ming. For good or for bad, these routes prevented northwestern Fujian from being isolated.

In terms of agriculture, although much of the Jianning area is mountainous, it was considered a rice-exporting area in imperial China. Rice was grown on both paddies and dry land, and varieties of early-ripening rice specially adapted to poor soil have been cultivated since the Northern Song.[54] Until recently, it was customary in Jianning to grow only one crop of rice per year. The reason is uncertain, but it cannot be the climate—the growing season allows two crops, the other usually being winter wheat.[55]

Another important Minbei agricultural product has been tea, which has been cultivated on hills and moutainsides since the Tang.[56] Tea was grown first in Jian'an, where the famed Beiyuan 北苑 was established around the beginning of the tenth century. During the Tang, Song, and Yuan, the highly prized tea from this area was subject to a government monopoly.[57] Tea also began to be a major product in the Wuyi Mountains during the Yuan. Minbei tea continued to play a role in the regional economy during the Ming, but it was only in the mid-Qing that it attained international fame and economic importance.[58]

Of the forestry products, the lumber from conifers, especially China fir (*shan* 杉), and pine, constituted the most important exports; firwood was particularly favored in the construction of ships and houses.[59] No records note deforestation in the Minbei area, although this occurred in regions nearer the coast.[60] Apparently, by the late Ming, if not earlier, a small number of people, some of whom were from outside the Minbei region, had bought up large tracts of forest. Much the same story applies to bamboo, another important Minbei product.[61]

There were a number of silver and iron mines in the mountains of Minbei. The mining of silver began in the Tang.[62] In the late fifteenth century, silver mines were in operation in Chongan, Jianyang, Zhenghe, and Shouning, and iron mines and works in Jian'an, Ouning, Pucheng, Songxi, and Zhenghe.[63] Apparently, the amounts extracted were never very large, and most of the silver went directly to the government. Indeed, in the late Ming, silver was being imported from the coast to the Minbei region, partly to pay taxes. Many of the miners and foundry workers were from Jiangxi or Zhejiang across the border; the miners had a long tradition of participation in rebellions, including the one led by Fan Ruwei 范汝爲 (1130–32) during the early Southern Song and another led by Ye Zongliu 葉宗留 (1442–48) in the Ming, which was started by miners in the Xianxia mountains along the Fujian-Zhejiang border.[64]

Finally, the heterogeneous set of dialects spoken in Minbei serves as another proof of its long and complex history of interaction with the outside world. For example, although most of the dialects belong to the Western Min group, that of Pucheng is unique and cannot be classified any more specifically than a "Southern Chinese" dialect.[65] And the Western Min dialect of Shaowu differs from those of Jianyang, Jian'ou, Chongan, and others in the pronounced Gan-Kejia influence on it, which is not surprising given Shaowu's proximity to Jiangxi and the route between the two areas over Shan Pass. Even the other Western Min dialects, such as those spoken within the Jianning area, differ from one another in ways that may reflect not only interaction with outside regions but also the uneven distribution of roads and waterways within the region.

The peculiarities of the Minbei area are evident even from this cursory overview of its geography. Administratively, it has been part of Fujian for over a millennium, but its economic, social, and cultural ties with the Jiangnan region have been extremely important. It was a relatively remote area, accessible only through difficult mountain and water routes, and yet it maintained numerous ties with the outside world throughout the late imperial period. It was, except during the Southern Song and Yuan, a cultural and economic backwater, but nevertheless it managed to sustain one of the most important printing industries in the country. In many ways, the geographic and historical contradictions of Minbei are mirrored in the Jianyang book trade. In exploring the publishing industry in the next six chapters, we can also gain a better understanding of the area as a whole.

2

The Physical Appearance
of Jianyang Woodblock Imprints

No study on the history of the publication and consumption of the block-printed book can neglect examining the materials and techniques of its production and its physical appearance. Understanding the physical nature of the book is essential in turn to knowing how publishers produced their imprints and how readers were affected by their reading materials—the ways they looked at, read, punctuated, and skimmed the pages of these books. All too often, however, such information has remained the purview of rare book experts and has been relegated to entries in bibliographies and book catalogues for use in identifying a particular edition. Even the vocabulary of this body of knowledge, necessary for discussing the history of the Chinese book, is relatively unfamiliar to many China scholars (and for this reason is introduced below). The purpose of this chapter, however, is not to repeat information found in great detail in the literature[1] but to discuss technical matters specifically relevant to Jianyang imprints, such as the paper, ink, woodblocks, block carving, as well as such aspects of the appearance of these works as the format and layout of the text, calligraphic styles, punctuation, and illustrations. Much of this information comes from examining the imprints themselves, an essential exercise in the traditional Chinese connoisseurship of books (*banben xue*) but not one that has been employed in correlation with other historical and modern sources to provide an understanding of the socioeconomic history of Chinese books and printing, something this chapter will try to do by focusing on Jianyang.

Moreover, as this study shows, developments in the technology of book production and in the form and appearance of the Chinese imprint are useful indicators of changes in the book market and readership throughout the late imperial period. An awareness of these changes will in turn help us understand the practices of commercial publishers and, on a broader level, the involvement of these publishers and their customers in the cultural, social, and economic trends of their times. Specifically, the discussion below, based largely on the history of the Jianyang book trade, argues that the exigencies of the book trade led to changes in the production and the physical appearance of these books more often than did technical developments in paper-making, block carving, and printing, which were relatively rare after the Song. Indeed, the evidence suggests that technological modifications, far from determining changes in book production and appearance, were in fact themselves driven by commercial and cultural trends.

Consequently, this chapter falls into two distinct parts. The first deals with the materials and techniques of book production, which were much the same throughout China in any given period and in many ways had reached the peak of technical advancement in the mid-eleventh century. Thus, much of what this section says about Jianyang imprints is also applicable to books published elsewhere in China, and the historical continuities are more obvious than the changes. The second part discusses the features of a Chinese block-printed page, with special attention to those frequently found in Jianyang imprints. We will consider not only how the nature of woodblock printing in general affected the appearance and arrangement of the text and image but also how commercial publishers in particular designed and modified the elements of the printed page to suit their various purposes. Here, in addition to brief descriptions of some relevant historical developments, we will raise a number of issues about the publishing, selling, and reading of books, to which we will return in subsequent chapters.

Materials Used in Book Production

Paper

According to relatively late sources, such as the 1886 work *Min chan lu yi* 閩產錄異 (Record of Fujianese products) of Guo Bocang 郭伯蒼, almost all Jianyang books, from the beginning in the Northern Song, were printed on paper made from bamboo.[2] Although no pre-Ming source specifically mentions bamboo paper-making in the Minbei region, a few works from the late Tang and Song talk of bamboo paper in Guangdong, Jiangsu, and Zhejiang.[3] Paper-making was probably introduced by the late Tang or Five Dynasties into Fujian, where it became important in a number of mountainous areas in which bamboo was plentiful.[4] Although paper could be and had been made since earlier times from various basts (hemp, jute, ramie, rattan) and tree barks (mulberry and paper mulberry), in Minbei these materials were apparently used mainly to make other products, including clothing, bedding, and mosquito nets, for which bamboo paper was deemed unsuitable. Moreover, because these plants were less naturally abundant and required more attention to cultivate and to turn into pulp, bamboo became by far the chief paper-making material in much of southern China.[5] Indeed, even the higher-quality bark paper was often not made entirely from paper mulberry; bamboo and sometimes rice stalks were mixed in as well.[6] Similarly, "bamboo" paper was sometimes a mixture of bamboo and rice straw pulp, as is obvious from the rice hulls present in the paper in some Jianyang imprints.[7]

The paper made from bamboo by the traditional Chinese method has a yellow to brown tinge, mostly due to the lignin remaining in the pulp.[8] Probably because of this and because of the relatively low quality of much of the bamboo paper made in imperial China (a tendency to tear, a rough surface), books printed on bamboo paper were disdained by bibliophiles, who much preferred white or pale yellow paper made from other materials.[9] One kind of bamboo paper made mainly for printing in inland Fujian, including the Minbei area, was known commonly as *yukou zhi* 玉扣紙 (jade knot paper) or *shu(ji) zhi* 書(籍)紙 (book paper). Its quality varied from place to place because of differences not only in paper-making technique but also in the kinds of bamboo used.[10] In general, this was a thin (about 0.05–0.08 mm) paper whose color ranged from pale yellowish tan to medium brown.[11] The density of extraneous fibers and other materials on the surface of the sheet and its brittleness varied from book to book and sometimes from leaf to leaf in a single volume. In many of the poorly produced imprints, not only are the sheets extremely thin, but their thickness is visibly uneven, and there is almost no paper along the chain and laid lines.[12] This thinness causes problem in taking an impression from the woodblock.[13] Some care must be exercised not to tear the sheet when rubbing the back of it on the inked woodblock, but if the rubbing is too lightly done or the block is worn, the resulting impression will not be sufficiently dark. Yet another problem is that with age the paper becomes increasingly brittle because of the substantial amount of lignin in this paper as well as other chemical changes. The resulting decrease in fold strength is obvious in the many books whose leaves are wholly or partially split along the centerfold, which receives the brunt of handling by the reader.

For reasons of economy, "spliced" paper was sometimes made using bamboo mixed with other materials. The quality of such mixed-pulp papers is especially hard to control and may, at least in the Jianyang imprints examined for this study, account for the noticeable deterioration of books produced in times of paper shortage, such as the end of the Yuan and the beginning of the Ming (late fourteenth to early fifteenth century).[14] Another frequent criticism of Jianyang imprints, especially those from this period, is that the impressions are not black but gray. Although this problem is blamed chiefly on the use of poorer inks (see below), the varying ability of different grades of paper to absorb ink is also a consideration. The same ink may appear more pallid and duller on inferior bamboo paper than it does on better-quality paper.[15]

Although the general technique for making bamboo paper is similar to that for paper made from other materials, it apparently took some time to master the art of producing bamboo paper of satisfactory quality in the Song. For example, Su Yijian 蘇易簡 (957–95) observed that nobody other than the recipient of a note written on bamboo paper dared open it up, because it would split upon refolding. And Cai Xiang 蔡襄 (1012–67), when serving as prefect of Quanzhou, forbade his staff to use bamboo paper because of its poor quality.[16] By the late eleventh or early twelfth century, however, the technique of making bamboo paper had vastly improved, and its use was widespread. For example, Su Shi 蘇軾 (1036–1101) noted that people in his time, unlike those of previous generations, used bamboo for paper-making. The Jiatai period (1201–4) edition of the Guiji 會稽 (Zhejiang) gazetteer also mentioned the newfound popularity of bamboo paper; the gazetteer reported that three superior grades suitable for calligraphy and official documents were produced in the region. In fact, the famous calligrapher Mi Fu 米芾 (ca. 1051–1107) wrote that he began to use bamboo paper from Guiji when he was fifty.[17]

The lack of mentions of bamboo paper from Minbei in any extant Song source despite its wide use in local imprints suggests that, unlike that produced in Guiji or elsewhere in Fujian, it was probably considered unsuited for calligraphy, painting, and the finest printed books.[18] But many Ming sources, including local gazetteers, encyclopedias (*leishu* 類書), and travel accounts, routinely mention the production of bamboo paper in the Minbei region and other parts of Fujian.[19] In the Wanli period, Wang Shimao mentioned paper-making only in passing, giving the impression it was too common to warrant a detailed description.[20]

In fact, few writers in any period were interested enough to record the technical details of paper-making. The notable exception, and the most complete account of paper-making from the Ming, can be found in *Tiangong kaiwu* by Song Yingxing. The similarities between Song's description and those of Yang Zhongxi in the Qing and two early twentieth-century observers suggest strongly that paper-making techniques had remained unchanged for three hundred years and most likely for much longer.[21] To produce the wide variety of papers for different applications that were possible using bamboo pulp, however, required variations in specific procedures. In addition to paper for calligraphy and painting, other grades were made for books, sutras, calendars, paper money, wrappers, firecrackers, and coat linings, largely for local consumption. Many of these different papers had distinct names, which varied from place to place.[22]

An examination of the paper used in many Jianyang imprints from the Song reaffirms the claim made above that the technology for making high-quality bamboo paper had already been perfected by the late eleventh century. In fact, the bamboo paper in the Song imprints is less discolored than the paper in many later ones. What accounts, then, for the plethora of later Jianyang books made of rough, brittle, badly discolored paper? To a large extent, deterioration over time depends on storage conditions, and Song imprints are most likely to have received the best care from later librarians and bibliophiles. But this explanation is insufficient. The paper in most of the Yuan and early Ming imprints, as well as a portion of the mid- and late Ming ones from Jianyang, is discolored. That many of the most deteriorated books are also the ones that received the least attention overall (editing and proofreading, if any, and printing) suggests a deliberate decision to use cheaper, lower-quality paper made by omitting certain steps in turning pulp into the final product. The rapid growth in the book market that began in the mid-Ming around the Jiajing period (1522–66) probably further encouraged this practice, but it may also have been spurred by printers' deliberate attempts to increase their market by producing a lower-cost product. Christian Daniels, in a recent study of paper-making in the Fujian area in the Ming and the Qing, argues that this was indeed the case, and that the procedure described in the *Tiangong kaiwu* represents how the pulp-processing and paper-making process *should* be done.[23] The widespread use of lower-quality bamboo paper is therefore a clear example of a technology that is modified, or simplified, as a result of commercial demand.

The kind of attention Ming literati paid to paper-making reveals something of their response to the expansion of commercial publishing and the lowering of production quality. From the Wanli period to the end of the

Ming, a number of treatises on *objets d'art*, including the four treasures of the scholar's studio (paper, ink, brush, and inkstone), were written. In comparison to similar works of the Song and Yuan, the late Ming writings are even more suffused with the spirit of the art connoisseur and amateur, who might be deeply involved in supervising the practical details of having paper made for his use in calligraphy and painting, of which there were many different kinds. For example, a particular style of calligraphy required that the characters run slightly on the sheet to give a "spilled ink" (*bomo* 波墨) effect, for which only one kind of paper with just the right amount of sizing was suitable.[24] This meticulous attention, however, was rarely paid to paper intended for printing, perhaps because it was generally perceived as a mechanical technique rather than an art and one far less demanding of (and more indifferent to) the kind of paper used. Even in the detailed descriptions of the *Tiangong kaiwu*, there is no discussion of different grades of paper made from a given material. As we will see, this same lack of interest and disdain pervaded other technical aspects of book production, including the ink, calligraphy, and illustrations. Those literati who referred to Jianyang imprints, for example, tended to be highly critical of everything about the books, including the paper.[25] Although such comments were not new in the Ming, the heightened discrimination regarding those arts claimed by the literati (and aspirants to this group) to be their own was a means of distancing themselves from "lower" forms, such as commercial publishing. Other aspects of book production, discussed below, also reveal similar developments dictated by commercial and cultural rather than by strictly technological trends.

Ink

Like paper, the ink used for printing was of a lower quality than that for calligraphy and painting. Although the making of highly prized ink cakes has been described appreciatively and in great detail and the names of master inkmakers recorded,[26] little is known about the production of cheaper inks. According to the *Tiangong kaiwu*, the lampblack produced by burning pine wood in a bamboo chamber is divided into several grades and "that from the first one or two sections is scraped and sold only as low-grade lampblack; it is further pounded and ground by printers and used [in printing books]."[27] At least some of the ink produced in Jianyang and the neighboring counties must have been made in this way.[28] Moreover, since printing ink need only be sufficiently dark and adhere to the paper without smudging but need not fulfill the aesthetic requirements of ink for painting (e.g., "to make a clear tone which has expressive spirit—'penetrating to the bone'"),[29] it was composed of

far fewer ingredients. Two descriptions, from the eighteenth and early twentieth centuries, are quite similar. After being beaten and sifted through a sieve,
ten parts of the soot were mixed with one part of cowhide glue and added to
water and wine to form a thick paste. To dispel its bad odor and improve its
qualities, the paste was stored in a jar for at least three summers. When it was
to be used, it was mixed with enough water to make a liquid and strained
again.[30]

Judging from Chinese block-printed books in general, this ink was quite
adequate for printing. The only noticeable defect, evident in a number of
Jianyang commercial imprints from all periods, is the pale color—dark gray
rather than black—of the impressions, which probably resulted from over-
diluting the ink paste with water as a cost-cutting measure.

Woodblocks for Printing

Traditional Chinese woodblocks are made from plankwood (cut along the
grain), which, for a given tree trunk, yields larger pieces than the end-grain
wood (cut against the grain) and allows the cutter to avoid the problematic
knotty heartwood.[31] The unplaned blocks are then seasoned for up to several
years, until they have dried and shrunk and warped as much as they are likely
to.[32] Finally, the blocks are planed, oiled, and polished.

Generally, an even, close-grained, and relatively hard wood was preferred.[33] The choice of wood depended on the kind of material being printed
(text or pictures) but more often on the availability and cost of the wood. The
woods used for block printing in China include camphor, catalpa, boxwood,
Chinese honey locust, and fruitwoods like pear and Chinese date (jujube).
Catalpa (*zi* 梓) was so widely used that the character acquired a second
meaning—to print; it appears in many printer's colophons. Similarly, in Jianyang imprints, the character *li* 梨 (pear) also came to mean print in a number
of printer's colophons. Pearwood is a relatively hard wood and can be used
for general-purpose woodblock printing. The oldest surviving woodblocks in
Jianyang date from the late nineteenth and early twentieth centuries and are
made of pear wood. Local tradition says that pear wood was used extensively
in earlier times as well—plausible, but unproven.[34]

Contrary to the mistaken notion that has spread to Western works on
Chinese printing,[35] soft banyan wood most likely was *not* used in Jianyang
woodblocks since banyan trees do not grow so far north. The blurry nature of
many Jianyang imprints is much more likely due to printing too many copies
from a woodblock and/or printing more than 200–300 copies without letting

the woodblock "rest" from several hours to a day. Without a pause, the block would swell up as it absorbed the water-based ink and to a lesser extent from the continual rubbing to transfer the impression to the paper. This was probably a widespread problem among commercial printers anxious to print as many copies of a book as quickly as possible, but it remains almost unmentioned in the traditional literature on rare books and printing, since presumably such a flaw would not have afflicted the higher-quality books valued by bibliophiles.[36] The number of satisfactory impressions that can be pulled off a woodblock depends on the hardness of the wood, its water absorbency, weather conditions, and the standards of the printer. According to two modern publishing houses, two thousand to three thousand copies can be made from pearwood blocks before minor repairs need to be made.[37] Finally, a certain amount of care and time is required to obtain clear pages even from new blocks. For example, often in a poor imprint part of the impression on a page would come out quite clearly, whereas another part would be faint or blurred, indicating a problem with either the printing block itself and/or with the impression.[38] A commercial printshop either in a hurry to beat its competitors to the market with a cheap edition or unable to pay for repairing old blocks or engraving new ones would ignore such considerations and might simply keep making impressions until they were nearly illegible. Figure 1 shows an impression pulled off a worn block, in which the strokes of characters carved in relief (black on white, or *yangke* 陽刻) become fatter and coarser, and the characters carved in intaglio (white on black, or *yinke* 陰刻) become somewhat thinner.[39]

Many surviving copies of Jianyang imprints from the Yuan and the Ming were late impressions produced from woodblocks that were not only worn from numerous impressions but split and never repaired (or originally made from split blocks and not well pinned together).[40] Figure 2 shows an example of a split block. Woodblocks were sometimes transferred from one printer to another (either borrowing or buying), sometimes over relatively long distances. For example, from the mid-Ming on, a number of Jianyang printers operated in Jinling (Nanjing) and probably other big cities in the Jiangnan area, and they may have carted the blocks between Fujian and various places in Jiangnan, despite the arduousness of such transports. Judging from the imprints, the resulting damage to the blocks was often not repaired. One such case was that of the blocks for the *Lu banjing* 魯班經 (Classic of Lu Ban). One modern scholar has shown that the same blocks were used by a Suzhou printer and a Jianyang printer and argues that the blocks were moved from Suzhou to Jianyang.[41] Another case, a well-documented one, is that of the

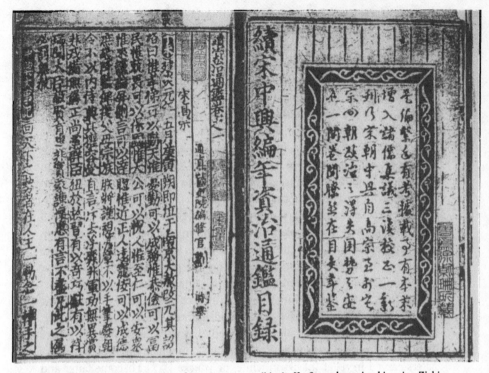

Fig. 1 Example of an impression from a worn woodblock. *Xu Song zhongxing biannian Zizhi tongjian* 續宋中興編年資治通鑑. Yuan. Publisher: Chen family Yuqing tang.

large Song encyclopedia, *Cefu yuangui* 冊府元龜 (Prime selections from the storehouse of literature), which was printed under official auspices in Jianyang in 1642 by the county magistrate. Upon leaving office, he carted the blocks home to Xinchang county in Jiangxi, where many of them were destroyed in a fire in 1660.[42]

Fire was an ever-present danger. For example, a disastrous fire in 1500 swept through Shufang destroying the printing blocks for many works.[43] In addition, chaos and destruction in times of political turmoil, such as the Yuan-Ming and Ming-Qing transitions, resulted in the loss of many woodblocks. This may explain the noticeable but temporary decline in the printing industry during the early Ming and its final demise at the beginning of the Qing. For example, the 1703 edition of the Jianyang county gazetteer noted that the woodblocks for 157 of 237 works by Jianyang authors and printed in Jianyang were missing or damaged.[44]

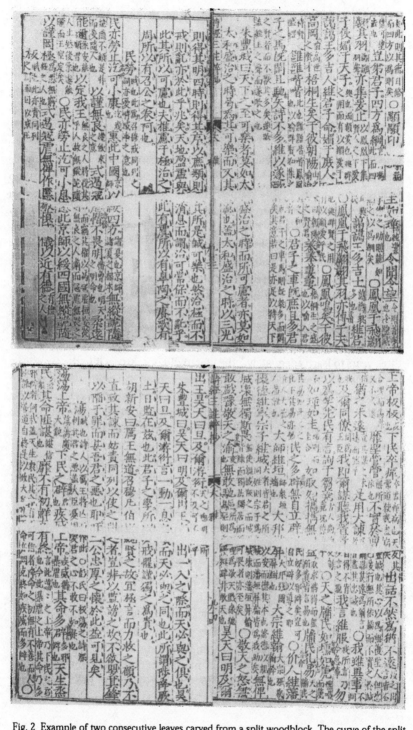

Fig. 2 Example of two consecutive leaves carved from a split woodblock. The curve of the split shows that the two leaves were carved in the same up and down direction. *Shijing san zhu cui chao* 詩經三註粹抄. 1590. Publisher: Yu family Cuiqing tang.

Woodblock Carving

Of the various processes required for producing a Chinese woodblock book, the one calling for the most skill is the carving of the characters and images. Thus the majority of the terms that have come to mean publishing a woodblock imprint refer to the engraving process: *kan* 刊, *ke* 刻, *diao* 雕, *juan* 鐫, *qie* 鍥, *qin* 鋟, *ming* 銘.[45] These words are also quite fitting since once the woodblocks for a book are carved, they are permanent in a way that movable type composed in a frame is not. For woodblock imprints, the idea of an "edition" and its date more properly relates to when the blocks were carved rather than to the date when the impressions were made, which could be any time after the blocks have been cut. Thus a work described in library catalogues and bibliographies as a *Song kanben* 宋刊本 is printed from blocks carved in the Song. In the absence of any evidence such as repairs that can be dated, materials added subsequently (including owners' seals), or possibly the printing paper, it would be hard to know when an impression was made from the blocks. In fact, as already noted, many extant copies of old Chinese books are late impressions made from woodblocks engraved much earlier.[46]

Although woodblock carving was a skill that required at least two to three years to learn adequately,[47] the literati did not respect it in the same way, for example, as they did seal-carving. Indeed, nearly all written references to blockcarvers tell of their careless, irresponsible, and sometimes even criminal attitude toward their craft. For example, Hong Mai 洪邁 (1123–1202), who was prefect of Jianning in 1175–80 and had at least one part of his huge collection, the *Yi Jian zhi* 夷堅志 (Records of Yi Jian), printed there, tells the story of carvers who were struck by lightning when they changed the wording of prescriptions in a medical text. Another engraver was forced by an official to make blocks for forging paper money.[48] In some imprints, the blockcarvers recorded their names, usually on the bottom part of the centerfold; one main purpose of this practice was to identify the person responsible for errors. In fact, in a series of the Classics published by Jianning prefecture during the Jiajing period, a note at the beginning of each work (Fig. 3) states this intention explicitly and cites the number of shoddy, error-filled commercial editions, many from the Jianning area itself.[49]

Another reason a blockcarver might inscribe his name on the centerfold of the leaf (Fig. 4a)[50] was for accounting purposes. Since he was paid according to the number of characters carved, this figure might be recorded along with his name on each leaf, or the total number of characters would be noted at the end of a section (Fig. 4b). Often the carver would not inscribe his full name. Thus Ye Chengmao 葉成茂 may simply carve "Ye" 葉, or

福建等處提刑按察司為書籍事照得五經四書士子第一切要
之書舊刻頗稱善本近時書坊射利改刻袖珍等板款制褊狹字
多差訛如巽與訛作巽語由古訛作猶古之類豈但有誤初學雖
士子在塲屋亦訛寫被黜其寫誤亦已甚矣該本司看得書傳海
内板在閩中若不精校另刊以正書坊之謬恐致益誤後學議呈
巡按察院詳允會督學道選委明經師生將各書一遵
欽頒官本重複校雙字畫句讀音釋俱頒明的書詩禮記四書傳說
欽制如舊易經加刻程傳恐只窮本義涉偏頗也春秋以胡傳為
主而在八公穀三傳附焉資條考也刻成令鐵刊市寫此牒仰本府
眷落當該官吏即將鈔去各書轉發建陽縣拘各刻書匠戶到官
每給一部嚴督務要照式翻刊縣仍選委師生對同方許刷賣書尾
就刻匠戶姓名查考再不許故違官式另自改刊如有違謬拿問
重罪追板刻毀决不輕貸仍取匠戶不致違謬結狀同依准繳來
嘉靖拾壹年拾貳月　日故牒建寧府

Fig. 3 Notice in front of each of the series of Classics published by the Jianning Prefecture government during the Jiajing period (1522–66) in the Ming, criticizing badly produced commercial editions and requiring the blockcarvers for this edition to record their names in the center strip.

(a)

Fig. 4 Recordings of blockcarver's name and number of characters carved.

(*a, left*) Blockcarver's name at the bottom of the center strip on leaves of the *Zhouyi jingzhuan zhuanyi* 周易經傳傳義. The same blockcarver, Yu Benli 余本立, was responsible for carving four leaves (1–4), which means that he carved two blocks (on both sides) in sequence, a common work practice. Publisher: Jianning Prefecture government. Ming Jiajing period (1522–66).

(*b, below*) *Chunqiu jingzhuan jijie* 春秋經傳集解. Southern Song. Publisher: Yu Renzhong of Wanjuan tang (National Central Library [Taipei] Rare Book Collection, no. 00580).

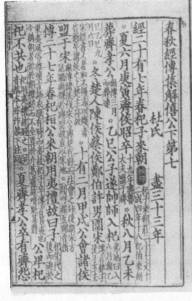

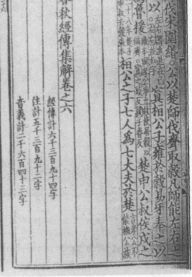

(b)

"Chengmao" 成茂, or "Ye Cheng" 葉成, or "Mao" 茂, or identify himself as "Ye wu" 葉五 (i.e., "Ye Number Five"); a certain amount of deduction and luck is needed to determine whether these variants refer to the same person. For example, since the carver usually worked on the text on both sides of a block, two consecutive leaves would have the same carver's name. Furthermore, it is not unusual that the same carver would work on two or occasionally three blocks of consecutive text. Thus if Ye Chengmao happened to have recorded his full name on one leaf, "Ye wu" on the next, and "Ye Mao" on the third, the identification is straightforward.

The recording of the engravers' names in an imprint is useful to scholars for several reasons. First, it is possible to date an imprint approximately if the name(s) of engraver(s) match those of another imprint with a known date. Second, in much the same way, the provenance of an imprint may be determined if it has the same group of carvers as another imprint whose place of origin is known.[51] Finally, by knowing how many different carvers worked on a given text, it is possible to estimate the minimum time required for producing the imprint, since the carving is the slowest step in the overall process. For example, in the Jianning prefecture set of the Classics mentioned above, each work had over 110 different carvers. Since each carver can cut 100 characters a day,[52] the shortest period that a work with 300 characters per leaf and 200 leaves could be carved would be about six days. Actually, the time required was much longer, since the evidence indicates that not all the carvers worked at the same time, and errors in the text had to be corrected.

In general, those imprints that recorded blockcarvers' names are those published by the central or regional governments and large religious works such as the Tripitaka and the Daoist Canon put out by temples (sometimes in collaboration with private donors or a government agency). Carvers' names are also recorded on certain high-quality imprints by private individuals. A survey of Song and Yuan imprints from the Jianning area (Appendix A) from two modern sources shows that those works (nos. 2, 7, 14, 27, 32, 33, 39, 41, 49, 64, 73, 79) recording blockcarvers' names tended to be published under official or semi-official auspices or by the Cai 蔡 family in particular.[53] For example, the *Zhouyi benyi* 周易本義 (The basic meanings of the *Zhouyi*; no. 2 in Appendix A) lists Wu Ge, a prefect of Jianning in the Xianchun period (1265–74) as the publisher. Another Jianning prefect of the Xianchun period, Wu Jian, published at least two works, including the *Zhangzi yulu* 張子語錄 (Recorded sayings of Master Zhang; no. 49).[54] Similarly, the *Yude tang zouyi* 育德堂奏議 (Memorials from the Yude tang; no. 41), was probably published by the Jianning prefectural office since it lists another Jianning prefect, of the Jiading period (1208–24), as the author and records the names of a number of blockcarvers who worked on an imprint published by the Jian'an prefectural school. The *Tao Jingjie xiansheng shizhu* 陶靖節先生詩註 (Poems of Tao Qian with commentaries; no. 73), annotated by a Fujian provincial official, was probably an edition reprinted in Jianning around 1265, to judge from the names of blockcarvers.[55] In 1180, while Hong Mai was prefect of Jianning, the first four parts of his *Yi Jian zhi* 夷堅志 (no. 64) were published at Jian'an, probably at some prefectural office or school.[56] Of the remaining works in Appendix A that have blockcarvers' names, two were printed by the Cai family (nos. 27 and 33) and one other (no. 39), which gives no printer, was collated (*jiaozheng* 校正) by one Cai Wenzi. The Cai family was noted for its publications from the Southern Song onward and seems to have been exceptional in recording blockcarvers' names in its products.

How many blockcarvers were working in a major printing center like Jianyang? We have no figures for the Song or Yuan, but the Jianning prefecture set of Classics from the Jiajing Period implies that in the mid-sixteenth century perhaps a few hundred carvers were in the Jianyang area at any given time, due to the opportunities for employment from government agencies, commercial printers, and private individuals. It is doubtful, however, that a single commercial printshop or an individual had the financial resources to employ anywhere close to a hundred blockcarvers at one time, and piecework employment was probably the norm.

For Jianyang commercial imprints in general, however, we encounter two major problems in learning about the blockcarvers. First, few works from any period recorded the carvers' names. It is therefore quite difficult to determine details such as exactly how many carvers worked on a given text for how long. There are several possible reasons for this omission of the carvers' (and copyists') names from the imprints. First, the quality of the books was such that the publishers were not concerned about holding the carvers and copyists responsible for their work. Second, these printshops operated on a sufficiently small scale that the owners probably deemed it unnecessary to record the carvers' names (although the number of characters per leaf or per section *was* sometimes recorded, as shown in Fig. 4b). Third, many carvers were either relatives or local men and women[57] well known to the publisher. The first possibility cannot be ruled out, but it seems an insufficient explanation, since carvers' names are absent from commercial imprints of all qualities. The second and third reasons are equally likely. For example, analysis of the lists of carvers' names recorded in any imprint from the Jianyang area reveals that many of them had the same surnames as a number of the Jianyang commercial publishers and were probably related to the latter. Unfortunately, this tie cannot be proven, because extremely few names of these blockcarvers appear in the Jianyang genealogies examined for this study. This absence may reflect the compilers' attitude that such men were not worthy of inclusion in the genealogy, since they were likely among the poorer and less educated members of the descent group.[58] Furthermore, men who worked as block-carvers often traveled throughout the country or even abroad and may not have returned to their homes, so that perhaps they were not remembered for long, if at all, in their family's records.[59]

In conclusion, the technique of carving both text and image on wood-blocks has changed very little for the thousand or more years that Chinese books have been produced. Block carving is the rate-determining step in the physical production of imprints, and it is probably the costliest in terms of material and labor. Thus, that block printing remained the dominant tech-nique for most of the late imperial period shows that it was an economically viable method for commercial book production for all this time. Of the two developments that became widespread in the Ming, color printing and the use of the calligraphic style known as *jiangti* (see Chapter 6), the former was an extension of the potential of woodblock printing, and the latter made carving more efficient and allowed more text to be packed onto a page with-out seeming too cramped or illegible. In fact, these modifications in block-carving techniques can be seen largely as responses to the pressures of a rap-idly expanding book market in the mid- and late Ming. In the following dis-cussion, some of the important changes and continuities in the appearance of the block-printed book are discussed, including two topics closely related to block carving: developments in calligraphic styles and in illustrations.

The Design of the Jianyang Block-Printed Book

Traditional connoisseurship and bibliographies of block-printed books de-voted much effort to recording the visual appearance of the product itself, in-cluding its size; the amount of text on a page; the calligraphic style; the ar-rangement of the main and auxiliary texts; the different reading aids, including running titles and punctuation; and the *tu* 圖, a term that refers to images, maps, diagrams, and tables.[60] These elements have not, however, been utilized to create what D. F. McKenzie designates as bibliography in its broadest sense, a "sociology of texts" that studies them "as recorded forms, and the processes of their transmission, including their production and re-ception."[61] And although we should not hastily and unquestioningly borrow concepts used in the study of the Western book, such as page layout, typog-raphy, *mise en page*, and paratext,[62] they can help us develop a sociology of the Chinese text. The following discussion is by no means a comprehensive treatment of this subject; rather, it describes how the various features listed above constitute a Chinese—and specifically, a Jianyang—block-printed book. The remainder of this chapter focuses, largely from the viewpoint of publishers, on the "*text* as a complex structure of meanings which embraces every detail of its formal and physical presentation in a specific historical context."[63] This discussion introduces some basic terminology and looks at Jianyang imprints from different periods to see how text and image were arranged and speculates on why publishers adopted such page designs. In later chapters, as we examine the Jianyang book trade in different historical periods, we will return to these issues and broaden the discussion to consider the readers as well as the producers of these imprints.

Manuscript and Imprint: The Continuing Bond

The components of a woodblock-printed book reflect the continuing bond between manuscript and imprint in China. An awareness of this relationship will help us gauge more accurately the ways print affected the presentation and reception of text and image and avoid attributing as innovations in print those elements of the *mise en page* already found in the pre-print manuscript. For instance, the practice of interlineal commentary, which is placed after the relevant portion of the main text (*zhengwen* 正文), long predates printing; it already existed in handwritten copies of the Classics.[64] So did punctuation of manuscript texts (sometimes in black and vermilion) by the scribe or emendator (rather than the reader). In fact, two-colored punctuation did not appear in printed editions until the Ming.[65] The dearth of extant manuscript copies of non-religious works (other than small fragments) makes it difficult to provide much further evidence for this argument, but we must be wary of distorting the impact of printing on the visual appearance of the Chinese book.

It is, instead, more useful to examine how the functions of that feature evolved and expanded in print. For example, the "picture above, text below" (*shangtu xiawen* 上圖下文) format, with an illustration on the top part of a page above the related text, was used in different kinds of Buddhist works, both handwritten and printed, from the Tang on. Surviving examples include prayer sheets, illustrated narratives, and charms, as well as sutras.[66] As non-religious printing began to flourish in the Song, this format was then used for other kinds of works, including the Confucian classics and popular encyclopedias, as well as the historical fiction known as *pinghua* 平話 (plain tales), of which the only extant examples are from the Jianyang area and date to the Yuan (Figs. 5a, b). By the Ming, the *shangtu xiawen* format was utilized in nearly all works intended for readers of varying literacy.

Fig. 5 Examples of illustrated historical fiction in the *shangtu xiawen* format from Jianyang.

(*a, right*) *Xinkan quanxiang Qin bing Liu guo pinghua* 新刊全相秦併六國平話. Yuan Zhizhi period (1321–23). Publisher: Yú family Wuben tang.

(*b, below*) *Quanxiang pinghua Sanguo zhi* 全相平話三國志. Yuan Zhizhi period (1321–23). Publisher: Yú family Wuben tang.

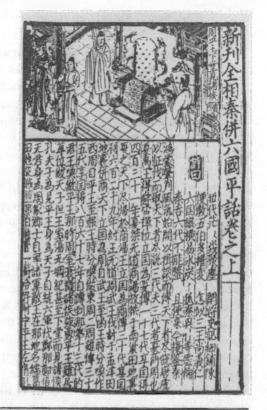

(a)

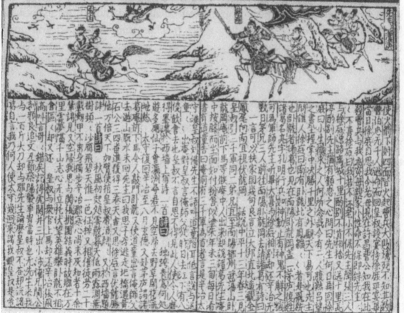

(b)

Moreover, the process of printing by facsimile woodcuts in which the original handwritten copy is pasted face down on the block to be engraved made the bond between the manuscript and the final printed version far more intimate than was the case in Western typographic printing, in which both the text and image could diverge drastically from the manuscript original and did so increasingly with time. Consequently, in woodblock printing it was a matter of course to borrow formats found in pre-print manuscripts. And conversely, as imprints became more widespread, manuscripts formally produced for public use would be "composed" in the format of printed works. Among the obvious examples are two huge works produced under imperial auspices: the *Yongle dadian* 永樂大典 (Yongle encyclopedia; compiled 1403–8) and the *Siku quanshu* 四庫全書 (Complete library of the four branches of literature; compiled 1773–82).

This link between printing and handwriting encouraged the persistent attitude that the finest imprint was one that most closely approximated a fine manuscript. Indeed, since the printed version is produced by a knife cutting through wood, the unavoidable jaggedness of the printed characters can only approach, however closely, the smooth brush stroke of the handwritten counterpart. Thus, in contrast to the Western typographic imprint, there never developed a set of aesthetics for evaluating the look of a Chinese woodblock imprint different from that applied to the look of a manuscript. Although certain styles of characters used nearly exclusively for printing did gradually develop, they were always measured against handwriting styles and found wanting.[67] Why the printing styles of characters developed and how they were utilized by the printers will be discussed below and in later chapters.

Looking at a Jianyang Imprint

Size. Throughout the thousand-plus years of the Chinese block-printed book, the appearance of the leaf or folio (ye 頁 or 葉) remained relatively constant (see Fig. 6).[68] The dimensions of such a leaf, which could vary widely, are usually measured by the framed area within the single- or double-ruled border, the size of the main text characters, the number of columns per page or half-leaf (*banye* 半頁/葉), and the number of characters per column. Broadly speaking, the page of an "average" Jianyang imprint from the Song through the Ming is approximately 20 cm high x 13–14 cm wide.[69] The "average size volume" (*zhongzi ben* 中字本) would have about 10 columns per page and 15–25 characters of main text per column; a large-character volume (*dazi ben* 大字本), fewer than 10 columns per page and usually fewer than

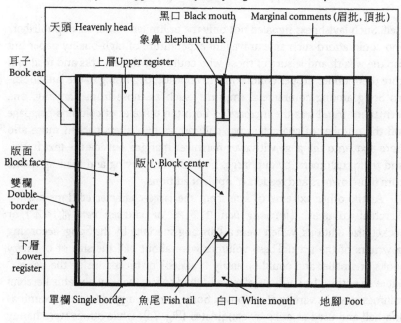

Fig. 6 Format of a leaf in a block-printed Chinese book.

15 characters per column); and a small-character volume (*xiaozi ben* 小字本), 14 to 15 columns per page and 25 to 30 characters per column.[70] Even a small character volume would have been quite legible.[71] In addition, the size of the book was such that it could be easily held in the hand. Of the extant Jianyang imprints from the Song on, the vast majority conforms to these average-frame measurements and are average-character volumes.[72]

　　Even without seeing a particular block-printed book, we can often size up its likely quality by the dimensions of the characters and the leaf. There are relatively few large-character editions of Chinese books, and those that qualify as such were either published under official auspices or by private individuals rather than by commercial printers. Deluxe editions produced by government offices, such as the large-character editions from the Northern Song Directorate of Education or even the handwritten *Yongle dadian* of the Ming made their official prestige manifest. Indeed, it is in such works that we can best appreciate the function of blank, white space. More of it highlights the individual black characters, endowing each with a distinctiveness missing when they are so jam-packed that they form an indifferent gray mass. In a choice edition, the blank space above and below the text frame is luxuriantly broad, making the overall height of the leaf half again as high as the block face itself. Such lavishness signaled not only the unlimited resources of publishers who could afford such an extravagant expenditure of high-quality paper but also the wealth and leisure of those who could buy these works and read and store them under proper conditions. In contrast, beginning in the late Southern Song among commercial imprints, such as those from Jianyang, one permanent trend was the increase in both the number of columns per page and the number of characters per column, as publishers packed more and more text onto the page with ever narrower margins outside the text frame. And their customers, by and large, had different buying and reading habits from those owners and readers of opulent editions.

At the other extreme of size from the large-character editions are the "kerchief volumes" (*jinxiang ben* 巾箱本 or *xiuzhen ben* 袖珍本), or pocket-size editions, which were a Jianyang specialty by the Song, according to writers of the time. These volumes were about half the size of ordinary books or smaller and could be easily "palmed" or tucked inside the sleeve.[73] But even within the confines of such limited space, the very portable kerchief volumes served a variety of purposes. Some were smuggled into the examination hall and used as cribs by candidates (Fig. 7a), while others were handy references or casual reading during travel (Fig. 7b).[74] In fact, their popularity increased with time, and by the mid-Ming nearly every kind of work, scholarly or popular, had been published in a pocket edition.

Components of a Jianyang imprint. Generally speaking, a traditional Chinese block-printed book has some or all of the following features:[75]

1. Front matter, including cover page (*fengmian ye* 封面頁); prefaces (*xu* 序 or 敘, *ti* 題, *yin* 引, *shuo* 說, among other terms); a statement of general editorial principles (*fanli* 凡例 or *fanyan* 凡言); supplementary or introductory materials (essays, maps, genealogies, list of personages mentioned in the main work, list of editorial credits, bibliography or sources cited, and the like); table of contents (*mulu* 目錄) and sometimes also an overall table of contents (*zongmu* 總目); and publisher's colophon and notes (which may also be placed at the end of the entire work).

2. Main contents, including the basic and auxiliary texts, as well as tables, charts, diagrams, pictures, maps.

3. Back matter, including postfaces (*ba* 跋, *houti* 後題, *houxu* 後序).

The following discussion is organized around the functions these various components serve, with illustrated examples to clarify the descriptions. A diachronic rather than a synchronic account will show how commercial publishers, as exemplified by those of Jianyang, redesigned and reorganized the

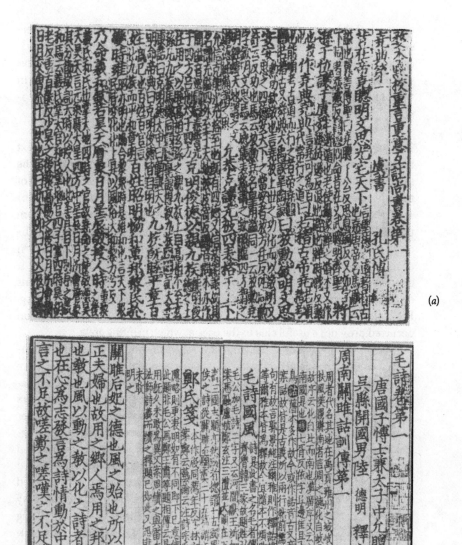

(a)

(b)

Fig. 7 Examples of kerchief volumes from the Song. (*a, top*) *Wuben dianjiao chongyan chongyi huzhu Shangshu* 婺本點校重言重意互註尚書. Southern Song. Page 10.2 cm h x 6.9 cm w. (*b, bottom*) *Mao shi* 毛詩. Southern Song. Page 14.3 cm h x 10.2 cm w.

contents of their imprints to meet the demands of the book market at different times. The task of explaining such developments in their specific historical context will be taken up more fully in later chapters, but even this brief description will make it apparent that both the changes and the continuities in the look of the Chinese block-printed book were driven by cultural and economic rather than technological factors.

Text. One noticeable trend over time is the growing regularization of the text toward the same number of evenly spaced characters in each column and the same spacing for the larger characters of the main text and the smaller ones of the interlineal commentary. Thus, whereas many Song imprints (e.g., Fig. 4b) are less consistent in this regard, far more from the Yuan and nearly all from the Ming are. This practice obviously made the production process more efficient, since it facilitated the design of the page, proofreading, and calculation of the copyists' and blockcarvers' pay based on the number of characters. It also expedited the preparation of other editions, even if there were deletions or additions, since such changes were easier to track in copying and proofing. For historians of the Chinese book, the period over which this regularization occurred provides a useful clue to the pace at which printing grew.

We have already noted the tendency, especially among commercial publishers, to cram as many characters on a page as possible, certainly far more than is normally feasible on a handwritten page. Moreover, the full complement of punctuation, short glosses, and longer commentaries in characters usually smaller than, and interrupting or surrounding, the main text further blackened the page and rendered it far less readable. In many cheap commercial editions, punctuation and copious annotations signaled not careful and thoughtful editing but rather the remnants of such practices in a bowdlerized and pirated edition. And in any case, surely there were readers who objected to their own diminished authority over a text that came pre-punctuated. Why publishers persisted in producing these confected editions in ever increasing numbers is a complex subject that we will explore in later chapters. The following discussion concentrates on describing how punctuation and auxiliary texts were presented in a printed book.

Of course, punctuation (*quandian* 圈點) existed long before the development of print,[76] but as the number of printed works grew, various punctuation marks acquired standard meanings. In the Song, these included the jot ╲ to separate phrases or, if placed alongside the characters, to indicate emphasis; the small open circle ○ to separate phrases; the large open circle ○ to separate sections of the same text or the main text and the interlineal commentary; short vertical dashes on the right side of characters to indicate a quotation; longer vertical lines on the side for emphasis and other purposes; and rectangular, circular, or oval boxes enclosing characters to denote proper names, the start of a new section, and the like. By extension, we can include characters carved in intaglio that serve as section headers (e.g., Figs. 1, 4b, and 5a, b). What is important, however, is not only if and how the text was punctuated by the producers of the imprint (publisher, author, editor) or reader, but also what effect these conventions had on reading practices. For example, in a (sparingly) punctuated Jianyang imprint from the Song,[77] *Chunqiu jingzhuan jijie* 春秋經傳集解 (Collected commentaries for the *Spring and Autumn Annals*; Fig. 4b), the open circle serves to separate glosses from different sources rather to separate phrases in a single passage. Although the main text is only occasionally separated by open circles, it is in effect punctuated into phrases by the annotations themselves. This practice raises the question of the functions of punctuation. Why are the longer commentaries also not punctuated? It is true that these auxiliary texts are often easy to understand on first reading, but they at times include lengthy quotations from other sources, which may be just as hard as the main text to comprehend. Furthermore, since most of those who studied the Classics and Four Books had memorized large portions of these works in childhood and probably read a work for the commentaries more than for the main text, it would seem that it is the commentary that requires clarification through punctuation. Finally, Song and Yuan texts generally have less and simpler punctuation than mid- and late Ming texts, some of which are overpunctuated with a variety of symbols that can distract from a rapid reading of the text. But even this observation may be an overgeneralization, as we will shortly see.

Although punctuation serves as the most concise form of commentary on a text, a wide variety of commentaries in words are also found in Chinese imprints: before, after, between, and on the side of the main text, as well as above the text frame.[78] These commentaries range from terse glosses on the pronunciation and meaning of a character or phrase to brief citations of the sources of quotations and allusions to lengthy explications or critiques of the main text. Gradually, as the accumulation of commentaries threatened to obscure the legibility of the main text and of one another, they were spatially reorganized into two or more registers on the page (Fig. 8a) or placed at the end of the *juan* 卷.[79] Indeed, by the Ming, reading a Chinese work with its full critical apparatus of punctuation and commentaries (*pidian* 批點 or *pingdian* 評點) had become such an enterprise that a number of publishers or editors felt the need of an explanation of general editorial principles—the *fanli* 凡例 or *fanyan* 凡言 located in the front matter (Fig. 8b). In turn, the

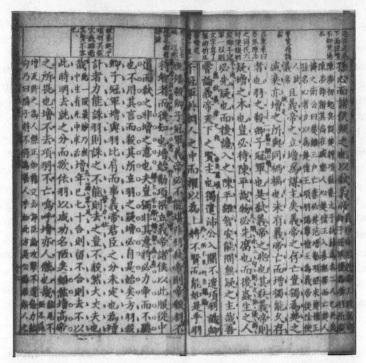

(a)

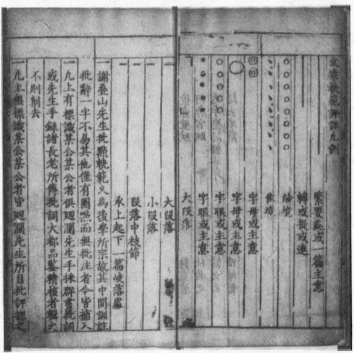

(b)

Fig. 8 Sample page of punctuated text and explanation of punctuation. *Xin hui Lan xiansheng ji baijia pingzhu wenzhang guifan* 新迴瀾先生集百家評註文章軌範. 1608. Publisher: Liu Longtian of Qiaoshan tang (Naikaku bunko, 360 函 7號).

hierarchy of texts indicated by the arrangement of the different kinds of commentaries in relation to the main text and to one another and by the different sizes of the characters in which they were printed, not to mention the rearrangements of these elements in later editions, form a supra-layer of commentary on the work itself, as well as the ways it was read in different periods.

We can also trace the elaboration of commentaries, and their inclusion in a growing variety of works over time. Although the tradition of appending lexical and exegetical commentaries belonged originally to the Classics and Histories, auxiliary texts were appearing in a variety of other works by the Song. The publisher's decision to incorporate commentaries depended on a number of factors. First, did a particular work traditionally have commentaries? The Classics, for example, were almost never printed without commentaries (*baiwen* 白文). Second, what need was there to explain a particular work to the intended reader (or listener)? Thus the publisher might deem short glosses identifying persons, places, and other terms in a collection of stories for schoolchildren as necessary as long commentaries and subcommentaries in a scholarly work. Third, commentaries (and punctuation) often were selling points in a competitive bookmarket. A buyer might see more of both (whatever the quality) as adding to the value of a book, as might the fact that the commentaries were (supposedly) written by famous authors of the time. Commentaries and elaborate punctuation could lend a certain cachet to the work—a cachet that changed with the times as well as reading conditions (and perhaps audience). For example, whereas the historical "plain tales" published in a running illustration format during the Yuan in Jianyang had neither punctuation nor commentaries (Figs. 5a, b), late Ming fictional works in the same format from Jianyang publishers sometimes had both. By the mid-sixteenth century, such confected editions were common, whether they were the lower-quality Jianyang ones or the fancier productions with full-page illustrations and far handsomer page layouts that came out of Nanjing or Suzhou. Clearly, commercial publishers of the Ming thought certain types of fiction worthy of commentary and punctuation. On the other hand, the lavishly produced late Ming editions of dramas and drama miscellanies often boasted of a panoply of (sometimes multicolored) commentaries and punctuation, while cheaper contemporary editions had at most some sparse punctuation. Economics is one reason for this difference, but at least as important are the different circumstances under which the two types of publications were read—the lavish editions were intended to be perused leisurely and nuances of the text savored with the help of the commentaries and the accompanying full-page or full-leaf illustrations, while the cheaper and often smaller editions may have served as reading for the road. Finally, a reader might welcome the commentaries and punctuation as instruction in educated taste or guides to the correct interpretation for the government examinations. The punctuating or annotating of a text in print "thus extends from a very personal level designed for private consumption all the way to a highly professionalized degree of commentary writing and diversification in terms of markets."[80]

Several features of the imprint that served as practical aids for the printer or reader remained largely unchanged throughout the history of the block-printed book. Information given in the center strip or *banxin* 版心 (Fig. 6) helps us to understand how the leaves of the imprint were produced and assembled. As noted above, the bottom of the strip may show the copyists' and the blockcarvers' names and occasionally the (abbreviated) name of the printshop, and the character count per leaf may be recorded at the top. In the middle of the strip, the *juan* and folio numbers and often a running title for that *juan* or section of the work would be recorded.

Other long-standing practices served not so much the reader's needs as the publisher's; they functioned chiefly to facilitate the assembling of the leaves into book form. For example, the foliation or numbering of leaves begins anew with each *juan* rather than continue seriatim from the previous *juan*. Furthermore, most books have a table of contents, but it never gives page numbers, although it may provide a detailed listing of the work's topics, down to subsections of each *juan*. Such an omission suggests that different *juan* were assigned to different copyists. It also made it easier for a publisher to add or drop a *juan* in his particular "edition." Finally, despite the use of the many other textual apparatuses described above, no traditional Chinese book (and too few modern ones) have an index.

The look of the *banxin* is also useful for identifying Jianyang imprints from different periods. Most Song imprints have one or two fish tails (*yu-wei* 魚尾) to help fold the leaf in half accurately, but few except Jianyang imprints had black strip(s) on the top or bottom of the *banxin* (Fig. 6). Because so many of these *heikou ben* 黑口本 were from Jianyang, this feature has been used to identify them as such. Indeed, a number of imprints of uncertain provenance have too readily been labeled *Jianyang heikou ben* in bibliographies without sufficient evidence. Nevertheless, the *heikou* in conjunction with other evidence is useful in determining whether a Song or Yuan imprint is from the Jianyang area.[81] During the Song and Yuan, the "elephant trunk" (*xiangbi* 象鼻) in Jianyang imprints was relatively thin or *xi* 細 (about 1 mm); those in Ming editions tended to be broader. But did these minutiae matter to any reader? Perhaps only a bibliophile would be fully alert to such details, but in a more impressionistic way, even a more casual peruser of the work could recognize a Jianyang imprint, for better or for worse, by glancing at the *banxin*, the style of the characters, and other elements of the page. And such recognition was valuable to commercial publishers.

Yet another convenience in many Song and Yuan (but far fewer Ming) Jianyang imprints is the ear (*erzi* 耳子 or *shuer* 書耳), outside the text frame, which serves much the same purpose as the running head on the top of pages of modern books. Although it cannot be proved conclusively, the *erzi* has sometimes been considered a Jianyang innovation, and perhaps it served as yet another attraction to potential customers.[82] As shown in Fig. 4b, the *erzi* is now on the inside edge and the centerfold is the exposed outer edge of the bound book, but the *erzi* was originally on the outside edge in butterfly and back-wrapped bindings. Upon rebinding into a thread-bound format, the positions of the centerfold and book-ear are reversed.[83]

Developments in calligraphic styles and their uses in different sections of a printed book tell much about the changing strategies of commercial publishers. For instance, a distinctive calligraphic style for the body text serves to identify the provenance of a Chinese imprint.[84] Thus during the Song, two prevalent styles of regular script (*kaiti* 楷體) were found in high-quality Jianyang imprints, which endowed these books with a characteristic look that distinguishes them from the despised *Mashaben*.[85] On the other hand, the far less lovely characters found in the inferior commercial imprints are also easily recognizable. By the late Southern Song and the Yuan, the styles of the characters had often become noticeably more utilitarian and economical and sparing of aesthetic considerations (Fig. 5). And by the late fifteenth century, commercial imprints produced throughout the country sported one version or another of the "craftsman styles" (*jiangti*), which allowed the characters to be written and carved far more quickly and efficiently.

The printer or publisher was identified in various ways, such as the colophon (*paiji* 牌記), which was sometimes enclosed within a distinctively decorated box (colophon block or cartouche), or the cover page (*fengmian ye*).[86] In Jianyang imprints, the publisher's colophon may be found at the end of the preface(s) or the table of contents, at the end of the work, or at the end of some or all *juan*. Some colophons, especially those in Southern Song publications, could be quite simple—one or two lines, giving the name of the printshop, sometimes of the individual printers as well, and the date when the blocks were engraved.[87] But in the Yuan and Ming, in the colophon or a more blatant advertising notice (*gaobai* 告白), a publisher would explain why he produced the work and, as commercial publishing became increasingly competitive, extol the merits of his edition and denigrate those of his competitors.

The publisher could also be identified in two other parts of the paratext. First, he might list his name or that of his shop alongside that of the author and collators at the beginning of the first *juan* (*juanduan* 卷端) and possibly all the *juan* as well. Second, within the prefaces and less often among the postfaces written in conjunction with a particular edition, the publisher's role might be mentioned, although nearly always in passing—for example, that the publisher had found and had revised the work in order to disseminate it (*yi guang qi chuan* 以廣其傳).[88] The explicit identification of a commercial publisher in an imprint is usually brief and almost incidental, other than in the colophon and advertisement. And even in these two sections, the information is severely limited and the sales pitch cliché-ridden. Commercial publishers, even the many from Jianyang, remain shadowy figures. Yet the features of the block-printed book argue for a publisher deeply involved in compilation, design, and printing. In fact, it is by closely examining these features that we can become best acquainted with these men, as we will do in the next four chapters.

Finally, commercial publishers may have preferred not to identify themselves in certain kinds of imprints, such as kerchief volumes that served as examination cribs, or editions that were patently and often sloppily plagiarized from earlier ones, or works that had been proscribed by the government. Or perhaps the printer had come by the blocks in such a way that he preferred not to record his name and would leave an unsightly blank within the cartouche. For such books, perhaps the publisher's name had no effect on sales.

Tu 圖. Features collectively known as *tu*—illustrations, maps, diagrams, and tables—are found in Chinese imprints from the Song onward.[89] They occupied anywhere from an entire leaf to part of a page and were usually carved together with the text on the same block. Thus, in a carefully designed page, the body text and the *tu* could be closely integrated, more so than in many early Western imprints when the illustration on a woodcut, wood engraving, metal engraving, or etching was a separate physical element from the text composed with movable type and locked into a form, even if they were printed together in a press.

Since the woodcut was the medium for *tu*, the images were overwhelmingly conceived as black-line figures with limited tonal gradations.[90] Although skilled cutters were capable of very fine and delicate carving, this black-line approach (which was required for the text) resulted in the rendering of images in certain ways and a development of an aesthetic "syntax" different from that for other media, such as painting and pottery. Unlike the master craftsmen who drew designs and engraved the blocks, the vast majority of blockcarvers did only the cutting. Indeed, the division of labor between the scribe preparing the paper copy and the blockcarver implies that the two must have reached some general understanding of how to translate text and image on paper into a standardized linear system to facilitate and routinize the carving. Hence there was less opportunity for technical and artistic innovation than was the case when the copyist/draftsman and carver were one and the same. In turn, the technical limitations of block-printed images in reproducing paintings in a way acceptable to connoisseurs may have prevented them from noticing *tu* in general or at least in discussing them at any length in their writings. On the other hand, comparatively simple, schematic expository pictures and diagrams in all kinds of works, as well as illustrations in more "popular" works, were easily accepted.

Although the quality of the images varied, those in commercial imprints were on the whole relatively simple, with no pretense to great artistic merit. Indeed, their very simplicity allowed them to be copied quickly from work to work.[91] For example, two different Southern Song imprints from Jianyang, *Shangshu tu* 尚書圖 (Illustrated *Book of Documents*) and *Mao Shi juyao tu* 毛詩舉要圖 (Illustrated essentials of the *Book of Poetry* with commentaries by Mao) have similar illustrations (Figs. 9a, b). In fact, even when printers of the Yuan and Ming claimed to have carefully collated the main text and commentaries and added new annotations, they still used the same *tu* as in the Song editions, a clear admission of their strictly utilitarian function. Rather than detailed pictures depicting what the musical instruments looked like, schematic representations of images already familiar to the reader are provided for quick recognition. Similarly, the pictures of the Grand Carriage of the Son of Heaven in *Shu jizhuan fu yinshi* 書集傳附音釋 (*Book of Documents* with collected commentaries and phonetic glosses) (Fig. 9c) and in two editions of *Xunzi* 荀子 (Figs. 9d–e) show how the same tableau can be inserted in different books.[92]

The pages illustrated in Figs. 9c–e are in the *shangtu xiawen* format, which commercial publishers exploited for a wide variety of books. For example, works of fiction with running illustrations above the text were printed in Jianyang by the Yuan, if not earlier, and became even more prevalent in the Ming (Figs. 10a, b). Indeed, the popularity of medical texts, school primers, fortune-telling manuals, household encyclopedias, drama miscellanies, and other kinds of works in this format during the Ming suggests that such imprints may have been looked at almost as often as they were read. Moreover, even for those reading the text, glancing at the pictures could provide relief from the crowded, unattractive text underneath.

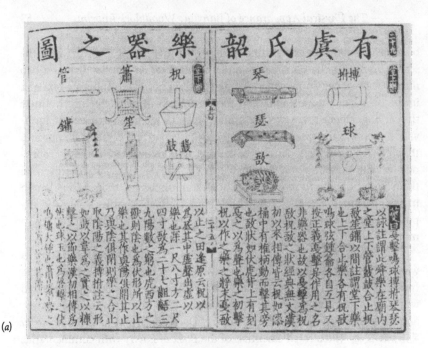

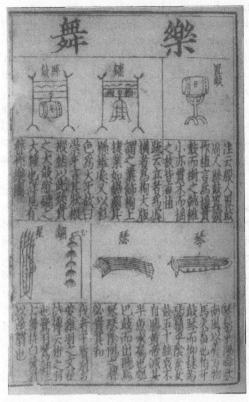

Fig. 9, pt. I Similar illustrations in two different Song Jianyang imprints.

(*a, above*) *Shangshu tu* 尚書圖. Southern Song Shaoxi period (1190–94). Publisher: Yú family.

(*b, left*) *Mao Shi juyao tu* 毛詩舉要圖. Southern Song (Seikadō bunko).

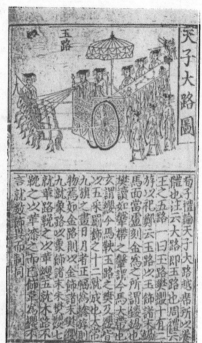

Fig. 9, pt. II. Similar illustrations of the Grand Carriage in Yuan and Ming imprints.

(*c, above left*) *Chongkan Ming ben Shu jizhuan fu yinshi* 重刊明本書集傳附音釋. Yuan.

(*d, above right*) *Zuantu huzhu Xunzi* 纂圖互注荀子. Early Ming reprint of Southern Song Jianyang edition.

(*e, right*) *Zuantu huzhu Xunzi* 纂圖互注荀子. Early Ming edition.

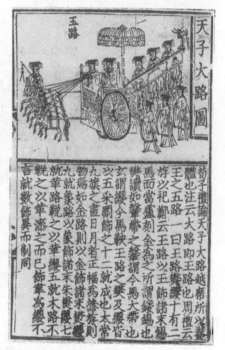

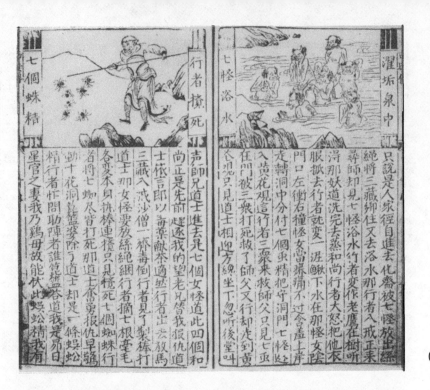

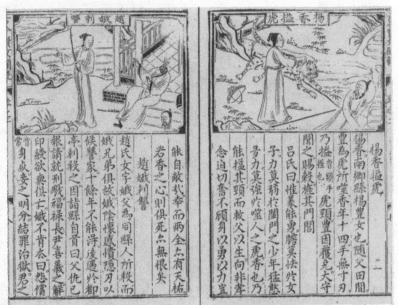

Fig. 10 Examples of Ming Jianyang imprints in the *shangtu xiawen* format. (*a, top*) *Dingqie quanxiang Tang Sanzang xiyou zhuan* 鼎鍥全相唐三藏西遊傳 (see also Fig. 41). Ming. Publisher: Liu Liantai. (*b, bottom*) *Guifan* 軌範. Ming Wanli period (1573–1619). Publisher: Zheng Yunzhai of Baoshan tang.

The insertion of *tu* in different registers on a congested page (Figs. 11a, b) served much the same purpose. Moreover, by the Ming, in many non-scholarly popular works, the relationship between the different registers on a single page may have been slight or nonexistent. We will see in Chapter 6 that this variegated deployment of textual and pictorial elements on their printed page was a popular tactic of commercial publishers to make their imprints more attractive and more entertaining, as well as to convince potential buyers that they were getting their money's worth.

As Craig Clunas points out, the functional *tu* that serve to illustrate the text or convey related information should be distinguished from the more highly regarded *hua* 畫, which also appeared in books.[93] The *tu*, which pre-date printing, were largely taken for granted, and publishers often failed to mention in a book's title that it contained *tu*, unless that was an important selling point. This is certainly true for many Jianyang commercial imprints that contained *tu*, including the Classics, dictionaries, histories, handbooks on family rituals, military treatises, medical texts, works on divination and the calendar, household encyclopedias, and the collected writings of individuals (*bieji* 別集). The notable exception was fiction and plays and ballads in the *shangtu xiawen* format, whose titles would often note that they were "completely illustrated" (*quanxiang* 全像).[94] Only a handful of the illustrations in Jianyang imprints aspired to any high aesthetic level. If anything, the publishers seem rather to have opted for efficiency and economy in producing these *tu* by replicating near identical illustrations from work to work.

In fact, a number of images—both pictures of actual objects and abstract figures—that had appeared in printed materials as early as the Tang continued to be found in imprints for centuries afterward. For example, the animals of the Chinese zodiac shown in a privately printed calendar for the year 877[95] are seen in a Yuan encyclopedia of the 1330s (Fig. 12a) and a Ming Wanli period compendium of commentaries on the *Book of Documents* (Fig. 12b). Moreover, that image and auxiliary text were thus lumped together shows how much they were considered part and parcel of the entire page or leaf along with the related main text, as is usually the case with materials that are block-printed. Finally, the same image, for example, a palm serving as a mnemonic device, could be used in different kinds of works, such as an arithmetic manual (Fig. 13a), a divination text (Fig. 13b), and a rhyming dictionary (Fig. 13c). Thus the power of print is not limited to the dissemination of exactly reproducible images but also extends to the transmission of similar images whose meanings can be easily transformed or traduced.[96]

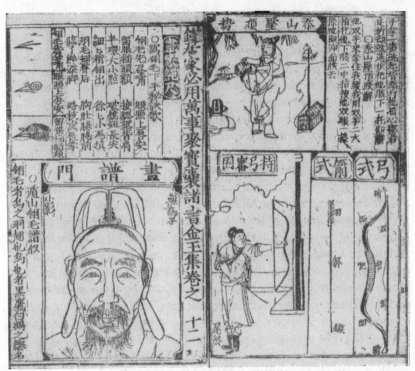

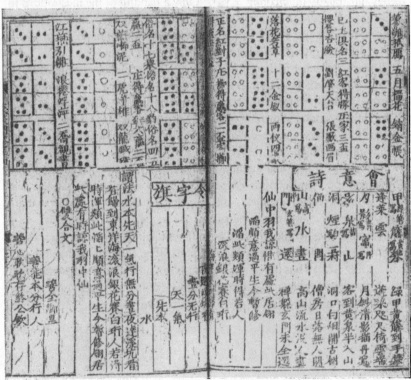

Fig. 11 *Xinkan simin bianyong bu qiu ren bolan quanshu* 新刊四民便用不求人 博覽全書.
Late Ming. Publisher: Xiong.

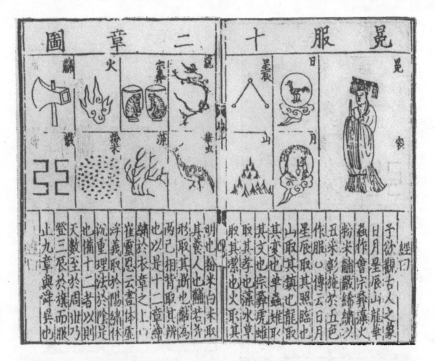

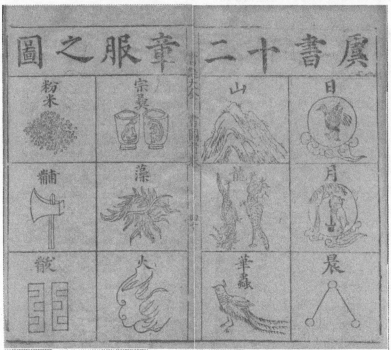

Fig. 12 Pictures of the animals of the Chinese zodiac from a Yuan and a Ming work (cf. the calendar of 877 in Fig. 1113, p. 153 of Tsien Tsuin-hsuen, *Paper and Printing*). (*a, top*) *Shilin guangji* 事林廣記. Yuan Zhishun period (1330–33). Publisher: Chunzhuang shuyuan. (*b, bottom*) *Shujing daquan* 書經大全. Ming Wanli period (1573–1619). Publisher: Yu family.

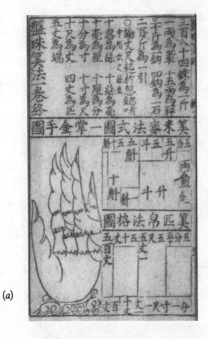

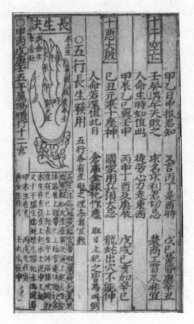

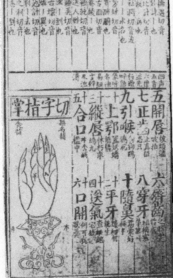

Fig. 13 Using the same image in three different contexts.

(*a, top left*) *Panzhu suanfa shimin liyong* 盤珠算法士民利用. Ming Wanli period (1573–1619). Publisher: Xiong Tainan (Naikaku bunko, 子 56 函 5 號).

(*b, top right*) *Duanyi shenshu* 斷易神書. Ming Wanli period. Publisher: Liu Longtian of Qiaoshan tang (Naikaku bunko, 305 函 284 號).

(*c, left*) *Yunhai pian zhengzong* 韻海篇正宗. 1598. Publisher: Yu Xiangdou of Santai guan.

The largely emblematic function of certain illustrations is made clear by their placement in an imprint and by the choice of details to include or omit. For example, a sixteenth-century artist's impression in drawing the (not very) "veritable portrait of Mr. Shantang" 山堂先生眞像 (Zhang Ruyu 章如愚, *js* 1196) to appear at the beginning of his encyclopedic compilation, *Qunshu kaosuo* 群書考索,[97] or of pre-eminent *Daoxue* thinkers of the Song (Zhu Xi and Cheng Yi 程頤) is deemed quite adequate. Zhu Xi, of course, is instantly recognizable by the seven warts, but these appear on opposite sides of his face in two imprints by the same publisher.[98] The commemorative purpose is served by the mere inclusion of these pictures, which need not resemble the subjects portrayed.[99]

In Chinese books, the uses of *tu* were determined not only by the nature of block-printing technology but also by the subservience of the *tu* to the text. That is, one reads a Chinese book for the words, which may or may not be illustrated by pictures and diagrams. The simpler and more schematic certain *tu* were, the more efficiently they served to clarify the text. Thus the *tu* in most books had neither the talismanic character nor the potential to induce meditation possessed by pictures in other printed materials such as religious images and New Year's pictures.[100] This characterization of the *tu* in block-printed books does not mean that these images and diagrams were not sometimes looked at (or "read") in preference to the text, nor that some *tu* transcended the usual limitations of their kind (as we will see in Chap. 6), but it does explain the purposes and limitations of *tu* as intended by their makers.

A historian of the book must read all its components in every possible way: the text and punctuation of the main work and its commentaries, of the front and back matters, of the publisher's notes, and of the captions and inscriptions for the illustrations; the images; and the blank space between the texts and images—and how all of them are arranged with respect to one another. Only with this comprehensive reading can we understand the nature of the book. In this chapter we have begun such a reading for Chinese block-printed books.

As we have seen, the most highly valued of Chinese block-printed books were those that displayed the same characteristics as well-made manuscripts—beautiful calligraphy printed or written with brilliantly black ink on high-quality white paper. Because woodblocks are carved by tracing handwritten characters and hand-drawn images, it is easier to remain faithful to the original, and there is less compelling reason to modify a block-printed book for production convenience than is the case with a movable-type book. Hence, such changes as modifications of calligraphic style or the page layout, when they occurred, resulted more often for non technological reasons such as economic pressures on commercial publishers to print more books more quickly, changing intellectual approaches to how to read and use a text, and growing aesthetic sophistication in looking at images. In this chapter, the economic factor has been fairly evident. Other factors are explored in their historical contexts in the next four chapters.

If the very wide propagation and multiplication of a given text is considered one of the most important functions of the printed book, it is ironic that in imperial China, the highest-quality books were most often produced by those who were not always concerned about this aspect of publishing—the central and regional governments and religious organizations sponsoring the printing of the Buddhist Tripitaka or the Daoist Canon. Often, their main concern was the preservation of the correct and well-collated version of a valuable text, which could be done by carving the text either in stone (as were the Classics) or on woodblocks for printing.[101] One can argue that the shift from stone to wood represented a change in technology but a continuity of purpose. Such well-produced texts did at times spur technological innovations, such as improving the technique of movable-type printing, which, however, may have been more costly and elaborate than existing methods of production.

In contrast, commercial publishers, whose main purpose was to profit from selling as many copies as possible of a work, often skimped on materials and economized with crowded page layouts. By squeezing as many characters per column and as many columns per page as possible and adding glosses and annotations in even smaller characters, they succeeded in producing many of the least legible books in Chinese history. At the same time, however, it would be hasty to conclude that improvements in the printed book owed nothing to these commercial publishers. The changes, for better or worse, in the way texts and images were read and looked at and the resulting changes in thinking about and responding to printed materials owe much to these men.

Part II

3

The Development of the
Jianyang Book Trade, Song-Yuan

Hong Mai, in his huge collection of anecdotes of strange occurrences, the *Yi Jian zhi*, tells the story of a young girl suddenly struck deaf and dumb who recovers after her uncle prays to the bodhisattva Guanyin for a month. To broadcast this miracle, the uncle has a broadsheet printed up (*lou ban yi guang qi chuan* 鏤板以廣其傳). In the next story, a man who has lost his only son visits a Buddhist temple. There, a monk gives him a picture of Guanyin that he claims is extremely efficacious and tells him to print it for distribution. As a result of this meritorious act, his wife gives birth to another son exactly one year after the death of their firstborn, and later the couple has two more sons. These stories illustrate two of the diverse uses of printing in China, a medium that was already some four hundred years old by the time the *Yi Jian zhi* was written. What was new in the Song, however, was not the printing of flyers or pictures of deities but the tremendous growth in the printing of books. The great popularity of the *Yi Jian zhi* itself was demonstrated by the printing of the work in installments in different parts of the country as Hong Mai was writing it. The preface to the 1180 Jianyang edition mentions earlier editions printed in Sichuan, Lin'an (Hangzhou), and Fujian (probably in Jianyang in 1166).[1]

The widespread printing of books in the Song, first by government and religious organizations and then by commercial publishers,[2] exerted an enormous impact on many aspects of Chinese culture that is only beginning to be explored.[3] During this period, books of all kinds were being printed, although both government and commercial publishers heavily favored the Classics, Histories, and reference works such as dictionaries and encyclopedias. The range of offerings of commercial publishers, however, was broader and included belles lettres, collections of anecdotes, and almost all works related to the government examination system that government offices would not publish. The larger repertoire covered by commercial imprints, as well as their lower prices, meant that they exerted at least as great an influence on the cultural life of the times as government publications. New ways of reading, writing, editing, presenting information on the printed page, and communicating an author's ideas and reputation to the world—not to mention cheating on examinations—resulted from the prevalence of commercial imprints.

The growth of commercial printing began in the Northern Song in the eleventh century but accelerated dramatically in the Southern Song. One scholar has estimated there were some thirty printing centers in the Northern Song and some two hundred in the Southern Song.[4] Although there is no simple clear-cut way to measure the relative importance of these places, it is clear that five areas of the country far outstripped the others in the quantity of books published.[5] Not surprisingly, the first, by a wide margin, was the Liangzhe circuit (modern Zhejiang and southern Jiangsu), the wealthiest and most populous area of the country in the Song. Hangzhou's importance as an official, religious, and commercial printing center had already been established by the mid–Northern Song and was enhanced when it became the Southern Song capital.[6] The second-ranking region was Fujian, which beat out the Jingji circuit (where the Northern Song capital, Kaifeng, was located), as well as two other prosperous and populous regions, Chengdu fu circuit in Sichuan and Jiangnan West circuit (modern Jiangxi and bits of Jiangsu, Hunan, and Anhui). In Fujian, several of the important printing centers were urban areas on or near the coast: Putian, Jinjiang/Quanzhou, Longqi/Zhangzhou, and most important of all, the circuit capital, Fuzhou. Dwarfing all of them by the mid–Southern Song, however, was Jianning prefecture[7] in northwestern Fujian, particularly Masha and somewhat later, Shufang[8] (both in Jianyang County),[9] Jian'an, and to a lesser extent, Chongan and Pucheng (see Maps 1 and 2).

This remote, mountainous area, bordering on Jiangxi and Zhejiang, was a haven for salt and tea smugglers, bandits, rebels, and vagrants. Officials appointed to serve there were of the opinion that it was ungovernable and that the natives were violent, superstitious, and rebellious. Except for the highly prized tribute tea from Beiyuan in Jian'an county, the central government largely ignored the region. How, then, did the Jianyang region become one of the largest commercial printing centers in the country? And why did this book trade continue unabated and even grow during the Yuan, contrary to the generally held view that literati culture with its vital dependence on education and official success was in abeyance? And why (though this part of the story is for another chapter) did the Jianyang printing industry revive spectacularly in the mid-Ming after a long lull, reach an unprecedented scale, and then die off suddenly in the early Qing? The answers to these questions are important, not only for learning about the exceptionally long-lived and far-reaching Jianyang book trade but also for understanding a book culture that spanned over eleven hundred years, numerous dialects, and varying literacies of many different readers.

This chapter discusses the rise and rapid growth of commercial printing in the Jianyang area during the Song and Yuan. During this period of some 250 years, some of the best Jianyang books were printed, and a number of the commercial practices that would develop further in the Ming were already quite evident. The Song and Yuan are treated together because of such important continuities as publisher families who operated during both dynasties and the kinds of books they produced. Despite some turmoil in Minbei during the Song-Yuan transition, the evidence suggests that the Jianyang book trade was not disrupted to any noticeable extent. On the other hand, although no abrupt changes occurred in the Jianyang printing industry between the Southern Song and the Yuan, there were some significant developments, partly attributable to or reinforced by the changing political and cultural climate. Thus, the nature of both the continuities and changes makes it useful to discuss the Jianyang publishing industry during the Song and Yuan together in this chapter. In contrast, the Jianyang book trade suffered a long decline at the beginning of the Ming, and when it recovered in the sixteenth century, it was significantly different.

We will begin with a brief description of Minbei during the Song and Yuan, with an emphasis on those aspects affecting the book trade. The next part concentrates on Jianyang publishers connected with commercial printshops, family schools, and private academies. Despite the important role these men played in transmitting the scholarly and popular cultures of their times, we know little about their intellectual and social background and their position in the literati world. This section uses the available information to sketch out the social history of some Jianyang publishers, particularly those from the Liu, Yu, and Xiong families, who were active in the book trade for several centuries. Publishers operating under official auspices, such as prefectural and circuit officials and government schools, are discussed in much less detail because their imprints do not necessarily reflect the characteristics of the evolving Jianyang book trade.

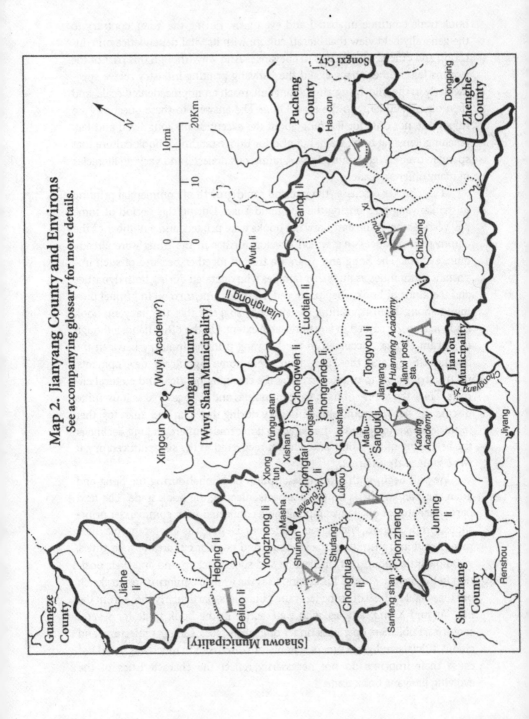

Map 2. Jianyang County and Environs
See accompanying glossary for more details.

N

10mi
20Km
10
0
0

Guangze County

Jiahe li

[Shaowu Municipality]

Beiluo li

Heping li

Yongzhong li

Xingcun

(Wuyi Academy?)

Xiong 'tun

Masha

Shuinan

Yungu shan

Xishan

Dongshan

Mayang Xi

Chongtai li

Shufang

Chonghua li

Likou

Houshan

Shufang

Chonan County
[Wuyi Shan Municipality]

Jiangzhong li

Chongwen li

Chongrende li

Luotian li

Tongyou li

Jianyang Huanfeng Academy

Jianxi post sta.

Kaoting Academy

Matou

Sangu li

Chonzheng li

Junting li

Sanfeng shan

Shunchang County

Renshou

Jiyang

Jian'ou Municipality

Chongyang Xi

Chizhong

Nanpu Xi

Xi

Sanqu li

Wufu li

Pucheng County

Hao cun

Songxi Cty.

Dongping

Zhenghe County

J I A N Y A N G

Map 2 Glossary

Feature	Location/description
Aofeng Academy 鰲峰書院	in Xiong tun, Chongtai district, Jianyang county
Beiluo li* 北雒里	district in Jianyang county
Chizhong, Houjing cun* 池中、後井村	in Shuiji township 水吉鎮; important site of Jian pottery kilns in the Song
Chongan xian* 崇安縣	in Jianning prefecture; now Wuyi Municipality
Chongchuan 崇川	in Chonghua district, Jianyang county
Chonghua li* 崇化里	district in Jianyang county
Chongtai li* 崇泰里	district in Jianyang county
Chongzheng li* 崇政里	district in Jianyang county
Da Tan shan 大潭山	just west of Jianyang county seat
Dongping zhen* 東平鎮	township in Zhenghe county
Dongshan* 東山	in Chongtai village district, Jianyang county
Haocun* 濠村	in Pucheng county
Heping li* 和平里	district in Jianyang county
Hualong Academy 化龍書院	at the base of Xishan (q.v.)
Huanfeng Academy* 環峰書院	in Tongyou district, Jianyang county
Jiahe li* 嘉禾里	district in Jianyang county
Jianxi post station* 建溪驛	Shuinan street 水南街, south of Jianyang county seat
Jianyang county* 建陽縣	
Jiyang zhen* 吉陽鎮	township in Jian'ou Municipality
Kaoting Academy* 考亭書院	at Sangui district, Jianyang county (south of Jianyang county seat)
Liyuan 梨園	in Tongyou district, Jianyang county
Lufeng Academy 廬峰書院	at foot of Yungu shan, Chongtai district
Lükou* 莒口	(modern) township, roughly corresponding to Chongtai district, west of Jianyang county seat
Mafu* 馬伏	in Chongtai district
Masha township* 麻沙鎮	in Yongzhong district, Jianyang county
Masha township Shuinan* 麻沙鎮水南	south of the Mayang river, across from Masha town
Nanshan Academy 南山書院	in Chongan county, on the Jiuqu stream in the Wuyi mountains at the foot of Tiger Roar Mountain
Nanxi zhangyin 南溪樟隱	in Masha town Shuinan—where Zhu Mu 祝穆 wrote and compiled his works
Pingshan Academy 屏山書院	at the foot of Pingshan, in Wufu district, Chongan county†

(*continues on next page*)

Map 2 Glossary, *cont.*

Feature	Location/description
Renshou* 仁壽	in Shunchang 順昌 county
Ruizhang Academy 瑞樟書院	in Masha town; one of the family schools of the Liu descent group
Sanfeng shan* 三峰山	on the border of Chongzheng and Chonghua districts
Sangui li* 三桂里	district in Jianyang county
Sanqu li* 三衢里	district in Jianyang county
Shufang/Shulin* 書坊/書林	in Chonghua district, Jianyang county
Tanxi Academy 潭溪書院	in Lükou, Chongtai district (also known as Tanxi jingshe 精舍)
Tongwen Academy 同文書院	in Chonghua district, Jianyang county
Tongyou li* 童游里	district in Jianyang county
Wufu village district* 五夫里	in Chongan county
Wuyi Academy/Hongyuan Academy* 武夷書院/洪源書院	beneath Pingshan, Wuqu stream, Wuyi Mountains, Chongan county (location on Map 2 approximate)
Xingcun* 星村	in Chongan county
Xingcun jingshe 星村精舍	in Xingcun on the Jiuqu stream, Wuyi Mountains, Chongan county
Xingxian shang li 興賢上里	in Jianyang county
Xiong tun* 熊屯	in Chongtai district, Jianyang county
Xishan* 西山	in Chongtai district
Xishan Academy 溪山書院	on Houshan street (後山街), Chongtai district, Jianyang county
Xishan jingshe 西山精舍	at the foot of Xishan, founded in the Southern Song by the *Daoxue* scholar Cai Yuanding 蔡元定
Yongzhong li* 永忠里	district in Jianyang county
Yungu Academy 雲谷書院	at the foot of Yungu shan, in Chongtai district, Jianyang county
Yungu shan* 雲谷山	in Chongtai district, Jianyang, bordering on Chongan county
Yunqu bridge 雲衢橋	at the south gate of Shufang
Yunzhuang Academy 雲莊書院	has shrine for Liu Yue 劉爚, at the foot of Taiping Mountain in Mafu, Chongtai district, Jianyang county

*Shown on Map 2.
†Another Pingshan Academy located south of the Jianning prefectural seat was renamed the Jian'an Government Academy.

Historical Background

Between the late Tang and the start of the Northern Song, the Minbei area was under the control of several regimes, including the Min (941–46) and the Southern Tang (946–75).[10] The Southern Tang, with its capital at Jinling (Nanjing), marked the persisting influence of the Jiangnan area on north-western Fujian. Apparently, this area was comparatively quiet and free from turmoil, and a sustained migration into the area began in the late Tang and continued through the Northern Song, from Jiangxi and Zhejiang or via these areas from further north.[11]

In reality, whatever the outside government that claimed jurisdiction over the Minbei area during the Tang-Song interregnum, it was ruled by various military leaders who were members of powerful local clans. At the same time, at least some of these groups were building a power base through education and official success. We do not know enough about Minbei society during this period to determine whether the local magnates belonged to the same families that began producing scholars and officials in significant numbers in the Song, but records do reveal tensions between local military leaders and officials appointed by the central government. Local leaders continued to be influential throughout the Southern Song, sometimes siding with government officials and sometimes with rebels and smugglers.[12] The high degree of local autonomy probably contributed to the court's view that Minbei was a difficult region to govern.[13]

In large part, the central and Fujian circuit governments ignored the Minbei region except for two of its products, tea and rice. The state monopoly over the highly prized Minbei tea began in the Tang and was strongest during the Song.[14] The highest grade of this tea was the imperial tribute tea, which was grown on government plantations and processed in government work-shops into tea cakes. These official tea gardens alone employed several thousand tea pickers, many of whom came over the mountains from Jiangxi.[15] Actually, nongovernment workshops far outnumbered the government ones. These private workshops probably processed tea grown by small peasant households or by Buddhist monasteries. Although the total tea production of Minbei in the Song was small[16] compared with those of other regions such as Jiangnan and Sichuan, the government's monopoly on the sale of Fujian tea was never relaxed, probably because of its high reputation at the imperial court and partly because of its importance in the northern border trade. As a result of this tight control, however, tea smuggling thrived. This illicit trade involved bandits, peasants, tea pickers, monasteries, and local magnates, as well as tea merchants. It is noteworthy that in a number of the rebellions that began in or spread to the Minbei area around the time of the fall of the

Northern Song, such as that led by Ye Nong 葉濃 in 1128, tea pickers and tea smugglers were among the recruits.[17] The Minbei tea monopoly continued under the Yuan, but it was much less important and was abolished in 1329–30.[18] Although the overall impact of the tea trade on the Minbei region in the Song and Yuan is difficult to assess, the important point is that it linked the region economically, socially, and politically with surrounding areas. Many of the tea merchants, tea pickers, and tea smugglers came from other areas of Fujian or from Jiangxi and brought with them licit and illicit commerce as well as social unrest.

The other Minbei product that received much official attention and was the source of social tension and unrest was rice. As noted in Chapter 1, Minbei for much of its history was considered a rice-exporting area. As a result, rice from the Jianning area would be requisitioned to relieve shortages in coastal regions, especially around Fuzhou, even when there was not enough for the Jianning area itself.[19] The resulting suffering and unrest in times of shortage was a serious problem that occupied the attention of local officials and community leaders. The problem was exacerbated by poor transportation within the area. Even when the towns in the region were adequately supplied with relief grain, bad roads meant that the outlying regions were unable to receive aid. Indeed, given the heavy dependence on water routes, it was easier to send rice from Jianning to Fuzhou down the Minjiang than to distribute it from a town to the countryside within the Minbei region.[20] The efforts of the local community leaders to deal with rice shortages resulted in the establishment of charitable granaries by communities[21] and by families.[22] The success of both institutions required the participation of local leaders, but apparently the Jianning community granary was defunct by 1219.[23] In contrast, some family granaries lasted into the Yuan and were re-established in the Ming, a testimony to the narrower idea of "community" and the longevity of the families that supervised them.

The Buddhist monasteries constituted another influential force in the Minbei region. They were among the largest landowners and probably had the greatest share of the tea estates next to the government. Whatever its economic power, however, Buddhism in Fujian seems not to have been noted as an intellectual force, and this may have been particularly true in the Minbei area.[24] Certainly, if the known Jianyang imprints are any indication, the monasteries seemed little or not at all involved in the printing business. Two of the Song dynasty Tripitakas were printed in Fujian when the Jianyang book trade was already in full swing, but both were printed in Fuzhou.[25] On the other hand, it is possible that the monasteries were involved in printing short sutras and religious pictures such as those mentioned in the Hong Mai story and that the distribution network for this much more ephemeral literature differed considerably from that for books printed in Jianyang.

Northern Fujian, then, was something of a cultural and political backwater until the Northern Song, when men from the region succeeded spectacularly in the government examinations: in numbers of *jinshi*, Jianzhou ranked first in the empire with 809 during the Northern Song and continued to do well in the Southern Song.[26] This rather sudden success can perhaps be attributed to the migration of families from the north who had official connections to the central government. The degree holders and other Minbei natives with official careers whose family background can be traced share several features. The genealogies of these men invariably claim that the family was descended from an ancestor who was a high civil or military official, came to the area during the late Tang or Five Dynasties period, and decided to settle there to avoid political turmoil in the north. Most families also claimed to have originated in Shaanxi or Henan,[27] and some genealogies record that the founding ancestor or some of his immediate descendants lived in Jiangxi before crossing the mountains to Fujian. Whatever the truth of such claims, it is clear that by the Southern Song these men increasingly sought to assert the legitimacy of their leadership in the area through government service or, in the case of noted thinkers such as Zhu Xi and his students, intellectual prominence on a national scale.[28] This in turn required success in the government examination system and therefore a heavy investment in education. By around 1080, every county in Jianzhou had at least one government school,[29] and many families had established schools for their members, with some wealthy families boasting more than one. By the time Zhu Xi and his students made the area a *Daoxue* stronghold in the late twelfth century, the Jianyang area had reached a cultural (and economic) level it has never again attained. From this perspective, the development of the printing industry in Jianyang seems a natural part of the whole story.

Several factors facilitated the growth of Jianyang as a major printing center during the Song. The area had most of the natural resources necessary for producing block-printed books. The heavily forested mountains provided the materials for the woodblocks and ink. Moreover, paper was made from the many varieties of bamboo that grew in great abundance in the mountains. Of the different types of paper produced in the area, one well-known product used for printing was called book paper (*shuji zhi*) or (jade) knot ([*yu*]*kou zhi*).[30]

It is quite likely that the book-printing industry grew out of and then coexisted with the printing of items for common use, such as calendars, almanacs, religious charms, and funeral money; this aspect of the printing industry undoubtedly continued. That the evidence for this other side of the printing industry is far scantier than for book printing should not lead us to assume that it did not exist. For instance, a similar situation obtained in Sichuan; one of the few hints we have of this is a ban in 835, recorded in the Song encyclopedia *Cefu yuangui*, on privately (and thus illegally) printed calendars, which were being issued before the official calendar.[31] Later, in 883, again in Sichuan, an official of the imperial secretariat noted that there most of the books for sale there dealt with divination, portents, dreams, and geomancy or were "character books," and elementary texts. These early block-printed books were apparently of very poor quality—smeared and blurred to the point of illegibility.[32] Official and scholarly use of woodblock printing thus apparently trailed religious and popular uses by a century or more. Only in 953, just before the establishment of the Song, were the Classics first printed. Thereafter, however, both official and commercial publishing grew apace.

The book trade took off so rapidly in Jianyang during the Song for a number of other factors as well. Its development was heavily influenced by the great importance placed on education and success in government examinations by the local elite. Consequently, during the Song, and to a lesser extent during the Yuan, the Classics and Histories constituted a significant portion of the titles published in Jianyang. The quality of Jianyang imprints seems to have been mixed from the start. In the late Northern Song, Ye Mengde noted that "many Sichuan and Fujian [books] are [printed] from blocks of soft wood, so that they are easily produced and quickly sold, but they are not well made. Fujian books are sold all over, just because they are produced with so little effort."[33]

Books from Jianyang were "sold all over" also because transporting *Mashaben* by water from Masha or Shufang to Jianyang, then north to Chongan or Pucheng and beyond, or downstream to Fuzhou, was relatively easy following the established trade routes. And merchants from other areas could travel via these same routes to buy cheap books, cheap paper, and other Minbei products. Thus, part of the apparent puzzle of an important book center existing in such a remote area is solved when we remember that the area was not uniformly remote and isolated.

Family schools and commercial printers produced most of the Jianyang imprints, an indication of the local government's relative lack of interest in publishing at this time.[34] This situation contrasted with the publishing activities of local and regional governments in areas such as Liangzhe and Jiangnan west circuits, and even other parts of Fujian, particularly Fuzhou. The hesitation of most (though not all) local officials to sponsor publications may reflect an unwillingness on their part to share in the opprobrium attached to "shoddy" Jianyang imprints. This unfavorable view apparently extended to the bamboo paper produced in the region as well. During the Song, districts such as Huizhou in Anhui, Tanzhou in Hunan, Nanchang in Jiangxi, and Jinhua and Shaoxing in Zhejiang were called upon to supply the government's enormous need for paper for books, proclamations, public records, and paper money.[35] These places were deemed to produce paper satisfying government specifications, which the bamboo paper of Minbei did not. In turn, however, this absence of official attention, together with the largely ineffectual attempts at controlling what was printed, meant that the Jianyang book trade had the freedom to develop in accordance with the increasingly varied demands of its customers. By the mid-Ming, both the prefectural and the county governments would take more advantage of the printing resources available in the Jianyang area, but by then commercial printing had attained a vigor that made it extremely difficult to control.

Jianyang Publishers

The scale of the Jianyang printing industry is apparent from the number of publishers. We know the names of about fifty private or commercial publishers in Minbei during the Southern Song and of about sixty during the Yuan. In comparison, we know of some twenty publishers in Hangzhou during the Southern Song, a number that decreased drastically to only four during the Yuan. Taking these numbers as rough approximations—and there are good reasons for doing so—we can conclude that the Jianyang publishing industry appears to have been as large as or larger than that in the country's capital during the Southern Song and that it continued unabated into the Yuan.[36]

A more precise pronouncement is difficult since a simple count of the number of publishers/printers does not take into account the number of titles produced. For example, the great majority of Minbei publishers have fewer than five titles attributable to them. Moreover, a number of these publishers may have been related to one another or connected through social and intellectual ties.[37] Publishers with the same surname may have worked together closely, perhaps under the aegis of the family school. Others may have lent or given another publisher woodblocks, and based on evidence of Chinese family business practices, woodblocks constituted an important part of the partible inheritance.[38] Thus fifty different names do not necessarily mean fifty separate publishing operations.

Table 1 summarizes statistics for Song and Yuan publishers from the Jianyang area;[39] the lengthier tables in Appendix B (pp. 279–306) give the

Table 1
Statistics for Known Jianyang Publishers and Printers of the Song and Yuan

Active period	Publishers/ printers	*Jiashu* 家塾	*Shuyuan* 書院/ *jingshe* 精舍	Total
Song only	34	10	3	47
Yuan only	40	1	8	50
Song and Yuan	6		1	7
Yuan and Ming	6		4	10
Song, Yuan, Ming	2		1	3

names of known publishers. Table B.1 lists commercial and private publishers; Table B.2, those affiliated with family schools; Table B.3, those affiliated with academies and halls of refinement (*jingshe* 精舍); Table B.4, printers working under official auspices, namely, regional government officials, prefects of Jianning, magistrates of Jianyang, and government schools.

As the names of the publishers in Table B.1 suggest, it is often difficult to tell if a particular establishment was a commercial printer or an individual who directed and financed on a one-time basis the publishing of a particular work. Moreover, there are many misleading names. For example, not all the publishers labeled *shuyuan* were academies, and at least one of the *jingshe* (Liu shi Cuiyan jingshe, Table B.3, no. 102) active in the Yuan and Ming had definitely became a commercial enterprise by Ming times. The term *jiashu*, at least for nine of the ten known examples in the Song, however, does refer to family schools recorded in the genealogies. As for terms such as *shutang* 書堂, *zhai* 宅, and *zhai* 齋, they may have referred to a commercial publisher, a private individual printing on a one-time or occasional basis, a family school, or possibly (but not likely) an academy.[40] Indeed, the traditional distinctions between commercial imprints (*fangke*) and private imprints (*sike*) sometimes are far from clear.

Enough information is available to show the problematic nature of the term *shuyuan* in referring to printers. Of the twelve *shuyuan* and one *shutang* in Table B.3, we have commemorative essays and/or descriptions in local gazetteers or genealogies for eight (nos. 101, 103–4, 106–8, 110–11). Several publishers, such as the Liu family's Pingshan shuyuan 屏山書院, Yunzhuang shuyuan 雲莊書院, and Hualong shuyuan 化龍書院, and the Xiong family's Aofeng shuyuan 鰲峰書院, were well-known academies established by prominent families with close ties to Zhu Xi and his disciples.[41] Others, however, may not have been *shuyuan* in the usual sense of "academy."[42] Still other publishers in Table B.3 present the opposite problem: what was definitely a well-documented academy, such as Xiong He's Wuyi shuyuan 武夷書院, is identified in its imprints as a *shutang* (no. 110), which probably refers specifically to the printing division associated with the school. Similarly, it is uncertain whether the Tongwen tang 同文堂 (Table B.1, no. 41) was the same as the famous Tongwen shuyuan (no. 107) established by Zhu Xi in Jianyang in the Qiandao period (1165–73).[43] The connection between printing activities and the cultural role of schools in the Jianyang area is explored below.

The data in Table 1 show that about one-fifth of the printers in the Song were apparently operating under the auspices of a family school. There is no way to know whether the books they produced were for the use of the school alone or were sold to outsiders as well. But since approximately four thousand candidates sat for the triennial prefectural examination in Jianning in the early Southern Song, and some ten thousand were taking it by 1186,[44] the market for educational books must have been substantial. The benefits of commercializing the printing activities of a school would have been obvious. In addition, some of the publishers not explicitly labeled *jiashu* may also have functioned (partly) as such, or at least have begun life as such. This practice continued into the Yuan. For example, a number of the books published by one of the best-known Jianyang printers at the time, Yu Zhi'an 余志安 of Qinyou tang 勤有堂 (Table B.1, no. 65), contain both "Printed by Qinyou tang" and "Printed by Yu Zhi'an at the Family School."[45]

Thus it would not be unreasonable to suggest that a significant part of the printing business in Jianyang originated in printshops for family schools. Even after these became commercial concerns, they continued to produce many of the same kinds of books—the Classics and Four Books with their commentaries, Histories, medical works, and literary collections. A large and reliable local market provided the foundation for the expansion of the Jianyang book trade. The pace of this expansion occurred is difficult to chart precisely, but it seems to have taken three-quarters of a century or less: the earliest extant dated Jianyang imprint is an edition of Sima Qian's *Shiji* 史記 (Record of history) from 1057, and before the end of the Northern Song in 1127, Ye Mengde was complaining about Fujian books.

A survey of the books produced by various types of Jianyang printers reveals little difference in titles between those who were *jiashu* printers and those who were not. Still, printers labeled as *jiashu* had virtually disappeared by the Yuan (see Table 1), by which time the Jianyang long-distance book trade was well established. The absence of *jiashu* in the Yuan can be explained by the abolition of the civil service examination system. Even after its restoration in 1313, the quotas for Chinese were tiny. But, as we shall see below, the

Classics continued to be printed in the Yuan and accounted for about the same proportion of the total number of titles as in the Song.

It is also noteworthy that several of the printing establishments begun in the Song or Yuan continued for over 200 years, including several of the best-known printer families: Liu (Table B.1, no. 36, and Table B.3, no. 102), Yang (Table B.1, no. 57), and Yu (no. 67). Furthermore, evidence from the genealogies and publishers' notes in books show that descendants of a printer might continue the business under a different name. For example, the Xiong family's Weisheng tang 衛生堂 (Table B.1, no. 55), which produced medical works, evolved into the better-known Zhongde tang 種德堂 (no. 56) under Xiong Zongli and his successors during the Ming.

Jianyang printing was a family industry as well as a family business. At least some of the blockcarvers belonged to the same families as the publishers. For example, of twenty-two blockcarvers surnamed Liu, Yu, or Xiong who worked on imprints from the Jianyang area, six can tentatively be identified as members of the printers' families.[46] The utilization of family members would have kept labor costs competitively low. This as well as the use of locally produced cheap paper and ink may explain why Jianyang imprints were said to be among the cheapest in the country. There is little information on the size of such family operations and no reason to assume that there was a typical scale of operation. The Liu genealogy mentions that the Liu shi Rixin tang 日新堂 (Table B.1, no. 36) had sixteen persons working on the physical production of the books and another sixteen involved in collating and proofreading.[47] The Rixin tang, one of the best-known and most prolific printing businesses, was probably much larger than other shops.

There is also evidence that different publishers cooperated in the editing and collating of a text, if not the printing. For example, the *Hou Han shu* 後漢書 (History of the Later Han) printed by Huang Shanfu jiashu 黃善夫 家塾 and Liu Yuanqi jiashu 劉元起家塾 (Table B.2, nos. 95–96) have almost identical prefaces and postfaces, although the blocks for the two editions were different.[48] Given the social and intellectual relationships among publishers (the subject of the next section), such cooperative ventures are not unusual. As we will see, the intellectual and political allegiances of many publishers, both commercial and official, were influenced by *Daoxue*, and these interests led them to focus on publishing the Classics, Histories, and some philosophers. An even broader unifying factor during the Song was the growing examination culture, which apparently absorbed the energies of so many educated men in the Jianyang area. Some of them channeled this preoccupation into publishing works for examination candidates.

Most of the early publishers apparently were residents of Jianyang county, in or around Masha zhen (town) 鎮. Somewhat later, in the late Southern Song or Yuan, printshops became common in Shufang (or Shulin) in Chonghua li (village district) 崇化里 (see Map 2). Both Masha and Shufang (literally, "book quarter") were situated upstream from the county seat and were close to a number of academies. Thus many of the publishers listed in Tables B.1–3 and their successors in the Ming identified themselves as "of Masha" or "of Shufang/Shulin (in Chonghua)." Others referred to themselves or their establishment as located in "Tancheng 潭城 / Tanyang 潭陽 / Tanyi 潭邑," an old name for Jianyang. Others located themselves more specifically as being "of Chongchuan 崇川," a local stream in Chonghua village district, or "of Yunqu 雲衢," near a bridge of that name also in Chonghua. Some others identified themselves more generally as establishments of Jianning fu (prefecture); Jian'an (the prefectural seat); Fusha 富沙, an old name for Jianning; or Zhicheng 芝城, an alternative name for Jian'an. Finally, others specified only a provincial or regional location: Min-Jian 閩建, Minsha 閩沙, or Minzhong 閩中. Evidence from genealogies and imprints indicate, however, that despite the vagueness of some of these locations, most of these publishers were located in Jianyang. The descriptions of academies in local histories usually identify at least a subcounty district in which they are located; occasionally more precise information is given, placing them near a mountain or stream. The positions of a number of the places shown on Map 2 are conjectural, based on available information.

The Liu, Yu, and Xiong Families of Publishers

What of the publishers themselves—those whom we know by name or by that of their printing establishment? Few of the individuals listed in Tables B.1–3 were well known on the national or even the regional level. Only two claimed to have had official degrees or to have served in office (Liu Tongpan 劉通判, no. 27, and Liu Junzuo 劉君佐, no. 102).[49] Indeed, an overwhelming number of them are not mentioned in local gazetteers, and only a few show up in genealogies.[50] Moreover, as already noted, when such men are mentioned in the genealogies, their printing activities almost always go unnoticed, unless one of the works they printed and/or compiled was the genealogy itself. What evidence we can glean from the genealogies, however, suggests that the publishers tended to come from the less prominent branch(es) of their descent groups.

For instance, according to the extant editions of genealogies for branches of descent groups surnamed Liu in the Jianning area,[51] six of the eleven commercial publishers in the Song and two of nine in the Yuan (Tables 2a, b)[52] claimed descent from one ancestor, Liu Ao 翱. More prominent Liu men of the Song and Yuan, such as Liu Yue 爚, a Zhu Xi disciple and nationally renowned *Daoxue* scholar and official,[53] the encyclopedist Liu Yingli 應李,[54] as well as Liu Mianzhi 勉之,[55] Zhu Xi's father-in-law, claimed as their ancestor one of Liu Ao's younger brothers (Table 2c).[56] The two brothers Liu Zihui 子翬 and Liu Ziyu 子羽,[57] two of Zhu Xi's guardians and teachers, traced their ancestry to another younger brother of Liu Ao (Table 2d). Since just two Liu genealogies have been discovered, we can only guess at the comparative economic, political, and academic success of each branch of the descent group. Evidence, mainly from genealogical records and local histories, suggests that Liu men certainly contributed to the overall success of Minbei in producing *jinshi*. The most spectacular record belonged to the Xizu nanpai (Table 2c), where success begot success for at least three generations between 1172 and 1274.

In contrast, noticeably fewer degree and office holders are recorded for the Liu Ao branch of the family than for the other two branches. The one known *jinshi* from the Ao branch during the Song is Liu Chongzhi 崇之 (*js* 1175).[58] Two other possible *jinshi* are Liu Fuyan 復言 (Tongpan)[59] and Liu Junzuo. It is possible that certain branches of various descent groups chose to specialize in printing, even while pursuing examination degrees. This may explain, for example, why the greatest number of printers surnamed Liu came from one sub-branch of the descent group. For the Song and Yuan, however, the evidence is inconclusive. First, other than the Liu, we can identify very few Jianyang printers in the genealogies. Second, information for the Liu printers suggests that their branch of the family, like their more prominent relatives, emphasized scholarship and academic success. The examination success of the Xizu nanpai, which boasted three or more *jinshi* for several generations running in the Southern Song, is extraordinary by any standard and overshadows the accomplishments of their printer relatives in the Xizu beipai.

More useful than a mere tally of degree and office holders, however, is an examination of the printing activities of these men and their close relatives. Liu Chongzhi was a student of Zhu Xi and the son of Liu Zhongji 仲吉, brother of Liu Lizhi 立之, and nephew of Liu Zhongli 仲立 (Table 2b), all three of whom were publishers. The nature and the high quality of their four extant imprints bespeak both the wealth and the willingness to produce such work. Three were large works: the *Xin Tang shu* 新唐書 (New history of the Tang), the *Hou Han shu*, and the 150-*juan* literary anthology of Song prose,

Table 2a

Simplified Family Tree of Liu Descent Groups in the Jianning Area

Xizu beipai 西族北派
(settled in Masha 麻沙)
Liu Ao 劉翺 (858-936)

Wei 暐
(Heng fang) 亨房
Xiao 曉
(Yuan fang) 元房
Ye 曄
(Li fang) 利房
Sao 噪
(Zhen fang) 貞房

See Table 2b

Xizu nanpai 西族南派
(settled in Jianyang Mafu 建陽馬伏)
Liu Bin 劉豳

See Table 2c

Dongzu 東族
(settled in Chong'an Wufu li 崇安五夫里)
Liu Xiang 劉翔

See Table 2d

Table 2b
Simplified Family Tree of the Liu Xizu Beipai 劉氏西族北派

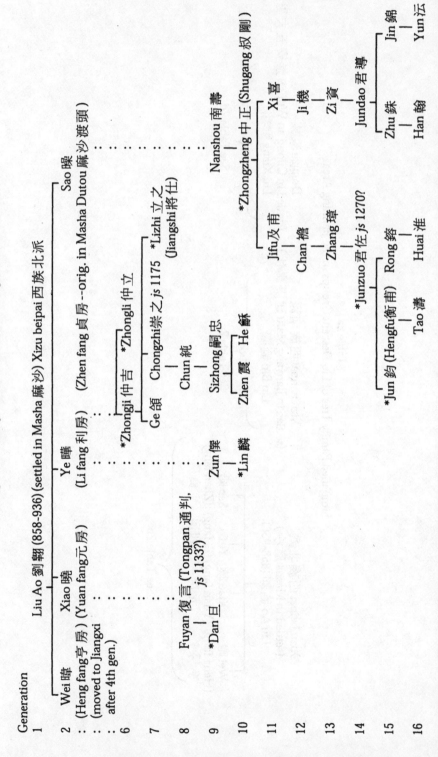

Li fang 利房

Gen						
16						
17						
18						
19						
20						
21						
22						
23	*Guangqi 光啓			*Dajin 大金 (Yutian 玉田) (1557-1639)		
24	*Kongnian 孔年	Kongye 孔業		*Dayi 大易 (Longtian 龍田) (1560-1625)		
25	*Shunchen 舜臣 (1597-1653)			*Kongjing 孔敬 (js 1625)	*Kongdun 孔敦	
26				*Zhaoqing 肇慶 (1608-74)		
27						

Yun 沄 — Tong 桐 — Shou 壽 — Gou 狗

Han 翰 — Bo 伯 — *Kuan 寬 — *Lei 壘 — *Mu 塋 (兌常) — *Hui 輝 (Zongqi 宗器?)

Tao 濤 — Tong 橦 — *Yan 剡 — Lu 壚 — Yin 銀 — Gong 釭

Huai 淮 — Shun 順 — Xuan 垹 — *Wenshou 文壽

*Shizhong 仕中

*Hong 洪 (Hongyi 弘毅) — Shiqi 仕奇 — *Chonglin 崇林 (雙松?) — Chongsen 崇森

Shicheng 世承

*Yongmao 永茂 ?? — (Liantai 蓮台) — Chengwei 成威 — Zigao 子高

Tiansi 天泗 — *Hong 洪 — Yude 餘德

Fuqi 福榮 — Xuewu 學武 — Youci 有慈

*Guohao 國好 (Suming 素明) — *Zhaogan 兆感 — *Yuansong 元頌 (Yafu 雅夫, 1670-1760)

Notes: 1. An asterisk (*) before a name indicates that the person was involved in some aspect of book publishing.
2. Missing from extant part of genealogical table, but also of the Xizu beipai is the printer Liu Jinwen 劉錦文 (zi Shujian 叔簡) of Rixintang 日新堂. See biographical sketch in JYXZ (1553 ed.), 12.18b-19a (name misprinted as 劉文錦).

Table 2c

Xizu nanpai 西族南派

(settled in Jianyang Mafu 建陽馬伏)
Liu Bin 劉鬵

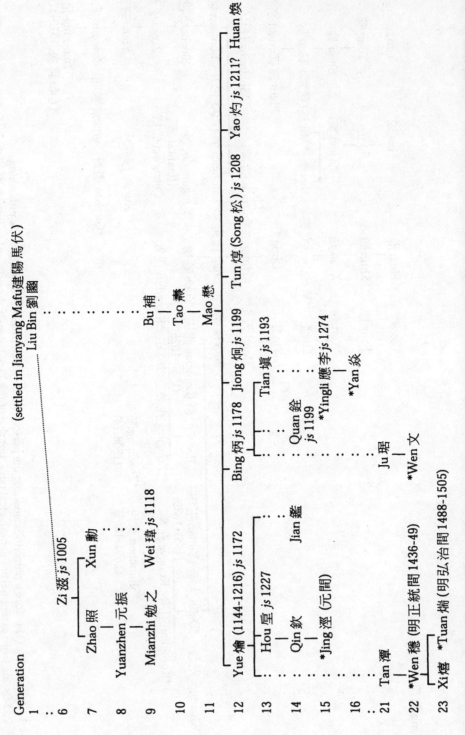

Generation

1
..:
6 Zi 滋 js 1005
7 Zhao 照 Xun 勳
8 Yuanzhen 元振
9 Mianzhi 勉之 Wei 瑋 js 1118
10
11
12 Yue 爚 (1144-1216) js 1172   Bing 炳 js 1178 Jiong 炯 js 1199   Tun 焞 (Song 松) js 1208   Yao 灼 js 1211? Huan 煥
13 Hou 垕 js 1227   Jian 鑑   Tian 塤 js 1193   Bu 補
14 Qin 欽   Quan 銓 js 1199   Tao 檩
15 *Jing 涇 (元聞)   *Yingli 應李 js 1274   Mao 懋
16 *Yan 俟
..:
21 Tan 潭   Ju 琚
22 *Wen 穩 (明正統間 1436-49)   *Wen 文
23 Xi 僖   *Tuan 端 (明弘治間 1488-1505)

Table 2d

Dongzu 東族 (Wufu li in Chongan county 崇安五夫里)

Generation			
1	:		
:	:		
:	:		
7	Liu Xiang 劉翔	Minxian 民先	
8	Ji 楫	Yun 藴	Ge 齡 js 1094
9	Tang 棠	Zixiang 子翔 / Zihui 子翬	Ziyu 子羽 / Ziyi 子翼
10	Ruyu 如愚 js 1142	Zhen 瑱 · Jin 瑾 · Ping 玶 · Bi 琿	Gong 珙 js 1142 · Chang 瑺 · Xun 珣 · Chong 玩
11	Shen 琛	Xueji 學箕	Xuegu 學古 · Xueqiu 學裘 · Xueya 學雅
12	Wei 韡		
13			
14		Li 里	
15		*Zhang 張 (元至正間 1341-67)	
16		You 祐 · Li 禮 · Xi 禧 · Zhen 禎 · Zhi 祉	

Huangchao wenjian 皇朝文鑑. The fourth work was a collection of the prose writings of the Northern Song poet Huang Tingjian 黃庭堅, widely revered for his literary talent. The family's affiliation with Zhu Xi is also reflected in a tribute (*xiangzan*) Zhu Xi wrote for Liu Zhongji. Neither this piece nor Zhou Bida's 周必大 eulogy (*muzhiming* 墓誌銘), however, refers to Zhongji's publishing activities.

Liu Fuyan's *zi* appears in the name of a printshop, the Liu Tongpan zhai, which was run by his son, Liu Dan 旦. The three extant imprints from this shop consist of one Daoist classic, the *Daode jing*, an illustrated Legalist classic, the *Yangzi fayan* 楊子法言, and an illustrated edition of the Confucian classic, the *Xunzi* 荀子, the last of which Liu Dan is given credit for the collation (*jiao* 校). On Liu Dan himself, there is no information except a note in the genealogical table that both he and his wife were buried near Buddhist temples.

For Liu Junzuo, we have a bit more information. He was the great-great-grandson of another printer, Liu Zhongzheng 中正 (Table 2b) and the first publisher of the Cuiyan jingshe (Table B.3, no. 102), which continued to put out works until the late sixteenth century. According to the genealogy, he received a *jinshi* degree and served as an official in Nan'en circuit in Guangdong.[60] It is uncertain whether he served under the Song or the Yuan government or both, but based on his preface (dated 1301) to the edition of the genealogy he revised, Liu Junzuo probably was one of a number of Minbei men who retired from public life when the Yuan conquered south China. In the preface, he noted that each time the genealogy was revised, it was printed, and a copy was given to each branch of the *fang* 房. But since the blocks had been destroyed in 1276 when Yuan troops first invaded the region, he had assumed the task of producing a new edition.[61] It is possible that his printing activities were spurred by his work on the genealogy. He also moved from Masha, which probably was extensively damaged in the invasion, to Shulin (Shufang) and therefore is considered the ancestor of the Shulin branch of the family and of many later Liu printers of the Yuan and Ming (see Table 2b).

Aside from the genealogy, five other works were probably printed by Liu Junzuo through the Cuiyan jingshe from 1294 to 1328.[62] Two of the works were reprints of the Classics with commentaries by Zhu Xi. The first, *Cheng-Zhu er xiansheng Zhouyi chuanyi* 程朱二先生周易傳義 (Meaning of and commentaries on the *Zhouyi* by Cheng Yi and Zhu Xi), is dated 1314, a year after Zhu Xi's commentaries were declared the official interpretations for the civil service examination. The second work, the *Shi jizhuan* 詩集傳 (*Book of*

Poetry with collected commentaries), printed in 1327, was an elaborate production that included a series of old prefaces, a map, a table of personages in the *Book of Poetry*, a bibliography, and new sub-commentaries. The authorial/ editorial credit is given to Hu Yigui 胡一桂 (Hu Tingfang 胡廷芳), a well-known *Daoxue* scholar of the Yuan who also taught and collaborated with Xiong He and Liu Yingli at the Hongyuan shuyuan in Wuyi shan (see below).[63] It is therefore highly likely that Liu Junzuo, like these other men, was a strong *Daoxue* adherent.

In addition, a preface written for this edition testifies to the availability of such works in the Yuan. It states that since commercial *dacheng* 大成 editions of the *Book of Poetry* (that is, complete compendia with collected commentaries, sub-commentaries, maps, tables), which had once been very common, had become hard to find, this edition was printed to fill the gap. The author closed by noting that he wrote it at the "Cuiyan Liu shi jiashu" 翠巖劉氏家塾 (family school of Mr. Liu of Cuiyan). There is no suggestion that the lack of demand in the first few decades of Yuan rule in the south may have been responsible for the dearth of copies, and the overall tone of the preface is little different from those written in the Southern Song. One reason may be that the influence of *Daoxue* in the Jianyang area remained an afterglow in the Yuan, perpetuated by men who retired from public life after 1279 and devoted themselves to teaching, writing, and, in some cases, printing as well. To them, the task of keeping their moral, intellectual, and social traditions alive, by revising genealogies and collating and contributing their own annotations and commentaries to scholarly works, was made more urgent by the destruction during the dynastic transition and by the indifference of the new government. Yuan officials in Minbei, like most of their Song predecessors, apparently failed to take advantage of the area's publishing resources.

As for the eight Yu 余 printers from the Song and Yuan whom we know by name, only one, Yu Zhi'an, can be identified with fair certainty in the genealogy, *Tanxi Shulin Yu shi zupu* 潭西書林余氏族譜 (Genealogy of the Yu descent group of Shulin in Tanxi; see Table 3).[64] It is possible, however, to find a bit of information about him and about an earlier printer, Yu Renzhong 余仁仲, from their imprints.

Yu Renzhong, the printer of Wanjuan (shu)tang 萬卷 (書) 堂 (Table B.1, no. 61), was active during the Southern Song. His name appears neither in the county, prefectural, or provincial gazetteers consulted nor in the Yu genealogy. Of his fourteen known imprints, the six that are datable come from the last two decades of the twelfth century. Based on the eleven imprints that are editions of the Classics and their commentaries, Yu seems to have

Table 3

Simplified Family Tree of the Tanxi Shulin Yu shi 潭溪書林余氏世系

1	Huan 煥 (settled in Fujian, 530)
.. : 14	Tongzu 同祖
15	Xi 皙
16	Chende 辰德
17	Daoshun 道順 (991-1063)
18	Wan 完 (1024-?) (founder of 上萃房)
19	Yong 庸 (1056-?)
20	Shi 適
21	Yunwen 允文 (1112-?)
22	Yugong 禹功 (1148-?)
23	Qing 慶 (1200-41)
24	Wenxing 文興 (1237-1309) (勤有居士)
25	*Anding 安定 (1275-1347) (=Zhi'an 志安?)
26	*Zi 資 (1313-58)
27	Xuan 烜 (1344-1416)
28	Qi 琪 (1389-1464)

Dao'an 道安 Daochun 道淳

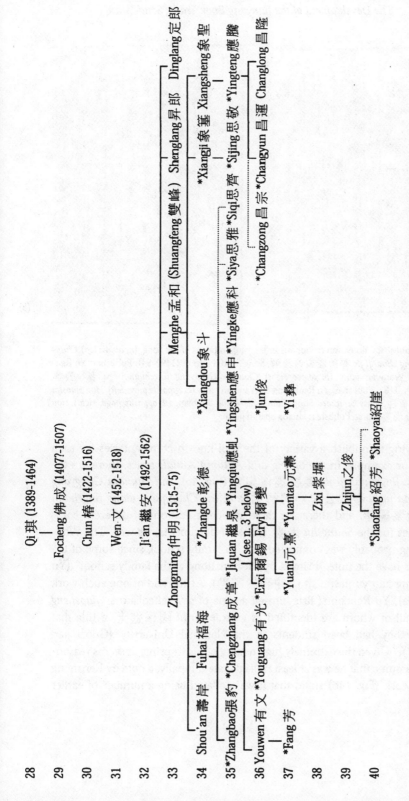

28	Qi Qishi (1389-1464)
29	Focheng 佛成 (1407?-1507)
30	Chun 椿 (1422-1516)
31	Wen 文 (1452-1518)
32	Ji'an 繼安 (1492-1562)
33	Zhongming 仲明 (1515-75)
34	Shou'an 壽岸 Fuhai 福海 Menghe 孟和 (Shuangfeng 雙峰) Shenglang 昇郎 Dinglang 定郎
35	*Zhangbao 張豹 *Chengzhang 成章 Jiquan 緝泉 *Yingqiu 應虬 *Yingshen 應申 *Yingke 應科 *Xiangji 象鑒 Xiangsheng 象聖
36	Youwen 有文 *Youguang 有光 *Erxi 爾錫 Eryi 爾變 *Xiangdou 象斗 *Siya 思雅 *Siqi 思齊 *Sijing 思敬 *Yingteng 應騰
37	*Fang 芳 *Yuani 元熹 *Yuantao 元燾 *Jun 俊 *Changzong 昌宗 *Changyun 昌運 Changlong 昌隆
38	Zixi 紫墀
39	Zhijun 之俊 *Yi 彝
40	*Shaofang 紹芳 *Shaoyai 紹崖

Notes: 1. Names of men known to be involved in publishing are marked by an asterisk (*). Other men also active in publishing are known from information in imprints but their names do not appear in the genealogy.
2. Conjectures are indicated by ——————

3. In several instances, I have based my reconstruction of the genealogical tree on information from the imprints, which differ from that given in the genealogy. For example, Yu Zhangde 彰德 (34th generation) is the same as Yu Siquan 泗泉, even though the genealogy has Zhangde as the father of Siquan. I deduced that Zhangde's son was probably named Jiquan 緝泉 (or Yingliang 應良).

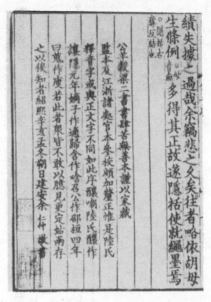

(a)   *(b)*

Fig. 14 Publishers' notes and colophons in Jianyang imprints of the Song. (*a, above left*) *Chunqiu Guliang zhuanji jie* 春秋穀梁傳集解. Song Shaoxi period (1190–94). Publisher: Yu Renzhong of Wanjuan tang. (*b, above right*) *Chunqiu Gongyang jingzhuan jiegu* 春秋公羊經傳解詁. 1191. Publisher: Yu Renzhong of Wanjuan tang. (*c, opposite page, left*) *Hou Hanshu zhu* 後漢書注. Early Southern Song. Publisher: Wang Shubian. (*d, opposite page, right*) *Hou Hanshu* 後漢書. Song. Publisher: Huang Shanfu jiashu.

been trying to publish a variety of the well-known commentaries for each work. For example, in the *Spring and Autumn Annals* series, there are the *Chunqiu jingzhuan ji jie* 春秋經傳集解 (Fig. 4b), the *Chunqiu Gongyang jingzhuan jiegu* 春秋公羊經傳解詁, and the *Chunqiu Guliang jingzhuan* 春秋穀梁經傳, and there are three surviving editions of different commentaries for the *Shangshu* 尚書 (Book of documents) as well. The Wanjuan tang probably was connected to a Yu family school, since some of the imprints have the note "Printed by Yu Renzhong at the family school" (Yu Renzhong kan yu jiashu 余仁仲刊於家塾). At the end of one such work (Fig. 14a), Yu Renzhong lists himself as one of several collators (*jiaozheng* 校正), all of whom are identified as *guoxue jinshi* 國學進士, a title that implies they had been students in the National University (Guozi jian 國子監).[65] Given the extremely high quality of his imprints, it seems reasonable to assume that he was at least well educated. Finally, a note by Renzhong in this work (Fig. 14b) states that it was collated using a number of earlier

(c)

(d)

editions, including those of the Directorate of Education owned by his family. The evidence strongly suggests that Yu Renzhong came from a family with a scholarly tradition, and the high quality of his imprints suggests access to the wealth necessary for such efforts.

Even more prolific than Yu Renzhong was Yu Zhi'an of Qinyou tang (Table B.1, no. 65), for which some 29 imprints are extant, dating from around 1314 to 1344. The name Yu Zhi'an is not found in *Tanxi Shulin Yu shi zupu*, but a modern scholar has convincingly identified him with a Yu Anding 余安定 (1275–1347) in the twenty-fifth generation of the genealogical table (Table 3).[66] If this identification is accurate, then at least thirteen Yu printers of the Ming are descended from Yu Zhi'an.[67] The entry for Yu Anding in the genealogy's *shixi* gives no information beyond his dates, the surname of his wife, and the location of his gravesite. As usual, information on Yu Zhi'an as a printer must be extracted from his publications.

Eleven of the Qinyou tang's imprints were new editions of the Classics and their commentaries. Two others were commentaries on the Four Books; their publication reflects the *Daoxue* emphasis on these works that became prevalent in the thirteenth century.[68] One of these, the *Si shu tong* 四書通 written by the Yuan scholar Hu Bingwen 胡炳文, was unusual in that it is the only work known to have been commissioned by a government office to be printed by a commercial printer in Jianyang during the Yuan. This information is given in an afterword, which says that the education commissioner of the Jiangzhe circuit had ordered the work to be printed in Jianyang.[69] Another work that *may* have been commissioned by a government official or a private individual is the beautifully produced *Gu lienü zhuan* 古烈女傳 (Lives of exemplary women from antiquity) in a running illustration (*shangtu xiawen*) format. Two other works dealt with law and legal practice: the *Tang lü suyi* 唐律疏議 (Tang law code) and a forensic treatise, the *Xiyuan lu* 洗冤錄 (Washing away of wrongs) by Song Ci 宋慈, a Jianyang native.[70] Three other Qinyou tang imprints were medical texts; one was a reprint of the large Song official compendium, *Taiping huimin heji ju fang* 太平惠民和劑局方 (Prescriptions from the Pharmacy Bureau for the people's welfare of the Taiping era). Of the three literary collections, there was one reprint each of the ever-popular poems of Li Bo and of Du Fu. The third, *Linxi ji* 麟溪集, a poetry anthology, is noteworthy because it shows how readily Jianyang printers produced works of contemporary authors; Yu Zhi'an's edition seems to have appeared within a few years of the collection's compilation during the Zhizheng period (1341–67).[71] Another contemporary work was the *Guochao mingchen shilüe* 國朝名臣事略 (Deeds of famous officials of the [present] dynasty) by Su Tianjue 蘇天爵, a collection of biographies of early Yuan officials and generals. The Qinyou tang edition is dated 1341, six years after the original edition.[72] Finally, not all the Qinyou tang's imprints were high quality. A Daoist work from the Song, *Bai xiansheng zazhu zhixuan bian* 白先生雜著指玄編, is notable for its poor calligraphy and pictures and crowded page layout.[73]

Because the other publishers surnamed Yu cannot be identified as belonging to the same descent group as Yu Zhi'an, we do not know if they were related to him or to one another. All of them, however, as well as other Yu shi 余氏 printing establishments list themselves as "of Jian'an" 建安.[74] Whether they were related or not, there is evidence from their imprints that they collaborated with (or stole from) one another, as well as other Jianyang printers. For instance, a 1318 Qinyou tang edition of the *Book of Documents* with commentaries by Zhu Xi was reprinted in a near identical edition by the Yu shi Shuanggui tang 余氏雙桂堂. In a second case, it is very obvious that the blocks for the classified and annotated verse collection of the Tang poet Du Fu (*Ji qianjia zhu fenlei Du Gongbu shi* 集千家註分類杜工部詩) originally cut by the Qinyou tang in 1312 had been transferred to Ye Rizeng 葉日增 of Guangqin tang 廣勤堂. Ye proceeded to efface all identifications of the original printer and substitute those of the Guangqin tang, including a picture of a bell with the four characters *Sanfeng shutang* 三峰書堂 and a tripod with the characters *Guangqin tang* after the table of contents. A little later on, there is the note, "Newly printed by the Guangqin tang" (*Guangqin tang xinkan* 廣勤堂新刊)! Actually, the Guangqin tang did add two more *juan*, including a *nianpu* 年譜 (biographical chronology), but these supplements were noticeably inferior in calligraphy to the original. The blocks may have been transferred to the Guangqin tang by Yu Zhi'an or by his son Yu Zi 資, whose wife was surnamed Ye.[75] A third, rather confusing example is a compilation of examination literature from the Yuan, *Sanchang wenxuan* 三場文選 (Selected essays from the three sessions [of the examination]), which has two title pages giving Yú[76] shi Wuben (shu)tang/zhai 虞氏務本 (書)堂/齋 as the publisher for several of the subcollections but Yu shi Qinde tang 余氏勤德堂 for others. The publishers' notes indicate that various parts of the compilation were printed in the late Yuan, between 1335 and 1341.[77] It is possible that two publishers decided that collaboration was cheaper than competition for a fairly large work that they thought might be popular.[78]

The commercial publishers from the Xiong family, judging from their imprints, began operating during the Yuan (Table B.1, no. 52–56). None of their personal names were recorded in their publications, but those associated with the Weisheng tang were probably the ancestors of the Ming publishers of the Zhongde tang. Furthermore, certain social patterns among the Xiong resemble those for the Liu publishers. First, of the eleven Xiong *jinshi* during the Song, none apparently belonged to the Rang house of the West branch (Xizu Rangfang 西族讓房) of the descent group, from which all the identifiable printers of the Ming came (Table 4).[79] The men about whom we have some information, including Xiong Ke 克 (Table B.1, no. 51), Xiong He 禾 (Table B.3, no. 110), Xiong Jie 節, and Xiong Gangda 剛大, came from different, apparently more prominent branches of the descent group than the Ming printers.[80] Second, like the Liu, a number of the well-known Xiong men were closely associated with the *Daoxue* movement, as students of Zhu Xi or of other well-known *Daoxue* proponents who were natives or had been officials in Minbei, such as Huang Gan 黃榦 (1152–1221), Cai Yuanding, and Zhen Dexiu 眞德秀 (1178–1235).

Xiong Ke (*js* 1157 or 1160)[81] of the East branch (*Dongzu* 東族) is probably best known as the author of the *Zhongxing xiaoli* 中興小歷 (Minor chronicles of the restoration), which recounts events in the reign of the Southern Song emperor Gaozong (r. 1127–62). He is also credited with publishing four books, including his father's *Xuanhe Beiyuan gongcha lu* 宣和北苑貢茶錄 (Record of Beiyuan tribute tea in the Xuanhe period), one of

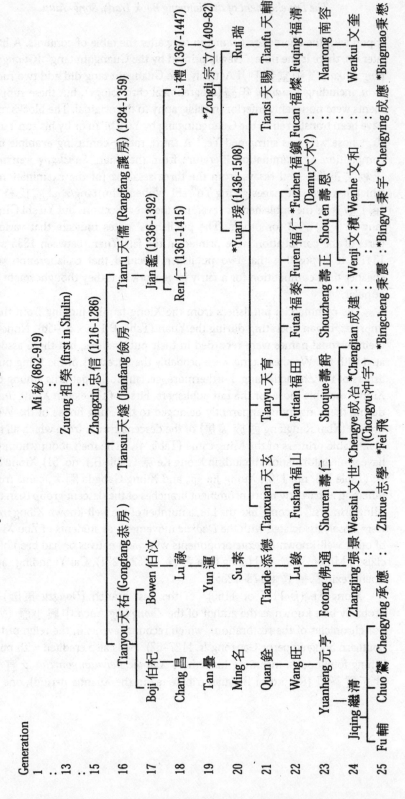

Table 4
Simplified Family Tree of the Xiong shi Xizu 熊氏西族世系 *

Generation										
1	Mi 祕 (862-919)									
:	:									
13	Zurong 祖榮 (first in Shulin)									
:	:									
15	Zhongxin 忠信 (1216-1286)									
16	Tianyou 天祐 (Gongfang 恭房)		Tiansui 天綏 (Jianfang 儉房)		Tianru 天儒 (Rangfang 讓房) (1284-1359)						
17	Bowen (伯汶)	Boji (伯杞)	Tiande 添德	Tianxuan 天玄	Tianyu 天育	Tianxi 天賜	Tianfu 天輔	Fuqing 福清			
18	Chang 昌	Lu 祿	Lu 錄	Fushan 福山	Futian 福田	Li 禮 (1367-1447)	Fuzhen 福鎮 Fucan 福燦 (Damu大木?)	Nanrong 南容			
19	Tan 曇	Yun 運	Wang 旺			Ren 仁 (1361-1415)	Futai 福泰 Furen 福仁	Wenkui 文奎			
20	Ming 名	Su 素	Yuanheng 元亨	Shouren 壽仁	Shoujue 壽爵	*Yuan 瑗 (1436-1508)	Shouzheng 壽正 Shou'en 壽恩				
21	Quan 銓		Jiqing 繼清	Zhangjing 張景	Wenshi 文世	Jian (1336-1392)	*Chengye 成冶 *Chengjian 成建 Wenji 文積 Wenhe 文和	*Bingmao 秉懋			
22	Wang 旺		Chuo 鷟	*Chengying 承應	Zhixue 志學	*Zongli 宗立 (1409-82)	(Chongyu沖宇)	*Bingyu 秉宇 *Chengying 成應			
23	Fotong (佛通)										
24	Chengying 承應				Rui 瑞			*Bingcheng 秉震 : *Bingyu 秉宇			
25	Fu 輔				*Fei 飛						

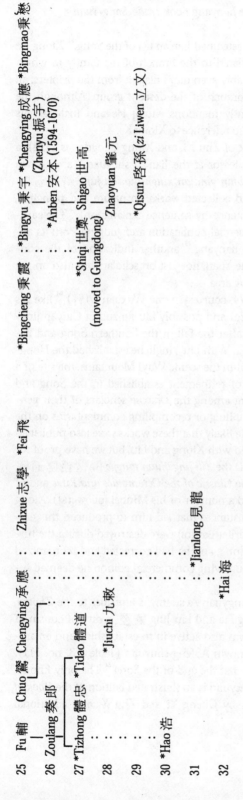

25 Fu 輔
26 Zoulang 奏郎
27 *Tizhong 體忠 *Tidao 體道
28 *Jiuchi 九敕
29
30 *Hao 浩
31
32

Chuo 騡 騺   Chengying 承應   Zhixue 志學   *Fei 飛

*Bingcheng 秉震   *Bingyu 秉宇   *Chengying 成應   *Bingmao 秉懋
(Zhenyu 振宇)
*Anben 安本 (1594-1670)
*Shiqi 世蘷 Shigao 世高
(moved to Guangdong)
Zhaoyuan 肇元
*Qisun 啓孫 (zi Liwen 立文)

Jianlong 見龍

*Hai 海

Notes: 1. An asterisk (*) in front of a name designates person's involvement in some aspect of the publishing industry.
2. A few minor errors have been corrected from a similar table in Fang Yanshou 方彥壽, "Jianyang Xiongshi keshu shulüe" 建陽熊氏刻書述略, Guji zhengli yu yanjiu 6 (1991), 202.

over a dozen works on the much-esteemed Jian'an tea of the Song.[82] Xiong Ke must have been only distantly related to the branch of the family to which Xiong He belonged and was probably even more distant from the printers, all of whom belonged to the West branch of the descent group. Although the West branch's genealogy frequently mentions Xiong He and includes his commemorative essays, it makes no reference to Xiong Ke.

Xiong Jie (*js* 1199), a student of Zhu Xi, and Xiong Gangda (*js* 1214), a student of Huang Gan and a professor at the Jian'an shuyuan,[83] are known chiefly for their work on the *Xinbian yindian xingli qunshu jujie* 新編音點性理群書句解 (Newly compiled collected works on nature and principle, with pronunciation guide and sentence-by-sentence explanation).[84] The earliest extant edition is a Yuan commercial publication and, judging from its appearance, almost certainly from Jianyang,[85] another indication of the continuing influence of *Daoxue* in the Yuan, not just on scholars but also on the publishing industry in the Jianyang area.

Xiong He (1247–1312, *js* 1274, courtesy name Wuxuan 勿軒),[86] like his affinal relative Liu Yingli (Table 2c) and possibly Liu Junzuo of Cuiyan jingshe, retired to his native Minbei after the fall of the Southern Song and became active as a teacher and writer. With Liu Yingli, he established the Hongyuan Academy (Table B.3, no. 110) in the scenic Wuyi Mountains, the site of a number of academies and halls of refinement established in the Song and Yuan. Both men were pre-eminent among the *Daoxue* scholars of their generation and were involved in compiling or recompiling commentaries on the Classics and Four Books. It is quite likely that these works were also published by one of the academies connected with Xiong and Liu, but we have proof for only a few of these, one of which is the *Yili jingzhuan tongjie* 儀禮經傳通解 (The complete explanations of the *Classic of the Ceremonies and Rites* and of the commentaries [by Zhu Xi and a number of his Minbei followers]). Xiong He's preface describes the circumstances that led him to produced this edition: the printing blocks for an earlier edition were destroyed during the turmoil at the end of the Southern Song, and he had corrected and reorganized the contents, based in part on a surviving commercial edition he deemed inadequate.[87]

One work printed by the Hongyuan Academy is a primer to the *Zhouyi*, which contains prefaces by Xiong He and Liu Jing 劉涇, a distant cousin of Liu Yingli (Table 2c). Xiong He was also active in re-establishing and enlarging the family's older and well-known Aofeng shuyuan (Table B.3, no. 111), most of which had been destroyed at the end of the Song.[88] The only known Yuan imprint from the Aofeng shuyuan is an illustrated edition of the *Book of Changes* with the commentaries by Cheng Yi and Zhu Xi and additional commentaries by Xiong He. This work is entitled *Wuxuan Yixue qimeng tuzhuan tongyi* 勿軒易學啓蒙圖傳通義 (Wuxuan's illustrated "mind-opener" for studying the *Book of Changes*, with complete commentaries).[89] This long-winded title would have done justice to the commercial imprints produced in the same area. But what is notable is the "mind-opener" (*qimeng*), a term that referred to works meant to serve as an introduction or primer; such works became popular with both academy and commercial publishers in the Yuan.

Extant Jianyang imprints from academies and halls of refinement date mainly from the Yuan rather than the Song. Although it is possible that Song editions and printing blocks had been destroyed, it is more likely, based on the activities of men such as Xiong He, that they considered it part of their responsibilities to maintain the intellectual tradition that had been so prominent in Minbei during the Song.[90] The decrease in the number of family schools may reflect their role in preparing their students for the civil service examinations, but the *shuyuan* and *jingshe* in the area, many established by Zhu Xi and his associates, remained open and even flourished with little government interest.[91] Ironically, Zhu Xi's idea that education should be freed from the strictures of studying for the government examinations was practiced in the private academies of the Jianyang area in the Yuan, due in large part to the efforts of scholars like Liu Junzhuo, Liu Yingli, Liu Jing, and Xiong He.

Among the commercial Jianyang printers not formally associated with schools in the Yuan, two trends are clear. First, they continued to publish many of the same books as their predecessors had during the Song, including the Classics and Histories, with an emphasis on *Daoxue*-approved works. Their other publications, however, suggest that they were diversifying their offerings. Popular works, such as collections of medical prescriptions, household reference manuals, and illustrated historical fiction became increasingly important in their repertoire.[92] One reason for this widening of publishers' lists was the decline in the demand for scholarly works, as the chances of passing the examinations became dismally small.

This same factor may well have also led to changes in career choices for men in printer families already in the Song. The number of Jianyang area men engaged in some aspect of the publishing industry can be seen as part of an important social phenomenon that was widespread by the Southern Song, namely, a surplus of educated men compared to the quotas for the government examinations and the number of official positions. In Jianning prefecture, this certainly seems to have been the case, an ironic though not surprising result of the great examination successes of men from this area throughout the Song.[93] These men certainly deemed themselves sufficiently well educated to publish a variety of scholarly works. It was necessary to possess (or at least to claim) scholarly competence since producing such editions involved not merely the mechanical reproduction of a worthy text but also the intellectually demanding tasks of acquiring reliable exemplars, collating them, and producing a new edition that was cleansed of mistakes but retained textual variants for the judgment of their readers. Such intentions were expressed by them or for them in the books' prefaces and postfaces or more brashly and succinctly in printers' notes. The high quality of many extant Jianyang imprints from the Song and some from the Yuan support their publishers' claim to erudition. Indeed, for those whose families had not yet attained notable success in government office, their activities as editors, collators, and publishers served to legitimize their claim to be gentlemen-scholars. In addition, the prominence of imprints from family schools during the Song suggests that the publishers or others in their families were also teachers.

On the other hand, the tiny kerchief albums and the whole corpus of examination-related literature argue the sound business sense of at least some of the same printers. Whether Jianyang men opted out of the long and highly uncertain path to official success or simply never succeeded despite repeated attempts, working in some capacity in the publishing industry, as author, editor, proofreader, or printer, became a viable means of earning a living using their years of education. In his *Yuan shi shi fan* 袁氏世範 (Precepts for social life; first published in 1179), Yuan Cai 袁采 (ca. 1140–ca. 1195) suggests that "of those without the ability to pursue the *chin-shih*, the best can become clerks and work with documents, the next best can practice punctuating reading for children and become their tutors."[94] Although Yuan Cai does not explicitly mention publishing as an alternative for those who cannot be scholar-officials, we can argue that through their books, the Jianyang printers were teaching and punctuating texts for all their readers and, in the case of their notorious kerchief editions, stealthily accompanying the candidates into the examination halls to give them dishonorable aid.

During the Yuan, however, the lower demand for examination literature would have led to a decline in the Jianyang printing industry if the publishers had persisted in producing only the same works as they had in the Song. There was probably also a decreasing demand for teachers; certainly the drop from ten *jiashu* involved in printing in the Song to only one in the Yuan (Table 1) would support this conjecture. As a result, men from the printer families either had to diversify their lists of publications or had to engage in new income-earning work, such as professional writing and medicine.[95] This factor in turn explains the increase in medical texts and popular fiction among Jian-yang imprints, which we will survey in the next chapter.

It is noteworthy that for the Liu, Yu, and Xiong families—the three descent groups for which we have the most evidence—almost all the men involved in commercial publishing in the Ming who can be identified directly or indirectly in their genealogies are descended from printers of the Song and Yuan. Some of the Ming men were also well-known professional writers and editors in the publishing industry; some also were noted for their medical knowledge. This clearly suggests that by the mid-Ming it had become quite common for some branch(es) of a descent group to specialize in the book trade and other activities deemed respectable. What persisted, as suggested by the resounding silence of the genealogies on such matters, was the tension between the commercial aspects of the printers' work and their aspirations to be gentlemen-scholars.

4

Jianyang Imprints
of the Song and Yuan

In this chapter, we will examine the imprints themselves, first by considering what their visual appearance can tell us about the printing industry of the times. The second section is devoted to *Mashaben*, the name commonly given to shoddy Jianyang editions. Ironically, because most extant Jianyang books from the Song and many from the Yuan are among the best woodblock imprints ever produced and not *Mashaben*, information on these excoriated volumes must be obtained indirectly, from sources such as contemporary government documents and private writings. Lastly, in a discussion organized by types of works, we will survey a number of Jianyang imprints of the Song and Yuan.

Visual Appearances of Jianyang Imprints of the Song and Yuan

In all, there are about 190 extant Jianyang imprints from the Song.[1] Many of them are easily identified as such since the publisher recorded his name or that of his establishment and its location. Based on the distinctive appearance of these works, it is possible to identify others as likely to be imprints from the same area. Examples of Jianyang imprints from the Southern Song that belie the area's reputation for low-quality books are shown in Figs. 4b and 14–17. In contrast, the two popular works in Fig. 18, although equally recognizable as Jianyang products, are visibly inferior in terms of page design.[2] Indeed, by the late thirteenth century, the quality of *Jianben*, the uses to which they were put, and the nature of the publishers who produced them varied considerably, and these differences are reflected in the looks of the imprints. In this section, we will examine a number of these imprints and consider in more detail how readers of the times might have perceived a *Jianben*.

As noted in Chapter 2, a distinctive calligraphic style can help date and place an imprint. The two styles of the regular script prevalent in Jianyang imprints are illustrated in Figs. 15 and 16. Figure 15 shows examples of a slender, elegant style that one modern source describes as approximating the "slender gold style" (*shoujin ti* 瘦金體) of Emperor Huizong 徽宗 (r. 1101–26).[3] Figure 16 illustrates the bold, muscular influence of the "Yan style" (*Yan ti* 顏體),[4] based on the writing of Yan Zhenqing 顏眞卿, one of the three highly influential Tang calligraphers.[5] Although scholars of rare books agree that the distinctive calligraphies found in Song imprints from the Jianyang area make them easy to identify, they disagree on how to describe these styles.[6] One source of the disagreement is that they speak in general terms without reference to specific examples; another is the subjectivity always exercised in judging calligraphic styles. Because those used in imprints tend to be *more or less* in the style of a given calligrapher (or calligraphers), it is difficult and not very useful to classify the style in an imprint as, say, just *Yan ti*, or even a mixture of styles. In this discussion, I will refer to specific examples rather than attempt to label the style as definitively akin to any of the famous models.

For example, although the calligraphy in the pages in Fig. 15 can be seen as approximating the slender gold style, it could also be labeled the "Ou style" (*Ou ti* 歐體), modeled after the style of the Tang calligrapher Ouyang Xun 歐陽詢. It can also be thought of as a stylistic precursor to the bolder style, usually considered to be the Yan style, of the imprints shown in Fig. 16. Rare book experts most frequently associate these full-bodied characters composed of thick vertical strokes and thinner horizontal ones with the Jianyang imprints of the Song. Another distinguishing feature is the horizontal stroke growing in thickness as it slants upwards from left to right and ending in a tiny downward hook, similar to the common *pinggou* 平鉤 stroke. These features, already present in the brush strokes of the Yan style, are exaggerated and embellished by the knife stroke as the characters are carved in wood. The marked contrast between thick and thin strokes, however, means that only larger characters can be carved in this style to great effect. Smaller characters,

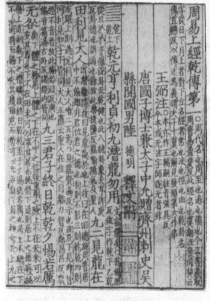

(a)

(b)

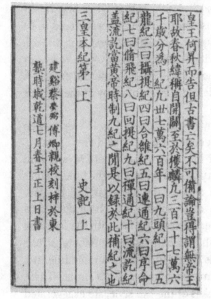

(c)

Fig. 15 Examples of Song Jianyang imprints showing a calligraphic style resembling the "Slender Gold Style" of the Emperor Huizong.

(*a, above left*) *Zhouyi zhu* 周易注. Early Southern Song.

(*b, above right*) *Hou Hanshu zhu* 後漢書注. Early Southern Song. Publisher: Wang Shubian.

(*c, left*) *Shiji jijie suoyin* 史記集解索引. 1171. Publisher: Cai Mengbi.

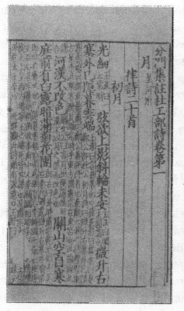

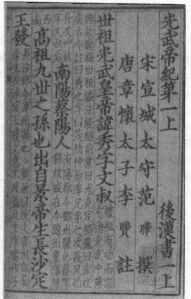

Fig. 16 Examples of Song Jianyang imprints showing the *Yan ti* calligraphic style.

(*a, above left*) *Fenmen jizhu Du Gongbu shi* 分門集註杜工部詩. Southern Song.

(*b, above right*) *Hou Hanshu* 後漢書. 1208. Publisher: Cai Qi of Yijing tang (Seikadō bunko).

(*c, right*) *Minggong shupan qingming ji* 明公書判清明集. Southern Song (Seikadō bunko).

such as those for the commentary sections, although also beautifully written and carved, look much less distinctive. In general, it seems that a number of publishers in the Jianyang area were deliberately cultivating a look for their imprints to distinguish them from those produced elsewhere in the country. These prime examples of Southern Song Jianyang imprints have been used as exemplars for subsequent editions or reprinted in facsimile by government agencies, bibliophiles, and modern publishing companies. This is not to say that deceptive commercial practices are not present in some of the loveliest volumes. For example, as Ming-sun Poon points out, the Jian'an publisher Wei Zhongju's (Table B.2, no. 97) editions (ca. 1200) of the collected works of Liu Zongyuan 柳宗元 (773–819) and of Han Yu 韓愈 (768–824) contained a "ghost bibliography" listing nonexistent works.[7]

As lovely as the calligraphy is, the relatively cramped layout detracts from the overall beauty of the page.[8] The main reason for this is the inclusion of glosses and commentaries, as well as the occasional overpunctuation of the main text. In the *Collected Commentaries for the Spring and Autumn Annals* (Fig. 4b), the main text is quite easy to read, but the intertextual commentary and glosses are printed in a smaller, thinner style and less legible. Although the use of intaglio characters for section headers helps the reader navigate through the text, the sheer mass of smaller-character text can be daunting, especially when it fills an entire page. This problem in legibility was aggravated in the Yuan and Ming when the characters of both the main text and the commentary became smaller and less well written.

A number of high-quality imprints produced in the Jianyang area look noticeably different from the previous examples. These works (Fig. 17) were often printed under official auspices or by private individuals who specified the design of the book and had the means to publish in more expensive formats. The spacious look of these imprints results from fewer characters per column and fewer columns per page, which qualifies them as medium-(*zhongzi ben*) or large-format (*dazi ben*) editions. Moreover, they were, as well, often printed on superior paper. But what is most significant is that they do not have a recognizably Jianyang "look," which suggests that their publishers intentionally distinguished them from the imprints produced by the commercial publishers and/or family schools. Quite possibly, then, although a few Song government officials were perfectly willing to exploit the resources available for book printing in Minbei, they also wanted to maintain their distance from the local industry and the opprobrium associated with at least part of it. For example, Wu Jian, who served as prefect of Jianning sometime during the Xianchun period (1265–74), stated in a colophon at the

張子語錄中
溫良恭儉遜何以盡夫子之德人只爲少他名
道德之字不推廣見得小溫良恭儉遜聖人
惟恐不能盡此五德如夫子之道忠恕而已
聖人惟憂不能盡忠恕聖人豈敢自謂盡忠
恕也所求乎君子之道四是實未能道也
聖人之心則直欲盡道事則安能得盡如博
有盡聖人人也人則有限是誠不能盡道也
施濟狠堯舜寶病諸堯舜之心其施直欲至
于無窮方爲博施言朔南暨聲教西被于流

育德堂奏議卷第一
淳熙輪　對劄子一　十四年十一月
臣聞有高世之德必有高世之功仰惟　陛下
明有以照萬數志有以運四海持之以恭儉達
之以寬仁而充之以樂善無我二十六年之間
日新而無倦　聖德之盛上符帝王而非漢唐
諸君所可望矣夫有是德斯有是功而　陛下
方慊然於大功之未立　聖明之所獨見者猶
蔽於群議之難合　聖志之所獨存者猶牽於

夷堅甲志卷第一　十九
孫九鼎
孫九鼎字嵩嶺忻州人政和癸巳爲太學七夕
日出訪鄉人段浚儀於竹柵巷汴北岸而行
忽有金紫人騎從甚都呼之於稠人中遠下馬
曰國鎮父旦安樂別視之乃婦夫張珖也指街
此一酒肆曰可見遯於此少從容孫曰公富人
也豈可令窮措大買酒自我錢不中使遂坐肆
中欲唱自如少頃孫方悟其死問之曰公死已

Fig. 17 Examples of non-commercial Jianyang imprints from the Song.

(*a. above left*) *Zhangzi yulu* 張子語錄. Southern Song Xianchun period (1265–74). Publisher: Wu Jian (prefect of Jianning).

(*b, above right*) *Yude tang zouyi* 育德堂奏. Song.

(*c, right*) *Yi Jian zhi* 夷堅志. 1180; repaired in the Yuan. Original publisher: Jianning Prefectural School (Seikadō bunko).

end of the *Zhangzi yulu* 張子語錄 (Recorded sayings of Master Zhang [Zai 載]) (Fig. 17a) that he had had the work printed at the office of the Fujian Fiscal Commission (*kan yu Fujian Caozhi* 刊于福建漕治), although he did not mention its location.[9] Other imprints that do mention Jianning, Jian'an, or Jianyang state clearly that they were published at the prefectural or county office or school. Yet despite this insistence on an official imprimatur, many of these works were printed for a complex blend of public and private reasons. For example, as mentioned in Chapter 2, the first four sections of Hong Mai's *Yi Jian zhi* (Fig. 17c) were printed, probably at the prefectural school, in 1180, the last year of Hong's tenure as prefect of Jianning.[10] Given the immense popularity of this work even as it was being written, Hong Mai probably thought it sensible to have it printed where he could supervise the production. The possible profits from selling the work would have benefited the prefectural government as well as the author himself.[11]

What did the denigrated *Mashaben* look like? In general, *Mashaben* referred to imprints like the kerchief volume shown in Fig. 7a, as well the two works in Figs. 18a–b. The work in Fig. 18a, *Xinbian hunli beiyong Yuelao xinshu* 新編婚禮備用月老新書 (New edition of the new handbook of the Old Man of the Moon for marriage preparations), is a writing manual (see below). It fits contemporary writers' description of the typical *Mashaben*: its cramped pages are packed with plenty of information, accurate and inaccurate, and the extant copy looks as if it had been pulled off blocks that had already been used for several thousand copies. The work shown in Figure 18b is the earliest known edition of the historical narrative *Xinbian Xuanhe yishi* 新編宣和遺事 (New edition of *Bygone Events of the Xuanhe period*). Although the calligraphy is not bad, it certainly lacks the distinction of the best imprints. In addition, the page layout is more cramped, and simplified characters and shorthand are used (e.g., the symbol 〈 to indicate a repeated character). The visual style of these two works, which originated by the late Southern Song, became prevalent among Jianyang imprints during the Yuan and early Ming. The cheaper, lower-quality commercial imprints are particularly tricky to date precisely, because the publishers were not overly concerned to provide such works with a distinctive look; they knew what they could skimp on in producing books for a growing market. Once they had settled on a workable format, they continued using it for a long time, until other economic imperatives dictated a change. Indeed, contrary to the belief of writers from the Ming and Qing who attributed the work to the late Southern Song, recent scholars believe that the *Xuanhe yishi* was written in the early Yuan, and this particular edition must date from that period or later.[12]

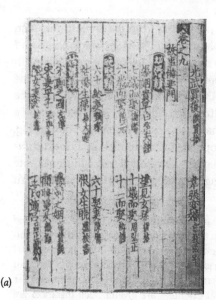 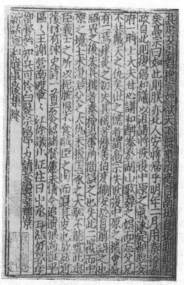

(a)   (b)

Fig. 18 Two imprints of popular works from Jianyang, Southern Song–Yuan. (*a, left*) *Xinbian hunli beiyong Yuelao xinshu* 新編婚禮備用月老新書 (National Central Library [Taipei] Rare Books Collection, no. 07929). (*b, right*) *Xinbian Xuanhe yishi* 新編宣和遺事. Yuan (National Central Library [Taipei] Rare Books Collection, no. 08592).

Certain important continuities and changes in the Jianyang printing industry from the Southern Song to the Yuan are worth noting. First, books such as dictionaries, medical texts, and illustrated historical fiction may also have been published in the Song, but since we have few or no certain examples, they will be discussed in this section on the Yuan. Second, a number of publishers active in the Song continued operating in the Yuan, and in a few cases, into the Ming as well. Moreover, the region's reputation for shoddy imprints persisted and probably became more deserved. Of the extant Jianyang imprints from the Yuan, there is a much larger portion of low-quality ones than from the Song.[13] For example, the bamboo paper used in books was noticeably worse and has discolored much more, and the page layout for many works became even more cramped. The calligraphy to some extent reflected the influence of the well-known Yuan calligrapher and painter Zhao Mengfu 趙孟頫.[14] Not surprisingly, elements of the Zhao style (*Zhao ti* 趙體) were mixed in with other styles and with the commercial printers' pragmatic concern to cram as much text as possible on a page. The result was thinner, smoother characters which were also smaller than the bold, square *Yan ti* characters in many Song imprints of Jianyang.

Some of the changes in Jianyang publishing from the Song to the Yuan are clearly illustrated in printers' colophons. Figs. 14a–d show colophons and printers' notes from Jianyang imprints of the Song, which are relatively plain and sober: either one or two lines, sometimes enclosed in a box, giving the name of the printshop, sometimes of the individual printers as well, and the date the blocks were engraved.[15] Sometimes, in addition to, or in the place of a colophon, the publisher may list his name or that of his shop. Thus, in Fig. 14a, before Yu Renzhong's stylized colophon, he lists himself as a *Guoxue jinshi* and collator, along with four other men. Occasionally, an additional note may mention the reasons for producing the book, such as that written by Yu Renzhong (Fig. 14b):

Good editions of the *Gongyang* and *Guliang* [commentaries on the *Spring and Autumn Annals*] have not been available in the bookstores. I have collated the edition of the Directorate of Education in my family's collection with other Jiangnan and Zhejiang local government editions and made many corrections. But the characters in phonetic annotations by Master Lu [Lu Deming 陸德明, 556–627] sometimes differ from those in the text proper. . . . [Several examples are given.] Such instances are many, and I dare not make changes according to my own humble judgment. For the time being, I have kept both readings and wait for the [opinion of the] learned. Written by Yu Renzhong of Jian'an on the first day of the first month of winter in the 2nd year of Shaoxi [1191].

Fig. 14c shows another note in a similar but more assertive vein by the printer Wang Shubian: "This establishment has now carefully collated and printed a large-character, error-free edition of the Histories of the Former and Later Han. We implore the enlightened attention of the eminent. Respectfully, Wang Shubian of Qiantang." As Ming-sun Poon notes, Wang probably felt that it was good publicity to note that he was originally from the capital, Hangzhou, whose imprints had a better reputation.[16]

Later in the Yuan, colophons and publishers' notes would become more elaborate, and more aggressive and full title pages, often with decorations or illustrations, would be added as well. Figure 19 shows a Jianyang edition of the *Qian jin yao fang* 千金要方 (Essential prescriptions worth a thousand pieces of gold) from the Yuan. The publisher's name is not recorded in extant copies of this edition, but it is quite similar in appearance to other medical imprints from Jianyang. At the end of the table of contents, the printer inserted the following note:

There are not a few medical books, but the *Essential Prescriptions Worth a Thousand Gold Pieces of the Perfected Master Sun* cannot be neglected. The "*qianjin*" in its title indicates its great worth. If one understands its discussions on pulse analysis, acupuncture, moxibustion, and regulation of poisons, then there is nothing more.

Fig. 19 Yuan imprint of medical prescriptions: *Chongkan Sun zhenren beiji qian jin yao fang.* 重刊孫眞人備急千金要方 (Seikadō bunko).

Recently we obtained an early Song government edition from Sichuan, which we dare not keep private. [Thus] we have collated it anew and printed a fine edition to present to the public, worthy of a Bian Que or a [Wang] Shuhe [famous physicians of the past]. Can we not say that this is a great boon to [the cultivation of] good health?

The eye-catching style of such advertisements, often written in running script or grass script and enclosed in a decorative frame, also became increasingly popular.

Three examples of the best Jianyang imprints from the Yuan are shown in Figs. 20a–c. The first is an edition of the *Book of Poetry, Shi jizhuan tongshi* 詩集傳通釋 with annotations by Zhu Xi and later elucidations by Liu Jin 劉瑾, a nephew of Liu Zihui[17] and a distant relative of the publisher, the Liu family's Rixin tang, which continued to produce works into the early sixteenth century. The calligraphic style, the use of intaglio characters to mark new sections, and the uniformity of the number of large and small characters have become identifying marks of Jianyang imprints from the Yuan. Figure 20b is the annalistic history of the Northern Song by Li Tao, the *Xu Zizhi tongjian* 續資治通鑑, printed by the Chen family's Yuqing tang 陳氏餘慶堂, probably in the early fourteenth century.[18] Another historical work (Fig. 20c), a collection of biographical sketches of famous early Yuan officials and

(a)

(b)

(c)

Fig. 20 Examples of superior Jianyang imprints of the Yuan.

(a, above left) *Shi jizhuan tongshi* 詩集傳通釋. 1352. Publisher: Liu family Rixin tang.

(b, above right) *Xu Zizhi tongjian* 續資治通鑑. Yuan. Publisher: Chen family Yuqing tang.

(c, left) *Guochao mingchen shilüe* 國朝名臣事略. 1335. Publisher: Yu Zhi'an of Qinyou tang.

generals, was printed in 1335 by the well-known Qinyou tang of Yu Zhi'an. All three works, as beautiful as they are, look very different from the superior Jianyang imprints of the Song (Figs. 14–16), particularly in their sense of economy in crowding more text onto a page.

During the Yuan, the number of medical texts printed in Jianyang increased, for reasons suggested above. Most were famous works written in earlier periods and revised and enlarged in the Song and Yuan, such as the *Qianjin yaofang* (Fig. 19). A number of them were illustrated, such as the work on acupuncture and moxibustion, *Zhenjiu cisheng jing* 針灸次生經 (Second classic of acupuncture and moxibustion; Fig. 21a). This edition was produced by the Guangqin tang of the Ye family 葉氏廣勤堂, which also published the third-century classic on pulse analysis by Wang Shuhe, *Xinkan Wang shi maijing* 新刊王氏脈經 (Master Wang's classic on pulse analysis, newly printed; Fig. 21b). Another kind of medical work popular with different printers was the compilation of medical prescriptions, such as the *Shi yi dexiao fang* 世醫得效方 (Effective prescriptions of physician families), which appeared in a 1345 edition, soon after it was compiled (Fig. 21c).[19] Although it was probably produced under some kind of official auspices—one Chen Zhi, a superintendent of the Jianning route's Medical Bureau, was listed as its publisher—it was probably sold much like any commercial imprint. In fact, the mediocre calligraphy and the poor paper of this edition makes it inferior to the better Jianyang commercial imprints of the time.[20]

The number of commercially printed dictionaries also increased in the Yuan. For example, in Jianyang alone, the famous rhyming dictionary, *Guangyun* 廣韻 (Expanded rhymes), was reprinted in at least six different editions, and the *Libu yunlüe* 禮部韻略 (Outline of rhymes from the Ministry of Rites) in three different editions (shown in Figs. 22a–c). The first was printed by the Chen family's Yuqing tang in 1355, the second by the Liu family's Rixin tang in the same year, and the third (which does not list a publisher) probably about the same time. Although they look nearly identical and demonstrate the printers' efficient strategy of producing facsimile editions, a close examination of the characters on a number of different pages proves that they were printed from different blocks. Another work (Fig. 22d) is not a dictionary but a sample book of Song Emperor Gaozong's grass script characters arranged according to the rhyming scheme of the *Guangyun*; it was also reprinted at least twice in Jianyang.[21]

As noted in Chapter 2, many early examples of commercial works in the *shangtu xiawen* (running illustration) format date from the Yuan. One rather

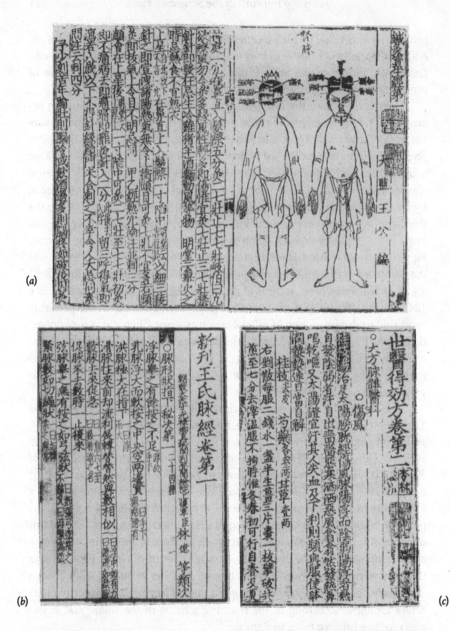

Fig. 21 Medical works from Jianyang during the Yuan. (*a, top*) *Zhenjiu cisheng jing* 針灸次生經. Yuan. Publisher: Ye family Guangqin tang. (*b, bottom left*) *Xinkan Wangshi maijing* 新刊王氏脈經. Ca. 1330. Publisher: Ye family Guangqin shutang. (*c, bottom right*) *Shi yi dexiao fang* 世醫得効方. 1345. Publisher: Chen Zhi, superintendent of the Jianning Prefecture Medical Bureau.

unique example, mentioned earlier, is the *Lives of Exemplary Women from Antiquity* printed by the Yu family's Qinyou tang, probably in the first half of the fourteenth century. Like the plain tales (*pinghua*) shown in Figs. 5a–b, the illustrations run across the full width of the leaf, but occupy half the height of the page. The blocks for this edition were probably cut by copying a late Song edition, from which only a preface dated 1214 survives.[22] If the fourteenth-century edition was indeed a copy of the Song edition, this is more indirect evidence for the existence of non-Buddhist *shangtu xiawen* works in the Song, of which we have very few extant examples.

As for historical fiction in this format, the imprints from Jianyang are the only extant examples from the Yuan.[23] These works are the forerunners of the illustrated historical novels, story collections, and drama miscellanies that became the Jianyang printers' specialties in the mid- and late Ming. The Yuan works are not deluxe editions, and the text portion, with its cramped page layout and nondescript calligraphic style, resembles that in many other ordinary Jianyang imprints of the time. The unexceptional quality of the text in these works probably owes more to economics than to the competence of the blockcarvers. The more impressively executed illustrations, which are full-leaf in width, are superior to many in Ming works, which are nearly all half-leaf in width. In contrast, the text is quite bare, without punctuation and without glosses or annotations. In fact, the only variation *within* the text for the reader's eye is the occasional use of intaglio characters, such as "the verse says" (*shi yue* 詩曰), to mark a few stanzas of verse. The pictures above the text therefore serve, among other purposes, as visual relief from the cramped text.

In the series of plain tales published by the Yú family's Wuben tang 虞氏務本堂 in the Zhizhi period (1321–23), each work advertises on the title page that it is fully illustrated (*quanxiang* 全相). Fig. 5a shows the first half-leaf of the first *juan* of the *Xinkan quanxiang Qin bing Liu guo pinghua* 新刊全相秦併六國平話 (New edition of *The Plain Tale of the Unification of the Six States by the Qin*). As in all the other works, the carver recorded his name (here, Huang Shu'an 黃淑安) just beneath the caption on the right side of the picture.[24] The illustration in Fig. 5b from the *Quanxiang pinghua Sanguo zhi* 全相平話三國志 (Plain Tale from the *Chronicle of the Three Kingdoms*) manages to utilize the long horizontal space across an entire leaf to convey a feeling of distance or separation between the pursued figure and his pursuers. Another edition of this work is a *Sanfen shilüe* 三分事略, printed by the Jian'an shutang 建安書堂, possibly dating from 1294,[25] and even earlier works may yet be discovered.[26]

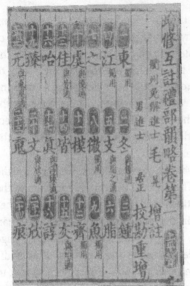

(a)   (b)

Fig. 22 Yuan editions of rhyming dictionaries from Jianyang. (*a, above left*) *Zengxiu huzhu Libu yunlüe* 增修互註禮部韻略. 1355. Publisher: Chen family Yuqing tang (Seikadō bunko). (*b, above right*) *Zengxiu huzhu Libu yunlüe* 增修互註禮部韻略. 1355. Publisher: Liu family Rixin shutang (National Central Library [Taipei] Rare Books Collection, no. 01084). (*c, opposite page left*) *Zengxiu huzhu Libu yunlüe* 增修互註禮部韻略. Yuan (Seikadō bunko). (*d, opposite page right*) *Caoshu Libu yun bao* 草書禮部韻寶. 1288. Publisher: Jian'an Xiaozhai (National Central Library [Taipei] Rare Books Collection, no. 01076).

Given the popularity in the Song of historical tales in both oral and written forms, it is quite likely that this running illustration format was used for such works by the Southern Song. Indeed, there is evidence to support this speculation. First, we have one extant work of fiction from a Southern Song bookstore located in an entertainment quarter of Hangzhou.[27] Second, as we noted in Chapter 2, the running illustration format had been used in other kinds of works, including the Classics and Buddhist sutras. Third, the style of the illustrations in the Jianyang *pinghua* was not unique to imprints alone, but it showed up in other media, including pottery, especially ceramic headrests and vases from Cizhou 磁州.[28] In fact, these illustrated ceramic pillows date from the thirteenth century and were produced in northern China under the Jin and Yuan dynasties. Art historians have pointed out that these pictures were inspired by dramas or modeled after those in paintings and woodblock prints.[29] Jianyang imprints and Cizhou ware are alike in several ways. Both were often considered popular wares; they appeared with little or no official supervision, they were produced over a long period, and they were sold

(c)

(d)

throughout a large geographical area. In any case, if scholars' conjectures are correct, then either the *shangtu xiawen* historical romances and possibly dramas were published in places other than Jianyang, or Jianyang imprints reached a wider area than can be attested. Furthermore, judging from Yuan dynasty blue and white porcelain vases depicting scenes from dramas, such as the *Xixiang ji* 西廂記 (The story of the western chamber), it seems likely that illustrated editions of dramas were also published in the Yuan, although we have no extant copies.[30] The style of the picture on the vases is quite similar to that in a *shangtu xiawen* edition of the play published in 1498, over 150 years later, by a commercial house in Beijing.[31]

The *pinghua* and other commercial imprints from the Yuan, which were presumably aimed at many readers with varying degrees of literacy, contain many simplified characters. This practice, as well as the use of variant forms for a given character in a printed text, was not new, however, as even a cursory examination of religious and secular materials from the Tang and early Song shows. But they became widespread during this period for a number of reasons, including the oft-cited one that the Mongols and the other non-Han ethnic groups present in greater numbers in Yuan China had difficulty mastering Chinese and so preferred to use simplified characters.[32] In any case, since there was no standard set of simplified characters, the copyists, and probably the blockcarvers as well, commonly produced an approximation not of the proper character but of a frequently used version of the simplified character. This unprecedented increase in the number of variants, correct and incorrect, for a given character probably made scanning a text somewhat more difficult.[33]

In the Yuan there was a broadening readership who wanted not an impeccable text that was the fruit of a tremendous scholarly labor involving the collation of earlier versions but a text that was more or less correct, useful for the information or entertainment it conveyed. What is significant is that this rather slapdash and utilitarian attitude also permeated scholarly works in general, and not just examination cribs or pocket-size references. This represents a dramatic about-face from the beauty of Song imprints, whatever their scholarly quality.

Thus, although extremely few technical innovations appeared in Chinese block-printed books in the Southern Song and Yuan, the gradually increasing range of commercial imprints and the growing commercialization of publishing were important developments. For Jianyang, these trends were also related to the rapid expansion of its long-distance book trade, which must have been well established by the late thirteenth and early fourteenth centuries. *Mashaben* went everywhere, even Korea and Japan.

Mashaben

A story that went the rounds among Song literati and is recorded in at least three Song works goes as follows. A professor in the Hangzhou prefectural school asked his students: "[The hexagram] *Qian* 乾 corresponds to metal, and *Kun* 坤 also corresponds to metal, how is that?" (乾爲金坤亦爲金何也). Upon checking their Directorate of Education edition of the *Yijing*, the students responded, "Sir, you must be using a *Masha* edition, because the Directorate edition says that *Kun* corresponds to *fu* 釜 [i.e., receptacle]." Embarrassed, the instructor had to admit his mistake and withdraw his question.[34]

The imprints of the known publishers discussed above are not on the whole the notorious *Mashaben* condemned by Song and Yuan writers. Indeed, a number of the books shown in the preceding illustrations are now counted among the most prized possessions of the libraries fortunate enough to own them. Even among the Jianyang publications whose publishers are unidentifiable and are listed in catalogues simply as *Jiankanben*, some (though not all) come close to the high quality of the works of the well-known publishers.[35] What, then, was a *Mashaben*? Clearly, bad physical quality—poor paper, pallid ink, a cramped page layout with badly printed characters, a smudgy impression—was associated with *Mashaben*. Moreover, critics of *Mashaben* frequently railed at the bad editing and misprints as well as the bowdlerization and forging of portions of the texts. Although any badly printed work from Jianyang could be condemned as a *Mashaben*, nearly all the known examples from the Song and Yuan are scholarly works, and many of these are examination literature of some kind.[36]

Were *Mashaben* as ubiquitous as Song and Yuan writers claimed? The answer is yes, and several kinds of sources give evidence of this. First, there are the imprints themselves, since fortunately for later scholars, a few of these shoddy *Mashaben* did survive. Second, there are a number of bibliographies, especially descriptive library catalogues of the times, such as the *Junzhai dushu zhi* 郡齋讀書志 (Reading notes from the prefectural studio) of Chao Gongwu 晁公武 (?–1171) and the *Zhizhai shulu jieti* 直齋書錄解題 (Annotated book catalogue of the Zhi Studio) of Chen Zhensun 陳振孫 (ca. 1190–after 1249).[37] A third kind of material consists of official documents, such as memorials, decrees, edicts, and legal restrictions on publishing of various kinds of works, which can be found in sources such as the *Song huiyao jigao* 宋會要輯稿 (Draft of essential documents of the Song) and the histories, including the *Song shi* 宋史 (Dynastic history of the Song), the *Xu Zizhi tongjian (changbian)* 續資治通鑑（長編）([Collected materials for] A continuation of the *Comprehensive Mirror for Governing*), and *Jianyan yilai xinian yaolu* 建炎以來繫年要錄 (Essential records of events since the start of the Jianyan period [1127–30]). Corresponding Yuan sources are far fewer, although a little information, such as few general prohibitions on books, can be gleaned from the *Yuan dianzhang*. Finally, by dint of much searching, we can find among the collected writings of individuals an occasional observation or anecdote that reveals something of the lively and competitive book trade that had evolved by the Southern Song.

An idea of the competitiveness of the book market for works like the *Mashaben* can be gained by tallying the number of different editions of a given work. For example, one writer extremely popular with the commercial publishers and so presumably with their customers was the Northern Song scholar-official and poet Su Shi. There were in the Southern Song, from Jianyang alone, at least five different editions of the *Wang zhuangyuan ji baijia zhu fenlei Dongpo xiansheng shi* 王狀元集百家註分類東坡先生詩 (Poems of Master Dongpo with collected commentaries edited by First Scholar Wang), first printed in the latter part of the twelfth century. Judging by the worn impressions of some extant copies, the blocks were used many times, and at least one other edition was printed by the Xiong family in the Yuan. To entice customers, three of these editions also offered an additional *juan* giving Su Shi's chronological biography (*nianpu*), and one of these, from the Yú Pingzhai Wuben tang, was billed as an "enlarged and collated" (*zengkan jiaozheng* 增刊校正) edition. Such elaborate titles promising (though often not delivering) all sorts of enhancements of the original text were almost *de rigueur* among commercial editions and are a quick way to identify them.[38] The editorial credit was falsely attributed to Wang Shipeng 王十朋 in the hope that his fame as the top-ranking *jinshi* of his year would lend credit to the work. There was also at least one Jianyang edition of Su Shi's (supposedly) complete works. As Chen Zhensun rather waspishly noted, not only was the Jianyang edition incomplete (it lacked Su's verses written on imperial order or *yingzhao* 應詔) and full of mistakes, but a certain Mr. Zhang in Jizhou had reprinted this edition without making corrections.[39]

A useful way to learn about the workings of the book market in the Song is to look at how commercial printers responded to, anticipated, and even created demand for their books among students preparing for the civil service examinations and how the government attempted to regulate this trade. As large as the potential local market was for such imprints in Jianyang (see above), the publishers early on had, by all accounts, tapped into the national market. In theory, they were competing for the largest well-educated group of customers of the time—probably several hundred thousand by the mid–Southern Song.[40]

For the preliminary prefectural and the departmental examinations leading to the *jinshi* degree,[41] students had to study the Classics and commentaries, as well as history and works on poetry. Among the important texts, depending on the intellectual and political climate of the particular period, were the *Three Histories* (*Shiji*, *Han shu*, *Hou Han shu*), the *Xin Tang shu*, Sima Guang's 司馬光 *Zizhi tongjian* 資治通鑑, and Confucian works such as the *Xunzi* and *Yangzi fa yan*.[42] Works emphasized by *Daoxue* scholars or written/compiled by them were in favor in certain periods and gained a permanent ascendance in the last few decades of the Southern Song when Zhu Xi's commentaries for the *Four Books* gained official recognition.[43] Other works needed for preparing for the examinations included philological works, chronicles of historical events, biographies, geographies, and works on government institutions.

By the mid-eleventh century, all the Classics, the *Four Books*, seven of the dynastic histories, and a number of newly compiled or revised dictionaries had been printed by the Directorate of Education.[44] Although the Directorate editions were distributed to regional government academies and could be sold to the public, they were prohibitively expensive, especially the original large-character editions.[45] The records of donations of Directorate editions to schools apply only for the Northern Song, a fact that suggests the practice stopped when cheaper commercial editions became available.[46] According to the Southern Song writer Li Xinchuan 李心傳 (1166–1243), officials serving in the capital would buy a complete set of Directorate editions for several *thousand* strings of cash.

In addition to basic texts and references, other works, which were not published by the government,[47] included collections of examination essays, either those written by successful candidates or model ones on anticipated topics, were in great demand. Furthermore, entire genres of examination literature, popularly referred to as *shiwen* 時文 (current writings),[48] flourished. Other than examination essays, there were digests of historical and philosophical works, guides to improving one's writing style, and topically arranged books (*leishu*) on a wide range of subjects, many conveniently organized for examination use.[49] Finally, crib copies of all these books, the tiny kerchief volumes,[50] for smuggling into the examination hall, constituted the profitable low end of examination-related literature. All publishers, including regional and local governments as well as commercial printers, stood to profit from this market. Furthermore, because even the highly esteemed Directorate editions were far from flawless and because printing had generally increased the number of works available, Song scholars enthusiastically took up the practice of collating texts.[51] In the case of the commercial publishers, the results were a very mixed bag.

As Ming-sun Poon points out, there are after all only nine Confucian classics and the Four Books, a rather limited corpus of works for publishers needing to maintain and, if possible, enlarge their market. One obvious way, of which we have seen several examples, was to offer various features to explain the main text. For example, there are at least five different (i.e., printed from different woodblocks) Jianyang editions from the second half of the twelfth century of the typically titled *Zuantu huzhu chongyan chongyi Zhou li* 纂圖互注重言重意周禮 (*The Rites of Zhou*, illustrated and cross-referenced [to other works on this title], cross-referenced for repeated words and phrases, cross-referenced for synonyms). The only edition whose publisher is known, and which delivers all the features promised in the title, is that of Yu Renzhong's Wanjuan tang. The other four, which seem to have been based on the Wanjuan tang edition, either add, or more frequently, subtract some of these features. One edition omits the punctuation (of the main text) present in the Wanjuan tang imprint, but has extra *chongyan chongyi*. Another provides much smaller and more crudely executed illustrations. A fourth, which has added phonetic glosses (the standard ones by the Tang scholar Lu Deming) is as well produced as the Wanjuan tang's version and has a few blockcarvers' names recorded in it. The fifth is a kerchief edition that omits most of the illustrations. Similar examples of false advertising can be found among Jianyang editions of the other Classics. Nor were the more reputable Jianyang printers free from exaggerated or false claims. For example, the *Han shu* printed jointly in 1195 by Huang Shanfu and Liu Yuanqi claims that its collation notes are by the famous Northern Song scholar Song Qi 宋祁, a claim that has been questioned by modern scholars.[52]

It is in the titles not published by government offices, however, that we see the greatest proliferation of commercial imprints and the government's largely ineffective attempts to control them. Based on the summary in Table 5 of Song memorials, edicts, decrees, and other government documents dealing with examination literature published by commercial printers throughout the country, especially those in Jianyang, we can make a number of observations.[53] First, it is quite obvious from the complaints and suggestions repeatedly made in the memorials and petitions and the responding decrees that the market for printed examination-related literature was so well established by the early twelfth century[54] at the very latest that the government was fighting a losing battle. Second, commercial printers apparently produced these materials with impunity. The punishments as stated in the legal documents varied: the offending imprints and their printing blocks were to be destroyed, and the printers and booksellers could be fined, beaten, or exiled. The severity of the punishment depended on the specific materials. For example, according to the *Qingyuan tiaofa shilei* 慶元條法事類 (Classified paragraphs of the law of the Qingyuan period [1195–1200]), the penalty for printing examination essays in general was 80 blows of the stick; publishing a work on border affairs merited a penalty of exile to a distance of 3,000 *li*.[55] We do not know if such punishments were consistently carried out. The only example in Table 5 is the incident in 1177 when Masha printers were arrested and beaten severely for printing essays "emphasizing false learning."[56] In contrast, some twenty years later, in 1198, local officials reported on the audacity of another Masha printer who had reproduced in the *Taixue zong xinwen ti* 太學總新文體 (New general essays from the Imperial University), three pieces supposedly written by one Guo Mingqing, the first-place candidate in the university's entrance examination in the spring of 1197, according to the publisher. Official investigation showed that not only had Guo not been admitted to the university, but also he did not write the essays![57] Despite the usual recommendations that the printing blocks and the unsold copies be destroyed, the printer seems to have continued operating. Either he or others in the area went on to more ambitious projects, forging examination essays attributed to well-known scholars.

Table 5

Summary of Government Memorials, Edicts, Decrees Dealing with
Privately and Commerically Produced Examination-related Literature

Date	Issue
1005	Bureau of Examinations, Ministry of Rites, charges in a memorial that students often bring handwritten copies of literary works into the examination halls
1009	Emperor Zhenzong's edict reprimanding authors of works with unorthodox ideas and frivolous literary styles; the Fiscal Authorities are to be assigned the task of examining printed works and works applying for authorization and are to report to the throne those deemed publishable
1012	Emperor Zhenzong stops the practice of strip-searching examination candidates—as a result, 18 candidates are found guilty of bringing along unauthorized books, and 93 guarantors are implicated
1057	Ouyang Xiu's memorial describing the procedure of smuggling notes into the examination halls
1101	Officials petition to burn all printed examination essays together with their printing blocks except those on the Classics compiled by the government
1108	Circuit Educational Superintendent Su Yue suggests that commercial editions of examination essays that are printed merely for profit and do not conform to the "Way of the kings of antiquity" be replaced by well-edited government editions
1112	Memorial complaining about the smuggling into examination halls of "small books with characters as minute as the heads of flies. After the examination was over, the leftover literature piled up [like a mound]. In addition, booksellers prints small books . . . which can rest in the palm of the hand. Candidates rush to buy these small books, such as the *San jing xinyi* 三經新義 [by Wang Anshi] and explanations of the *Zhuangzi* and *Laozi* for use in the examination"; proposal to prohibit these books approved
1114	In response to a memorial from Circuit Educational Superintendent Huang Qianshan about the harm done to scholars by bookstore editions of examination books like *Jueke jiyao* 決科機要 (Important tips for succeeding in the examinations), which lazy students simply memorize without understanding, Emperor Huizong offers rewards for information leading to the prosecution of criminals and the destruction of printing blocks
1117	Suggestion similar to that of Huang Qianshan made in another memorial, which mentions examination aids with titles such as *bianti* 編題 and *leiyao* 類要; the memorialist notes that there have been many prohibitions of such items in the past and advocates stricter enforcement

(*continues overleaf*)

Table 5, cont.

Date	Issue
1145	Memorial from Sun Zhongao, director of the National University, on the prevalence of unauthorized bookstore editions of unorthodox thoughts and styles, despite repeated warnings and prohibitions; Sun suggests publishing regulations be enforced; bookstores should submit manuscripts they want to print to local officials and instructors in government academies for screening and authorization
1147	Memorial charging that bookstores throughout the country are printing unorthodox works without official authorization; the Fiscal Authorities should investigate the situation and immediately destroy the printing blocks for such works
1155	A prefect, Cai Di, suggests that, other than texts from the Directorate of Education, no books should be printed without authorization. In response, Emperor Gaozong comments that private printing, especially in Fujian and Sichuan, should be prohibited and that the Ministry of Rites should be responsible for this task
1156	Henceforth all reference works needed during an examination will be provided by the examiners; measure not carried out consistently
1159	Edict warns bookstores to refrain from printing books without an authorization from the Directorate of Education
1171	Directorate of Education compiles essays that meet the criteria for the entrance examination to the Imperial University
1177	(1) Petition from the Directorate of Education reports on the illegal printing of examination essays that "emphasize false learning" 似主張偽學 in Masha and proposes that the Fiscal Authority of Fujian should confiscate printing blocks together with unsold books for burning by the Directorate and should arrest the printers and booksellers involved and beat them severely (2) Proposal similar to those made in 1114 and of 1117 mentions that bookstores in Jianning Prefecture are printing forged examination essays; emperor issues edict prohibiting this
1180	Edict stressing prohibition of unauthorized printing by bookstores
1190	(1) In response to a memorial, edict issued prohibiting Jianning printers from publishing editions of examination essays (2) Department of Ministries proposes that the government compile a selection of examination essays, apparently to counteract commercial editions; opposed by Peng Guinian, a professor at the National University

Table 5, cont.

Date	Issue
1195–1200	Regulations in the *Qingyuan tiaofa shilei, juan* 17, on publishing and owning forbidden works
1198	Local officials report unauthorized printing of examination essays by bookstores in various places; petition for immediate destruction of printing blocks and prohibition of the books to be supervised by Department of Ministries and Ministry of Rites
1199	Memorial by Huang Yu, an official in the Ministry of Rites, proposing that examination essays be inspected by instructors in academies before being printed by bookstores
1201	Petition from officials proposing that forged books, private works, and examination essays not authorized by the Directorate of Education be destroyed
1205	Proposal by Xiao Kui of the Ministry of Rites that the government compile examination essays on the Classics and poetry presented since the Shaoxing period (1131–62)
1216	Petition states that small-print books intended for examinations include digests and topical discussions of the Classics and Histories and entire *fu* 賦: "Cunning candidates succeed by chance, at the expense of the truly learned scholars who fail"
1223	Memorials from Yang Lin, professor at the Directorate of Education, and Hu Gangzhong, professor at the National University, attack examination misconduct, mentioning the popularity of pocket editions of all kinds (*jing zi shi ji shilei* 經子史集事類), and suggest that the printing blocks of small editions be burned and sales of the books be strictly prohibited. Enforcement of the prohibition should begin in Hangzhou and then be extended to all prefectures of the empire. The memorial was referred from the Ministry of Rites to the Directorate of Education for discussion and investigation
1253	Edict issued reasserting prohibition against smuggling texts into the examination halls

SOURCES: 1005: Hong Mai, *Rongzhai suibi, juan* 3, p. 31; 1009: *Song shi* (*SS*) 7: 140; 1012: Peng Baichuan, *Taiping zhi ji tong lei*, p. 1898; 1057: Ouyang Xiu, *Quanji*, 2: 872; 1101: Xu Song, *Song huiyao jigao* (*SHY*): *xuanju* 選舉 (*XJ*), 4/3; 1108: *SHY: xingfa* 刑法 (*XF*), 2/48; 1112: *SHY:XJ*, 3/56, 4/7, 6/27; 1114: *SHY:XF*, 2/62; 2/67; 1117: *SHY:XF*, 2/67; 1145: *SHY:XF*, 2/151; Li Xinchuan, *Jianyan yilai xinian yaolu* (*JYYL*), *juan* 154, p. 2496; 1147: *SHY:XF*, 2/151; 1155: *JYYL, juan* 168, pp. 2744-45; 1156: *JYYL, juan* 172, p. 2827; 1159: *JYYL, juan* 182, p. 3037; 1171: *SHY:XJ*, 5/40–41; 1177: *SHY:XF*, 2/129; 1180: *SS*, 35: 672; Bi Yuan et al., *Xu Zizhi tongjian* (*XZZTJ*), p. 935; 1190: *SHY:XF*, 2/124; Peng Guinian, *Zhitang ji, juan* 1, pp. 2-4; 1195–1200: *Qingyuan tiaofa shilei, juan* 17; 1198: *SHY:XF*, 2/129; 1199: *SHY:XJ*, 5/19; 1201: *SHY:XJ*, 5/24; 1205: *SHY:XJ*, 5/3; 1216: *SHY:XJ*, 6/25; 1223: *SHY:XJ*, 6/49-50; 1253: *XZZTJ*, p. 4736.

The legal decrees commonly had a provision that informants reporting printers of forbidden works would receive a reward (from the confiscated property) of 30–100 strings of cash. This enticement may have been efficacious to some extent and thus partially explains why so few of these imprints are extant. On the other hand, their very function would have precluded a long life; if the petition of 1112 is correct, the cribs must have been inexpensive enough that their owners would throw them away on leaving the examination hall.[58] In theory at least, those printing and selling examination literature were subject to severer punishments than their customers. After all, there was no law against reading such works outside the examination hall, and those caught using small editions in the examinations were not subject to corporal punishment. In fact, as Poon has pointed out, it was quite easy to smuggle such materials into the examinations since candidates were allowed to bring reference works such as dictionaries. To prevent this, in 1156, the examination authorities were ordered to provide such books, but the measure apparently was not consistently carried out.[59]

Third, the contents of some of the examination cribs, according to the petition of 1216, consisted of digests, topically arranged discussions of the Classics and Histories, and excerpts from commentaries—everything but the main text. This makes perfect sense, since a candidate who had not memorized the Classics by the time of the examination would have little use for the text, whereas the materials that were contained in the cribs were eminently plagiarizable. Indeed, many cribs sensibly provided exactly what its owner needed to write. Those who chose the poetry track for their examinations had books with exposition essays (*lun* 論), complete *fu* 賦 (poetic expositions) and *shi* 詩 (regulated poems), as well as policy essays (*ce* 策). Those opting for the "meaning of the Classics" track had essays on the Classic of their specialty and exposition and policy essays and could easily have tucked into their sleeve cribs containing a generous selection of such pieces.

Fourth, the frequent proposal that a government agency compile the best examination essays seems not to have been carried out very frequently. Officials' fears that students would succumb to trendy but unorthodox ideas that would help them pass the examinations and no longer study the true meaning of the Classics led to numerous memorials, like that of Circuit Educational Superintendent Su Yue in 1108, proposing that only the government be allowed to issue approved examination essays. But the many attempts of the state to win back its authority and control over the diffusion of examination literature were never very effective. For instance, both the memorials of 1199 and 1205 ask that essays from around the time of the Shaoxing period (1131–62)—some forty or more years earlier, be compiled, commentaries added, and published. Even when this was done, they were rather limited in number and scope, emphasizing the Classics. Moreover, since the main criteria were orthodoxy and elegant style, using them as models was a rather uncertain proposition given that political and literary trends could swing drastically. Finally, even if a government office compiled and printed a collection of such essays, they would most likely be relatively expensive and thus spawn a whole slew of cheaper commercial editions, each of which would entice customers by offering the usual added features discussed above. The entire process would just begin again.

Yue Ke 岳珂, in the early thirteenth century, summed up the situation as follows:

Ever since the country began to recruit officials through examinations, generations have given priority to studying for them. Thus works that are topically arranged, or itemized, or outlined and summarized in order to facilitate reading are today so numerous [lit., that they would cause cattle moving them to sweat]. The Jianyang bookstores compile them by the day and print them by the month, and their contents continuously change. . . . I have investigated the situation and found that from the time peace came to the country [i.e., the start of the dynasty], such works have been prohibited. . . . Today, these books are everywhere and are a hundred times as numerous as the Classics, Histories, and other works. Indeed, to prohibit and destroy them is impossible. But they are not capable of deceiving the truly learned scholar.[60]

In instituting the examination system, the Song government had helped generate an examination culture that would become increasingly embedded in the society and decreasingly under the state's control. The production, publication, and use of examination-related literature, perhaps more than any other kind of books, clearly demonstrate this. Even works first compiled or collated and issued by the government in a very short time became common intellectual property. In a society in which printing had become such a pervasive medium of text transmission, it was also bound to become a great leveler of textual authority. Much of the examination-related literature deserved its quick demise, but not all. For example, some excellent *leishu* were compiled.[61] And in an intellectual tradition in which the inescapable presence of the great classics of the past so often compelled scholars to channel their energies into recollating or writing yet another subcommentary or study on these works, or compiling excerpts from them, the potential of print allowed scholars to hope that their outpourings would reach readers in their own times and even survive down the ages.

In conclusion, from the Northern Song on, *Mashaben* may exemplify all the abuses mentioned above, but their vigorous growth with time argues a certain inevitability about the ways in which commercial printing would develop, especially in an area distant from the largest book markets in the cities.

The Jianyang publishers by no means had a monopoly on shoddily produced books, but the survival of the Jianyang book trade probably depended increasingly on the poorer-quality imprints. These works could be produced more cheaply and transported with less financial risk than superior editions, and most important, they could command a wider market. Indeed, the increase of *Mashaben* among Jianyang imprints in the Yuan may well reflect the growing importance of the long-distance book trade.

Jianyang Imprints: A Survey

This survey of Jianyang imprints begins with a discussion of the kinds of books published in Jianyang in the Song and Yuan and then takes a closer look at selected titles in order to understand trends during these three centuries, when commercial publishing became such an important part of Chinese culture. Table C.2 classifies extant imprints dating from the Song,[62] Yuan, and Ming according to the traditional *siku* classification.[63] The table is based on a bibliography of over 2,000 Jianyang imprints compiled in the course of this study, as described in Appendix C. It follows, therefore, that the same caveats for the bibliography apply to the table and that the distributions and their changes over time are far more useful, than the absolute number given for each kind of imprint, for studying the historical development of the Jianyang book trade. The books of all publishers other than government offices are included, since little difference in the distribution of the kinds of books printed could be found among imprints from ostensibly commercial establishments, family schools (*jiashu*), or academies (*shuyuan*).

Other than Ming-sun Poon's data for various kinds of publishers in the Song,[64] there are no other distribution tables similar to Table C.2 Thus it is difficult to make conclusive comparisons between books commercially printed in Jianyang and those printed by other kinds of publishers or in other areas of China. Because of the wide geographical scope of the Jianyang book trade from the Song on, however, we can use the information in Table C.2 to extrapolate to a much broader perspective on the book culture of the entire country during the Song and Yuan (the Ming is discussed in the next two chapters).

In general the order of this discussion reflects the *siku* order in Table C.2. Occasionally, however, I have regrouped certain kinds of works because of the logic of the discussion. For example, since many works in the Confucianist (*rujia* 儒家) subcategory in the "Philosophy" section (*zibu* 子部), that is, mainly works by later Confucian scholars, will be discussed in conjunction with the Classics and the Four Books. not only because their contents are related but also because the trends in publishing such works were the same during the Song and Yuan.

Classics (*jingbu* 經部)

Classics, Four Books, and Confucianist works. The ancient Confucian classics were staples of the Jianyang printing industry in the Song and remained so through the Yuan. A comparison of the outputs of the two dynasties show that they remained roughly the same fraction of the total for each period. The obvious changes in the overall "Classics" section result partly from the greater number of works on the Four Books and, even more so, the dramatic growth in number of philological works printed in the later period.

The greater popularity of works on the Four Books in the Yuan reflect the increased emphasis on them (via-à-vis the Classics) in the government examinations and also their advocacy by the proponents of *Daoxue*, including personal disciples of Zhu Xi and some of his close friends in the Jianyang area, who perpetuated their teachings into the Yuan. Of the thirteen known Jianyang imprints on the Four Books, nine are definitely dated after 1313, when the Yuan government conferred official recognition on Zhu Xi's commentaries on these texts. (The precise dates for the other four are unclear.)

A similar situation prevails for the Classics and commentaries: of the 44 known Jianyang imprints, 30 are dated after 1313. Of the three works datable before 1313, one was printed by Xiong He's Hongyuan shuyuan in 1289 and the other by Xiong He's relative Xiong Jing 熊敬 in 1305.[65] The dates of these imprints suggest that by the Yuan the habit of studying classical works in connection with the civil service examination was a habit too deeply ingrained among Chinese literati to be broken, even when they confronted tiny examination quotas that promised little chance of official success.

We may argue that the works on the Classics and Four Books were written or compiled by scholars with little interest in taking the examinations or serving the Yuan government, but rather with the desire to preserve and propagate Chinese learning during a particularly bleak period for such studies. Certainly, there is evidence of Song loyalism and an inclination toward Confucian eremitism among Yuan literati.[66] This eremitic outlook was supported by notions of self-cultivation based on *Daoxue* ideas, particularly among men in the Jianyang area, one of the strongholds of Neo-Confucianism. This argument, however, would not explain why their works were printed commercially. The restoration of the examination system therefore accounts in part for the publication of these works.

Another reason why production of commercial imprints of the Classics and Four Books continued to be important in the Yuan has to do with the particular kinds of works produced. The 1289 publication from the Hongyuan shuyuan mentioned above is a primer for the *Book of Changes*, entitled *Yixue qimeng tongshi* 易學啓蒙通釋 (Primer with complete explanations for the study of the *Book of Changes*). In fact, among the books on the Classics printed in Jianyang by either academies or commercial publishers, primers, often called *qimeng* 啓蒙—or more descriptively, "texts to open the minds of the ignorant"—or *mengqiu* 蒙求, "seeking enlightenment," or, if the work was for children, *tongzi wen* 童子問, "(answers to) children's questions," figure more prominently among Jianyang imprints of the Yuan than the Song (and would be found in great profusion in the Ming). There is at least one primer apiece for the *Book of Changes*, the *Book of Poetry*, the *Rites of Zhou*, and the *Spring and Autumn Annals*, and two for the Four Books among Jianyang publications of the Yuan. Such a trend suggests the increasing willingness of scholars to write and printers to produce introductions to the Classics, which were probably used not just for teaching young children but also for enlightening older readers.[67]

Such a trend in the Yuan is visible not only in Jianyang but also in other parts of the country.[68] For example, a small primer on the Classics 428 characters long, arranged in four-character phrases, the *Xingli zixun* 性理字訓 (A primer of human nature and principles), was originally compiled by an associate of Zhu Xi. It was then annotated by another scholar in the late Southern Song and further expanded by a Yuan scholar in Xiuning (Huizhou). Finally another Xiuning scholar added commentaries. The work gives evidence of connections among scholars and publishers in Huizhou and Jianyang. First, in a preface to the *Yixue qimeng tongshi* published by the Hongyuan Academy, Xiong He wrote that it was revised by the son of the author (Hu Fangping 胡方平, another Huizhou scholar of the late Southern Song) when the former visited the Wuyi Mountains. Second, one other Huizhou scholar, Ni Shiyi 倪士毅, after finishing the compilation of the *Chongding Si shu jishi* 重訂四書輯釋 (Revised compilation of annotations for the Four Books), sold the manuscript to a famous Jianyang commercial publisher, Liu Shujian of Rixin tang (Table B.1, no. 36), who brought out an edition in 1341 and a revised edition the following year.[69]

The important point is not that scholars began to consider such works worth writing only in the Yuan—some of the primers and guides to the Classics published in the Yuan had been written in the Southern Song—but that political, social, and cultural conditions brought about by the Mongol conquest not only did not impede but may well have stimulated the writing and

publishing of these texts. On the other hand, would such works have prolifer-
ated had Song China not come under Mongol domination? If we look ahead
to the state of commercial publishing in the late Ming, when these primers
and guides (as well as all other kinds of examination literature) would
become main staples of the book trade, the answer to this hypothetical question may well be yes. The growing importance of these works in the Yuan represents not so much a break from Song developments in books and publishing but the intensification of a pre-existing tendency that would continue into
the Ming.

The rather interesting variety of the extant Confucian[70] works printed in
Jianyang in the Song is not representative of any single intellectual school of
the day. For example, although there is at least one edition of the *Jinsi lu*
近思錄 (Reflections on things at hand), the *Daoxue* primer compiled by Zhu
Xi and Lü Zuqian 呂祖謙 (1137–81), there is also a *Xiangshan xiansheng
yulu* 象山先生語錄 (Recorded sayings of Master Xiangshan) by Lu Jiuyuan
陸九淵 (1139–92).[71] There are two editions of the *Yangzi fayan*, three of the
Xunzi, and one of the *Wenzhong zi* 文中子. What many of these imprints
had in common was their relevance to the government examinations; Hilde
de Weerdt found in her survey of three anthologies of examination essays that
the last three works were among the more popular choices for the exposition
question in the examinations.[72] As for the Zeng family's edition of the *Jinsi lu*,
with the full title 文場資用分門近思錄 *Wenchang ziyong fenmen Jinsi lu*
(*Reflections on Things at Hand*, [re]classified for examination use), it was
coupled with an anonymous *Jinsi hou lu* 近思後錄 (Continuation of the *Reflections on Things at Hand*), which was organized in a similar fashion.[73]

The Yuan imprints of Confucian works reflected the growing influence of
· *Daoxue*, especially in the Jianyang region. Indeed, other than a *Xunzi*, all the
other works in this category were clearly written by *Daoxue* adherents or were
texts emphasized by them. There was a basic *Daoxue* anthology, the *Zhuzi
chengshu* 朱子成書, a *Hui'an xiansheng yulu* 晦庵先生語錄 (Recorded
conversations of Zhu Xi), the *Xingli qunshu* compiled by Xiong Jie with commentaries by Xiong Gangda described in the previous chapter, and at least
two *Kongzi jiayu* 孔子家語 (School sayings of Confucius), a work that
would be very popular with Jianyang printers in the Ming.

Philological works (xiaoxue 小學). The increasing number of philological
works published in Jianyang during the Yuan exhibit some rather different
trends.[74] In the fourteenth century, there were seven editions from Jianyang
alone of the *Daguang yihui Yupian* 大廣益會玉篇 (Expanded and im-
proved *Leaves of Jade*). The original *Yupian* was compiled in the sixth century,

but all the Song and Yuan imprints are based on the 30-*juan* edition revised in the Northern Song under official auspices.[75] The Jianyang versions, while organized in 30 *juan*, were actually an abridgement of the official edition, a fact not noted in the imprints. Nevertheless, three of them offered an additional guide to using the dictionary and two annotations correcting errors in the official [Song] edition. Equally popular was the rhyming dictionary, *Guangyun*, which had also been officially revised in the Northern Song. Not all of the seven known Jianyang editions from the Yuan can be dated exactly, but at least three of them were published within a ten-year period, a clear sign that printers kept a close watch on the book market. It is also interesting that whereas the one Song printing was of the unabridged edition of 1008 revised under imperial auspices, the Yuan imprints were copies of a later abridged edition.[76] Another rhyming dictionary, the *Libu yunlüe*, compiled and later revised in the Northern Song, was reprinted at least five times in Jianyang during the Yuan.[77] Examination of three of them (Figs. 22a–c) shows that the printers adopted the efficient strategy of copying an older edition; the resulting imprints are nearly identical.

Although such works were considered important tools for studying classical works, they were also useful general references for reading and for writing, including versification, from couplets to short poems to dramatic songs in a play. Indeed, arguments about such uses contributed to the compilation and publication of newer works. For example, Zhou Deqing 周德清 (ca. 1270–after 1324) criticized the use of the *Guangyun* in composing *qu* 曲 (dramatic arias) because it allowed southern pronunciations of the rhymes, whereas his own work, the *Zhongyuan yinyun* 中原音韻 (Songs and rhymes of the central plain; 1324) admitted only northern pronunciations because the *qu* form had originated in the Beijing area. Selections from a compilation of *qu* published in Jianyang, the *Yuefu xinbian Yangchun baixue* 樂府新編陽春白雪 (Sunny spring and white snow: a newly compiled [collection] of Music Bureau songs), were held up by Zhou as examples that violated his rule of northern pronunciations only. But surely the proliferation of commercial editions of the *Guangyun* promoted new possibilities for composing *qu* by encouraging the use of rhymes in the southern pronunciation.[78]

History (*shibu* 史部)

During both the Song and the Yuan, dynastic and annalistic histories, as well as abridgments and outlines of these works, dominated the historiographical offerings of Jianyang publishers. A closer look at these imprints, however, shows important differences between the two periods. First, about half the Song period Jianyang imprints in the History category were actual dynastic histories. Furthermore, eleven of the twenty were printed by family schools (*jiashu*). At first, it may seem puzzling that Jianyang publishers produced so many dynastic histories, since they were substantial works that may not have commanded as large a market as shorter works that students may have found more immediately useful in preparing for the government examinations. The explanation probably has to do with the role of the *jiashu* printers, who consistently issued the best Jianyang publications—usually well collated and well printed—because they possessed both the financial and the intellectual resources for such publication efforts.

The Jianyang editions of the *Shiji* from the Song provide support for this argument. The earliest, dated to 1057, is a *Shiji suoyin* 史記索隱, with annotations by Sima Zhen 司馬貞 and phonetic glosses by Lu Deming, both of the Tang, but it does not contain the entire text of the *Shiji* itself.[79] It predates all other printed editions with the Sima Zhen annotations, which were not included in the various Directorate editions that contained the *jijie* 集解 (collected explanations). Moreover, of the five later imprints of the *Shiji*, which included both the *jijie* and the *suoyin*, two were published in Jianyang.

This plurality of texts means that as influential as the Directorate editions were—and we certainly should credit them with inspiring later editions of the same works—the influence was not always direct. That is, by launching its own full-scale publishing effort, the Song state spurred nonofficial publishers to issue works for which no authoritative government edition existed. The three Jianyang *Shiji* with the *suoyin* annotations may well have been published in collaboration with local scholars who owned old manuscript copies of the work, considered it part of the scholarly tradition of the *Shiji*, and felt that it was as important to disseminate it in print as the *jijie*. The two Southern Song Jianyang editions of the *Shiji jijie suoyin* were issued by publishers who identified themselves as part of family schools. Such publishers were able to recollate texts based on Directorate and other government editions and participate in the popular Song scholarly activity of trying to produce an error-free text. As Susan Cherniack points out, private printers often had greater opportunity for such work and could even, as in the colophon for Huang Shanfu edition of the *Hou Han shu*, invite readers to notify the publisher of any errors they might find.[80]

The importance of the government examinations also meant that commercial publishers brought out works most in demand by the students. It is interesting that there is a rough correspondence between the dynastic histories published in Jianyang and those from which the topics of exposition questions in the examination were drawn. There were four Jianyang editions of the *Qian Han shu*, five of the *Hou Han shu*, and three of the *Xin Tang shu*.[81]

"Detailed abridgments," or *xiangjie* 詳解／詳節, of both dynastic and annalistic histories abounded. There were at least two editions of the *Shiqi shi xiangjie* 十七史詳節 (Detailed abridgment of the seventeen dynastic histories), as well as one each for the parts corresponding to the *Shiji* and the *Sanguo zhi* 三國志 (History of the Three Kingdoms), by Lü Zuqian, one of the most popular teachers of literary composition in the Southern Song. He is also credited with the pronunciation glosses for a Jianyang edition of the *Donglai xiansheng yinzhu Tang jian* 東萊先生音註唐鑑 (Mirror [for Aid in Government of] the Tang), by Fan Zuyu 范祖禹 (1041–98) of the Northern Song. As Ming-sun Poon points out, Lü may not have intended his notes for publication as such and probably derived no benefit from it.[82] A similar situation prevailed among the annalistic histories: for one Jianyang edition of Sima Guang's original *Zizhi tongjian*, there were five *xiangjie*. It is also telling that nearly all the publishers of these detailed abridgments did not identify themselves by name in their imprints. One publisher whose name we do know was Zhan Guangzu (Table B.1, no. 77), who in the Chunyou period (1241–52) printed the *Zizhi tongjian gangmu* 資治通鑑綱目 (Outline of the *Comprehensive Mirror for the Aid of Government*), the drastic reworking of Sima Guang's work by Zhu Xi and his students. By the mid-thirteenth century, *Daoxue* was gaining important official recognition,[83] and Zhu Xi's works were printed more and more often.

During the Yuan, as almost all the *jiashu* printers in Jianyang disappeared, the number of dynastic histories printed dropped drastically.[84] In fact, of the three Yuan works listed in the dynastic histories category, only one—a *Qian Han shu*—was definitely a new Jianyang commercial edition. Another was a facsimile reprint of a Jianyang Southern Song edition of the *Xin Tang shu*, and the third consisted of textual analysis (*kaozheng* 考證) of the two *Han Histories*.

There are two noteworthy trends in the increase in the number of annalistic histories and related works. The first continues from the Song in that although there was only one Jianyang edition each of the *Zizhi tongjian* and of Zhu Xi's *Zizhi tongjian gangmu*, there were three *xiangjie* and one *jieyao* 節要 (abridged essentials). The second may have to do with the publishers' anxiousness to offer histories of the Song Jianyang publishers issued at least two eighteen-*juan*(!) editions of a *Xu (Song biannian) Zizhi tongjian* 續 (宋編年) 資治通鑑, supposedly by Li Tao 李燾 but was instead a rather strange concoction dealing with the entire Northern Song; the collation is credited to a certain Liu Shenyuan of Wuyi, which suggests that the work was compiled at the behest of the Jianyang printers.[85] At least one Jianyang publisher coupled this work with two other annalistic histories of the Southern

Song—the *Xu Song Zhongxing biannian Zizhi tongjian* 續宋中興編年資治
通鑑 (Continuation of the *Comprehensive Mirror* for the Song after 1127) by
Liu Shiju 劉時舉, covering the years 1127–1224, and the anonymous *Song ji
san chao zhengyao* 宋季三朝政要 (Important official events of the last three
reigns of the Song), which deals with the years 1225–78.[86] Finally, although the
publisher is unidentified, there is a Yuan edition of the *Song shi quan wen xu
Zizhi tongjian* 宋史全文續資治通鑑 (Complete history of the Song, supplementing the *Comprehensive Mirror*). Judging from its appearance, it is
quite possibly a Jianyang product. Since all these Song annalistic histories
were printed in the Jianyang area starting around 1312, prior to any official
compilation of the dynasty's history, Song loyalism may have been behind
these publication efforts, just as Southern Ming loyalism would inform certain Jianyang imprints over 300 years later.

Philosophy (*zibu* 子部)

In this rather disparate category, the largest subcategories are the works of
Confucian thinkers (already discussed together with the Classics and Four
Books), medical works, and *leishu* (classified works).

Medical works (*yijia* 醫家). During the Song, the central government sponsored the writing, compilation or recompilation, and printing of some 38 editions of medical texts,[87] and commercial publishers in the Song and to a lesser
extent in the Yuan often adopted the expedient practice of printing their own
editions of government publications. The combined efforts of both official and
commercial publishers apparently contributed to the impression that the Song
scholarly medical tradition consisted mainly of collections of prescriptions
(*fangshu* 方書), pharmaceutical works (*bencao* 本草), and discussions on cold
damage disorders (*shanghan lun* 傷寒論), a tradition that influential medical
authorities later on in the Jin and Yuan periods would criticize and revise.[88]

The many reprintings of medical books by commercial publishers, especially large compendia of prescriptions, attest to their popularity in the Song
and even more so in the Yuan. First, five of the nine medical works from the
Song, and twelve of the nineteen from the Yuan are collections of prescriptions,[89] all of them reprints of well-known works. In the latter half of the
fourteenth century, there were at least four editions of the *Taiping huimin heji
ju fang*, compiled under imperial auspices (1107–10).[90] A sixth Jianyang version from about the same time is a composite printing using blocks from two
other editions, even though it declares itself a new edition.

Two other books from the Song and two from the Yuan are pharmaceutical works, or *bencao* (which also contain prescriptions). From the Yuan, there are also two books on acupuncture, one brief discussion of pulse analysis (*chamai* 查脈), and another short work on cold damage illnesses. There is only one medical classic—an edition of the *Huangdi neijing suwen* 黃帝內經素問 (Plain questions of the Yellow Emperor's classic of internal medicine).[91] Nearly all the medical books are ones with portions that could easily be read and used by a lay person without much special medical experience. Although a greater variety of medical books were printed in Jianyang during the Ming, nearly a quarter of them were still prescription collections or pharmaceutical works.

The great number of medical works published in Jianyang may have reflected a greater professional interest in medicine among the publishers or their relatives. It certainly seems to be the case among the Xiong, whose Weisheng tang (Preserving life hall) was apparently renamed the Zhongde tang (Hall of cultivating virtue) and would publish many more medical works in the Ming.

Classified books (leishu). Leishu, often translated "encyclopedia," are topically arranged compilations of passages from a number of sources. Sometimes the compiler's contribution in the form of commentaries on the selected passages or summaries at the end of each topic or section is just as valuable as his work as an anthologizer in selecting and organizing the excerpts. The *leishu* category encompasses a variety of books ranging from everyday household manuals to writing manuals to dictionaries of quotations to examination essays to story collections to works truly encyclopedic in their scope. Because these works often cover so much material and are useful for a broad range of purposes, it is often hard to organize them further into subcategories.[92]

Although the first *leishu* was compiled around 220 CE, *leishu* in the Song took on more and more functions. As printing made more works generally available, it became easier for scholars, as Hoyt Tillman puts it, "to systematize existing knowledge into formats for methodical comprehension"[93] largely for classical studies and governance. Not only did the widespread use of printing make the task of compiling *leishu* easier for more scholars, but it also ensured the compilers that their labor would be rewarded by a larger readership than in the days of only handwritten copies. Second, *leishu* were, of course, a great convenience for readers who lacked access to a vast array of original sources[94] and/or did not have the time or inclination to plow through so much material. This feature is especially evident in collections of essays used by students preparing for the examinations.[95] Many contemporary scholars felt that this feature epitomized the broad but shallow approach to reading or, in the case of examination essays, reading only to memorize the text. Nevertheless, these critics were fighting a losing battle against a method of reading broadly that was becoming feasible for many more people because of the greater availability of books through printing. Naturally, the commercial printers were instrumental in this process.

None of the monumental encyclopedias compiled in the Song or Yuan, such as the *Cefu yuangui, Taiping yulan* 太平御覽 (Imperially reviewed [encyclopedia] of the Taiping period), and *Wenxian tongkao* 文獻通考 (Complete investigation of [important] documents), were reprinted in Jianyang until the Ming, and then only under official auspices. These omissions suggest that in the Song and the Yuan, the Jianyang printers perhaps had difficulty obtaining copies of such massive works and in any case were probably reluctant to spend the time, money, and labor needed to print them. Furthermore, it is no surprise that a number of the *leishu* published in Jianyang were essentially topically arranged literary anthologies or dictionaries of phrases drawn from well-known works and readily spawned more of the same. Even a quick comparison of ten of these works show that they often cited the same passages. This may be because many of these collections were merely "recompiled" (i.e., copied) from older collections, a cheaper and faster method than compiling a totally new edition from a large number of original sources that were hard to come by for a compiler or printer, even in a large bookproducing center like Jianyang.

All the *leishu* printed in Jianyang during the Song were compiled or substantially revised during the dynasty. Those useful for examination studies include the *Xinbian Gujin shiwen leiju* 新編古今事文類聚 (New compilation of *Classified Facts and Writings of the Past and Present*) of Zhu Mu 祝穆, a native of Jianyang,[96] at least two commercial editions of the *Leishuo* 類說 (Classified extracts), a collection of excerpts from early fiction,[97] the *Huang Song shibao leiyuan* 皇宋事寶類苑 (Classified collection of the words and deeds [of eminent men of the Northern] Song), which culled passages from the *xingzhuan* 行傳 (life and deeds) of famous Song men, and *Chongxiu shiwu ji yuan* 重修事物紀原 (Record of the origins of things, revised edition).

There are extant Jianyang editions from the Yuan of a Song *leishu* with a pronounced *Daoxue* emphasis, the *Xinjian jueke gujin yuanliu zhilun* 新箋決科古今源流至論 (The best essays, old and new, with new commentaries for the examinations).[98] This collection, completed around 1237, contains detailed essays on the history of political and social institutions useful in preparing for the government examinations. The Jianyang edition of 1367 is a typical example of the widely deplored *Mashaben*; its cramped page layout squeezes fifteen columns of 25 characters each onto a page. Such collections were a specialty of the Jianyang book trade, and judging from the extremely worn impressions of an extant copy,[99] they sold very well. Finally, given the intellectual inclination of the work, it is not surprising that both this and an earlier Jianyang edition appear to have been issued by publishers with *Daoxue* connections.[100]

Although these *leishu* may have been intended by their authors or compilers to help students prepare for the government examinations, several of them apparently remained popular for centuries as handy references and source books for writers. For example, despite the fact that Zhu Mu himself stressed the uses of the *Gujin shiwen leiju* for moral cultivation and although his 1246 preface rather coyly stated that his purpose in collecting the excerpts from works of prose and poetry was simply to aid his weak memory, the work in its expanded form with supplementary installments (*ji* 集) was published at least five times in Jianyang during the Ming, probably as much for its usefulness as a writer's aid as for any other reason.[101]

Evidence to support this conjecture comes from a survey of the majority of the Jianyang *leishu*, which reveal an emphasis on works that served as aids to composition, including phrase dictionaries and writing manuals.[102] These books, like several of the general literary collections discussed below, illustrate the many aspects of printed literary production for sale. In addition to Zhu Mu's *Shiwen leiju* and the *Leishuo* mentioned above, two other Song imprints from Jianyang concentrated on presenting and explaining expressions that could be used either verbatim or modified in a reader's own writing: the *Tang-Song Bo-Kong liu tie* 唐宋白孔六帖 ("Memory Questions" compiled by Bo [Juyi] of the Tang and Kong [Chuan] of the Song),[103] and of *Donglai xiansheng fenmen shilü wuku* 東萊先生分門詩律武庫 (Classified arsenal of versification methods by Lü Zuqian). Although these works obviously were intended for highly educated readers, the publisher's pitch for the *Classified Arsenal* is quite telling: "Recently we have obtained a manuscript copy of the Lü family school's *Arsenal*. As a weapon in versification battles, it can be used to direct one's forces and fiercely vanquish one's opponents. Not wishing to keep it to ourselves, we have printed it to disseminate it." One wonders how the publisher managed to obtain yet another set of Lü Zuqian's notes, if indeed they are such. Moreover, while all literati learned from youth to write regulated poems (*lüshi* 律詩), the blurb's bellicose approach to literary composition uses language more often found in advertisements for examination literature and in these texts themselves. Thus this work may have appealed particularly to those practicing *shi* for the poetry track in the examinations.

A number of writing manuals provided not just choice phrases but sample compositions that could be copied or closely imitated. These were compiled in the late Song or Yuan and were printed in Jianyang, sometimes in several editions from the late thirteenth century on. A representative example is the *Xinbian tongyong qi zha jie jiang wang* 新編通用啓箚截江網 (Newly compiled river net containing official letters and notes in general use), which not only provides the correct formulas for and examples of various types of official writing (letters, memorials) but also verses that could be used for many different occasions.[104] The compilation is attributed to a Xiong Huizhong 熊晦仲, about whom we have no other information. What is most interesting is the preface by a Chen Yuanshan 陳元善 dated 1313, which complains about two recent commercial editions of a *Hanmo qi zha* 翰墨啓箚 for including one thing but leaving out another.

This criticism almost certainly is a reference to the *Hanmo quanshu* 翰墨全書 (The complete book on the art of writing) by Xiong He in collaboration with Liu Yingli as the compiler. Xiong He's 1307 preface to this work begins with a similar complaint about the abuse of *qi* 啓 and *zha* 箚, which were originally official forms of communication, but by Xiong's time were utilized by the literati in their communications with each other, a trend abetted by the commercial publishers.[105] Ironically, Xiong He's attempts to rectify what he considered incorrect writing and cultural practices were undermined by commercial editions of his own work, which incorporated materials that would perhaps not have met with Xiong's approval. As Chen Yuanshan's preface and the welter of extant copies show, the *Hanmo quanshu* itself became one of the more popular offerings of the Jianyang commercial publishers almost immediately after it appeared. It remained popular at least through the Ming: my conservative estimate is six, perhaps seven, Jianyang editions or partially revised reprints during the Yuan and Ming.[106]

Writing manuals lacking Xiong's literary and cultural agenda were also published in the Yuan. These include the *Xinbian shiwen leiyao qizha qingqian* 新編事文類要啓札青錢 (Collected treasures of classified essentials of facts and composition, newly edited),[107] whose 1324 edition includes five installments (*ji*). These additions strongly suggest that it was an expanded version of a popular earlier work. There were also a number of poetry-writing manuals, such as the *Zengguang shilian shixue dacheng* 增廣事聯詩學大成, a large poetry compendium of which there were three Jianyang editions in the Yuan.

A more specialized work was the late Song / early Yuan Jianyang imprint entitled *Xinbian hunli beiyong Yuelao xinshu* (Fig. 18a).[108] Among other things, this manual describes how to conduct betrothal and wedding ceremonies, how to word invitations to these ceremonies and feasts, and how the betrothed couple and their families should comport themselves. Again, it is a typical *Mashaben*, packing plenty of information (accurate and inaccurate) into cramped pages, and the extant copy looks as if it had been pulled off blocks that had already been used for several thousand copies.

Several other Jianyang *leishu* printed in the Yuan could be considered as more general encyclopedias and forerunners of those published in the Ming. One was the *Shilin guangji* 事林廣記 (Comprehensive record of many things), compiled by a native of the Minbei area, Chen Yuanjing 陳元靚, in the early thirteenth century[109] and printed at least twice in Jianyang during the Yuan.[110] The value of this work is enhanced by copious illustrations. Another such work, the earliest extant one printed in Jianyang, was the *Jujia biyong* 居家必用 (Household essentials),[111] which would be reprinted in variously supplemented editions in the Ming.

This lengthy survey of *leishu* demonstrates the diverse works grouped under this category. Although *leishu* predate imprints, it is easy to understand why printing would have spurred a growing variety of such works. Not only were *leishu* increasingly popular as convenient references for classical studies and for government administration, but also phrase dictionaries and writing manuals in particular became common compositional aids for writers, a trend similar to the evolving uses of rhyming dictionaries discussed above.

Such developments are most clearly seen in the commercial editions of *leishu*. The importance of carefully edited, error-free, complete texts, not to mention the original compiler's intellectual, ideological, and literary priorities, gave way to the need to produce omnium-gatherums quickly. It is interesting that even in the *Daoxue* stronghold of Minbei, the commercial publishers opted for breadth rather than ideological consistency in the contents of their *leishu*. Furthermore, the multiplication of categories and the addition of installments to supplement the original compilation served to persuade readers that they were getting ever more up-to-date information. We have already seen this practice in other kinds of books—for example, the Song Jianyang edition of the *Jinsi lu*, with Zhu Xi's original thirteen categories reorganized into 121 headings, for examination use. But it is with *leishu* that such practices became *de rigueur*. This was hardly the broad learning (*boxue* 博學) that many scholars strove for. Rather, it was a pragmatic attempt to make available an increasing amount of information to the reader, through categorization, with new materials often tucked under traditional and comfortably recognizable subject headings. Indeed, my overall impression of the writing manuals from Jianyang of the Song and Yuan is that more of the contents were excerpted from contemporary writings than from earlier texts. Finally, although none of the *leishu* published in the Song and Yuan can be considered "popular" works for the non-literati, their classification schemes, which ranged from the heavens to earth to man, would continue to be employed, but informed by somewhat different contents in the Ming *leishu*.

Buddhist works (*shi jia* 釋家). As noted above, very few Buddhist works seem to have been printed in the Jianyang area. Of the two extant books from the Song, one is a copy of the *Lotus Sutra*, probably published by a private individual, and the other is an annalistic chronicle of Buddhist history, to judge from the title, *Lidai biannian Shishi tongjian* 歷代編年釋氏通鑑.[112] The single Yuan work is the *Dabao jijing* 大寶積經, issued by the Houshan Bao'en wanshou tang 後山報恩萬壽堂; the printing of each chapter (or several pages thereof) was financed by a different contributor.[113] At least for the five extant chapters, none of the contributors is a Minbei native but come from Guangzhou and Jiangxi. Perhaps they had been in Jianyang, or the Bao'en wanshoutang may have been a commercial printer who actively solicited subscribers not only from the local area but from nearby provinces. The paucity of such imprints is rather puzzling, since the geographic distribution of the subscribers in the *Dabao jijing*, as well as the availability of cheap printing facilities in the Jianyang area, suggests a happy combination of demand and supply for these works. It may be that we have stumbled on the tiniest surviving trace of a distribution network for Buddhist sutras and other popular religious works that was different from that for the other books examined in this chapter. Such religious materials may well have constituted an even more perishable kind of imprint than secular books.

Belles lettres (*jibu* 集部)

Literary collections. The majority of Jianyang imprints in this category consist of collections of individual authors (*bieji* 別集) and general collections incorporating the works of two or more authors (*zongji* 總集). The *bieji* titles are interesting in what they suggest about the Jianyang book trade: a few works were repeatedly reprinted, especially the best-known exponents of *guwen* 古文 (ancient-style prose), whose writings often served as models for examination essays. For instance, there were at least eight Jianyang editions from the Song and Yuan of Han Yu's collected writings collated by Zhu Xi and five of Liu Zongyuan's collected writings glossed by a multitude of commentators (*wubai jia zhuyin bian* 五百家注音辨). *Guwen* masters of the Song were even better represented, with Su Shi being the most published (six editions of his poetry and two of his prose collection), Su Xun 蘇洵 (two editions), Su Che 蘇轍 (one),[114] Huang Tingjian (three), Wang Anshi 王安石 (one), and Zhang Lei 張耒 (one).

A look at what seems not to have been printed in Jianyang is also instructive, as long as we keep in mind the hazards of random survival. First, selectivity based on what was most in demand meant that although Lü Zuqian's writings most relevant to the examinations were printed over and over again (see above), there is no known Jianyang edition of his collected prose or verse works. Similarly, Yang Wanli 楊萬里 (1127–1206) is represented not by his complete works but by two imprints of excerpts from his writings, at least one of which was compiled by a Jian'an man.[115] There are also Jianyang imprints of a selection of letters of Sun Di 孫覿 (1081–1169), well known for his writing skills, and a collection of the four-six parallel prose of Li Liu 李劉 (*js* 1214), a master of this style. Finally, only three *Daoxue* proponents, all with Minbei associations, had their collected works printed in the Jianning area, not by commercial publishers but by the Jianning prefectural school (Zhu Xi) or by academies associated with their family schools (Liu Yue 劉爚 and Liu Xueji 劉學箕).[116]

As for the general collections, there is an even greater emphasis on works useful for the examinations. For example, ten of the fourteen Song imprints from Jianyang consisted of collections of examination literature, and it is probably no coincidence that several of these credited Minbei men as their compilers.[117] Three other works were well-known literary anthologies; their publishers counted on a sufficiently large market that would include potential examination candidates or their teachers: Lü Zuqian's *Huangchao wenjian* 皇朝文鑑 (The mirror of literature from our dynasty), *Wanbao shi shan* 萬寶詩山 (The ten thousand gem mountain of verse), and the sixth-century work *Wenxuan* 文選 (Anthology of literature).[118]

Not surprisingly, among the Yuan publications from Jianyang were fewer examination anthologies, although there were a small-size edition of the *Wanbao shi shan* and a collection of actual examination essays, an edition apparently issued by two different Jianyang publishers. The new development is a number of literary anthologies compiled in the Yuan, perhaps an indication of the direction of both the literati's and the publishers' energies during that period. The *Huang Yuan fengya* 皇元風雅 (Elegant pieces of the Yuan dynasty) was compiled by a Jianyang man,[119] and at least two later installments were printed there during the Yuan.

Fiction (*xiaoshuo changpian* 小說長篇). It is quite possible that works of fiction had been printed by the late Southern Song. Indeed, for two such publications from Jianyang, it is difficult to determine precisely the date either of composition or of printing: the *Xinbian Xuanhe yishi* (Fig. 18b),[120] and the earliest extant edition designated by its publisher as a *pinghua* or vernacular historical narrative, the *Xinbian Wudai shi pinghua* 新編五代史平話, with stories of famous men from the Five Dynasties. The other *pinghua* are the series with running illustrations on top and text on the bottom published by the Yú family's Wuben tang (Fig. 5).

The texts in these publications, while almost certainly shaped to some extent by oral story-telling traditions, were (re)written almost entirely for reading, and of course, the stories came originally from the dynastic histories. For example, the *Xuanhe yishi* derived much of its materials from other Song books popular enough to have been printed several times, such as Chen Jun's 陳均 *Huangchao biannian gangmu beiyao* 皇朝編年綱目備要 (Essential digest of the annals of the imperial court), Lü Zhong's 呂中 *Huangchao dashi jiangyi* 皇朝大事講義 (Explanations of the significance of great events of the Song), Zhu Xi's *Tongjian gangmu*, casual jottings, such as Zhao Yushi's 趙與峕 *Bintui lu* 賓退錄 (Recorded after the guest's departure), and many of popular Song (and Tang) verse.[121] Although gathering all these sources to compose a work like the *Xuanhe yishi* was not impossible before the spread of printing, the greater availability of books certainly made it far easier. Not only were these historical narratives a new genre of the late Southern Song and the Yuan, but they owed their very existence to the growth of printed books in general.

Summary and Some Contrarian Conclusions

Why did Jianyang develop into one of the largest printing centers of the Song and Yuan? Briefly, we can point to three factors: (1) the availability of all the natural resources necessary for woodblock printing; (2) the location of Jianyang, Jian'an, Chongan, Pucheng, and other Minbei towns on waterways that made them important entrepôts for the trade between Fujian and the Jiangnan area; and (3) the intellectual tradition that led to the dazzling examination success of the region and that had its full flowering in the contributions of Minbei men to the *Daoxue* movement. No one of these factors by itself was necessary or sufficient, but the combination of them provides a plausible explanation of the growth of Jianyang book trade into one of national scope in less than a century.

With the drastically reduced importance of the examination system in the Yuan, it would seem that the major market for Jianyang imports was lost. But the Jianyang publishing industry continued to thrive for several reasons. First, the intellectual tradition that flourished in the Song simply was too strong to die out in less that a century, especially in regions like Minbei, where a number of Song loyalist scholars who retired from public life were instrumental in keeping alive *Daoxue* ideas, by teaching and, to a lesser extent, by printing works they wrote or edited. These men also had a close relationship with other printers in the area, with whom they shared a similar intellectual outlook. Indeed, the continuing importance of the Classics, Histories, and related works among Jianyang publications suggests that we should not overestimate the connection between scholarly efforts devoted to textual analysis and emendation and the government examinations. Certainly during the Song, the examination system fueled editorial and authorial efforts of all quality. Its much diminished influence in the Yuan, however, lets us see more clearly by itself the great general impetus created by the spread of the printed text, with its unprecedented potential for broadcasting and preserving, if only through sheer numbers alone, the efforts of a writer. And nothing in the Yuan diminished the power of print.

Other factors just as important as the continuation of classical learning explain the evolution of the Jianyang book trade in the Yuan—the large number of medical works, especially collections of prescriptions, and nonscholarly works, such as household encyclopedias and illustrated historical fiction. Although similar medical texts and probably the other kinds of works as well were being printed by the late Southern Song, their greater importance among Jianyang imprints of the Yuan argues that the printers were tapping into a large market with diverse readers, a market that would be their mainstay in the Ming.

Consistent with these observations is another overall change from the Song to the Yuan: the relatively smaller number of superior editions of all kinds of work in the Yuan. My impression from examining imprints from both periods is that in general, the page layout for Yuan editions was more cramped, squeezing more of the main text and even more of the smaller character commentary and annotation into each column of a page. Texts of many different kinds of works were now easily available to be reprinted cheaply if badly. But this general devaluation of imprints may have led to a larger market—customers who otherwise would not have bought a book might buy an inexpensive edition of a prestigious work, to display rather than to read.

The example of Jianyang helps us to begin to understand that large and important part of commercial publishing that went on in rural areas and rivaled that which took place in large cities for nearly the entire period that block-printed books dominated China.[122] Were the printers in the rural areas producing books for different audiences, or did they simply find operating outside the large cities more economical, even considering the costs of transport? Based on what we know of the Jianyang book trade, the economic factor seems more likely. Certainly, no easy and simple distinctions can be made between the publishing industries in the urban and rural areas.

There is, however, an important distinction worth making—that between the high- and low-quality imprints. A nagging question arises when we look at the beautifully produced imprints from Jianyang, which have gained the admiration and solicitous care of book collectors and libraries for nearly a millennium. That is, what fraction are they of all the books printed in the Jianyang area during the Song? From the early eleventh century onward, we hear numerous complaints about the inferior *Mashaben* that were flooding the market but almost nothing about the high-quality imprints from the same area, and, indeed, sometimes from the same publisher. Although probably not as expensive as, say, the prestigious Directorate imprints, copies of superior Jianyang editions must have been significantly costlier and fewer in number than *Mashaben*. Copies of high-quality Song editions have survived despite their relative scarcity because they have been cherished by their owners through the centuries. But during the Song, such works had a limited circulation, and the bibliophiles and other scholars who had access to them constituted a small elite among the book buyers and readers at that time.

It does not necessarily follow, however, that fewer printed copies of a better edition made it less "influential"—after all, if the scholars involved in collating, editing, reading, and being influenced by them were themselves influential, then the effect of these editions may be great. Moreover, original copies of relatively scarce imprints could be reproduced either by hand-copying or reprinting and thus indirectly wield an influence disproportionate to their numbers. Thus the impact of a printed work cannot be gauged simply by the number of copies produced; its particular history of dissemination must be considered.

As for cheaply and often shoddily produced *Mashaben*, their overall impact also cannot be understood merely by considering the number of copies for a given work. First of all, we do not even have such numbers, so that an observation like Yue Ke's that examination literature was "a hundred times as numerous as the Classics, Histories, and other works" leaves us multiplying one unknown by a hundred to yield another unknown. Second, we should consider the negative impact of such *Mashaben*. In reacting to what they perceived as textual outrages perpetrated in low-quality imprints, different groups of readers often had to confront the task of defining and delimiting more clearly the proper ways to write, edit, publish, and read printed texts. For scholars deeply concerned with the transmission of uncorrupted texts and dissatisfied even with Directorate of Education editions, *Mashaben* obviously represented versions of works beyond textual redemption. But faced with the plethora of such imprints, they had to admit the impossibility of achieving their ideal of a perfect, error-free text. Paradoxically, the uncertain survival of even once widespread works also forced on editors and publishers the pragmatic step of resorting to extant *Mashaben* to help them produce a new edition. The Song state also had to acknowledge, if indirectly, its inability to regulate the transmission of scholarly texts, as exemplified particularly in the literature for the examination system that it itself had instituted. Private individuals wishing to broadcast their own writings or those of family members or associates through printing also discovered that the very work they wanted to publish could be distorted in a cheaper pirated edition full of errors.

As it turns out, the section on *Mashaben* has been devoted largely to works written for and by the highly educated. It is time to face some unresolved and perhaps unresolvable questions having to do with imprints that qualified equally as *Mashaben* but did not survive. Where, for instance, are the works for more "popular" consumption, which may also have been read and written by the literati, but not exclusively so? Where are the almanacs and calendars, character books, school primers, and divination texts—materials that had been printed since the Tang? Surely they continued to find a steady or growing market in the Song and Yuan. And the extant writing manuals and *leishu*, such as the *Shilin guangji*, may represent the average-quality editions of works whose cheapest and shoddiest versions have vanished completely. The problem is that we have neither extant examples of these imprints nor clear descriptions of them from the Song and Yuan. Some Ming editions of such works are extant, including those written in the Song and Yuan, and it would be foolhardy to assume that it did not occur to commercial publishers to print them until the Ming.

We will return to the issue of this near-total absence of extant popular types of imprints in the next two chapters, but there is an important point to be made now. And that is a dominance of literati culture in print that began in the Northern Song. Although neither the state nor the educated elite was the first to exploit the power of print to transmit and broadcast texts, most of the imprints that have endured throughout the centuries and so have prevailed as recorded history are those that proclaim the values of the state and the elite. This does not mean that there was only one such set of values, as the political, cultural and moral battles fought in black and white on the printed page clearly show. But the big difference between what is lost and what remains is the difference between elite and nonelite traditions.

Thus we are reminded of not only the generative power of print but also its fixative, transformative, *and* extinctive powers. Over its three centuries of existence, the Song went from a society with very few printed books to many more printed books, all against a background of printed ephemera—broadsheets, private almanacs and calendars, thin divination texts, instruction manuals of all sorts. These materials have vanished completely, except as they were captured, fixed as parts of larger printed *books*. But as such, these texts often were not only culled but also revised from a far wider repertoire of printed ephemera, manuscripts, oral tradition, and actual practice. So whereas the compilation of a *leishu* that drew on a range of booklets on, say, wedding rituals, preserved something of its original sources, it also often distorted and perhaps discouraged the preservation of these materials in their original forms.[123]

That the originally more abundant cheap editions are less likely than the scarcer expensive ones to survive for very long—a phenomenon reflected in the inverted distribution of the two in modern collections—should make us more cautious in drawing conclusions about commercial printing for any given period. We can argue, however, that in terms of the book trade, the original editions of high-quality editions were less important than the cheaper and usually inferior editions. Furthermore, there were probably more works that were primarily or exclusively published as common, inexpensive editions: some of the writing manuals we described, many manuals on divination techniques, and possibly more works of fiction in the running illustration format. We believe that they were printed, either from contemporary notices or from their extant precursors from the Tang. It is impossible to tell how many copies of each work were printed, and it is dangerous to assume that they must have been numerous just because they were relatively cheap. After all, how many customers were there for a manual on geomancy? On the other hand, perhaps there were plenty of buyers of a simple character dictionary. Based on what we have learned about *Mashaben* for this period, however, perhaps we are nearer the truth in believing that the publishing and selling of popular works partook of the cultural and economic efflorescence of the Song and continued undiminished in the Yuan.

This is a conclusion contested by scholars who believe in the unprecedented explosion of print starting around the mid-sixteenth century in the Ming.[124] They correctly point out, for example, the very small percentage of printed books in both imperial and private libraries throughout the Song, the complaints of Song writers about the difficulty of procuring a desired work in print (or manuscript), and the generally high cost of paper in the Song and Yuan compared to the (later) Ming. While acknowledging the validity of these scholars' basic argument, I still wish to redress the balance somewhat for the earlier periods. First, as Joseph McDermott admits, this "ascendance of the imprint" in the Ming is necessarily based mainly on literati uses of print, since we have so little information of other uses. But in focusing on the literati and the books that they were most likely to read and/or catalogue in their collections, we miss out on the bulk of the book trade. That is, we are missing information on all the imprints that the literati might also have read but did not bother noting, including popular or "utilitarian" works, which also constituted most of the reading material for nonliterati groups. Second, at least as apt a comparison of the Song and Yuan with the late Ming is of the earlier two periods with the late Tang and Five Dynasties. And for the latter comparison, there is no question about the dramatic increase in the uses of print and the number of works published. And an even more useful juxtaposition may be that between the Northern and the Southern Song. The testimony of contemporary writers attest to a keen awareness of the increasing uses and abuses of print. Perhaps, in the final analysis, this appreciation is as important as the actual quantity of printed works in gauging the impact of print on a society.

Still, the materials for examining these issues, however, are maddeningly limited, especially for the Song and Yuan, even if we take into account all the known imprints of the period. Quite predictably, we end with many more questions than answers, but we have also learned better how to mine the available sources to obtain some answers, an advance that will help us extract even more information from the comparative wealth of Ming sources, including over 1,600 Jianyang imprints, some of which are discussed in the next two chapters.

Part III

Part III

5

The Jianyang Book Trade
During the Ming

By the beginning of the Ming, the Jianyang book trade had been in existence for over three hundred years, and the region's publishers had produced some of the finest imprints in the history of Chinese bookmaking. The lengthy decline in the publishing industry starting at the very end of the Yuan and lasting for over a century into the Ming justifies breaking the story between the Song-Yuan and the Ming periods. Such a division does not deny important continuities; yet we can justifiably view the book trade in the Ming as a notably distinct development, characterized by the increasing uses of the printed book by different social groups. And as we shall see, a further subdivision into the early and late Ming proves meaningful since the book trade in central and south China broke out of its stagnation toward the end of the fifteenth century and grew enormously thereafter.

As measured by the surviving quantity and variety of imprints, the revived Jianyang book trade flourished through the end of the Ming dynasty. During this resurgence, Jianyang produced many works that resembled those from the Jiangnan area, where many customers of the Minbei publishers were found. In addition to continuing to print a large number of texts of the Classics and the Histories or works related to them, as well as some perennially best-selling literary collections, the Jianyang publishers diversified into other kinds of works, especially medical texts, divination manuals, merchant route books, household encyclopedias, collections of plays and ballads, and illustrated fiction.

Some of the Jianyang publisher families that had begun operating in the Song or Yuan expanded their business in the Ming, and members of these and other Minbei families moved into the large cities of Jiangnan, particularly Nanjing. The emigrants included publishers, editors, and well-known master blockcarvers/calligraphers. Their migration was one indication of the continuing growth of the vibrant book trade in the highly cultured and urbanized Jiangnan area. Although many Jianyang imprints retained characteristics that identified them as such, equally significant are the characteristics they shared with imprints from other areas. Indeed, by the late Ming, the book trade in central and south China could be considered a unified market, whose most important publishing centers were Suzhou, Nanjing, and Hangzhou in the Jiangnan area—and Jianyang.

This chapter begins with a brief historical description of Minbei during the Ming, touching on factors that affected the book trade. It then discusses the activities of several well-known families who were responsible for the overwhelming share of the Jianyang imprints that are known today. We will examine not only these publishers' commercial imprints but also their involvement with the publishing operations of local government offices. Next, using quantitative data based on the known Jianyang imprints of the Ming, as well as anecdotal evidence, we will chart the changes in the region's book trade throughout the dynasty. Lastly, I will offer some speculations on the practical details of the Jianyang publishing industry, based on the evidence presented and on judicious extrapolations from information about the book trade in other parts of China during later periods. The imprints themselves are the focus of the following chapter.

Historical Background

Circumstantial evidence suggests that under the Ming Minbei experienced social unrest and economic depression until the late fifteenth century. Records on the Yuan-Ming transition in this area are rare, and there are only hints of the extent and nature of the destruction that occurred.[1] Unlike the Fujian coastal area, Minbei suffered from relatively few rebellions at the end of the Yuan.[2] The most notable event was the entry into the region through the Shan Pass and the two sieges of the Jianning prefectural seat in 1361 by Chen Youliang, Zhu Yuanzhang's most serious rival.[3] Nevertheless, refugees from the more disturbed areas of Jiangxi and Jiangnan apparently migrated into northern Fujian, as others had during the ninth-century Southern Tang period, but on a much smaller scale. Such was the motive of the ancestor of at least one of the leading publisher families, the Xiao 蕭 (see below), according to its genealogy.

Although the general decline in Minbei may have begun with the tumultuous Yuan-Ming dynastic transition, it was exacerbated by a number of factors during the first hundred years or so of the Ming. The story of the Minbei tea industry exemplifies the generally lackluster economy of the region in this period. In 1391, the first Ming emperor, Taizu, ordered that Jianning's famed *longtuan* cake tea need no longer be made and that only leaf tea be accepted as imperial tribute.[4] Although Ming Taizu's expressed intentions were to relieve the people from the onerous burden of manufacturing cake tea in favor of the less costly leaf tea, his decree may have contributed to the stagnation of the Minbei tea industry. In fact, Minbei leaf tea was generally unimportant in the regional economy and inferior to that produced in other areas of China during the Ming. Zhou Lianggong 周亮工 (1612–72), in his mid-seventeenth-century travel account of Fujian, noted that the monasteries, which still owned much of the tea-growing lands in Minbei, were steaming their tea leaves rather than firing them and had to invite monks from Huizhou to teach them the Songluo method of firing the leaves.[5]

Two serious rebellions during the first half of the fifteenth century may well have hindered Minbei's recovery from the disturbances of the Yuan-Ming transition. The first was the uprising in the Xianxia Mountain area bordering Zhejiang started by silver miners and led by Ye Zongliu.[6] In the six years (1442–48) before Ye was defeated, he rallied workers in mines and foundries throughout the Jianning area and besieged some of the most important towns, including Pucheng and Jianyang. Both Minbei natives (some serving their corvée) and outsiders made up the rebel forces, who numbered a thousand at the most. Apparently, one reason it took so long to defeat this relatively small force was that government troops did not arrive in any number until 1447. After Ye Zongliu, there was no serious rebellion among Minbei miners, but they continued to be regarded by officials as an unsettled and potentially troublesome group.

In 1448, the remnants of Ye's troops joined forces with the peasant rebels led by Deng Maoqi 鄧茂七 in what would become the most serious uprising in Fujian during the Ming.[7] Although the rebels were based in Sha and Youqi counties in Yanping prefecture, to the south of Jianning, they made sorties into neighboring areas that roused local militias into action. For instance, two Jianyang men managed to gather and lead a force of a thousand to fight the insurgents.[8] The relatively rapid mobilization of local forces may have been a reaction to Ye Zongliu's earlier rebellion and the seriousness of the second uprising, as well as the tardiness of the government troops in responding to both uprisings. In any case, Deng Maoqi was defeated by a combination of local militias and troops sent from Nanjing in 1449.

Even when the area recovered toward the end of the fifteenth century, the economy remained relatively stagnant, especially in contrast to the prosperity of southern coastal Fujian.[9] This stagnation in net growth, however, did not prevent significant changes in the region's agricultural economy. For example, in northern Fujian, the drive to exploit mountain lands (*pan shan* 拚山) was the equivalent of the coastal efforts to reclaim alluvial lands. The mountain lands were used for cash crops such as indigo, tobacco, ramie, and tea or harvested for lumber and bamboo. Indeed, lumber from the remoter interior regions of Fujian, including Jianning, Shaowu, and Yanping prefectures, became increasingly important as the regions more accessible to water transport nearer large rivers and the coast became deforested. These increasingly valuable mountain lands became the property of wealthy men from outside the region with the capital to buy and exploit them. Thus land in Minbei was increasingly owned by absentee landlords from coastal Fujian or from Jiangxi or Zhejiang, and Minbei natives themselves did not profit as much as they might have from the exploitation of the area's resources.[10] In addition, many of the poverty-stricken shack dwellers (*pengmin*) cultivating the mountain lands came from outside Minbei and, like the miners, were viewed with unease by government officials. Under such circumstances, it seems perhaps surprising that so few uprisings occurred in Minbei.

Another reason for the stagnation of the Minbei economy was the nature of the trade flow between the interior and the coast. In exchange for lumber, bamboo, paper, books, certain cash crops like indigo and ramie, and, above all, rice, Minbei received ironware, sugar, fruits, overseas goods, and, most important, salt and silver (for tax payments) from the coast. As Chang Pin-tsun observes, to obtain the salt and silver, it was sometimes necessary for people in the interior to export rice and live on cheaper foodstuffs—an economic necessity resulting from the government's insistence on designating the Minbei a rice-exporting region.[11] Despite the increasingly unfavorable balance of trade with coastal Fujian and Jiangnan during the mid- and late Ming, Minbei towns such as Jianning, Jianyang, and Pucheng remained important as entrepôts for the trade both into Jiangxi and Zhejiang and down the Minjiang to Fuzhou.

In some ways, the Jianyang book trade in the Ming reflected the region's general economic fortunes. In the first part of the Ming, it suffered a long decline. Of the nearly 1,700 known Jianyang imprints from the Ming, only about 11 percent are dated to before 1500, figures that actually represented a downswing less drastic than the countrywide trend in official and commercial publishing. Commercial printing revived around the beginning of the sixteenth century, and its increasing momentum resulted in the publishing boom of the late Ming. If, as seems likely, the Jianyang book trade in the Song and the Yuan depended seriously on the Jiangnan area for customers, then economic and demographic conditions in Jiangnan would affect the Jianyang book trade. Certainly, in the late Ming, when the Jianyang publishers were outproducing everyone else, the otherwise stagnant economic and cultural conditions in Minbei itself would also argue the book trade's dependence on central and south China. If the economic, demographic, and political conditions of this wider region in the early Ming were markedly worse than before and after this period, then the Jianyang book trade would have suffered accordingly.

The abundant Jianyang imprints of the late Ming apparently came mostly from Shufang in Chonghua district (Map 2), since Masha's printing industry never revived after being destroyed in the Yuan. Furthermore, a disastrous fire at Shufang at the beginning of 1500, when over 2,000 houses burned, is said to have destroyed most of the woodblocks there, an event that may well explain the dearth of pre-sixteenth-century Jianyang imprints.[12] Nevertheless, publishing not only recovered in Shufang but continued to grow thereafter in the Ming. The compilers of the 1553 Jianyang county gazetteer proudly noted that buyers came from all over for the book fair held on the first six days of each month in Chonghua. Indeed, some fifty years later, the 1601 edition of the gazetteer noted that although other markets in Jianyang remained periodic, the one in Shufang had become permanent.[13] Merchants bought not only books but also other goods such as paper and tea; they probably also brought books from other regions to sell. According to one modern scholar, there were more printshops in the Jianyang area than in Nanjing, the southern capital and the largest urban printing center in the country.[14]

How do we account for the existence of this flourishing book trade in an area that was otherwise economically and culturally listless? Part of the answer lies in the possibly fortuitous interest and sponsorship of a number of local and regional government officials in the first half of the sixteenth century. A far more important reason, however, lies in the scope of the Jianyang book trade, which, more than ever, depended vitally on outside markets, particularly in Jiangnan. In fact, not only Jianyang publications but also Minbei printers and blockcarvers traveled across the mountains to Nanjing and other cities, perhaps to settle there as sojourners. Thus, in considering the Jianyang book trade of the Ming, we are considering a broad segment of the scholarly and popular cultures of south and central China.

This situation changed drastically at the end of the Ming, and the Jian-yang book trade all but disappeared. One cause was political: Minbei was a Southern Ming stronghold, and Jianning was very briefly the seat of the Longwu 隆武 emperor. As a result, the prefectural seat and several other towns were razed by Qing forces, and the general devastation of the region, for reasons yet to be fully understood, led to a permanent decline that has lasted to the present day. During this period, the commerce that had formerly been the economic and cultural lifeline of the region decreased precipitously, and except for the tea trade, Minbei became an isolated as well as remote inland area. Although the area recovered to a certain extent beginning in the eighteenth century and continued to export tea and rice in the Qing and Republican periods, virtually no more books were produced.[15]

Commercial and Government Publishers of Jianyang

If anything, Jianyang played an even greater role in commercial publishing in the Ming than it had in the Song and Yuan. During the Ming, the number of printing establishments in Jianyang (based on a count of *tangming* 堂名) was roughly the same as that in Nanjing, significantly greater than in other important Jiangnan urban book centers such as Suzhou and Hangzhou, and greater by far than that in Beijing.[16] Table B.5 lists over 100 printshops and over 400 individuals recorded as the printers of one or more books produced in Jianyang.[17] As it turns out, the three families—Yu, Liu, and Xiong—who had already been conspicuously active in the Southern Song and Yuan publishing, continued to dominate the Jianyang printing industry in the Ming. Together with publishers from eleven other Minbei families (see Table 6) involved in the book trade, these men accounted for nearly 90 percent of the commercial imprints from the region. Although most of the individual publishers, authors, editors, illustrators, and carvers remain as shadowy as their Song and Yuan predecessors, the greater abundance of imprints provides far more information about their intellectual and business connections with one another and with publishers in other parts of central and south China. Consequently we have a clearer idea of the Ming publishers' probable business strategies, including what they chose to print and why, as well as where they set up shop. The essential role such men played in transmitting and broadcasting both scholarly and popular culture in Ming China can therefore be understood in greater detail.

We will first examine in some detail the activities of the Yu, Liu, and Xiong, for whom we have more information than for the other Jianyang publishers, mostly from genealogies and their imprints. We will then look briefly

Table 6
Jianyang Publisher Families,
Ranked by Number of Attributable Imprints

	Surname	Song	Yuan	Ming
1	Yu 余	20	43	371
2	Liu 劉	21	57	342
3	Xiong 熊	0	10	174
4	Zheng 鄭	0	6	112
5	Yang 楊	0	2	105
6	Chen 陳	(4)	(10)	85
7	Zhan 詹	1	5	83
8	Ye 葉	1	6	62
9	Xiao 蕭	0	0	43
10	Huang 黃	(6)	0	42
11	Wang 王	(5)	0	39
12	Zhang 張	0	(3)	24
13	Zhu 朱	0	4	12
14	Yú 虞	5	12	1

MING TOTAL   1,495

Notes: Ranking is based on the number of Ming imprints. For a given
surname, a number in parentheses indicates that it is not possible to prove
that the publishers in the Song or Yuan were related to those in the Ming.
The numbers of imprints are, of course, approximate.

at the activities of other Minbei families: the Zheng, Chen, Ye, and Xiao.
Next, we will explore the role of various regional and local officials in the
Minbei printing industry and their connections to the commercial publishers.
This chapters then ends with some speculations on the practical details of the
Ming book trade in central and south China, of which Jianyang was a vital
part.

Yu Publishers

During the Ming, about forty men surnamed Yu are listed as printers, and
some ten more as authors, editors, or collators in books from Jianyang. At
least seventeen of them can be identified definitely in the genealogy of the
Shulin Yu descent group (*Shulin Yu shi zongpu*) as descendants of the Yuan
period printer Yu Zhi'an (see Table 3). Many of the men not mentioned in
the genealogy were probably relatives of the seventeen listed, to judge from

the shared generational names (both the *ming* 名 and *zi* 字) and the periods when they were active.[18] This is particularly true from the second half of the sixteenth century onward until at least the end of the Ming, as shown by the number of Yu men involved in printing from the thirty-fifth to the thirty-seventh generations. Moreover, the surnames of wives, which are usually given in the genealogical table, suggest frequent intermarriage between the Yu and other Jianyang publisher families. For example, both the grandfather and father of Yu Chengzhang (thirty-fifth generation) married women surnamed Xiong, and Chengzhang married a woman surnamed Liu.[19]

Because the genealogy is so reticent, we cannot compare the social and economic fortunes of the Shangxiang House 上庠房, to which the printers belonged, with those of other branches of the descent group, but the absence of certain information may be telling. The absence of officeholders among Shangxiang men from the Southern Song until the mid-fifteenth century suggests a general decline in family fortunes. Second, the genealogy contains no essays commemorating the founding or refounding of ancestral halls, clan schools, and other institutions like those seen in many other Minbei genealogies. By the mid-fifteenth century, the situation improves: the increase in the number of Yu printers roughly coincides with an increasing number of clan members with some modest official titles such as *shengyuan* 生員. The reasons for the decline in the late Yuan–early Ming of the Yu family have yet to be understood, but this situation seems to reflect a general social trend in Minbei that is shared to a large extent by the Liu and Xiong descent groups.

Although the late Ming represented the heyday of the Yu printers, they apparently became almost inactive by the early Qing. A few works were reprinted during the Shunzhi (1644–61) and Kangxi (1662–1722) periods from old Ming blocks, but hardly any new titles by a Yu printer appeared.[20] One immediate reason for the Yu family's decline in the Qing, as for the region as a whole, was probably their overt Southern Ming loyalism. At least two Yu imprints have Southern Ming dates.[21] In addition, it is quite likely that the members of the Yu clan who had moved to Jiangnan during the late Ming now saw no reason for returning and continued their work in the book trade elsewhere.

Among the Yu printers, Yu Xiangdou is the most famous and the only Jianyang publisher to have rated an entry in the *Dictionary of Ming Biography*, in which his authorial and editorial efforts are discussed in some detail.[22] The information in the extant genealogy about Yu is limited to a few words in the *shixi* giving the names of his father and his son. Even the surname of his wife is missing, but from his father's entry, we know that Yu's mother was a

Liu, and may well have come from one of the publisher families; he seems to have received the printing blocks for several of his imprints from the Liu. From the birth and death dates of his grandfather and from the dates of his books, Yu was probably born in the 1550s or 1560s and began printing in the mid- or late 1580s, after having failed the government examinations a number of times. The latest imprint likely to be his is dated 1637.[23] The approximately 70 extant titles attributable to him[24] are a representative sampling of the kinds of works produced in Jianyang in the late Ming.[25]

In many of his publications, Yu credited himself as author, annotator, or editor as well as publisher, a common practice in the mid- and late Ming. To mention his works of fiction alone, Yu compiled and revised two collections of Daoist stories,[26] compiled and partially wrote three collections of court-case stories (*gongan* 公案), and provided commentaries and annotation to two, possibly three different editions of the *Sanguo zhizhuan* 三國志傳 (Chronicle of the Three Kingdoms; see below). Moreover, his 1594 edition of *Shuihu zhuan* 水滸專 (The water margin) has uncredited additions written by him, the poor literary quality of which has led one modern scholar to term them "the hasty, slipshod writing of a relatively illiterate bookseller."[27] Yu also listed himself as the compiler of a treatise on poetry, at least two household encyclopedias, and several works on divination. These claims may not be entirely true; convincing evidence shows that at least parts of one of the encyclopedias are from blocks originally cut by Liu Longtian, quite possibly Yu's relative by marriage and another productive Jianyang printer of the late Ming.[28]

Another common practice of commercial publishers like Yu Xiangdou was to modify works to attract more customers and then take the authorial credit themselves or give it to someone other than the original writer. Xiong Damu 熊大木, a well-known writer of historical fiction in the mid-sixteenth century and a relative of the Xiong publishers of Jianyang, was a victim of such a ploy. Two of his works, the *Tang guo zhizhuan* 唐國志傳 (Chronicle of the Tang) and the *Da Song zhongxing Yue Wang zhuan* 大宋中興岳王傳 (Chronicle of Yue Fei and the restoration of the Song), were reprinted by Yu Xiangdou's Santai guan; the books list Yu Ying'ao 余應鰲, possibly a nephew of Xiangdou, as the author.[29]

Rare among commercial publishers, however, were Yu's more personal expressions of himself in his imprints. For example, at least three different portraits of himself are inserted into a number of his publications (see below). In addition, in some twenty of his books, Yu wrote prefaces to which he signed his own name.[30] Finally, in the *Dili tongyi quanshu* 地理統一全書, a 1628 collection of works on geomancy jointly published by Yu Yingqiu 應虬 and

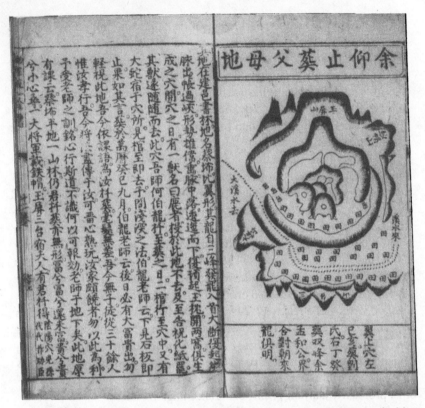

Fig. 23 A Ming geomancy text from Jianyang. *Dili tongyi quanshu* 地理統一全書. Ming Chongzhen period (1628–44). Publishers: Yu Yingqiu and Yu Yingke.

Yu Yingke 應科 and compiled by Yu Xiangdou, Yu managed to involve both his living and his dead relatives.[31] Some eight living relatives are listed as collators or editors at the beginning of many of the *juan*, and there are four full-page pictures showing the burial sites of Yu's parents (Fig. 23) and other ancestors to illustrate various geomantic factors. Yu also provided an account of the arrival of the Yu lineage in Chonghua district of Jianyang county and of the supposed origins of publishing in Shufang.

In the west of Jianyang county, about eighty *li* [40 km] from the county seat, is the district called Chonghua, which is today's Shufang [Bookquarter]. . . . Originally, when Shufang was settled, there were only three lineages, the Fu 傅, the Liu 柳, and the Ruan 阮. The Fu lived in the what is now the Rear Alley, the Liu in today's Luo Family Alley, and the Ruan in today's Ruan Settlement Alley. . . . All of them tilled the land and wove cloth to make their living. In the Song, after retiring from office, my ancestor Yu Tongzu, who was a native of Xin'an county [Henan] and had been a Grand Master for Consultation and Military Commissioner of Guangxi, [came here and] determined by siting to settle in this place. He was accompanied only by his nephew Zhisun and his brother-in-law Fan De. . . . At that time, there were only five or six lineages and about eighty to ninety households, although their homes were scattered all over. Zhisun was an expert in siting. Traveling around in his leisure, he determined that the area would later become one of culture and learning and exhorted the people to establish a Confucian temple at a site called "The Commanding Dragon Inclining Its Head," in order to gain the [site's] full benefit. He also encouraged people to print books for a living, . . . and all the people heeded his advice. At that time, printing was not used to disseminate information and only the people of Shufang perceived the benefits of blockprinting. Families that were well-to-do printed books in order to study; families that were poor engraved blocks in order to print books. The people in the region rejoiced in their craft, and not one out of a thousand wandered away to seek work for his living. All this resulted from the geomantic skill of Zhisun. From then on, the people and homes of Shufang multiplied. During the Song, when Zhu Xi determined by siting the location for Kaoting [Academy], he came to Shufang. Seeing the beauty of the landscape and the luxuriantly growing forests, he re-established the Confucian Temple and founded Tongwen Academy. He collated and printed the collected commentaries for the Five Classics and Four Books, all the histories, and the writings of many philosophers, for dissemination everywhere. These works were reprinted in the capital, in areas west of Zhejiang, and other places.[32]

Very shrewdly, Yu summarized in this passage various traditional stories about the publishing industry of Shufang, which must have been in common circulation in the area long before the late Ming. Thus it was the Yu, and by extension the other well-known publisher families to whom the Yu were related, who, when they came to the sparsely settled Chonghua district, recognized by their skill in geomancy, its potential as a place of culture and learning. By heeding Confucian traditions and by showing the inhabitants the benefits of blockprinting, they realized Shufang's promise. Admittedly, Yu Xiangdou was exceptional among commercial publishers in his unabashed self-advertising in his imprints, but in this excerpt, we get a rare glimpse of how Yu and other commercial publishers must have perceived themselves—as scholars worthy of association with Zhu Xi and his disciples and, like him, skilled in geomancy and engaged in dissemination of learning through printing. Yu thus endowed the Jianyang publishers with an intellectual respectability that they may not have attained in many of their imprints.

Yu's statements about himself, textual or pictorial, aimed at portraying him as a refined scholar capable of writing elegantly or enjoying the pleasures normally associated with a literatus or as a model of filial piety through his efforts to have his parents buried at the best site possible. Were such pretensions inconsistent with his commercial printing enterprises in general and with wanting to popularize various kinds of works in particular? Probably not. First, by the attitudes expressed in his printer's notices and prefaces, he was broadcasting quite orthodox and traditional ideas and values in his imprints of the Classics and histories. Second, his popularized works of fiction allowed a commercial publisher to introduce less refined but more "genuine" literature to readers educated enough to comprehend the language and allusions in the text.[33] Such an attitude was shared by a number of more famous late Ming scholars and authors, such as Feng Menglong and Li Zhi 李贄 (1527–1602). Yu's authorial, editorial, and publishing efforts may not have been on the same level as those of these men, but all of them reflected a pronounced trend in the late Ming that emphasized the value not only of disseminating the popular and naïve in the arts, but also of teaching morality and history through popular fiction.[34] The main distinction between Yu and more famous writers is that he was interested in purveying all the knowledge (or misknowledge) he could sell in print.

Another prolific Jianyang printer was a first cousin of Yu Xiangdou, Yu Zhangde 彰德 (*zi* Siquan 泗泉),[35] whose printshop, the Cuiqing tang 翠慶堂, was active at the same time as Yu Xiangdou's, in the late Wanli period (ca. 1590–1618), and produced close to 70 titles. Two of Yu Zhangde's sons, Jiquan 繼泉 and Yingqiu, and their cousin Yingke 應科 (see Table 3) are credited as editors and annotators and sometimes as publishers in many of Cuiqing tang's imprints.[36] In addition, Yu Yingqiu also served as an editor for publishing houses in Nanjing and printed a number of books using the printshop name Jinsheng tang 近聖堂.

The close collaboration among Yu men is also evident in their joint printing ventures. In addition to the geomancy work showing Yu family gravesites mentioned above, another example that illustrates the efficient use of woodblocks is the rhyming dictionary *Gujin yunhui juyao xiaobu* 古今韻會舉要小補 (Basics of rhymes old and new with slight revisions). Some extant copies list Yu Xiangdou and Yu Zhangde as the joint printers, and two others list Xiangdou alone, and yet another copy cites Zhou Shixian 周士顯, then the magistrate of Jianyang, as the publisher (see below).

Although the Cuiqing tang produced books of all kinds, about a third of them were literary—collections of individuals' writings, anthologies of occasional pieces, drama miscellanies, and collections of anecdotes. In many of the anthologies, the name Deng Zhimo 鄧志謨 or one of his sobriquets appears as the author, compiler, or annotator. Both Deng's role as a writer and the quality of his work are suggestive of the ways late Ming commercial printshops operated. A native of Raozhou 饒州 in Jiangxi, Deng wrote many fanciful essays, at least three novels, and a number of lyric dramas (*chuanqi* 傳奇).[37] According to one modern source, he was a tutor in the Yu household[38] as well as house writer for the Cuiqing tang, which printed about a dozen of his works. None of Deng's writings, at least those put out by the Cuiqing tang, is a literary masterpiece. Rather, they show his marketable skill as a quick producer of entertaining middle-brow pieces that sold well in the book markets, especially if they were packaged with some care. One example is the "Contest" series of occasional pieces printed by the Cuiqing tang in the Tianqi period (1621–27), which are discussed later in this chapter.

Liu Publishers

The earliest known publishers from the Liu descent group date to the Song, and the last to the early Qing.[39] In terms of longevity, the Liu publishers were at least the equals of the Yu, and in terms of total output, slightly behind them, judging by the extant titles (Table 6). During the Ming, most of the commercial printers named Liu apparently belonged to the Zhen house of the Northern branch of the Western lineage (Xizu Beipai Zhenfang—see Table 2a, b), as they had in the Song and Yuan. According to Table 2, of the 35 Liu men whom we know to have been involved in printing as authors, editors/collators, printers, and master blockcarvers, 28 can be identified as members of the Zhen house; five others were members of others lines in the Northern branch. By and large, the few members of the Southern branch of the Western lineage (Xizu Nanpai, Table 2c) and the Eastern lineage (Dongzu, Table 2d) who engaged in printing activities worked either on the clan's genealogy or on the works of their illustrious ancestors.[40]

The local histories and the Liu genealogy suggest that the fortunes of the Liu descent group in general and the sub-branch to which the printers belonged declined during the early Ming, possibly for reasons similar to the Yu printers. First, nearly all of the Liu men belonging to this descent group who merited a biographical sketch in the local gazetteers are from the Song and Yuan, rather than the Ming.[41] Second, there are only two *jinshi* surnamed Liu from Jianyang during the Ming. Although the far more competitive examination for this degree in the Ming makes comparisons with the Song problematical, the low number of *juren* 舉人 (three from Jianyang, with two of them being men who also received the *jinshi* degree), and only ten yearly tribute students (*sui gongsheng* 歲貢生) supports the argument that the Liu descent group was far less successful in the Ming. Third, the Zhen house seems to have been rather destitute until some time toward the end of the fifteenth century. For example, a biographical note for Liu Yan 剡 (Table 2b), a printer and editor in the Yongle period (1403–24) and the great-great-grandson of the Yuan printer Liu Junzuo, mentions his family's poverty.[42] Moreover, at least some branches of the descent group in Shulin (Shufang) were subject to corvée, from which they presumably would have been exempt if there were officials in the family. The writer of a preface to a Ming edition of *Si shu wenmu* 四書問目 by Liu Bing 炳, a renowned Song scholar of the Southern branch of the Western clan (Table 2c), condemned the attempts of some Liu men from Shulin to evade corvée by claiming close kinship with the more il- lustrious Eastern lineage or by changing their name.[43] Quite probably, the members of the Eastern lineage were exempt from labor service because they were classified as official households (*guan hu* 官戶) or because their ranks included a number of students and examination graduates.[44] In contrast, the less privileged Liu men from Shulin were liable for labor service. For example, Liu Hongyi 弘(洪)毅,[45] who produced some of the finest imprints from Jianyang in the Ming, was excused from one year of corvée in acknowledg- ment of his work on the large Song encyclopedia, *Qunshu kaosuo* 群書 考索 (Inquiry into a multitude of books).[46] In this publication and in several others, Liu Hongyi listed himself as "Shu hu Liu shi Shendu zhai" 書戶劉氏 慎獨齋 (Shendu Studio of the Liu book household), so it is likely that his particular labor service entailed the production of imprints for local govern- ment offices.[47] In fact, from the end of the fifteenth century through the 1530s, a period when both Jianyang county and Jianning prefectural government of- ficials were heavily involved in publishing, several other Liu printing houses, including Liu Shizhong 劉仕中 at the Anzheng tang 安正堂 and the Liu family's Mingde tang 明德堂 mentioned their status as *shu hu*.[48]

To judge from many of the books the Liu printed or edited, neither the possible decline in their economic fortunes nor their obligation to perform labor service necessarily meant the publishers were poorly educated—or saw themselves as anything less than scholars. Liu Hongyi's editions of the stan- dard histories, for example, are generally considered among the best from the Ming.[49] Moreover, the family's fortunes had improved significantly by the mid-sixteenth century at the latest. Liu Kongjing 孔敬, the elder son of an- other well-known and prolific printer, Liu Longtian 龍田 (1560–1639), was a *jinshi* of 1625, and several other members of the family were tribute students around the same time. These achievements argue a successful pursuit of the common strategy among families in late imperial China of using their learn- ing to earn a living while investing money in educating sons in the hope that a few of them would succeed in the examinations. For the Liu, especially for members of the Zhen house, work in the book trade as printers, authors, edi- tors, and blockcarvers was a long family tradition. Some of those involved in publishing, such as Liu Yan 剡 (Table 2b), also possessed medical expertise, which could be applied to editing and printing the many medical texts the family published.

Two of the printing houses operated by Liu publishers, the Cuiyan jingshe and the Rixin tang, had been founded in the Yuan in the late thirteenth century. The Cuiyan jingshe apparently continued into the late sixteenth century, printing mainly works on the Four Books, histories, and a few medical texts and collected writings of individuals.[50] The Rixin tang, which produced similar works, was in business into the early sixteenth century. These two printing houses were among the few that operated and produced most of their works in the fifteenth century. Some of their works were reprints from blocks cut in the Yuan. Other works, however, were newly edited and printed for the first time in the Ming. For example, a 1428 edition of a digest of the *Zizhi tongjian* printed by Liu Wenshou 文壽 (Table 2b) of the Cuiyan jingshe lists his distant cousin Liu Yan as a collator.[51] A sequel to this work printed four year later lists the then-magistrate of Jianyang, Zhang Guangqi 張光啓, as the editor. In 1437 the same printshop produced a short medical work on pulse analysis by the young Xiong Zongli, who would become a well-known publisher in his own right.

Of the Liu family printing houses that began in the Ming, three were particularly prolific. First, Liu Hongyi's Shendu zhai, noted for its superior editions of the standard histories and large literary anthologies, produced some 45 imprints from about 1498 to 1534. Among the largest works printed by Liu Hongyi were a reprint of the official geography *Da Ming yitong zhi* 大明一統志 (Comprehensive gazetteer of the Great Ming; 1505); the encyclopedia *Qunshu kaosuo* (1508), with Yuan and Ming supplements to the original Song version; *Shiqi shi xiangjie* 十七史詳節 (1516) by the Song scholar Lü Zuqian; *Wenxian tongkao* (1516–19), the Yuan encyclopedia by Ma Duanlin 馬端林; and *Shiji daquan* 史記大全 (The great compendium on the *Record of History*; 1521), an edition of Sima Qian's work with a very complete set of commentaries. All of these except the *Da Ming yitong zhi* were clearly printed under official auspices or commissioned by wealthy local literati. For example, as Figure 24 shows, the magistrate of Jianyang, Ou Yu 區玉, was listed as the publisher of the *Qunshu kaosuo* at the beginning of each *juan*, and Liu Hongyi and seven other men were variously credited as collators of different *juan*. Various colophons throughout the work name the Shendu zhai as the printshop. Similarly, both the *Shiji daquan* and the *Wenxian tongkao* list the Jianyang magistrate, Shao Bin 邵圖 (*zi* Zongzhou 宗周), as the publisher and Liu Hongyi as the collator and/or printer. Considering the near simultaneous production of these large works, it is unlikely that Liu had the

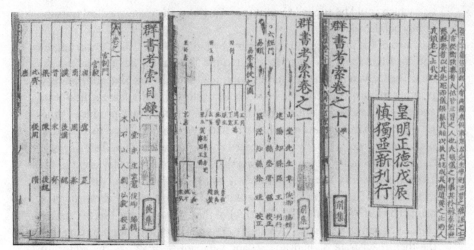

Fig. 24 *Qunshu kaosuo* 群書考索. 1508–18. Publisher: Ou Yu (Jianyang county magistrate). Printer: Liu Hongyi of Shendu zhai.

financial and material resources to undertake their production by himself. Several of the works produced under official auspices were reprinted shortly after their first publication, and notes in the later editions provide some interesting information. For example, *Liji jishuo* 禮記集說 (*Record of Rites*, with collected discussions), originally published in 1504, was reprinted with corrections of 2,585 characters, or roughly 1 percent of all the text. The *Wenxian tongkao*, a much larger work, was first published in 1519 and then reprinted after 11,221 characters were corrected (about 0.5 percent of the total number). Without similar data for other imprints, it is impossible to tell how typical these numbers are. If we suppose that the Liu Hongyi was more concerned about proofreading and correcting his original blocks than other Jianyang printers, then *their* percentage of wrong characters would be higher.[52] Again, the stern note placed at the front of each of the Classics published by the Jianning prefectural government (Fig. 3) might indicate that the county and prefectural officials in Minbei were particularly strict at this time and demanded that the Shendu zhai make the corrections noted.

There are no known imprints from the Shendu zhai after 1534, perhaps because Liu Hongyi found no successor willing to maintain the blocks and print such large works. Or perhaps the blocks were dispersed, many being carted off by officials when they left their offices in Jianyang (see below).[53]

With the Anzheng tang and the Qiaoshan tang 喬山堂, we come to two printshops the variety and quality of whose outputs were typical of Jianyang in the late Ming. The Anzheng tang was associated with at least five printers[54] and produced some 80 imprints from the beginning of the sixteenth century through the second decade of the seventeenth century. The Qiaoshan tang, which published some 70 titles, was run by Liu Longtian and his elder brother Liu Yutian 玉田, and later by Longtian's younger son, Kongdun 孔敦 (Table 2b), from the second half of the sixteenth century into the second decade of the seventeenth century. Both shops produced a wide variety of texts, including the Classics, histories, household encyclopedias, medical works, and illustrated works of fiction.

Like other Jianyang men engaged in the book trade, the Liu publishers often functioned as authors and editors as well and often collaborated not only with other Liu family printers but also with other shops, both in Jianyang and in more distant places, especially Nanjing. For example, Liu Kongdun is credited as a collator and editor for at least five works produced by the well-known Nanjing publishing houses of the Zhou 周 family: the Daye tang 大業堂, the Renshou tang 仁壽堂, and the Wanjuan lou 萬卷樓. In fact, Liu Kongdun's connections with the Zhou printers went beyond just working for them: his 1628 edition of the illustrated pharmaceutical work *Tuxiang bencao mengquan* 圖像本草蒙筌 was printed using the same blocks as the edition by Zhou Ruquan 如泉 at about the same time. Because the Zhou imprint is not dated, it is difficult to say which "edition" is earlier. Liu and Zhou may have agreed to share the blocks with each putting his own name in the printer's colophon.[55]

For different printers to use the same printing blocks either simultaneously or successively seems to have been a fairly common practice. The blocks for another work edited and printed by Liu Kongdun, the *Chongding Xiangzhai zaofu quanshu* 重訂相宅造福全書 (Complete book on generating good fortune for homes; 1628), were used by another Jianyang printer, Yang shi Sizhi guan 楊氏四知館, and by the Suzhou printer Yan Shaoxuan 嚴少萱. Since neither of these editions is dated, it is not possible to determine the sequence in which the three printers used the blocks. As mentioned in Chapter 2, one modern scholar has suggested that the blocks themselves were transported between Jianyang and Suzhou,[56] although it is also possible that the printing for two or all three editions was done at the same place, with the block(s) for the title page or printer's colophon modified as needed. Such collaborations support the argument that by the mid-sixteenth century, the book trade in south China, especially in Fujian and the Jiangnan area, was essentially unified. Works were produced by the same authors, editors, printers, and blockcarvers, many of whom moved from place to place in this widespread publishing network.

Fig. 25 *Wuyi zhilüe* 武夷志略. 1619. Publisher: Sun Shichang of Chongan (Jianning).

Another example of a well-traveled Jianyang man engaged in the printing industry was Liu Suming 素明, a well-known blockcarver of the late sixteenth and early seventeenth centuries, who often also drew (painted) the illustrations he carved. In many of these illustrations, he is recorded as the carver and sometimes the calligrapher as well. Liu Suming and at least five of his relatives were engravers and illustrators who attained the same level of professional recognition as members of the Huang family from Anhui, with whom they sometimes collaborated in Nanjing.[57] The twenty or so imprints on which Liu Suming worked were published in such diverse places as Jianyang, Hangzhou, Suzhou, and Wuxi, suggesting that he, like so many other engravers, traveled throughout Fujian and the Jiangnan area. The landscape from the *Wuyi zhilüe* 武夷志略, a 1619 gazetteer published privately in Chongan, has "Shulin Liu Suming kexiang" 書林劉素明刻像 (Drawn and engraved by Liu Suming of Shulin) on a vertical rock face (right half-leaf; see Fig. 25). Like the Xiao family (discussed below), the Liu engravers also worked with other Jianyang men who established themselves in the publishing industry in Jiangnan.

Xiong Publishers

Compared with the Yu and Liu, the Xiong family's commercial printing activities began late, probably in the late Yuan, and most of their imprints date from the Ming.[58] As noted in Chapter 3, most Xiong printers of the Ming belonged to the Western lineage (Xizu) of the Xiong descent group in the Jianyang area. There are four known Yuan imprints from this family, one of which is dated 1357. Thereafter followed a hiatus of few decades, and the earliest datable Ming imprint is from 1408. It is possible that the Xiong family went through a decline like the Yu and the Liu at the beginning of the Ming.

From the beginning, medical texts dominated the lists of several Xiong printing houses, especially the Zhongde tang 種德堂,[59] operated by Xiong Zongli and several of his direct descendants. Some twenty Xiong men involved in the book trade during the Ming and early Qing can be identified in the family's genealogy (Table 4), and there were at least six others who are not.

As in the Yu and Liu families, many of the Xiong men functioned not only as printers but also as authors, editors, and collators. Xiong Zongli's medical knowledge enabled him to edit a number of medical classics and to write several popular introductions to these works. His editions of such well-known medical works as the *Furen daquan liangfang* 婦人大全良方 (Complete effective prescriptions for women's diseases) and the *Taiping huimin heji ju fang* were reprinted or served as the basis for several subsequent editions.[60] Xiong rated a biographical note not only in his family's genealogy but also in the Jianyang county gazetteer, both of which mentioned his medical expertise and his editorial efforts but not his printing activities.[61] According to the genealogy, Xiong was a student of Liu Yan, another Jianyang man engaged in printing and presumably in medicine (see above). As we have seen, this combination of medicine and publishing seems not to have been uncommon in Jianyang by the mid-Ming. Indeed, in the short biographical account found in *Riji gushi* 日記故事 (Stories for daily notice) by Xiong Damu (Zongli's great-grandson), the merit accumulated by Zongli in helping people through his medical skills was similarly earned for two more generations, by Zongli's elder son Yuan 瑗 and Yuan's oldest son Yiqing 一清 (*zi* of Tianxuan 天玄—see Table 4), who also became physicians.[62] Other descendants of these men worked in the publishing industry.

As exemplified by the efforts of Yu Xiangdou and his relatives, members of Jianyang printer families took to writing works of fiction. The most famous author of fiction from Jianyang was Xiong Damu, whose wrote in the mid-sixteenth century.[63] Since no imprints list Xiong Damu as the publisher, it is possible that he worked mostly as an author and editor. His extant works include four historical novels and the *Riji gushi* mentioned above.[64] In addition, he is credited as the compiler of a *leishu*-type literary anthology. Seven of the extant editions of his works were issued by well-known publishers in Nanjing, Hangzhou, or Suzhou in the 1550s and 1560s; of the three Jianyang editions printed in the seventeenth century, one is a reprint of a Hangzhou edition. These facts again support the argument that Jianyang was part of a larger book market encompassing Fujian and the Jiangnan region.

Among the Xiong publishers of the late Ming, none was more prolific than Xiong Chengye 成冶 (Table 4, twenty-fourth generation), another descendant of Zongli. His 45 or so imprints produced under the Zhongde tang name span nearly the entire Wanli period, from 1573 to about 1612, and are quite representative of the offerings of the Jianyang publishers of the time: Classics, examination literature dealing with the histories, medical texts, including reprints of earlier Zhongde tang editions, works on geomancy, and different kinds of *leishu*, including household references, writing manuals, and collections of moralistic tales. Along with these simple anecdotes, Xiong Chengye also printed about five primers on various Classics for beginning readers. Finally, his one known foray into historical narratives was a *Sanguo zhizhuan*, one of about four similar editions produced by Xiong publishers during the late sixteenth and early seventeenth centuries.

The Xiong family seems to have continued printing books into the Qing, although in a much reduced fashion. One reason for the decline was their pronounced Southern Ming sentiments, which seem to have been shared by their distant relatives in the Eastern lineage of the family as well as those in Jiangxi. One extant Xiong imprint boldly gives a date of Longwu 2 (1646), and at least one Xiong man actively supported the Longwu emperor.[65] After the Qing subdued the Minbei area, several members of the clan who had held office under the Ming retired to teach, but they printed very few books.

Another possible reason for the decline was that a number of Xiong men simply emigrated from the area to escape the devastation and the turmoil caused by the Ming-Qing transition. Some of them apparently remained in close contact with their family and other printers in Jianyang. Thus Xiong Chengying 成應, of the twenty-fifth generation, who is noted in the genealogy as having moved to Nanjing, printed books both there and in Jianyang. The genealogy also records that two generations later Xiong Shiqi 世崎 moved permanently to Guangdong, where he opened a bookstore, but it does not mention any descendants.

Finally, in a very belated change of practice, the compilers of the last extant edition of the Xiong genealogy notes that one Xiong Jianlong 見龍 (1716–69) was a bookseller, and one Xiong Hai 海 (1716–83) became a printer after having no success in the official examinations. But by then, the Minbei area had fallen into the general decline of which the Jianyang book trade was a most notable victim.

Zheng Publishers

After the Yu, Liu, and Xiong, the most prolific Jianyang publishers were those from the Zheng 鄭 family. Despite the twenty-odd men known by name and over 100 imprints, however, there is frustratingly little information about the Zheng. Most of what we know comes from correlating information found in their publications and from a recently discovered tomb tablet for one of the most productive of the late Ming printers, Zheng Shikui 鄭世魁 (1545–1602). According to the tomb epitaph, the Zheng had settled in Minbei by the Southern Song,[66] although we have no evidence of the family's involvement in publishing until the early fourteenth century during the Yuan, when about six imprints were issued by the Zongwen tang 宗文堂.

As with all the other Jianyang families involved in the book trade, the overwhelming majority (at least 104 out of 112) of the Zheng publications appeared from the Jiajing period onward. Moreover, the three datable to the early fifteenth century may have been reprints using blocks carved in the Yuan. The trajectory of the Zheng publishers' activities is thus consistent with the broad historical trends in commercial publishing in the Fujian and Jiangnan areas. It is also possible that for the Zheng, even more than for the Liu, Yu, or Xiong, the revival of their printing operations during the Zhengde and Jiajing periods was connected with the interest of local officials and their financial sponsorship. More than half of the twenty-odd Zheng imprints from this time are editions of the Classics, histories, Confucian works, and medical texts.

By the start of the Wanli period, however, the publications from the Zongwen tang and other Zheng printers were far more typical of Jianyang commercial offerings. For example, they issued at least ten editions of popular story collections, which were topically arranged, simply retold anecdotes from the Classics and histories, with a moral tacked on to each.[67] In addition, three different Zheng publishers contributed their own edition of the *Sanguo zhizhuan* in the printing frenzy surrounding this work during the last years of the Wanli period, when Jianyang publishers managed to produce at least twenty different editions (see below). Finally, the Zheng publishers offered their fair share of examination literature, including digests of the Classics and Histories, and various literary anthologies.

Many of these imprints attest to the Zheng's collaboration with other Jianyang publishers. Perhaps borrowing from Yu Xiangdou was inevitable; in any case, at least the edition of the *Sanguo zhizhuan* printed by Zheng Yizhen 以禎 was chock-full of verse from Yu's 1592 edition of the work. Around the same time, a collection of *gongan* stories compiled and previously published by Yu were reprinted by the Zheng's Zongwen tang. When the latter printed its edition of the story collection *Gushi baimei* 故事白眉, it included the notes by Deng Zhimo, who had quite possibly written them for the earlier version from Yu Wenxi 余文熹, since Deng was often employed as a house writer by several of the Yu publishers.

Only one imprint provides evidence that the Zheng may have set up business in Nanjing; the 1601 edition of the political history *Gushu poutan* 孤樹裒談 by Li Mo 李默 (d. 1556) was published by the Zheng's Zongwen shushe 宗文書舍 in Nanjing.[68] Other possible clues pointing to Nanjing connections are far more tenuous: there are similarities between the Zheng Yizhen twelve-*juan* edition of the *Sanguo zhi* and the earlier (and better-produced) edition by Zhou Yuejiao 周曰校, the famous Nanjing publisher.[69]

Chen Publishers

According to a tomb epitaph for the Ming publisher Chen Yuwo 陳玉我 (1580–1650), his family belonged to a descent group that had settled in Minbei during the Shaoxing period (1131–62) of the Southern Song.[70] There is no evidence, however, to link the several Jianyang printers surnamed Chen in the Song with the Yuan and Ming printers of this name. By the early fourteenth century, the Chen family's Yuqing tang 餘慶堂 had begun printing books, a few of which would be reissued in the early Ming under the same *tangming*. By the early sixteenth century, during the Zhengde period (1506–21), the Chen had published at least eighteen medical texts—quite possibly a continuation and expansion of the interest of their Yuan predecessors and one encouraged by local and regional government officials.

Apparently, like Xiong Zongli, some of the Chen men, like Chen Yuwo's father, Chen Qiquan 奇泉, had a wide knowledge of medicine, as well as of calendrical calculations and geomancy, and by the Wanli period had published over a dozen works on various forms of divination. This may have been popular combination of interests among Jianyang publishers for which we lack solid evidence. Since in the Yuan and Ming these men enjoyed less success as scholar-officials, they may well have resorted to a combination of medicine, divination, and publishing to maintain their claim to a cultural and intellectual position in local Minbei society.

One man, Chen Jingxue 陳敬學, from whom we have one known publication, was the son-in-law of Zhu Bingtie 朱秉鐵, a twelfth-generation descendant of Zhu Xi and possibly connected with the Zhu family's Jianyang publishing house, Yugeng tang 與耕堂.[71] More connections between Chen publishers and other Jianyang men can be found in the Chen imprints. For example, Yu Yingkui 余應奎, who is listed as the collator of a philological work printed by several Jianyang publishers, receives similar credit for two medical works published by Chen Qiquan's Jishan tang 積善堂 during the Wanli period. Finally, the only drama issued by a Chen publisher was a joint publication by Chen Hanchu 含初 and Zhan Linwo 詹林我, a member of another Jianyang publishing family.[72] Indeed, this work is closer in appearance to publications of Nanjing, where the two men might have been in business.

Ye Publishers

Like many of the Jianyang families discussed in this section, the printing activities of the Ye 葉 may have begun in the Southern Song, although the evidence is very thin—one popular anthology of examination poetry from the Guangqin tang 廣勤堂.[73] The four Yuan imprints from the fourteenth century and the three Ming imprints from the first three decades of the fifteenth century provide clearer evidence of the Ye publishers' activities. Indeed, the Guangqin tang published works through the mid-sixteenth century, while the Zuode tang 作德堂, operated by other Ye publishers, also produced imprints until about the same time.[74] Lastly, that of the fifty-three or so imprints attributable to various Ye printers so few were produced in the early Ming is consistent with the general trend in commercial publishing in the Fujian and Jiangnan areas. Not until the late fifteenth century did most of the Ye publishers' books appear in both Jianyang and Nanjing.

These later imprints yield most of the detailed information about how the publishers operated. For example, a 1582 imprint of a philological work, *Hai pian xin jing* 海篇心鏡, published by Ye Rulin 葉如琳 credits Yu Yingkui as the collator (*jiaoding* 校訂).[75] In a later edition of the same work published by Ye Huiting 會廷 in 1596, a Liu Kongdang 劉孔當, possibly a son or nephew of the Jianyang publisher Liu Longtian, was listed as the collator. Information in a 1581 edition of the *Xinke zengbu quanxiang xiangtan Lizhi ji* 新刻增補全像鄉談荔枝記 (Newly engraved, fully illustrated edition in local dialect of the *Tale of the Lizhi*), a drama in the Chaozhou dialect, suggests the transfer of blocks from the family of the original publisher, Ye Wenqiao 葉文橋 of Nanyang tang 南陽堂, to the Zhu family of Yugeng tang, or possibly a collaboration between the two publishing houses to finance the carving of the blocks.[76]

Ye publishers operated not only in Jianyang, but also in Nanjing and in Sanqu 三衢 in Zhejiang. During the Wanli period, Ye Gui (Jinshan) 葉貴 (近山) published about a dozen imprints, in which he identified his print shop as "Jinshan tang of Ye Gui from Jianyang on Sanshan Street in Jinling" (金陵三山街建陽葉貴近山堂). Sanshan Street was located in the area of Nanjing that was home to most of the city's best-known commercial publishers.[77] Ye Gui's collaboration with other publishers is demonstrated clearly in the divination work *Xinkan Han Zhuge Wuhou mi yan qin shu* 新刊漢諸葛武侯秘演禽書 (Newly engraved book of divination by Lord Zhuge of the Han), identical editions of which were issued by him and by the Wenlin ge 文林閣 of the prominent Tang 唐 family publishers of Nanjing.[78] Not surprisingly, Ye Gui also maintained connections with Jianyang publishers. His 1602 edition of the philological work *Hai pian zhengzong* 海篇正宗 was a reprint of the one compiled and published earlier by Yu Xiangdou himself.

The connections between the Ye publishers of Sanqu in western Zhejiang (near modern day Changshan in Quzhou, bordering on northern Fujian) and those in Jianyang and Nanjing are more difficult to prove unequivocally. The collected prose of the famous Ming author Tang Shunzhi 唐順之, *Tang Jingchuan xiansheng wenji* 唐荊川先生文集 (Collected prose of Tang Jingchuan) was issued in 1553 by both the Ye Baoshan tang in Sanqu in Zhejiang (浙江葉寶山堂) and Ye Jinshan in Nanjing's book district (書林葉近山); except for the printers' colophons, the two editions are identical.[79] The colophon of another work states that a "Mr. Hu" (Hu shi 胡氏) of Sanqu printed the work in Piling (in modern Changzhou, Jiangsu), but the advertisement (*gaobai*) at the front of the imprint is written by a Ye Jinquan 葉錦泉 of Sanshan Street in Nanjing, who is also noted as the work's publisher.[80] We can tentatively untangle these relations by suggesting that the Ye family was originally from Jianyang and continued to operate a publishing business there. It established branches in Sanqu and Nanjing, while collaborating with the Hu publisher(s) of Sanqu who also did business in Piling. Although it is highly plausible that the peripatetic publishers from the smaller printing centers in south and central China established a network of branch shops throughout the region, we have little specific evidence other than these scraps of information for the Ye (and Hu) publishers.

Xiao Publishers

Compared to the other Jianyang families, the Xiao 蕭 appeared to be late-comers to the publishing industry. According to their genealogy, *Xiao shi zupu* 蕭氏族譜, a Xiao Qiyin 蕭啓殷 settled in Minbei at the end of the Yuan, but it was not until the mid-sixteenth century that the family began printing, under the name Shijian tang 師儉堂. There is one sliver of evidence that the Shijian tang continued to operate until the end of the seventeenth century,[81] but most of the imprints from the Xiao publishers date from the late Ming.

Among what was probably the first generation of publishers was Xiao Mingsheng 鳴盛 (*hao* Jingwei 儆韋; 1575–1644), who achieved some official success as a *juren* and served twice as a county magistrate.[82] It is the next generation, however, in particular, Xiao Shixi 世熙 (Shaoqu 少衢/渠, 1570–1621) and his younger brother Xiao Tenghong 騰鴻 (*hao* Qingyun 慶雲, 1586–?), who produced the most imprints. The clear differences both in content and in appearance between their publications strongly suggest that while Shixi operated primarily in Jianyang, Tenghong was based in Nanjing.[83] Xiao Shixi's imprints exhibited the variety typical of late Ming Jianyang imprints and include editions of the Classics, a geomancy text, and about ten literary anthologies designed for examination study. Xiao Tenghong, in contrast, is best known for his illustrated plays, produced in the style of other such works from Nanjing.

On the upper right corner of a full-leaf illustration from a Nanjing edition of the play *Xiuru ji* 繡襦記 (The story of the embroidered jacket) is "Engraved by Liu Suming" *Liu Suming juan* 劉素明鐫, followed by his seal, on which is carved "Drawn by Suming" *Suming tushu* 素明圖書 (see Fig. 26a).[84] What is also noteworthy is that other than the commentator, who is the famous Ming literatus Chen Jiru 陳繼儒,[85] the other three men listed on the first page of the first *juan* are all Jianyang men (Fig. 26b). The publisher is Xiao Tenghong. Yu Wenxi 余文熙, who is credited as the proofreader, was a cousin of Yu Xiangdou, but also worked extensively in Nanjing, judging from the imprints that credit him as a collator or editor. Finally, the collator Xiao Mingsheng (see above), possibly an uncle of Xiao Tenghong, worked in both Jianyang and Nanjing. Thus, three of the most important Jianyang families involved in the book trade are represented in one imprint produced in Nanjing.

(a)

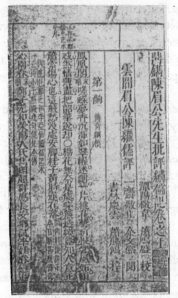

(b)

Fig. 26 Imprint by Jianyang men working in the Nanjing printing industry. *Xiuru ji* 繡襦記. Ming Wanli period (1573–1619). Publisher: Xiao Tenghong.

(*a, above*) Full-leaf illustration drawn and carved by Liu Siming.

(*b, left*) First page of the work listing Xiao Tenghong as the publisher and Yu Wenxi and Xiao Mingsheng as collators.

Local and Regional Government Involvement
in Jianyang Publishing

For the Ming, far more than for the Song and Yuan, there is evidence of local and regional officials involved in publishing in Minbei. Some of these activities were attempts by government offices to regulate the quality of scholarly publications in the Jianyang area, especially the Classics and the Histories; others were efforts by individual officials to have works printed in which they had a personal interest. Especially during the Zhengde and Jiajing periods, some Jianyang county magistrates, Jianning prefects, and Fujian circuit officials became deeply involved in publishing in Minbei and were responsible for over thirty imprints. Many of these imprints were scholarly works—the Classics, Histories, large examination *leishu*, and a number of individual and general literary collections—although one of the last known such works was a play, *Kunlun nu* 昆侖奴 (The Kunlun slave), published in 1615 by the Jianyang magistrate, Liu Yunlong 劉雲龍.[86]

The central government evinced its interest in Fujian publishing very early in the Ming, as part of its search for good editions of works that had apparently disappeared or become perilously rare, a usual concern of the state at the start of a new dynasty. Thus in 1390, apparently spurred by the Fujian provincial administrator's presentation of several editions of histories published in the province, the court ordered the Board of Rites to buy books throughout the country and to have printing centers (*shufang*) make impressions from their existing blocks. In the following year, two students from the Imperial University went on an official mission to Fujian to buy books. The Nanjing government's actions were quite timely, since in 1404, the Jianning prefecture's Confucian school and temple, where many editions of the Classics and their printing blocks were stored, burned down. Perhaps not coincidentally, the prefect who requested land for rebuilding was also one of the first officials in Minbei to publish a work there.[87]

Apparently, the dearth of imprints was still a problem that worried the central government some 40 years later. In 1439, no less than the then–chief descendant of Confucius recommended that the Board of Rites obtain not just books but blocks from Jianyang and have new copies printed.[88] It seems not unreasonable to infer that at that time good editions with relatively complete commentaries of the Classics and Four Books and probably other Confucian works were still relatively rare, even in Nanjing and Beijing, as well as in Qufu, the ancestral home of the Kong lineage group. Thus Gu Yanwu's 顧炎武 (1613–82) remark that at the end of the Zhengde period, only the

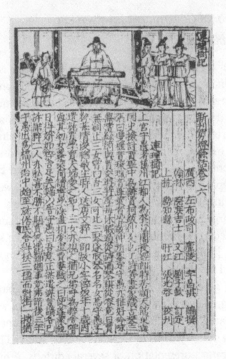

Fig. 27 *Xinkan Jian deng yu hua* 新刊剪燈
餘話. 1433. Publisher: Zhang Guangqi (Tenri
Central Library).

principalities, some government offices, and Jianning had printing blocks is
quite plausible.[89]

Another early local official who collaborated with Jianyang publishers
and scholars was Zhang Guangqi, who served as the Jianyang county magistrate during the Xuande period (1426–35).[90] Probably his best-known editorial contributions are those to the digests of various annalistic histories
published originally by the Liu family's Cuiyan jingshe (see above). These
works, which figured prominently in the studies of examination candidates,
were reprinted at least six times in Jianyang alone during the Ming. Another
well-known, but very different work, for which Zhang was listed as the
publisher is the 1433 edition of *Jian deng yu hua* 剪燈餘話 (More tales while
trimming the lampwick; Fig. 27).[91] This work, written by the scholar-official
Li Zhen 李禎 (1376–1452, *zi* Changqi 昌祺), was inspired by an earlier
collection, *Jian deng xin hua* 剪燈新話 (New tales while trimming the
lampwick; author's preface dated 1378), by Qu You 瞿祐. According to the

preface in the 1433 edition by Li Zhen's friend, Liu Jing 劉敬 (1368–1454, *zi* Ziqin 子欽), another high-level scholar-official of the early Ming, Zhang had requested the manuscript copy of *More Tales* from Liu, who had been his teacher, in order to have it printed. It is likely that Zhang intended to take advantage of the printing resources available to him in Jianyang, and quite possibly this work in the *shangtu xiawen* format was indeed published there, but by the time it came out, Zhang had moved south to assume the magistracy of Shanghang 上杭 county in southwestern Fujian, as noted at the start of *juan* 6 (shown in Fig. 27).

Nor is this the end of the story of the publishing of the *Jian deng* collections. In 1442, the head of the Directorate of Education condemned recently written meretricious stories on strange and sensational events, naming in particular the *New Tales*, and advanced the usual proposal that such works be burned and that those who printed, read, or owned them be punished according to the law.[92] Such developments suggest that Zhang's motive in publishing *More Tales* (as stated in his preface) did indeed rise from the admiration for the work that he shared with Liu Jing. Zhang probably felt that printing such a book that heretofore had limited circulation in manuscript form was worth defying the disapproval of other, more conservative officials. In any case, the virulent objections to the story collections apparently elicited no government actions against them, or at least none that were effective. From Jianyang, there were at least one commercial edition of *More Tales* in 1487 and two editions containing both collections in the sixteenth and seventeenth centuries.

In 1500, the disastrous fire that destroyed so many printing blocks in Shufang caused enough concern in Nanjing that a Fujian regional inspector was dispatched to Jianyang to assess the damage.[93] Apparently the publishing industry revived enough, perhaps with contributions from government officials, so that by 1526 concern for the spread of shoddy imprints from Jianyang led to the establishment of a government supervisory office there, with several high-level provincial officials in charge, including Wang Dian 汪佃, a member of the Hanlin Academy who was appointed regional judicial commissioner and charged with collating and checking the texts prepared for publishing.

During the Jiajing period, the Jianning prefectural government was actively concerned about the poor quality of the commercial Jianyang editions. This is apparent in the notice at the beginning of each of the series of Classics published by the Prefectural Office at that time (Fig. 3):

Proclamation of the Fujian Provincial Surveillance Commission. Be it known that the *Five Classics* and the *Four Books* are the most indispensable [works] for students. The old editions are considered well printed, but in recent times, commercial publishers, who aim solely at profit, issue pocket editions in small print and with many errors, such as *sun yu* 巽與 incorrectly given as *sun yu* 巽語, and *you gu* 由古 as *you gu* 猶古. Not only is this harmful to beginners, but many candidates for degrees have been disqualified because of the mistaken texts they have used, which is indeed a serious matter. This office deems it necessary that all works published in this province [lit., *Minzhong* 閩中, implying Jianyang Shufang] for circulation throughout the empire, if they have not been carefully collated, must be re-engraved to rectify the errors committed by the commercial printing establishments. Therefore this office has petitioned the judicial commissioner to appoint competent instructors and students to collate all the texts carefully. Characters, punctuation, and commentaries—all should be made correct....

Standard texts are accordingly to be printed and distributed in Jianyang to serve as guides. All works must be checked before they are sold. Names of the block carvers are to be placed at the end of books to make possible the tracing of any mistakes committed. Booksellers should not deviate from the standard texts issued by the officials.

Anyone who disregards this regulation will be punished and will have his blocks destroyed. No lenience will be shown. All printers are required to file a statement promising to comply with this regulation.

Twelfth month of the eleventh year of the Jiajing period [1532–33][94]

Indeed, the editions of the Classics published by the prefectural government, as well as those it reprinted, meticulously recorded the carvers' names, although not at the end of the works, but at the bottom of the center strip (Fig. 4a).

Also noteworthy is the number of different sets of Classics that were published, partly or wholly, in Jianyang during the Jiajing period. In addition to the set from which the notice shown in Figure 3 comes, there was another set that originally listed the Fujian regional inspector (*xun'an* 巡按) Ji Cheng 吉澄 as publisher. This same set seems then to have been reprinted under the direction of Yang Yi'e 楊一鶚, who was the prefect of Jianning at the time.[95] One possible explanation for this apparent surfeit is that the regional governments or the officials themselves presented or sold such editions to schools that lacked these essential works to signify their concern and generosity.[96]

Not surprisingly, a number of the same officials involved in publishing were credited with the compilation of the local histories. For example, the 1540 edition of the Jianning prefectural gazetteer names among its compilers Wang Dian 汪佃 and Zhu Xing 朱幸, a professor in the Confucian school in Jianning county (in Shaowu Prefecture). That the listing of their names in the Jianning prefectural gazetteer may not have been merely honorific is suggested by their publication of a poetry collection by a Tang poet Li Pin 李頻, who was a Minbei native. Another official involved both in compilation of the

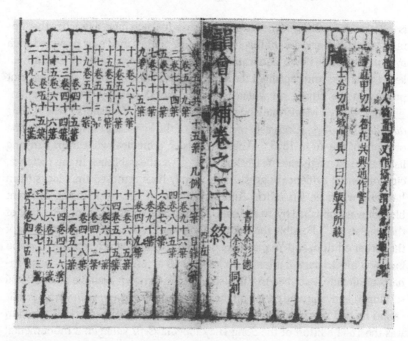

Fig. 28 *Gujin yunhui juyao xiaobu* 古今韻會舉要小補. 1606. Publisher: Zhou Shixian (Jianyang county magistrate).

local history and in other publications was Feng Jike 馮繼科, magistrate of Jianyang, who published a work of Ji Ben 季本, a student of Wang Yangming. Since there is little information about Feng himself,[97] it is hard to know his motivations for publishing this work.

Whether the commercial publishers worked willingly with these government officials is unclear. The 1504 supplement to an earlier Jianyang local history contains is a terse statement about the arbitrary confiscation and occasional destruction of printing blocks by the Jianning prefectural government.[98] Moreover, in the most productive of such "collaborations," that between officials and Liu Hongyi of Shendu zhai (see above), there is some hint of coercion in the statement that Liu was released from his *corvée* for working on the monumental encyclopedia, *Qunshu kaosuo*. Another imprint that may have caused some tension between the government official and the printers involved is the rhyming dictionary *Gujin yunhui juyao xiaobu* 古今韻會舉要小補, which credits the Jianyang magistrate of the time, Zhou Shixian 周士顯, as the publisher (see Fig. 28).[99] At the end of the work, two well-known and prolific commercial publishers of the late Ming, Yu Xiangdou and Yu Zhangde (Siquan), receive modest recognition as the joint "printers." This is followed by a listing of the number of leaves for each *juan*, a practice that implies official supervision of this imprint since neither men ever provided such information in his own publications. Apparently one or both of the Yu men kept the blocks and reprinted the work. One extant copy has a title page, not present in the others, on which is stated "Blocks held by the Santai guan" 三台館藏板.[100] Magistrate Zhou also headed the list of collators in the *Wujing daquan* 五經大全 (Complete compendia of the Five Classics) printed by one or more of the Yu in 1605.[101] A few years later, a medical work from Jianyang listed the next magistrate, Ye Dashou 葉大受, as the publisher. In this instance, circumstantial evidence suggests that Ye may have removed the blocks from Jianyang when he left office. Another edition of the work (using different blocks) was published by Yu Siquan's Cuiqing tang, probably soon after that of the magistrate.[102] Possibly the Cuiqing tang was involved in the production of the earlier edition, and Yu may have deemed it a work worth republishing and had new blocks carved after he no longer had access to the original ones. Finally, as already described in Chapter 2, the best-known example of an official serving in Jianyang who carted off the printing blocks of a work in whose publication he had been involved is Huang Guoqi 黃國奇. The work in question was the 1642 edition of the Song encyclopedia *Cefu yuangui*, a monumental work for which Jianyang publishers may well have felt they lacked the resources to engrave new blocks, even if the area's printing industry had not been disrupted by the turmoil accompanying the fall of the Ming in 1644.

Charting the Jianyang Book Trade During the Ming

Given the vicissitudes of time, it is not surprising that more books have survived from the Ming than from the Song and Yuan. For Jianyang imprints, Tables C.1 and C.2 show the skewed distribution by dynasty.[103] It may not be possible to determine the reasons for the overwhelming dominance of Ming imprints. Does it result simply from the greater survival rates of more recent publications? Or was there an increase in the number of publications? Or were there changes in the book-reading, -buying, and -collecting habits of different social groups,[104] or even different acquisition practices by Chinese, Korean, Japanese, and the few European book buyers of that period?[105] The sampling problems are compounded in at least two ways. First, the extant imprints from each period may not accurately reflect the distribution of titles actually published. For example, although Song sources note the ubiquity and abundance of low-quality *Mashaben*, far fewer of them have survived than the finest Jianyang imprints from that period, which have received the loving care of bibliophiles through the ages. Second, the low survival rate of the cheaper printed books, such as leaflets on how to write letters and official documents, or almanacs and calendars, and the even lower survival rates of printed ephemera like public announcements, tax forms, contracts, broadsheets, of which we have virtually none from any period, render even rough quantitative comparisons for such materials across time nearly impossible.[106]

Scholars who see an unprecedented publishing boom from the mid-Ming on and those reluctant to acknowledge such a phenomenon tend to divide according to their period of specialization. In fact, there is not (and may never be) enough quantitative data to yield a conclusive answer, and the qualitative evidence amassed so far has largely served only to fuel both sides of the argument. Because of the problems just described, even the information on the Jianyang book trade, which has the longest continuous history and the largest number of surviving imprints of any area in China, does not suffice to shift the debate significantly toward either view.

Although quantitative comparison between the book trade of earlier dynasties and of the Ming tend to be inconclusive, the relative wealth of surviving Ming imprints from Jianyang can help us answer some more specific questions concerning the changes in the book trade within the Ming. For example, is there evidence for the belief among modern scholars that there was an explosive increase in commercial imprints starting around the mid-sixteenth century as compared to the earlier Ming? And if so, how can we characterize this increase? Did it entail mainly production of many more of the same kinds of works published earlier, or was there also a wider variety of works available? Were there changes in the ways commercial publishers operated? Were they based primarily in one location or did they rely on increasingly widespread production and distribution networks that spread across provinces? If the publishing industry was truly interregional, was the book trade in these areas homogeneous? Recently, a number of scholars have presented convincing anecdotal evidence for a change in the publishing industry countrywide between the earlier and the later Ming.[107] We will examine these issues by counting Ming commercial imprints from Minbei and by speculating on the business operations of Jianyang publishers.

Growth in Ming Commercial Publishing—Some Estimates and Their Credibility

Even a casual perusal of the catalogues of the major Chinese rare book collections in Chinese libraries[108] or of the important Qing private collections would reaffirm the impression that the number of books printed in the later half of the Ming far exceeded those from the earlier part of the dynasty. But is there a way of measuring, even approximately, the number of commercially printed editions from Jianyang in different periods of the Ming?

First, by dividing the dynasty exactly in half (conveniently at the end of the Hongzhi period in 1505),[109] we find that out of a total of some 1,660 known titles published by commercial and private Jianyang publishers,[110] only about 179 (11 percent) were produced in the first 138 years.[111] Indeed, this ratio may actually be further skewed in favor of the later Ming since a number of imprints attributed to the early Ming were actually reprints using woodblocks cut during the Yuan. Even so, as noted above, the Jianyang publishing industry was comparatively more lively than that in much of the rest of the country. Thus, until at least the beginning of the sixteenth century, printed editions of many works were so scarce that the central, regional, and local governments took advantage of the blocks available in Jianyang. In addition, a similar estimate for all imprints from the various large Jiangnan printing centers (Nanjing, Suzhou, Wuxi, and Hangzhou) shows that slightly under 10 percent of these titles were printed in the first half of the dynasty.[112] The similar numbers for the various Jiangnan book centers and for Jianyang alone argue that the ratios are not due solely to a "naturally" lower survival rate for the earlier imprints; historical circumstances were similarly contributing to the decline in the book trade in both Jiangnan and Jianyang.

In any case, would correcting for the survival rates of imprints greatly alter this disparity between the earlier and later periods? Several bibliographies contain information that can help us obtain some idea of the survival rate of Jianyang imprints for the first two hundred years or so of the Ming. Two of these are particularly useful—one of 384 titles in the 1553 edition of the Jianyang county gazetteer, and the other of 368 titles in *Gujin shuke* 古今書刻 (Blockprinted books, old and new), a bibliography organized by geographic area compiled around 1570 by a scholar, Zhou Hongzu 周弘祖.[113] A comparison of these lists with my own bibliography of known Jianyang imprints for the appropriate dates gives a survival rate of about one-third in both cases.[114] This figure likely reflects in part the loss of woodblocks in the 1500 fire in Shufang, a conjecture supported by the lack of blocks noted in a different book list in the 1601 edition of the Jianyang county gazetteer.[115] The blocks destroyed probably included those carved in the Song and Yuan, as well as ones from the earlier Ming. Such a large-scale disaster might well have stimulated the active official participation in reviving the Jianyang printing industry. Furthermore, we do not know for any particular title whether reprinting required the carving of new blocks because of substantial revisions to the text or because the old blocks were no longer available. The second reason is in general more likely, since the contents of many of the works listed by the 1553 gazetteer and Zhou Hongzu remained largely unchanged from edition to edition. The implication, again, is that the lifetime of the blocks was dictated more often by circumstances other than being worn out from too many impressions.

In any case, if we correct for the one-third survival rate and assume the actual number of works published in Jianyang up through 1505 to be three times the known figure (3 x 179 = 537), and if we further assume a highly unlikely 100 percent survival rate of post-1505 publications, then the percentage of works published in the first half of the dynasty increases, but only to 36 percent. This would mean that the number of commercial titles published in Jianyang in the second half of the dynasty was still nearly twice that of the first half. These quantitative estimates therefore support the argument that there was a significant growth in commercial publishing in Jianyang in the late Ming.

Other, rather different kinds of evidence also attest to the growth of commercial publications in the latter half of the Ming. For example, although Ming writers seldom compared imprints produced in different periods of the dynasty, the few remarks they did make confirm the disparity between the early and late Ming.[116] Thus, Lu Rong 陸容 (1436–94), writing in the Hongzhi period, noted:

> At the beginning of the dynasty, only the National Academy had printing blocks, and the regional and local government offices in the provinces apparently did not. In the Xuande [1426–35] and Zhengtong [1436–49] reign periods, books and printing blocks were still not widespread. Today, the daily growth of printing blocks signals an esteem for learning far greater than before. . . . All the high officials give [imprints] as presents and often have all kinds of books printed. Some government departments are quite extravagant in this regard.[117]

Although Lu was speaking mainly about official publications, by the end of the fifteenth century, when he wrote this, commercial publishing was also beginning to take off. Nearly a century later, Hu Yinglin 胡應麟 (1551–1602) wrote:

> I met an old scholar who in his youth could not obtain the *Shiji* or the *Han shu*. When he finally had the good fortune to do so, he copied the complete texts and recited them day and night and was anxious to learn them by heart. But in recent times, people in the cities have taken to getting all kinds of scholarly works trace-copied, using up to ten thousand sheets a day in the process. Now the abundance of and easy access to books by students is such that there are five times as much literature and scholarship available as there was in the past, but those who have passed the examinations bundle up their books and do not look at them anymore.[118]

Hu's reproaching of his contemporaries for failing to appreciate the unprecedented wealth of learning available to them echoes the view of numerous earlier writers in different periods and therefore should not be taken entirely at face value.[119] It is interesting, however, that Hu complained of the abundance not just of printed books, but also of copies made by tracing a text, apparently by the numerous copyists found in the cities. Some of these copyists were most likely employed by commercial publishers as well, to write the texts to be transferred onto the woodblocks, so that they worked in two different sectors of the business purveying recorded information.

Looking back on his youth, Li Xu 李詡 (1505–93) wrote that he and his friends would pay two to three cash for each sheet of trace-copies of examination literature. They did so because they could not afford the good editions printed using woodblocks or movable type published by private individuals or academies, and the cheap commercial editions that abounded at the time he wrote this comment in the late Wanli period were not yet available.[120] By the Wanli period, there was no lack of commercially printed examination literature, as Shen Defu 沈德符 (1578–1642) noted. The most successful examination essays were immediately published without any corrections.[121]

Finally, the bibliographic notes of rare book collectors in the Qing and Republican periods show that the great majority of the Ming nongovernment publications they valued were produced from the mid-sixteenth century onward.[122] For example, Sun Congtian 孫從添, a bibliophile of the mid-Qing, commenting on private and commercial editions from the Ming, made particular note of ten publishers, all of whom were active after 1500.[123] Only one title on Ye Dehui's 葉德輝 (1864–1927) list of over 30 select Ming imprints dates to before 1500, as do only fourteen on his list of more than 100 noteworthy private and commercial Ming imprints.[124]

Once more, indications are that there was a revival of commercial printing around the beginning of the sixteenth century and that its increasing momentum resulted in the publishing boom of the late Ming. Moreover, a comparison of the number of Jianyang imprints from the late Yuan and the early Ming strongly suggest that the decline in the book trade did not occur until the start of the Ming. At least 60 of the 220 Yuan imprints listed in Table C.2 are dated to the last reign period; moreover, Jianyang imprints were produced as late as 1367, facts suggesting that the rate of printing in Jianyang did not slack off in the late Yuan. It is beyond the scope of this study to explain in detail why the decline occurred in the early Ming, but a few points are worth noting. First, my impression is that the decline in the publishing industry was less severe in Jianyang than in Jiangnan. The figures cited above suggest that both areas' commercial publishing suffered to the same extent, but the decrease in official publishing, which was far more important in Jiangnan, would have rendered the overall despression in book production more severe in

Jiangnan. Second, Jianyang's long-term dependence on the Jiangnan book market meant that the Minbei printing industry could not recover to any appreciable extent until Jiangnan's own economy, especially in the urban centers, recovered as well.[125] And if the Jianyang publishers depended on a closely linked market throughout much of central and south China, then their prosperity actually reflected the region's economy rather than Minbei's.

Characterizing the Late Ming Book Trade of Jianyang

Not everyone was entirely pleased with the resurgent publishing industry of the late Ming. The noted bibliophile Xie Zhaozhe 謝肇淛 (1567–1624) bemoaned the deteriorating quality of commercial imprints from the Jiangnan area as well as Jianyang.

Of block-printed books of the Song, those from Hangzhou were the best and then [those from] Sichuan, with those from Fujian being the worst. Today, Hangzhou imprints are not commendable, but the best block engravings done in Jinling [Nanjing], Xin'an [in Huizhou], and Wuxing [Huzhou] are not inferior to that of the Song. Those from Hunan and Hubei and Sichuan are all unexceptional. The bookstores of Jianyang put out the most books, but the printing and paper are wretched, because they are meant to make money and not to be transmitted through the ages. In general, books printed for the purpose of making a profit cannot be well produced, so they are not worth the cost of their printing [lit., throwing away twice the cost of the book (by buying it)]. Lately, books from Wuxing and Jinling have been succumbing precipitously to this malady.

Recently, imprints such as *Feng shi shiji* 馮氏詩記, *Jiao shi leilin* 焦氏類林, and all the books printed in Xin'an, such as the *Zhuang[zi]* and the *[Li]sao*, are of the best workmanship and not inferior to those from the Song. The publishers also take pains to proofread the texts, and so errors are extremely rare. [But] the imprints of Mr. Ling of Wuxing, who is anxious to make a profit, are worse than works that are plagiarized—and no wonder. When he collates the works, he gets the characters wrong. In contrast, books such as *Shuihu [zhuan]* 水滸[傳], *Xixiang [ji]* 西廂[記], *Pipa [ji]* 琵琶[記], *Mo pu* 墨譜, and *Mo yuan* 墨苑, which are meticulously produced with heavenly workmanship and utterly exquisite, are nothing but romances and other works to gratify the ear and eye—what a pity as well!

Lately something of the Suzhou school of engraving and printing has been introduced into central Fujian, but only in my area [Fuzhou]. There are no more than three to five who have the calligraphic skill and no more than ten or so who can do the engraving. Moreover, the woodblocks are thin and brittle and liable to crack after a while, so that the characters lose their true form. This is the cause of problems with books from Fujian.[126]

Thus, according to Xie, fine imprints were produced, but the mass printing of mediocre or poor-quality works was a pervasive problem. It was not that the

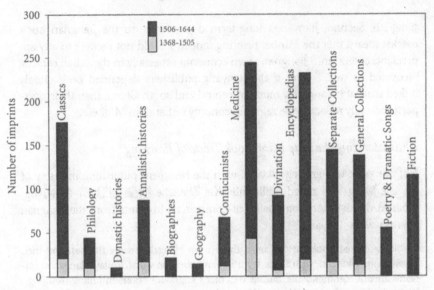

Fig. 29 Comparison of number of Jianyang imprints in selected categories, early to late Ming.

publishers did not have careful collators or skilled calligraphers and engravers at their disposal, but that in printing for profit, they stinted on quality while devoting much care to nonscholarly works such as story and drama collections and art albums. Such complaints, rarely heard before the mid-sixteenth century, became a litany in later times.

The changes from the early to late Ming in commercial publishing entailed not only a huge growth in the numbers of books produced, but also a far greater variety. Figure 29 charts the increases for Jianyang imprints in a number of different categories in the *siku* system. The lighter, lower portion of each bar represents the number of imprints for the earlier half of the Ming through the Hongzhi reign period (1368–1505), and the darker upper portion the number of imprints for the second half of the dynasty (1506–1644).[127]

What can we conclude from Figure 29? First, in every category shown, more books were published in Jianyang during the second half of the Ming than in the first half. Second, several kinds of works—the Classics,[128] Confucian works, and medical books—were published in relatively the same proportions even as their absolute numbers grew in the later Ming. Among the categories of Jianyang imprints that had been relatively unimportant in the early Ming but later became publishing staples are divination texts, encyclopedias, collections of poetry and dramatic songs, and fiction. In fact, in the case of drama and fiction, almost nothing was published prior to the sixteenth century of what would become primary offerings of the Jianyang booksellers in the late Ming. In short, the kinds of imprints that grew conspicuously in both relative and absolute terms are mainly nonscholarly books that the more conservative literati like Xie Zhaozhe disliked and considered frivolous. Xie probably also deplored the low-quality divination texts on geomancy, physiognomy, astrology, and the like as well as household manuals. Indeed, the text and illustration in many of these publications would not have gratified the reader's eye. The point, however, is that the late Ming book trade was catering to purchasers of many of the works criticized by men like Xie Zhaozhe or Hu Yinglin. Without the many customers who bought the cheap, low-end works, the late Ming publishing boom would not have occurred, any more than the earlier one in the Song and Yuan.

Some Speculations About the Jianyang Book Trade

Despite the more than 1,600 known Jianyang imprints from the Ming, and despite the information we can glean from them and other sources about commercial publishers, we have in truth little information on such practical details as the size of a commercial printshop or the circumstances under which a publisher employed editors, collators, blockcarvers, printers, and book binders. We also do not know whether a commercial publisher also sold the works he printed, what variety of printed materials he produced, how imprints were sold outside Minbei, and what the price of a given imprint was. Consequently, the following speculations about these important and interesting questions are based on the information presented above and on judicious extrapolations from what we know about Chinese printing and bookselling in later periods and in other parts of the country.[129]

First, it seems likely the larger and more long-lasting Jianyang publishers of the Song, Yuan, and Ming not only controlled the carving of the woodblocks and the printing and binding of the sheets but also sold their own imprints in Jianyang. We have almost no information on the size of printing establishments in Jianyang.[130] We do, however, know a bit more about one of the most famous and certainly most prolific private publisher's operations of the late Ming—the Jigu ge of Mao Jin (1599–1659) 毛晉及古閣 in Changshu (Jiangsu), which was active from the Chongzhen period (1628–44) through the early years of the Qing and printed some 600 titles.[131] Mao owned over 100,000 blocks and at one point employed about twenty carvers and printers, among others.[132] The total output of the Jigu ge exceeded that of even the largest Jianyang publishers of the late Ming, such as the Liu family's Qiaoshan tang, Yu Xiangdou's business, or Yu Siquan's Cuiqing tang, none of which produced more than 80 (known) titles, even though they were in existence for nearly as long as Mao. Most likely, therefore, a Jianyang publishing business would not have employed more carvers and printers than the Jigu ge.

How many such workers were there in Minbei? As discussed in above, the blockcarvers' names recorded at the bottom of the center strip of each leaf in the Jiajing period editions of the Classics sponsored by the Jianning prefectural government provide a way to guess at the number of blockcarvers in the area, since over 100 blockcarvers were involved in each work. Because commercial publishing was reviving in Jianyang during this period, and because some printers like Liu Hongyi were issuing large works, it is quite probable that several hundred blockcarvers worked in the area.[133] Female workers in the publishing business[134] were likely to have been either permanent or at least regular local employees, unlike male blockcarvers, who might have traveled outside Minbei. In any case, many of these workers, men or women, were ordinary blockcarvers, unlike the famous ones such as Liu Suming, who was known as both an illustrator and carver. Similarly, the pulling of impressions was the task that required the least skill in the book production process and may have been handled primarily by women or even children from Shufang or nearby areas.

As for the authors, editors, and collators who prepared the texts for publication, there is evidence that some of them worked regularly with a particular publisher. We have already noted, for example, the association between the writer Deng Zhimo and Yu Siquan's Cuiqing tang. Moreover, several Jianyang imprints of the late Ming have highly informative lists of the Minbei men who worked as compilers, editors, and collators. One such work, the *Si shu qianbai nian yan* 四書千百年眼 (Notes on the Four Books through the ages; preface dated 1633), lists Yu Yingke[135] as the main editor (*jigao* 輯稿) and another Minbei man, Zhang Gongli 張恭禮, as the collator, together with one Liu and one Xiong as associate collators (*jiaoding sheyou* 校訂社友), as well as ten members of the Yu family as associate editors (*tong zai jigao* 仝在輯稿), all of whom were known to have done similar work on other imprints.[136] Such lists provide some of the clearest evidence of the collaboration among the various publisher families in Jianyang.

These publishers also collaborated in the carving of blocks for various imprints. Despite the fierce competition among publishers, which led them to produce nearly identical editions of the same work almost simultaneously, once a set of blocks was cut, it could be lent or given to anyone who wanted to print more copies of the work; this practice would account for the presence of the colophons of two or more different publishers in a single work.[137] Another possibility is that several publishers invested jointly in the carving of blocks for an especially large work.[138] Although we have no solid evidence of this practice in Minbei, the blank space where the publisher's name would usually be found in over twenty Jianyang imprints I have examined suggests such collaborations. It also may explain why in some imprints, a publishing house is listed as holding the blocks (*cang ban* 藏板) rather than having cut the blocks. In still other instances, a commercial publisher may have kept the blocks originally cut under official auspices and perhaps later reprinted the work under his own name.

In contrast to the larger, better-known commercial publishers, some smaller-scale printing operations may have functioned primarily as block-carving shops (*kezi pu/dian* 刻字鋪/店) and concentrated on everyday printed matter, such as legal documents and forms (contracts, deeds), cheap (and illegal) copies of calendars, religious charms, and pictures (New Year's pictures or *nianhua* 年畫, images of popular deities such as the kitchen and door gods). These printshops may well have doubled as stationery stores selling various paper products, including paper stencils, funeral money, paper horses, and superior quality paper for calligraphy and painting.[139] Moreover, such printshops may have done contract work for the larger printers/ publishers, who mainly produced books and might sometimes need the services of more carvers or binders than they directly employed. Again, although we have neither surviving samples nor contemporary descriptions of these printed materials from earlier periods, we have examples of both for the Qing and the early Republican periods. In Minbei, which was noted for its bamboo paper production, shops dealing with paper goods were possibly plentiful, and in the Jianyang area in particular, the link between purveying such merchandise and blockprinting would have been quite natural.

How were Jianyang imprints sold? In Shufang, other than direct sale by the publishers themselves, books may have been sold by smaller printshops and by bookstores or book stalls set up during the periodic markets in Masha, Shufang, Jianyang, and other towns in Minbei, in addition to the bookfair held monthly in Chonghua district. Buyers from outside the region may not have come expressly to buy books but also the other goods for which Minbei was known, including rice, tea, paper, bamboo shoots, and iron- and copper-wares. These traveling merchants, whose profits depended on their mastery of arbitrage, would then resell their goods as they traveled to other parts of the country.[140] On the other hand, some of the book buyers who came to Jianyang may have been old customers who were provided with room and board (and entertainment) by the larger publishers.[141] It is far more difficult to know how Jianyang imprints were sold outside Minbei. Presumably the traveling merchants who bought imprints in Jianyang would have sold them, either directly to individual buyers or to booksellers outside Minbei. In addition, Jianyang natives who operated as publishers in cities like Nanjing may have distributed imprints produced by their relatives and associates back in Fujian.

Although Jianyang was a major publishing center in its own right, it may also have produced blocks and printed sheets and/or the finished bound imprints for publishers elsewhere. After all, the various steps in printing and publishing a book did not have to be done in a single place, and printed sheets or even the blocks themselves might have been moved to the place of publication after they were produced. This is particularly true in areas with readily available water transport, such as Minbei.[142] Thus although Fuzhou was a large publishing center, possibly the cheaper production costs in Jianyang or simply the need for more printing blocks than local blockcarvers could supply, may mean that some books "published" in Fuzhou were physically produced in Jianyang. This division of labor among different localities may explain certain puzzles that arise when we attempt to trace the provenance of an imprint based on the blockcarvers' names recorded in it. Moreover, as peripatetic as many blockcarvers might have been, quite possibly the blocks or the printed sheets for certain works traveled equally great distances.

Finally, there is a frustrating lack of data on book prices. The very few prices recorded in block-printed works from the Ming or earlier are highly problematic, since we do not know when or where the price was set, and we lack comparable information to determine the meaning of an isolated price. Moreover, the few prices we do know by and large refer to works that were in some way special—a rare imprint from the Song or Yuan, or a deluxe, multicolor album, perhaps with particularly elegant illustrations, an attentively printed movable-type edition, or an especially large opus consisting of many fascicles, or books sold to foreign customers, especially Japanese and Korean (for whom the prices might well have been marked up).

With these caveats in mind, we can reach some tentative conclusions on the implications of prices recorded in some late Ming Jianyang imprints.[143] For example, during the sixteenth century, Jianyang publishers produced two different editions of the 90-*juan Comprehensive Gazetteer of the Great Ming* (*Da Ming yitong zhi*), originally published by the central government in 1461. The second Jianyang edition was published by the Yang family's Guiren zhai 楊氏歸仁齋 in 1559 and then reprinted by Liu Shuangsong's Anzheng tang 劉雙松安正堂 in 1588. On the cover page of a copy of this reprinting is stamped a red seal with a price of three silver taels.[144] If this price was indeed set by the Anzheng tang, then in the late sixteenth century such a relatively large work of around sixteen fascicles[145] commanded a rather steep price—

perhaps a fifth or a quarter of a county magistrate's monthly salary![146] We know the prices of two other Anzheng tang imprints, both literary *leishu*. A 1607 edition of the *Xinbian gujin shiwen leiju* with the original Song text by Zhu Mu and subsequent installments from the Yuan and Ming, amounting to close to 40 fascicles, sold for three silver taels. A 1611 edition of the Yuan writing manual by Liu Yingli, the *Xinbian shiwen leiju hanmo daquan*, cost two silver taels. From the Chongzhen period, the *Shiji pinglin* 史記評林 (*Record of History*, with collected commentaries) from the Xiong family's Zhongde tang, approximately 50 fascicles, cost one tael seven *fen*, less than the other works, but still not cheap. Even more startling is the price of one tael given in a copy of the seven-*juan Tangshi xunjie* 唐詩訓解 (Tang verses, explicated) published in 1618 by Yu Yingke's Juren tang 居仁堂, which consisted of only four fascicles. Again, to attempt to explain and reconcile these prices would be a fruitless task; but they are comparable to those in imprints from other large publishing centers like Nanjing, Suzhou, and Hangzhou of the same period. Thus, Jianyang imprints were not invariably cheaper than those from Jiangnan, despite the oft-quoted passage by Hu Yinglin that "ten Fujian imprints are cheaper than seven from Zhejiang, which are cheaper than five from Suzhou, which are cheaper than three in Beijing."[147] Moreover, *if* the Jianyang prices mentioned indicate even within an order of magnitude the cost of imprints in the late Ming, then surely book collecting was the privilege of the wealthy few. It may also explain why hand copies remained in great demand, and scribal production remained competitive even when printed editions were readily available: a reader who could not afford to buy the entire work might find it cheaper to have a portion copied.

Most of the works whose prices we noted so far are large, multivolume works for scholarly use. What about smaller works or those for nonscholarly popular use? Unhappily we have even fewer prices for these works. Shen Jin mentions a song miscellany, of arias from plays, in three fascicles, the *Xindiao wanqu changchun* 新調萬曲長春 (Newly engraved everlasting spring of new airs and myriad songs), selling for one *qian* two *fen* (一錢二分), one-tenth the price of the works mentioned earlier. This is perhaps a believable price, but in the absence of comparable figures it is difficult to put in historical context. Presumably the demand for such songbooks from readers and listeners, including those interested in performing the songs themselves, would have been greater than that for scholarly works, but we do not know how much greater. Furthermore, when considering who could and would buy a printed book, we must differentiate the works not only by price but also, for a given price range, by the needs and priorities of those who could afford a book. Thus would a songbook selling for about the same price as a household

encyclopedia or writing manual have more buyers? According to James
Hayes's observations on the uses of written materials in villages in the
New Territories in the twentieth century, heavy reliance on the expertise of
specialists such as religious clerics, letter writers, diviners, and even entertain-
ers meant less dependence by the common people on printed works providing
some of the same information, even if they were sufficiently literate.[148]
Cautious extrapolation to earlier periods would suggest a similar situation and
that possibly a song miscellany or a story collection in the running illustration
format would have sold more copies than a handbook on physiognomy
or a writing manual, but, again, this remains speculation until we find more
evidence.

6

Jianyang Imprints of the Ming

An examination of the visual appearance of the important types of Jianyang imprints will help us understand some of the dominant trends in Ming commercial publishing. Since an exhaustive study of each and every type of book published in Jianyang is beyond the scope of this work, the discussion will concentrate on those printed in especially great abundance in the Ming, particularly their contents, their distribution, and their likely audiences, in order to derive important information on the scholarly and popular cultures of Ming China.

The Visual Appearance of Ming Jianyang Imprints

Some notable changes in the appearance of Jianyang imprints occurred between those from the first century of the dynasty and those of the mid- and late Ming. The similarities between Yuan and early Ming imprints demonstrate that book printing continued in Jianyang despite the turmoil that accompanied the dynastic change. Some of these resemblances, however, may simply reflect continued use of blocks carved in the Yuan and repaired as needed; it may well be that publishers carved blocks for relatively few works at a time when the book trade was rather stagnant. Certainly, the number of early Ming Jianyang imprints is much lower than those for the mid- and late Ming, and it was not until the early sixteenth century that we see a revival of the Jianyang book trade. In terms of the visual appearance of the printed book—the calligraphy, use of punctuation, the page layout, and the sophistication and range of illustration—major changes became evident in the middle of the sixteenth century.

This section examines the changes in the appearance of Jianyang imprints with an eye to uncovering what commercial publishers thought was important in designing a product that would sell. Proportionately fewer extant Jianyang imprints from the Ming match the beauty of the finest examples from the Song, nor are they as well collated or edited. Since the best-produced works generally had the greatest chance of survival, this implies that by the late Ming, Jianyang publishers by and large had truly earned the poor reputation they have among rare book experts (although they did not have a monopoly on poor imprints). At the same time, the market for commercial imprints was large and firm enough that Jianyang publishers added recognizable trademarks, such as showy colophons, to their works as selling points.

In terms of calligraphy, early Ming imprints from Jianyang retained many of the characteristics of Yuan works—thin, slender characters packed into tight columns and printed on poor to mediocre paper, such as the *Shiqi shi zuan gujin tongyao* 十七史纂古今通要 (Compilation of essential excerpts, old and new, from the Seventeen Histories), an early imprint from the Xiong family (Fig. 30). This easily recognizable style shows the influence of several famous calligraphies (see Chap. 3) and, with time, developed into a variety of regular script that was looser and more pliant than the monumental style of Song imprints. Figures 31a–b show two examples of the different calligraphic styles that appeared in Jianyang imprints. The first work (Fig. 31a), *Zuantu huzhu Yangzi fayan* 纂圖互註揚子法言 (Model sayings of Master Yang, illustrated with cross-commentaries), claims to be based on a Song Directorate of Education edition, and the characters of the main text attempt to imitate the original calligraphic style but result in a different, less distinctive look. The other work (Fig. 31b), *Zengxiu fuzhu Zizhi tongjian jieyao xubian* 增修附註資治通鑑節要續編 (Continuation of the digest of the *Mirror for Government*, augmented and revised with commentary), was printed by the Wang family's Shanjing tang 王氏善敬堂 in 1452. Both the large characters of the main text and the small characters of the commentaries tend toward a more mechanical and stiffer style. Even the colophon text is executed in an unexceptional seal script. Finally, an early sixteenth century printing of the ever-popular *Guangyun* by the Zhan family's Jinxian tang 詹氏進賢堂 used blocks carved in at least three different periods, the Yuan and the late fifteenth and early sixteenth centuries. The difference between the Yuan characters (Fig. 32 left) and a later (Fig. 32 right) calligraphic style clearly reveals the move toward more rigid characters.[1]

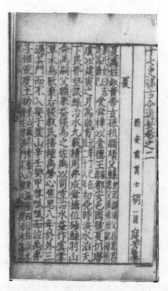

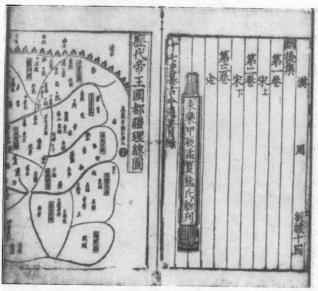

Fig. 30 *Shiqi shi zuan gujin tongyao* 十七史纂古今通要. 1424. Publisher: Xiong (Naikaku bunko, 297 函 152 號).

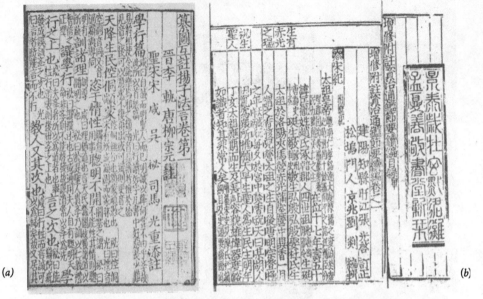

Fig. 31 Examples of two different calligraphic styles in Jianyang imprints of the Ming. (*a, left*) *Zuantu huzhu Yangzi fayan* 纂圖互註揚子法言. Early Ming Jianyang imprint. (*b, right*) *Zengxiu fuzhu Zizhi tongjian jieyao xubian* 增修附註資治通鑑節要續編. 1452. Wang family Shanjing tang.

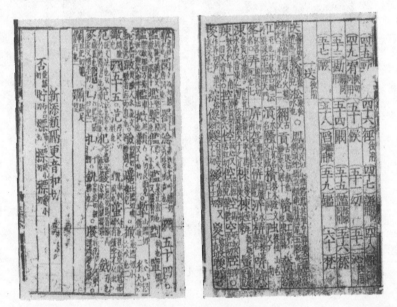

Fig. 32 *Guangyun* 廣韻. 1519. Publisher: Zhan family Jinxian tang (National Central Library [Taipei] Rare Books Collection, no. 01065).

Some Jianyang imprints of the Ming did, of course, exhibit excellent calligraphy. The *Shiji* printed in 1518 by the Shendu zhai of Liu Hongyi (Fig. 33a) is one such work.[2] An example of a story collection in the *shangtu xiawen* format with better than average calligraphy is the *Xin zengbu xiang jiandeng xinhua* 新增補相剪燈新話 (New stories told while trimming the lampwick, newly expanded and supplemented with illustrations), reprinted in 1511 by the Yang family's Qingjiang shutang 楊氏清江書堂 (Fig. 33b). A third example (Fig. 33c) is a 1590 imprint, *Shijing sanzhu cuichao* 詩經三註粹抄 (Excerpts from three commentaries on the *Book of Poetry*), by the well-known Cuiqing tang of Yu Siquan.

Of mechanical, nondescript calligraphy in Jianyang imprints, however, there are many more examples. Indeed one and the same publisher was capable of producing both lovely works and ones looking totally uninspired. Thus, the mediocre calligraphy of the story collection *Yanju biji* 燕居筆記 (Jottings in a leisurely life; Fig. 34a) was also produced by the Cuiqing tang. Equally nondescript is an anthology of Ming prose and poetry produced in 1529 by the Zongwen tang, another well-known Jianyang printshop of the mid- and late Ming (Fig. 34b). Finally, the calligraphy in a literary anthology printed by the Cuiqing tang during the Wanli period (Fig. 34c) is typical of late Ming Jianyang imprints.

As briefly described in Chapter 2, many of these nondescript calligraphic styles were known as "workman styles" (*jiangti*), but more specifically by the late Ming *jiangti* meant the "Song style" (*Songti* 宋體) illustrated in Fig. 35. This was supposedly based on the calligraphic style of some Song imprints, but in the late Ming it had transmogrified into the straight, rigid, and mechanical style composed of thick vertical and thin horizontal, completely level strokes—a "hard style" (*yingti* 硬體)—so familiar in modern Chinese books. It is easier to pack more such characters into a column and more columns onto a page without seeming as overcrowded as using calligraphic styles that are "soft" (*ruanti* 軟體). Moreover, because the strokes were so straight, the text posed little challenge even to a copyist of mediocre calligraphic ability, and the characters could then be carved at a more efficient pace than the older, more flowing calligraphic styles (*xieke* 寫刻). This style was used by all kinds of publishers—private, government, and commercial—throughout the country. The result was a widening gap between books employing an older calligraphic style and those in some form of *jiangti*, and an even wider gap between imprints and manuscripts.

Accompanying these developments, however, was a backhanded acknowledgment of the value of elegant calligraphy. In an attempt to bridge the

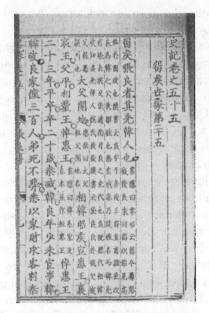

(a)

(b)

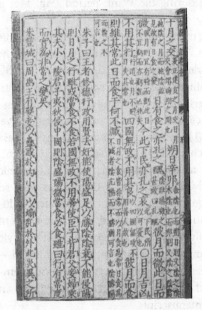

(c)

Fig. 33 Examples of better calligraphic styles in Jianyang imprints of the Ming.

(*a, above left*) *Shijii* 史記. 1518. Publisher: Liu Hongyi of Shendu zhai.

(*b, above right*) *Xin zengbu xiang Jiandeng xinhua* 新增補相剪燈新話. 1511. Reprinted by the Yang family Qingjiang shutang.

(*c, left*) *Shijing sanzhu cuichao* 詩經三註粹抄. 1590. Publisher: Yu Siquan of Cuiqing tang. (National Central Library [Taipei] Rare Book Collection, no. 00277).

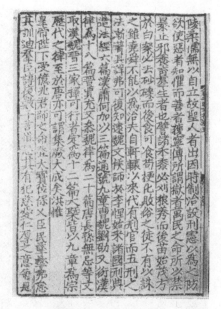

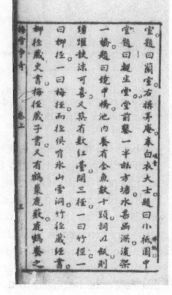

Fig. 34 Examples of mediocre calligraphic styles in Jianyang imprints of the Ming.

(a, above left) Xinke zengbu quanxiang Yanju biji 新刻增補全相 燕居筆記. Ming Wanli period (1573–1619). Publisher: Yu Siquan of Cuiqing tang (Naikaku bunko, 附5函7號).

(b, above right) Huang Ming Wenheng 皇明文衡. 1529. Publisher: Zongwen tang.

(c, right) Meixue zhengqi 梅雪爭奇. Ming Tianqi period (1621–1627). Publisher: Yu family Cuiqing tang.

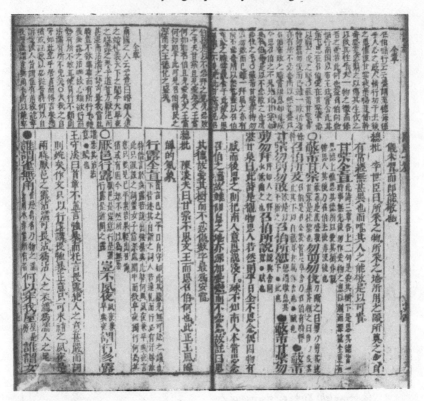

Fig. 35 Example of a page in *jiangti* (workman style). *Xinke daxiao Feng xiansheng shoushou Shijing* 新刻大小馮先生手授詩經. Late Ming. Publisher: Yu Yuansu of Yuejian shan fang (Naikaku bunko, 273函 218號).

gap between the printed and written word, publishers would use more distinctive calligraphic styles for the sections set off from and sometimes more prominent than the main text, such as the cover page, the prefaces, the publishers' colophons and notices, and inscriptions within illustrations. In fact, publishers often specifically noted that the prefaces and postfaces by famous men were executed as *xieke*; that is, they were carved by faithfully emulating the author's handwriting in grass, running, or clerical script. In addition, the use of these varieties of calligraphies flattered a potential reader by implying that he or she belonged to the educated elite with the learning to decipher these more difficult styles. In the Wanli imprint of the literary collection *Yunpi* 運甓, for example, the publisher uses three different calligraphic styles for the three prefaces, all very different from that in the main text (Fig. 36). This trend is seen in books by all kinds of publishers. The difference

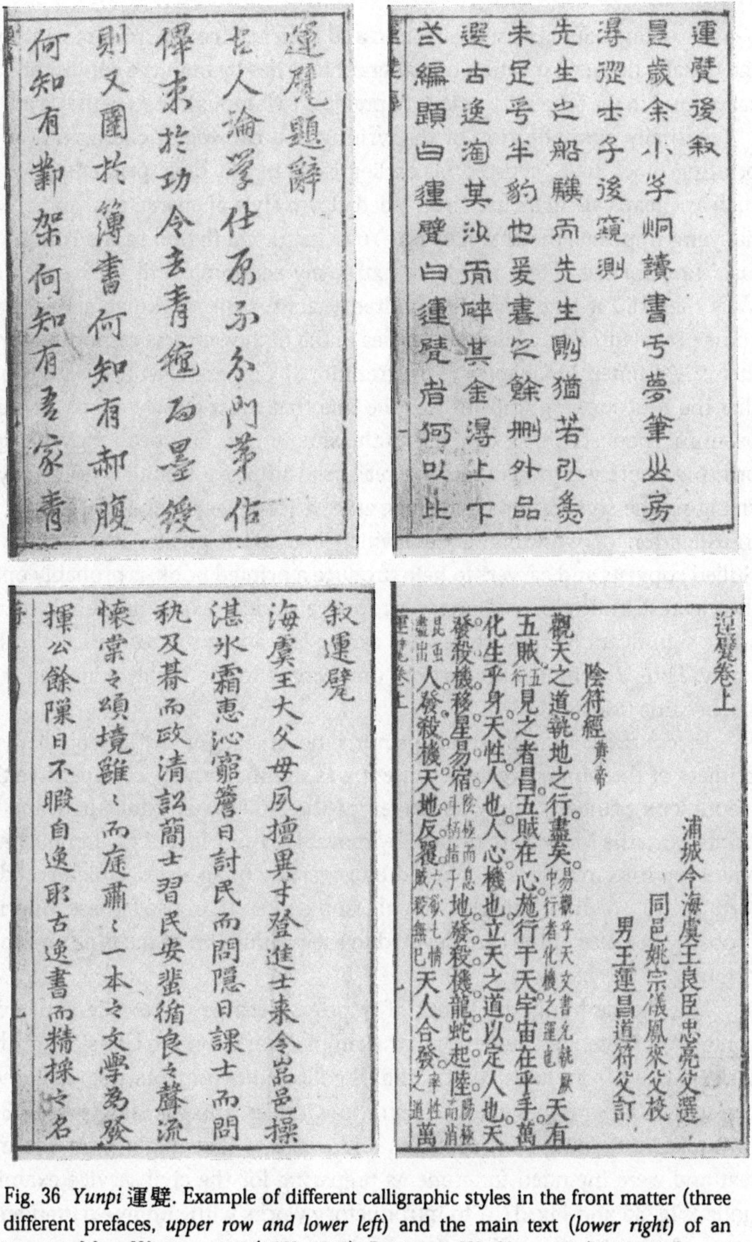

運甓後敘
是歲余小子炯讀書于夢筆山房
得從士子後窺測
先生之船艤而先生則猶若臥㥯
未足乎半豹也爰書之餘删外品
選古逸淘其沙而淬其金得上下
二編題曰運甓曰運甓者何以比

運甓題辭
古人論學仕原不分門第佔
俾求於功令去青纏而墨綬
則又圖於簿書何知有郝腹
何知有鄴架何知有書家青

敘運甓
海虞王大父毋夙擅異才登進士來令嵩邑操
湛氷霜惠沁窮簷日討民而問隱日課士而問
執及暮而政清訟簡士習民安蜚循良之聲流
懷棠之頌境雖之而庭肅之一本之文學為發
揮公餘隙日不暇自逸取古逸書而精採之名

運甓卷上
浦城令海虞王良臣忠亮父選
同邑姚宗儀鳳來父校
男王運昌道符父訂
陰符經 黄帝
觀天之道執天之行盡矣天有五賊見之者昌五賊在心施行于天宇宙在乎手萬化生乎身天性人也人心機也立天之道以定人也天發殺機移星易宿地發殺機龍蛇起陸人發殺機天地反覆天人合發萬

Fig. 36 *Yunpi* 運甓. Example of different calligraphic styles in the front matter (three different prefaces, *upper row and lower left*) and the main text (*lower right*) of an imprint. Ming Wanli period (1573–1619). Publisher: Wu Yanming (National Central Library [Taipei] Rare Books Collection, no. 13849).

between a high-quality private edition and a cheaper commercial reprint lay in the usually poorer execution of calligraphic styles by both the copyist and the carver and in the false attributions of prefaces to famous literati of the day.

Actually, simplification of the writing and carving of characters for the printing block had occurred far earlier. Even in the Tang, printed ephemera such as cheap calendars used a stripped-down style of characters,[3] and among Jianyang imprints, the characters in Yuan historical fiction in the running illustration format (Figs. 5a, b) are extremely economical in their execution. Why then did it take over six hundred years for the workman styles to become prevalent? Part of the answer lies in the highly adverse response of most literati. As noted in Chapter 2, the traditional Chinese view had always been that the best-looking imprint was the one that most closely approximated a beautiful manuscript. In contrast to the situation in European movable-type printing, there was no compelling reason to improve technical efficiency by changing the style of the characters, at least for a very long time. Hence, the introduction of workman styles, which enabled a greater number of less skilled copyists and carvers to help produce a printed book, is probably one of the clearest indications of pressures from a rapidly expanding book market and a significant increase in readers caring less about the aesthetics of calligraphy. Thus a technical innovation, unwelcome to the highly educated readers, became universal.

In contrast, movable-type printing never caught on among Jianyang printers of the Ming, largely because it was significantly more expensive than woodblock printing.[4] Only about ten of the 1,600-plus extant Jianyang imprints from the Ming were printed by movable type. Most of the famous movable-type imprints were sponsored by government agencies, which could afford to do so. Interestingly enough, some literati praised these imprints, probably because of the care devoted to the production of the type and to the printing.[5]

During the Ming, the layout of imprints became more differentiated by content and intended audience. For example, works on the Classics and Histories ranged from large compendia of collected commentaries, replete with prefaces, bibliographies, maps, illustrations, tables, and genealogies (Fig. 37a), to books containing commentaries and exegeses that might omit the main text and were intended for students preparing for the civil service examinations (Fig. 35 and Fig. 37b) to introductory works with simply-written annotations for beginning students (Fig. 37c).

The use of two or three registers on the page was common in Ming imprints. The contents of the various registers depended on the subject of the

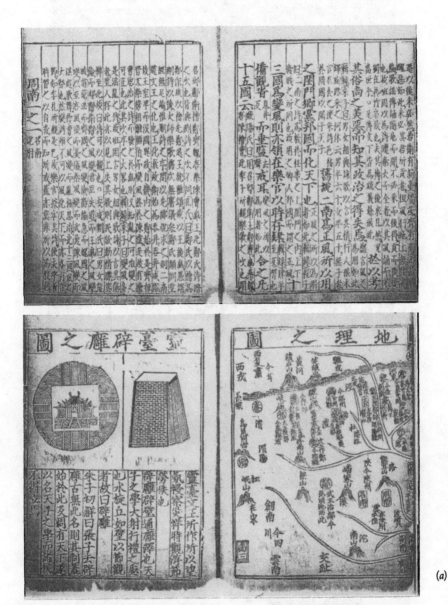

Fig. 37 Different Jianyang imprints on the *Book of Poetry*. (*a, both panels*) *Shijing suyi huitong* 詩經疏義會通. 1523. Publisher: Liu family Anzheng tang. (*Fig. 37 continues overleaf*)

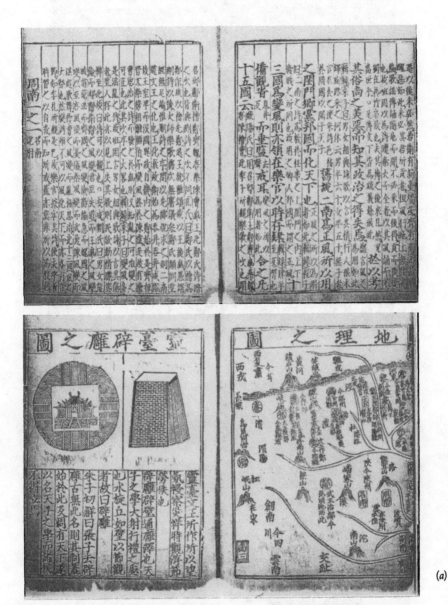

(a)

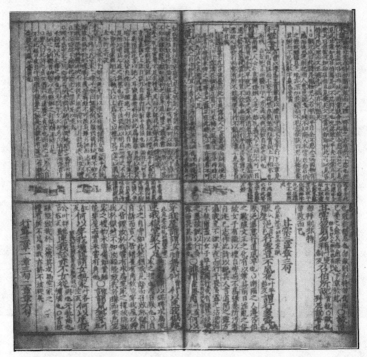

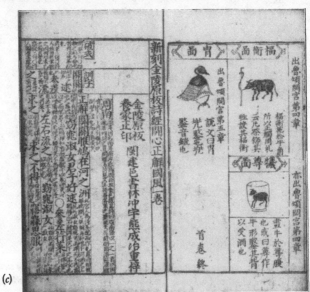

Fig. 37, *cont.* (*b, top*) *Xinqie Jin Yun xiansheng Shijing chanmeng yanyi jizhu* 新鍥晉雲 先生詩經闡蒙衍義集註. 1595. Publisher: Zhan Chongquan of Jingguan tang (Naikaku bunko, 274 函 219 號). (*c, bottom*) *Xinkan Jinling yuanban Shijing kaixin zhengjie* 新刻金陵 原板詩經開心正解 (see also Fig. 39). Ming Longqing period (1567–72). Publisher: Xiong Chengye (Naikaku bunko, 273 函 208 號).

book. In many scholarly works, the bottom, or basic, register contains the text and the most important commentaries. For example, in editions of the Four Books, Zhu Xi's commentaries, because of their importance for the civil service examinations, had by the Ming attained the status of a classic in their own right and were printed in characters smaller than the main text but larger than other commentaries. These texts, as well as phonetic and semantic glosses, may appear in the uppermost or middle register. Sometimes the zeal for annotations extended even to prefaces, showing up in a narrow upper register or in small characters next to the main text. In works of fiction or drama, the top register was usually used for glosses and comments of literary criticism or appreciation for a particularly well-written or affecting passage in the main text (Fig. 26b). In household encyclopedias, the two registers may simply contain two separate texts on the topic of the section in question. Thus, in the household encyclopedia shown in Fig. 11a, the top register of the page on the right offers a discussion and illustration of a wrestling technique, while the text and picture in the bottom register deals with archery. On the opposite page, the top register deals with painting a bird's head, and the bottom with painting the hair on a human face. Similarly varied discussions on games, from a different *juan* of the same work, are shown in Fig. 11b.

Punctuation, as pointed out in Chapter 2, also became increasingly widespread in Ming works and was advertised in the titles of many commercial imprints (*pidian*) and explained in "general principles" *fanli* (Fig. 8b) for works particularly cluttered with punctuation marks and annotations (Fig. 8a). Publishers, however, seem not to have had a consistent policy on which kinds of works to punctuate. Thus in three quite similar Jiajing editions of the *Zhouyi jingzhuan* 周易經傳 (*Zhouyi* with commentaries), the preface written in 1099 by the Northern Song *Daoxue* scholar Cheng Yi was punctuated but without annotations in the edition published by the Jianning prefecture (Fig. 38a), punctuated but with unpunctuated lengthy notes in one Jianyang commercial edition from 1536 (Fig. 38b), and finally with both main text and notes punctuated in a second Jianyang commercial edition (Fig. 38c).[6] Since Cheng Yi's preface, like Zhu Xi's commentaries on the Four Books and the Classics, had achieved the status of a minor classic, the commercial publishers probably felt that the text deserved detailed commentaries of its own, which would also make their offerings that much more attractive to a potential buyer.

Another trend in the Ming was the growing use of *tu* (illustrations, charts, tables) in Jianyang commercial imprints, such as the Classics (Fig. 39a), dictionaries, histories, handbooks on family rituals (Fig. 39b), military

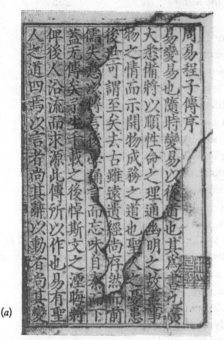

(a)

(b)

(c)

Fig. 38 Variously punctuated preface in three editions of the *Zhouyi* of the Ming Jiajing period (1522–66).

(*a, above left*) *Zhouyi* 周易. Publisher: Jianning prefecture (National Central Library [Taipei] Rare Books Collection, no. 00032).

(*b, above right*) *Zhouyi zhuanyi daquan* 周易傳義大全. 1536. Publisher: Ye family Zuode tang (National Central Library [Taipei] Rare Books Collection, no. 00071).

(*c, left*) *Zhouyi zhuanyi daquan* 周易傳義大全. Publisher: unknown (Jianyang) (National Central Library [Taipei] Rare Books Collection, no. 00069).

classics (Fig. 39c), medical texts (Fig. 39d), works on divination (Fig. 23) and calendrical calculations (Fig. 39e), household encyclopedias (Figs. 11a, b), and fiction collections (Fig. 39f). Many of the images were not new, but they were deployed in an unprecedented variety of books and displayed easily distinguishable differences in drawing and carving styles.

The *tu* often occupied only part of a page or a register and were usually situated as close to the related text as possible. One example of this layout, the *shangtu xiawen* format, was used not only for single works of fiction and story collections (Figs. 10a, b) but for nonfiction works as well, such as the simple handbook on infant care shown in Fig. 40a and the work on physiognomy in Fig. 40b.[7] Depending on the kind of work, however, the *shangtu xiawen* format could serve different purposes. For example, in physiognomy manuals, medical works, and household encyclopedias, the pictures not only illustrate the text but also can function somewhat independently as pictorial references for a "reader" who dispenses with the text because the person is illiterate or because the image (possibly with captions) supplies adequate information.

Somewhat different in purpose are the pictures in story collections and single works of fiction, which can serve as visual distraction, in the sense of both entertainment and relief from the often hard to read text below. Whether these *tu* work as running illustrations that can intelligibly carry the entire narrative by themselves is questionable.[8] In any case, the majority of these pictures have captions—a reversal of the usual roles since here the text explicates the image. With or without captions, however, it is doubtful that a reader could comprehend the story as well as a reader of modern comics. On the other hand, the conventions of the pictures often help to propel the story forward and give a sense of a temporal as well as a spatial flow. Thus a series of scenes of depicting riders on horseback or a battle scene tend to maintain, say, a consistent right to left direction, along with the text beneath. Or repetitions of some story device or scene in the text are conveniently illustrated by the same or very similar images. Even certain images that at first seem inane may work as visual cues for contemplating some fairly abstract discourse in the text (Fig. 41).

In the Ming, just as the growing use of the workman styles for the characters in the body text of an imprint led to a re-introduction of more elegant calligraphy in other sections, there also developed a trend to incorporate full-page or full-folio *tu*.[9] Occasionally Jianyang publishers would produce works in which the *tu* were better executed than usual. For example, one kind of anthology popular in the late Ming gathered short prose and verse pieces on a

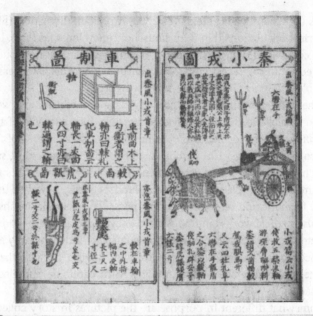

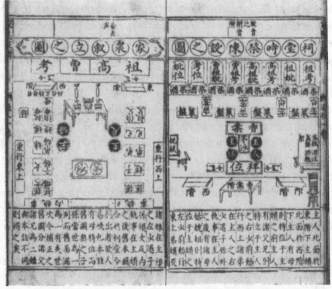

Fig. 39 Examples of *tu* (illustrations, tables, figures) in Jianyang imprints of the Ming. (*a, top*) *Xinkan Jinling yuanban Shijing kaixin zhengjie* 新刻金陵原板詩經開心正解 (see also Fig. 37). Ming Longqing period (1567–72). Publisher: Xiong Chengye (Naikaku bunko, 273 函 208 號). (*b, bottom*) *Jia li zhengheng* 家禮正衡. 1599. Publisher: Yu Mingwu of Zixin zhai (Naikaku bunko, 經 13 函 7 號) (*Fig. 39 continues on next two pages*).

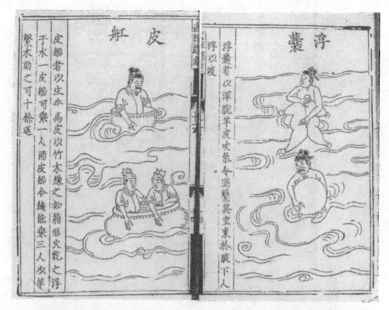

(c)

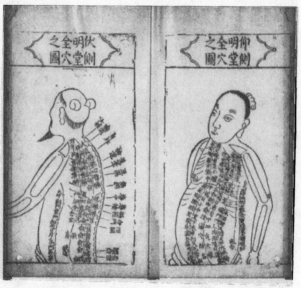

(d)

Fig. 39, cont. (c, top) *Wu jing zongyao* 武經總要. Ming. Jianyang imprint (National Central Library [Taipei] Rare Book Collection, no. 05717). (d, bottom) *Zhenjiu dacheng* 針灸大成. Late Ming. Publisher: Xiong Chongyu of Zhongde tang (Naikaku bunko, 304 函 281 號) (*Fig. 39 continues overleaf*).

(e)

(f)

Fig. 39, *cont.* (*e, top*) *Xinke taijian lifa zengbu ying fu tongshu* 新刻太監曆法增補應福通書. Ming Wanli period (1573–1619). Publisher: Xiong Chongyu of Zhongde tang (Naikaku bunko, 305 函 288 號). (*f, bottom*) *Dingjuan quanxiang Yijian shangxin bian* 鼎鐫全像一見賞心編. Late Ming. Publisher: Yu of Cuiqing tang (Naikaku bunko, 309 函 50 號).

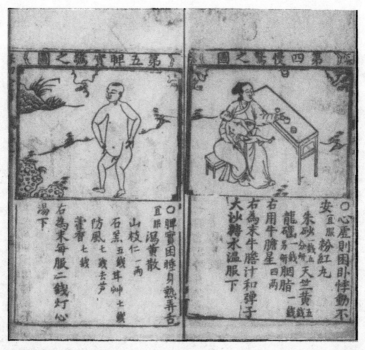

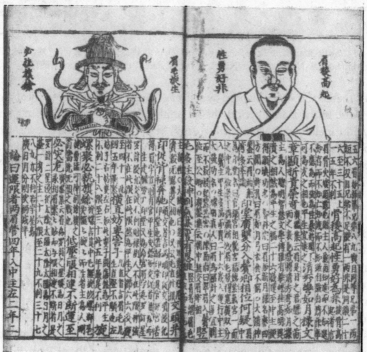

Fig. 40 Nonfiction works in the *shangtu xiawen* format. (*a, top*) *Xiao'er tuina fa* 小兒推拿法. Ming Wanli period (1573–1619). Publisher: Liu Longtian of Qiaoshan fang (Naikaku bunko, 303 函 289 號). (*b, bottom*) *Xinkan tuxiang renxiang bian* 新刊圖像人相編. 1585. Publisher: Qingjiang shutang (Naikaku bunko, 305 函 290 號).

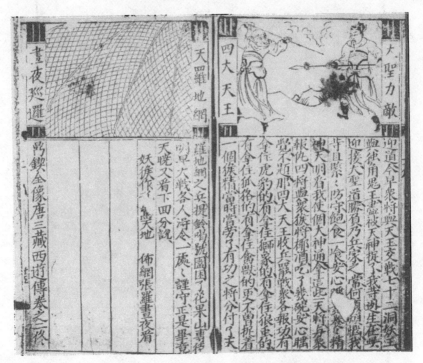

Fig. 41 *Dingqie quanxiang Tang Sanzang Xiyou zhuan* 鼎鍥全相唐三藏西遊傳. Ming. Publisher: Liu Liantai (National Central Library [Taipei] Rare Book Collection, no. 08617).

given theme and was enhanced by full-page illustrations scattered throughout the work. In the Tianqi period, the Yu family's Cuiqing tang published a series of works including *Shuguo zhengqi* 蔬果爭奇 (The contest of the vegetables and fruits; Fig. 42). Although the calligraphy and the illustrations did not equal the best produced in this period, they are among the better published Jianyang imprints of the late Ming (Fig. 42).

Differences and similarities in the execution of *tu* within a given format can provide some interesting insights into the workings of Ming commercial publishing.[10] For example, compare the illustrations in the four *shangtu xiawen* editions of the historical narrative *Sanguo zhizhuan*.[11] The first (Fig. 43a), published around 1592 by Yu Xiangdou,[12] shows pictures in a style in common use in Jianyang since the Yuan; they are also reminiscent of illustrations in imprints from other parts of the country, such as *The Record of Hua Guan Suo*, one of the chantefables (*shuochang* 說唱) published in the Chenghua period by the Yongshun tang 永順堂 in Beijing.[13] The illustrations in three other Jianyang editions of the same work (Figs. 43b–d) have more in

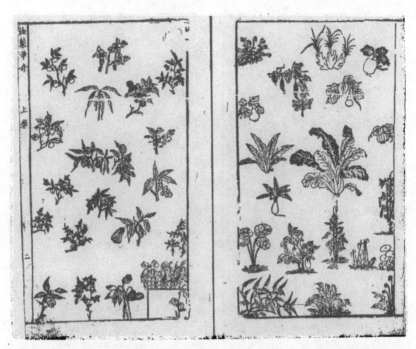

Fig. 42 *Shuguo zhengqi* 蔬果爭奇. Ming Tianqi period (1621–27). Publisher: Yu Siquan of Cuiqing tang.

common with book illustrations of the Wanli and later periods. Furthermore, the last two not only closely resemble each other—and the illustrations in at least four other late Ming Jianyang editions—but they are executed in much the same style as the full-page pictures found in a number of Jianyang imprints of the same time, including that shown in Figures 39f and 44.

Several important conclusions emerge from these comparisons. First, there were no exclusive regional styles of illustration.[14] The distinctive styles are better attributed to individuals and specific groups working as illustrators and carvers. Second, we cannot even associate with a particular publisher a distinct look for illustrations in a given format in his imprints. Competition among different publishers often encouraged them to produce editions with near-identical texts and illustrations, as demonstrated by Figures 43c–d. Indeed, financial considerations meant that commercial publishers might prefer using a set of already carved blocks, on which they could record their names somewhere, to making a considerable investment in new blocks. The *Quan Han zhizhuan* 全漢志傳 (Record of the two Han dynasties), another Jianyang work in the *shangtu xiawen* format, was originally published by

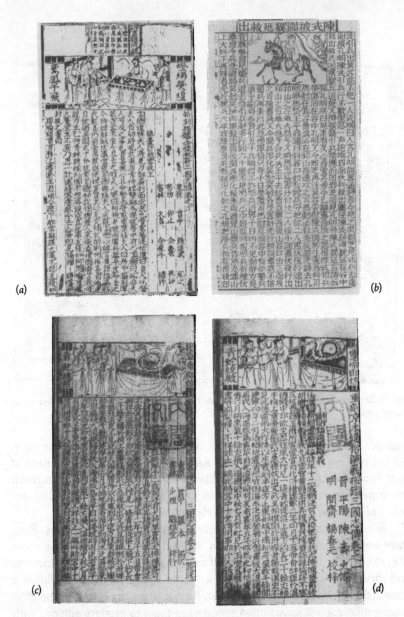

Fig. 43 Illustrations from four different Jianyang editions of the *Sanguo zhizhuan*. (*a, top left*) *Xinkan an Jian quanxiang piping Sanguo zhizhuan* 新刊按鑑全像批評三國志傳. Ca. 1592. Publisher: Yu Xiangdou (Württembergische Landesbibliothek). (*b, top right*) *Jing juan an Jian quanxiang dingzhi Sanguo zhizhuan* 精鐫按鑑全像鼎峙三國志傳. Late Ming. Publisher: Liu Rongwu Liguang tang (British Library Indian and Oriental Office, 15333 e6). (*c, bottom left*) *Xinqie Jingben jiaozheng tongsu yanyi an Jian Sanguo zhizhuan* 新鍥京本校正通俗演義按 鑑三國演義. 1605. Publisher: Zheng Shaoyuan of Lianhui tang (Naikaku bunko, 附1函9號). (*d, bottom right*) *Chongke Jingben tongsu yanyi an Jian Sanguo zhizhuan* 重刻京本通俗演義按鑑三國志傳. 1610. Publisher: Yang Chunyuan (Naikaku bunko, 配436b 308 函 258號).

Fig. 44 Full-page illustration from a late sixteenth-century Jianyang imprint. *Da kui Shujing jizhu* 大魁書經集注. Ming Wanli period (1573–1619). Publisher: Yu Mingwu of Keqin zhai.

Yu Shiteng of Keqin zhai 余世騰克勤堂 (Fig. 45a),[15] and apparently was later reprinted by Liu Shizhong of Airi tang 劉世忠愛日堂 (Fig. 45b) and Yang Minzhai's Qingbai tang 楊閩齋清白堂 (Fig. 45c).

In a number of commercial imprints from both the Jianyang and the Jiangnan areas, particularly fiction and plays, the full-page or full-folio *tu* were grouped into a single fascicle (*ce* 冊) separate from the text. Thus although the pictures in these works serve as illustrations and are not solely self-referencing as true *hua* were supposed to be, their physical separation from the text suggests that they could be appreciated on their own. They often imitated actual paintings both in their artistic styles and in the inclusion of seal impressions and inscriptions. These pictures therefore occupied a middle

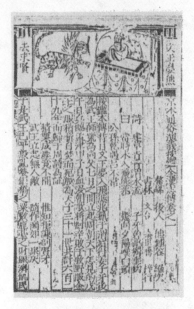

(a)

(b)

(c)

Fig. 45 Three different publishers recorded in a single Jianyang imprint. *Jingben tongsu yanyi an jian Quan Han zhizhuan* 京本通俗演義按鑑全漢志傳. Ca. 1588 and later (Hōsa bunko).

(*a, above left*) Publisher: Yu Shiteng.

(*b, above right*) Publisher: Liu Shizhong of Airi tang.

(*c, left*) Colophon of Yang Minzhai's Qingbai tang added in reprinting.

ground between the functional and often simply executed *tu* and the more aesthetically oriented *hua* and represented an attempt by commercial publishers to attract a clientele among the literati (or those aspiring to belong to that group).

Evidence of the commercial publishers' confidence in their position in the book market of the mid- and late Ming can be found among their books: in colophons, title pages, publishers' notes, and, even very occasionally, portraits of themselves. The design of the cover title page depended on the work, but it often had pictures and advertisements (Fig. 46). The title page of this household encyclopedia states that it was printed by Yu Wentai (Yu Xiangdou). As noted above, some of the blocks for the work probably belonged to his relative by marriage, Liu Longtian. Yu, however, had no hesitation in appropriating credit for both compiling and printing the work and even asserted the superiority of his edition in the note on the title page.

Among commercial printshops all sorts of books are printed, but many are copied from old works and take one part while throwing away ten, discard the grain while keeping the chaff. Scholars everywhere are aware of it. This printshop has recently published the book entitled *The Handbook for Myriad Uses*, which is topically arranged and fully laid out for all uses, so one need not look for other (editions). We ask the buyer to keep the Santai [guan] in mind.

Shulin Yu Wentai

Such notes in fact are quite commonly found among Jianyang imprints and are in general as truthful as the one in this encyclopedia.

In addition, the colophon block, or cartouche, with a lotus leaf design had become a familiar trademark, in many variations, of Jianyang imprints by the late Yuan or early Ming (Figs. 45c, 47, and 48).[16] Like the Yang family's Qingbai tang, a publisher sharing or inheriting woodblocks sometimes inserted its own colophon at the end of a work originally issued by another publisher. Sometimes a later publisher had no hesitation about effacing the name of his predecessor and putting his own name and a later date in the colophon block. For example, the Zhan family's Yi zhai 詹氏易齋 printed the *Liang Han juanyan* 兩漢雋言 (Critique on excerpts of the *Han Histories*) in 1587 (Fig. 48a); in 1608 the Cuiqing tang used the same blocks to reprint the work and merely substituted its name in the cartouche (Fig. 48b).

Finally, a few Jianyang publishers of the Ming have left portraits of themselves in their imprints.[17] Xiong Zongli, the fifteenth-century Jianyang publisher noted for his medical expertise and his editorial work in collating medical classics (see Chapter 5), portrayed himself as a scholar among his books (Fig. 49a). Yu Xiangdou of the late Ming displayed himself much as he

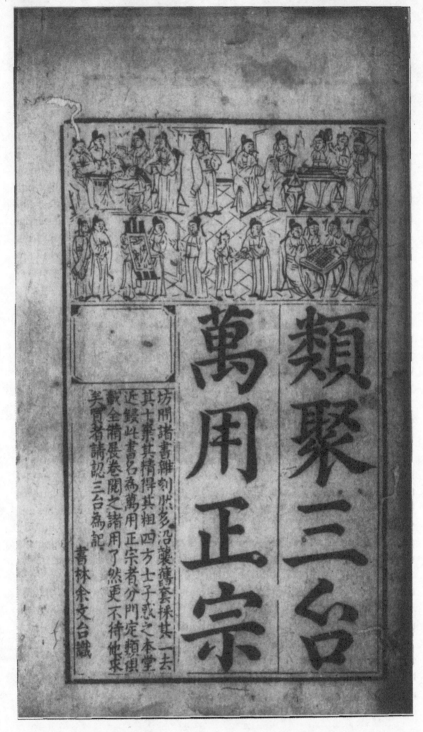

類聚三台萬用正宗

坊間諸書雜刻狀多沿襲舊套採其一去
其十棄其精得其粗四方士子惑之本堂
近鐫此書名為萬用正宗者分門定類俱
載全備展卷閱之諸用了然更不待他束
美實者請認三台為記

書林余文台識

Fig. 46 Title page of a Ming Jianyang imprint. *Wanyong zhengzong bu qiu ren quanbian* 萬用正宗不求人全編. 1607. Publisher: Yu Wentai (Yu Xiangdou).

(a)   *(b)*

Fig. 47 Examples of lotus leaf colophon blocks in Ming Jianyang imprints. (*a, left*) *Quan Han zhizhuan* 全漢志傳. Original printing 1588 by Yu Shiteng of Keqin zhai. Colophon of Yang family Qingbai tang added in reprinting (Hōsa bunko). (*b, right*) *Xuke Wenling si taishi pingxuan gujin ming wen zhuji* 續刻溫陵四太史評選古今名文珠璣. 1595. Publisher: Yu Liangmu (Shaoyai) Zixin zhai.

(a)   *(b)*

Fig. 48 Two different printers' colophons for copies for a work from the same set of blocks. (*a, left*) *Liang Han juanyan* 兩漢雋言. 1587 colophon: Zhan family Yi zhai (Naikaku bunko, 290 函 90 號). (*b, right*) 1608 colophon: Cuiqing tang (Naikaku bunko, 290 函 98 號).

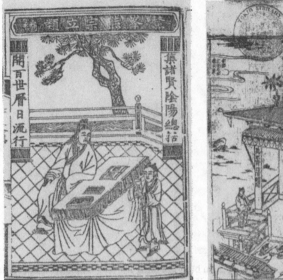

(a)

(b)

Fig. 49 Portraits of Jianyang publishers in their own publications. (*a, left*) *Leibian lifa tongshu daquan* 類編曆法通書大全. Ming Jianyang imprint. (*b, right*) *Santai tongshu zhengzong* 三台通書正宗. 1638. Publisher: Yu Yangzhi (Yu Xiangdou) (National Diet Library [Tokyo], no. 205–6).

wanted to be seen, as a gentleman-scholar viewing the moon, rather than as a compiler, printer, and purveyor of mediocre Jianyang imprints that is Yu's reputation among rare book scholars (Fig. 49b). Both portraits support the argument that by the mid-Ming, if not earlier, men such as these two were fully confident of their position and power as commercial publishers in a society with an ever-increasing demand for printed books.

A Selective Survey of Jianyang Imprints of the Ming

Some notable changes occurred over time in the relative distributions of the kinds of books printed in Jianyang. First, the overall proportion of the Classics decreased significantly from the Yuan to the Ming, although the absolute number of imprints increased. Such numbers, however, tell almost nothing of the real story, which must take into account the changing contents and styles of books produced. For example, there was a greater variety of each kind of book within this category, such as the simple introductions for children to the Classics and Four Books. These abounded in the late Ming, but there are extremely few examples from either the Song or Yuan among Jianyang publications. Similarly, during the Ming books in the History category represented a smaller percentage of the overall output than in the previous dynasties, but there were many more of them printed. The discussion below will suggest why some kinds of books, such as annalistic histories and geographies, were so popular. Some of the greatest changes are found in the very diverse Philosophy section, including a significant increase in both the percentage and the absolute number of imprints. Specifically, much of this increase results from the printing of medical texts and *leishu*, as well as to a smaller, but no less significant extent, the publishing of divination texts, of which there were almost none earlier. In the Belles Lettres category, collections of individual authors and general collections continued in importance, but the number of fictional narratives and of collections of plays and ballads, of which we have few examples from the Song and Yuan, grew significantly.

Thus, the commercial book trade in southern China during the Ming differed considerably from that of the Song and Yuan. Two caveats should be noted, however. First, the bulk of Ming imprints from Jianyang (about 90 percent) date from the mid-fifteenth century or later, and it is possible that a similar analysis of the imprints from one of the major Jiangnan publishing centers or from Fuzhou for the earlier Ming may show that these important changes had already occurred to some extent in the first century of the dynasty. Second, although this chapter emphasizes the differences between Ming and pre-Ming commercial imprints, we cannot ignore continuities in the evolution of the book trade in late imperial China. For example, the increase in the number of *leishu* from the Song to the Yuan and the even greater increase in philological works suggest changes in the kinds of book buyers as well as in their approaches to these and other texts. In addition, the illustrated historical romances in the *shangtu xiawen* format that were a Jianyang specialty in the late Ming were already being printed in the Yuan. As we noted above, the earliest example may be from 1294, a date sufficiently early to suggest that such works may well have first been printed in the Southern Song. Indeed, as we will see from the discussion below, by keeping in mind the developments that began before this period, we are better able to understand the changes in the book culture and book trade in the later Ming.

Classics

Ming editions of the Classics and the Four Books printed in Jianyang often came accompanied with a large and elaborate critical apparatus, incorporating material written by Ming authors as well as commentaries and annotations from earlier periods. This was true particularly of the "complete compendiums" (*daquan* 大全 or *dacheng*大成), which constituted a significant proportion of the texts for each Classic. For example, 10 out of 22 works on the *Book of Changes*, 5 out of 19 for the *Book of Documents*, 6 out of 21 for the *Book of Poetry*, 10 out of 22 for the *Book of Rites*, 10 out of 32 for the *Spring and Autumn Annals*, and 11 out of 32 for the Four Books were complete compendiums. Although it may seem surprising that the Jianyang commercial publishers produced so many such works, they probably thought to profit from printing much cheaper editions than, for example, the Directorate of Education editions from Nanjing or the original series of Complete Compendiums edited by Hu Guang 胡廣 and others.

There were also other kinds of aids to reading the Classics. For example, information on persons mentioned in the Four Books (in the main texts as well as in other writings) was offered in four different works. Other works were relatively short (one volume) and consisted of a writer's thoughts on one or more of the Classics, the basic text of which would be omitted entirely. Still others were introductions to the Classics with relatively simple commentaries, annotations, and glosses, as well as illustrations.

Pages from six different Jianyang commercial imprints of the *Book of Poetry* are shown in Figs. 35, 37, and 50. They share a number of similarities despite their different calligraphic styles: the page is divided into two or three registers, with the main text in large bold characters (except for Fig. 50b, which dispenses with the main text altogether), the text layouts are cramped—ten or more columns per page and about 25 characters or more per column for the commentary. The intertextual commentaries, annotations, and glosses tend to present more specific information to aid in resolving the meaning of the text. Often, well-known, older commentaries such as those by Zhu Xi or the Cheng brothers immediately follow the main text and are further elucidated as if they had grown to be part of the Classic itself. The top panel usually has more general comments, sometimes a précis or a digest of the passage below. Judging by readers' punctuation marks, the upper section was often the only part read, especially by examination candidates who would already have memorized the main text and would be looking for explications that they could reproduce on their examination essays. Although such arrangements of the main text and the critical apparatus are common in commercial, private, and official editions, the cramped layout and the often mediocre and nondescript calligraphy are marks of the cheaper commercial imprints.

It is also interesting to note that not all these editions were punctuated. Indeed, the main text itself, being already "punctuated" (set off) by copious commentaries and annotations, requires no punctuation marks. The text in

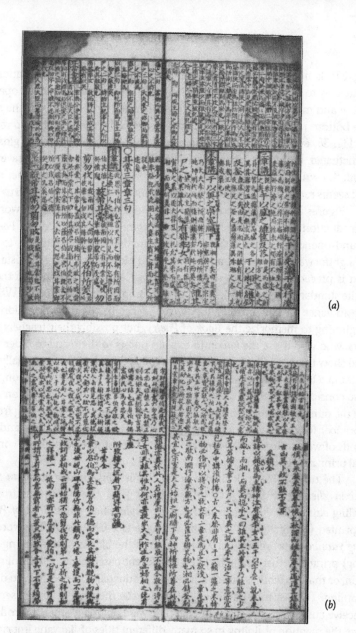

Fig. 50 Examples of works on the *Book of Poetry* (cf. Figs. 35 and 37a–c). (*a, top*) *Shijing jiezou* 詩經節奏. 1595. Publisher: Liu Shuangsong of Anzheng tang (Naikaku bunko, 273 函252 號). (*b, bottom*) *Wei Zhongxue xiansheng Shijing mai jiangyi* 魏仲雪先生詩經脈講意. Late Ming. Publisher: Yu Yingqiu of Jinsheng ju (Naikaku bunko, 273 函210 號).

Fig. 37b is not punctuated at all, but the commentaries and annotations are quite easy to understand. The text in Fig. 50b is punctuated by small open circles ○ and marked by jots ヽ. Another set of open circles alongside the text in the bottom register indicates that the passage is discussed in the top register. In Fig. 35, everything but the main text and the small-character glosses is punctuated. In the texts shown in Fig. 50a, there is no punctuation save some reader's own. Based on these examples, a printer's decision to punctuate or not seems rather arbitrary and not dependent on the nature of the text.

Figures 37c and 39a show one of the more attractive of the six works, an introduction (for a relatively advanced beginner) to the *Book of Poetry*, a "mind-opener" (*kaixin* 開心), as noted in the title. In addition to clear, straightforward, and useful annotations and glosses in all three registers, the text is preceded by a series of illustrations of objects mentioned in the text, quite standard in these works (and in the complete compendiums). Who was the audience for such introductory works? Most likely not young children just beginning to memorize the *Book of Poetry*, but possibly their teachers or tutors, who would use the *kaixin* to explain points to them and to older pupils and show them the illustrations. More advanced students and especially those without a teacher, and others who with only limited classical education, might also consider such books a useful substitute for formal personal tuition. Based on the number of *kaixin*, *mengquan* 蒙筌, and *qimeng* 啓蒙 (freeing from ignorance) for the Classics and Four Books, histories, medical texts, and other kinds of works during the Ming, these books constituted a staple of commercial printers everywhere.

The title of the work shown in Fig. 37c is *Xinke Jinling yuanban Shijing kaixin zhengjie* 新刻金陵原板詩經開心正解 (New [re]print from the Jinling edition of the *Primer and Correct Explanation of the Book of Poetry*), reprinted (*chongzi* 重梓) by Xiong Chengye (see Chapter 5). The words *Jinling yuanban* may mean that Xiong received the blocks from a Jinling (Nanjing) printer, or that Xiong had new blocks cut based on an older Jinling edition, or that the work is purely a Jianyang product and has nothing to do with Nanjing. The last may be quite likely, since the mention of Jinling served to deceive customers into thinking that they were buying a superior product. In fact, the mention of Jinling in so many different titles of Jianyang imprints has led some Chinese scholars to assume almost automatically that a work mentioning *jing* 京 in its title (*jingben* 京本, *jingban* 京板, etc.) came from Jianyang.[18] Although they may be correct more often than not, the facts that so many Jianyang natives in the book trade worked in Nanjing and that by the mid-sixteenth century the provenance of many imprints, especially the cheaper ones, could not be identified by their physical appearance alone make these assumptions less certain.

The last section in the Classics category is *xiaoxue* 小學, or philology. Here, the Jianyang printers continued producing the rhyming dictionaries that apparently sold well in the Yuan. Of the 44 works in this category, about 20 are rhyming dictionaries, such as the *Guangyun*, which had been revised and expanded during the Northern Song, or similar later works, including the *Gujin yunhui juyao*, compiled in the late thirteenth century. Not surprisingly, all Jianyang editions of the *Guangyun* were of the condensed Yuan version; the *Yunhui juyao* was based on the larger work *Libu yunlüe* for the purpose of supplying scholars with a short, convenient-to-use rhyming dictionary. In fact, no unabridged edition of any rhyming dictionary seems to have been produced by the Jianyang printers, who did, however, go to the trouble of excerpting all the entries from the *Hongwu zhengyun* 洪武正韻 (Correct rhymes of the Hongwu period; compiled in 1375 under imperial auspices) with quotations from the Classics. These works were popular since the entries for each character gave not only the pronunciation(s) and definitions but also brief excerpts from famous works to illustrate the meanings. As with the introductory texts to the Classics and Four Books, these rhyming dictionaries may have appealed to an ever increasing number of students who lacked teachers to guide their readings.

The Jianyang publishers' commercial considerations show up clearly in about sixteen dictionaries variously titled but all containing the phrase *hai pian* 海篇, roughly translated as "leaves from a sea [of words, phrases, or rhymes]" in their name. The *hai pian* is reminiscent of two famous earlier dictionaries, the *Yu pian* 玉篇 (Leaves of jade), originally compiled in the sixth century, and the *Lei pian* 類篇 (Classified leaves), compiled in the eleventh century. The *hai pian* is also confusingly similar to the *Si sheng pian hai* 四聲篇海 (Sea of leaves [classified] by the four tones) compiled in the thirteenth century, of which there is also one error-ridden late Ming Jianyang edition.[19] Among the various *hai pian* is the work published by Ye Rulin 葉如琳 (1582 preface), entitled *Hanlin chongkao zi yi yun lü Hai pian xin jing* 翰林重考字義韻律海篇心鏡 (*Mirror of the Mind's Leaves from the Sea* arranged by the characters' meanings and regulated rhymes, collated by Hanlin Academy scholars), with material derived from a number of earlier dictionaries. It was certainly not collated by any Hanlin scholars but by two men related to Jianyang publishers. It is the arrangement of its contents, however, which gives a clue to its popularity. Each *juan* presents its information in two registers, and the entire work is organized largely according categories of knowledge, like many *leishu*. Furthermore, in each *juan*, the two registers do not necessarily offer related information. For example, in *juan* 6, the lower register has characters related to devices and machines, and the upper register explains "difficult characters" from the *Book of Poetry*. A fairly detailed table of contents makes finding a particular character easier, but readers may also have derived enjoyment from browsing through the work.

History

Jianyang commercial editions of the standard histories (*zheng shi* 正史), the annalistic histories (*bian nian* 編年), and the miscellaneous histories (*za shi* 雜史) show their publishers' sensitivity to the demands of their customers, who, for these works, were overwhelmingly students preparing for the government civil examinations. As Benjamin Elman has pointed out, the dominance during much of the Ming of the Cheng-Zhu *Daoxue* approach to historiography, with its moralistic emphasis, resulted in privileging the annalistic works over the standard and miscellaneous histories, and more specifically, the outlines (*gangmu* 綱目) modeled after the *Zizhi tongjian gangmu* 資治通鑑綱目, a redaction and rearrangement of the Sima Guang's work compiled by Zhu Xi and his followers.[20] Thus nearly nine times more annalistic histories and related works were published than standard histories. Indeed, the poverty of editions of the standard histories is particularly clear—only two were published—the *Shiji* twice and the *Qian Han shu* once. Furthermore, one of the *Shiji* was printed by the Shendu zhai, with its proprietor, Liu Hongyi, listed only as the collator and the Jianyang magistrate of the time as the publisher (see Chapter 5). The other eight works counted among the standard histories in Table C.2 are not the histories themselves but shorter works of commentary and essays on the histories. The Jianyang imprints in the miscellaneous histories category show a similar trend: five of the twelve titles are actual histories and the other seven are commentaries on and explanations of them. Lastly, for those readers who needed some access to the other standard histories, a number of excerpts together with lengthy commentaries and critiques were available.

The publishers' preference for works explaining the actual histories also extend to the annalistic works. For example, there was no Jianyang edition of Sima Guang's massive 204-*juan Comprehensive Mirror for Aid in Government*, but there were at least eight of the corresponding *Gangmu*. Supplementary *tongjian*, such as the *Qianbian* 前編 by Jin Lüxiang 金履詳 (two editions), the *Song-Yuan tongjian* by Chen Jing 陳桱 (three), and the *Huang Ming zizhi tongji* 皇明資治通紀 by Chen Jian 陳建 (two) were far outnumbered by the corresponding *gangmu*.[21] The *tongjian* and their *gangmu* in turn spawned *jieyao* 節要 (digests), *huibian* 彙編 (compilations), *zuanyao* 纂要 (essential compilations), *daguan* 大觀 (overviews), and *jingchao* 精抄 (choice excerpts), as well as mind-numbing combinations of such offerings. For several related reasons, two of the most popular of such works were the essential digests for Sima Guang's history (eleven editions) and for the continuation for the Song and Yuan by Chen Jing (seventeen). Most editions of the digest of the *Comprehensive Mirror* credit it to a Mr. Shaowei (少微先生), that is, Jiang Zhi 江贄, who was a follower of Sima Guang and, more important, a native of Chongan in Minbei. In truth, this work, as well as the digest for Chen Jing's history, was probably produced by Liu Yan, a direct descendant of the Yuan publisher Liu Junzuo of Cuiyan jingshe (see Chapter 5). Furthermore, Zhang Guangqi, the magistrate of Jianyang county in the Xuande period, was credited as the collator. These Minbei affiliations, as well as the purpose of the works themselves, probably account for their popularity among the Jianyang publishers.

Perhaps the most amusing set of imprints of annalistic histories are those produced by Yu Xiangdou in the early seventeenth century. Yu offered at least three differently entitled works whose contents were mostly the same and consisted of portions from various *tongjian* and *gangmu*. The authorship of these *Scholarly Outlines of the Annalistic Histories* (*Dafang gangjian* 大方綱鑑 or *Dafang tongjian* 大方通鑑) was variously attributed to Li Tingji 李廷機 (*js* 1583, d. 1616) or Yuan Huang 袁黃 (1533–1606, *js* 1586). Li was a native of Jinjiang in southern Fujian and a Grand Secretary in the early seventeenth century who placed first in the provincial and metropolitan examinations and second in the palace examination of 1583. More examination literature was attributed to him by Fujian's commercial publishers than he could possibly have written. Yuan Huang, best known for his advocacy of "ledgers of merit and demerit," which served, among other uses, to help an examination candidate's keep track of his chances of success, had indeed written a number of works for examination study. In the 1610 edition, which credited Yuan Huang with the compilation, Yu Xiangdou includes a preface supposedly by Yuan dated 1606 (the year of his death) and another preface dated 1610 that mourns his passing. A third man who shared the dubious distinction of having spurious authorship or editorship thrust upon him was Ye Xianggao 葉向高 (1562–1627), also a Grand Secretary and Jinjiang native. In fact, Ye and Li were often paired together in Jianyang imprints, as in the 1612 work from Xiong Chongyu, the *Lichao jiyao gangjian* 歷朝紀要綱鑑 (Essentials of the outline of chronicles of past reigns).[22]

Nevertheless, it is among the historical works that some of the best Jianyang imprints of the Ming are found, particularly the superior editions of standard and annalistic histories and geographies produced by the Shendu zhai of Liu Hongyi. As noted in Chapter 5, Liu probably printed at least some of these works—especially the large ones—under official auspices, and various officials were listed as the publisher, editor, or collator. They may well have taken the printing blocks away with them when they left office. There is indirect evidence for this practice. In the 1601 edition of the Jianyang county gazetteer, of the books probably printed by Liu, only three or four are listed, and the one most certainly by Liu, the *Wenxian tongkao*, is listed as missing its printing blocks.[23] Given that the book trade of the time was so market-driven and glutted with more examination-type literature than full-length scholarly works, the chances of obtaining a copy of this important and useful reference would have been slim. Consequently, one of the officials involved probably found the opportunity to cart off the blocks irresistible. Whether the officials listed participated in the collating of these works is difficult to tell, but given Liu's own record of impressive imprints, he himself most likely did much of this work in addition to supervising the printing.

Of the remaining kinds of books in the History category, those in the geography (*dili* 地理) section make for an interesting mix—there are at least four gazetteers of the Wuyi Mountains region, two superior reprints of the famous administrative guide *Da Ming yitong zhi*, a merchant route book, and several other travel guides or administrative guides. An examination of the last three kinds of works, however, reveals that they seem to consist of excerpts from the *Da Ming yitong zhi* or some other comprehensive administrative guide, for, as modern scholars have pointed out, all contain much the same information.[24] Yet there must have been a strong demand for these guides and route books judging from the many different commercial editions, such as the one by Liu Longtian's Qiaoshan tang (Fig. 51). The question is why buy a merchant route book that indiscriminately lists government post routes along with routes truly usable for commercial transport, and "local products" that mainly mention tribute goods rather than mercantile products? The answer may be that they still contain enough useful information for travelers of all kinds, and they were certainly cheaper than the official editions of the large administrative guides. We have already seen many examples of commercial printers' purveying information (or misinformation). Their ability to continue doing this profitably depended to a large extent on their customers' need for such information, which otherwise would have been hard to obtain—by buying more expensive books, hand-copying books, or relying on word of mouth. Compared with these methods, perhaps the printed word and image even as produced in a cheap commercial edition printed on inferior

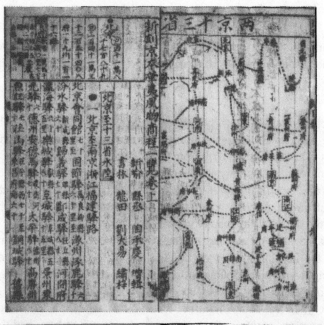

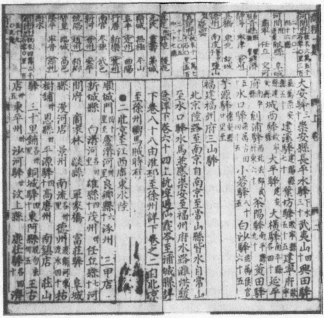

Fig. 51 Example of a merchant's route manual. *Shang cheng yilan*
商程一覧. Ming Wanli period (1573–1619). Publisher: Liu Longtian of
Qiaoshan jingshe (Naikaku bunko, 史 123 函 5 號).

paper and blighted by nondescript calligraphy and a cramped page layout had an authority and appeal that modern readers can imagine only with difficulty.

Philosophy

It is in certain works in the Philosophy category that we find some of the most notable differences between editions from the Ming and those from earlier periods. The number of Confucian (*rujia*) works increased, but by far the most impressive growth was in the number of medical works; books on divination, of which there had been extremely few previously; and the different types of books grouped under the rubric *leishu*. Again, it is not possible within the scope of this chapter to analyze each type of book in these categories, but the remarks below are meant to suggest lines for further research.

In the Confucian category, the Jianyang publishers produced works resembling the imprints dealing with the Classics and Four Books. There were large compendiums, including six different editions of the *Xingli daquan* 性理大全 (Great compendium of Neo-Confucianism) and seventeen condensed versions of this work or commentaries on it. The latter had the usual two- or three-register page layout for commentaries on the Classics and Four Books, and many were clearly written for use by students studying for the government examinations. In addition, a number of introductory Confucian texts meant for children and other readers were often illustrated. For example, the text of Zhu Xi's *Xiaoxue* 小學 (Elementary learning), a work highly popular with the Jianyang printers, was preceded by a set of portraits, ranging from figures of classical antiquity to famous *Daoxue* scholars. Jianyang editions of the *Kongzi jiayu* 孔子家語 (School sayings of Confucius) also began or ended with a series of ten or so full-page illustrations from the life of Confucius. Finally, one edition of Lü Kun's 呂坤 *Guifan* 軌範 (Standards for women) is a superior example of the *shangtu xiawen* format that was a trademark of Jianyang works (Fig. 10b). The punctuated text is written in a large, clear style, and the illustrations are comparatively good for this format.[25]

The greatest number of books printed in Jianyang during the Ming— nearly 15 percent—consists of medical texts, of which a far greater variety was published than was the case in the Song and Yuan. As noted in Chapter 3, part of this increased diversity resulted from critiques and revisions by medical scholars of earlier works, a process that had begun in the Jin and Yuan and continued into the Ming. Furthermore, the central government was far less engaged in the Ming than in the Northern Song in publishing medical works and left the initiative partly to regional governments and various principalities but mainly to private individuals and commercial publishers. The last developed a repertoire of publications that encompassed different trends in medical ideas and practice, both scholarly and popular, and this eclecticism in turn was probably driven largely by the demands of the book market. Indeed, the topical distribution of Jianyang medical imprints in Table C.3 shows just how varied the publications were.

In Chapter 3, I mentioned that some Jianyang men engaged in both publishing and medicine in the late Southern Song and Yuan, a connection that continued in the Ming. A brief examination of the publishers who produced medical texts shows that although nearly all the well-known publishing families of Jianyang printed such works, certain members of a given publishing family appear to have had a particular interest in medical topics and used a *tangming* devoted to printing such works. These include the Liu family's Puji yao tang 溥濟藥堂 (Hall of universally beneficial medicine) and Mingde tang 明德堂, the Yu family's Xiyuan shutang 西園書堂, and the Xiong family's Weisheng tang 衛生堂, which later became the well-known Zhongde tang.[26]

Since we know—with the exceptions of Xiong Zongli and Chen Qiquan (see Chapter 5)—nothing about the individual publishers of medical works from Jianyang, we can only guess, based on patterns in the imprints, at how they were engaged with medicine. That is, were they also practicing physicians, did they identify or associate with professional physicians from a particular medical lineage (*shiyi* 世醫) or as Confucian doctors (*ruyi* 儒醫), a growing number of whom belonged to the ranks of scholar-officials or associated with them? Or were the publishers more interested in popular, non-scholarly medical traditions, such as acupuncture, moxibustion, ophthamology, and surgery?[27]

For at least two important publishing families, the Xiong and the Chen, there is a clear connection between a serious interest in medicine and in divination in their imprints in these two fields. For example, out of the 40 or so imprints produced by Xiong Zongli himself, about 32 were medical works and six were works on divination, mainly geomancy and numerology. This correlation suggests an approach to medical theory and practice somewhat different from that of the professional or Confucian doctors. These distinctions do not imply that some Jianyang men, like Xiong Zongli, were not highly knowledgeable in the scholarly traditions of medicine; rather, they might have been more eclectic in their interests. Thus Xiong Zongli published a number of medical works, including classics in the field like the *Huangdi neijing* 黃帝內經 (Yellow Emperor's classic of internal medicine) and the *Nanjing* 難經 (Classic on difficult issues), the *Shanghan lun* 傷寒論 (Treatise on cold damage disorders), the *Furen daquan liang fang* 婦人大全良方 (Complete effective prescriptions for women's diseases), the *Maijing* 脈經 (Classic on pulse [diagnosis]). In all of these publications, he incorporated his own substantial annotations and commentaries, adding to and subtracting from earlier commentaries, as did other medical writers of the time. Sometimes he also wrote introductions to explain what he felt to be esoteric and difficult to understand passages in the medical classics as well as in newer works. For instance, his edition of the *Classic on Pulse* was entitled *Wang Shuhe Mai jue tuyao su jie* 王叔和脈訣圖要俗解 (Wang Shuhe's discussion on pulse analysis with essential illustrations and popularized explanation).[28] Moreover, Xiong also published at least one work apiece on the less esteemed subjects of surgery and acupuncture, to which Confucian doctors and most professional physicians paid little attention.

It seems unlikely that the Jianyang publishers were themselves professional doctors. Although some titles claimed, like many from other publishers, that the work revealed the secretly transmitted traditions of a certain family or school of physicians, none claimed to be from the Jianyang area. Quite possibly, Xiong Zongli was exceptional in his own family for his dual interest in medicine and publishing. His son and grandson who, according to *Riji gushi* (see Chapter 5), were physicians but did not engage significantly in publishing, while his other descendants apparently did not practice medicine.

By the early sixteenth century, Xiong's own descendants and a number of other Jianyang printshops were reprinting Xiong's editions as well as other medical works, many of which were illustrated with pictures, diagrams, and charts (Fig. 39d). The quality of these illustrations varied widely, many having been copied and recopied from previous works with their inaccuracies and mistakes intact. Others, especially pharmaceutical works, offered well-drawn, detailed pictures clearly showing the different varieties of a plant (Fig. 52)— as well as some totally inaccurate or uninformative picture of an animal or a mineral.

Some of the publishing practices described can be illustrated by various works on *fuke* 婦科 (gynecology) and, in Chinese traditional medicine, the closely related fields of *chanke* 產科 (obstetrics), *erke* 兒科 (pediatrics), and *douzhen* 痘疹 (smallpox [treatment]).[29] There were nine Jianyang imprints on *fuke* during the Ming. One, published probably in the early seventeenth century, was a work entitled *Furen maifa* 婦人脈法 (Pulse diagnosis of women); it was coupled with the *Yinchan quanshu* 胤產全書 (Complete book on childbirth), both by a famous late Ming scholar-official and medical authority, Wang Kentang 王肯堂 (1549–1613). The other eight publications on *fuke* were editions of the Song classic by Chen Ziming 陳自明, *Furen daquan liang fang*, with substantial commentaries and supplementary materials

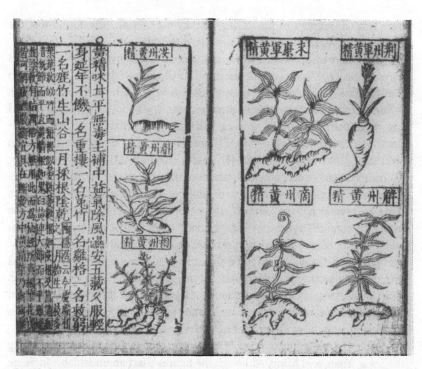

Fig. 52 A copiously illustrated pharmaceutical work. After a description of the properties and suitable applications of *huangjing* 黃精 (Solomon's seal), a number of prescriptions and recipes are given. *Beiyong bencao* 備用本草. 1579. Publisher: Yang Xianchun of Guiren tang (National Diet Library [Tokyo] 特 1-393).

by various Ming authors.[30] Four of the eight Jianyang editions, all published in the fifteenth and first half of the sixteenth centuries, contain additions by Xiong Zongli; the other four editions contain the revisions of the government medical official, Xue Ji 薛己 (1487–1559).[31] The first edition with Xue Ji's commentaries was published in 1547. A commercial edition from the famous Nanjing commercial publisher, Tang Fuchun 唐富春, appeared the following year, and its close similarity in layout and text organization to at least one of the Jianyang editions further supports the probability of collaboration between publishers in the two printing centers. Commercial publishers, therefore, seemed aware of trends in medical ideas, because either they themselves or their associates were knowledgeable about the field. On the other hand, it is curious that whereas even later Ming medical writers moved beyond Xue Ji's revisions, the Jianyang editions did not. For some reason, they failed to keep up to date with the newer ideas, which might have circulated among a relatively limited number of physicians, or they may simply have found that the editions with Xue Ji's revisions sold sufficiently well.

Next to medical works, *leishu* represented the Jianyang printers' largest output—nearly 14 percent. As discussed in Chapter 4, the term *leishu*, often translated as "encyclopedia," encompasses a wide variety of books whose common feature is their topical arrangement. In the following discussion, I have organized *leishu* into nine categories, based primarily on their functions: (1) general encyclopedias, (2) works primarily devoted examination literature, (3) writing manuals, (4) poetry manuals, (5) literary references, (6) compilations of surnames, (7) stories and anecdotes, (8) household references, and (9) primers on a variety of subjects. Such a classification, similar to those in several modern works,[32] is not perfect—there is inevitably some overlap among the categories. For instance, much of the material in a "general" encyclopedia or in a writing manual could be highly useful for examination study; the great majority of the story collections served as children's primers; and most of the household encyclopedias included brief sections on writing verse, legal documents, or letters. Nevertheless, subdividing *leishu* into these different categories helps us to talk more clearly about the changes through time in the works produced by the Jianyang commercial publishers.

Table C.4 shows the number of different *leishu* printed in Jianyang during the Song, Yuan, and Ming. Although the figures chart an undeniable increase in both the quantity and the variety of such works in the Ming, it is worth noting that some of the Ming imprints represent the earliest extant editions of works from previous eras. On the other hand, certain kinds of *leishu*, such as the story collections and the household manuals, truly came into their own only in the Ming, a development crucially linked to the spread of education among groups other than the literati elite. According to Sakai Tadao, the growth of the country's economy in the later Ming benefited non-elite groups, including petty merchants, landowning peasants, and even itinerant workers who had no fixed residence or permanent economic position. Such individuals not only aspired to greater prosperity and security but also became interested in acquiring at least some relatively simple and popular understanding of traditional Confucian values, social skills, and even amusement through suitable reading. This argument is manifestly borne out by the existence of many *leishu* that offered moral anecdotes or practical knowledge and advice, or served as writing manuals, as well as other kinds of works, including certain medical texts, divination manuals, literary anthologies, and the wealth of illustrated fiction produced by many of the same Jianyang publishers.

As in the Song and Yuan, few of the monumental general encyclopedias were printed in Jianyang during the Ming, probably for much the same reasons. The exceptions, such as the *Wenxian tongkao* (from the Shendu zhai) and the *Cefu yuangui*, were printed under official auspices. On the other hand, some printshops produced well-known large works intended to help students write examination-type essays or poems, such as the *Qunshu kaosuo*, the *Gujin shiwen leiju*, and the *Gujin yuanliu zhilun*. There are at least three Jianyang editions from the Ming of each of these works. Other, shorter collections of model examination essays were even more numerous. The Jianyang editions mostly were cheap, inferior texts with a cramped page layout, squeezing fifteen columns of 25 characters each on a page. Such collections constituted one of the specialties of the Jianyang book trade, and, judging from the extremely worn impressions of extant copies, they sold very well.

Topically arranged literary anthologies and dictionaries of phrases drawn from well-known works, first printed in the Song, continued to be popular. During the Ming, the Jianyang publishers either reprinted (sometimes using old Yuan blocks) these works or supplemented them with new sections but without efforts to update the original ones. For example, in the geography section of some *leishu*, Jianning continued to be referred to as a route (*lu*) as it was designated in the Yuan, rather than a prefecture (*fu*), its proper designation in the Ming.

By far, the greatest number of *leishu* published in Jianyang during the Ming—nearly a quarter of the total—were collections of moralistic anecdotes, aimed, according to the prefaces, at young children and their teachers. Such anthologies were hardly new in the Ming, being modeled after earlier compilations, including the first *Mengqiu* 蒙求 (Youth inquires) written in the mid-eighth century.[33] Like much of traditional Chinese children's literature, these collections recognize the value of rhymed verse; each piece begins typically with a four-character couplet, followed by the actual anecdote, which is often accompanied by simple lexical and phonetic glosses. Judging by the Jianyang editions, several collections proved to be particularly popular. There were some nine editions of the *Shuyan gushi* 書言故事, which had been compiled in the Southern Song,[34] eight of the *Gushi baimei* 故事白眉 (Stories from white eyebrows), five of the *Jinbi gushi* 金璧故事 (Gold and jade stories), two of the *Gushi huangmei* 故事黃眉 (Stories from yellow eyebrows), and some eleven collections containing different assortment of stories, all with *Riji gushi* (Stories for daily notice) in their titles.

Different editions of a given compilation offered, or claimed to offer, different commentaries. For example, Deng Zhimo, the late Ming professional author active in writing and annotating for commercial publishers of the period, is credited with collating or supplementing seven of the eight versions of the *Gushi baimei*. Probably spurred on by the popularity of the collection, Deng also wrote his own sequel, the *Gushi huangmei*, which he hoped, as he stated in the preface, would outsell the earlier work. A number of Jianyang men involved in publishing also appear as compilers or annotators of these story collections. One of the earlier collections, the *Xinkan dazi fenlei jiaozheng riji gushi* 新刊大字分類校正日記故事 (Newly engraved, large-character, topically arranged, collated stories for daily reading), was collated by Xiong Damu.[35] The *Jinbi gushi* lists as its compiler one Zheng Yiwei 鄭以偉, who was probably a brother or cousin of the Zheng publishers. Yu Yingqiu of the Cuiqing tang collaborated with Deng Zhimo on the *Pangxun siliu gushi yuan* 旁訓四六故事苑 (Garden of annotated stories with accompanying admonitions in four-six prose).[36]

Publishers sometimes made efforts to format their compilations to quite specific audiences. For example, a 1601 imprint from Huang Zhengfu 黃正輔 consists of two collections aimed at two different levels of readers. In the first, *Bianmeng ershisi xiao riji gushi* 便蒙二十四孝日記故事 (Twenty-four stories on filial piety for daily reading made easy for beginners), the verse sections are clearly set off from the story, which is punctuated but lacks annotations. Two panels of illustrations are provided on each page, in a *shangtu xiawen* format. The second collection, *Xinjuan Hui jun yuan ban jiaozheng huixiang zhushi bianlan xing xian riji gushi* 新鐫徽郡原板校正繪像註釋便覽興賢日記故事 (Stories on sages for daily reading, newly engraved [based on a] Huizhou edition, annotated, illustrated for convenient reading), is designed for somewhat more advanced, though by no means sophisticated readers: the text is unpunctuated but accompanied by simple glosses giving the sources or dates of the stories, and not every page has an illustration.

Nevertheless, it is debatable whether children constituted the exclusive or even chief readership for these stories. The simplicity of the prose, the easily remembered verse, the illustrations, and the clearly presented moral message all would have made such collections enticing to readers who lacked the education for more sophisticated reading but enjoyed working through a volume whose contents were already familiar from oral sources and to listeners for whom a more complex literary style would have been less comprehensible and less enjoyable. In effect, such stories provide the pleasure of recognition in print of a literature and a culture with which readers were already acquainted. In these ways, the *leishu* story collections shared some of the appeal of other Jianyang publications, such as illustrated fiction and drama miscellanies, which are discussed below.

Yet another class of *leishu*, offered in some 30 Jianyang editions, are household encyclopedias. These manuals for everyday living presented information in the forms of calendrical, astronomical, and astrological charts and tables specifying auspicious and inauspicious days for different activities; and on agriculture (when to plant which crops, to cultivate silkworms,); rules of deportment and the proper forms of address for one's superiors and inferiors; the correct form for legal contracts; divination methods, including geomancy, palmistry, chronomancy, oneiromancy, numerology, physiognomy, and astrology; pictures and diagrams of Daoist charms; the many ways of writing auspicious characters; abbreviated writing manuals; a list of the hundred family names; the four styles of calligraphy; rules of games; proverbs and short homilies in a popular Confucian style; word puzzles and jokes; and the routes and distances between important places in the country (Figs. 11a, b).[37] In essence, these household manuals offered abridged versions of other works, including almanacs (*tongshu* 通書),[38] route books, and other types of *leishu*. They may therefore have appealed to a potential book buyer as something of a bargain. These household manuals have been studied by modern scholars for their wealth of information,[39] some of which can be found in no other extant sources. On the other hand, many of these books—certainly the Jianyang imprints from the Ming—are near duplicates of one another in the information (text and image) they offer. And more often than not, as with the travelers' route books discussed above, the information in them had been copied from previous sources, such as administrative guides and literary anthologies. More research needs to be done before we can judge the reliability of the information, but the argument for the popularity of the travelers' route books offered above may be even more valid for these household encyclopedias.

Who was the audience for such works? Perhaps fairly well educated householders who needed such references. But these works may also have been bought by less educated, possibly semi-literate or even illiterate, customers who could then produce the work for the ready reference of a literate person answering their questions or providing a service like writing a letter. Inexpensive printed books, therefore, could answer the need for information of the literate and illiterate alike.

In fact, in the titles and prefaces of many *leishu*, the Ming publishers declared their desire to reach a broad audience from different socioeconomic groups. The well-known Yu Xiangdou publication of 1599, *Xinke tianxia simin bianlan Santai wanyong zhengzong* 新刻天下四民便覽三台萬用正宗 (Santai's orthodox instructions for myriad uses for the convenient perusal of all the people in the world, newly engraved), again declared in its preface that the work was "meant for the practical use and convenience of all people."[40] This emphasis that the contents of household encyclopedias were meant for the use of both the elite and the non-elite developed in the Ming, as is shown by Sakai's examination of two Yuan and six Ming editions of the *Shilin guangji*, which had been compiled in the late Southern Song.[41] Sakai found that over time the accretions, both in the tables of contents as well as the contents themselves, showed a tendency of the publishers to offer more material useful to the non-elite.[42]

Did this tendency to cater to a readership drawn from a wide, heterogeneous cross-section of society mean that the Jianyang publishers thought of themselves as Sakai's "lower-class scholars"? From all the evidence presented in this chapter, it seems far more likely that they counted themselves among the well-educated, with good reason. Some of them or their relatives attained one of the lower government degrees, and on rare occasion—such as Liu Longtian's older son, Kongjing—the *jinshi* degree. Some of the publishers— certainly Xiong Zongli—considered themselves scholars cum physicians, fully qualified to write and edit works on medicine and other subjects. Thus, in addition to sound business sense, the publishers' declared purpose of printing works to serve the needs of all kinds of people most probably reflected the late Ming philosophical and literary trend of appreciating elements of non-elite culture and at the same time popularizing Confucian, Daoist, and Buddhist teachings to instruct the common people. Many of these developments are reflected in the various kinds of *leishu* published in the late sixteenth and early seventeenth centuries, especially those from Jianyang.

Moreover, seen in this context, it is not surprising to find links between several of the Jianyang publishers and Yuan Huang, the scholar-official and well-known advocate of morality books as well as of *sanjiao* syncretism.[43] At least six works written or compiled by Yuan Huang were published in Jianyang. One of them, the *Si shu xun er su shuo* 四書訓兒俗說 (Instructions for sons and plain talk on the Four Books) published by the Yu family's Santai guan 余氏三台館 in 1607, contains a preface signed "Student [of Yuan Huang] Yu Yingxue" (Mensheng Yu Yingxue 門生余應學). Yingxue was either a son or nephew of Yu Xiangdou, the proprietor of the Santai guan and publisher of three of Yuan Huang's works, as well as a medical work by Yuan's great-grandfather.[44] Another connection between Yu Xiangdou and the Yuan family comes in the form of a preface written by Yuan Huang's son, Yan 儼, for a work on geomancy written by Yu and published in 1628 by two of his nephews, Yu Yingke and Yu Yingqiu. Finally, Yuan Huang's compilations of examination literature would have made him popular with the Jianyang publishers in any case. His outline of history, *Lishi gangjian bu* 歷史綱鑑補, was also published by Yu Xiangdou, while his *Gujin wenyuan juye jinghua* 古今文苑舉業精華 (Choice selection of examination writings, past and present) was issued by Yu's marriage relative, Liu Longtian.

A final item in the *leishu* category is the over 90 works on various divination (*shushu* 術數) techniques published in Ming Jianyang. Of the types of divination works listed in Table C.5, the most popular are books on geomancy (*xiang zhai xiang mu* 相宅相墓) and on fate determination and physiognomy (*ming shu xiang shu* 命書相書). Many of these contained at least some portions that were more comprehensible and accessible to the lay reader, at least compared to works on numerology, divination by the *Book of Changes*, and other more esoteric methods. Nevertheless, of the divination works I have examined, very few seemed aimed chiefly at the nonprofessional, and my sense is that the abbreviated divination sections in the household encyclopedias were sufficient for most lay readers, either to peruse or to have around the house should a professional be consulted. On the other hand, it is telling that a number of Jianyang publishers most active in the production of household encyclopedias (and other kinds of *leishu*) also produced the bulk of the divination texts: eighteen from Yu Xiangdou and the Yu family's Cuiqing tang, fourteen from various Xiong publishers, fourteen from various Chen publishers, and ten from the Liu family's Qiaoshan tang. Furthermore, both the Xiong and Chen families had long histories of printing medical works and had men who were known to be skilled both in medicine and divination—Xiong Zongli, of course, and Chen Qiquan. Again we are seeing a kind of intellectual and professional syncretism not at all surprising for the later Ming.

Belles lettres

In the belles lettres section, the importance of individual (*bieji*) and general collections (*zongji*) among Jianyang imprints continued in the Ming. The individual collections are rather disparate, ranging from the works of the most famous authors of the past and well-known Ming writers to the writings of relatively unknown men from Minbei. Not surprisingly, it is among the individual collections that we find the largest percentage of privately published works. Although these are still few compared to the commercial imprints in this category, private individuals, whether or not natives of Minbei, took advantage of the publishing resources available to them. Of the approximately fifteen collections privately printed, at least six of them list as their publishers men who were serving in some government office in the Jianning area.

Among the general collections, several kinds were particularly popular, including writing manuals,[45] general literary anthologies for a given period or across time, poetry anthologies, model essays, collections of "literary gems," and explicit examination literature. One striking pattern is the repetition of certain popular titles in each of these categories, and the appearance of the same literary pieces in collections that were supposedly different. The majority of the approximately ten well-known large anthologies printed in Jianyang, including two editions of the *Wenxuan* 文選, one of the *Song wenjian* (or *Huang chao wenjian*) 宋文鑑, and similar Ming compilations, such as a *Liang Han wenjian* 兩漢文鑑 (Han literary anthology), and a *Wanshou Tangren jueju* 萬首唐人絕句 (Ten thousand Tang "stopped-short lines"),[46] the majority of them tended to be published under official auspices. There were also at least 25 Jianyang editions of six different titles of model essays— whose purpose was to teach good writing by example. One of these, the *Wenzhang guifan* 文章軌範 (Model compositions), compiled in the Song, was often coupled with a Ming sequel, the *Xu Wenzhang guifan*. The four extant Jianyang editions from the Wanli period constitute only a small fraction of the total number of editions printed in the mid- and late Ming.[47] These works are replete with critical commentaries and glosses interspersed among, above, and after the main text (Fig. 8), much like the text for many a Classic or History. In addition, the *fanli* of many editions clearly explain the punctuation marks and compilation principles. Finally, certain collections that had been popular centuries earlier in the Song continued to be popular in the late Ming among the Jianyang publishers: sixteen out of the 36 poetry anthologies were Tang collections, and Jianyang imprints included eight collections of prose works by the three Su (Su Shi, Su Xun, and Su Che) of the Northern Song.

Another kind of anthology popular in the late Ming was the collection of short prose and verse pieces on a given theme, enhanced by full-page illustrations scattered throughout the work. For example, in the Tianqi period, Yu Zhangde of the Cuiqing tang published a series of occasional pieces: *Hua niao zhengqi* 花鳥爭奇 (The contest of the flowers and birds), *Meixue zhengqi* 梅雪爭奇 (The contest of the plum and snow; Fig. 34c), *Shanshui* 山水爭奇 (The contest of the mountain and water), *Shuguo zhengqi* 蔬果爭奇 (The contest of the vegetables and fruits; Fig. 42), and *Fengyue zhengqi* 風月爭奇 (The contest of the wind and moon).[48] These collections consisted of prose and verse works, some by famous authors of the past and present, and some by Deng Zhimo, Yu Yingqiu, and other writers probably employed by the Cuiqing tang. In each collection, following a preface in rather purple prose and printed in a mediocre grass script, the punctuated pieces are presented along with a number of very good full-page or full-leaf illustrations that rival some of the better ones in books printed in Nanjing, Hangzhou, and Suzhou. Apparently the works sold quite well, and in Yu

Yingqiu's preface to the *Contest of the Flowers and Birds*, he notes that further collections were being compiled to meet the readers' demands.

One wonders what kind of audience Yu and Deng had in mind. Presumably these books were more costly than a *shangtu xiawen* work of comparable length and would appeal to those wealthy enough to indulge in their (aspirations to) literary and artistic connoisseurship. In addition, the producers of these works apparently were trying to appeal to a broader audience than just the very highly educated. This is suggested by the glosses (sufficiently few to keep the text on the page from looking cramped), almost all of which give the pronunciation and meaning of a character or phrase, identify allusions, or paraphrase a passage to elucidate its meaning. There are hardly any notes on the literary style and composition of the text, and none of the marks by the side of the main text was used to denote a particularly important or well-written passage or to call the reader's attention to more notes in an upper register.[49] The text is quite simply punctuated with open circles. The *Contest* series was quite popular, if the prefaces to the later works are to be believed, and the Jianyang printers seemed to have succeeded in tapping into a market of connoisseurs (or would-be connoisseurs) willing to splurge on such works.

Also popular with the Jianyang printers were drama and song miscellanies.[50] These differed from editions of complete plays in that they included only excerpts, such as song sequences from the plays (Yuan and Ming *chuanqi* 傳奇), as well as lyric verses (*sanqu* 散曲), poems (*shige* 詩歌), popular songs (*xiaoqu* 小曲), drinking songs, songs in dialect, songs to tease courtesans from different regions (*shua hai* 耍海), jokes, riddles, and even lists of the names of provinces, prefectures, counties, and cities. The page was usually divided into two or three registers, each devoted to a different text, sometimes with illustrations (*chatu* 插圖) of the same quality as in the *shangtu xiawen* texts. The organization of the various kinds of pieces was sometimes loose or nonexistent—the dramatic arias for a given play might be scattered haphazardly among arias from other plays or folk songs. In short, the contents of these works suggest that they were meant to appeal to a large and diverse audience, including theatergoers (and those who heard excerpts from their friends or street performers) who wanted copies of the latest and most popular arias to sing themselves or have performed for them at home, courtesans and their clients, and all kinds of listeners who appreciated songs in their own dialect. This was also an audience with an insatiable appetite for novelty and variety, which explains why all the offerings in these miscellanies were described as "new," "latest and most popular," and "currently in fashion." Perhaps the random arrangement of the pieces was an attempt to give the impression of even greater variety. And in the spirit of anything goes in a work intended for diversion, even irrelevant if useful information such as lists of place-names was included.

Starting in the mid-sixteenth century, these miscellanies seem to have been printed and sold everywhere throughout the country, and the Jianyang printers produced their share. At least two of these works from Jianyang included excerpts of plays in southern Fujian (Minnan) vernaculars (Quanzhou and Chaozhou dialects).[51] Neither was an original edition, and therefore the Jianyang imprints testify to their popularity and to the unity of the book trade in much of Fujian and Jiangnan. In a sense, it is not too important whether they were sold in the Jianyang area to traveling Minnanese or transported to southern Fujian for sale.[52]

The vast majority of the numerous collections of stories and the historical chronicles the Jianyang printers poured onto the book market were in the *shangtu xiawen* format (see also Chapter 2 and Figs. 10 and 43). The cramped layout typically meant some fifteen columns per page and over 25 characters per column (≤ 0.4 cm in height). The pictures were for the most part mediocre to crude, drawn from a stock repertoire of images repeated again and again from book to book—two warriors fighting on horseback, several men kneeling before an official seated at a table, beheadings. Even small details, such as the folds of a tablecloth are nearly identical from picture to picture. The illustrations, however, did provide a visual relief from the text beneath and served as visual markers for a reader (or looker) searching for a particular place in the work. In addition, there was the occasional illustration that succeeded in fully utilizing the visual potential of a rectangular space about 6 x 9 cm in size. Most important to the printers, however, was that the illustrations were a strong selling point, since these works, like the drama miscellanies described above, were not only read privately by individuals but also read aloud to a listening audience to whom the pictures would be shown. In addition, the caption placed on either side of the illustration was often a catchy couplet that would be recited out loud and memorized.

Who then read, looked at, or listened to these works? The identities of some of the intended audiences are obvious. In addition to the collections of anecdotes exhorting children to filial piety and other virtues, such as the *Riji gushi* (see above), there were similar stories aimed partly at women, such as Lü Kun's *Guifan* described above (Fig. 10b). The stories are quite short, usually 50–60 characters, often followed by several lines of verse that can be memorized. Indeed, since so many different kinds of works could be printed in a *shangtu xiawen* format, the audience was potentially unlimited.

The *gongan* (court-case) story collections constitute only about one-tenth of all fictional works[53] printed in Ming Jianyang, but they are worth examining for what they suggest about their publishers' business strategies. These tales involve an upright magistrate[54] who always solves the case and gives a lengthy judgment at the end of the story. A collection would be divided topically—homicide, sexual transgressions, theft and robbery, violent disputes. One suspects that one important reason for the popularity of the *gongan* stories was their sensationalism, particularly as depicted in the illustrations, which were full of violence (heads being chopped off, beatings, forced drownings), and sex, violent and nonviolent (Figs. 53a, b). Indeed, many Ming readers seem to have obtained their quota of vicarious violence and sex from such books. The text is generally not difficult and often not very well-written, and none of the Jianyang editions are punctuated, which suggests that little attention was paid to the editing of these stories.

Judging from some of the extant copies, the blocks for a given work were used by several printshops. Each would identify itself at the beginning of a *juan* or in a printer's colophon, and there are often two or more different printers listed in the imprint. For example, a two-*juan* work entitled *Huang Ming zhusi lianming qipan gongan* 皇明諸司廉明奇判公案 (All kinds of court cases from the Ming dynasty, marvelously and righteously judged) lists as publishers both the Zheng family's Zongwen tang and the Cuiying tang 萃英堂.[55] Its stories are also not entirely the same as those in the 1598 four-*juan* collection by the same name published by Yu Xiangdou's Shuangfeng tang 雙峰堂. Moreover, copies of these collections reveal that the blocks would often be used until they were worn to the point of illegibility. These stories must have enjoyed a tremendous popularity, judging from the spate of "editions" that generously borrowed materials from one another.[56]

As scholars have pointed out, the late Ming *gongan* collections seem to have been produced within a relatively brief period, with a Jianyang edition of 1594 being the first definitely datable imprint[57] and other collections from Jianyang and Nanjing through the early seventeenth century. Nevertheless, court-case materials have appeared since at least the Southern Song, in various oral and written literary genres including plays, *chantefables*, and stories where court scenes figured without being the main setting.[58] Thus as Y. W. Ma put it, the commercial publishers of the late Ming *gongan* story collections would have been well acquainted with "a common tradition from which anyone could draw freely to compose his own works."[59] Nevertheless, the *gongan* stories borrowed from each type of source to a different degree. For example, it seems that the portrayal of Judge Bao in many of the stories

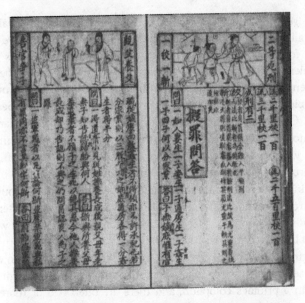

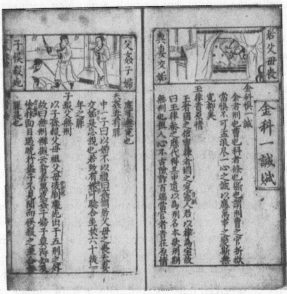

Fig. 53 Illustrated court-case stories. *Gujin lütiao gongan* 古今律條公案. Ming Wanli period (1573–1619). Publisher: Xiao Shaoqu of Shijian tang (Naikaku bunko, 296 函81 號).

owes more to that found in the *chantefables* than to the Yuan and early Ming northern dramas. Patrick Hanan, in his analysis of the stories in the 1594 collection mentioned above, observes that those depicting Judge Bao standing up to the Emperor Renzong bear close similarity to the *chantefables*.[60] Moreover, if a large part of the audience for the *gongan* stories was the same as that for the *chantefables*, that is, in McLaren's words, "prosperous and pious members of the commoner classes, specifically, landholders, traders and merchants,"[61] then the borrowings from the earlier *chantefables* make much sense. It is also worth noting that the arrangement and style of the text and illustration in several *chantefables* printed in the 1470s by a Beijing commercial publisher closely resemble those in many Jianyang commercial imprints with either *shangtu xiawen* or the *chatu* layouts. The Jianyang publishers could easily have been inspired by the format as well as the contents of these *chantefables*, had they needed any incentive for such imitation.

The *gongan* collections, however, offered something else to these and other readers. At least one Jianyang edition included in the preliminary *shoujuan* 首卷 an entire section on the essentials of criminal law in very simple language, information not often found in other popular imprints, even the household encyclopedias (Fig. 53a).[62] Thus, this popularized, abbreviated, and perhaps ultimately not entirely reliable legal reference material served as another important selling point for the *gongan* anthologies.[63] A combination of seemingly practical information and entertainment recounting all sorts of sensational and outrageous crimes must have proved highly tempting to many book buyers.

These same attractions are found in *Jianghu qiwen dupian xinshu* 江湖奇聞杜騙新書 (New book of exciting tales on avoiding scams and swindles),[64] a collection of tales of how con artists and the like cheated, robbed, and killed travelers (see Chapter 5). Although not involving court-room scenes or wise magistrates, the stories resemble those in the *gongan* in their focus on the narrative and rudimentary descriptions of the stock characters, whose emotions and inner motives are taken for granted and almost never described. At the end of each tale, a commentary draws a cautionary moral, often emphasizing practical precautions for the reader, who is presumably a traveler needing such advice in case he encounters similar criminals. The tales often present specific details of the setting and the circumstances of the event, and one learns the name and background of the main character, his mode of travel (the kind of boat, for example), the merchandise he deals in, the name of the broker in Suzhou with whom he stays, and so on. Presumably the specificity of such information not only added an extra thrill to reading about the sordid (and hopefully vicarious) horrors of life on the road but also lent a certain authenticity that helped convince a reader to heed the stories' warnings. That is, the work served both as entertainment and as a reference manual on the myriad ways not to get cheated, robbed, and murdered when traveling.

Finally, there are the historical chronicles, or *zhizhuan*, and tales of marvels, such as the *Journey to the West*, which also enjoyed a wide and diverse audience. In fact, in addition to the *Journey to the West*, two other great Ming novels,[65] *Romance of the Three Kingdoms* and the *Water Margin*, were published numerous times in the *shangtu xiawen* format. The texts of these novels as they appear in this format varied from edition to edition, and publishers had no qualms about adding or deleting text. Yu Xiangdou is an obvious example. In contrast, another kind of Ming fictional historical narratives called *yanyi* 演義 (literally, elucidation and popularization), had full-page or full-leaf illustrations preceding or interspersed among the text, or no illustrations at all.[66] The *yanyi* editions generally were better produced, and the text more carefully collated and edited with annotations and glosses and commentaries that chiefly offer literary critiques and appreciations of the text absent from the simpler version. The *zhizhuan* editions were cheaper and usually written in simpler language, with less material directly drawn from histories and fewer set pieces of poetry. In addition, the text received less editorial attention. Conversely, a printer like Yu Xiangdou felt more at liberty to modify the "original" text in an effort to increase its selling potential.

Rather than attempt the task of analyzing every edition of each narrative published in Jianyang, I will focus on the imprints of the *Romance of the Three Kingdoms*. By the most recent count, there are about 32 extant editions of the *Romance of the Three Kingdoms*, of which 22 belong to the simple recension, and 19 of these are definitely Jianyang imprints.[67] Even among these simpler pictorial editions, however, there are some significant distinctions, largely because of the different commentaries offered. One of Yu Xiangdou's editions was aimed at readers possessing a rather basic education, judging from the simple phonetic and lexical glosses and textual citations.[68] As for a second work, the *Xinke an Jian quanxiang piping Sanguo zhizhuan* 新刻按鑑 全像批評三國志傳 (The *Record of the Three Kingdoms*, according to the *Zizhi tongjian gangmu* [of Zhu Xi], fully illustrated, with commentaries, newly engraved), printed by Yu Xiangdou in 1592,[69] Anne McLaren argued in her recent study that it was intended for readers interested in military strategy, given the illustrations, captions, and interlinear commentary with memorable aphorisms that provide a text in easily digested segments focusing on tactics and strategies. These "applied" commentaries are quite different from those written by literati figures for other editions of *The Three Kingdoms*, which deal instead with rhetoric and aesthetic coherence.[70] Similarly,

Wilt Idema, in discussing a set of Jianyang *shangtu xiawen* historical chronicles from the Yuan, suggests they were directed toward a "wealthy, yet limitedly literate public," including Mongols and other non-Han, and Chinese military officials and their families.[71]

In any case, there were probably many lookers and listeners as well as readers of the works. Kin Bunkyō, in his recent book on the *Sanguo zhi*, cites a story recounted by Chen Jitai 陳際泰 (1567–1641), a professional writer of examination essays and the son of a Jiangxi businessman. When Chen was a boy, the family lived in Wuping in Fujian, not far from Jianyang. His maternal uncle gave him a copy of a *Sanguo zhizhuan*, which he read avidly. His mother berated the uncle, saying that the boy was so befuddled looking at the book's pictures of men and horses fighting that he would not even eat. Jitai replied that he was not looking at the pictures but reading the words below them.[72] His protest suggests that many others *did* only look at the pictures (Figs. 43a–d).

By the mid-Ming, such illustrated imprints probably constituted the lower end of the range of editions of historical narratives, while editions in the sophisticated literary version constituted the high end. The cheaper works could and probably did command a larger market, which nevertheless overlapped with the market for the higher-priced works.[73] The *shangtu xiawen* works of fiction in the Ming, therefore, enjoyed an audience that ranged from military officials to children to older students, who found them a less demanding way to learn their history,[74] to all those who enjoyed reading or listening to the same tales told by storytellers on the street. Finally, we should not discount the overlapping audiences for each version of a given narrative. After all, much of the pleasure of the text comes from rereading, either the same or a reformulated version in which the publisher, commentator, and reader join their imaginative forces to draw new meanings and enjoyment out of the same basic narrative. The rich details of such a work as the *Sanguo* make multiple readings, sometimes even within a single version, nearly inevitable.

The Qing Aftermath

Given the amazing scale of commercial publishing in Jianyang through the end of the Ming, its rather quick and irreversible decline by the beginning of the eighteenth century, at the latest, is a great mystery. Rather than a sudden cessation of printing, the little evidence available points to the publishers' inability to recover from the Ming-Qing transition. As mentioned at the start of this chapter, Minbei was a Southern Ming stronghold in 1645 and 1646 and for nine months the headquarters of the Longwu emperor.[75] Until 1651, in-fighting among various Ming loyalist groups, the conquest of the area by Qing forces, and the depredations of local militias and bandits contributed to the destruction of towns in Minbei. The few books known to have been printed during this time show that at least some of the publishers harbored ardent Southern Ming sentiments. One work, compiled by Yu Yingqiu and published in 1645 was the *Wuku* 武庫 (Military arsenal), alternatively and optimistically entitled *Juan gujin zhongxing choulüe* 鐫古今中興籌略 (Old and new military stratagems for the [dynastic] restoration). Yu seized the political moment and claimed that Zheng Zhilong 鄭芝龍, the southern Fujianese pirate-merchant and supporter of the Longwu emperor, by whom Zheng had just been appointed the Marquis of Pinglu 平虜侯, had approved the publication (*Pinglu hou Zheng jian ding* 平虜侯鑒定) and had written a preface for it.[76] In a very short time, this political expediency must have backfired as the Qing gained control of Minbei.

It is quite possible that lingering Ming loyalist sentiments in Minbei made the newly appointed Qing officials in the area suspicious of the publishers and their potential for producing anti-Manchu materials. Several Xiong men made clear their feelings. For example, one of Xiong He's descendants reprinted He's works and indicated his anti-Manchu sentiments not just by using the Southern Ming reign period to date the book (Longwu 2, i.e., 1646) but also by publishing the writings of a well-known Southern Song loyalist who had declined to serve in the Yuan government.[77] Two years later, Xiong Zhixue 志學, a descendant of the Ming publisher Xiong Zongli, printed the works of two distant cousins from Jiangxi; all three men were known as Ming loyalists. Although there is no known case of censorship and harsh punishment similar to the Ming history case in Zhejiang in 1661,[78] the new Qing officials in the Jianyang area probably kept watch over what was published there. Their vigilance may have prevented the printing industry from recovering, as it had from natural and man-made disasters in the past.

In more general terms, there are indications that Minbei economy did not ever revive fully after the troubles of the Ming-Qing transition in the 1640s.[79] The Jianyang commercial publishers probably lost an important market along the Fujian coast, where the Zheng family's naval forces continued to harass the Qing until the early 1680s and the Rebellion of the Three Feudatories was not subdued until 1683. Even more serious might have been the disruption of trade across the mountains to Jiangnan, which probably lasted for at least the first few decades of the Qing.

Nevertheless, printing activities continued to some extent in Jianyang. Zhou Lianggong, who served in several high-level posts in Fujian from 1647 to 1654, visited Shufang and noted later that publishers were up to their old tricks, producing error-ridden editions of the Classics. Indeed, one of their mistakes had made its way into a candidate's paper in the palace examination of 1659! Zhou therefore argued that all Jianyang printing blocks should be burned.[80] A more tolerant later visitor was Pan Lei 潘耒, a disciple of Gu Yanwu, the famous and influential early Qing scholar. Having re-edited Gu's *Rizhi lu* 日知錄 (Knowledge gained day by day) after his death, Pan then took his manuscript to Jianyang. With the help of an acquaintance who was then the assistant magistrate of the county, he found blockcarvers to carve the new 32-*juan* edition and had it printed around 1695.[81]

There are some indirect clues, however, that the surviving Jianyang publishers were by and large reprinting from pre-existing blocks rather than having new ones carved. One example, noted earlier, is the re-issue of a poetry study by Yu Xiangdou, complete with a preface by Xiangdou dated 1697, long after his death.[82] Some seven other works were also early Qing reprints using Ming blocks. Only about 25 Jianyang imprints were first published in the Qing, and about half of them were produced by private individuals rather than by the commercial establishments of Shufang. Most notable among these private editions were local histories of the Wuyi Mountains, some of which recorded the blockcarvers' names at the bottom of the center strip, thereby providing evidence that at least through the end of the seventeenth century there continued to be a concentration of blockcarvers in the area.

By the first half of the eighteenth century, however, the Jianyang publishing industry was definitely a thing of the past. Other than reprints from old blocks, there are no more commercial imprints. By 1775, when the Qianlong emperor dispatched officials to investigate the books printed by Yu Renzhong of the Qinyou tang during the Song, there was a sense of wonder and rediscovery of Jianyang as a great printing center.[83] As the Qing bibliophile Huang Pilie 黄丕烈 (1763–1825) said of a book printed in Pucheng (located in Minbei on the most important route to Jiangxi), "Because the way is far and transport difficult, merchants who accidentally obtain [a book from Minbei] take it to be a strange thing," a far cry from Zhu Xi's oft-quoted comment that there was no place, however far, that Jianyang books did not reach.[84]

There is no single compelling reason for the permanent decline of Jianyang as one of the country's largest printing centers. All the factors discussed above played a role. Whatever the actual causes, a look back from the perspective of the Qing and Republican periods shows that Jianyang publishing belonged to an older mode of that industry, when it was dominated by a few large printing centers. Despite the supposedly lower quality of Minbei imprints, Jianyang ultimately had more in common with the major book centers of Jiangnan in the periods when they dominated the national book market than it did with smaller, lesser-known places that also produced imprints, but in smaller numbers and with perhaps a more limited distribution network. Thus, as more of the printing industry spread to smaller centers throughout the country in the Qing and early Republican eras, the older, mostly urban centers lost some of their importance. In the case of Nanjing or Suzhou, this decline was only partial, and a lesser but still vital publishing industry survived into the Qing, because of these cities' location in the economically and culturally vibrant Jiangnan area. In contrast, the general economic decline of the more remote Minbei area killed off the Jianyang book industry, which had less chance to recover and resume operation. Indeed, in contrast to other rural book centers emerging in many parts of the country, no printing industry along the new patterns developed in Minbei.

Recapitulation

When we assess the Jianyang printing industry during the Ming, it is also useful to consider the kinds of books it did *not* produce. Of publications using technical developments like color printing and bronze movable type, there are only a few examples among Jianyang imprints. Moreover, the unprecedented variety of books printed in Ming China included geographies that described other countries in Asia fairly accurately, technical works (on, among other things, agriculture, sericulture, military science, engineering, mining, crafts such as carpentry, cooking manuals), collectanea, picture albums, catalogues of ink-sticks, and works for amusement (fiction, drama, songs, games), as well as an ever-increasing number of medical books and household encyclopedias. Among the over 1,600 known Jianyang commercial imprints, there are few geographies, two on military science, one on carpentry (possibly a reprint), less than five collectanea, no picture album, and no ink-stick catalogue. There are, however, many medical works, household encyclopedias, and works for amusement.

The repertory of Jianyang imprints clearly was determined by the commercial nature of the area's publishing industry. As noted above, in the history category, for example, Jianyang publishers issued outlines, explications, and digests of original scholarly work in great numbers, in contrast to the high-quality imprints of Liu Hongyi's Shendu zhai, which were often produced under official auspices. This comparison is true of Jianyang imprints on almost any other topic. Being almost entirely market-driven, commercial publishing survived by producing examination literature, popular reference manuals on all subjects, and works for entertainment. Publishers found ways to make these works profitable by streamlining both the contents and the physical production process and by shrewdly calculating the optimal size of a "run" and determining the likeliest markets to maximize their profits. Such works contributed to the hardiness of the Jianyang book trade. Examination literature in particular helped it through the lean years of the early Ming. In contrast, lengthy scholarly works, such as the complete *Daoxue* compendia, dynastic and annalistic histories, and large encyclopedias on government administration and institutions or on literary subjects, were not reprinted often by anyone, because of the high expenses and relatively low demand. Of course, the dearth of such works was particularly acute in the early Ming, and the exceptional (and infrequent) efforts of certain government offices such as the Directorate of Education, some of the Ming principalities,[85] and printers working under official sponsorship only highlight the problem. But even into the late Ming, such scholarly works could be hard to obtain, either because they remained relatively expensive or because they were not widely distributed. Thus, in reading Ming writers' laments about the unavailability of many important scholarly works,[86] we must remember that the scarcity of certain kinds of printed works may have more to do with the dominance of commercial publishing rather than a lack of scholarly interest or technological inadequacies.

In any case, the general pattern is clear: the Jianyang book trade survived—and thrived—by concentrating on books that could be produced cheaply and entailed less of a financial risk if lost while being transported to markets in Jiangnan or on the Fujian coast. As a result, Jianyang printers avoided costly printing processes, such as color-printing by *taoban* 套版 (using several blocks for different colors) and movable type (which entailed a relatively large initial outlay, especially for bronze type). Thus, books produced using these methods, including geographies with multicolored maps, ink-stick catalogues with color illustrations, and works with the commentaries and annotations printed in a different color from the main text, were not produced in Jianyang. Picture albums containing original paintings along with well-designed text printed in a superior calligraphic style were also absent from Jianyang imprints.

Moreover, it would be difficult to gauge the philosophical and intellectual trends of the times or of new developments in medicine and technology by consulting the contents of most Jianyang imprints. For example, the inclusion of an essay by Wang Yangming in an anthology of model prose writing or a collection of examination essays published in Jianyang is less an indication of the compiler's interest in Wang's philosophical ideas and more a recognition of Wang's marketability as one of the best-known and most influential thinkers of the day. His name sold books, and that was what mattered to Jianyang printers. Similarly, among the plethora of medical works published in Jianyang in the late Ming, including the Xiong family's reprints of works written or edited by Xiong Zongli, many reflect old-fashioned ideas rather than the latest ones in medical theory and practice. Even manuals for everyday use tended to reprint sections again and again from older books, some dating from the Song or Yuan. When Jianyang publishers ventured to print important new works, such as Song Yingxing's comprehensive technological treatise, *Tiangong kaiwu*,[87] or well-produced works like novels with full-leaf illustrations, they tended to be copied or facsimile-reprinted from editions originally published elsewhere.

We can argue therefore that the Jianyang publishers' choices of what to print were in some ways quite conservative and did not represent the most notable, "new dimensions" of Ming printing. This view, however, overlooks important developments in the growth of medical texts, books on family ritual, works on divination, encyclopedias, novels, story collections, and drama miscellanies. Although we have a few examples of each kind of these works from the late Song and the Yuan, their numbers grew from a trickle in the earlier periods to a torrent in the late sixteenth century. The demand for them, even as (or because they were) cheap reprints, must have been high, since printers produced so many of the same works in a short time. Moreover, as the evidence in this chapter suggests, the audience for these works came from a wide cross-section of society and was made up of readers of varying degrees of literacy. Although some books were read in their entirety, others, such as those on family ritual and the household encyclopedias, were consulted when needed. Still others may have been possessions to be displayed, and others may have catered to the literary pretensions of those lacking a thorough classical education. In short, new and significant developments in the history of publishing and reading can occur even as old texts are reprinted and repackaged between new covers.

As we have seen, by the Song printing was used by many different groups in Chinese society. Chapter 4 described the impact of the printed book on the educated elite and noted the widespread use of printed money, broadsheets, religious charms and sutras, funeral money, cheap calendars, and school primers. But evidence for the impact of the printed *book* on the less educated—most women, merchants, shopkeepers—is largely lacking until the mid- or late sixteenth century. Although we cannot yet determine how much greater was the extent of this impact in the Ming, we can point to important qualitative changes in commercial imprints between the Song–Yuan–early Ming and the later Ming. A full explanation of this phenomenon would require a thorough investigation into the growth of literacy during this period, the growing awareness of groups other than the literati of the uses of information in the printed book, and the connection of these developments to the general growth of the private economic sector in late Ming China.

For this study, the question is whether we can extrapolate the details of the Jianyang book trade to the story of books in Ming China in general and to still broader cultural, social, and economic issues. I believe we can. First, the evidence throughout this chapter clearly points to the broad regional scope of the Jianyang book trade. Ironically, the books produced in Jianyang during the Ming tell us more about south central China as a whole than about the Minbei backwater where they were printed. Second, it is significant that the vicissitudes of the Jianyang book trade during the Ming—the long initial decline from the end of the Yuan and the subsequent spectacular renaissance during the sixteenth century—reflects the story of printing for the country as a whole.[88] Furthermore, an impressionistic survey of the books printed in the large urban printing centers, such as Beijing, Nanjing, Suzhou, and Hangzhou, suggests that these places also produced, on the lower end of the scale, much the same kinds of books as those from Jianyang. The difference is that we have so many more Jianyang imprints, and this chapter has shown some of the ways we can mine the information in them.

7

Conclusion

During the Yongxi 雍熙 period (984–87) of the early Song, a printed edition of a book of prophecies, the *Tui bei tu* 推背圖, by the Tang mathematician and astrologer Li Shunfeng 李淳風, was selling very well in the Kaifeng book market. Angered because astrological works should be available only to approved government personnel (for state security reasons), the second Song emperor, Taizong, ordered that a hundred copies containing patently false predictions be printed and put on sale. A Gresham's law of books prevailed, and even the commercial edition lost favor with book buyers.[1] Clearly by the late tenth century, printing was already a well-known technology used for a variety of purposes, and a sophisticated, not to say cynical, appreciation of the power of print existed not only among publishers and readers throughout Chinese society, but also among the highest echelons of a state just starting its own ambitious compilation and publication efforts.

The six-century-long history of Jianyang publishing thus did not start with the invention of xylography in China, and its demise in the early Qing preceded the general decline of woodblock printing by at least two centuries. But the story of Jianyang imprints does coincide with the glory days (or centuries) of woodblock printing in China. Thus this study has shown what information on the social history of the Chinese book can be obtained by focusing on the books printed in this area and how to extract that information from a variety of sources. As a result, we can formulate more precisely some of the questions that have dominated this field: the impact of printing on various groups in Chinese society as exemplified by the many different uses they have made of the printed text and image, the response of commercial publishers to customers' demands, the changes over time in the visual appearance and contents of commercial imprints, the differences between a predominantly woodblock print culture and one shaped, at least for the first few centuries, by movable type in Europe. Although these issues have fascinated China scholars for a long time, there has been a general impression that the sources simply could not yield the information necessary to address any of them adequately. The findings of this study argue that such an assumption is unduly pessimistic.

Of course, many aspects of book culture in imperial China cannot be investigated even by considering such a long-lived and wide-ranging book trade as that of Jianyang. Nevertheless, as the chapters in this study show, much can be learned. One part of the story is the continuities. There were, for example, relatively few advances in the techniques of block-printing from its beginnings in the eighth century through the nineteenth and twentieth centuries, when it was supplanted by other printing methods. The page layout of the Chinese block-printed book remained much the same, even if methods of folding and binding the leaves improved somewhat. Certain kinds of books, such as the Classics and Four Books, dictionaries, some histories, collections of medical prescriptions, and writings of the best-known authors, remained steady sellers for over a millennium (and some are still going strong). The criteria for judging the quality of an imprint remained tied to its resemblance to a beautiful manuscript—superior paper and good calligraphy. The intentions expressed by most publishers, either private or commercial, for printing a work remained unchanged—to make available to readers a rare work or a better edition of a worthy text.

Another part of the story is, however, the changes in the uses of the Chinese printed book. For example, the order in which different social groups began to adopt printing for their own use suggests how difficult it is to determine, except perhaps with hindsight, when the "right" time for a technology has come, and for whom. Woodblock prints were first used for religious purposes, such as Buddhist sutras and Daoist charms. By the late eighth century, we have evidence of crudely printed calendars, school primers, and dictionaries in Sichuan and the lower Yangzi valley, where the abundance of the natural resources needed for printing facilitated its development. It is only in the Song, however, that the government and educated elite began to utilize printing to any considerable extent.

Political, cultural, and economic conditions in the Song spurred the use of printing by central and local governments and the literati throughout the country in general and contributed to the growth of the printing industry in a region like Jianyang in particular. Some of the reasons why Jianyang became such an important printing center were explored in Chapters 3 and 4. Like Sichuan and the lower Yangzi area, Minbei had an abundance of the necessary raw materials needed for woodblock printing. Perhaps as important was the general growth of commerce in the Song, so that areas not necessarily the foremost political and cultural centers could become important economically with the right natural resources and location. The towns of Minbei served as entrepôts along some of the most important inland trade routes connecting Fujian and the Jiangnan area; there was ready access to the most important markets for Jianyang books. Another development during the Song essential to the growth of printing was the evolution of the scholar-official elite and the attendant book culture that was encouraged by the government's active interest in compiling, collating, and publishing scholarly works and made inevitable (or, as some would argue, debased) by the government examination system. All these factors contributed to the rapid rise of the Jianyang book industry in the Song, as exemplified by the prominence of the publishers associated with their family or clan schools. Starting in the Song, the reverence for scholarship together with the government examination system generated a surprisingly large number of people[2] who possessed a thorough knowledge of the Confucian elite culture and subscribed to its values, even if few of them ever reached the high ranks of the politically and culturally powerful. Many of them, despite their obscurity, became the crucial transmitters and purveyors of this elite culture. In the case of the commercial publishers, their aggregate influence proved to be as great as any representative of these ideas and values.

In Jianyang, these publishers produced some of the best imprints of the Classics and Histories that have survived from the period and belie the region's already widespread reputation for shoddy imprints. Still, other evidence also suggests that commercial printing was already well developed in Jianyang by the Southern Song, and that the much-deplored *Mashaben*, whose contents ranged from bowdlerized editions of the Classics to examination essays to literary collections, circulated widely throughout much of the country. The Jianyang commercial printers put out everything that would sell, and the books did sell, not only in China but also in Japan and Korea.

The strongly commercial character of the Jianyang printing industry explains why it remained so active in the Yuan. In addition to scholarly works, books for everyday use and for entertainment became an important portion of the Jianyang output during the Yuan, a trend that would become overwhelming in the Ming. In fact, the existence of such books as medical texts, household encyclopedias, and illustrated novels in the Yuan and possibly in the late Southern Song should be a warning against the idea that books for popular use were a new development in the Ming. Too many uncertainties, especially the lower survival rate of such works from the earlier periods, make such pronouncements unjustifiable.

Moreover, in certain ways, the countrywide decline in the activities of official, private, and commercial printers during the first century or so of the Ming serves as a caveat against assuming an unbroken monotonic increase with time in the quantity and variety of books produced in China. Specifically, for Jianyang, only 10 percent of the imprints for the Ming were produced in the first half of the dynasty (up to about 1500), and the full flowering of the Minbei book trade did not occur until the third quarter of the sixteenth century. In fact, since the Jianyang book trade seems to mirror some of the general trends in the history of the Chinese printed book, especially in the Ming, we can extrapolate from the information in the over 1,600 known imprints of this period, to social and cultural conditions in south central China, especially the culturally and economically advanced areas of Jiangnan and coastal Fujian. As already noted in Chapters 5 and 6, it is ironic that Jianyang imprints of the Ming reveal more about the larger region than about Jianyang itself.

Finally, the permanent demise of the Jianyang printing industry in the mid-seventeenth century remains something of a mystery. The turmoil and destruction suffered in Minbei during the Ming-Qing transition seems an insufficient explanation. Also unsatisfactory is the suggestion that nonurban printing centers declined in the face of overwhelming competition from those in large cities—there is too much evidence to the contrary. The answer may well lie in the overall economic stagnation that had prevailed in the area since at least the start of the Ming and was exacerbated by a decline in interregional commerce passing through the Minbei area. Without this trade, the Jianyang book industry lost the competitive edge it enjoyed over the large urban book centers, especially in Jiangnan and on the Fujian coast.

In some important respects, the story of publishing in Jianyang is unique. First, although cheap, mediocre, or shoddy imprints were expected from rural book centers in imperial China, the Jianyang publishers' offerings ran the entire gamut, from superior deluxe editions to chapbook-quality works. Also unique was the enormous output of Jianyang publishers, who far outdistanced publishers in any other rural printing center during the centuries they were active and competed successfully with the greatest urban book centers of the country. Nevertheless, close attention to some of the factors contributing to the long-lived success of the Jianyang book trade can help us understand the development in general of Chinese woodblock publishing.

What made for a successful publishing center in imperial China? First, given the relatively high cost of transport throughout this long period, location in an area with an abundance of the natural resources needed for printing was essential. Second, in the absence of a large local market for books, the area must be located along important trade routes leading to markets necessary to the sustain the book trade. Neither of these conditions requires that the area be an urban center or of great cultural and political significance.[3] In its early days, the Jianyang printing industry was no doubt stimulated by the intellectual activity that made the area one of the most successful in the government examinations and a stronghold of Neo-Confucianism during the Song. But what sustained the book trade later in the Yuan and the Ming after the area's cultural decline were the geographic and economic factors just enumerated. For a book-printing center, success requires only that books as a commodity be profitably produced and marketed, not that they be "consumed" locally, as the success of cheaper ordinary-quality imprints in late imperial China demonstrates.

Suggestions for Future Research

The following suggestions by no means exhaust the possible subjects for research on the history of the Chinese book, but they are ones that came to mind in the course of this study, either as ways of expanding on the issues explored here or as alternative approaches to topics for which little or no information can be obtained through the kinds of methods used in this book to study the earlier periods of Chinese woodblock printing.

Several topics relate specifically to the Jianyang printing industry. First, for the categories of books of which we have a sufficiently large sample, individual works warrant closer analysis. For example, can we discern more precisely patterns in the kinds of Confucian works printed in Jianyang during the Song and the Yuan, when the area was a stronghold of the Neo-Confucianism advocated by Zhu Xi and his followers, and how did they differ from the works published in the Ming, when the region was not noted for adherence to a particular philosophical school? Second, a very different set of books, the story collections illustrated in the *shangtu xiawen* format, can also be examined in greater detail. Other works in the same format, such as historical narratives and the *gongan* detective stories, have been analyzed to some extent for their literary style, contents, and possible intended audiences, and much the same can be done for the collections of anecdotes classified as *leishu* produced in Jianyang during the late Ming.

A number of local literati and local officials have been credited with the writing, editing, and publishing of books in Jianyang. It should be possible to

gain a better understanding of the cultural life of the region and of why official interest in sponsoring printing projects there began in a serious way only
during the mid-Ming, when the central and regional governments were
much less active in compiling and printing large works. Such a study could
be done by culling information found in local histories, genealogies, and the
imprints themselves. In particular, prefaces may prove to be a valuable
source of information, since they often discuss something of the history of
the work, including earlier editions. They sometimes mention the reasons
why the book was printed and discuss those involved in writing and editing
the work or initiating the printing project.

Moreover, it would be instructive to compare the prefaces and postfaces
in surviving imprints with those of nonextant works. This is feasible since we
have many more prefaces than books, in the collected writings of individuals,
in the literary sections of local histories, or in other surviving editions of the
same work. Examination of prefaces in general would serve both to expand
our knowledge of the history of the handwritten and printed book and to
doublecheck the reliability of our deductions based on surviving imprints.
For instance, we could obtain a fuller idea of the attitudes of the literati in
different periods toward the uses of the printed book. A specific example
would be the prefaces to collections of examination essays. During the late
Ming, when the writing and publishing of such works was a high-growth industry, their prefaces often noted the fine literary style and erudition found
in the essays, even though the authors had never succeeded in passing one or
more of the government examinations. There are enough such prefaces to
collections by rather well-known and respected scholars to suggest that not
all of these works were viewed with the contempt that later scholars impute
to the Ming literati in general.

Another aspect of the Jianyang book trade for which we have some information is the connection between the Minbei publishers and those in
large cities in the Jiangnan area, particularly Nanjing. The evidence in Jianyang imprints shows that men from this area worked as editors, blockcarvers, and probably printers in Jiangnan, but it may be possible to fill out the
picture by starting at the other end. For example, there is so far no study of
the well-known Zhou 周 family printers or the equally famous Tang 唐 family, both of whom operated a number of printshops in Nanjing. We may be
able to arrive at a better understanding of the relationship between Liu
Kongdun and the Zhou printers with whom he and his father, Liu Longtian,
collaborated, as described in Chapter 5. The details of how the Tang family's
Shide tang edition of the *Journey to the West* was reprinted in a facsimile edition by Xiong Yunbin 熊雲濱 in Jianyang might be revealed if we know

more about the Shide tang's other publications. Given the number of print-shops in Nanjing and the imprints of the late Ming, a systematic study including a bibliography of all known imprints would be extremely useful for the history of the book in this period.[4] Similar studies for other Jiangnan printing centers such as Suzhou and Hangzhou could also be done.[5]

A number of other issues come to mind mainly because of the frustrating lack of information for Jianyang publishing. One important set of questions deals with the economic aspects of the book trade. We know very little about the size of "print runs" of commercial imprints or about production and labor costs, particularly for pre-Qing times. These lacunae are not limited to the Jianyang book trade, but exist for the country in general. The small bits of isolated information are enticing but difficult to interpret without a context: the price of one tael of silver for the literary encyclopedia printed by the Liu family's Anzheng tang in 1611 is not very useful without knowing how much other books (and other goods) cost. One source of information can be found in editions of the Buddhist Tripitaka, in which the monetary amounts contributed by donors and occasionally the production and labor costs are recorded at the end of each *juan*. By correlating this information with general price data for the corresponding period, it should be possible to get a good idea of the finances of printing a very large religious work and to extrapolate to the usually smaller-scale commercial printshops of the same period.

The publishing activities of private academies can also be examined more fully. So far, the work that has been done has focused on the bibliographic aspects of such imprints.[6] Although a number of academies in the Jianyang area printed the Classics and Histories during the Song and Yuan, neither the general histories nor the publishing activities of these schools have been examined in any detail. In addition, the histories of famous academies in other areas, however, such as the Xihu Academy in Hangzhou during the Yuan and the Chongzheng academies (one in Wuxi, one in Guangdong) during the Ming, are known in some detail and may be worth studying in connection with their publishing activities.

In late imperial China, there were a number of printing centers outside the large cities. As already noted, none of them produced as many imprints as Jianyang nor approached it in terms of the longevity and wide geographic scope of its book trade. One, however, that of Huizhou in Anhui, thrived in an area that was similar in some respects to Jianyang. First, it was also a hilly region that possessed the natural resources necessary for printing. From the Song onward, it was known for producing the highly esteemed paper known as *xuanzhi*, superior ink, and inkstones. Second, culturally and economically,

Huizhou achieved a national importance that lasted through much of late imperial China. By the mid-Ming, both private and government schools in the region were noted for the scholars they produced. The merchants from the area became longtime sojourners active in the community affairs of the places in which they settled. At the same time, their strong ties to their families at home were reflected in the elaborate and long-lived kinship organizations of Huizhou, as documented in their many genealogies. During the Ming, Huizhou became known for its superior imprints, including multicolored catalogues of ink-sticks and picture albums. It was also known for the great skill of its blockcarvers and for the Huizhou style of woodcut illustration.[7] One family of blockcarvers in particular, the Huang, were active during the late Ming, and we know something about both the men and their work.[8] The availability of these sources, as well as numerous local histories, suggest that a detailed study of Huizhou printing, particularly during the Ming, would be both feasible and informative.

Aside from Huizhou and Jianyang, most of the printing centers in nonurban areas in late imperial China were much smaller in scale, and they produced works mainly for local or nearby markets. These local publishing centers are worth studying because they represent an essential part of the woodblock-printing culture in imperial China to which the least educated had the most direct access in the countryside. In addition to relatively simple and crudely made books such as school primers, morality books, brief instruction manuals (on family ritual, divination, contracts, and letters), these printers also produced cheap calendars, funeral money, religious charms and pictures, and other printed items for practical use. In fact, if James Hayes's findings for a modern town in the New Territories reflect some of the conditions in late imperial China, these kinds of printing ephemera may have been, unsurprisingly, much more important than books for the largely illiterate segment of the population.[9] Unfortunately, this means that the likelihood of any such materials surviving from even the Qing is extremely low. It is difficult to determine exactly how many such printing centers existed, since almost all of them have disappeared and have left few records or imprints. Fortunately, a few have left sufficient traces to allow historians to study them in some detail. One such place is Sibao Changting, in the southern Fujian interior. Again, because it was a nexus of the trade routes in the region and because some of its imprints and the genealogies of the two most important printer families are extant, Cynthia Brokaw's current research on the area may contribute significantly to our understanding of these small printing centers, which probably existed in all parts of the country. Another promising site is the area around Shaoyang Municipality 邵陽市 (Baoqing prefecture 寶慶府 during the Qing) in Hunan, which boasted of nearly 40 print-shops in the Qing and Republican periods. In north China, long thought to be even harder to study because of the lack of sources, a preliminary survey for Shandong reveals that it will be possible to trace printing activities in small towns (in addition to those in the major cities) for the Qing and Republican periods.[10]

An even more compelling reason for studying these often small, rural printing centers is that they seem to have grown in both number and aggregate importance, starting possibly in the late Ming and early Qing, and represented a significantly different mode of commercial publishing from the older one dominated by a relatively few large book centers. That is, throughout the Qing and into the early Republican periods, the diffusion of both elite and popular cultures through woodblock printing continued but in an even broader fashion. Of course, research on such printing centers can differ greatly from that on earlier ones. For example, more of the physical evidence may have survived—the woodblocks, the imprints, and sometimes even the printshops themselves and their business records. In places still involved in publishing and selling books in the Republican period, it may even be possible to interview informants. On the other hand, the survival rate of most of the imprints from these places have been extremely low. Disdained by libraries and private collectors, who have not made the effort to collect such tattered and tatty works, the importance of these imprints to the history of the Chinese book remains largely unrecognized. Still, a better understanding of the late stage of woodblock printing in China requires that we investigate these printing centers and their publications as much as possible. Indeed, some of these imprints, mostly from the late nineteenth and early twentieth centuries, can still be bought at flea markets in China today. And even if most such places can no longer be studied fully, it would still be worthwhile to attempt to estimate their number, locations, and periods of activity and determine their sometimes surprisingly far-flung distribution networks.

One of the more neglected areas in the history of the printed Chinese book is the development of the woodcut illustrations collectively known as *tu*, in particular, pictures, maps, and abstract designs and diagrams that, together with charts and tables, refer to and expand on the information conveyed in the text. An examination of the *tu* in some six hundred years of Jianyang imprints reveals the continuity and increasing dissemination of images. In large part, this can be explained by the nature of woodblock printing, which facilitates both facsimile carving or carving from a near-identical copy of the original page or image. What awaits further exploration is how old and how widespread these printed images are. Did they first appear in print or were they translated from some other medium like religious paintings or sculptures or bronzes? Did they occur in calendars and household pictures of popular deities and folk heroes as well? If so, can we detect systematic differences among the various representations? Can we trace the history in print of one particular image?

Because both text and image continued to be printed on woodblocks during most of imperial China, the technological differentiation found in the West between illustrations in better-quality books produced by metal etching or engraving techniques and those in cheaper popular books printed from woodblocks did not exist.[11] Rather, in China, the differentiation was between the more utilitarian and more simply and less artistically rendered *tu* and the more aesthetically esteemed self-referencing *hua*. In more general terms, in adapting printing to their own uses, different groups in imperial China had to devise means to express these diverse uses within the confines of one commonly used medium. Over twelve hundred years of Chinese printing shows that such differentiations were very feasible, but some notable common features, such as recurring images, have also endured for all that time. As the history of the Chinese book continues to be written, we will understand more but marvel no less at all that can be conveyed on a woodblock impression.

Appendixes

Appendix A

Selected List of Song and Yuan Jianyang Imprints

Notes About the Table

1. Printer: "Jiankanben" 建刊本, means that the printer is not identifed in the work, but evidence such as the calligraphy, paper, etc., strongly suggests that it was printed in the Jianyang area.

2. Date: given as precisely as the evidence allows.

3. *siku*: see Table C.2, which gives the *siku* classification corresponding to the number in the table.

4. Dimensions: given in height of the block frame x width of the half-leaf (page) in cm.

5. *shukou*: indicates whether centerfold has a black strip (*heikou* 黑口) or is blank (*baikou* 白口)—see Fig. 6.

6. Carver: "y" means that there are carvers' names recorded in the imprint.

7. References: refers to the collection from which the imprint comes:

Seik #: *Seikadō bunko Sō-Gen pan zuroku* 靜嘉堂文庫宋元版圖錄. Tokyo: Kyūko shoin, 1992. Number refers to entry in the catalogue.

ZBK #: Beijing tushuguan, ed., *Zhonggguo banke tulu* 中國版刻圖錄. Beijing: Beijing wenwu chubanshe, 1961. Number refers to the figure in the work.

Table A.1
List of Selected Song and Yuan Jianyang Imprints

	Publisher	Title	Date	siku	Dimensions (cm)	shukou	Carvers	References
1	Jiankanben 建刊本	周易注 魏王弼, 晉韓康伯撰	南宋初	1-1	18.1 x 12.7, 半葉12行21-22字, 注文雙行28字	白口		ZBK 159
2	Jianningfu zhifu Wu Ge 建寧知府吳革	周易本義	宋咸淳間 (1265-74)	1-1	24.0 x 15.5, 半葉6行15字, 注文雙行同	白口	y	ZBK 200
3	Liu Junzuo Cuiyan jingshe 劉君佐翠嚴精舍	尚書輯錄纂深6卷 附書序1卷 元董鼎撰	元至正14 (1354)	1-1	19.6 x 12.6, 半葉11行20字, 注文雙行24字	黑口		Seik 129
4	Jiankanben 建刊本	毛詩舉要圖	南宋	1-3	17.7 x 11.4, 半葉13-14行26字	細黑口		Seik 3
5	Jiankanben 建刊本	纂圖互注毛詩20卷 附舉要圖1卷	宋紹興間 (1131-62)	1-3	19.9 x 12.6, 半葉10行18字, 注文雙行24字	細黑		ZBK 185
6	Jiankanben 建刊本	新刊直音傍訓毛詩句解 20卷宋李公凱撰	宋末元初	1-3	18.4 x 11.9, 半葉13行23字, 注文雙行24字	細黑口		Seik 2
7	Jiankanben 建刊本	附釋音毛詩註疏 20卷漢毛亨傳, 鄭玄箋 唐孔達疏 陸德明音義	元初刊明正德遞修	1-3	18.8 x 12.5, 半葉10行18字, 注文雙行23字	白口	y	Seik 130
8	Liu Junzuo Cuiyan jingshe 劉君佐翠嚴精舍	韓魯齊三家詩攷 6卷 宋王應麟撰	元泰定4 (1327)	1-3	19.2 x 12.7, 半葉11行22字, 注文雙行22字	細黑		Seik 133

Publisher	Title	Date	siku	Dimensions (cm)	shukou	Carvers	References
9 Liu Junzuo Cuiyan jingshe 劉君佐翠巖精舍	詩集傳附錄纂疏 20卷, 詩序附錄纂疏1卷; 詩傳綱領附錄纂疏 1卷; 語錄輯要 1卷 元胡一桂撰	元泰定 4 (1327)	1-3	19.8 x 12.7, 半葉 11行 20字, 注文雙行 24字	細黑口		Seik 131
10 Liu shi Rixin tang 劉氏日新堂	詩集傳通釋 20卷 綱領通釋外綱領1卷 宋朱熹集傳 元劉瑾通釋	元至正 12 (1352)	1-3	19.8 x 12.8, 半葉 12行 21字, 注文雙行 21字	細黑口		Seik 132
11 Yu Renzhong Wanjuan tang 余仁仲萬卷堂	禮記注 20卷 漢鄭玄撰 唐陸德明音義	宋紹興間 (1131-1162)	1-4	17.8 x 12.9, 半葉 11行 19字, 注文雙行 27字	細黑口		ZBK 171-72
12 Jiankanben 建刊本	禮記舉要圖 1卷 漢鄭玄注 唐陸德明釋文	南宋	1-4	17.8 x 11.5, 半葉 13-16行 約25字, 注文雙行 約 25字	細黑口		Seik 8
13 Jiankanben 建刊本	周禮(附音重言重意互註本)漢鄭玄註	南宋	1-4	13.9 x 9.0, 半葉 12行 23字, 注文雙行 23字	細黑口		Seik 5
14 Jiankanben 建刊本	纂圖互註周禮 12卷 漢鄭玄註 唐陸德明釋文	南宋	1-4	18.4 x 11.7, 半葉 12行 21字, 注文雙行 25字	細黑口	y	Seik 6
15 Jiankanben 建刊本	纂圖互註禮記 20卷 禮記舉要圖 1卷 漢鄭玄註 唐陸德明釋文	南宋	1-4	17.8 x 11.7, 半葉 11行 21字, 注文雙行 約25字	細黑口		Seik 7

Table A.1, *cont.*

Publisher	Title	Date	siku	Dimensions (cm)	shukou	Carvers	References
16 Yu Renzhong Wanjuan tang 余仁仲萬卷堂	春秋公羊經傳解詁 12卷 漢何休撰 唐陸德明釋文	宋紹熙 2 (1191)	1-5	17.8 x 12.0, 半葉 11 行 19 字, 注文雙行 27 字	細黑口		ZBK 169-70
17 Jiankanben 建刊本	音註全文春秋括例始末左傳句讀直解 宋林堯叟撰	元	1-5	15.5 x 10.5, 半葉 11 行 21 字, 注文雙行 21 字, 等	細黑口		Seik 142
18 Chen shi Yuqing tang 陳氏餘慶堂	增修互註禮部韻略 5卷 宋毛晃增註 毛居正重增	元至正 15 (1355)	1-10	21.8 x 13.8, 半葉 11 行 14 字, 注文雙行 28 字	細黑口		Seik 161
19 Liu Junzuo Cuiyan jingshe 劉君佐翠巖精舍	廣韻 5卷 宋陳彭年等輯	元至正 16 (1356)	1-10	19.0 x 11.7, 半葉 13 行 30 字, 注文雙行 30 字	黑口		ZBK 325-26
20 Jiankanben 建刊本	增修互註礼部韵略 5卷 宋毛晃增註 毛居正重增	元末	1-10	21.8 x 13.7, 半葉 11 行 28 字, 注文雙行 28 字	細黑口		Seik 160
21 Jiankanben 建刊本	史記集解 劉宋裴駰撰	南宋初	2-1	18.6 x 12.3, 半葉 13 行 27 字, 注文雙行	白口		ZBK 164
22 Wang Shubian 王叔邊	後漢書注 唐李賢撰	南宋初	2-1	18.2 x 13.1, 半葉 13 行 23-4 字, 注文雙行約28 字	細黑口		ZBK 160-61
23 Jiankanben 建刊本	晉書 唐房玄齡等撰	南宋初	2-1	18.3 x 12.5, 半葉 14 行 27 字	細黑口		ZBK 165
24 Jiankanben 建刊本	北史 存 81卷 唐李延壽撰	南宋中	2.01	20.7 x 12.7, 半葉 10 行 18 字	細黑口		Seik 34

Publisher	Title	Date	siku	Dimensions (cm)	shukou	Carvers	References
25 Cai Mengbi jiashu, Jianxi Sanfeng 建溪三峰蔡夢弼家塾	史記集解索隱 130卷 漢司馬遷撰 劉宋裴駰集解 唐司馬貞索隱	宋乾道 7 (1171)	2-1	19.3 x 13, 半葉 12 行 22 字, 注文雙行 22 字	白口		ZBK 162-63
26 Liu Yuanqi (Liu Zhiwen) Jiashu 劉元起(劉之問)家塾	漢書注 100卷 唐顏師古撰	宋慶元元年 (1195)	2-1	18.8 x 12.5, 半葉 8 行 18 字, 注文雙行 24 字	細黑口		ZBK 181-82
27 Cai Qi Yijing tang 蔡琪一經堂	後漢書存 75卷 劉宋范曄撰 唐李賢注 晉司馬彪撰 梁劉昭注補	宋嘉定元年 (1208)	2-1	21.1 x 13.1, 半葉 8 行 16 字, 注文雙行 21 字	細黑口	y	Seik 23
28 Huang Shanfu jiashu zhi jingshi, Jian'an 建安黃善夫家塾之敬室	史記集解索隱正義 130卷 漢司馬遷撰 劉宋裴駰集解 唐司馬貞索隱 張守節正義	南宋	2-1	19.9 x 12.6, 半葉 10 行 18 字, 注文雙行 22-3 字	細黑口		ZBK 175-76
29 Jiankanben 建刊本	新唐書 225卷 宋歐陽修, 宋祁等撰	南宋	2-1	19.3 x 13.2, 半葉 14 行 24 字, 注文雙行 29 字	白口		ZBK 166
30 Huang Shanfu jiashu zhi jingshi, Jian'an 建安黃善夫家塾之敬室	後漢書註 90卷 劉宋范曄撰 唐李賢註	宋	2-1	19.5 x 12.6, 半葉 10 行 18 字, 注文雙行 24 字	細黑口		ZBK 177-78
31 Cai Qi Yijing tang 蔡琪一經堂	漢書集註 100卷 漢班固撰 唐顏師古註	宋	2-1	21.1 x 13.1, 半葉 10 行 16 字, 注文雙行 21-2 字	細黑口		ZBK 183-84

Table A.1, *cont.*

Publisher	Title	Date	siku	Dimensions (cm)	shukou	Carvers	References
32 Jiankanben 建刊本	新唐書（中字本）225卷 首目2卷 歐陽修等奉勑撰	元天曆2 (1329)	2-1	19.0 x 12.3, 半葉 10行 19字, 注文雙行 23字	白口	y	Seik 170
33 Cai shi jiashu 蔡氏家塾	增修陸狀元集百家注 資治通鑑詳節 宋司馬光撰 宋陸老集注	南宋中	2-2	18.5 x 12.9, 半葉 13行 22字, 注文雙行 27字	白口	y	Seik 38
34 Jiankanben 建刊本	資治通鑑釋文 30卷 宋史炤撰	南宋	2-2	20.4 x 12.7, 半葉 12行 22字, 注文雙行 30字	細黑口		Seik 39
35 Chen shi Yuqing tang 陳氏餘慶堂	宋季三朝正要（通鑑三種之三）附 共6卷 撰者未詳 宋陳仲微錄	元皇慶元年 (1312)	2-2	18.2 x 12.5, 半葉 13行 22字	細黑口		Seik 179
36 Zhu shi Yugeng tang, Jian'an 建安宋氏 勇耕堂	續資治通鑑 18卷 提年李燾撰	元皇慶間 (1312-13)	2-2	19.2 x 12.6, 半葉 13行 22字	細黑口		Seik 180
37 Chen shi Yuqing tang, Jian'an 建安陳氏 餘慶堂	續宋中興編年資治通鑑 15卷 宋劉時舉撰	元皇慶間 (1312-13)	2-2	18.5 x 12.5, 半葉 13行 22字, 注文雙行 28字	細黑口		Seik 177–78
38 Zhang shi 張氏	宋季三朝政要 附 共6卷 撰者未詳	元至治3 (1323)	2-2	20.8 x 13.0, 半葉 15行 24字	細黑口		Seik 181
39 Jiankanben 建刊本	增修陸狀元集百家注 資治通鑑詳節 宋司馬光撰 宋陸老集注	元末	2-2	17.7 x 12.6, 半葉 13-14行 23字, 注文雙行 27字	細黑口	y	Seik 174
40 Jiankanben 建刊本	契丹國志	元	2-4	17.6 x 11.6, 半葉 12行 21字	黑口		ZBK 331

Publisher	Title	Date	siku	Dimensions (cm)	shukou	Carvers	References
41 Jianning kanben 建寧刊本	育德堂奏議 3 卷 宋蔡幼學撰	宋	2-6	22.2 x 14.6, 半葉 9 行 18 字	白口	y	ZBK 197
42 Yu Zhi'an Qinyou shutang, Jian'an 建安余志安勤有書堂	國朝名臣事略 15 卷 元蘇天爵撰	元元統 3 (1335)	2-7	19.1 x 12.3 (Seik), 19.4 x 12.1 (ZBK), 半葉 13 行 24 字, 注文雙行	粗黑口		Seik 185, ZBK 318-19
43 Jiankanben 建刊本	新編排韻增廣事類氏族大全 10 集 (甲集--癸集) 編者不詳	元	2-7	18.4 x 12.3, 半葉 17 行 28 字	細黑口		Seik 218
44 Jiankanben 建刊本	重刊宋朝南渡十將傳	元	2-7	16.4 x 10.7, 半葉 11 行 21 字	黑口		ZBK 330
45 Jiankanben 建刊本	東萊先生標注三國志詳節 20 卷	宋紹熙間 (1190-94)	2-10	19.5 x 12.5, 半葉 10 行 18 字, 注文雙行 23 字	細黑口		ZBK 186
46 Jian'an kanben 建安刊本	新編方輿勝覽 70 卷 宋祝穆撰, 祝洙增補	宋咸淳 3 (1267)	2-11	17.2 x 11.3, 半葉 14 行約 15 字, 注文雙行 23 字	細黑口		Seik 54
47 Yu Zhi'an Qinyou shutang, Jian'an 建安余志安勤有書堂	故唐律疏議 30 卷 唐長孫無忌等撰 算例 12 卷	元至順 3 (1332)	2-13	18.8 x 12.4, 半葉 14 行 21 字, 疏議低一格, 行 24 字	黑口		ZBK 327-28
48 Liu Junzuo Cuiyan jingshe 劉君佐翠嚴精舍	註陸宣公議 15 卷 唐陸贄撰	元至正 14 (1354)	2-13	18.2 x 11.8, 半葉 12 行 23 字, 注文雙行 23 字	細黑口		Seik 184
49 Fujian Caozhi keben 福建漕治刻本	張子語錄	宋	3-1	20.7 x 14.7, 半葉 10 行 18 字	白口	y	ZBK 198-99

Table A.1, *cont.*

	Publisher	Title	Date	siku	Dimensions (cm)	shukou	Carvers	References
50	Jiankanben 建刊本	名公書判清明集 零本 不分卷	南宋	3-3	19.0 x 11.8, 半葉 9 行 16 字	細黑 口		Seik 61
51	Zheng Tianze Zongwen shutang 鄭天澤宗文書堂	經史證類大觀本草 31卷 宋唐慎微撰 本草衍義 20卷 宋寇宗奭撰	元大德 6 (1302)	3-5	20.2 x 13.9, 半葉 12 行 20 字, 注文雙行 25 字	粗黑 口		Seik 199
52	Ye shi Guangqin tang 書坊葉氏廣勤堂	新刊王氏脈經 10卷 晉王叔和撰	元天曆 3 (?) (1330?)	3-5	18.7 x 12.8, 半葉 12 行 24 字, 注文雙行 24 字	黑 口		ZBK 314-15
53	Nanxi shuyuan 南谿書院	新刊惠民御藥院方 20卷 元御藥院編	元	3-5	18.5 x 11.8, 半葉 12 行 22 字	粗黑 口		Seik 204
54	Ye shi Guangqin tang, Shulin 書林葉氏廣勤堂	針灸資生經	元	3-5	19.6 x 12.4, 半葉 12 行 21 字	黑 口		ZBK 329
55	Jiankanben 建刊本	太平惠民和劑局方	元	3-5	19.7 x 12.8, 半葉 14 行 23 字	黑 口		ZBK 332
56	Jiankanben 建刊本	孫眞人備急千金要方 30卷 唐孫思邈撰 宋林億等校	元刊後修	3-5	18.1 x 11.8, 半葉 12 行 22 字, 注文雙行 22 字	細黑 口		Seik 198
57	Ye shi, Jian'an jun zhai 葉時,建安君齋	類說 60卷 宋曾慥撰	宋寶慶 2 (1226)	3-10	15.2 x 10.6, 半葉 10 行 16 字	細黑 口		ZBK 188

Publisher	Title	Date	siku	Dimensions (cm)	shukou	Carvers	References
58 Yu Renzhong Wanjuan tang 余仁仲萬卷堂	重修事物紀原 20卷首目 2卷 宋高承撰	宋慶元 3 (1197)	3-11	18.0 x 12.5, 半葉 21行 14字	白口		Seik 79
59 Jiankanben 建刊本	唐宋白孔六帖 42卷 存 宋孔傳續 唐白居易撰	宋	3-11	20.1 x 13.3, 半葉 10行 16-17字, 注文双行 23字	細黑口		Seik 76, ZBK187
60 Jiankanben 建刊本	新編通用啓劄截江綱 10集 68卷 宋熊晦仲編	南宋元初	3-11	15.3 x 10.3, 半葉 14行 24字, 注文雙行	細黑口		Seik 82
61 Jiankanben 建刊本	東萊先生分門律詩 庫前集 15卷後集 15卷 宋呂祖謙撰	南宋末元初	3-11	18.2 x 12.3, 半葉 11行 19字	細黑口		Seik 89
62 Zheng shi Jicheng tang 鄭氏積誠堂	纂圖增新群書類要事林廣記	元至元 6 (1340)	3-11	18.6 x 11.8, 半葉 16行 25-27 字不等	黑口		ZBK 320-21
63 Yang shi (?) Qingjiang shutang 楊氏(?)清江書堂	新增說文韻府群玉 20卷 元陰時夫編	元	3-11	21.0 x 12.6, 半葉 10行字數不定 注文雙行 29字	大黑口		Seik 217
64 Jiankanben 建刊本	夷堅志 (甲志-丁志 20卷) 宋洪邁撰	宋淳熙 7 (1180)	3-12	20.2 x 14.6, 半葉 9行 18字	白口	y	Seik 84
65 Longshan shutang 龍山書堂	揮麈錄 宋王明清	宋	3-12	19.5 x 13, 半葉 11行 20字	細黑口		ZBK 189-90
66 Yu shi jiashu 虞氏家塾	老子道德經章句 2卷	宋	3-14	19.3 x 12.5, 半葉 10行 17字, 注文雙行 24字	細黑口		ZBK 191-92

Table A.1, *cont.*

Publisher	Title	Date	siku	Dimensions (cm)	shukou	Carvers	References
67 Jiankanben (orig. Wu Yan publ.) 建刊本 (吳炎刻本)	新校正老泉先生文集 宋蘇洵撰	宋紹熙4 (1193)	4-2	19.5 x 12.8, 半葉14行25字, 注文雙行22字	黑口		ZBK 173-74
68 Jiankanben 建刊本	杜工部草堂詩箋 宋蔡夢弼撰	宋紹熙間 (1190-94)	4-2	18.9 x 12.6, 半葉11行19字, 注文雙行25字	細黑口		ZBK 168
69 Huang Shanfu jiashu zhi jingshi, Jian'an 建安黃善夫家塾之敬室	王狀元集百家注分類東坡先生詩25卷 東坡紀年錄1卷	南宋	4-2	19.9 x 13.2, 半葉13行22字, 注文雙行27字	細黑口		ZBK 179-80
70 Jiankanben 建刊本	分門集註杜工部詩 殘存3卷	南宋	4-2	19.5 x 12.8, 半葉11行20字, 注文雙行22字	細黑口		ZBK 193
71 Jiankan jinxiangben 建刊巾箱本	箋註陶淵明集10卷 晉陶潛撰	南宋末	4-2	15.3 x 11.0, 半葉9行16字, 注文雙行16字	細黑口		Seik 223
72 Jiankanben 建刊本	新刊五百家註音辯昌黎先生詩集 宋李公煥箋註	宋	4-2	20.4 x 12.6, 半葉10行18字, 注文雙行23字	細黑口		ZBK 194
73 Jianning kanben 建寧刊本	陶靖節先生詩註	宋	4-2	18.9 x 13.0, 半葉7行15字, 注文雙行同	白口	y	ZBK 196
74 Yu Zhi'an Qinyou shutang, Jian'an 建安余志安勤有書堂	分類補註李太白詩25卷	元至大4 (1311)	4-2	19.6 x 12.7, 半葉12行20字, 注文雙行26字	細黑口		Seik 224

Publisher	Title	Date	siku	Dimensions (cm)	shukou	Carvers	References
75 Yu Zhi'an Qinyou shutang, Jian'an 建安余志安勤有書堂	集千家註分類杜工部詩 25卷 宋徐居仁編 黃鶴同注	元皇慶元年 (1312)	4-2	19.8 x 12.7, 半葉 12行 20字, 注文雙行 26字	大黑口		Seik 226
76 Zheng Tianze Zongwen shutang 鄭天澤宗文書堂	靜修先生文集 22卷 元劉因撰	元至順元年 (1330)	4-2	18.6 x 11.9, 半葉 13行 21字	黑口		ZBK 316-17
77 Liu shi Rixin tang 劉氏日新堂	伯先生詩續編 3卷 元虞集撰 題葉氏 四歧堂氏1卷	元後至元 6 (1340)	4-2	16.1 x 10.3, 半葉 10行 15字	黑口		ZBK 322-23
78 Jiankanben 建刊本	聖宋名賢五百家播芳大全粹	宋紹熙間 (1190-94)	4-3	18.8 x 12.8, 半葉 14行 25字	白口		ZBK 167
79 Jiankanben 建刊本	汪齋先生標注崇古文訣 20卷 宋樓昉輯	宋	4-3	18.7 x 11.9, 半葉 12行 23字	白口又 細黑口	y	Seik 121
80 Yu shi Fuben shutang, Jianan 建安 虞氏服本書堂	趙子昂詩集 7卷 元趙孟頫撰	元至元元年 (1335)	4-3	17.0 x 10.1(Seik), 16.8 x 9.9 (ZBK), 半葉 11行 20字	細黑口		Seik 233, ZBK 324
81 Yu shi Qindetang/ Yu shi Wuben tang 余氏勤德堂/虞氏務本堂	新刊類編歷舉三場文选庚集 8卷 辛集? 元劉貞輯	元至正元年 (1341)	4-3	16.0 x 10.3, 半葉 14行 24字	細黑口		Seik 251
82 Jiankanben 建刊本	增廣音註唐郢州刺史訂卯詩集	元	4-3	19.4 x 12.0, 半葉 10行 19字	黑口		ZBK 333

Table A.1, cont.

Publisher	Title	Date	siku	Dimensions (cm)	shukou	Carvers	References
83 Jiankanben 建刊本	詳註周美成詞片玉集 宋周邦彥撰	宋	4-5	17.8 x 11.3, 半葉 10行 17字, 注文雙行 17字	細黑口		ZBK 195
84 Jiankanben 建刊本	朝野新聲太平樂府	元	4-5	16.4 x 10.2, 半葉 16行 28字	黑口		ZBK 334
85 Jiankanben 建刊本	梨園按試樂府新聲	元	4-5	19 x 11.9, 半葉 17行 30字	黑口		ZBK 336
86 Jiankanben 建刊本	樂府新編陽春白雪	元	4-5	16.3 x 11.3, 半葉 16行 27字	黑口		ZBK 335

Appendix B

Lists of Jianyang Publishers

Table B.1
Jianyang Printers and Publishers of the Song and Yuan
(*Note: The number in the last column is the estimated
number of attributable imprints. S = Song, Y = Yuan.*)

	Publisher/Printer	Date	Books
1	Bao'en wanshou tang Chen Juelin, Jianyang 建陽報恩萬壽堂陳覺琳	元延祐 2 (1315)	1
2	Cai Meixuan 蔡梅軒	元後至元 6 (1340)	1
3	Cai Qi Chunfu Yijing tang, Jianning shupu 建寧書鋪蔡琪純父一經堂	南宋 (ca.1200)	2
4	Cai shi, Jian'an 建安蔡氏	元	1
5	Chen Balang shupu/zhai, Jianyang Chonghua 建陽崇化陳八郎書鋪/宅	南宋	2
6	Chen shi 陳氏	宋	1
7	Chen shi Liugeng tang, Jian'an Shuangbi 建安雙璧陳氏留耕堂	元	2
8	Chen shi Yuqing tang 陳氏餘慶堂	元–明	7 (Y)
9	Dexing shutang 德星書堂	元	1
10	Fan Diao or Shengdiao, Jian'an 建安 范刁/生刁	南宋	1
11	Fu Zi'an, Jian'an 建安傅子安	元後至元 2 (1336)	1
12	Gao shi Rixin tang, Jian'an 建安高氏 日新堂	元至正 26 (1366)	1

Table B.1, *cont.*

	Publisher/Printer	Date	Books
13	Huang Sanbalang shupu, Jianning fu 建寧府黃三八郎書鋪	宋乾道間 (1165–73)	2
14	Jian'an Shutang 建安書堂	元	1
15	Jiang Zhongda Qunyu tang, Jian'an 建安江仲達群玉堂	宋	1
16	Jishan tang 積善堂	元	1
17	Li Dayi, Jianning 建寧李大異	宋嘉定3 (1210)	1
18	Li shi Jian'an shutang 李氏建安書堂	元	1
19	Liu Chengfu 劉誠甫	宋淳祐9 (1249)	1
20	Liu Chengfu, Jian'an 建安劉承父	元至元 20 (1283)	1
21	Liu Jiangshi zhai, Masha 麻沙劉將士宅	南宋	1
22	Liu Kechang, Shulin 書林劉克常	元至正27 (1367)	1
23	Liu Lin 劉麟	宋宣和6 (1124)	1
24	Liu Rixin zhai Sangui tang 劉日新宅 三桂堂	宋開禧元年 (1205)	1
25	Liu Shilong zhai 劉仕隆宅	宋	1
26	Liu Shugang zhai Yijing tang 劉叔剛宅 一經堂	南宋 (ca.1175)	4
27	Liu Tongpan zhai Yanggao tang (operated by Liu Dan 劉旦) 劉通判宅 仰高堂	南宋	3
28	Liu Yingdeng 劉應登	元至元 24 (1287)	1
29	Liu Zhiming, Masha 麻沙劉智明	宋	1
30	Liu Zhongji zhai, Mashazhen Shuinan 麻沙鎮水南劉仲吉宅	南宋 (ca.1160–73)	2
31	Liu Zhongli 劉仲立	宋隆興2 (1164)	1
32	Liu shi, Shufang 書坊劉氏	宋淳熙間 (1174–90)	1
33	Liu shi Jian'an 建安劉氏	元	1
34	Liu shi Mingde tang 劉氏明德堂	元–明	2 (Y)
35	Liu shi Nanjian shutang 劉氏南澗書堂	宋/元	1
36	Liu shi Rixin tang (Yuan: Liu Jingzhao, Liu Jinwen, Liu Shujian, etc.) 劉氏 日新堂 (元間：劉京兆, 劉錦文, 劉叔簡等)	元–明	25 (Y)
37	Liu shi Shusi, Jianyang 建陽劉氏書肆	元至正23 (1363)	1
38	Liu shi Xueli tang 劉氏學禮堂	元	1
39	Longshan shutang 龍山書堂	宋	1

Table B.1, *cont.*

	Publisher/Printer	Date	Books
40	Quanwen tang, Yunqu 雲衢全文堂	元	1
41	Tongwen tang, Jian'an 建安同文堂	元至正 11 (1351)	1
42	Wang Mao Fuguitang, Jian'an 建安王懋甫桂堂	宋	1
43	Wang Pengfu 王朋甫	宋乾道淳熙間 (1165–89)	1
44	Wang Shubian 王叔邊	南宋初	1+
45	Wang shi Shihan tang, Jianyi 建邑王氏世翰堂	宋嘉祐 2 (1057)	1
46	Wei Xianwei zhai, Jian'an 魏縣尉宅, 建安	宋慶元年 (1195)	1
47	Wei Zhongqing 魏忠卿	宋	1
48	Wu shi Dexin shutang, Fusha Biwan 富沙碧灣吳氏德新書堂	元至元 3 (1337)	1
49	Wu shi Youyu shutang, Masha 麻沙吳氏友于書堂	元 (1324–39)	2
50	Xiong Jing 熊敬	元大德 9 (1305)	1
51	Xiong Ke 熊克	宋乾道淳熙間 (1165–89)	3
52	Xiong shi, Jian'an	元	1
53	Xiong shi Boya tang 熊氏博雅堂	元–明	1 (Y)
54	Xiong shi Wanjuan shutang 熊氏萬卷書堂	元	1
55	Xiong shi Weisheng tang 熊氏衛生堂	元	1
56	Xiong shi Zhongde tang 熊氏種德堂	元–明	1 (Y)
57	Yang shi Qingjiang tang 楊氏清江堂	元–明	2 (Y)
58	Ye shi Guangqin tang 葉氏廣勤堂	宋–元–明	1 (S), 4+ (Y)
59	Yiyou shutang 益友書堂	元	1
60	Yu Gongli 余恭禮	宋嘉定 9 (1216)	1
61	Yu Renzhong Wanjuan tang 余仁仲萬卷堂	南宋 (ca.1180–1200)	14
62	Yu Tangqing Mingjing tang 余唐卿明經堂	宋寶祐 2 (1254)	1
63	Yu Tengfu 余騰夫	南宋	1
64	Yu Yanguo Lixian tang 余彥國勵賢堂	宋/元	2
65	a. Yu Zhi'an Qinyou shutang 余志安勤有書堂	元 (ca.1314–44)	27
	b. Yu shi Qinyou tang, Jing'an 靖庵余氏勤有堂	元	2

Table B.1, *cont.*

	Publisher/Printer	Date	Books
66	Yu Zhuo 余卓	元	1
67	Yu shi Qinde tang 余氏勤德堂	宋/元–明	1 (S), 4 (Y)
68	Yu shi, Chongchuan 崇川余氏	宋/元	1
69	Yu shi, Jian'an 建安余氏	元	1
70	Yu shi Shuanggui tang 余氏雙桂堂	元	4
71	Yú Pingzhai Wuben shutang (Yú Yewen, etc.) 虞平齋務本書堂 (虞壄文等)	宋–元	1 (S), 4 (Y)
72	Yú Qianli, Masha zhen Nanzhai 麻沙鎮 南齋虞千里	宋乾道 5 (1169)	1
73	Yú Shuyi zhai, Jianning fu Masha zhen 建寧府麻沙鎮虞叔異齋	宋	1
74	Yú Xinheng zhai 虞信亨宅	元	1
75	Yú shi, Jian'an 建安虞氏	宋紹熙前後 (1190–94) –元	1 (S), 5 (Y)
76	Yuyong shutang, Jian'an 建安玉融書堂	元至正 17 (1357)	1
77	Zhan Guangzu Yueyai tang, Wuyi 詹光祖 月崖堂, 武夷	宋淳祐間 (1241–52), 元大德 6 (1302)	1 (S), 1 (Y)
78	Zhan Huan, Jian'an 建安詹環	元	1
79	Zhan shi Jinde shutang 詹氏進德書堂	元	1
80	Zhang shi 張氏	宋	1
81	Zhang shi Jiyi shutang, Yunqu 雲衢張氏 集義書堂	元至治 3 (1323)	3
82	Zheng Mingde zhai 鄭明德宅	元天曆 1 (1329)	1
83	Zheng Tianze Zongwen shutang 鄭天澤 宗文書堂	元 (ca.1302–20)	3
84	Zheng shi, Jian'an 建安鄭氏	元	1
85	Zheng shi Jicheng tang 鄭氏積誠堂	元至元 6 (1340)	1
86	Zhu shi Biwan shutang 朱氏碧灣書堂	元至正7 (1336)	1
87	Zhu shi Yugeng tang, Jian'an 建安朱氏 與耕堂	元–明	3 (Y)
88	Zhu shi, Jian'an 建安祝氏	宋嘉熙 3 (1239)	1

Table B.2
Jiashu 家塾 Publishers in the Song and Yuan

	Publisher/Printer	Date	Books
89	Cai Mengbi Fuqing jiashu, Jianxi Sanfeng 建溪三峰蔡夢弼傅卿家塾	南宋 (ca.1171–94)	1+
90	Cai Ziwen Dongshu zhi jingtang 蔡子文東塾之敬堂	宋治平3 (1066)	1
91	Cai shi jiashu 蔡氏家塾	南宋中	2
92	Chen Yanfu jiashu 陳彥甫家塾	宋慶元2 (1196)	1
93	Chongwen shushu 崇文書塾	元泰定2 (1325)	1
94	Huang Jifu jiashu 黃及甫家塾	宋	1
95	Huang Shanfu jiashu zhi jingshi 黃善夫家塾之敬室	南宋	4
96	Liu Yuanqi (Liu Zhiwen) jiashu 劉元起 (劉之問)家塾	宋慶元間 (1195–1200)	2
97	Wei Zhongju, Wei Zhongli jiashu 魏仲舉, 魏仲立家塾	南宋	4
98	Yú shi jiashu 虞氏家塾	宋	1
99	Zeng shi jiashu 曾氏家塾	南宋	2

Table B.3
Shuyuan 書院 and *jingshe* 精舍 Publishers in the Song and Yuan

	Publisher/Printer	Date	Books
100	Chunzhuang shuyuan, Jian'an 建安 椿莊書院	元泰定 2 (1325), 明	1 (Y)
101	Huanxi Shuyuan 環溪書院	南宋-元	4 (S), 1 (Y)
102	Liu Junzhuo, Liu Hengfu Cuiyan jingshe 劉君佐, 劉衡甫翠巖精舍	元-明 (ca.1294-1588)	15(Y)
103	Liu Wen Hualong shuyuan (Liu Yingli) 劉文化龍書院 (劉應李)	元-明	1 (Y)
104	Liu shi Pingshan shuyuan 劉氏屏山書院	元至正間 (1341-67)	2
105	Liu shi Tianxiang shuyuan 劉氏天香書院	南宋	1
106	Liu shi Yunzhuang shuyuan 劉氏雲莊書院	(宋?)-元-明	1 (Y)
107	Tongwen shuyuan 同文書院	元末明初	1
108	Wuyi jingshe 武夷精舍	南宋	1
109	Xiang shi Jiangyin, Jian'an Shuyuan 項氏 江陰建安書院	宋寧宗間 (1195-1224)	1
110	Xiong He Wuyi shutang/Hongyuan shutang 熊禾武夷書堂/洪源書堂	元至元 26 (1289)	1+
111	Xiong shi Aofeng shuyuan 熊氏鰲峰書院	元至正 13 (1353)	1+
112	Yu shi Xiyuan jingshe 余氏西園精舍	元	2
113	Yú shi Mingfu zhai/Nanqi jingshe 虞氏 明復齋/精舍	元至正間 (1341-67)	2
114	Zhan shi Jianyang shuyuan 詹氏建陽 書院	元大德間 (1297-1307)	1
115	Zhang shi Meixi shuyuan, Jianyang 建陽張氏梅溪書院	元-明	3 (Y)
116	Zongwen jingshe/shuyuan 宗文精舍/書院	元	2

Table B.4
Publishers Working in the Jianning Area Under
Official Auspices in the Song and Yuan

	Publisher/Printer	Date	Books
1	Fujian Caozhi Wu Jian 福建漕治吳堅	宋 (ca.1265)	5
2	Han Yuanji (Jianning prefect) at Jian'an Junzhai 韓元吉建安郡齋	宋淳熙 2 (1175)	1
3	Jian'an Caosi Hui Zhao 建安漕司惠詔	宋紹興 17 (1147)	1
4	Ye Shi, Jian'an juan zhai 葉時, 建安君齋	宋寶慶 2 (1226)	1
5	Jianning fu Jian'an Shuyuan 建寧府建安書院	宋咸淳 1 (1265)	1
6	Jianning fu fuxue 建寧府府學	宋淳熙 7 (1180)	1
7	Jianning fu zhifu Wu Ge 建寧府知府吳革	宋咸淳 1 (1265)	1
8	Jianning junzhai 建寧郡齋	宋嘉定-寶慶間 (1208–26)	2
9	Jianyang xian zhixian Zhao Yuxun 建陽縣知縣趙與洵	宋淳祐 12 (1252)	1
10	Jianning lu Guanyi tiling Chen Zhi 建寧路官醫提領陳志	元至正 5 (1345)	1
11	Jianning lu Jian'an Shuyuan 建寧路建安書院	元至正 11 (1351)	1

Table B.5
Commercial and Private Publishers and Printers in the
Jianyang Area During the Ming
(*Note: The names of a few men related to publishers, who are listed
as collators or annotators are also included in this table.*)

	Publisher/Printer	Date	Books
1	An Rukun 安如坤	明萬曆 23 (1595)	1
2	Bao shi, Siming 四明包氏	明嘉靖 36 (1557)	1
3	Baoshan tang 寶善堂	明萬曆間	3
4	Baoyan tang 寶顏堂	明間	1
5	Baozhu tang 寶珠堂	明萬曆間	1
6	Bowen tang, Jian'an Shulin 建安書林 博文堂	明洪武–嘉靖 (1368–1566)	3
7	Cai Dangmian, Jianning fu 建寧府蔡當勉	明間	1
8	Cai shi Daoyi tang, Masha 麻沙蔡氏道義堂	明嘉靖 30 (1551)	1
9	Cai Yisuo 蔡益所	明末	2
10	Cai Youkun 蔡有鵾	明萬曆間	1
11	Cai Zhenghe, Jianyang Shulin Airi tang 建陽 書林愛日堂蔡正河	明萬曆間	1
12	Changgeng guan, Shulin 書林長庚館	明間	2
13	Chen Bangzhan 陳邦詹	明萬曆間	1
14	Chen Bangzhong 陳邦忠	明萬曆間	1
15	Chen Dezong (Yaowu) Cunde shushe, Shulin 書林陳德宗 (耀吾) 存德書舍	明萬曆間	5
16	Chen Errun, Shulin 書林陳爾潤	明崇禎間	1
	Chen Gongjing (Huaixuan/Yixin)—*see* Chen shi Cunren tang		
17	Chen Guojin, Tanyang 潭陽陳國晉	明萬曆間	1
	Chen Guowang (Yuwo)—*see* Chen shi Jishan tang		
	Chen Hanchu (Xiling)—*see* Chen shi Cunren tang		
18	Chen Hua 陳華	明正統 9 (1444)	1
19	Chen Huang 陳璜	明間	1
20	Chen Jingxue Dexing tang 陳敬學 德星堂	明嘉靖 19 (1540)	1
	Chen Kunquan Jishan tang—*see* Chen shi Jishan tang		
	Chen Lie—*see* Xie Tingjie		
21	Chen Qi 陳琦	明嘉靖 11 (1532)	1
22	Chen Qiao 陳喬	明間	1

Table B.5, *cont.*

	Publisher/Printer	Date	Books
	Chen Qiquan (Sunxian) Jishan tang—*see* Chen shi Jishan tang		
	Chen Shihuang Cunde tang—*see* Chen shi Cunde tang		
23	Chen Sun'an, Tanyang Shulin 潭陽書林 陳孫安	明天啓間	1
	Chen Xian (Yunxiu) Jishan tang—*see* Chen shi Jishan tang		
24	Chen Yingxiang, Shulin 書林陳應翔	明間	2
25	Chen Zhongxiu, Minsha 閩沙陳鐘秀	明嘉靖17 (1538)	1
26	—Chen shi Cunde tang 陳氏存德堂	明正德–萬曆 (1506–1619)	15
	—Chen Shihuang Cunde tang 陳世璜 存德堂	明正統3 (1438)	1
27	Chen shi Cunren tang 陳氏存仁堂		
	—Chen Gongjing (Huaixuan/Yixin) Cunren tang, Minzhong Shulin 閩中 書林陳恭敬(懷軒/以信)存仁堂	明末	5
	—Chen Hanchu (Xiling) Cunren tang, Shulin 書林陳含初 (錫齡) 存仁堂; one work co-published with Zhan Linwo 詹林我	明萬曆間	2
28	—Chen shi Jishan tang 陳氏積善堂	明間	16
	—Chen Guowang (Yuwo) Jishan tang 陳國旺(玉我)積善堂	明崇禎間	4
	—Chen Kunquan Jishan tang, Tanyang Shulin 潭陽書林陳崑泉積善堂	明萬曆間	3
	—Chen Qiquan (Sunxian) Jishan tang, Longxi tang 陳奇泉 (孫賢) 積善堂, 龍溪堂	明萬曆–天啓 (1573–1621)	8
	—Chen Xian (Yunxiu) Jishan tang 陳賢 (雲岫) 積善堂	明萬曆間	7
29	Chen shi Yuqing tang, Jian'an 建安陳氏 餘慶堂	元–明	3 (M)
30	Chen shi shutang 陳氏書堂	明洪武6 (1373)	1
31	Chongwen tang 書林崇文堂	明崇禎間	3
32	Chunzhuang shuyuan, Jian'an 建安椿莊 書院	元–明	2 (M)
33	Deju tang, Min Jian Shulin 閩建書林 德聚堂	明末 (1573–1643)	6
34	Dong Zuhe, Jianning 建寧董祖和	明崇禎8 (1635)	1

Table B.5, *cont.*

	Publisher/Printer	Date	Books
35	Fang Ruiquan, Min Jian 閩建方瑞泉	明萬曆28 (1600)	1
36	Fu Jishan, Zhuju Shulin 書林築居傅繼山	明末	1
37	Fu Ruochuan Jianqi jingshe 傅若川建溪 精舍	明洪武15 (1382)	1
38	Gong Chengjian et al., Jianyang 建陽 龔承薦等	明天啓 4 (1624)	1
	Huang Canyu (Yiwo), Jianyi Shulin—*see* Huang shi Cuncheng tang		
	Huang Cibo Jiyi shutang—*see* Huang shi Jiyi tang		
	Huang Erzhao Cuncheng tang, Yilin—*see* Huang shi Cuncheng tang		
39	Huang Qisheng Yizheng tang, Jianyang 建陽黃啓勝亦政堂	明萬曆32 (1604)	1
40	Huang Renpu (Yuanshu), Minzhong Tanyang 閩中潭陽黃仁溥 (元叔)	明萬曆40 (1612)	1
41	Huang Shibiao, Huang Shizheng 黃師表, 黃師正	明崇禎3 (1630)	1
	Huang Taifu, Tanyang—*see* Huang Zhengxuan		
42	Huang Xiuyu Xingzheng tang, Jianyi Shulin 建邑書林黃秀宇興正堂	明間	1
43	Huang Yaoyu (Zhengda) 書林黃耀宇 (正達)	明萬曆間	3
44	Huang Zhengbin 黃正賓	明崇禎13 (1640)	1
	Huang Zhengci Jiyi shutang—*see* Huang shi Jiyi shutang		
45	Huang Zhengfu Wenzong tang 黃正輔 文宗堂	明萬–天啓 (1573-1627)	4
46	Huang Zhengse 黃正色	明崇禎17 (1643)	1
47	Huang /Zhengxuan (Taifu), Shulin 書林 黃正選 (台甫／輔)	明	2
48	Huang Zhengzong Xingzheng tang, Xiuyu tang, Shulin 書林黃正宗興正堂, 秀宇堂	明萬曆間	1
49	Huang Zhizhai 黃直齋	明萬曆間	1
50	—Huang shi Cuncheng tang 黃氏存誠堂	明末	4
	—Huang Canyu/Yiwo, Jianyi Shulin 建邑 書林黃燦宇 (裔我)	明末	6
	—Huang Erzhao Cuncheng tang, Yilin 藝林 黃爾昭存誠堂	明末	2

Table B.5, *cont.*

	Publisher/Printer	Date	Books
51	—Huang shi Jiyi tang 黃氏集義堂	明弘治–崇禎 (1488–1644)	5
	—Huang shi Lewu shuxuan Jiyi tang 黃氏樂吾書軒集義堂	明萬曆 26 (1598)	1
	—Huang Cibo Jiyi shutang, Shulin 書林 黃次白集義書堂	明萬曆 32 (1604)	1
	—Huang Huai Jiyi tang 黃淮集義堂	明弘治 16 (1503)	1
	—Huang Zhengci Jiyi shutang 書林 黃正慈集義書堂	明萬曆間	2
52	Huang dian, Jianning cheng qu quan 建寧城衢泉黃店	明嘉靖 11 (1532)	1
53	Jian'an shutang (shusi) 建安書堂 (書肆)	明洪武間	4
54	Jiang Yi 江沂	明成化 (1465–87)	1
55	Jiang shi Mingya tang 江氏明雅堂		
	—Jiang Xiuquan, Shulin Mingya tang 書林 明雅堂江秀泉	明間	1
	—Jiang Yunming Mingya tang 江雲明 明雅堂	明萬曆間	1
56	Jiang shi Zongde tang, Shulin 書林江氏 宗德堂	明弘治–正德 (1488–1521)	3
57	Jin Kui (Gongtang), Min Jian Shulin 閩建 書林 金魁 (拱唐)	明萬曆間	1
58	Jinglun tang, Shulin 書林經綸堂	明萬曆 43 (1615)	1
59	Jiyou zhai, Min Shulin 閩書林芨郵齋 (in collaboration with Liu Longtian Qiaoshan tang—q.v.)	明萬曆間	1
60	Lan Ren (Lanshan shuyuan) 籃仁 (籃山書院); Lan Chu, Chong'an 崇安藍鋤 (reprint)	明建文 2 (1400)/ 明嘉靖 5 (1526)	1
61	Langhuan zhai, Min cheng 閩城瑯嬛齋	明間	1
62	Li Chunxi 李春熙	明萬曆間	1
63	Li shi jia, Jian'an 建安李氏家	明隆慶 6 (1572)	1
64	Li shi Jian'an shutang 李氏建安書堂	明洪武間	2
65	Liangcai tang, Jianning 建寧亮采堂	明間	1
66	Lin Yizhong 林一中	明成化 18 (1482)	1
	Liu Chaoguan (Shuangsong)—*see* Liu shi Anzeng tang		
67	Liu Chaojue Hezhi zhai, Shulin 劉朝爵合志齋	明間	1

Table B.5, *cont.*

	Publisher/Printer	Date	Books
68	Liu Chaozhen (collator) 劉朝箴 (校閱)	明萬曆36 (1608) preface	1
69	Liu Ciquan (Tingli), Shulin 書林劉次泉 (廷禮)	明萬曆38 (1610)	1
70	Liu Dahua (Yingxi), Tanyang Shulin 潭陽 書林劉大華 (應襲)	明萬曆元年 (1573)	1
71	Liu Heng Pingshan tang 劉亨屏山堂	明隆慶6 (1572)	1
72	Liu Hongyi (Hong) Shenduzhai 劉弘毅 (洪) 慎獨齋	明弘治-嘉靖 (1488-1566)	45+
73	Liu Huaichuan, Shulin 書林劉懷川	明天啓5 (1625)	1
74	Liu Huaishu 劉懷恕	明萬曆間	3
	Liu Hui—*see* Liu shi Mingde shutang		
75	Liu Jinxian (Junli), Shulin 書林劉近賢 (君麗)	明萬曆間	1
	Liu Kongdun—*see* Liu shi Qiao(mu) shan tang		
	Liu Kongjing—*see* Liu shi Qiao(mu) shan tang		
	Liu Kongnian (Sishan)—*see* Liu shi Qiao(mu) shan tang		
76	Liu Kuanyu 劉寬裕	明宣德10 (1435)	1
	Liu Liantai—*see* Liu shi Anzheng tang		
	Liu Longtian (Dayi, Shaogang)—*see* Liu shi Qiao(mu) shan tang		
77	Liu Puqing, Shulin 劉溥卿, 書林	明萬曆7 (1579)	1
	Liu Qin'en (Rongwu)—*see* Liu shi Liguang tang		
78	Liu Qizong 劉起宗	明嘉靖33 (1554)	1
	Liu Shizhong—*see* Liu shi Anzheng tang		
	Liu Shunchen (Biyu)—*see* Liu shi Qiao(mu) shan tang		
	Liu Taihua (Yingxi)—*see* Liu shi Mingde shutang		
79	Liu Tingbin 劉廷賓	明成化14 (1478)	1
80	Liu Tingji 劉廷吉	明成化15 (1479)	1
	Liu Tingqu—*see* Liu shi Mingde shutang		
81	Liu Wen Hualong shuyuan 劉文化龍書院	元, 明初	2 (M)
82	Liu Wen, Liu Tuan (Wenxiang) Yunzhuang shuyuan 劉穩, 劉端 (文祥) 雲莊書院	明正統-成化 (1436-65)	3
	Liu Wenshou—*see* Liu shi Cuiyan jingshe		
83	Liu Xingwo, Shulin Fusha 書林富沙劉興我	明崇禎間	2
84	Liu Xishu, Shulin Jingzhao 書林京兆 劉禧叔	明萬曆31 (1603)	1
	Liu Xixin (Yuanchu)—*see* Liu shi Anzheng tang		

Table B.5, *cont.*

	Publisher/Printer	Date	Books
85	Liu Yafu, Jianyi Shulin 建邑書林劉雅夫	明間	1
86	Liu Yan 劉剡	明正統 5 (1440)	1
87	Liu Yuanren, Shulin 書林劉元任	明間	1
	Liu Yutian (Dajin)—*see* Liu shi Qiao(mu) shan tang		
88	Liu Ze 劉澤	明正德7 (1512)	1
	Liu Zhaolin—*see* Liu shi Liguang tang/ge		
89	Liu Zhaoqing 劉肇慶	明間	1
	Liu Zongqi—*see* Liu shi Anzheng tang		
90	Liu shi Anzheng tang 劉氏安正堂— includes: Liu Shizhong, Shuhu 書戶 劉仕中, Liu Chaoguan (Shuangsong) 劉朝琯 (雙松), Liu Liantai 劉蓮台, Liu Xixin (Yuanchu) 劉希信 (元初), Liu Zongqi 劉宗器	明弘治-萬曆 (1488-1619)	80+
91	Liu shi Bencheng tang 劉氏本誠堂	明間	2
	—*see* also Liu shi Mingde shutang: Liu Tingqu		
92	—Liu shi Cuiyan jingshe 劉氏翠巖精舍	元,明	12(M)
	—Liu Wenshou Cuiyan jingshe 劉文壽 翠巖精舍	明宣德-景泰 (1426-1456)	3
93	Liu shi Huaide tang 劉氏懷德堂	明-清初	5+
94	Liu shi Huoyou tang 劉氏活幼堂	明正德 5 (1510) preface	1
95	—Liu shi Liguang tang/ge 劉氏藜光堂/閣	明末	2
	—Liu Qin'en (Rongwu) Liguang tang 劉欽恩 (榮吾) 藜光堂	明末	5
	—Liu Zhaolin Liguang ge, Tanyang 潭陽劉肇麟	明崇禎間	3
96	—Liu shi Mingde shutang 劉氏明德書堂	元,明弘治- 萬曆 (1488-1619)	18+ (M)
	—Liu Hui 劉輝	弘治-嘉靖 (1488-1522)	5
	—Liu Taihua (Yingxi), Tanyang Shulin 潭陽書林劉太華 (應襲)	明萬曆間 (1573-1619)	3
	—Liu Tingqu, Minshan tang/Bencheng tang 劉廷衢閩山堂/本誠堂	明嘉靖間	3
97	Liu shi Pujiyao shi 劉氏溥濟藥室	明宣德-成化 (1426-87)	2

Table B.5, *cont.*

	Publisher/Printer	Date	Books
98	Liu shi Qiao(mu)shan tang, Zhongxian tang 劉氏喬(木)山堂,忠賢堂, includes: Liu Longtian (Dayi, Shaogang) 劉龍田 (大易,少崗), Liu Yutian (Dajin) 劉玉田(大金), Liu Kongdun 劉孔敦, Liu Kongjing 劉孔敬, Liu Kongnian (Sishan) 劉孔年 (似山), Liu Shunchen (Biyu) 劉舜臣 (弼虞)	明末 (1573–1644)	70+
99	Liu shi Qingyuan shutang 劉氏慶源書堂	明弘治14 (1501)	1
100	Liu shi Rixin tang 劉氏日新堂	元,明嘉靖間	24 (M)
101	Liu shi Wenming shutang 劉氏文明書堂	明弘治14 (1501)	1
102	Liu shi Yi'an tang, Shulin 書林劉氏遺安堂	明間	1
103	Liu shi Yongde tang 劉氏永德堂	明嘉靖14 (1535)	1
104	Luo Shaozhu, Tancheng 潭城羅少竹	明間	1
105	Luo Yongzheng, Min Jian Shulin Duanyuan, 閩書林端源羅永正	明萬曆35 (1607)	1
106	Luo shi Jixian shutang 羅氏集賢書堂	明末	2
107	Mingshi shutang 明實書堂	明間	2
108	Mingya tang, Minjian 閩建明雅堂	明萬曆間	3
109	Qingxin tang, Shulin 清心堂, 書林	明萬曆15 (1587)	1
110	Qingyou tang, Jian'an 建安慶有堂	明間	1
111	Rongyu tang 容與堂	明	3
112	Shao shi Caoxuan tang, Masha 麻沙 邵氏草玄堂	明萬曆間	1
113	Shiqing tang, Tancheng 潭城世慶堂	明天啓2 (1622) preface	1
114	Shude tang 樹德堂	明萬曆間 (1573–1619)	1
115	Sizhi guan, Shulin 書林四知館	明末	2
116	Suihanyou, Shulin 書林歲寒友	明間	1
117	Sun Shichang, Chongan 崇安孫世昌	明萬曆47 (1619)	1
118	Tiandetang, Shulin 書林天德堂	明天啓–崇禎 (1621–44)	4
	Wang Huiyun—*see* Wang shi Sanhuai tang		
119	Wang Ji, Tanyang (collator) 潭陽王基 (校閱)	明間	1
120	Wang Jiejue (Xijiu) 王介爵 (錫九)	明間	1
	Wang Kunyuan—*see* Wang shi Sanhuai tang		

Table B.5, *cont.*

	Publisher/Printer	Date	Books
121	Wang Shuangquan (Jingren), Shulin 書林王雙泉 (景仁)	明隆慶 3 (1569)	1
	Wang Taiyuan—*see* Wang shi Sanhuai tang		
122	Wang Yangting Jiyu tang 王仰庭積玉堂	明萬曆間 (1573–1619)	2
123	—Wang shi Sanhuai tang 王氏三槐堂	明間	5
	—Wang Huiyun Sanhuai tang 王會雲 三槐堂	明萬曆 28 (1600)	1
	—Wang Kunyuan Sanhuai tang, Shulin 書林王崑源三槐堂	明末	1
	—Wang Taiyuan Sanhuai tang, Shulin 書林王泰源三槐堂	明間	1
	—Wang You, Min Shulin 閩書林王祐	明萬曆間	2
124	Wang shi (?) Shanjing tang 王氏 (?) 善敬堂	明正統–萬曆 (1436–1619)	11
125	Wang shi Qinyoutang 王氏勤有堂	明洪武間	2
126	Wang shi, Shulin Shuangxi 書林雙溪王氏	明間	1
127	Wei Binchen (Bang'ao), Tanyang 潭陽 魏斌臣(邦翱)	明間	1
128	Wei Qifeng, Shulin 書林魏岐鳳	明間	1
129	Wei jia, Shulin 書林魏家	明初	1
130	Wei shi Renshi shutang, Shulin 書林魏氏仁實書堂	明景泰–天啓 (1450–1621)	12
131	Wei shi, Jianxi 建溪魏氏	明萬曆 40 (1612)	1
132	Wencui tang, Shulin 書林文萃堂	明末	2
133	Weng Shaolu, Nancheng Shulin 南城書林 翁少麓	明末	8
134	Weng shi, Shulin Jianxi 書林建溪翁氏	明萬曆間	1
135	Wu Shiliang, Jianyang Shuhu 建陽書戶 吳世良	明萬曆間	2
136	Wu Yanming, Jianyang Shufang 建陽 書坊吳彥明	明萬曆間	1
137	Wu shi Sanyou tang 吳氏三友堂	明萬曆 10 (1582) preface	1
138	Xia Xiang, Jianyang Sanquli 夏相, 建陽 三衢里	明嘉靖 31–35 (1552–56)	1
139	Xia Zhenyu 夏振宇	明間	1

Table B.5, *cont.*

	Publisher/Printer	Date	Books
140	—Xiao shi Shijian tang 蕭氏師儉堂	明末 (1573–1644)	4
	—Xiao Mingfeng 蕭鳴鳳		2
	—Xiao Mingsheng (Jingwei) 鳴盛 (徹韋)		2
	—Xiao Zhiwei 簫徵韋		1
	—Xiao Shaoqu (Shixi) 蕭少衢/渠 (世熙) and Xiao Bingyi 蕭秉彝		20
	—Xiao Tenghong (Qingyun) 騰鴻 (慶雲)— mainly in Nanjing		17
141	Xie Tingjie 謝廷傑 and Chen Lie 陳烈	明隆慶 6 (1572)	1
142	Xie Zhaoshen, Jianning 建寧謝兆申	明萬曆 45 (1617)	1
143	Xiong Anben (Xianchu) 熊安本 (咸初)	明萬曆間	5
144	Xiong Bin 熊斌	明成化間	3
145	Xiong Bingchen 熊秉宸	明萬曆–崇禎 (1573–1644)	4
146	Xiong Bingmao (editor) 熊秉懋 (輯)	明萬曆間	1
	Xiong Chengjian (Shengnan)—*see* Xiong shi Zhongde tang		
	Xiong Chengye (Chongyu)—*see* Xiong shi Zhongde tang		
147	Xiong Damu 熊大木 (author, editor)	明嘉靖–萬曆間	4
148	Xiong Fei (Chiyu) Xiongfeiguan 熊飛 (赤玉) 雄飛館	明天啓–崇禎 (1621–44)	3
149	Xiong Fu, Shulin 書林熊輔	明間	1
	Xiong Fugui—*see* Xiong shi Zhongzheng tang		
150	Xiong Jianhua, Xiong Liangyan 熊劍化, 熊良彦	明萬曆 35 (1607)	1
151	Xiong Jianshan, Shulin 書林熊建山	明末	2
152	Xiong Jiuxiang (Jiuchi) 熊九香 (九敕)	明崇禎 9 (1636)	1
153	Xiong Liangcheng, Shulin 書林熊梁成	明間	1
	Xiong Longfeng Zhongzheng tang—*see* Xiong shi Zhongzheng tang		
154	Xiong Longfeng and Yu Yunpo 熊龍峰, 余雲坡	明末	1
155	Xiong Qingbo Chengde tang 熊清波誠德堂	明萬曆 24 (1596)	1
156	Xiong Renhuan, Shulin Yanshiju 書林燕石居 熊稔寰	明萬曆間	6
	Xiong Rongwu—*see* Xiong shi Zhongde tang		
157	Xiong Shaoquan, Shulin 書林熊少泉	明萬曆 11 (1583)	1
158	Xiong Tai'nan 熊台南	明萬曆元年 (1573)	1

Table B.5, *cont.*

	Publisher/Printer	Date	Books
159	Xiong Tidao 熊體道	明間	1
160	Xiong Xinshun, Jianyi Shulin 建邑書林 熊心舜	明萬曆間	1
161	Xiong Xinyu 熊心禹	明萬曆 24 (1596)	1
162	Xiong Xiu 熊繡	明成化 23 (1487)	1
163	Xiong Yanming (editor) 熊彥明 (輯)	明初	1
164	Xiong Yuan 熊瑗	明天順間	2
165	Xiong Yuqian shi jia 熊雨錢世家	明間	3
	Xiong Zhenyu—*see* Xiong shi Zhongde tang		
166	Xiong Zhizhang 熊之璋	南明隆武 2 (1646)	1
	Xiong Zongli Zhongde tang—*see* Xiong shi Zhongde tang		
167	Xiong shi Aofeng shuyuan 熊氏鰲峰書院	元,明	3 (M)
168	Xiong shi Boya tang 熊氏博雅堂	元,明	2 (M)
169	Xiong shi Dongxuan 熊氏東軒	明嘉靖 26 (1547)	1
170	Xiong shi Feilaishanren 熊氏飛來山人	明間	2
171	—Xiong shi Hongyuan tang 熊氏宏遠堂	明萬曆 23 (1596)	1
	—Xiong Yunbin (Tizhong) Hongyuan tang 熊雲濱 (體忠) 宏遠堂	明萬曆間	11
172	Xiong shi Houde tang 熊氏厚德堂	明正德 8 (1513)	1
173	Xiong shi Weisheng tang 熊氏衛生堂	元,明	2 (M)
174	Xiong shi Yifengcao tang 熊氏一峰草堂	明嘉靖 32 (1553)	2
175	—Xiong shi Zhongde tang 熊氏種德堂	元,明	8+ (M)
	—Xiong Zongli Zhongde tang (Zhonghe tang) 熊宗立種德堂 (中和堂)	明正統-成化 (1436–1487)	25+
	— Xiong Chengye (Chongyu) Zhongde tang 熊成冶 (沖宇)	明萬曆間	45
	—Xiong Chengjian (Shengnan) Zhongde tang 熊成建 (省南) 種德堂	明萬曆 29 (1601)	1
	—Xiong Zhenyu 熊振宇	明萬曆間	3
	—Xiong Rongwu, Shulin 書林熊榮吾	明末	1
176	—Xiong shi Zhongzheng tang 熊氏忠正堂		2
	—Xiong Longfeng Zhongzhengtang 熊龍峰 忠正堂	明萬曆間	7
	—Xiong Fugui Zhongzheng tang 熊彿貴 忠正堂	明萬曆 31 (1603)	1
177	Xiong shi □wu shushe 熊氏 □吾書舍	明間	1

Table B.5, *cont.*

	Publisher/Printer	Date	Books
178	Xiong shi, Tanyang Shulin Qianxi 潭陽書林前溪熊氏	明間	2
179	Xiuzhen tang 秀振堂	明崇禎16 (1643) preface	1
180	Xu Qiu'e, Jianning 建寧徐秋鶚	明萬曆9 (1581) preface	1
181	Xu Yingyuan (Renhe) 許應元 (仁和)	明嘉靖39 (1560)	1
182	Xu Zhongzhen, Min yi 閩邑徐鐘震	南明隆武間 (1645–46)	1
183	Yang Bingzheng 楊秉正	明萬曆46 (1618)	1
184	Yang Biqing 楊璧卿	明末	2
185	Yang Chunrong (Taizhai) 楊春榮 (泰齋)		
	—Huanwen tang, Shulin 書林煥文堂	明萬曆間	1
	—with Sanqu Shulin Wang Yingjun 三衢書林王應俊	明萬曆43 (1615) preface	1
	—Tongren zhai Sizhi guan 同仁齋四知館	明萬曆32 (1604)	1
186	Yang Chunyuan (Minzhai, Qiyuan), Jianyi Shulin 建邑書林楊春元 (閩齋,起元)	明萬曆間	9
187	Yang Dingjian 楊定見	明間	1
188	Yang Diqing, Shulin 書林楊帝卿	明間	1
189	Yang Fawu Shouren zhai 楊發吾守仁齋	明萬曆間	2
	—with Yu Wentai 余文台		1
	Yang Jiang—*see* Yang shi Qingbai tang		
	Yang Jucai (Suqing fu)—*see* Yang shi Qingbai tang		
190	Yang Kuixian 楊奎先	明萬曆間	1
191	Yang Liquan 楊麗泉 (Jin 金/Junlin 君臨) of Qingbai tang 清白堂 and Sizhi guan 四知館	明萬曆間	3
192	Yang Maoqing, Shulin 書林楊懋卿	明末	2
193	Yang Meisheng, Shulin 書林楊美生	明萬曆間	2
194	Yang Mingfeng, Shulin 書林楊明峰	明萬曆間	2
	Yang Qinzhai—*see* Yang shi Qingbai tang		
195	Yang Suqing (Ricai) 楊素卿 (日彩)	明末	2
196	Yang Taipu and Zhang Mingyu 楊太僕, 張明欲	明嘉靖間	1
197	Yang Wengao, Shulin 書林楊文高	明間	1

Table B.5, *cont.*

	Publisher/Printer	Date	Books
198	Yang Xianchun (Xinquan) Guiren tang, Qingbai tang 楊先春 (新泉) 歸仁堂, 清白堂	明末 (ca. 1579– ca. 1631)	10
199	Yang Xiaomin, Shulin 書林楊小閩	明間	1
200	Yang Yingchun, Shulin 書林楊應春	明萬曆間	2
201	Yang Yingzhao, Huayang shuyuan 華陽 書院楊應詔	明嘉靖 43 (1564)	1
	Yang Yongquan—*see* Yang shi Qingbai tang		
202	Yang Yuanshou Guiren zhai, Shulin 書林 楊員壽歸仁齋	明隆慶間	1
203	Yang Zhangfei Sizhi guan 楊彰飛四知館	明間	1
204	Yang shi Guiren tang 楊氏歸仁堂	明間	10+
205	—Yang shi Qingbai tang 楊氏清白堂	明間	5+
	—Yang Jiang Qingbai tang 楊江清白堂	明嘉靖 32 (1553)	1
	—Yang Jucai (Suqing fu), Shulin 書林 楊居寀 (素卿父)	明末 (1620–44)	5
	—Yang Qinzhai Qingbai tang 楊欽齋 清白堂; one title co-published with Yilin Jishan tang 藝林積善堂	明萬曆間	2
	—Yang Yongquan Qingbai tang 楊湧泉 清白堂	明嘉靖間	1
206	Yang shi Qingjiang tang 楊氏清江堂	明間	20+
207	Yang shi Sizhi tang 楊氏四知堂	明萬曆 39 (1611)	1
208	Yang shi Suichu shuwu, Jian'an 建安楊氏遂初書屋	明隆慶 6 (1572)	1
209	Yang shi Tongren zhai 楊氏同仁齋	明萬曆 28 (1600)	1
210	Yao Kui, Zhicheng 芝城姚奎	明嘉靖間	2
	Ye Cai—*see* Ye shi Guangqin tang		
211	Ye Huiting (Tianxi) Baohe tang, Jianyang Shulin 建陽書林葉會廷 (天熹) 葆和堂	明萬曆間	2
212	Ye Jinshan (Gui), Jinling Sanshan jie Jianyang 金陵三山街建陽葉近山 (貴)—in Jianyang and Nanjing	明嘉靖–萬曆 (ca. 1553–ca. 1597)	20+
213	Ye Jianyuan, Jianyang Shulin 建陽書林 葉見遠	明萬曆 36 (1608)	1

Table B.5, *cont.*

Publisher/Printer	Date	Books
Ye Jingkui—*see* Ye shi Guangqin tang		
214 Ye Jixuan Nansong tang, Minjian Shulin 閩建書林葉繼軒南松堂	明末	1
215 Ye Qing'an, Shulin 書林葉清庵	明萬曆2 (1574)	1
216 Ye Rulin (Jianquan), Shulin 書林葉如琳 (澗泉)	明萬曆10 (1582)	1
217 Ye Shun Tanxiang guan, Jianyi Shulin Cunxuan 建邑書存軒林葉順檀香館	明萬曆間	2
218 Ye Wanxing Quannan shushe 葉晥星泉南 書舍	明萬曆2 (1574)	1
219 Ye Wenqiao Nanyang tang 葉文橋南陽堂	明	1
Ye Xiu (Jingzhai)—*see* Ye shi Zuode tang		
220 Ye Yingzu, Shulin/Ye Junyu Juxing tang/ Ye Shulian 書林葉應祖/ 葉均宇 聚星堂/葉樹廉	明萬曆間	1
Ye Yiting (Yilan)—*see* Ye shi Zuode tang		
221 Ye Zhiyuan, Fujian Shulin 福建書林葉志元	明萬曆間	1
222 Ye shi Cuiqing tang 葉氏萃慶堂	明	2
223 —Ye shi Guangqin tang 書林葉氏廣勤堂	宋-元-明	7 (M)
—Ye Cai Guangqin tang 書林葉材廣勤堂	明間	1
—Ye Jingkui Guangqin tang 書林葉景逵 廣勤堂	明正統-成化 (ca. 1443–73)	3
—Ye shi Cuixuan Guangqin tang 書林葉氏 翠軒廣勤堂	明嘉靖間	2
224 Ye shi Nanshan tang, Shulin 書林葉氏南山堂	明嘉靖間	1
225 Ye shi Zuode tang 葉氏作德堂	明嘉靖間	
—Ye Xiu (Jingzhai) Zuode tang, Shulin 書林靜齋葉秀作德堂		1
—Ye Yiting (Yilan) Zuode tang 葉儀廷 (一蘭) 作德堂		8+
226 Yijing tang 一經堂	明崇禎間	1
227 You Jingquan, Shulin 書林游敬泉	明萬曆間	2
Yu Biquan Keqin zhai—*see* Yu shi Keqin zhai		
Yu Cangquan (Liangjin) Yiqing tang, Xin'an tang—*see* Yu shi Yiqing tang		
228 Yu Changgeng 余長庚	明末	1
229 Yu Changzong (author) 余昌宗 (撰)	明萬曆間	1

Table B.5, *cont.*

	Publisher/Printer	Date	Books
230	Yu Changzuo (Erxi) Zhifang tang 余昌祚 (爾錫) 直方堂	明萬曆-天啓 (1573–1627)	4
231	Yu Chaolong 余超龍	南明隆武2 (1646)	1
	Yu Chengzhang (Xianyuan)—*see* Yu shi Yiqing tang		
232	Yu Dongquan (Shangxun) 余東泉 (尚勳)	明末	2
233	Yu Gongren (Rengong, Yuanchang) Daran tang 余公仁 (仁公, 元長) 達然堂	明末-清初	3+
234	Yu Guangxi, Shulin 書林余光熹	明	1
235	Yu Heng 余恒	明萬曆47 (1619) preface	1
	Yu Hongchen—*see* Yu shi Zhengtian tang		
236	Yu Huiquan 余會泉	明	1
237	Yu Jing'an 余靖庵	明	1
238	Yu Jingyu 余敬宇	明萬曆間	1
	Yu Jinquan—*see* Yu shi Keqin zhai		
239	Yu Jiquan (Yingliang, Zhenru) 余繼泉 (應良, 眞如)	明萬曆間	2
	with Yu Xiangwo 余祥我		1
240	Yu Jiyue 余季岳	明	1+
241	Yu Kai 余楷	明末	1
	Yu Kaiming Santai guan—*see* Yu Xiangdou		
242	Yu Liangcai 余良才	明萬曆間	1
	Yu Liangjin (Cangquan) Yiqing tang, Minzhong—*see* Yu shi Yiqing tang		
	Yu Liangmu (Shaoyai) Zixin zhai—*see* Yu shi Zixin zhai		
	Yu Liangshi (Xiufeng) Yiqing tang—*see* Yu shi Yiqing tang		
243	Yu Mingquan, Minnan Shulin 閩南書林 余明泉	明萬曆間	1
	Yu Mingtai (Chengfu) Keqin zhai—*see* Yu shi Keqin zhai		
	Yu Mingwu (Liangxiang) Zixin zhai—*see* Yu shi Zixin zhai		
244	Yu Nanfu 余南扶	明萬曆間	2
245	Yu Qiru 余杞孺	明萬曆14 (1586)	1
246	Yu Shaojiang, Shulin 書林余少江	明末	1
	Yu Siquan (Zhangde) Cuiqing tang—*see* Yu shi Cuiqing tang		
247	Yu Siyai 余泗崖	明萬曆間	1
248	Yu Songxuan 余松軒	明萬曆間	1
	Yu Taiyuan Zixin zhai—*see* Yu shi Zixin zhai		

Table B.5, *cont.*

	Publisher/Printer	Date	Books
249	Yu Tingfu 余廷甫	明成化-弘治 (1465–1505)	2
	Yu Wanchu—*see* Yu shi Yiqing tang		
	Yu Wenjie Zixin zhai—*see* Yu shi Zixin zhai		
	Yu Wentai—*see* Yu Xiangdou		
250	Yu Xiancheng, Shulin 書林余憲成	明間	1
251	Yu Xiangdou 余象斗 (Wentai 文台) Santai guan 三台館, Shuangfeng tang 雙峰堂		70+
	—with Yu Siquan 余泗泉	明萬曆 34 (1606)	1
	—Yu Kaiming Santai guan 余開明三台館	明崇禎間 (1628–44)	4
252	Yu Xiangkui, Shuangfeng tang 雙峰堂余象奎	明間	1
	Yu Xiangwo (Yingxing), Shulin—*see* Yu shi Keqin zhai		
253	—Yu Xianke (Yingkong) Juren tang, Santai guan 余獻可 (應孔) 居仁堂, 三台館	明萬曆 46 (1618)	1
	—Yu Xianke Jingguan shi, Shulin and Zhan Shengmo Maozhai Jingguan shi 書林余獻可靜觀室, 詹聖謨茂齋	明萬曆 28 (1600) preface	1
254	Yu Xianyuan, Yu Yusheng Yiqingtang/Yongqingtang—*see* Yu shi Yiqingtang		
255	Yu Xiufeng Yiqing tang—*see* Yu shi Yiqing tang		
256	Yu Xiyu Zhongqing tang, Min Jian Shulin 閩建書林余熙宇忠慶堂	明萬曆 37, 39 (1609, 1611)	2
257	Yu Yinbo 余寅伯	明間	1
258	Yu Yingke 應科 (Yigeng 夷庚, Junhan 君翰, Qianji 謙吉) (editor) (輯)	明崇禎 6 (1633) preface	1
259	—Yu Yingqiu (Youlong) Jinsheng tang 余應虬 (猶龍) 近聖堂 (also involved with Yu shi Cuiqing tang)	明末-南明	16
	—with Yu Yingke, 余應科合刊	明崇禎元年 (1628)	1
260	Yu Yingyang Jingxian tang, Shulin 書林余應陽敬賢堂	明嘉靖-隆慶 (1555–69)	2
261	Yu Yingzhao Santai guan 余應召三台館	明末	2
262	Yu Youtang fengshan Shulin Jingshe 余有堂風山書林精舍	明嘉靖 3 (1524)	1
263	Yu Yuantao (Gongzhao) (editor) 余元熹 (公炤) (編)	明崇禎 17 (1644)	1

Table B.5, *cont.*

	Publisher/Printer	Date	Books
264	—Yu Yuanxi (collate) 余元熹 (參)	明崇禎9 (1636) preface	1
	—Yu Yuanxi (Dungu zhai) 余元熙 (敦古齋)	明末	2
	—with Yu Yuntai 余運泰	明末清初	1
265	Yu Yunbo, Shulin 書林余雲波	明末	2
	Yu Yunxi Zixin zhai—*see* Yu shi Zixin zhai		
	Yu Yusheng—*see* Yu shi Keqin zhai		
266	—Yu shi, Shulin 書林余氏	明正統6 (1441)	1
		明正德15 (1520)	1
	—Min Zhicheng Jianyi/Jianyang Shulin Yu shi 閩芝城建邑/建陽書林余氏	明萬曆間	9
267	—Yu shi Cuiqing tang 余氏翠慶堂	明末	13
	—Yu Siquan (Zhangde) Cuiqing tang 余泗泉 (彰德) 翠慶堂		57
268	Yu shi Jingxian tang 余氏敬賢堂	明嘉靖間	2
269	Yu shi Keqin zhai 余氏克勤齋		
	—Yu shi Keqin shutang, Shulin 書林余氏 克勤書堂	明正德4 (1509)	1
	—Yu Biquan 余碧泉	明萬曆間	10
	—Yu Chengzhang (Xianyuan) 余成章 (仙源)	"	10
	—Yu Jinquan, Shulin 書林余近泉	明間	4+
	—Yu Mingtai (Chengfu) 余明臺 (成富)	明萬曆間	4
	—Yu Xiangwo (Yingxing) Junfa tang, Yanqing tang 余祥我 (應興) 瀋發堂, 衍慶堂	明萬曆間	9
270	Yu shi Qindetang 余氏勤德堂	元, 明	2 (M)
	Yu shi Santai guan—*see* Yu Xiangdou		
271	Yu shi Shuangguitang 余氏雙桂堂	元, 明	4 (M)
272	Yu shi Shurui tang 余氏書瑞堂	明間	1
273	Yu shi Xin'an tang 余氏新安堂	明成化-嘉靖	4
	—*see* also Yu Cangquan (Liangjin) Yiqing tang, Xin'an tang		
274	Yu shi Xingwen tang 余氏興文堂	明嘉靖-萬曆 (1522–1619)	2
275	Yu shi Xiyuan (shu)tang/jingshe, Jianyang Shulin 建陽書林 余氏西園 (書) 堂/精舍	元-明	6 (M)

Table B.5, *cont.*

	Publisher/Printer	Date	Books
276	—Yu shi Yiqing tang 余氏怡慶堂	明萬曆間	5
	—Yu Cangquan (Liangjin) Yiqing tang, Xin'an tang 余蒼泉 (良進) 怡慶堂, 新安堂	明萬曆 30 (1602)	6
	—Yu Chengzhang (Yu Xianyuan) 余成章 (余仙源)	明萬曆間	7
	—with Yu Yusheng Yongqing tang 余郁生永慶堂		5
	—Yu Liangshi (Xiufeng), Jianyi Shulin 建邑書林余良史 (秀峰)	明末	15
	—Yu Wanchu 余完初	明萬曆 43 (1615)	1
277	Yu shi Yuejianshan fang 余氏躍劍山房	明末	4
278	—Yu shi Zhengtian tang 余氏正塡堂	明間	1
	—Yu Hongchen 余洪晨	明嘉靖7 (1528) 序	1
279	—Yu shi Zixin zhai 余氏自新齋	明	11
	—Yu Yunxi 余允錫	明嘉靖間	2
	—Yu Liangmu (Shaoyai) 余良木 (紹崖)	明萬曆間	14
	with Yu Taiyuan and Yu Wenjie 余泰垣, 余文杰	"	1
	—Yu Mingwu (Liangxiang) 余明吾 (良相)	"	3
	—Yu Mingwu and Yu Liangmu 余明吾, 余良木	"	3
	—Yu Taiyuan 余泰垣	"	5
	—Yu Wenjie 余文杰	"	3
280	Yú shi Wuben shutang, Jian'an 建安虞氏務本書堂	明洪武 21 (1388)	1 (M)
281	Yuanqing tang, Shulin 書林爰慶堂	明末	2
282	Yuantai tang, Tanyang Shulin 潭陽書林源泰堂	明萬曆間	2
283	Yuming tang 玉茗堂	明-清	2
284	Zhan Boyuan (Renting) Shulin 書林詹伯元 (仁廷)	明萬曆間	1
285	Zhan Bozhen (Yiting) Wenshu tang, Tanyang 潭陽詹伯禎 (怡廷) 文樹堂	明	1
286	Zhan Changqing Jiuzheng zhai, Jianyang Shulin 建陽書林詹長卿就正齋	明嘉靖間	5
	Zhan Chenger—*see* Zhan shi Xiqing tang		

Table B.5, *cont.*

	Publisher/Printer	Date	Books
	Zhan Chongquan Jingguan shi—*see* Zhan shi Jingguan shi		
	Zhan Daojian Jinxian tang—*see* Zhan shi Jinxian tang		
287	Zhan Fomei, Fujian Shufang 福建書坊詹佛美	明間	1
288	Zhan Guangsheng 詹光陞	明萬曆40 (1612)	1
289	Zhan Guozheng, Shulin 書林詹國正	明嘉靖32 (1553)	1
290	—Zhan Hengyuan Chuxian guan 詹恒袁儲賢館	明萬曆間	1
	—Zhan Hengzhong Chuxian guan, Jianyang Shulin 建陽書林詹恒忠儲賢館	明萬曆36 (1608)	1
291	Zhan Liang, Min-Jian Shulin Yizhai 閩建書林易齋詹諒	明萬曆間	2
	Zhan Linsuo—*see* Zhan shi Jinxian tang		
	Zhan Linyu (Shengze)—*see* Zhan shi Jingguan shi		
292	—Zhan Shengmo (Maozhai), Jianyang Shulin 建陽書林詹聖謨(茂齋)	明末	2
	—with Zhan Yaowo 詹耀我	明末	1
293	Zhan Shengxue (Mianzhai), Jianyang Shulin 建陽書林詹聖學(勉齋)	明萬曆16 (1588)	3
294	Zhan Tianxiang, Wuyi 武夷詹天祥	明	1
	Zhan Xiumin (Zhangjing)—*see* Zhan shi Xiqing tang		
295	Zhan Yanhong, Min Jian Shulin 閩建書林詹彥洪	明萬曆16 (1588)	1
296	Zhan Yizhai, Shulin 書林詹易齋	明萬曆間	2
297	Zhan Zhongrui, Shulin 書林詹鐘瑞	明末	1
298	Zhan shi 詹氏	明間	2
299	Zhan shi Jinde jingshe/shutang 詹氏進德精舍/書堂	明初	7
300	Zhan shi Jingguan shi 詹氏靜觀室		
	—Zhan Chongquan Jingguan shi 詹沖泉靜觀室	明萬曆間	3
	—Zhan Guangyue Jingguan shi 詹光岳靜觀室	明萬曆41 (1613)	1
	—Zhan Linyu (Shengze) Jingguan shi, Zhicheng Shulin 芝城書林詹霖宇(聖澤)	明末	22

Table B.5, *cont.*

	Publisher/Printer	Date	Books
301	—Zhan shi Jinxian jingshe/(shu)tang 詹氏進賢精舍/(書)堂	明弘治-萬曆 (1488–1619)	14
	—Zhan Daojian 詹道堅	明萬曆間	1
	—Zhan Linsuo, Shulin 書林詹林所	明萬曆間	2
302	Zhan shi Jiuzheng zhai, Shulin 書林詹氏就正齋	明	1
303	—Zhan shi Xiqing tang 詹氏西清堂	明嘉靖-萬曆 (1522–1619)	5
	—Zhan Chenger Xiqing tang 詹承爾西清堂	明嘉靖間	1
	—Zhan Xiumin (Zhangjing), Jianyang Shulin 建陽書林詹秀閩(張景)	明萬曆間	3
304	Zhang Daofu, Shulin 書林張道輔	明	1
305	Zhang Daye, Min Shulin 閩書林張大業	明萬曆間	1
	Zhang Mingyu—*see* Yang Taipu		
	Zhang Minyue, Shulin—*see* Zhang shi Xinxian tang		
306	Zhang Qipeng, Shulin 書林張起鵬	明萬曆間	4
307	Zhang Shiyong, Jianyang 建陽張世用	明成化 18 (1482)	1
308	—Zhang shi Xinxian tang, Shulin 書林張氏新賢堂	明嘉靖-萬曆 (1522–1619)	8
	—Zhang Minyue, Shulin 書林張閩岳	明萬曆間	2
	—Zhang Yixuan, Jianyi Shulin 建邑書林張裔賢	明萬曆間	3
309	Zheng Bishan, Jianyang Shulin 建陽書林鄭筆山	明萬曆間	1
	Zheng Jihua Zongwen tang—*see* Zheng shi Zongwen tang		
310	Zheng Mingshi, Min Shulin 閩書林鄭名世	明萬曆 37 (1609)	1
311	Zheng Mingxiang (Renwu), Min shulin 閩書林鄭名相(任吾)	明萬曆 44 (1616)	1
312	Zheng Neng Langhuan zhai, Mincheng 閩城鄭能瑯嬛齋	明萬曆間 (ca. 1603–19)	1
313	Zheng Ruiwo 鄭瑞我	明萬曆 44 (1616)	1
314	Zheng Shangxuan Renruitang, Fusha Shulin 富沙書林鄭尚玄人瑞堂	明崇禎間	5
315	Zheng Shaocong, Shulin 書林鄭少聰	明萬曆 14 (1586)	1
	Zheng Shaoyuan (Chungao)—*see* Zheng shi Lianhui tang, Shulin		
	Zheng Shaozhai—*see* Zheng shi Zongwen shutang		
	Zheng Shikui Zongwen tang—*see* Zheng shi Zongwen tang		
	Zheng Shixi (Dongsheng) Zongwen tang—*see* Zheng shi Zongwen tang		

Table B.5, *cont.*

	Publisher/Printer	Date	Books
	Zheng Wangyun—*see* Zheng shi Zongwen tang		
	Zheng Xishan—*see* Zheng shi Zongwen tang		
	Zheng Yihou—*see* Zheng shi Zongwen tang		
316	Zheng Yiqi, Tanyang Shulin 潭陽書林鄭以祺	明末	2
317	Zheng Yizhen, Tanyang Shulin 潭陽書林 鄭以楨	明萬曆間	1
318	Zheng Yunlin (Shirong) 鄭雲林 (世容)	明萬曆間	3
319	Zheng Yunting (Ziming), Shulin 書林 鄭雲亭 (子明)	明隆慶間	2
	Zheng Yunzhu (Shihao)—*see* Zheng shi Zongwen tang		
	Zheng Zhiqiao (Ziyi)—*see* Zheng shi Guangyu tang		
320	Zheng Zong 鄭熜	明嘉靖間	1
321	—Zheng shi Baoshan tang 鄭氏寶善堂	明間	2
	—Zheng Yunzhai (Shikui) Baoshan tang 鄭雲齋 (世魁) 寶善堂	明萬曆間	12
322	—Zheng shi Guangyu tang 鄭氏光裕堂	明萬曆間	3
	—Zheng Yihou (also Zongwen tang) 鄭以厚 (宗文堂)	明萬曆間	7
	—Zheng Zhiqiao (Ziyi) 鄭之僑 (子翼)	明萬曆 38 (1610)	1
323	Zheng shi Jiashu 鄭氏家塾	明嘉靖 14 (1535)	1
324	Zheng shi Juyuan shushe 鄭氏聚垣書舍	明萬曆間	1
325	—Zheng shi Lianhui tang, Shulin 書林鄭氏 聯輝堂	明萬曆 30 (1602)	1
	—Zheng Shaoyuan (Chungao) Lianhui tang/Sanyuan tang, Shulin 鄭少垣 (純鎬) 聯輝堂/ 三垣堂	明萬曆間	2
326	—Zheng shi Zongwen tang 鄭氏宗文堂	明正統–萬曆 (1436–1619)	32
	—Zheng Jihua 鄭繼華	明萬曆間	1
	—Zheng Shaozhai Zongwen shuyuan 鄭少齋宗文書院	明萬曆間	2
	—Zheng Shixi (Dongsheng) 鄭世襲 (東昇)	明嘉靖 38 (1559)	1
	—Zheng Wangyun 鄭望雲	明萬曆間	2
	—Zheng shi Wangyun lou, Shulin 書林鄭氏 望雲樓	明萬曆 6 (1578)	1
	—Zheng Xishan 鄭希善	明嘉靖 24 (1545)	1
	—Zheng Yunzhu (Shihao) 鄭雲竹 (世豪)	明萬曆間	23

Table B.5, *cont.*

	Publisher/Printer	Date	Books
327	Zhou Wenyi, with Liu shi Rixin shutang 周文儀, 劉氏日新書堂	明正德15 (1520)	1
328	Zhu Cangling, Zhitan 芝潭朱蒼嶺	明間	1
329	Zhu Meichu, Jianyang Shulin 建陽書林 朱美初	明崇禎6 (1633)	1
330	Zhu Renjing, Fujian 福建朱仁儆	明萬曆4 (1576)	1
	Zhu Renzhai—*see* Zhu shi Yugeng tang		
331	Zhu Shize 朱世澤	明萬曆間	2
332	Zhu Taoyuan and Zhu Mingwu, Shulin 書林朱桃源, 朱明吾	明萬曆間	1
333	Zhu Xun 朱詢	明間	1
334	Zhu Ying 朱瑩	明泰昌元年 (1620)	
335	—Zhu shi Yugeng shutang 朱氏與耕書堂	元-明	2 (M)
	—Zhu Renzhai, Shulin 書林朱仁齋	明萬曆間	2
336	Zhu shi Zunde shutang 朱氏尊德書堂	明宣德9 (1434)	1

Appendix C
Compiling the Bibliography
of Jianyang Imprints

Method of Compilation

The bibliography currently consists of 2,190 Jianyang imprints from commercial and private publishers, as well as those published under some kind of official auspices (e.g., Jianyang county, Jianning prefecture, Fujian circuit/province, etc.), from the Song, Yuan, Ming, and early Qing (Table C.1 below).

I have combined the publications of the commercial and "private" publishers, since it is often difficult to differentiate between these two categories. This is especially true since the clearly commercial Jianyang publications covered such a broad variety of subjects and ranged widely in the quality of editing, proofing, and physical production. Thus I have included the publications of the family schools (*jiashu*) and of the private academies (*shuyuan*) and halls of refinement (*jingshe*) of the Song and Yuan. In any case, they amount to only about 10 percent of the total for each period. In the Ming, since many Jianyang publishers apparently produced only a few imprints, the question arises whether they were "commercial" or "private." Usually examination of the imprints will resolve this uncertainty, and most of them clearly were products of the commercial printing industry. Finally, imprints produced under official auspices include those with some internal indication that they were issued by a government office, as well as those designating a government official (e.g., county magistrate of Jianyang, fiscal intendant of the Fujian circuit) as the publisher. I have included all the imprints that qualify according to this criterion, although whether a work was published for an official purpose or for arguably private motives by the official(s) involved is sometimes difficult to ascertain. The chances are that even if the official had a work printed for private reasons, he used the government resources available to him, and the resulting imprint would be comparable in quality and appearance to other publications issued by the same government agency.

The bibliography includes both extant works and those described in some detail in the annotated bibliographies of famous collections of Chinese rare books. It has been compiled using the printed or card catalogues of seventeen libraries in China, eleven in Japan, three in Taiwan, five in the United States, three in England, over 100 annotated bibliographies, an on-line Chinese rare books catalogue,[1] as well as a small number of titles in European libraries. Since 1992, I have spent some 36 months in China, Taiwan, Japan, the United States, and England, where I examined the original copies of 47 Song, 86 Yuan, and 735 Ming imprints. I have also examined over 200 facsimile reproductions (either of several leaves or of the entire extant work) of Jianyang imprints. These reproductions were most useful for Song and Yuan imprints, since access to the originals is particularly limited.[2]

As noted in Chapter 1, the bibliography is not complete, but I believe that it includes almost all the Song imprints (about 95 percent) and an overwhelming portion (over 90 percent) of the Yuan and Ming imprints. The most serious omission of which I am aware is probably the uncatalogued Jianyang imprints in European libraries. Moreover, the published catalogues of some Chinese libraries with major rare book collections are somewhat out of date, and/or the card catalogues are accessible only to the library staff, but this probably results in only a very small number of Jianyang imprints missing from the bibliography.[3] Yet another reason why the bibliography represents an undercount of known Jianyang imprints is that in the catalogues of libraries and private collections compiled over the centuries, a number of imprints are simply listed as *Jiankanben* 建刊本, since information from their physical appearance and from their contents (prefaces, colophons, etc.) does not allow a more precise characterization. Still other imprints are even more vaguely described as *heikouben* 黑口本.[4] Unless I found the evidence from examining the original imprint or from the description of the work in a bibliography to be sufficiently convincing, I have not included such works in my bibliography. Ultimately my decision whether or not to consider such a work a Jianyang imprint is based on my educated guess made after consulting Chinese rare book experts, when possible.

Other problems arise from uncertainties in dating the publication of many works or, more precisely, the carving of the printing blocks. Internal evidence, including a date in the printer's colophon, dates for the latest prefaces and postfaces, as well as physical features (style of the printed characters, the binding, the kind of paper, various features of the blockface) serve as the best guides for dating an imprint. When few of these clues are available, I had to resort to the best educated guess. The resulting margin of uncertainty may mean that an imprint can be no more precisely dated than as "late Southern Song or Yuan" or "late Yuan/early Ming." Of course, this uncertainty demonstrates how artificial a distinction is imposed by a mere change in dynasty. Consequently, to arrive at the numbers in the tables in this appendix, I had to make some arbitrary decisions about classifying such imprints in a given historical period. Again, this means that the figures in the tables serve far better as indications of publishing trends than as absolute counts of the number of imprints for a given category in a given period.

Finally there is the vexing problem resulting from copies of a work most probably printed from the same set of blocks, but with colophons of publishers from different locations, including Jianyang. The *Lu banjing* (see Chapter 2) with blocks apparently shared by printers in Suzhou and Jianyang (and possibly elsewhere) is one example. In that particular case, I did include this imprint in my bibliography, on the grounds that it indicated a kind of work that a Jianyang publisher felt was worth producing, as did his Suzhou counterpart (as well as something of the "homogenization" of the book trade in central and south China).

The bibliography has been compiled as a computer relational database using the program FoxPro,[5] so that it can be searched for publisher, title, author, subject (currently according to the *siku* classification), date, and library. Each entry also includes a "Memo" field with miscellaneous information. (See sample printouts below.) Using the database, I have been able to extract information very quickly, such as the number of imprints attributable to a particular publisher, and the topical distribution of imprints for a particular printer or historical period. Indeed, without the bibliography, this study would not exist.[6]

Use of the Siku Classification

Nearly all traditional Chinese bibliographies since the third century order their entries using some form of the *siku* system with its four major divisions of the Classics, Histories, Philosophy, and Belles Lettres. Thus, although the *siku* system (Table C.2 below) has a number of drawbacks, I decided to keep it for ease of reference since so many bibliographic sources (traditional annotated catalogues of various collections, card catalogues for the Chinese rare book collections of many libraries, as well as the on-line RLIN Chinese Rare Books Catalogue) also use it. Certain subcategories included under each of these divisions may seem anomalous compared with other systems of classifying knowledge, so that "Philosophy" includes what would be considered as sciences (e.g., medicine) or religions (Daoism and Buddhism). Nevertheless, using the subdivisions as given by the *Siku quanshu* editors and the further subdivisions by modern Chinese cataloguers,[7] the *siku* system is quite adequate for the sorting and searching the bibliographic database. The fineness of these subdivisions allows for great flexibility in regrouping works for any particular purpose. Furthermore, an extra "field" in the database can be used to designate imprints with a particular characteristic (e.g., examination literature) and made searchable. Consequently there is no reason why the major *siku* categories that seem totally incongruous according to modern Western bibliographic approaches should pose any obstacle to using the database of Jianyang imprints.

There are no universally recognized English translations of the names of the *siku* categories, but for most of them I have used those found in a number of well-known sources, such as the *Sung Bibliography*. In a few instances, I have differed from the organization used by the editors of the *Siku quanshu* project. For example, in the *xiaoshuo* 小說 category (3-12) under "Philosophy," I have placed only works known as "random jottings" (*biji*筆記/*suibi* 隨筆), which include many anecdotal works. Fictional works, which constitute a very different genre, have been classified as *xiaoshuo changpian* 小說長篇 under "Belles lettres." Thus in addition to the novel-length works, I have also included in this last category other varieties of fiction, such as the collections of court-case stories (*gongan*).

Table C.1
Summary of Statistics for Jianyang Imprints Bibliography

Type of publisher	Song	Yuan	Ming	Qing	Total
Commercial and private	192	220	1,664	ca. 30	2,106
Under official auspices	14	2	58	ca. 10	84
GRAND TOTAL					2,190

Table C.2
Distribution of Jianyang Commercial Imprints by Dynasty,
Ordered by the *Siku* System

Category	Song #	Song %	Yuan #	Yuan %	Ming #	Ming %
1-1 易 Book of Changes	7	3.6	8	3.6	24	1.4
1-2 書 Book of Documents	9	4.7	6	2.7	22	1.3
1-3 詩 Book of Poetry	6	3.1	12	5.5	21	1.3
1-4 禮 Book of Rites	10	5.2	3	1.4	28	1.7
1-5 春秋 Spring & Autumn Annals	9	4.7	10	4.5	34	2.0
1-6 孝 Book of Filial Piety	0	0.0	2	0.9	0	0.0
1-7 五經總義 Works on the Classics	1	0.5	3	1.4	8	0.5
1-8 四書 Four Books	3	1.6	13	5.9	39	2.3
1-9 樂 Music	0	0.0	0	0.0	0	0.0
1-10 小學 Philology	2	1.0	19	8.6	44	2.6
1 經部 Classics (TOTAL)	47	24.5	76	34.5	220	13.2
2-1 正史 Standard histories	20	10.4	3	1.4	10	0.6
2-2 編年 Annalistic histories	7	3.6	12	5.5	87	5.2
2-3 紀事本末 Narrative histories	0	0.0	0	0.0	0	0.0
2-4 別史 Separate histories	0	0.0	0	0.0	0	0.0
2-5 雜史 Miscellaneous histories	1	0.5	1	0.5	12	0.7
2-6 詔命奏議 Decrees & memorials	1	0.5	2	0.9	2	0.1
2-7 傳記 Biographies	2	1.0	4	1.8	21	1.3
2-8 史鈔 Historical excerpts	5	2.6	1	0.5	35	2.1
2-9 載記 Contemporaneous records	0	0.0	0	0.0	0	0.0
2-10 時令 Chronography	0	0.0	0	0.0	0	0.0
2-11 地理 Geography	3	1.6	3	1.4	14	0.8
2-12 官職 Bureaucracy	0	0.0	1	0.5	4	0.2
2-13 政書 Works on government	1	0.5	2	0.9	14	0.8
2-14 目錄 Bibliographies	0	0.0	0	0.0	1	0.1
2-15 史評 Historical criticism	2	1.0	0	0.0	23	1.4
2 史部 History (TOTAL)	42	21.9	29	13.2	223	13.4
3-1 儒家 Confucianists	9	4.7	6	2.7	67	4.0
3-2 兵家 Strategists	0	0.0	0	0.0	15	0.9
3-3 法家 Legalists	2	1.0	0	0.0	4	0.2
3-4 農家 Agronomists	1	0.5	0	0.0	0	0.0
3-5 醫家 Medicine	9	4.7	19	8.6	244	14.7
3-6 天文算法 Astronomy & mathematics	0	0.0	0	0.0	13	0.8
3-7 術數 Divination	0	0.0	1	0.5	92	5.5
3-8 藝術 Arts	0	0.0	0	0.0	10	0.6
3-9 譜錄 Catalogues	1	0.5	0	0.0	2	0.1

Table C.2, *cont.*

Category	Song		Yuan		Ming	
	#	%	#	%	#	%
3-10 雜家 Miscellaneous schools	4	2.1	1	0.5	35	2.1
3-11 類書 Encyclopedias	9	4.7	28	12.7	232	13.9
3-12 小說 Anecdotists	4	2.1	1	0.5	17	1.0
3-13 釋家 Buddhists	2	1.0	1	0.5	2	0.1
3-14 道家 Daoists	5	2.6	3	1.4	27	1.6
3-15 Collectanea 叢書	0	0.0	0	0.0	6	0.4
3 子部 Philosophy (TOTAL)	46	24.0	60	27.3	760	45.7
4-1 楚辭 *Elegies of Chu*	0	0.0	2	0.9	1	0.1
4-2 別集 Separate collections	39	20.3	30	13.6	144	8.7
4-3 總集 General collections	14	7.3	11	5.0	138	8.3
4-4 詩文評 Literary criticism	0	0.0	1	0.5	12	0.7
4-5 詞曲 Ci poetry & dramatic songs	2	1.0	5	2.3	55	3.3
4-6 小說長篇 Fiction	2	1.0	6	2.7	110	6.6
4-7 叢書 Collectanea	1	0.5	0	0.0	1	0.1
4 集部 Belles lettres (TOTAL)	57	29.7	55	25.0	461	27.7
TOTAL	192		220		1664	100.0

Table C.3
Medical Imprints from Jianyang in the Ming

	Category	No.		Category	No.
1	Medical classics 醫經	19	7	Prescriptions 方書 —General	9
2	Discussion of basic theories 基本理論	10		—Jin and Tang 晉唐 方書	1
3	Cold damage disorders 傷寒金匱	30		—Song and Yuan 宋元方書	9
				—Ming 明代方書	16
4	Methods of diagnosis 診法 (including 脈 診, pulse analysis)	16	8	Various medical fields 監證各科 —General discussions 監證綜合	26
5	Acupuncture, moxibustion, massage 針灸推拿 —Acupuncture 針灸通論 —Massage 推拿按摩	13 2	8.3 8.4 8.42	Internal medicine 內科 Gynecology 婦產科 Obstetrics 產科	7 8 5
6	Materia medica 本草 —Works with annotations and commentaries 本草注釋	1	8.5 8.52 8.6 8.8	Pediatrics 兒科 Smallpox 痘疹 Surgery 外科 Ophthalmology 眼科	16 12 5 5
	—General	1	10	Case studies 醫案醫話醫論 —Notes (on case studies) 筆記雜錄	1
	—Five Dynasties and earlier 五代以前本草	3			
	—Song, Jin, and Yuan 宋金元本草	2	11	Historical literature 醫史	3
	—Ming 明本草	5	12	Collectanea 綜合性 著作	13
	—Mnemonic verses and songs and handy references 歌括便讀	8	13	Veterinary medicine 獸醫	2
	—Diet therapy 食療 本草	1		TOTAL	244

NOTE: The medical categories used above are based on those in the *Quanguo Zhongyi tushu lianhe mulu* 全國中醫圖書聯合目錄, edited by the Library of the Research Institute for Chinese Medicine (Zhongguo zhongyi yanjiuyuan tushuguan) (Beijing: Zhongyi guji chubanshe, 1989).

Table C.4
Types of *leishu* from Jianyang in the Song, Yuan, and Ming

	Type	Song	%	Yuan	%	Ming	%
1	General	4	44.4	2	7.1	26	11.2
2	Exam 科業	2	22.2	3	10.7	21	9.1
3	Writing manuals 啓箚	2	22.2	6	21.4	33	14.2
4	Poetry 詩賦詞澡			11	39.3	39	16.8
5	Literary phrase references			1	3.6	22	9.5
6	Surnames 姓氏			2	7.1	4	1.7
7	Stories & Anecdotes 故事					54	23.3
8	Daily use 日用			3	10.7	31	13.4
9	Primers 啓蒙	1	11.1			2	0.9
	TOTAL	9		28		232	

NOTE: See Chapter 6 for explanation of *leishu* categories.

Table C.5
Divination Works from Jianyang in the Ming

	Category	No.
1	Numerology 數學	1
2	Metereology 占候	3
3	Geomancy 相宅相墓	36
4	Divination by *Yijing* 占卜	8
5	Fate, physiognomy 命書相書	30
6	Yin-yang, five agents 陰陽五行	9
7	Oneiromancy, etc. 雜術	5
	TOTAL	92

NOTE: Types of divination works based on and modified from those given in the *Siku quanshu tiyao* 四庫全書提要.

Table C.6
Sample Printout of a Page from the Jianyang Bibliography,
Showing Publishers Surnamed Chen, Arranged by Name and Then by *Siku* Order, for All Periods

Publisher	Title	Date	siku	Libraries	References
Chen Kunquan Jishan tang 陳崑泉積善堂	新刊京本伊洛淵源 14 卷 宋熹撰	明萬曆 4 (1576)	2-7	C541	中國善本書目史部 #4600
Chen Dezong/Yaowu Cunde shushe 陳德宗/耀吾存德書舍	六訂歷朝捷錄百家評林 5卷明顧充評無評趙秉忠輯評	明萬曆 29 (1601)	2-15	C140, C301	山東省特藏 #3762; 中國善本書目史部 #15550; LC 2000.25-36
Chen Guowang 陳國旺	新刻陳徐二先生評選史記則 8卷 明陳繼儒, 徐蕭穎撰	明崇禎間	2-15	C002	中國善本書目史部 #15604
Chen shi Cunde tang 陳氏存德堂	新鐫歷朝評林捷錄 4卷明顧充撰	明萬曆間	2-15	C721	中國善本書目史部 #15535
Chen Balang shupu 建鄴府陳八郎書鋪	賈誼新書 10卷	宋間	3-1		書林清話 3.25a; see NCL list for a 陳八郎宅 imprint; 後顧堂題跋 6.2a-b
Chen shi Jishantang, 陳氏積善堂	新刊校正京本武子本義3卷	明嘉靖間	3-2	J002	內閣文庫 p. 178b, 子 10函 8 號 ; LC 23.14-18
Chen shi Jishan tang 陳氏積善堂	無冤錄 3卷 元王與撰	明萬曆 3 (1575)	3-3	C193	中國善本書目子部 #1524 存 2卷 (中,下)
ChenDezong/Yaowu Cunde tang 陳德宗/耀吾存德堂	鐫圖註八十一難經圖4卷明張世賢補正撰明註王叔和脈訣鐫圖琮瑱5卷明張世賢圖解	明萬曆 34 (1606)	3-5	C590	中國善本書目子部 #1775; cf.懷德堂 edition; 中醫目錄 00224?

Table C.7
Sample Printout of a Page from the Jianyang Bibliography,
Showing Ming Philological Works (*siku* category *xiaoxue* 小學), Arranged by Name of Publisher

Publisher	Title	Date	*siku*	Libraries	References
Chen Qiquan, Shulin 書林陳奇泉	洪武正韻16卷 洪武正韻玉鍵1卷	明萬曆間	1-10	C2009, C2381	中國善本書目經部#5030
Chen Sun'an, Tanyang Shulin 潭陽書林陳孫安	刻太古遺蹤海篇 集韻大全31卷 明鄒書滽滽輯	明天啓間	1-10	C1642,...	杜信孚4.76a; 中國善本書目經部#4645
Huang Zhengci jiyi shutang, Shulin 書林黃正慈集集義書堂	大廣益會玉篇30卷 王篇廣韻指南 梁顧野王撰 唐孫強增字 宋陳彭年重修	明弘治17 (1504)	1-10	C001, U017	杜信孚5.27b; 北圖 p. 171, #7968; Edgren collection
Jianyang xian zhixian Zhou Shixian 建陽縣知縣同士顯	古今韻會舉要小 補30卷 明方日升撰	明萬曆34 (1606)	1-10	T001, U001, U004	NCL p. 86, #01120M3; 杜信孚3.18a); LC 20.62—same as 余彭德宗豢汁同刻 edition; Gest #TA166/696, Ch'ü 78; RLIN NJPX89-B3806; FYS 1988 says 1606, but dif. from LC 7.20-23; 王重民661b;福師大885.CW61; see also 鄭氏宗文堂 (嘉靖) FYS 1988.2: 222
Liu Hui Mingde shu tang 劉輝明德書堂	廣韻5卷	明間	1-10		
Liu Hui Mingde shu tang 劉輝明德書堂	大廣益會玉篇 30卷 梁顧野王撰 唐孫強增字 宋陳彭年重修	明弘治 (1488-1505)	1-10		杜信孚3.11a; FYS 1988.2: 221
Liu Longtian Qiaoshan tang 劉龍田喬山堂	鼎刻臺閣考正達 古韻律海篇大成 20卷 明曾六德	明萬曆32 (1604)	1-10	C852, J002	FYS 1988.2: 223; 杜信孚5.26a; 內閣文庫 p. 48b, 278函207號; 中國善本書目#4672

Reference Matter

Notes

Chapter 1

1. To cite but a few well-known works: Ye Dehui, *Shulin qinghua*; the essays on Chinese books in *Nagasawa Kikuya chosaku shū*; Tsien, *Paper and Printing*; and Zhang Xiumin, *Zhongguo yinshuashi*.

2. The two main printing centers in northern Fujian were Masha 麻沙 and Shu-fang 書坊, both located in Jianyang county in Jianning 建寧 prefecture. During the Song and Yuan, some commercial printers, schools, and private individuals in other places in Jianning, such as Chongan 崇安 in the Wuyi Mountains, and Jian'an 建安, were also active. Traditionally, however, imprints from the Minbei area have been called *Jianyang ben* 建陽本, or *Jian(kan)ben* 建刊本, or, usually in a derogatory sense, *Mashaben* 麻沙本; I use "Jianyang" to denote all books produced in this area.

3. My estimate is that Jianyang imprints constitute about one-seventh of all known books printed in China from the Song through the Ming dynasties.

4. Norman, "The Kienyang Dialect of Fukien"; Rawski, *Agricultural Change and the Peasant Economy of South China*; and Gardella, *Harvesting Mountains: Fujian and the China Tea Trade, 1757–1937*.

5. Of these two regions, only Sibao Changting is the subject of a systematic investigation that promises to yield important information for the history of the book in traditional China. See Brokaw, "Commercial Publishing in Late Imperial China: The Zou and Ma Family Businesses." Although certain aspects of Huizhou publishing have ben examined (e.g., Bussotti, *Gravures de Hui*), there has so far been no overall study.

6. A note on terminology: as used in this work, "printer" and "publisher" have the following meanings. If an individual or an establishment in charge of physically producing the woodblocks is also in charge of selecting, preparing, and marketing the

books produced, then he or it is not only the printer but also the publisher. This is usually the case for the commercial publishers referred to in this study. Sometimes, however, the printers were working for a private individual or government office, which made the production and distributing decisions, and that it would be more appropriate to designate that individual or office as the publisher. Although making this distinction between publisher and printer, I will use the two terms in a loosely interchangeable fashion throughout this work to avoid monotony.

7. The *tangming* often does little except to obfuscate the issue. Commercial printers in traditional China have called their printshops "hall" ([*shu*]*tang* [書]堂), "study" (*zhai* 齋), "house" (*zhai* 宅), "school" (*shuyuan* 書院), "hall of refinement" (*jingshe* 精舍), "pavilion" (*lou* 樓), and the like. It is best to consider other evidence about the work in deciding what kind of printer produced it.

8. Ming-sun Poon ("Books and Printing in Sung China," pp. 147–49) severely limits the number of "private" printers in Song China, as opposed to private-turned-commercial printers, among whom he numbers the family schools.

9. This is not the place for a review of the social history of the book in the West, a field that has grown enormously in the past four decades. Just an extensive listing of the bibliographic surveys would swell this note to several pages. Darnton's three essays reprinted in "The Printed Word" in *The Kiss of Lamourette* remain useful discussions of the field through the mid-1980s. Two more recent surveys are "Select Bibliography," in Cavallo and Chartier, *A History of Reading in the West*, pp. 443–71; and Rose, "The History of Books: Revised and Enlarged." The many studies that I found helpful in developing the ideas in this work include Febvre and Martin, *The Coming of the Book*; Eisenstein, *The Printing Press as an Agent of Change*; idem, *The Printing Revolution in Early Modern Europe*; Chartier, *The Culture of Print*; Chrisman, *Lay Culture, Learned Culture: Books and Social Change in Strasbourg, 1480–1599*; Hirsch, *Printing, Selling and Reading 1450–1550*; Martin, *Print, Power, and People in 17th-Century France*; Spufford, *Small Books and Pleasant Histories*. Other works will be cited in the course of this study.

10. For some interesting speculative observations on the earliest uses of print in China, see Strickmann, "The Seal of the Law: A Ritual Implement and the Origins of Printing"; Barrett, "The *Feng-tao k'o* and Printing on Paper in 7th-Century China"; and idem, "The Rise and Spread of Printing: A New Account of Religious Factors."

11. See Tsien, *Paper and Printing*, pp. 146–59. Because the surviving samples of such works are extremely few, we cannot say how numerous or widespread they were. Moreover, indications are that printing of popular works in the late Tang had some way to go before attaining the level of Song imprints. On the other hand, some Buddhist works, such as the *Lotus Sutra* (*Jin'gang jing* 金剛經), dated 868, were very well produced.

12. See Cherniack, "Book Culture and Textual Transmission in Sung China" for a detailed account of these events.

13. For brief sketches and primary references about these and other printers, see Febvre and Martin, *The Coming of the Book*, pp. 143–51.

14. See Wing-Tsit Chan, *Chu Hsi: New Studies*, pp. 77–81. Zhu Xi, who lived in various places in Jianning prefecture for much of his life, is claimed by the region as a quasi native son.

15. For Plantin, see Vöet, *The Golden Compasses: A History and Evaluation of the Printing and Publishing Activities of the Officina Plantiniana at Antwerp*. On the Crombergers, see Griffin, *The Crombergers of Seville: The History of a Printing and Merchant Dynasty*; on Manutius, M. Lowry, *The World of Aldus Manutius*; and on the Amerbachs, Hartmann and Jenny, *Die Amerbachkorrespondenz*. Admittedly the bulk of studies on individual publishers and publishing houses in the West, as well as the vast amount of materials yet to be examined, deal with those of more recent times, from the eighteenth century onward. For Chinese publishing history, a few pioneering studies give hope that for the past four centuries or so, we may also be able to construct a more detailed picture than for earlier periods. See, e.g., Widmer, "The Huanduzhai of Hangzhou and Suzhou: A Study in Seventeenth-Century Publishing"; Reed, "Gutenberg in Shanghai," on printing and publishing in Shanghai during the nineteenth and twentieth centuries; and the preliminary survey of surviving materials on publishing, printing, and bookselling businesses for the nineteenth and early twentieth centuries in Brokaw et al., "Mapping the Book Trade: The Expansion of Print Culture in Late Imperial China."

16. Both Liu Hongyi and Yu Xiangdou are discussed in Chapter 5 below. See Fig. 49b for one of these portraits of Yu Xiangdou.

17. It is worth noting that these sources tend to avoid matters concerning money in general, and no information is ever explicitly given on whether a man's income came from officeholding, land, teaching, printing, or any other activity.

18. Shen Jin's recent article, "Ming dai fangke tushu zhi liutong yu jiage," presents a number of prices for late Ming works, including a few from Jianyang. These numbers, however, may be problematic, not only because some of them seem out of line with what we know about Ming valuations of such works but also because most of the prices might have been set for Japanese buyers.

19. Darnton, "What Is the History of the Book," in *The Kiss of Lamourette*, esp. pp. 111–13. Indeed, although this article is useful as a preliminary framework for studying the history of the book in the West, consideration of publishers in late imperial China shows how we must modify Darnton's model for non-Western print cultures.

20. See Ivins, *Prints and Visual Communication*, pp. 47, 49–50. The differences between metal plate and woodblock illustrations are more complex than described here. See Chapter 2 for further discussion.

21. This is not always true, especially for better-quality books, such as albums with special full-leaf pictures. For two recent works that discuss illustrations in Chinese books of the Ming and Qing, see Clunas, *Pictures and Visuality in Early Modern China*; and Hegel, *Reading Illustrated Fiction in Late Imperial China*.

22. See, e.g., Inoue Susumu, "Zōsho to dokusho" and "Shoshi, shoko, bunjin"; and McDermott, "The Ascendance of the Imprint in Late Imperial Chinese Culture."

23. See Rose, "Rereading the *English Common Reader*," for just one critique of assuming an "implied reader." The number of works on readership and audiences for Chinese books has been growing recently, and relevant ones will be cited throughout this study.

24. For some regions other than Western Europe, studies of the history of the book, including the uses of print, have begun to appear in the past two decades. See

Rose, "The History of Books: Revised and Enlarged," for citations. In the case of Japan, Kornicki's recent study, *The Book in Japan*, traces a history of books very different from that for China, despite China's profound influence on Japan.

25. See, e.g., Johnson et al., *Popular Culture in Late Imperial China*, which includes several essays that give a good idea of the work being done on the social history of the Chinese book; as do the articles in *Late Imperial China* 17, no. 1 (1996), an issue devoted to print culture. For a brief survey of recent works on books and printing in late imperial China, see Brokaw, "On the History of the Book in China."

26. The bibliography is not complete, but I estimate that it includes almost all Song imprints (about 95 percent) and an overwhelming portion (over 90 percent) of the Yuan and Ming imprints. For details of the compilation of this computer database, see Appendix C.

27. For these genealogies, see Part B of the Works Cited, pp. 397–98.

28. In this study, the term *zu* 族 is translated "descent group," meaning a group of persons living in the same geographic region, sharing a surname, and claiming descent from one or several closely related ancestors. This deliberately loose description is preferable since it is nearly impossible to authenticate the earliest parts of these genealogies, and there is little information about any corporate activities among member of a given descent group. To avoid the monotony of using the term "descent group" too often, I will use the term "family" to mean the much the same thing. *Fang* 房 and *pai* 派 refer to branches and sub-branches of a clan, as set out in the genealogical tables.

29. The simplified family trees of the Liu, Yu, and Xiong printer families presented in Chapter 3 are based on the *shixi* in these genealogies.

30. For example, the well-known Liu shi Cuiyan jingshe was started by Liu Junzuo in the early Yuan and operated continuously until the mid-Ming (last dated imprint 1588). Fang Yanshou, in his study of the Liu genealogy ("Jianyang Liu shi keshu kao," pt. I, p. 207), was able to show that the Liu Hengfu mentioned as the printer of a late Yuan "Liu shi" edition most likely carried on the operation of the Cuiyan jingshe, since in the genealogy, he was mentioned as Liu Jun, *zi* Hengfu, and second son of Liu Junzuo. See also Table 2b in Chapter 3.

31. This reluctance to mention the printing activities of family members in the genealogies is not universal in China. For example, the activities of Sibao men involved in writing, printing, and selling books are mentioned explicitly in *their* genealogies. See Brokaw, "Commercial Publishing in Late Imperial China."

32. It is possible that the publishers belonged to branches of the descent groups other than those whose genealogies I examined. While I was in Jianyang, several people in positions to know told me that many genealogies had been destroyed during the Cultural Revolution, often by the families themselves. Nevertheless, there are probably extant genealogies in the Minbei area that are still in the families' possession and not yet discovered by scholars.

33. Liao Yingzhong actually lived and worked in Shaowu commandery, which borders on Jianning prefecture. His descendants moved to Jianyang, and the genealogy is still in the family's possession.

34. These are the counties under the administration of Jianning prefecture in the Ming. The number of counties and their boundaries changed from the Song through

the Republican era, but the boundaries of Jianning prefecture were largely unchanged for this period.

35. On Xiong, see *Jianyang xianzhi* (hereafter *JYXZ*) (1601 ed.), 8.17a; on Liu, *JYXZ* (1703 ed.), 6.69a.

36. On book collections, see *JYXZ* (1504 supplement of the 1453 ed.), *Dianji* section; 1553 ed., 5.19b–20a; 1601 ed., 2.18a–b; 1703 ed., 8.1a–13b. On the book market, see 1553 ed., 3.6a; for native products, see ibid., 4.33a.

37. For government prohibitions in the Yuan and Ming, see Wang Liqi, *Yuan-Ming-Qing san dai jinhui xiaoshuo xiqu shiliao*, pp. 3–18.

38. Shaowu was a commandery (*jun* 軍) during the Song and was raised to prefectural (*fu* 府) status in the Ming. The boundaries of Jianning and Shaowu have remained largely unchanged since the Song. The boundaries of Yanping (Nanjian 南劍) changed somewhat from the Song to the Yuan. All three areas were known as routes (*lu* 路) in the Yuan.

39. Actually, the average figure is not too useful since the annual rainfall is anywhere from 1,600 to 2,700 mm, depending on the specific location. See *JYXZ* (1994 ed.), pp. 90–92.

40. Richardson, *Forestry in Communist China*, pp. 3–5, 27.

41. In modern Jianyang county, forests occupy 69.6 percent of the mountains and 56.8 percent of the total area (Yang Shuixin and Huang Shou'en, "Jianyang zaozhi gujin tan," p. 13).

42. Hu Sanxing's commentary to the *Zizhi tongjian*, 275.12b–13a; quoted in Schafer, *The Empire of Min*, pp. 10–11n66. Hu's starting point is unclear—probably Jian'an (modern Jian'ou) or Yanping (Nanping).

43. Song Yingxing, *Tiangong kaiwu*, 2.36a; trans. from Sun and Sun, *T'ien-kung kai-wu*, p. 179.

44. For an account of a river journey from Shaowu to Fuzhou, see Franck, *Roving Through Southern China*, pp. 164–75. The six days from Fuzhou to Yanping was recorded by Beard, "The Foochow-Kienning Twentieth Century Limited," p. 15. For details of another upstream journey (from Fuzhou to Shaowu), see Bliss, *Beyond the Stone Arches*, pp. 4–10.

45. See Su Jilang (Billy Kee-long So), "Songdai Quanzhou ji qi nei lu jiaotong zhi yanjiu," for maps and a review (pp. 185–241) of primary sources relating to land and water routes from the Minbei region to Jiangnan and to other parts of Fujian. These routes are given in detail, with the names of stops every few tens of *li*, in the merchant route books of the Ming and later. One Jianyang edition (a reprint of an earlier work) is the *Shang cheng yilan* 商程一覽 printed in the Wanli period (1573–1620) by Liu Longtian's Qiaoshan jingshe (see Fig. 51, p. 229). For the routes described in the text, see Tao Chengqing, *Shang cheng yilan*, 1.2a–b, 2.54a, 2.56a–b.

46. Ashida, "Min Kampon ni okeru Binbon no ichi," p. 102.

47. Chen, "Yuan dai Fujian beibu ji qi linjin diqu suo shuchu de taoci qi," pp. 24–26.

48. Parker, "A Journey from Foochow to Wenchow Through Central Fukien," p. 89.

49. During the Qing and early Republican Periods, Hekou was the great black tea emporium, with merchants from all over China, large inns, tea firms, and ware-

houses. Ashida, "Min Kampon ni okeru Binbon no ichi," p. 99, notes the presence of a shrine to Tian Hou as well as *huiguan* for natives of Guizhou, Huizhou, and Ji'an (Jiangxi) in the early Republican period and possibly earlier. See also Fortune, *Two Visits to the Tea Countries of China*, 2: 160-61 and 223-24 for Hekou and chaps. 8-17 for the entire account of his journey from Ningbo to the Wuyi Mountains and Pucheng.

50. Wang Shimao, *Minbu shu*, p. 205.

51. Bielenstein, "The Chinese Colonization of Fukien Until the End of the T'ang," pp. 113-16. The series of maps in this book depicting the colonization of Fujian over time shows that the earliest settlers essentially followed the routes described in the text. See also Clark, *Community, Trade, and Networks*, pp. 7-18.

52. Clark, *Community, Trade, and Networks*, pp. 252-54.

53. See Chia, "Debatable Land: The Fujian-Jiangxi-Zhejiang Border Region During the Song."

54. A wide variety of early- and late-ripening rice has been grown in the Jianning region from the Northern Song onward. It was a Jian'an native who introduced dryland drought-resistant rice (*handao* 旱稻) from Jian'an to Lushan county in Ruzhou (Henan) while he was serving as magistrate there (Ho Ping-ti, "Early Ripening Rice in Chinese History," p. 208). The various local histories of the Minbei region (from the Ming) list a variety of rice, including a *lanni zao* 爛坭早 for soft mud, a *chigu he* 赤穀禾 suitable for growing on poor soil, and a *shoutian dao* 瘦田倒 (*sic*; the last character should be 稻) suitable for poor and mountainous land (*JYXZ* [1601 ed.], 3.26a-b).

55. Rawski (*Agricultural Change and the Peasant Economy of South China*, pp. 37-38), has suggested that perhaps this cropping arose because land rent was based only on rice and not on the wheat crop. According to *JYXZ* (1994 ed.), p. 201, double rice-cropping has been practiced since 1949, with good results from 1980 on.

56. Lu Yu in his *Cha jing* (ca. 780) mentioned northern Fujian tea favorably but gave no details.

57. For an overview of pre-Qing Minbei tea production and tea trade, see Robbins, "The Inland Fukien Tea Industry: Five Dynasties to the Opium War"; and Gardella, "Fukien's Tea Industry and Trade in Ch'ing and Republican China: The Developmental Consequences of a Traditional Commodity Export," pp. 25-67. (This material is not included in Gardella's recent book on the Minbei tea trade.) See also Chapter 3 below for more details.

58. See Gardella, *Harvesting Mountains*.

59. Chang Pin-tsun ("Chinese Maritime Trade: The Case of 16th Century Fuchien," p. 109) notes that in the sixteenth century China fir was very popular in Fujian for building houses.

60. Chang Pin-tsun (ibid., pp. 108-9) mentions deforestation of Longyan and Ningyang counties in Zhangzhou prefecture by the late Ming-early Qing; merchants (mostly from Zhangzhou and Quanzhou) had to go further inland in search of fresh supplies of timber.

61. On bamboo, see Chapter 2 of this work; and Chia, "Printing for Profit" (diss.), app. 2.

62. See Schafer, *The Empire of Min*, p. 63.

63. *Ba Min tongzhi* (hereafter *BMTZ*), *juan* 124, pp. 506–7. See also Zhu Weigan, *Fujian shigao*, 2: 57–63.

64. See Chia, "Debatable Land"; and Zhu Weigan, *Fujian shigao*, 1: 309–29 for Fan Ruwei, and 2: 129–31 for Ye Zongliu.

65. See Norman, *Chinese*, pp. 228–43, for an introduction to dialects spoken in Fujian. Norman argues that Min dialects are better divided into Eastern and Western groups rather than the older Northern and Southern groups.

Chapter 2

1. The technical aspects of Chinese woodblock printing have been treated in a fairly comprehensive fashion, mainly in Chinese, Japanese, and English works. The fullest bibliography of such studies (up to the early 1980s) can be found in Tsien, *Paper and Printing*, pp. 389–450; and a supplement by Tsien, "Zhongguo yinshua shi jianmu."

2. Guo Bocang, *Min chan lu yi*, 1.17b.

3. For a summary of Tang and Song references to bamboo paper, see Tsien, *Paper and Printing*, pp. 60–61; and Pan Jixing, *Zhongguo zaozhi jishu shigao*, pp. 89–92.

4. Ye Dehui (*Shulin qinghua*, 2.13a and 6.19b) mentions the Yu 余 family of Jian'an as papermakers during the Northern Song. The first remark says that an ink scroll by the Northern Song calligrapher Mi Fu contains the printed mark (*yinji* 印記) *Qinyou* 勤有. Qinyou tang was the name of the famous printshop run by Yu Zhi'an 余志安 in the Yuan. It is possible that the Yu family was engaged in papermaking or printing this early. The earliest dated extant imprint of the Qinyou tang is 1180.

5. Among the 840 or so Jianyang imprints I have examined, only about ten have paper that is cream-white and may have been made from pulp that was at least partly paper mulberry.

6. Song Yingxing, *Tiangong kaiwu*, *juan* 2, section 13 "Shaqing," p. 73a.

7. Rice straw paper (*caozhi* 草紙 or *daozhi* 稻紙) is listed as a common local product in Minbei local gazetteers (e.g., *Jianning fuzhi* [hereafter *JNFZ*] [1493 ed.], 10.7b). Although much less work is required to pulp rice straw than other materials, it forms a much weaker sheet with higher water retentivity than bamboo or other pulps. Thus, straw pulp is usually used in China in combination with some other pulp, largely to lower the cost.

8. Without modern chemical bleaching, it is not possible to produce bamboo paper as white as that from, say, paper mulberry (*chu* 楮) or blue sandalwood (*qingtan* 青檀), the chief material in *xuanzhi* 宣紙 traditionally produced in the Xuancheng 宣城 area in Anhui. The significantly greater proportion of lignin in bamboo fibers not only results in a paper initially yellow to dark brown in color but also accelerates the discoloring process accompanying aging. It also means that the natural bleaching by exposure to the sun used for *xuanzhi* is not useful and may be counterproductive, since the lignins would be photochemically induced to turn into darker compounds. Neither would the traditional way of airing and sunning books be healthy for those made from bamboo paper. See Chia, "Printing for Profit" (diss.), app. 2 for further details.

9. Here, we are talking specifically about aesthetic criteria for printing paper: white, off-white, or pale yellow paper that was relatively smooth (without extraneous bits of "chaff"), was flexible, and accepted ink without bleeding through the sheet. Although bamboo paper that meets these standards *can* be produced, the general prejudice against this material probably arose from the often lower quality control exercised during its production. In contrast, a more costly pulp from paper mulberry, mulberry, or blue sandalwood probably would have been subjected to a more careful treatment. Many local gazetteers in late imperial China were printed on bamboo paper. As a result, it took some time for scholars to overcome their prejudice and realize the value of these works for historical research.

10. Guo Bocang (*Min chan lu yi*, 1.17a–18b) talks about several kinds of paper made in inland Fujian, all called *kou zhi*. *Shu zhi* is routinely mentioned in Minbei local gazetteers; see, e.g., *JYXZ* (1553 ed.), 4.33a. Few sources mention which, if any particular kind(s) of bamboo was (were) preferred for paper-making in Fujian. The *Ba Min tongzhi, juan* 25 (p. 536), mentions *kuzhu* 苦竹 used for this purpose. Guo in *Min chan lu yi* (1.17a) says that in the four areas of Fujian that made paper, *huangzhu* 篁竹, *mazhu* 麻竹, *mianzhu* 綿竹, and *jianzhu* 椻竹 were also used. Christian Daniels has told me that modern papermakers in the area favor *mao zhu* 毛/茅竹 for paper-making, probably because its core cellulosic material occupies a proportionately larger amount of the stock than that of many other kinds of bamboo.

11. Terms to describe the colors of bamboo paper include dark/light tea-yellow (*shen/dan chahuang* 深/淡茶黃) and tan (*hehuang* 褐黃). See, e.g., Li Qingzhi, *Gushu banben jianding yanjiu*, tables 2–3, pp. 142–48.

12. In the usual Chinese method of paper-making by hand, a dipping or laid type of mold is used to catch the pulp from the vat. The mold is made of bamboo strips tied together with thread or animal hair. The indentations on the sheet made by the bamboo strips are known as laid lines and those by the thread or hair, chain lines. For a discussion and pictures of paper-making in general and "laid" molds, see Hunter, *Papermaking*, pp. 77–94.

13. Printing paper for traditional Chinese books is much thinner than that used in Western books. This is possible because the paper is printed on one side only and then folded in half. Thus the problem of the text from one leaf showing through another is not significant, even with cheap imprints.

14. Examples of Jianyang imprints using spliced paper include *Shi yi dexiao fang* 世醫得效方, 20 *juan* (1345 ed., Library of Congress call no. V G146.66 W42) and *Bai xiansheng zazhu zhixuan bian* 白先生雜著指玄編, 8 *juan* (Yuan ed., Naikaku bunko, 別 63 函 5號).

15. Sizing, as it is used in Western paper, was not generally applied to Chinese paper; the exceptions were papers intended for special purposes. Instead, ingredients added to the ink, such as animal and vegetable glue, served the same purpose as sizing in preventing the ink from running and spreading in uncontrolled fashion.

16. Su Yijian, *Wenfang si pu*, 4.10b. Su's remark is also the earliest Song reference to bamboo paper-making in the Jiangzhe region (4.7a). Cai Xiang, *Cai Xiang ji, juan* 34: "Wenfang si shuo," p. 632.

17. Su Shi, *Dongpo zhi lin*, p. 43; *Guiji zhi*, 17.42a; Mi Fu, *Shu shi*, p. 21. Zhang Xiumin (*Zhongguo yinshua shi*, p. 226) says that Mi Fu was the first to refer to paper from Fuzhou, but I have not been able to track down the reference.

18. Cai Xiang mentions paper from Jiqi in Anhui, as well as Fuzhou, Gutian, and Huizhou (all in Fujian), but not the Minbei region, in *Cai Xiang ji, juan* 34: "Wenfang si shuo," p. 628. The Fuzhou gazetteer of the late twelfth century, *Sanshan zhi, juan* 41, p. 8083, also mentions locally produced bamboo paper, which was used for printing some famous works, including the Pilu Tripitaka (1112–72). In general, mention of native products for a particular region in various pre-Ming sources are of limited use since they tend to list only tribute goods and products for which the region was famous (or infamous). Thus, a *leishu* compiled in the Yuan mentions for Jianning only books from Masha and Chonghua, tribute tea from Beiyuan, green-red brocade (another tribute good), paper quilts (probably from paper mulberry bark), and the famous rabbit fur black pottery. See *Shiwen leiju Hanmo quanshu* 事文類聚 翰墨全書, *Yiji* 乙集, 10下, p. 19b (1324 Wu shi Youyu tang 吳氏友于堂 ed., National Central Library [Taipei], Rare Book Collection no. 07932). Important though less interesting exports from Jianning, such as paper, rice, and lumber, are not mentioned. The ordinary, cheap Minbei bamboo paper seems to have been a long-lasting tradition; Guo Bocang (*Min chan lu yi*, 1.17b) in the Qing claims that for over two hundred years (when the Jianyang book industry no longer existed) buyers from Wuzhong (Taihu area around Suzhou) had annually ordered in advance all the following year's supply, leaving none for the Fujianese themselves. Recently, a book dealer from Hangzhou reminisced that prior to World War II he would go to Sanming 三明 and Ninghua 寧化 in inland Fujian (both south of Jianning) to buy cheap paper. When asked why he did not go to some other paper-producing area in Fujian, he replied that because he happened to have connections in those two areas, he could order the quantity needed, which would then be shipped to Hangzhou by train (Chia, interview notes for Yan Baoshan, July 8, 1999). Finding and buying paper (or any other commodity in large quantity) quite often depended on a fortuitous combination of circumstances having to do with availability, price, and business connections, something that has been true for many centuries in China.

19. Gazetteers include *JYXZ* (1553), 4.33a–b on paper and books as native products and 4.55a–b listing 23 kinds of bamboo; *JYXZ* (1601), 3.29b–30a listing kinds of bamboo and 3.35a giving different kinds of paper products; *JYXZ* (1832), *juan* 4, pp. 192–93 on bamboos and p. 196 on paper products; *JNFZ* (1493), 10.5b, listing 27 kinds of bamboo and 10.7a–b on paper and paper products; *BMTZ, juan* 25, p. 534 on paper and paper products and p. 536 on bamboo. Finally, detailed colored illustrations of bamboo paper-making in southern China from the mid-Qing period are reproduced in Schlieder et al., *Chinesische Bambuspapier Herstellung: Ein Bilderalbum aus den 18. Jahrhundert.*

20. Wang Shimao, *Minbu shu*, pp. 204, 205.

21. Song Yingxing, *Tiangong kaiwu* (1637 ed.), *juan* 2, section 13, "Shaqing"; Yang Zhongxi, *Xueqiao shihua xuji*, chap. 5, pp. 315–16. The two modern works are Hunter, *Papermaking*, esp. pp. 77–94 and 203–16; and McClure, *Chinese Handmade Paper*. McClure's book and another book of Hunter's, *Old Papermaking in China and Japan*, are useful mainly for the paper samples pasted in them. See Chia, "Printing for

Profit" (diss.), app. 2, for a review of the traditional technology of bamboo paper-making.

22. A number of these applications are listed in the local gazetteers' *chanwu* 產物 section. See note 9 to this chapter, and the descriptions of the paper samples in McClure, *Chinese Handmade Paper*.

23. In "16~17 seiki Fukken no shushi shōzō geijutsu," Christian Daniels argues that the great increase of demand for paper in the mid- and late Ming exerted pressure to economize on all aspects of the paper-making process.

24. For a general discussion of the literature of late Ming connoisseurship, see Clunas, *Superfluous Things: Material Culture and Social Status in Early Modern China*, chap. 1. For making paper for use in calligraphy and painting, see Corsi, "Scholars and Paper-Makers: Paper and Paper-Manufacture According to Tu Long's Notes on Paper." The *bomo* effect is mentioned in Corsi, p. 88n79. I am indebted to Harriet Zurndorfer for bringing this article to my attention.

25. See, e.g., Xie Zhaozhe, *Wu za zu*, 12.16a and 13.21a–b (for a translation of the second passage, see p. 185 of this work); and Hu Yinglin, *Shaoshi shanfang bicong* (*jia bu*). Hu says that for printing, Fujian paper ranks last, below Shunchang paper. By "Fujian," Hu is probably referring to Jianyang paper, since Shunchang is also in Fujian, just south of Jianyang.

26. See Tsien, *Paper and Printing*, pp. 240–51; and Zhang Xiumin, *Zhongguo yinshua shi*, pp. 38, 222–24, 333–34, and 536–38, for brief references to these works, almost all of which deal with ink for calligraphy and painting, but not printing.

27. Song Yingxing, *Tiangong kaiwu, xia juan*, section 16, *Danqing*, p. 44a, trans. by Sun and Sun, *T'ien-kung k'ai-wu*, p. 287.

28. Ink (*mo* 墨) is listed as a native product of Jianyang and other counties in Jianning in a number of gazetteers, including *JNFZ* (1493 ed.), 10.7b, and *JYXZ* (1553 ed.), 4.33b. Printing ink was most likely made from pine soot, which is cheaper than the lampblack made from various oils (tong, sesame, etc.), also produced in Jianyang, and results in an ink with a flat, dark black color.

29. Yu Feiyin, *Chinese Painting Colors*, p. 38.

30. du Halde, *The General History of China*, 2: 437; Lu Qian, *Shulin biehua*, p. 9. In contrast to inks for painting and calligraphy, I have found very few discussions of printing ink written in any period.

31. See Tsien, *Paper and Printing*, pp. 196–201, for a brief discussion of wood-blocks and carving techniques.

32. The actual process differs from place to place. Today, at both the Jinling kejingchu 金陵刻經處 (Nanjing) and the Jiangsu Guangling guji keyinshe 江蘇廣陵古籍刻印社 (Yangzhou), blocks of pearwood (*tangli* 糖梨) from Anhui are boiled to remove the sugar and other substances and then left to dry. Drying, ideally in a cool, airy place away from light and heat, is the essential step in the seasoning process. Carved blocks should be stored under the same conditions, standing upright, with a slight gap between adjacent blocks to allow the circulation of air. Vertical storage allows moisture and heat to penetrate the two carved surfaces equally and renders a block less liable to mechanical abrasions than if it were lying flat.

33. Although a harder wood is often preferable because it allows for the cutting of finer lines and more impressions, an extremely hard wood like maple or birch that

is very difficult and slow to cut is neither practical nor economical for the quantity of blocks required in book production.

34. In any case, a number of the woods commonly used for printing blocks are routinely listed in the local gazetteers. For example, camphor (*zhang* 樟), Chinese honey locust (*zaojia* 皂筴), boxwood (*huangyang* 黃楊) are listed in the *JYXZ* (1553 ed.), 4.56a–58b, pear (*li* 梨) on 4.39a, and Chinese date (*zao* 棗) on 4.42a.

35. See, e.g., K. T. Wu, "Ming Printing and Printers," p. 233; and Twitchett, *Printing and Publishing in Medieval China*, p. 46.

36. I learned about this problem from the book production department at the Jiangsu Guangling guji keyinshe, but the two related references in the literature that I have seen deal with wooden movable type rather than woodblocks. The first is in Jin Jian 金簡, *Wuyingdian juzhenban chengshi* 武英殿聚珍版程式: "If the weather turns hot and humid during the printing, the type will soak up ink and expand a little. In this case, stop work temporarily, place the forms in the open air for a time, and then resume printing" (trans. in Jin Jian, *A Chinese Printing Manual*, p. 12). The second reference is in the preface of Zhai Jinsheng 翟金生 to his own work *Niban shiyin chubian* 泥版試印初編 (1844). He talks of the superiority of his clay movable type over wooden type, which would give blurred impressions after just 200 copies, whereas the clay impression remained distinct after 100,000 copies (cited in Zhang Xiumin, *Zhang Xiumin yinshua shi lunwen ji*, p. 200).

37. This figure of 2,000–3,000 copies given by both the Guangling keyinshe and the Jinling kejingchu is quite low compared to the figure given by Tsien, *Paper and Printing*, p. 201, which says an initial 15,000 prints can be made and then another 10,000 after slight touching up. But Tsien does not specify the kind of wood. Actually, the equivalent of a "press run" usually was a much more modest number—between 20 and 200 copies. Since woodblocks lend themselves easily to printing on demand, it made better economic sense not to use ink, paper, and labor to produce more copies than can be sold at a given time. An excellent example is the use of blocks in a temple's possession to print one or more copies of a sutra on a donor's request. Finally, although woodblocks may seem permanent once carved, they are all too subject to the ravages of insects, fire, water, and changes in humidity and temperature, as well as damage by humans. Woodblocks are thus far more liable to destruction long before they wear out from too many impressions. At the Rongbao zhai 榮寶齋 art shop in Beijing today, frequent repairs are made even within 30–50 years, with about 10–20 percent of the blocks having to be replaced during that period of time.

38. Several considerations are important in making an impression by inking the block with a soft brush and then rubbing the back of the paper with a round stuffed pad. First, overinking should be avoided since it may result in ink accumulating in wells in the incised areas and/or smearing of areas that should print white. Second, overrubbing can damage both the paper and the block, especially if the latter is already worn or badly carved. On the other hand, the manual nature of this process in China means that it is more flexible and forgiving than the use of printing presses in the West to print from woodblocks.

39. Sometimes it is difficult to distinguish between a poor impression pulled off relatively unworn blocks and an impression from worn blocks. The characteristics

described above are usually reliable tests. For another example of impressions from worn blocks, see Fig. 7a.

40. Ideally, in an impression pulled from a printing block made of two or more pieces of wood held together by glue, nails, or dowels, the joint should not be visible. Blocks may be made from more than one piece of wood because the size of the leaf is unusually large, or because the original block is broken or partly destroyed and adding a new piece is easier than recarving the entire block.

41. See Ruitenbeek, "The *Lu Ban jing*: A Fifteenth-Century Chinese Carpenter's Manual," pp. 141–42 and plates 13–15. Whether the blocks were carted between these two places is uncertain, since each printer could have printed his "edition" at the same place and simply changed the part of the block with the printer's colophon.

42. These blocks were later repaired and served as the basis of the modern 1960 reprint. See the preface by Chen Yuan in this reprint edition. In addition to copies printed in or about 1642, there are more extant copies of the 1672 reprint by the magistrate's descendant Huang Jiuxi 黃九錫 at the family's Wuxiu tang 五繡堂.

43. *Fujian tongji* (hereafter *FJTZ*) (1922), *Fujian banben zhi*, 3a–b. See Chapter 5 for further discussion.

44. *JYXZ* (1703 ed.), "Yiwen zhi" 藝文志 section, 8.1a–8b.

45. These terms began to be prevalent in the Song. During the Tang and Five Dynasties, the term *yin*(*shua*) 印 (刷) seems to have been more common. After metal movable type printing prevailed starting in the late Qing, *yinshua* again became the usual term for printing. For other terms meaning a block-printed book, see Nagasawa Kikuya, "Kanpon no shurui to sono shōko," in *Nagasawa Kikuya chosaku shū*, 2: 25–26.

It is interesting that in the early period in Europe just after the advent of movable type, "cutting a book" (i.e., cutting the metal punches for the type) meant producing a book. Again the cutting of the punches was considered the operation that required the most skill in all the steps toward producing a movable-type book.

46. This creates an additional problem in determining when and where an extant work was printed. There is no routine way to resolve it, and each book has to be examined carefully before making any judgment on its likely date and place of printing.

47. This information is from the blockcarvers working today at the Jinling kejingchu and the Jiangsu Guangling guji keyinshe.

48. Cited by Cherniack, "Book Culture," p. 5 and note 1. For the forgery story, see Yang Lien-sheng, "The Form of the Paper Note *Hui-tzu* of the Southern Sung Dynasty," pp. 365–73; and Edgren, "Southern Song Printing at Hangzhou," pp. 46–51.

49. Aside from the part about punishing careless blockcarvers, the note reads somewhat like the advertising notes in commercial imprints, which also denounced competing editions for their sloppy production practices. See Chapter 5, pp. 177–78, for a translation of the note.

50. In Fig. 4a, notice that the same blockcarver, Yu Benli 余本立, was responsible for carving four leaves (1–4), which means that he carved two blocks (on both sides) in sequence. It was a common work practice for a carver to be assigned the engraving of several consecutive blocks.

51. This method is not foolproof since blockcarvers might have traveled as well as worked in groups. For a brief discussion of the problems encountered in using

blockcarver names in bibliographic analysis, see Edgren, "Southern Song Printing at Hangzhou," pp. 49–54.

52. Although 100 is a suspiciously round number, my observations of the block-carvers at the Jinling kejingchu and the Jiangsu Guangling guji keyinshe confirm that it is an estimate good to about ±10 percent. The best carver I observed carved about ten characters and repaired three in 50 minutes; a ten-hour workday would yield about a hundred characters.

53. The two sources are Beijing tushuguan, *Zhongguo banke tulu* (*ZBK*); and Seikadō bunko, *Seikadō bunko Sō-Gen pan zuroku*; both show a generous variety of Jianyang imprints for the Song and Yuan and provide information such as the dimensions of the block frame. As for the Cai family publishers' penchant for recording blockcarver names in the imprints, I have not yet found an explanation. The recent index for Song and Yuan imprints edited by Wang Zhaowen, *Guji Song-Yuan kangong xingming suoyin*, bears out the generalization that few Jianyang commercial imprints for these periods had blockcarvers' names. For the Ming, the *Mingdai kangong xingming suoyin* edited by Li Guoqing shows much the same tendency, again for Jianyang works. (Neither of these works are comprehensive for the periods they cover, but they do contain sufficient data on blockcarvers to permit generalizations.)

54. See Fig. 17a and further discussion of Wu Jian's imprints in Chapter 4. All five of Wu Jian's known publications (four extant) bear exactly the same colophon. See Edgren et al., *Chinese Rare Books*, entry 14, pp. 72–73, which shows the *Shaozi guanwu* 邵子觀物. Since this work has been severely trimmed and remounted on rebinding, no blockcarvers' names are shown.

55. See the notes to *ZBK*, fig. 196.

56. See Chapter 3 for further discussion.

57. Evidence for women blockcarvers in Jianyang is extremely rare. One unequivocal reference is found in a preface of a rhyming dictionary published in 1606, in which the writer states that women blockcarvers from a Jianyang printshop/bookshop engraved the blocks for the work 建陽故書肆婦人女子咸工剞劂. See the "Zai shu" 再叔 by Li Weizhen 李維楨, p. 8b, in *Gujin yunhui juyao xiaobu* 古今韻會舉要小補. Copies of this work are available in the rare book collection of a number of libraries, including the Library of Congress, Princeton Gest, and National Central Library (Taipei).

58. That the carvers engraved characters in wood for a living did not necessarily mean that they were literate. Judging from the way many of them rudely (mis)carved their names on the block (in several different ways), they were semi-literate at best. There is an anecdote about how an illiterate carver was paid with several copies of the finished imprint, which he promptly sold, in order to buy medicine (Brook, "Censorship in Eighteenth-Century China: A View from the Book Trade," p. 182).

59. Exceptions to this general anonymity of blockcarvers prove the rule. Those whose full names have been recorded tended to be masters of their craft, often capable of designing and drawing the illustrations that they then carved. In the page from the Yuan historical "plain tale" (Fig. 5a), the carver, Huang Shu'an, has recorded his name just beneath the caption on the right side of the picture. (It is unclear whether he carved both the pictures and the text or just the pictures.) For a discussion of Liu

Suming, a Jianyang native and well-known carver who worked during the late Ming, see Chapter 5.

60. A number of works deal with the basic aspects of the bibliographic analysis of traditional Chinese books. One standard work is the collection of essays by Nagasawa Kikuya, *Wa-kanjo no insatsu to sono rekishi* (reprinted as vol. 2 of *Nagasawa Kikuya chosaku shū*). A recent work in Chinese is Cao Zhi, *Zhongguo guji banben xue*. A brief work packed with information is Wei Yinru and Wang Jinyu, *Guji banben jianding congtan*. A work with much useful analysis of the rare books in the National Central Library collection is Li Qingzhi, *Gushu banben jianding yanjiu*. For other works, see Tsien, *Paper and Printing*, pp. 20–21.

61. McKenzie, "The Book as an Expressive Form," the first of the Panizzi Lectures, in idem, "Bibliography and the Sociology of Texts," p. 4. See also his essay, "Typography and Meaning: The Case of William Congreve."

62. There is no universal agreement on the definition of these terms. "Page layout" refers to the spatial arrangement of the text matter (number of characters per line, number of lines per page, size of the margins, indentations, justification). "Typography" in a broad sense refers to elements of book design such as the kinds and styles of letter type, the page layout, the organization of the main text and front and back matters, titling, etc. This is the sense in which the term is used by the English printer and graphic designer, Joseph Moxon, in his *Mechanick Exercises on the Whole Art of Printing* and by McKenzie in "Typography and Meaning." "Mise en page," which refers to much the same features as typography but with perhaps a greater emphasis on reading practices than on book design, is discussed by Laufer in "Les Espaces du livre" for imprints and "L'Espace visuel du livre ancien" for manuscripts. Even more comprehensive is "paratext," as used by Genette in *Paratexts* (p. 3) to mean that which links the author's intention, mediated by the book designers and producers, with the reader's response. All these concepts, after necessary modifications, are useful to a discussion of the Chinese imprint.

63. McKenzie, "Typography and Meaning," p. 89.

64. See fig. 1062 in Tsien, *Paper and Printing*, p. 44, which shows the "earliest extant version of the *Confucian Analects*" (dated 716); the interlineal commentary is written in smaller characters in a double column following the main text, which is written in a single column. It is possible, although not likely, that this arrangement was derived from very early imprints of other kinds of works. And as far as we know, the Confucian classics were first printed in the mid-tenth century, separately in Kaifeng and in Chengdu (Carter, *The Invention of Printing in China and Its Spread Westward*, pp. 67–81).

65. For references to the use of two-colored punctuation in the Tang, see Rolston, *How to Read the Chinese Novel*, p. 47; and also Mair, *T'ang Transformation Texts*, p. 138. It is interesting that a similar "blackening of the page" occurred in Western Europe during the fifteenth and sixteenth centuries, when the multicolored confected manuscript editions gave way to the largely unrelieved black of the early printed page; see Saenger and Heinlein, "Incunable Description and Its Implication for the Analysis of Fifteenth-Century Reading Habits," pp. 253ff.

66. See Zhou Wu, *Zhongguo banhua shi tulu*, figs. 6–10, for printed prayer sheets in a *shangtu xiawen* format; fig. 23 for a volume of "Efficacious charms from the

Tianzhu Temple" of Hangzhou (1232); and fig. 20 for a dazzling sutra, *Foguo Chanshi wenshu tuzan* 佛國禪師文殊圖讚 (dated 1210). This last work is discussed in Edgren, "Southern Song Printing at Hangzhou," p. 34 and shown in pls. 12–13. For an illustrated narrative in a Dunhuang manuscript (Stein 6983), see the International Dunhuang Project website, http://idp.bl.uk/bookbinding/chooser-frameset.html. Finally, Victor Mair has shown the intimate connection between pictures and transformation texts (*bianwen* 變文), although there are, strictly speaking, no surviving illustrated transformation text in the *shangtu xiawen* format; see Mair, *T'ang Transformation Texts*, pp. 17–27, for a list of what he considers *bianwen*.

67. Practices in the preservation and dissemination of manuscripts in times before printing, as described by Drège (*Les Bibliothèques en Chine au temps des manuscrits*), continued in much the same way after the growth of printing. In fact, not only did manuscript publishing survive into the Ming and Qing, but its interactions with print publishing also provide insights into what some of the literati elite perceived to be cultural limits to the uses of print, in contrast to the very different view of commercial publishers. Of course, there are clear and not so clear distinctions to be made between texts that existed only in one manuscript copy and those that were deliberately handcopied for dissemination (or publishing). But especially in the late Ming and Qing, a number of works, including now well-known novels such as *Jing Ping Mei* 金瓶梅 (The golden lotus) and *Shitou ji* 石頭記 (The story of the stone) circulated in manuscript form for some time before they were printed. The possibility remains that the authors or some of the manuscript readers may have been reluctant to see such works in print for a variety of reasons, including the loss of exclusivity among the happy few.

68. Here, as throughout this work, such generalizations apply to non-religious printed materials.

69. Traditionally, the size of the text area in a Chinese imprint is given in terms of the half-leaf or page. These measurements are good only to about ±0.4 cm since this is the average variation in the size of the carved block frame.

70. These guidelines are given in Wei Yinru and Wang Jinyu, *Guji banben jianding congtan*, p. 51. The number of characters refer to the main text. The commentary usually appears in smaller characters half the width of those in the main text and written in double columns (*shuanghang* 雙行). My examination of various texts leads me to believe that there was a general aesthetic ideal that the number of columns per page should be half the number of characters per column. See also the discussion on book size and format in Hegel, *Reading Illustrated Fiction*, pp. 78–97.

71. For example, consider a page 20 cm high x 13 cm wide, with 15 columns and 30 characters per column, and a center strip 1 cm wide. Each column would be $(13-0.5)/15 = 12.5/15 = 0.83$ cm wide. Assuming a generous 0.1 cm spacing on each side, each character would be $0.83-0.2 = 0.63$ cm wide. Since the column often begins with a blank space about 1 cm high, and assuming a generous spacing of 0.1 cm between characters, this means each character can be $[20-1-30(0.1)]/30 = 0.53$ cm high. Thus, even the commentary characters would be about 0.5 cm high x 0.3 cm wide and quite legible.

72. Appendix A lists 86 Song and Yuan *Jianben* for which these measurements are available. For comparison, see the dimensions of Song, Yuan, and Ming imprints given in tables 3.2–4 in Hegel, *Reading Illustrated Fiction*, pp. 83–84, 87, 88–95.

73. Zhang Xiumin, *Zhongguo yinshua shi*, pp. 161–62, gives dimensions of one work as 3.5 *cun* high and 2 *cun* wide (11.7 x 6.7 cm). Zhang also mentions smaller Song pocket editions, one measuring 8 by 4 cm.

74. That the original purpose of small editions was for convenience is mentioned by the Song writer Zai Zhi in *Shupu*, p. 27. Moreover, Chinese book connoisseurs through the ages have recognized that there are both well- and badly produced *jinxiang ben*. See, e.g., Sun Congtian, "Jianbie" 鑒別 (Discrimination) in his *Cangshu jiyao*, 3a, where he ranks most highly the very early pocket-size edition of the Thirteen Classics produced in Sichuan in the mid-tenth century. See also Ye Dehui, who notes the existence of manuscript pocket editions predating the printed ones in "Jinxiang ben zhi shi" 巾箱本之始, 2.2a–3a in *Shulin qinghua*.

75. Rolston (*How to Read the Chinese Novel*, pp. 65–66) gives a similar list for his "Paradigm of the Complete Commentary Edition" of a Chinese work of fiction.

76. Mair (*T'ang Transformation Texts*, p. 138) quotes from a note in a Dunhuang manuscript copy of the eighth chapter of the *Lotus Sutra* (Stein 2577) that states the emendator's concerns on what should or should not be punctuated, concerns that are equally relevant for printed texts.

77. Although punctuation marks occurred in Song imprints, few of the works from Jianyang were punctuated. For examples of punctuated Song imprints, see Ye Dehui, *Shulin qinghua*, 2.4a–5a; and Zhang Xiumin, *Zhongguo yinshua shi*, pp. 169–70. Zhang lists the various kinds of traditional Chinese punctuation marks found in Song imprints.

78. A useful and informative introduction to the critical apparatus in traditional Chinese texts is chapter 1, "Traditional Chinese Fiction Criticism," of Rolston, *How to Read the Chinese Novel*. For a discussion of the different kinds of commentaries, see esp. pp. 53–57. Since there are no standard translations for the various Chinese terms dealing with punctuation and commentary, I have adopted many of Rolston's translations: "marginal comments" (*meipi* 眉批 and *dingpi* 頂批) for those above the text frame, and "interlineal comments" for those placed after or on the side of the relevant passage of the main text.

79. *Juan* can be described as a chapter-like division of a book, although some scholars object to equating the Chinese and English terms.

80. Rolston, *How to Read the Chinese Novel*, p. 43. Although Rolston's remark refers specifically to literary works, it in fact applies far more broadly to all kinds of printed texts.

81. The lists of Song and Yuan imprints from different areas of China in tables 1 and 2 in Li Qingzhi, *Gushu banben jianding yanjiu*, pp. 92–108, do indeed suggest that the overwhelming majority of Jianyang imprints are *heikou ben*, in contrast to the *baikou ben* 白口本 from other areas. By the mid-Ming, *heikou ben* are too widespread to be of use in determining the provenance of an imprint. It is also interesting that of the *baikou ben* printed in Jianyang during the Song, most were probably *not* commercial imprints, i.e., they were published either by official agencies or by private

individuals. These same works are also the ones most likely to have blockcarvers' names recorded at the bottom of the *banxin*.

82. See, e.g., Xiao Dongfa, "Jianyang Yu shi keshu kaolüe," pt. 3, p. 239. Although this attribution is unproved, it is true that among Song editions, the ear is found frequently in Jianyang books. For an example of a Jianyang imprint in which the *erzi* gives the *juan* number, see the early Ming edition of *Zuantu huzhu Yangzi fayan* 纂圖互註揚子法言 in the Rare Book Collection of the National Central Library (Taipei), no. 05408.

83. Descriptions and illustrations of traditional kinds of Chinese bookbinding are available in a number of sources, including Martinique, *Chinese Traditional Bookbinding: A Study of Its Evolution and Techniques*; and the International Dunhuang Project's website, http://idp.bl.uk/IDP/bookbinding/chooser-frameset.html. As the website suggests, variations on the traditional methods of bookbinding that we now associate with printed fascicles were being employed for manuscripts by the Tang or perhaps earlier.

84. Of course, for later scholars, the calligraphy in an imprint is often most useful in dating the work as well.

85. Contrast, for example, the two kerchief albums in Figs. 7a and b. These calligraphic styles are further discussed in Chapters 4 and 6.

86. Strictly speaking, the term "colophon" refers to just the text within the colophon block or cartouche (if there is one). For *fengmian ye*, see Edgren, "The Chinese Book as a Source for the History of the Book in China." Of these cover pages, which might have been put on by the printer/publisher or bookseller, we have relatively few extant examples prior to the mid-Qing, since they would be the first sheet of the work to be torn off or damaged.

87. For Jianyang printers' colophons from the Song, see Figs. 14a–d. For other Jianyang printers' colophons and notices, see Poon, "The Printer's Colophon in Sung China," pp. 40–41, 46; some of these are reproduced in Tsien, *Paper and Printing*, p. 376. For brief discussions of the Chinese terms translated as "printer's colophon" or "printer's mark," see ibid., p. 39; and Ye Dehui, *Shulin qinghua*, 6.9a–10b. Poon (p. 49) suggests that unlike printers in other places (such as Hangzhou) who gave their address because their customers were mainly local, Jianyang printers did not since they had a nationwide distribution.

88. These prefaces may be written by the author (*zixu* 自序), an editor, the publisher himself (very rarely), an associate of any of these, or some well-known scholar or official. All too often in the last case, the preface may have been forged.

89. Although the many illustrations in printed Buddhist materials from the Tang on come immediately to mind, it is difficult to assess the prevalence of *tu* in non-Buddhist imprints before the Song because of their extreme scarcity. On illustrated works of fiction in late imperial China, see Hegel, *Reading Illustrated Fiction*, esp. chap. 4.

90. In Western art, "woodcut" refers to carving on the softer plankwood using knives and gouges, and "wood-engraving" refers to carving on the harder end-grain wood using gravers (burins), tools originally employed by metalsmiths. Generally speaking, woodcuts are characterized by bolder, stark black and white line figures, shapes or areas, often expressed by black lines. In contrast, wood-engravings are

marked by white-line designs and are capable of finer lines and greater subtlety of tonal gradations. Clearly, aesthetic considerations and the cultural and technological traditions in which a carver worked, as well as his/her own skill, must be taken into account. Technical and economic factors must have been decisive in the use of plankwood in Chinese block-carving of so much text. In turn, this meant that the *tu* incised on the same block would remain woodcuts.

It is interesting that when Thomas Bewick revived the art of wood-engraving in late eighteenth-century England, he achieved far better impressions using smooth "China" paper than the best available English book paper. Bewick originally obtained the paper from the packaging of tea from China. This certainly could not have been high-quality paper by Chinese standards and was probably made from bamboo. It became customary for wood-engravers to use "China," "India," or "Japan" paper for their proofs and their best impressions; see Ivins, *Prints and Visual Communications*, pp. 102–4 and Fig. 49.

91. This division of labor and consequent streamlining are not uncommon in graphic arts reproduction processes. The comment of Ivins (*Prints and Visual Communication*, p. 76), on a pragmatic statement about etching techniques by a seventeenth-century French manufacturer of prints is most apropos: "It would be hard to make a more practical definition of a tool for an average purpose, in which accuracy of representation of the personal characteristics of things was not as important as their reduction to an economically advantageous neatness of syntactical statement."

92. The *Book of Documents* (Fig. 9c) is from the Yuan and probably a Jianyang reprint of a Ningbo edition (Ming[zhou] ben 明[州]本). The first *Illustrated Xunzi with Various Commentaries* of Fig. 9d is a late Yuan–early Ming reprint of a Song edition from Jianyang, and the second one (Fig. 9e) is an early Ming imprint, probably from somewhere in Jiangnan. For another similar picture, see the reproduction from the Jin dynasty *Kongzi zuting guangji* 孔子祖庭廣記 in Zhou Wu, *Zhongguo banhua shi tulu*, fig. 83, p. 102.

93. See Clunas, "The Book Trade, Book Collection and the Dissemination of Knowledge in Late Imperial China," pp. 5–6; and idem, *Pictures and Visuality in Early Modern China*, pp. 104–11.

94. *Quanxiang* is written both 全相 and 全像, but the meaning is the same. The first is used in the Yuan *pinghua* from Jianyang and in some illustrated works from other areas in the Ming, and the second is used in the illustrated fiction and drama miscellanies from Jianyang during the Ming. The cover page for *Quanxiang pinghua Sanguo zhi* 全相平話三國志 from the Zhizhi reign period of the Yuan is reproduced in a number of works, including Zhang Xiumin, *Zhongguo yinshua shi*, front section; and Zhou Wu, *Zhongguo banhua shi tulu*, fig. 311.6. For further discussion of the historical *pinghua* from Jianyang, see Chapters 3–4.

95. See Tsien, *Paper and Printing*, fig. 1113, p. 153.

96. Of course this phenomenon is by no means limited to Chinese blockprinting. In Europe during the fifteenth and sixteenth centuries, stock woodcut illustrations were used again and again, within a single work, or in different imprints from the same publisher, or loaned by one printer to others; see Bland, *The Illustration of Books*, pp. 49–51. That both the text composed in movable type and the images

carved in woodblock could be printed together made this the most economical means of combining text and illustrations until the late sixteenth century.

97. See the *Qunshu kaosuo* printed by Liu Hongyi of Shendu zhai (1508–18); National Central Library (Taipei) Rare Book Collection, no. 07892.

98. There are portraits of both Cheng Yi and Zhu Xi in a primer on Confucian learning, the *Xiaoxue zhengmeng* 小學正蒙 (copy in the Naikaku bunko, 298 函 231號). The other Zhu Xi portrait is in *Zhu Wengong jiali zhengheng* 朱文公家禮正衡 (Naikaku bunko 經13函7號). Both works were published in the Ming Wanli period in Jianyang by Yu Mingwu.

99. By much the same logic, artists' imagined portraits of ancestors in genealogies served the important purpose of simply being included in the appropriate section of the compilation along with biographies and/or eulogies. Among the Jianyang genealogies I examined, the identical picture showed up as the portrait of an twelfth-century man of the You 游 descent group and of a fifteenth-century man of the Chen 陳 descent group. Apparently both men were Daoist adepts, since they are wearing Daoist headgear, the most notable feature of the illustration and probably the chief thing by which they were remembered. See "Zhen fu jiangjun Shilian gong xiang" 鎮撫將軍仕濂公像 in *Chen shi zongpu*, 2: 30b; and "Wen Qinglong tu Gejiuyan gong xiang" 文清龍圖閣九言公像 in *Guangping You shi zongpu*, 2.6b.

100. For a discussion on some of the contrasts between the more visually complex images in illuminated manuscripts and the visually simpler and more "reductive" woodblock prints in medieval and early modern Europe, see Camille, "Reading the Printed Image," in Hindman, *Printing the Written Word*, esp. pp. 266–74.

101. It is true, as Mark Halperin has reminded me, that at times "state and religious authorities also infused books with strong talismanic qualities," so that "producing massive amounts of texts brought considerable merit to the sponsors." But with the very notable exception that links the invention of block-printing with the dissemination of religious materials, such a motive for replicating texts seems to have contributed less to the evolution of the printed page than did non-religious commercial publishing.

Chapter 3

1. The two stories are "Wang Bai niang" and "Xu Xizai dao zi," Zhi zhi ding 支志丁, 1.1b–2a; for a summary and brief discussion, see Hansen, *Changing Gods in Medieval China, 1127–1276*, pp. 409–10. As Hansen notes, Hong Mai himself may well have learned about the events from flyers printed up to publicize them. The preface mentioning various places where the *Yi Jian zhi* had been printed is at the beginning of Yi zhi 乙志. A reproduction of the last part of the preface can be seen in the second plate for entry no. 84, of Seikadō bunko, *Seikadō Bunko Sō-Gen pan zuroku*, 2: 176.

2. See Chapter 1 for a discussion of the different kinds of publishers in imperial China.

3. There are a number of useful works on the history of Song (and to a lesser extent, Yuan) printing. Ming-sun Poon's 1979 dissertation, "Books and Printing in Sung China (960–1279)," presents a wealth of information on the subject, including a union catalogue of known Song imprints. Of the general histories on Chinese print-

ing, the most detailed discussions on Song and Yuan printing are Zhang Xiumin, *Zhongguo yinshua shi*, pp. 53–228, 280–333. The essays in Ye Dehui's *Shulin qinghua* remain basic reading for information and insights into traditional Chinese imprints. Part of K. Flug's 1959 book on Song printing has been translated by S. O. Fosdick into English as "Chinese Book Publishing During the Sung Dynasty (A.D. 960–1279)." One rich and insightful study is Susan Cherniack's "Book Culture and Textual Transmission in Song China." Thomas H. C. Lee's "Books and Bookworms in Song China: Book Collection and the Appreciation of Books" gives an overview of the topic. The coverage for the Yuan is much weaker. Aside from the sources already mentioned, K. T. Wu's 1950 article, "Chinese Printing Under Four Alien Dynasties" remains a useful reference.

4. Zhang Xiumin, *Zhongguo yinshua shi*, p. 59.

5. Poon, "Books and Printing in Sung China," pp. 8–27, gives some idea of the local distributions of imprints (official and nonofficial) in several ways, such as by the total number of known imprints for each circuit (table 1, p. 11), and by the number of printing centers in the three most prolific regions (Liangzhe, Fujian, and Chengdu fu circuits—maps 2–4, pp. 25–27). He also points out the problems of obtaining reliable distributions with the limited data available.

6. For the printing industry in Hangzhou during the Song, see ibid., esp. pp. 17–20, 156–62; Edgren, "Southern Song Printing at Hangzhou"; and Ichinose Yūichi, "Nan-Sō Rin'an no shoho ni kansuru ichi kōsatsu."

7. At the beginning of the Northern Song, the area was known as Jianzhou 建州, and then from 988 on as Jianning jun 建寧軍. In 1162 the local administration was upgraded to a superior prefecture, Jianning fu 建寧府. In the Yuan, the area was designated Jianning lu 建寧路; it reverted to Jianning fu in the Ming and Qing. The area covered by this prefecture was largely unchanged from the Southern Song on. For convenience, I will refer to the area as Jianning prefecture. For an outline history of the name and boundary designations of the Jianning area, see any of the prefectural gazetteers, such as *JNFZ* (1541 ed.), 1.1a–11b.

8. Based on the publishers' identification of themselves in their imprints and the histories of the printer families, the publishing industry in Masha was flourishing in the Song, but there is almost no mention of Shufang (or Shulin 書林) until the Yuan.

9. Other than for a brief period at the end of the Southern Song (1262–76), during which the county was renamed Jiahe 嘉禾, Jianyang county (with approximately the same boundaries) has existed since the late seventh century (*JYXZ* [1994 ed.], pp. 5–11).

10. Although the Southern Tang fell to the Song in 975, Fujian did not become a circuit under the Northern Song until 978. The history of the Minbei region during the Ten Kingdoms period is quite hazy. Some sources that touch on the subject are *FJTJ* (1922 ed.), *juan* 4–7; Schafer, *The Empire of Min*; Tanaka Seiji, "Goetsu to Binkoku to no kankei—Binkoku no nairan o chūshin ni shite"; and Clark, "The Consolidation of the South China Frontier: The Development of Ch'üan-Chou, 699–1126," pp. 130–76.

11. Very briefly, the number of households (*hukou* 戶口) in Jianning prefecture increased from 90,492 ca. 980 to 186,566 ca. 1080 to 196,566 ca. 1102. Figures are from various Song sources and can be found most conveniently in Liang Fangzhong,

Zhongguo lidai hukou tiandi tianfu tongji, pp. 135, 147, and 165. Figures from the Sui and Tang are not comparable since the boundaries of this area, variously known as Jian'an commandery (*jun*) and Jian prefecture (*zhou*), changed a number of times. The area's rapid population growth due to the influx of immigrants in the tenth and eleventh centuries leveled off by the late twelfth century.

12. In the late twelfth century, Zhu Xi even suggested that in times of food shortage, local officials might seek the assistance of local magnates to use their contacts with salt smugglers to obtain grain in eastern Guangdong and transport it over the mountains; see Zhu Xi, "Yu Jianning zhusi lun zhenji zhazi," in *Hui'an xiansheng Zhu Wengong wenji,* 27.4a–5a; cited in von Glahn, "Community and Welfare: Zhu Xi's Community Granary in Theory and Practice," p. 226.

13. For a discussion of the political and social conditions of this region in the Song, see Chia, "Debatable Land."

14. See Robbins, "The Inland Fukien Tea Industry"; and Gardella, "Fukien's Tea Industry and Trade," pp. 25–67.

15. The movement of the seasonal tea workers is suggested by Han Yuanji, who as prefect of Jianning sometime in the Chunxi period (1174–89) advocated that the local landlords put uncultivated land to use by persuading tea workers to become their tenants rather than dispersing each year; see his "Jianning fu (you) qin nong wen" in *Nanjian jiayi gao, juan* 18, p. 360 (trans. in part by Robbins, "The Inland Fukien Tea Industry," p. 131). See also Wang Zhongluo, "Cong chaye jingji fazhan lishi kan Zhongguo fengjian shehui de yi ge tezheng," p. 36; cited in Gardella, "Fukien's Tea Industry and Trade," p. 39.

16. Gardella, "Fukien's Tea Industry and Trade," p. 43, estimates that the Fujian tea tax in 1023 was only 2.74 percent of the national total.

17. Wang Zhongluo, "Cong chaye jingji fazhan lishi," p. 38; and *Wenxian tongkao* (hereafter *WXTK*): *zhengjue,* 5.22b.

18. Gardella, "Fukien's Tea Industry and Trade," pp. 55–56.

19. See von Glahn, "Community and Welfare," which gathers information from a variety of sources concerning the vicissitudes of rice production in the Jianning area in the Song. According to Chang Pin-tsun ("Chinese Maritime Trade," p. 160), the shipping of rice down the Minjiang to relieve shortages in the Fuzhou area continued in the Ming. Moreover, Minbei rice growers had to sell their rice to the coast in exchange for necessities like salt and silver (to pay their taxes) even if they had to subsist on poorer foods such as sweet potatoes.

20. See von Glahn, "Community and Welfare," p. 226.

21. Ibid., pp. 234–36.

22. According to Thomas H. C. Lee ("Neo-Confucian Education in Chien-yang, Fuchien, 1000–1400," p. 981), these family charitable granaries, or *yizhuang* 義莊, were related to the development of Neo-Confucianism and especially to Zhu Xi's social philosophy. The two charitable granaries he mentions were established by the Liu and the Xiong families in the thirteenth century.

23. Von Glahn, "Community and Welfare," p. 243.

24. Thomas Lee, "Neo-Confucian Education," pp. 961–64.

25. The two are the Chongning Tripitaka 崇寧大藏 (1080–1112) under the supervision of the Dongchan monastery 東禪院, and the Pilu Tripitaka 毘盧大藏

(1112–72) from the Kaiyuan Temple 開元寺; see Zhang Xiumin, *Zhongguo yinshua shi*, p.153.

26. Chaffee, *The Thorny Gates of Learning in Sung China*, pp. 149, 197.

27. Twelve of the sixteen families whose genealogies I examined claim Shaanxi or Henan as their place of origin.

28. The situation is less clear in the Northern Song. It could be that such men, like those from other regions, were more intent on establishing national rather than local networks, but we lack the evidence to substantiate this. Thomas Lee ("Neo-Confucian Education," pp. 954–61) argues that men from Jianyang had little national impact, politically or intellectually, in the Northern Song despite their examination success and that part of the reason may be due to their tendency to ally themselves with reformers, including Fan Zhongyan and later Wang Anshi. But again, the evidence seems too scanty to establish this for certain.

29. Chaffee, *The Thorny Gates*, p. 136. It seems, however, that at least some of the government schools suffered from neglect, at least by the Southern Song. Part of the reason may be due to the focus of local descent groups on their own schools. Zhu Xi, in a well-known essay, implies that it is rather ironic that although Jianyang imprints are sold everywhere, the county school lacks books, a situation being remedied by the donation of the magistrate; see "Jianning fu Jianyang xian xue cang shu ji," *Zhu zi daquan*, "Wen," 78.17a.

30. See Chapter 2 for a discussion of the materials used in woodblock printing.

31. Wang Qinruo et al., *Cefu yuangui*, 160.9a–b (2: 1192, in the Zhonghua shuju reprint).

32. Quoted in Carter, *The Invention of Printing*, p. 60.

33. Ye Mengde, *Shilin yanyu*, 8.7a.

34. There are about fourteen extant imprints published under official auspices in the Jianning area in the Song and only about two in the Yuan (see Table B.4, p. 285). This small number supports the argument that there was relatively little official interest in utilizing the resources for publishing available in the area.

35. Listed in Thomas Lee, "Books and Bookworms in Song China," p. 199.

36. Zhang Xiumin (*Zhongguo yinshua shi*, pp. 88–91) counts 37 Minbei publishers in the Song (all in the Southern Song except two) and 45 in the Yuan (pp. 290–91); for Hangzhou, he lists 20 in the Southern Song (pp. 70–71) and only four in the Yuan (p. 289). Gu Zhixing (*Zhejiang chuban shi yanjiu—Zhong-Tang Wudai Liang-Song shiqi*, pp. 106–56) gives about eighteen for Hangzhou for the Song and only four by name for the Yuan (*Zhejiang chuban shi yanjiu—Yuan-Ming-Qing shiqi*, pp. 62–67). Neither Zhang nor Gu gives an explanation for this drastic decrease, although their figure of four for the Yuan is most likely deceptively low, given other evidence of the continued publishing activity in that region. For the Southern Song, Edgren ("Southern Song Printing at Hangzhou," p. 4) lists eighteen, and Ichinose ("Nan-Sō Rin'an no shoho ni kansuru ichi kōsatsu"), twelve. The lower figures for Hangzhou compared with those for Minbei probably should not be taken too seriously. None of these studies counts Hangzhou publishers who designate themselves as *shuyuan* or *jingshe* or *jiashu*, probably on the assumption that these were not commercial establishments. Zhang, however, is inconsistent in counting such publishers for Minbei. My estimates include all such publishers.

37. This seems a common problem when studying the history of the Chinese book trade. For example, a similar difficulty occurs in trying to determine whether the various publishers or booksellers named Chen in Southern Song Hangzhou were related to each other; see Edgren, "Southern Song Printing at Hangzhou," pp. 36ff, and his Bibliography A.

38. While we have no evidence of this practice for Jianyang publishers, studies of commercial publishers in other areas in later periods prove this to be the case; see, e.g., Brokaw, "Commercial Publishing in Late Imperial China," p. 60.

39. The lists of Jianyang publishers during the Song and Yuan in Zhang Xiumin, *Zhongguo yinshua shi*, pp. 88–91, 290–91, tend to give as different publishers two names that vary only by the place attached to them—e.g., Jian'an Liu shi Nanjian shutang and Masha Liu shi Nanjian shutang. I have combined them on the grounds that many Jianyang area printers tended to be quite casual about place-names, and in many cases, the evidence from the imprints strongly suggests that the same printer may have used two slightly different names. Each name in Tables B.1–4 has at least one imprint that can be credited to it.

40. Because of the uncertain meanings of these terms, I retain the Chinese original rather than use an English term.

41. Thomas Lee, "Neo-Confucian Education," pp. 975–80; see also Walton, *Academies and Society in Southern Sung China*, pp. 38ff.

42. See Li Hongqi (Thomas Lee), "Jingshe yu shuyuan."

43. *JYXZ* (1832 ed.), *juan* 5, p. 225. Since the Tongwen tang (no. 41) was supposedly in Jian'an, it may not have had any connection to the academy of the same name (no. 107) in Jianyang County. For the latter, see Xiong He's 熊禾 commemorative essay on its re-establishment, "Chongjian Jianyang Shufang Tongwen shuyuan shu," in *Xiong Wuxuan xiansheng wenji*, 4.57–58. Note that this essay has one of the earliest references to Shufang (as opposed to Masha) in relation to the Jianyang book industry.

44. See Hu Yin 胡寅, *Peiran ji* 斐然集, 21.12b–13a, for the early Southern Song figure; and *Song huiyao: xuanju* 22.6b, for the 1186 figure.

45. See, e.g., the work *Yanshi shiji* 嚴氏詩緝 described in Wang Zhongmin, *Zhongguo shanbenshu tiyao*, pp. 11b–12a.

46. See Wang Zhaowen, *Guji Song-Yuan kangong xingming suoyin*. The numbers mentioned above may not appear impressive, but blockcarvers' names are listed in exceptionally few Song and Yuan Jianyang imprints, and these few are government or private publications. Although there is no general rule as to who was included in Chinese genealogies, the sixteen from Minbei that I examined rarely included persons lacking in education and some kind of economic and cultural standing. Given their low social status, it is a matter of extreme good luck even to find the blockcarvers' names in the genealogies. This is based on the usually terse comments in the genealogical tables section of the genealogy, the most likely place where the less distinguished members of the family would be noted. Of course, there is always the possibility that the blockcarvers either belonged to other branches of the descent groups than those of the publishers or were not related to the latter.

There were also women blockcarvers in the Song and Yuan, although we do not know if any of them were from Jianyang; see, e.g., Yang Shengxin, "Cong *Qishazang* keyin kan Song-Yuan yinshua gongren de ji ge wenti." See note 57 in Chapter 2 for a reference to women blockcarvers in Jianyang during the late Ming.

47. *Liu shi zupu,* 4.12–3. Those involved in the more scholarly aspects of producing a book, such as the editors, collators, proofreaders, and copyists, were less likely to be exclusively members of the printer's family.

48. See the bibliographic notices in Ye Dehui, *Shulin qinghua,* 3.20a–b; and Fu Zengxiang, *Cangyuan qunshu jingyan lu,* pp. 195, 196. The Huang Shanfu edition is shown in figs. 177–78 and the Liu Yuanqi edition in figs. 181–82 in *ZBK.*

49. Both men claimed to be *jinshi.* I am not including in this discussion prominent men like Xiong He and Liu Yingli, who belonged to the non-publishing branches of their descent groups, since they were best known as scholars, *Daoxue* adherents, and founders of academies in Minbei, rather than as publishers.

50. On the problems of finding or identifying a printer in a given genealogy, see Chapter 1. The two Liu genealogies I examined have yielded the greatest number of names: six of eleven printers in the Song and five of nine in the Yuan. Yu Zhi'an (Table B.1, no. 65), from the Yuan, is the only printer from that family who has been identified with fair certainty in the genealogy examined. Xiong He (Table B.3, no. 110) is found in the *Tanyang Xiong shi zongpu.* I have been unable to find other printers in the genealogies I examined. This may be because they are not recorded at all, or recorded under a different name, or belong to another branch of the descent group with a different genealogy.

51. *Liu shi zupu* 麻沙劉氏族譜 and *Jingzhao Liu shi Zhen fang zongpu* 京兆劉氏貞房宗譜, listed in Part B of the Works Cited. The first work consists of twelve volumes, the first ten being the genealogical tables for the Yuan 元 and Li 利 *fang* of the Liu descent group of Masha, and the last two volumes being the work "Jianzhou Liu shi zhongxian zhuan" 建州劉氏忠賢傳, which contains biographical sketches, prefaces to different editions, commemorative essays (e.g., on the founding of schools), etc. The other genealogy for the Zhen 貞 *fang* is incomplete; only five volumes are extant. The first volume has prefaces to earlier editions of the genealogy, commemorative essays, and the like, many of which are the same as those in the other genealogy. The other four volumes consist of genealogical tables for the Zhen *fang.* Table 2a showing the connections between the various branches and subbranches of the Liu descent group in the Jianning area was constructed using information chiefly from the essays in these two genealogies. The more detailed family tree of Table 2b for the Xizu beipai 西族北派 is based mainly on the Zhen *fang* genealogical tables.

52. The six Song publishers who come from the Ao branch are Liu Lizhi 立之 (Liu Jiangshi zhai, Table B.1, no. 21), Liu Lin 麟 (no. 23), Liu Shugang 叔剛 (no. 26), Liu Dan 旦 (the printer of Tongpan zhai 通判宅, no. 27), Liu Zhongji 仲吉 (no. 30), and Liu Zhongli 仲立 (no. 31). Their names (marked by an asterisk) can be found in the simplified family tree for the Xizu beipai in Table 2b. Liu Rixin (no. 24), one of other three Liu printers in Table B.1 is probably from the Xizu nanpai (Table 2c) or Dongzu (Table 2d), since his one known imprint has a preface by Liu Bing 炳 mentioning Rixin as a relative. There is insufficient information to determine whether the last two printers, Liu Chengfu 誠甫 and Liu Yuanqi 元起 (Table B.1, no. 19 and Table B.2, no. 96) are related to the other Liu men. The two Yuan publishers

from the Ao branch are Liu Junzuo and his son, Liu Jun 鈞 (Hengfu衡甫), of the Cuiyan jingshe (Table B.3, no. 102).

53. See *Song shi* (hereafter *SS*) 401: 12170–73; *Songren zhuanji ziliao suoyin* (hereafter *SRZJ*), 5:3914; and his biography in various local histories, such as *JYXZ* (1832 ed.), *juan* 11, pp. 424–25.

54. Liu Yingli is associated with the Liu Wen Hualong Academy (Table B.3, no. 103) as well as the Wuyi Academy (no. 110).

55. *SS* 459: 13462–63.

56. Some men from the more prominent branches of the Liu descent group were also involved to a small extent in printing. The few books they produced tended to be their own families' genealogies or works of one of their famous ancestors. These works were often published in collaboration with, or under the aegis of, an academy; see Fang Yanshou, "Minbei Liu shi deng shisi wei keshujia shengping kaolüe," pp. 223–30; and idem, "Minbei shisi wei keshujia shengping kaolüe," pp. 211–12.

It is likely that the earliest and possibly some later parts of the genealogies were forged. Thus I have been unable to find any record of Liu Ao or his two brothers in Tang sources (although biographical sketches of Liu Ao appear in several Ming and Qing editions of the Jianyang county gazetteer; see, e.g., p. 499 of the 1832 edition). All three brothers supposedly held high civil or military office—Liu Ao as prefect of Jianzhou in 896. The family came from Jingzhao 京兆 in Shaanxi and decided to stay in the Minbei area to escape the political turmoil of the north. Jingzhao appears occasionally as a choronym for Liu printers from the Song onward.

It is also unclear whether the various branches of the Liu descent group shown in Tables 2a–d were really related to each other. The important point, however, is that they were willing to claim kinship from the Song till at least the late Ming. For example, in a preface to the Masha Xizu beipai genealogy written in 1301, Xiong He, whose mother was a Masha Liu, states explicitly that both the Liu of Masha and the Dongzu Liu of Wufu were descended from the same ancestor(s), who came to Fujian in the late Tang. The latest extant preface to a genealogy revised by all three *zu* (Masha, Wufu, and Mafu) is dated Wanli 9 (1581) and can be found in the first volume of the *Jingzhao Liu shi Zhen fang zongpu* under the title "Liu shi zupu xi xu" 劉氏族譜系序. Prefaces dating to the Qing are for genealogies revised by branches of the Liu descent groups in Masha or Shufang.

57. *SS* 434: 12871–72 and 370: 11504–8, respectively. Nearly identical biographies of the two men appear in various local gazetteers; see, e.g., *JNFZ* (1541 ed.), 18.6b–7a for Zihui and 18.36b–39a for Ziyu.

58. See *JYXZ* (1832 ed.), *juan* 10, p. 360; and *BMTZ*, *juan* 49, p. 130.

59. Liu Fuyan is listed in the *Liu shi zupu*, vol. 2, as receiving his *jinshi* degree in 1133, a year when the departmental examination was not held. The date should perhaps be 1132, but there is no record in any other source that Liu Fuyan received a *jinshi* degree. The printing establishment known as Liu Tongpan zhai was actually operated by Liu Dan, Fuyan's son.

Similarly, Liu Junzuo supposedly received his *jinshi* degree in 1270, a non-examination year (the closest being 1271). This information is recorded in the genealogical table of the *Jingzhao Liu shi Zhen fang zongpu*, but neither he nor his marriage relative and friend, Xiong He, mentions this fact in their prefaces in the 1301 Liu genealogy revised by Junzuo. Junzuo himself appears in both the *xishi* and the biographical sections of the genealogy. It is possible that Song records somehow missed recording both Liu Fuyan and Liu Junzuo as *jinshi*. Both men were highly educated—Liu Fuyan served as assistant prefect (*tongpan*) of Zhangzhou in southern Fujian; Liu Junzuo's activities are discussed in the main text. Xiong He's preface to the *Masha Liu shi zupu* (slightly different from the version in the Liu genealogy) is included in his collected works, *Xiong Wuxuan xiansheng wenji*, 2.15–17.

60. *Jingzhao Liu shi Zhen fang zongpu*, "Xiangtu" 像圖 (vol. 2) and *juan* 3 of *xizu* "Bangli gong pai . . . ," 1a–2b.

61. "Liu shi chongxiu zupu xu" 劉氏重修族譜序, vol. 1 of *Liu shi zupu* in the Jianyang County Library, 4a–b.

62. The 1328 imprint has a preface by Junzuo dated the previous year. Fang Yanshou ("Jianyang Liu shi keshu kao," pt. I, pp. 205–6) argues reasonably that if Junzuo was young when he received his *jinshi* degree (as stated in the *Xiangtu* of the genealogy), then his probable dates are ca. 1250–ca. 1328.

63. See also Xiong He's two essays, both entitled "Song Hu Tingfang xu," in *Xiong Wuxuan xiansheng wenji*, 1.8–10.

64. The origins of the Yu lineage group in Minbei are unclear. Although *Tanxi Shulin Yu shi zupu* (see Table 3) claims that a Yu Huan settled in Fujian in 530, Yu Xiangdou claims that Yu Tongzhu (fourteenth generation), was a Northern Song official and a native of Xin'an county in Henan who settled in the Chonghua district after his geomantic calculations showed it to be an auspicious place. Yu Xiangdou's statement, from one of his publication on geomancy, *Dili tongyi quanshu* 地理統一全書, is translated in Chapter 5, pp. 158–59.

65. See Chaffee, *The Thorny Gates*, p. 103.

66. See Xiao Dongfa, "Jianyang Yu shi keshu kaolüe," pt. I, pp. 239–40. According to Xiao, (1) "Qinyou ju shi" 勤有居士 is the *hao* of Yu Anding's father, and it was a common practice among Jianyang printers to use the *hao* or *zi* of a father or grandfather for the *tangming*, (2) Yu Anding's dates are compatible with those for Qinyou tang's imprints, (3) the *Shu Cai shi zhuan ji lu zuanzhu* 書蔡氏傳輯錄纂注, an imprint of Liu Junzuo's Cuiyan jingshe (see above), credits Yu Anding as the editor/collator ("Jian'an houxue Yu Anding bianjiao" 建安後學余安定編校), and (4) Yu Zi 資, who is Yu Anding's son according to the genealogy, is listed as the editor/collator in a Qinyou tang edition of the *Tang lü suyi*: "Kaoting shuyuan Yu Zi bianjiao" 考亭書院余資編校. Yu Zi's connection to the Kaoting Academy, which was founded by Zhu Xi, provides more evidence of the Yu publishers' leanings toward *Daoxue*.

67. Thirteen is the lower limit, since there are at least five more printers/editors who share the same generational names as those found in the genealogy.

68. See de Weerdt, "The Composition of Examination Standards: *Daoxue* and Southern Song Dynasty Examination Culture," chap. 3, esp. pp. 249ff.

69. National Library of China (formerly Beijing National Library) Rare Book Collection, nos. 3370 and 7303 (incomplete).

70. Song Ci's preface of 1247 mentions blocks carved for the work, but no copy of this edition has survived. The earliest extant edition is that of the Qinyou tang,

which was reprinted in a Qing collectanea. See Song Ci (McKnight, trans.), *The Washing Away of Wrongs*, p. 30.

71. Ye Changchi, *Pangxi zhai cangshu ji*, 3.39b–40a, says the collection was compiled in the middle of the Zhizheng period, and Yu Zhi'an was active through perhaps 1350.

72. See Sekaidō bunko, *Seikadō bunko Sō-Gen pan zuroku* for notes on the Qinyou tang edition (no. 185), 1: 101–2. Another work, also edited by Su Tianjue, a large anthology of Yuan prose entitled *Guochao wenlei* 國朝文類, was printed by Liu Junzuo of Cuiyan jingshe in 1341. See K. T. Wu, "Chinese Printing Under Four Alien Dynasties," p. 474.

73. Judging from the discolored, coarse paper and the worn impression, the Naikaku bunko copy (別 63 函 5 號) I examined was probably printed in the early Ming. Nevertheless, as noted above, even an early impression would have shown up the mediocrity of the carving.

74. As discussed earlier, although Jian'an, strictly speaking, refers to Jian'an county, where the prefectural seat of Jianning was located, nearly all printers from the Song through the Ming listing themselves as "of Jian'an" were from Jianyang county—usually either Masha or Shufang/Shulin.

75. The blocks might have gone to Ye Rizeng after the death of Yu Zi in 1358, since the date given by the Guangqin tang for their printing is 1362. A number of copies of this work are extant. The National Palace Museum in Taipei has copies originally printed by the Qinyou tang and later by the Guangqin tang.

76. For clarity's sake, in referring to the Jianyang publishing families, I use "Yu" for the various 余 publishers and "Yú" for the 虞.

77. See the plates for entry 251 in Seikadō bunko, *Seikadō Bunko Sō-Gen pan zuroku*, vol. 2. See ibid., 1: 131, for a suggestion that the Qinde tang may have received the blocks from the Wuben zhai/shutang. But from the dates of publishers' notes in the various collections (*ji* 集), it is also possible that the two publishers were collaborating at the same time. One of the publisher's notes is dated 1341 and signed by a Yú Yewen 虞壄文, who was probably the proprietor of Wuben zhai.

78. Cynthia Brokaw (pers. comm.) has pointed out that in Sibao (southern Fujian), the printer who originally had the blocks cut might, by formal agreement, rent, sell, or bequeath the blocks to another printer, who could then substitute his own *tangming* 堂名. Similar arrangements are quite possible among printers in Jianyang, especially since many of them were related either as agnates or affines.

79. Through the late twelfth century, almost all members of the Xiong descent group in the Jianyang area claimed Chongtai li 崇泰里 (see Map 2) as their home. By then, however, they had already been divided into the East and West branches (東, 西族), which were further subdivided into *fang* 房. At Chongtai li (now the town of Lükou 莒口), about fifteen kilometers northwest of Jianyang county seat, there was a village named Xiong tun 熊屯, supposedly where the first Xiong settled in Minbei after immigrating from Nanchang in Jiangxi. In the twelfth and thirteenth centuries, several of the branches of Xiong descent group moved away from Chongtai li. For example, the branch that included the Xiong printers of the Ming moved to Shulin (Shufang); other branches moved even further, to Nanjing and Guangdong. For the

history of the Xiong descent group, see also Xiong Renlin, "Shixi heshi," in idem, *Hetai Xiansheng Xiong Shan wenxuan*, 16.3a–5a .

80. The extant genealogy, *Tanyang Xiong shi zongpu* 潭陽熊氏宗譜, covers several *fang* of the West Branch of the Xiong descent group in the Jianyang area. Since it does not mention any of the men with a *jinshi* degree in the Song—individuals most likely to be noted in genealogies—such men probably did not belong to the branch of the descent group from which the Ming printers came (and therefore their Song and Yuan predecessors). Only one Song man from the Rang *fang* of the West Branch is given a biography in a local gazetteer (*JYXZ* [1832 ed.], *juan* 13, p.492).

81. The first date is given by the *BMTZ*, *juan* 49, p. 129, and the second by various editions of the *JYXZ* (see, e.g., 1832 edition, *juan* 10, p. 360). Xiong Ke's biography can be found in the *SS*, *juan* 445, p. 13143–44, and in local histories, such as the *JYXZ* (1832 ed.), *juan* 11, pp. 412–13.

82. The dismal survival record of works (books, essays) on tea from the Song provides a lesson on the perils of assuming that certain works were not published simply because we no longer have copies. Of some eighteen such works (known because their prefaces survive or because they are mentioned in other, extant works), twelve concern the famous tribute tea from Beiyuan in Jian'an county, and at least ten of *these* were published in the Minbei area during the Song. But only two are extant—one is a Song edition, and another is a facsimile reprint from the Song edition in the 1273 collectanea *Baichuan xuehai* 百川學海.

83. For both men, see *JYXZ* (1832 ed.), *juan* 13, p. 481.

84. For a discussion of this work, see de Weerdt, "The Composition of Examination Standards," pp. 196–99.

85. The National Central Library (Taipei) has three copies (nos. 05546–48) of this edition, which does not identify the publisher. Since its dimensions are nearly identical to the Song edition(s) mentioned in works such as Lu Xinyuan, *Yigu tang tiba*, 6.14a–b, and *Tianyige shumu*, 3.2a, it might have been either a facsimile reprint of the earlier edition, or might simply have been mistaken as a Song edition by the bibliographies.

86. *JYZX* (1832 ed.), *juan* 10, p. 362, and *juan* 11, pp. 433–34; *BMTZ*, *juan* 49, p. 134, and *juan* 65, p. 536.

87. See Xiong He, "Kan Yili jingzhuan tongjie shu," in *Xiong Wuxuan xiansheng wenji*, 4.56–57. Xiong He revealed his ambivalent feelings toward the Jianyang printing industry in various pieces of his writings, in some of which he sometimes referred to Jianning as the "prefecture of books." On the other hand, in "Jian Tongwen shuyuan shang liang wen" (ibid., 5.64–65), he wrote that the real "Shulin" was the Kaoting Academy (and presumably other academies as well). If nothing else, this may suggest that these academies were more involved in book printing than the number of extant publications suggests.

88. *JYZX* (1601 ed.), 2.46b–48a; (1832 ed.), *juan* 1, pp. 151–52.

89. See Ding Bing, *Shanben shushi cangshu zhi*, 1.13a; and Lu Xinyuan, *Bisong lou cangshu zhi*, 3.9b–12a. Both refer to an old manuscript copy of the original imprint (probably the copy in the National Library of China Rare Books Collection, no. 6289). There are at least three imprints from the Aofeng Academy dated to the Ming Wanli period, two of which might have been reprints from the Yuan.

90. Lao Yan-shuan ("Southern Chinese Scholars and Educational Institutions in Early Yuan," p. 118) argues that during the Yuan academies in south China in general became more involved than they had been in the Song in printing books and acting as book repositories.

91. See Walton, *Academies and Society*, pp. 38ff and 105-6.

92. Such works may have been printed in the Southern Song, but of the three kinds mentioned, only collections of prescriptions are extant. I would argue tentatively that the relative importance of such popular works increased from the Song to the Yuan; the comparative survival rates from the two periods support this assertion.

93. The wide-reaching consequences of this social phenomenon on both the national and local levels have been the subject of many studies. Just to mention two recent studies in English, see Hymes, *Statesmen and Gentlemen: The Elite in Fu-chou, Chiang-hsi in the Northern and Southern Sung*; and Chaffee, *The Thorny Gates*.

94. From Section 2.58, "Occupations for Younger Relatives"; trans. from Ebrey, *Family and Property in Sung China: Yuan Ts'ai's* Precepts for Social Life, pp. 267-68.

95. Hymes, in "Not Quite Gentlemen? Doctors in Sung and Yuan," argues that among elite families in Fuzhou 撫州 prefecture in Jiangxi, being a medical doctor became an important option only in the Yuan, when educated men faced decreased opportunities for the traditionally preferred careers of a scholar-official and teacher.

Chapter 4

1. For statistical information on Jianyang imprints, see Appendix C. Table C.1 briefly summarizes the figures for Song, Yuan, and Ming publications. A breakdown of Jianyang imprints for the Song, Yuan, and Ming, arranged by *siku* order, is given in Table C.2. Almost all Jianyang imprints from the Song date from the late twelfth century and later; only two can be dated as possibly from the Northern Song: the *Yinchuan jirang ji* 尹川擊壤集, 20 *juan* (1066), printed by Cai Ziwen's family school (Table B.2, no. 90), and the *Shiji suoyin* 史記索隱, 30 *juan* (1057), printed by the Shihan tang of the Wang family (Table B.1, no. 45); see Luo Weiguo and Hu Ping, *Guji banben tiji suoyin*, 251.a–b and 494.a, for references to these two works. There is indirect evidence for a third work, *Yuan shi Changqing ji* 元氏長慶集. The extant Song edition from Sichuan has a preface dated 1124 by a Liu Lin of Jian'an, who printed the work earlier, but it does not say where; see Fu Zenxiang, *Cangyuan qunshu jingyanlu*, pp. 1080–81. See Appendix C for a discussion of the difficulties of precisely dating Chinese imprints.

2. And also in the paper and ink used. Cream-white paper and ink giving a black, glossy impression were used in printing the high-quality Jianyang works, which have deteriorated little to this day. In the lower-quality books, the paper was clearly tan-colored to begin with and has discolored noticeably over the ensuing centuries. The impression is in general less black. Still, some caution is called for in this comparison: extant copies of the lower-quality editions are most likely late impressions made off worn blocks and on mediocre paper; early impressions might have produced better copies.

3. See *ZBK*, figs. 159, 160, 164, and 165 and the related notes. Li Qingzhi (*Gushu banben jianding yanjiu*, pp. 53–54) argues that *shoujin ti* is not an accurate descrip-

tion, and based on surviving examples of Huizong's handwriting (ibid., p. 282), I would agree. Actually, a clearer example of the Slender Gold style can be seen in the printer's advertisement of Wang Shubian in Fig. 14c.

4. Yet another example of *Yan ti* can be seen in Fig. 4b.

5. The other two Tang calligraphers are Ouyang Xun 歐陽詢 and Liu Songquan 柳松權. For examples of the Yan, Ou, and Liu styles, see Li Qingzhi, *Gushu banben jianding yanjiu*, pp. 278–81; or most standard works on Chinese calligraphy.

6. For example, Wei Yinru and Wang Jinyu (*Guji banben jianding congtan*, p. 22) argue that Jianyang imprints are characterized by the Liu and Slender Gold styles; Tsien (*Paper and Printing*, p. 224) sees the influence of Yan and Liu; and Zhang Xiumin (*Zhongguo yinshua shi*, p. 159) says the Liu style is characteristic of Jianyang imprints.

7. Poon, "Books and Printing in Sung China," p. 175. On the other hand, these works number among the most beautiful Jianyang editions of the Song and were used as the basis for the modern reprints by the Commercial Press.

8. One rather unorthodox way to judge the quality of the calligraphy without the distraction of the page-layout is to look at the blank verso side of the leaf. Since the paper for many traditional Chinese books (especially Jianyang imprints) is relatively thin, the larger, darker characters of the main text come through more clearly than the smaller characters of the glosses and annotations and can be evaluated by themselves.

9. This would have been the office in Jian'an, the prefectural seat. Other than Wu Jian's publications, there is at least one other publication from this office, from the mid-twelfth century. As mentioned in note 54 to Chapter 2, Wu Jian's other publications all have the same colophon. For the *Zhangzi yulu*, see the editors' notes in *ZBK*, figs. 198–99. The blockcarvers whose names were recorded in the center strip of the work had also worked on a *Zhouyi benyi* 周易本義 in 1265 (*ZBK*, fig. 200) for the previous Jianning prefect. Apparently, a number of Fujian regional officials in the mid-thirteenth century employed approximately the same group of blockcarvers. For example, a four-*juan* collection of Tao Yuanming's poems, *Tao Jingjie xiansheng shi* 陶靖節先生詩 from about the Xianchun period (1265–74) lists a prefect of Fuzhou, Tang Han, as the publisher; see Chen Xingzhen, "Song ke Tao Yuanming ji liang zhong," p. 213, on the dating of this work.

10. There may also have been an earlier edition printed by the Jianning Prefectural School in 1166. The proof for this earlier imprint is indirect; see Fu Zengxiang, *Cangyuan qunshu jingyanlu*, pp. 791–92, and notes to this 1180 edition (entry no. 84) in the Seikadō bunko, *Seikadō bunko Sō-Gen pan zuroku*, 1: 48–49. The Seikadō copy was partly repaired in the Yuan.

11. For a discussion of local government and "semi-official" publishing in the Song, see Poon, "Books and Printing in Sung China," pp. 127–44.

12. William Hennessey ("The Song Emperor Huizong in Popular History and Romance: The Early Chinese Vernacular Novel *Xuanhe yishi*," pp. 12–15) argues that a reading of the work suggests its compiler was an eyewitness to the last days of the Southern Song; if so, a date of ca. 1300 is not unreasonable. He also makes a number of plausible speculations that the work was compiled as well as published in Jianyang (pp. 49–50). In any case, there was apparently a later, four-*juan* Ming edition from

Jianyang, published before 1540; see Gao Ru, *Bai chuan shuzhi*, under *shibu: zhuanji*; and Zhou Hongzu, *Gujin shuke*, p. 364.

13. Possible explanations include fewer surviving poor-quality imprints from the Song, a shortage of good paper in the Yuan, or the growth of the lower end of the Jianyang book trade in the Yuan. I believe that the last reason is most important.

14. Rare book scholars have argued that the Zhao style was prevalent among Jianyang imprints, but less so among those from other areas during the Yuan. Since a large percentage of extant Yuan works are Jianyang books, this has perhaps given an exaggerated impression of the influence of the Zhao style in this period; see Li Qingzhi, *Gushu banben jianding yanjiu*, p. 64. On the other hand, Zhao Mengfu and calligraphers influenced by him such as Shen Du and Shen Can of the early Ming exerted a huge impact on the calligraphy in Ming imprints in general; see Mote and Chu, *Calligraphy and the East Asian Book*, esp. pp. 111–32.

15. See note 87 in Chapter 2 for works discussing printers' colophons of the Song.

16. Poon, "The Printer's Colophon in Sung China," p. 45.

17. See the genealogy in Table 2d. Other than a listing in *Liu shi zupu*, 10.19a, I have only found one biography for him, in *JNFZ* (1541 ed.), 16.46a.

18. The Yuqing tang also printed *Song ji san chao zhengyao* 宋季三朝政要, a historical work on the events under the last three Song emperors. This 1312 edition looks very similar to the *Xu Zizhi tongjian* in Fig. 20b. These works are discussed later in this chapter.

19. The work contains a preface by the compiler, Wei Yilin, dated 1337.

20. See note 14 in Chapter 2.

21. Fig. 22d shows the edition from the Jian'an Xiaozhai 建安小齋 in the National Central Library (Taipei) collection; Seikadō bunko, *Seikadō bunko Sō-Gen pan zuroku*, fig. 162, shows a different Jianyang edition, possibly printed by the Zhu family's Yugeng tang 朱氏與耕堂.

22. See fig. 1170 in Tsien, *Paper and Printing*, p.258. for a folio from this work. Although Ye Dehui (*Shulin qinghua*, 7.3a) thought that the Qinyou tang edition was from the Song, Nagasawa Kikuya shows convincingly that it was from the Yuan. As he notes, at the end of several of the *juan*, there is a line that variously reads *Jing'an Yu shi moke* 靜庵余氏 模刻 or *Jing'an Yu shi moke* 靖庵余氏 模刻 or *Jian'an Yu shi moke* 建安余氏 模刻 or *Yu shi Qinyou tang kan* 余氏勤有堂 刊 or *Jian'an Yu shi mokan* 建安余氏模刊. The Qinyou tang operated in the Yuan and not the Song, and *moke* (facsimile-carved) supports the contention that its edition was based on an earlier Song one; see Nagasawa, "Eiri no Sō kampon ni tsuite," pp. 2–5, in *Nagasawa Kikuya chosaku shū*, vol. 3.

23. See also Hegel, *Reading Illustrated Fiction*, esp. pp. 20–28, 172–76, 217–21, for more discussion of and other illustrations from these *pinghua*.

24. It is unclear whether Huang Shu'an carved both the pictures and the text or just the pictures.

25. The cover title page of this work states "jiawu xinkan" 甲午新刊 (newly carved in [the year] *jiawu*). Zhang Xiumin (*Zhongguo yinshua shi*, pp. 323–24) argues that *jiawu* most likely refers to 1294, which is year 31 of the Zhiyuan 至元 period, since "Zhiyuan xinkan" 至元新刊 (newly carved in Zhiyuan) appears at the start of

the first *juan*. Other scholars, however disagree. Idema("P'ing-hua," p. 661) calls it a "later and inferior edition" of the *Sanguo zhi pinghua*. Given some of the omissions and great number of errors in the characters compared to the *Sanguo zhi pinghua* of the Zhizhi period, it seems that the later date of 1354 for the *Sanfen shilüe* is more likely. See Plaks, *The Four Masterworks of the Ming Novel*, p. 369n32, for brief comments on some of the discrepancies between the two editions.

26. In Beijing, Wei Yinru showed me the title page to a *Sanguo zhi*, that had been recycled as part of the wrapper of a later book. Wei suggested a date of around 1300 for this work.

27. The Zhang family (Zhang jia 張家) bookstore located in the Zhong wazi 中瓦子 area apparently produced a number of fictional works, including the *Da Tang Sanzang qu jing shihua* 大唐三藏取經詩話. This work and another version, also from Hangzhou around the same time, are not illustrated, but they can be classified as *huaben* 話本, as can the Jianyang works; see Edgren, "Southern Song Printing at Hangzhou," p. 32.

28. Roderick Whitfield ("Tz'u-chou Pillows with Painted Decoration," pp. 83-84) suggests that the pictures depicted may have been scenes from dramas or illustrated imprints. Yutaka Mino (*Freedom of Clay and Brush Through Seven Centuries in North China: Tz'u-chou Type Ware, 960-1600*, p. 146) juxtaposes another illustration from the *pinghua Sanguo zhi* with the picture of a porcelain pillow from Cizhou. For examples of illustrated Cizhou vases, see figs. 139-40 in Valenstein, *A Handbook of Chinese Ceramics*, pp. 144-45.

29. The potter's identification marks on many Cizhou pillows are similar to the printers' colophons seen in many Jianyang publications, both of which used the lotus leaf motif. This is best explained by the widespread dissemination of many symbols and images from folklore and religion—the flaming pearl, which was originally Buddhist, is another example. For an illustration of the Cizhou potter's mark, see Mino, *Freedom of Clay and Brush*, fig. 123, p. 116 (originally shown as fig. 16 in *Wenwu* 1964, no. 8: 14). Finally, as Whitfield ("Tz'u-chou Pillows," p. 77) points out, the lotus leaf canopy continued to be used on ceramics at least until the Qing Guangxu period (1875-1908).

30. Figure 1 of Clunas, "The West Chamber," shows a blue-and-white vase depicting a scene from *The Western Chamber*. This piece is dated "fourteenth century," and so it may, along with Clunas's other illustrations of porcelains and imprints, come from the Ming. But the blue-and-white vase shown in fig. 180 of *Zhongguo wenwu Jing-Hua* depicts a scene quite possibly from some version of the *Sanguo zhi*, one that might have been copied from a printed *pinghua*. I thank John Finlay for bringing this work to my notice.

31. Pages from this work are reproduced in a number of modern works, including the *ZBK*, figs. 382-83; Zhou Wu, *Zhongguo banhua shi tulu*, pls. 400.1-3; and Zhou Xinhui, *Mingdai banke tushi*, vol. 4, nos. 43-45.

32. See, e.g., Idema, *Chinese Vernacular Fiction: The Formative Period*, pp. xxiv-xxv, where he suggests that the *pinghua* might have "originated as educational texts for China's Mongol rulers."

33. It is uncertain how much more difficult. A miswritten Chinese character is probably no more distracting than a misspelled word, and perhaps less so—because

of the pictorial quality of the characters, rapid scanning of a text demands only an impressionistic recognition of the character.

34. Slightly different versions of this story are found in Ye Mengde, *Shilin yanyu*, pp. 73–74; Lu You, *Laoxue'an biji*, p. 47; Zhu Yu, *Pingzhou ke tan*, pp. 12–13; Shen Jiache, *Nan Song za shi shi zhu*, 3.11a; Zhu Guozhen, *Yongzhuang xiaopin*, p. 313. All versions set the story in Hangzhou at the beginning of the Yuanfu period (1098–1100), suggesting that *Mashaben* had achieved notoriety by the late Northern Song.

35. Jianyang imprints that cannot be associated with a particular printer make up about half of those from the Song and about a fifth of those from the Yuan. On the problems of ascertaining whether these works were from the Jianyang area, see Chapter 1 and Appendix C.

36. Again, the limited variety of extant Song and Yuan *Mashaben* most likely has to do with the greater chances of survival for scholarly works; they were also more likely to be mentioned by writers of the time. Later *Mashaben* from the Ming encompass a far greater variety of both scholarly and popular works. Even today some Chinese rare book scholars continue to confuse *Mashaben* with all Jianyang imprints. This disdain arises from a failure to examine Jianyang works in greater detail or from an especially narrow *banben xue* perspective that will not admit the importance of a social history of the Chinese book.

37. For a brief discussion of information on Jianyang imprints in traditional Chinese bibliographic sources, see Appendix C.

38. See Poon, "Books and Printing in Sung China," pp. 103–4, table 7, for a list of such special features and pp. 174ff for examples of elaborate book titles.

39. See Chen Zhensun, *Zhizhai shulu jieti*, 17: 474–75. Chen's remark is actually found in his note on the *Dongpo bieji* 東坡別集 published by Su Shi's great-grandson Su Jiao 蘇嶠 in Jian'an when he was serving as an official in the area.

40. Chaffee (*The Thorny Gates*, p. 35) gives the *Song huiyao* figure of 79,000 candidates at the prefectural-level examinations in 1099, 1102, and 1105; he estimates for southern China a corresponding figure of 400,000 in the mid-thirteenth century. To this should be added the number of students preparing for but not taking the examinations in a particular year.

41. Texts for the *zhuke* 諸科 degree (abolished in 1071) overlapped with those of the *jinshi* degree; see ibid., pp. 189–90. For the structure of the prefectural and departmental examinations in the Southern Song, see de Weerdt, "The Composition of Examination Standards," pp. 16–23.

42. As Thomas Lee (*Government Education and Examinations in Sung China*, pp. 110–11) notes, we have little detailed information on the curriculum of local schools during the Song and therefore must deduce, from the emphasis given them in examination questions, which works were most important. See also de Weerdt, "The Composition of Examination Standards," pp. 24ff and table I, "Supplementary Materials."

43. De Weerdt ("The Composition of Examination Standards," pp. 52–56, 325–37) argues that it was only in 1241 with Emperor Lizong's recommendation of Zhu Xi's commentaries for the *Four Books* and the writings of the five *Daoxue* masters of the Song (Zhou Dunyi, Zhang Zai, Cheng Hao, Cheng Yi, and Zhu Xi) that *Daoxue* achieved its intellectual dominance.

44. See Poon, "Books and Printing in Sung China," app. C, for a list of Song Directorate editions.

45. Li Xinchuan, *Jianyan yilai chao ye zaji*, p. 4 (cited in Poon, "Books and Printing in Sung China," p. 126). Customers could either buy the Directorate editions outright or supply the paper and ink, and rent the blocks. Some Directorate editions had information on the cost of renting the printing blocks and buying the paper and ink.

46. The restriction on printing of the Classics without the permission of the Directorate was lifted in the Xining period (1068–77) according to Luo Bi (twelfth c.) in "Chengshu deshu nan," *Lo shi zhiyi*, 1.3b (cited in Cherniack, "Book Culture in Sung China," pp. 28–29n54). The growing publishing activities of regional and local governments in the Southern Song may also have discouraged the Directorate from continuing their donations. See Poon, "Books and Printing in Sung China," pp. 127–40.

47. There were a few government compilations of the essays of the most successful candidates, but they could not compete with the commercial editions. See below.

48. That is, current styles of examination writings. The *shi* or "current" clearly signified the changing intellectual and political trends that affected the contents of the examination questions and the examiners' views.

49. See de Weerdt, "The Composition of Examination Standards," for a comprehensive treatment of these kinds of examination literature in the Song. For further discussion of *leishu*, see below.

50. See Fig. 7a in Chapter 2, p. 000. These small crib copies were also known by a number of other terms, such as *xiao ce* 小册, *xiao ben* 小本, and *jiadai ce* 夾袋册. *Xiuzhen ben* seems to have been a less derogatory term and referred to small-size editions made for convenience and portability. Interestingly, with the passage of time, these *jinxiang ben* have sometimes elicited later book connoisseurs' admiration, in contrast to Song disdain. Ye Dehui (*Shulin qinghua*, 4.2a–3b) admired the economy with which the publishers managed to fit substantial works into such small spaces and how finely the characters were carved ("like hair"). According to Ye (ibid., 9.11b–12a), there were editions of the *Book of Changes* in 21 leaves, the *Book of Documents* in 26 leaves, the *Book of Filial Piety* in 3 (!) leaves.

51. For imperfections in Directorate editions, see Cherniack, "Book Culture in Sung China," esp. pp. 57–78. See also the general discussion on Directorate editions in Poon, "Books and Printing in Sung China," pp. 113–27.

52. See Loewe, "Some Recent Editions of the Ch'ien-Han-shu," pp. 165–66.

53. Two important secondary sources on Song legal regulations regarding publishing are Zhu Chuanyu, *Songdai xinwen shi*, pp. 162–69 for examination essays and pp. 176–245 for publishing laws and regulations in general; and Niida Noboru, "Keigen jōhō jirei to Sōdai no shuppanhō" (The *Qingyuan tiaofa shilei* and Song publishing laws), and "*Sōkaiyō* to Sōdai no shuppanhō" (The *Song huiyao* and Song publishing laws), reprinted as chaps. 24–25 in idem, *Chūgoku hōsei shi kenkyū*. There are also useful discussions in Hok-lam Chan's "Sung Laws and Regulations on Publications and Circulation"; Poon, "Books and Printing in Sung China," esp. pp. 67–112; and Duan Xuanwu, *Songdai banke fazhi yanjiu*.

I have not included in Table 5 government documents prohibiting other kinds of printed materials such as calendars, astronomical works, works on litigation, unorthodox religious works, and discussions on border affairs since there are almost no known Jianyang imprints of such items.

54. It is quite possible that the report of 1005 talks of bringing unauthorized *handwritten* materials to the examinations because the technique of carving very small characters had not been perfected. But Ouyang Xiu's memorial of 1057 still describes handwritten examination cribs and says that transcribers can earn 20,000–30,000 cash for their work. See his "Tiaoyue juren huaijia wenzi zhazi" 條約舉人懷挾字箭子 in Ouyang Xiu, *Quanji*, vol. 2, 15: 872. The persistence of handwritten cribs for centuries afterward suggests their copyists worked at rates competitive with the printed editions, especially on rather unusual surfaces, such as the Qing period "cribbing garment," which has some 722(!) examination essays in minute script (in the Gest Oriental Library at Princeton University) written on it. Another example from the Qing, written on a piece of silk, is in the Schuyler Camman Collection in the Yale University Art Gallery.

55. *Qingyuan tiaofa shilei*, 17.19a. In general, the more drastic punishments were reserved for printing and selling works deemed to impinge on national security or to usurp the government's monopoly on that kind of material—edicts, decrees, imperial orders, memorials, veritable records, national histories, discussions on border affairs, calendars, and astronomical works.

56. Zhu Chuanyu (*Songdai xinwen shi*, p. 166) speculates that the "false learning" may have had political implications that made the case more serious, but the date does not fit any of the major political struggles of the Song, and the 1177 petition predates the well-known proscription of the Qingyuan period by nearly twenty years.

57. *SHY: Xingfa*, 2/129.

58. The anecdotal evidence yields a few bits of information about the prices of cribs and other printed examination literature. One story about the poet and official Xin Qiji 辛棄疾 (1140–1207) tells how, after defecting from the Jurchen court to the Southern Song, he had to pass the government examinations to become an official. Xin thought that would pose no hardship, since he could just buy a collection of *shiwen* for 300 cash and study it. Subsequently, after he had succeeded, Emperor Xiaozong (r. 1163–89) jokingly remarked, "This is the man who spent 300 cash to buy a government position"; see Wang Yun, "Xin Dianzhuan xiaozhuan" 辛殿撰小傳 in idem, *Yutang jiahua*, 2: 19. I thank Liu Hsiang-kwang for bringing this story to my attention.

Although an imprint costing 300 cash would not be considered expensive, we do not have sufficient information on book prices to know how cheap it was. There are very few such data for the Song, and they pertain mainly to larger and/or higher-quality works, such as Directorate editions; see Wang Zhongluo, *Jin ni yu xie congkao*, pp. 393–94, for some of these figures; and also Twitchett, *Printing and Publishing in Medieval China*, pp. 64–65.

59. Li Xinchuan, *Jianyan yilai xinian yaolu*, p. 2827; cited by Poon, "Books and Printing in Sung China," p. 110.

60. Yue Ke, *Kuitan lu*, 9: 78.

61. For a discussion of four such works, see de Weerdt, "Aspects of Song Intellectual Life." For more on *leishu* published in Jianyang, see the next section of this chapter.

62. Of the 192 imprints from the Song, nearly all are from the Southern Song, or more precisely, from ca. 1160 onward.

63. Despite the obvious difficulties in using the *siku* system, I have decided to retain it for Table C.2 and for the broad organization of this survey section in both the current and following chapters, since almost all bibliographies of traditional Chinese works use some version of the *siku* system. See the discussion in Appendix C.

64. See Poon, "Books and Printing in Sung China," table 8, p. 123, and table 12, p. 135, for the distribution of imprints according to the *siku* classification for central and local government agencies, respectively. All the Classics and commentaries are grouped together without further breakdown. See ibid., table 13, p. 154, for a total of seventeen imprints from eight private academies. For commercial imprints, see ibid., table 14, pp. 170–71, which gives only the subject coverage of 56 printers known by name but no numerical distribution and is based on a very conservative total of 128 imprints. Several older works, while not aspiring to a complete survey of known imprints for any region, kind of publisher, or period, are quite useful—see. e.g., Wang Guowei's *Liang-Zhe gu kanben kao*, and a number of Ye Dehui's essays in *Shulin qinghua*.

65. See the section on Jianyang publishers in Chapter 3 for a discussion of the Song loyalism and eremitic leanings of Xiong He and his associates.

66. See, e.g., Lao Yan-shuan, "Southern Chinese Scholars and Educational Institutions in Early Yuan: Some Preliminary Remarks."

67. It is no coincidence that many of these "primers" were written or promoted by *Daoxue* scholars. The first such compilation, the *Jinsi lu* 近思錄 compiled by Zhu Xi and Lü Zuqian in 1173, may be considered the model for subsequent works meant to introduce a reader to the Four Books and the Classics (ultimately for the purpose of moral self-cultivation). Thus men like Xiong He and Liu Yingli, as second-generation disciples of Zhu Xi, were following a tradition of producing such primers, some of which were aimed at quite advanced readers. Others were far simpler, and these are the works that became more popular in the Yuan.

68. For a description of such activities among Huizhou scholars in the Yuan, see Liu Hsiang-kwang, "Education and Society: The Development of Public and Private Institutions in Hui-chou, 960–1800," chap. 4.

69. *Siku quanshu zongmu*, vol. 1, *juan* 37, pp. 308–9. I am indebted to Liu Hsiang-kwang for this information.

70. These works are listed under section 3-1 in Table C.2.

71. In addition to the Confucian works counted in Table C.2, three were printed under some kind of official auspices by Wu Jian, a Fujian circuit transport official in the Song: *Zhangzi yulu* (of Zhang Zai 張載), *Guishan xiansheng yulu* 龜山先生語錄 (of Yang Shi 楊時), and *Zhuzi yulu* 朱子語錄.

72. De Weerdt, "The Composition of Examination Standards," p. 25, and "Supporting Materials," table I.

73. As de Weerdt (ibid., pp. 118–19) points out, this penchant for reclassification of the contents of works to facilitate studying for the examinations affected

Daoxue texts as well. The Zeng family editions probably were published in the mid-thirteenth century. Since there are no other editions of the *Hou lu*, it is possible that this work was compiled in the Jianyang area for the Zeng family publisher.

74. See the section above on *Mashaben* in this chapter and also the illustrations of dictionaries in Figs. 22a–c.

75. See Liu Yeqiu, *Zhongguo zidian shilüe*, pp. 70–75. For two other commercial editions (possibly also from the Jianyang area), see K. T. Wu, "Chinese Printing Under Four Alien Dynasties," p. 494.

76. For a brief general discussion of the *Guangyun*, see Zhao Cheng, *Zhongguo gudai yunshu*, pp. 43–53. K. T. Wu ("Chinese Printing Under Four Alien Dynasties," p. 495) lists three other commercial Yuan editions, one possibly also from Jianyang.

77. See Zhao Cheng, *Zhongguo gudai yunshu*, pp. 58–62. There were at least five commercial editions from areas other than Jianyang, according to K. T. Wu ("Chinese Printing Under Four Alien Dynasties," p. 495).

78. See the entry "Chung-yüan yin-yün" by William Dolby in the *Indiana Companion to Traditional Chinese Literature*, pp. 370–71.

79. See Diping xian chubanshe, *Shiji shulu* 史記書錄, for descriptions of different editions of the *Shiji*. The 1057 edition from Jianyang is described on pp. 34–39.

80. Cherniack, "Book Culture in Sung China," p. 73 and *n*188. The colophon leaf together with a transcription of the text is reproduced in Ozaki, *Seishi Sō-Genpan no kenkyū*, pp. 261–62.

81. See de Weerdt, "The Composition of Examination Standards," pp. 24–25, and "Supporting Materials," table I.

82. Poon, "Books and Printing in Sung China," p. 176.

83. See de Weerdt, "The Composition of Examination Standards," pp. 325–26.

84. Although this is a somewhat circular explanation, it seems more likely than any official obstruction. As K. T. Wu ("Chinese Printing under Four Alien Dynasties," pp. 463–69) points out, one of the most ambitious official projects in the Yuan was the printing of the Seventeen Histories, which was assigned to a number of schools in Jiangzhe route.

85. By the end of the Southern Song, large portions of Li Tao's long work were no longer extant, and more were lost during the Yuan (see Shiba Yoshinobu's entry on this work in Hervouet, *Sung Bibliography*, pp. 73–74). During the Yuan, it may have been difficult for publishers to obtain copies of even the portions that survived, so that they resorted to producing the eighteen-*juan* work, which dealt with the Northern Song, whereas the other two *tongjian* discussed above covered the Southern Song. That the collator was from Wuyi suggests that the specious work was compiled in the Jianyang area.

86. Copies of the editions printed by the Chen family Yuqing tang (Table B.1, no. 8) are extant. And the surviving copies of the Li Tao and the *Song ji san chao* from the Zhang family of Yunqu (Table B.1, no. 81) suggest that Zhang family produced all three works. The Zhu family's Yugeng tang (Table B.1, no. 87) apparently used the same blocks as those of the Yuqing tang. Several of these works are shown in Seikadō bunko, *Seikadō bunko Sō-Gen pan zuroku*, pls. 171–81, 2: 348–59.

87. Poon, "Books and Printing in Sung China," p. 123. Most of these imprints were produced in the Northern Song. The 38 editions published by various offices of

the Song central government consisted of about 25 different titles, some of them revised versions of previous publication. In addition, Poon (ibid., p. 135) lists 24 medical works printed by local governments in the Song.

88. See Leung, "Transmission of Medical Knowledge from the Song to the Ming," pp. 2–8, on the transmission of scholarly and nonscholarly medical knowledge in the Song, and ibid., pp. 8–19, on the Jin-Yuan reaction.

89. The *fangshu* not only were collections of prescriptions and recipes but also had general, somewhat more theoretical discussions of various aspects of medicine as well as more specific discussions on various diseases and ailments. Nevertheless, it is quite likely that such works were in demand more for their prescriptions and recipes, which could be used by everyone.

90. See Okanishi, *Song yiqian yiji kao*, pp. 765–87, for bibliographic information on different editions of this work.

91. Jianyang publications of medical classics would increase significantly in the Ming, due largely to Xiong Zongli, who edited, wrote, and published all kinds of medical books.

92. Two recent basic introductions to *leishu* are Hu Daojing, *Zhongguo gudai de leishu*; and Dai Keyu and Tang Jianhua, *Leishu de yan'ge*. On Song *leishu*, see Tillman, "Encyclopedias, Polymaths, and Tao-hsüeh Confucians: Preliminary Reflections with Special Reference to Chang Ju-yü"; and de Weerdt, "Aspects of Song Intellectual Life." On classifying *leishu*, see Zhang Dihua, *Leishu liubie*; Hu Daojing, *Zhongguo gudai de leishu*, esp. pp. 8–14; Teng and Biggerstaff's classifications in *An Annotated Bibliography of Selected Chinese Works*, pp. 82–128; and Wilkinson, *Chinese History: A Manual*, pp. 601–9.

Traditional bibliographies and library catalogues do not agree on what works should be considered *leishu*, even within the same *siku* system. For example, certain collections of anecdotes are catalogued as *leishu* because their contents are arranged topically, even though such works could just as reasonably be placed under *xiaoshuo* (anecdotists) or possibly the Belles Lettres *zongji* (general collections). On the other hand, some compilations, such as the *Leishuo* discussed above, are usually classified under *zajia* (miscellaneous schools), although this particular work could probably be more usefully considered a *leishu*.

93. Tillman, "Encyclopedias, Polymaths, and Tao-hsüeh Confucians," p. 91.

94. Although printing certainly helped to make more books available to more readers, it is difficult to measure with much precision the extent of this broadcasting of knowledge. For example, it is doubtful that most students preparing for the examinations would have the kind of access to works available to leading scholars who had large book collections or *entrée* to government and private libraries, especially in the capital.

95. Not all collections of examination essays can be classified as *leishu*, but some, including the valuable Southern Song work by Lin Jiong 林駉 and Huang Lüweng 黃履翁, *Gujin yuanliu zhilun* (discussed later in the main text), were quite comprehensive in their scope. For an analysis of this work, see de Weerdt, "Aspects of Song Intellectual Life."

96. The father of Zhu Mu (?–ca. 1246) moved from Xin'an in Anhui to Jianyang to study with Zhu Xi. It is uncertain where Zhu Mu was born, but the local and Fujian

provincial gazetteers claim him as belonging to Jianyang. See, for example, *JYXZ* (1832 ed.), *juan* 13, p. 478. As for the *Gujin shiwen leiju*, it is unclear whether the Jianyang edition dates from the late Song or early Yuan. It was printed by the Liu family's Yunzhuang shuyuan (Table B.3, no. 106). Since it includes not only Zhu Mu's original 60-*juan* compilation but also all the later supplements, it may have been a Yuan publication.

97. Evidence from descriptions in various catalogues, including Lu Xinyuan, *Bisong lou cangshu zhi*, 58.19a–20b; and idem, *Yigu tang tiba* 10.16a–b, 10.17a–b; and *ZBK*, entry 188, indicates that there were two different Jianyang commercial editions from the Southern Song. One of them was used by Ye Shi 葉時 to produce another edition in 1226 when he was prefect of Jianning. He resorted to this badly printed small-character edition, because apparently nothing else was available to him, yet another sign of the tenuous survival of even such a popular work.

98. See de Weerdt, "Aspects of Song Intellectual Life," esp. pp. 17–22.

99. National Library of China Rare Book Collection no. 880 (as well as an incomplete copy, no. 13342).

100. These are the Yuan Dade period (1297–1307) edition by the Zhan family's Jianyang shuyuan and the 1367 edition of Liu Kechang (Table B.1, no. 22). The Jianyang Zhan family seems to have been related to the Zhan publisher of Wuyi (Table B.1, no. 77) who printed a *Xinbian Hui'an xiansheng yulu leiyao* 新編晦菴先生語錄類要 (Newly edited classified essentials of the records of Zhu Xi's conversations) in 1302 and was connected to Xiong He. As for Liu Kechang's 1367 imprint, the blocks may have been cut earlier (1354) for the Cuiyan jingshe (Table B.3, no. 102), another Liu family printing establishment, whose founder, Liu Junzuo, was also associated with Xiong He, as noted above. For a discussion on one possible Song and three Yuan editions of this work, see de Weerdt, "The Composition of Examination Standards," the discussion of "Ultimate Essays on Origins and Development" in the "Notes on Primary Sources." The 1317 edition printed by the Yuansha shuyuan 圓沙書院 (National Library of China Rare Book Collection no. 3688) looks similar to the Liu Kechang edition, but we do not know the location of this academy.

101. See de Weerdt, "Aspects of Song Intellectual Life," pp. 7–8, 16.

102. For discussions and excerpts from a number of these works, see de Pee, "Negotiating Marriage," chap. 2.

103. The original work was compiled by the Tang poet Bo Juyi 白居易 and supplemented in the early Southern Song by Kong Chuan 孔傳; see Teng and Biggerstaff, *An Annotated Bibliography*, pp. 87–88. The "liutie" referred to memory questions on the Classics in the government examinations in the Tang and the Northern Song (until 1071), but the diverse wealth of materials in the work made it useful as an aid to writing in general.

104. Seikadō bunko, *Seikadō bunko Sō-Gen pan zuroku*, entry 82. The catalogue describes the imprint as late Southern Song / early Yuan.

105. Xiong He, *Xiong Wuxuan xiansheng wenji*, 1.5–7. The same preface also appears in several, but not all, of the Yuan and Ming editions of the work.

106. See de Pee, "Negotiating Marriage," pp. 144ff on the *Hanmo quanshu*, especially on the wedding section in a number of these works, and pp. 431–34 on various extant copies and the differences among their contents. Like de Pee, I also have

not seen a copy of the original edition by just Xiong He and Liu Yingli (if it is still extant). The title of the different "editions" vary somewhat: some are *Hanmo quanshu*, others are *Hanmo daquan* . . . 大全 (compendium). Every extant "edition" I know of gives the title as ". . . Shiwen leiju Hanmo . . ." 事文類聚翰墨, possibly the publisher's attempt to evoke the popular earlier work by Zhu Mu discussed above.

107. Ibid., pp. 121ff and 435 for discussions about parts of this work.

108. The appearance of the imprint does not allow for any more precise date other than the late thirteenth century. See de Pee, "Negotiating Marriage," pp. 97–114 and 437 for discussions of this work. As de Pee points out (pp. 98–99), the latest texts may date from around the mid-thirteenth century.

109. Of Chen Yuanjing, we know almost nothing, but most of the plausible speculations suggest that he was a native of Chongan county in Jianning prefecture and lived in the late twelfth and thirteenth centuries. An earlier work by Chen, *Suishi guangji* 歲時廣記, has prefaces by Liu Chun 劉純, who was the grandson of Liu Zhongji, a Jianyang publisher (Table B.1, no. 30) and son of a Zhu Xi disciple, Liu Chongzhi (Table 2b) and by Zhu Jian 朱鑑, a grandson of Zhu Xi. Chen therefore must have belonged to the literati elite of the area, although his *Shilin guangji* as we know it from Yuan and later editions does not have a *Daoxue* emphasis. For a summary of the surmises about Chen Yuanjing, see the introduction by Hu Daojing in the modern reprint of the Jian'an Chunzhuang Academy's edition from the Yuan Zhishun period (1330–32). The full title of this particular edition is *Xinbian zuantu zenglei qunshu leiyao shilin guangji* 新編纂圖增類群書類要事林廣記 (Comprehensive record of all matters, newly edited, illustrated, with expanded categories based on the classified essentials from many books).

110. See Morita Kenji, "Guanyu zai Riben de 'Shilin guangji' zhuben," pp. 272–74. The Chunzhuang Academy's edition seems to be the same as that of the Xiyuan jingshe, but it is definitely different from that of the Zheng family's Jicheng tang (Tables B.3, no 112 and B.1, no. 85, respectively).

111. The incomplete copy in the Rare Book Collection of the National Library of China (no. 18713) has a colophon giving the date (1339) and the publisher as the Youyu shutang (of the Wu family—Table B.1, no. 49), but there is also at the beginning of the table of contents of the first installment (*jia ji* 甲集) one line saying "newly printed by the Chunzhuang Academy" (Chunzhuang shuyuan xinkan 椿莊書院新刊). It could be that the two publishers collaborated or that one of them borrowed or inherited the blocks from the other but neglected to remove the latter's name.

112. See Fu Zengxiang, *Cangyuan qunshu jingyan lu*, p. 878, for brief notes on this work.

113. In the Rare Book Collection (no. 08666) of the National Central Library in Taipei.

114. There is also a prose collection of all three Su from the late Yuan as well.

115. Both Jianyang imprints are from the Yuan: *Pidian fenlei Chengzhai xiansheng wenkuai* 批點分類誠齋先生文膾 (Excerpts from Yang Wanli, annotated and classified), and *Chengzhai xiansheng si liu fa yi gao fu* 誠齋先生四六發遺菁馥, a selection of Yang's four-six prose. For the first work, the compiler was one Li

Chengfu from Jian'an. See de Weerdt, "The Composition of Examination Standards," pp. 120*n*105, 167, and "Supporting Materials," table IX B.

116. Zhu Xi's *Huian xiansheng Zhu Wengong wenji* 晦庵先生朱文公文集 was published by the Jian'an Academy in Jianning prefecture in 1256. Liu Yue's (see above and Table 2c) *Yunzhuang Liu Wenjian gong wenji* 雲莊劉文簡公文集 was published in the Yuan by the Liu family's Wen Hualong Academy (Table B.3, no. 103), possibly by Liu Yingli, one of Yue's collateral descendants. The *Fang shi xian jushi xiaogao* 方是閒居士小藁 of Liu Xueji (Table 2d) was published by the Liu family's Pingshan Academy (Table B.3, no. 104).

117. Several of these are discussed by de Weerdt in "The Composition of Examinations Standards": *Shi xiansheng aolun zhu* 十先生奧論註 (Awesome expositions from ten masters, with notes): p. 168 and "Supporting Materials: Notes on Primary Sources," VI and Table IX B; *Quandian Longchuan Shuixin xiansheng wencui* 圈點龍川水心先生文粹 (The best of Chen Liang and Ye Shi—with stress marks): pp. 166–67 and "Supporting Materials," table IX B; and *Lunxue shengchi* 論學 繩尺 (Standards for the study of the exposition).

118. See ibid., p. 151, for *Huang chao wenjian* and p. 29*n*32 for *Wanbao shi shan*. The latter work was published by the Ye family's Guangqin tang (Table B.1, no. 58) and it is possible that the compiler, one Ye Jingda 葉景達, was also the publisher or a relative.

119. See, e.g., the notes for this work in Ye Changchi, *Pangxi zhai cangshu ji*, 3.38b–39b.

120. See note 12 to this chapter.

121. See Hennessey, "The Song Emperor Huizong in Popular History and Romance," pp. 14–15, 22–23, 27–29, and various sections in his chap. 3, especially table I (pp. 42–43) listing parallel texts from other sources.

122. Indeed, if we are to explain this dominance, we should look to the factors that made commercial printing so prevalent at a very early stage of book printing in China and the importance of the nonurban printing industry. The argument that movable type is much less convenient for the several hundred thousand Chinese characters required for a complete font is not enough; the lesser importance of block-printing of books in Japan and even more in Korea needs to be explained. In addition, the fallacious technical argument that the usual water-based Chinese ink is ill-suited for metal type completely ignores the obvious existence of appropriate ink used in any number of movable-type imprints produced for centuries in China. Rather, the convenience and economy of block-printing for Chinese books ensured its longevity in China, where commercial printing constituted the largest segment of the industry. There are no known movable-type Jianyang imprints from the Song or Yuan, and only a handful from the Ming.

123. See de Pee, "Negotiating Marriage," which makes these points for writing manuals in chap. 2 and even more so for almanacs in chap. 4, esp. pp. 265ff. Drège ("Des effets de l'imprimerie en Chine sous la dynastie des Song") also notes the non-survival of nonscholarly printed books from the Song.

124. See, e.g., Ōki, *Minmatsu Kōnan ni okeru shuppan bunka no kenkyū*; Ko, *Teachers of the Inner Chambers*, esp. pp. 34–59; Inoue, "Zōsho to dokusho," and "Shoshi, shoko, bunjin"; and McDermott, "The Ascendance of The Imprint in Late

Imperial China." I thank Dr. McDermott for permission to cite from the draft version of his paper.

Chapter 5

1. Sources on both the Yuan-Ming transition and the Ming-Qing transition in Minbei are frustratingly limited. Nearly all the local gazetteers seem to suffer from historical amnesia, and private accounts are extremely few. For the Yuan-Ming transition, one indication of the extent of destruction comes from the numerous essays commemorating the repairing and/or refounding of an ancestral temple or clan school. Every genealogy I examined that includes such essays mentions the destruction of these places at the end of the Yuan.

2. See Zhu Weigan, *Fujian shigao*, 1: 461–67.

3. *FJTJ* (1922), "Jinshi zhi," 12.33a–35b.

4. See *Ming Taizu Gao huangdi shilu*, 22.56a; and He Mengchun, *Yudong xulu*, 10.24a. Although there was a tea monopoly in the Ming, the government's main concern was tea production in Shaanxi and Sichuan because of its importance to the northern border trade. In Fujian and much of central and south China, "the tea monopoly and tea taxation became virtually a dead letter" (Gardella, "Fukien's Tea Industry and Trade," p. 63).

5. Zhou Lianggong, *Min xiaoji*, p. 108. Songluo refers to a region in Huizhou where a new method of processing green teas was developed in the late Ming. These teas were becoming more popular as those from the Wuyi Mountains declined temporarily in general esteem.

6. See Zhu Weigan, *Fujian shigao*, 2: 129–31.

7. See ibid., 2: 132–38; and Li Longqian, "Ming Zhengtong nianjian Ye Zongliu Deng Maoqi qiyi jingguo ji tedian," pp. 227–51.

8. *JYXZ* (1832 ed.), 12: 461.

9. Rawski, *Agricultural Change and the Peasant Economy of South China*, esp. pp. 57–100.

10. For the Qing, this is suggested by the existence of *peitian* 賠田 contracts for the *peizhu* 賠主, an intermediary between the absentee landlord and the tenant, in several regions in interior Fujian, including Jianning; see Fu Yiling, *Ming-Qing nongcun shehui jingji*, pp. 44–59. Fu's work remains the basic study on the subject. Fu has no tenancy contracts from the Ming, but a comparison of the Qing contracts he discovered with the contract forms found in Ming *leishu* by Niida Noboru (*Chūgoku hōseishi kenkyū*, 2: 551–52) show them to be quite similar. See also Rawski, *Agricultural Change and the Peasant Economy of South China*, pp. 10–30, for a discussion of tenure of farm land in Fujian.

11. See Chang Pin-tsun, "Chinese Maritime Trade," pp. 158–64.

12. *JYXZ* (1553 ed.), 4.33a and 5.19a; *FJTJ* (1922 ed.): *Fujian banben zhi*, 1.3a-b. The latter gives the exact dates of the fire as the fourth to the sixth day of the twelfth lunar month of Hongzhi 12, which correspond to January 4–6, 1500, in the Western calendar.

13. *JYXZ* (1553 ed.), 3.6a; and *JYXZ* (1601 ed.), 1.43a.

14. Zhang Xiumin, *Zhongguo yinshua shi*, p. 383.

15. According to Jean Baptiste du Halde (*The General History of China*, p. 166), who traveled through the area in the 1720s, most of the houses of Jianning had been rebuilt after the Qing troops burned the city, but it was less impressive than before. On Jianning as a rice-exporting area in the Qing, see Yeh-chien Wang, "Food Supply in Eighteenth-Century Fukien."

16. Zhang Xiumin, *Zhongguo yinshua shi*, lists 13 commercial printers for Beijing (pp. 359-60), 24 for Hangzhou (pp. 365-66), 37 for Suzhou (pp. 369-71), 93 for Jinling (Nanjing; pp. 343-48), and 84 for Jianyang (pp. 378-83). These numbers are useful mainly as rough estimates for several reasons. First, some of the printers Zhang lists for Jinling were in fact Jianyang men who operated in both places. Second, a few of his attributions are questionable, since they are based on printer's colophons in the imprints, which state rather ambiguously "Printed by — of Shulin." The term *shulin* 書林 or *shufang* 書坊 can refer to commercial printshops in general or the area where they were situated, and cities like Nanjing, Hangzhou, and Suzhou had their own *shulin*. Thus, without other evidence (information from prefaces and postfaces, blockcarvers' names, physical characteristics of the book, etc.), it may not be possible to identify the provenance of the imprint.

17. In Table B.5, I have listed all the printers that can be reasonably considered commercial, largely based on the imprints themselves. Occasionally, as in the case of Liu Hongyi (see below in the main text), the printer was working on commission for an official or for a nonofficial group, but this is usually made clear in the imprint. For a discussion of the term "commercial publisher" as used in this study, see Chapter 1. In many cases, I have listed individuals under the printshop with which they were known to be associated. In many other cases, however, it is not possible to determine whether an individual *was* associated with a shop.

18. For example, Yu Sijing 余思敬 (*zi* Yuanyi 元翼), who appears in the thirty-fifth generation of the genealogical table along with his first cousins Yingshen 應申, Yingke 應科 (*zi* Yigeng 夷庚), and Yingteng 應騰 (*zi* Tianyu 天羽) and his second cousin Yingqiu 應虬, is quite possibly the brother or cousin of Siya 思雅, Siqi 思齊 (*zi* Yuanshu 元叔), and several other Yu men. The characters *si* 思, *ying* 應, and *yuan* 元 appear throughout the thirty-fifth generation of this part of the family (Table 3). Moreover, the character *yuan* here does not seem to denote either eldest son or the first male child in a generation, since a number of brothers all have *Yuan* in their *zi* and none of these men are noted as the first generation of a new sub-branch of the family.

19. We cannot prove that these women were related to the printers of the same name, but Yu Chengzhang's close collaboration with both Xiong and Liu printers suggests that he may well have been related to them by marriage.

20. An apparent exception was Yu Yuanchang 余元長 (*zi* Gongren 公仁 and also Rengong 仁公), who was active from the last few years of the Wanli period till around the first years of the Shunzhi period (1644-61). Although no Yu Yuanchang appears in the Yu genealogy I examined, he probably belongs to the thirty-seventh generation as counted in the *shixi*, since "Yuan" 元 was a generational name for three other men listed in the genealogy. For Yuanchang's publishing activities, see Richard Wang, "Creating Artifacts: The Ming Erotic Novella in Cultural Practice," pp. 37 (and

*n*38), 43–44, 68–69, 92–93, 329–33; and He Changjiang, "*Yanju biji* bianzhe Yu Gong-ren xiaokao."

21. One, the collected writings of Yu Jing 余靖, the northern Song official, *Wuxi ji* 武溪集, is dated Longwu 2 (1646), and the other, *Juan gujin Zhongxing choulüe* 鐫古今中興籌略, a rather apt collection of writings on military strategy edited by Yu Yingqiu, a second cousin of Yu Xiangdou and quite active as an author and editor in the late Ming.

22. Dell R. Hales, "Yü Hsiang-tou," in Goodrich and Fang, *Dictionary of Ming Biography* (hereafter *DMB*), pp. 1612–14. Other discussions of Yu's publishing activities include Sun Kaidi, *Riben Dongjing suo jian xiaoshuo shumu*, pp. 97–99; Xiao Dongfa, "Jianyang Yu shi keshu kaolüe," pt. 2, esp. pp. 213–16; Maruyama Hiroaki, "Yo Shōto-bon kōryaku"; Chen Xianghua, "Lüelun Yu Xiangdou yu qi *Piping Sanguo zhizhuan*"; and Richard Wang, "Creating Artifacts," esp. pp. 74–75, 85–90.

23. This 1637 work, *Wuke liqi zuanyao xiangbian Santai bianlan tongshu zhengzong* 五刻理氣纂要詳辯三台便覽通書正宗, is actually a reprint of three earlier works and may have been produced by Yu's younger relatives continuing his publishing activities. Yu achieved unusual longevity through his publications; the *Shilin zhengzong* 詩林正宗, with an original publication date of 1600, was reprinted by his descendants, who included a preface supposedly signed and dated 1697 by Yu! (Japan National Diet Library Rare Book Collection no. 180-78).

24. My count gives 72 imprints. Richard Wang ("Creating Artifacts," pp. 74–75) gives a higher figure of 81, which is similar to that of Maruyama Hiroaki ("Yo Shōto-bon kōryaku," p. 125). The difference probably results from my greater caution in attributing certain imprints to Yu Xiangdou, including at least one published by Yu Wenlong 余文龍. Yu Xiangdou used a number of other names, including Yu Junzhao 君召, Yu Shiteng 世騰, Yu Wentai 文台, Yu Xiangwu 象烏, Yu Yangzhi 仰止, and Yu Yuansu 元素; see Sun Kaidi, *Riben Dongjing suo jian xiaoshuo shumu*, p. 98; and Xiao Dongfa, "Jianyang Yushi keshu kaolüe," pt. 2, p. 216. In the case of some names for which I feel that there is insufficient evidence to identify with Yu Xiangdou, I have listed the imprints separately in Table B.5.

25. Thanks to Yu's penchant for self-advertising, we have a list of some of his imprints in his 1591 edition of *Xinqin Zhu zhuangyuan Yunchuang huiji bai dajia pingzhu Shiji pincui* 新鐫朱狀元芸窗彙輯百大家評注史記品粹, in the Rare Book Collection of the Zhongguo Kexueyuan library (Beijing). The list is given in its entirety by Xiao Dongfa, "Jianyang Yushi keshu kaolüe," pt. 2, pp. 213–14. The tone of the note accompanying the list alerts us to be cautious in accepting all the titles as actual publications by Yu Xiangdou.

26. These two works are commonly known as the *Journey to the North* (*Beiyou ji* 北遊記) and *Journey to the South* (*Nanyou ji* 南遊記). Given the internal evidence of the texts and the pattern of Yu Xiangdou's editorial efforts, he probably was *not* the original author of these works. The *Beiyou ji* has been translated into English by Gary Seaman as *Journey to the North: An Ethnohistorical Analysis and Annotated Translation of the Chinese Folk Novel* Pei-yu chi (Berkeley: University of California Press, 1987). The *Nanyuji* is the subject of a study by Ursula-Angelika Cedzich, "The Cult of the Wu-t'ung/Wu-hsien in History and Fiction: The Religious Roots of the *Journey to the South.*" As Cedzich points out, it is possible but as yet unproven that Yu Xiangdou also

compiled the *Journey to the East* and so put together, with some version of Wu Cheng'en's famous *Journey to the West*, the first printed edition of the *Four Journeys*.

27. Richard Irwin, *The Evolution of a Chinese Novel: Shui-hu-chuan* (Cambridge, Mass.: Harvard University Press, 1953), p 102; cited in the *DMB* entry for Yu Xiangdou, p. 1614.

28. In the 1599 *Dingqin Chongwen yue huizuan shimin wanyong zhengzong bu qiu ren quanbian* 鼎鍥崇文閣彙纂士民萬用正宗不求人全編 (35 *juan*), one line 萬曆新歲喬山堂劉少崗繡 [梓] appears at the end of *juan* 16; it was probably inadvertently left in by Yu. Liu Shaogang is Liu Longtian. In Yu's 1607 *Xinke tianxia simin bianlan Santai wanyong zhengzong* 新刻天下四民便覽三台萬用正宗 (43 *juan*), two characters in the printer's colophon seem to have been recut, and the picture of the child holding up the colophon is nearly identical to that in a number of Liu Longtian's imprints. Both works are in the Tōyō bunka Library in Tokyo University.

29. Sun Kaidi, *Riben Dongjing suo jian xiaoshuo shumu*, p. 32. Another relative (uncle?) of Yu Xiangdou, Yu Shaoyu 余邵魚, is listed as the author of *Lieguo zhizhuan* 列國志傳, a historical novel dealing with the Spring and Autumn Period (ibid., pp. 28–29). The *Lieguo zhizhuan* was reworked by Feng Menglong as *Xin lieguo zhi* 新列國志; see Hu Wanchuan 胡萬川, "*Xin lieguozhi* de jieshao," in Feng Menglong, *Xin lieguozhi*, 1: 1–9.

30. He would sign his *ming* and/or one of his sobriquets, e.g., "Santai shanren Yangzhi Yu Xiangdou (yan)" 三台山人仰止余象斗 (言). In other works that he printed, the evidence suggests that he wrote the preface(s) himself and then signed the names of famous scholars or officials, to whom editorial credit was spuriously given.

31. Yu is listed as the author and/or editor of every *juan* and seems to have been the moving spirit behind the work. Copies are held in the Naikaku bunko Chinese Rare Book Collection (291函 46號) and the Harvard-Yenching Rare Book Collection (T1747/8923).

32. *Ke Yangzhi zi canding zhengchuan dili tongyi quanshu* 刻仰止子參定正傳地理統一全書 (Engraved complete book of transmitted correct [principles of] geomancy, collated by Yangzhi zi [Yu Xiangdou]), 1.65b–66a. The book actually is a compilation of geomancy texts that Yu and a number of other men had either supplemented with comments or abridged. For Yu's ancestor Tongzu, see the fourteenth generation in the genealogy in Table 3. See also note 64 in Chapter 3 about discrepancies concerning the date of the Yu lineage's settlement in Minbei.

33. Cedzich ("The Cult of Wu-t'ung," p. 216) argues that "the *Journey to the South*, despite its plain vernacular style, required a comparatively high degree of literacy on the part of its readers." She suggests that Yu's intended audience were merchants, shopkeepers, and other sufficiently educated commoners, who, moreover, would approve of the modified views on the religious cult expressed in the novel.

34. This is an extremely oversimplified description of this late Ming–early Qing philosophical and literary "movement." For a brief summary and recent references, see Shelley Chang, *History and Legend: Ideas and Images in the Ming Historical Novels*, esp. pp. 22–27.

35. The table in the Yu genealogy mistakenly lists Yu Zhangde under his *ming* in the thirty-fourth generation (see Table 3) and as his own son under his *zi* Siquan.

Evidence from his imprints and from a funeral inscription or epitaph (*muzhiming*) for his son Yu Yingqiu, however, clearly shows that Zhangde and Siquan were one and the same person. The funeral inscription is "Shulin Jianju Yu Youlong muzhiming" 書林薦舉余猶龍墓誌銘 by Xiong Renlin 熊仁霖 in his *Hetai Xiansheng Xiong Shan wenxuan* (Naikaku bunko 314 函 89 號). Xiong Renlin, a native of Jiangxi, was a distant relative of the Jianyang Xiong. All of them were descended from ancestors who first settled in the Nanchang area of Jiangxi in the Southern Tang. Renlin also wrote epitaphs for several other Jianyang men that yield bits of otherwise unavailable information. The Fujian branch was started somewhat later by men from Jiangxi, a fact also mentioned in the prefaces of the Jianyang Xiong genealogy (see Chap. 3).

36. Thus the figure of 70 titles refers to imprints of Cuiqing tang, whose publishers included Yu Zhangde and his relatives.

37. I thank Kathryn Lowry for bringing some of this information to my attention.

38. Tan Zhengbi, *Zhongguo wenxue jia da cidian*, entry 4770, p. 1213.

39. There is one imprint by a Liu Lin (Table 2b, tenth generation) from the Northern Song (1124). Three Liu imprints are attributed to the early Qing in the catalogues of the libraries owning them.

40. For information on six of these men, see Fang Yanshou, "Minbei Liushi deng shisi wei keshujia shengping kaolüe."

41. This is based on a survey of the 1553, 1601, 1703, and 1832 editions of the Jianyang county gazetteer; the 1670, 1733, 1808, and 1924 editions of the Chongan county gazetteer; and the 1541, the Wanli period, and 1694 editions of the Jianning prefecture gazetteer.

42. The more complete biography of Liu Yan is "Taizhong gong Dacheng zhuan" 太中公大成專, in *juan* 1 of "Liu shi zhongxian zhuan" 劉氏忠賢專, which constitutes the last two volumes of *Liu shi zupu* 劉氏族譜 (1880), in the Fujian Normal University Rare Book Collection.

43. The preface "Chongkan Sishu wenmu xu" 重刊四書問目序 by Zheng Jing 鄭京 is included in "Liu shi zhongxian zhuan" (see preceding note), 4:22b–23a.

44. See Wang Yuquan, "Some Salient Features of the Ming Labor Service System," p. 18.

45. Both characters shown for "hong" in Liu Hongyi's name are recorded in his imprints.

46. The statement about the exemption reads "fu Liu yaoyi yi nian yi chang qi lao" 復劉徭役一年以償其勞 (to repay Liu for his work by [exemption of] one year's labor service). Presumably, since working on the imprint already constituted labor service specific to a *shu hu* 書戶, the exemption applied to some other obligation. The preface about Liu Hongyi is reproduced in the occasionally legible photofacsimile reprint of the *Qunshu kaosuo* published by Shumu wenxian chubanshe (1992). For more about this work, see below.

47. Wang Yuquan ("Some Salient Features of the Ming Labor Service System," pp. 25–29) does not list *shu hu* in his 47 household categories, which he culled from official Ming sources and which he himself notes is not complete. It seems reasonable

that the specific labor service obligations of *shu hu* related to various tasks of book production and that some unknown number of the Jianyang publishers were registered as *shu hu*, even though they did not state this, either in their imprints or their genealogies.

48. The only other Shufang *shu hu* that I have uncovered—that of Wu Shiliang 吳世良—is surprisingly late, in the Wanli period (one imprint dated 1574 and another 1609). For more on government publishing activities in the Minbei area, see the discussion below.

49. See, e.g., Ye Dehui, *Shulin qinghua*, 7.8b.

50. Most of the Cuiyan jingshe imprints of the Ming are from the fifteenth century; later imprints include one from 1519, another from 1522, and two from 1588. These four works may have been put out by printers not directly associated with the Cuiyan jinshe of the earlier period.

51. See Xie Shuishun and Li Ting, *Fujian gudai keshu*, pp. 262–64, for further discussion of the Cuiyan jingshe and Liu Yan.

52. Based on my examination of these imprints, it seems that the corrections the Shendu zhai made did not include characters that were popularly miswritten slightly, an omission quite commonly encountered among commercial blockprinted books.

53. The documented example of the blocks for the *Cefu yuangui* printed in Jianyang in 1642 has already been described in Chapter 2.

54. At least four of the printers, starting with Liu Hui 輝 (Table 2b), were in a direct father-son succession. See also Table B.5.

55. The Zhou Ruquan Wanjuan lou edition is in several rare book collections, including those of the National Diet Library and the Naikaku bunko in Tokyo and the Library of Congress in Washington. The Liu Kongdun edition is in the National Library of China.

56. Ruitenbeek, "The *Lu Banjing*: A Fifteenth-Century Chinese Carpenter's Manual," p. 142; see also note 41 in Chapter 2. The Liu Kongdun edition is in the rare book collection of the National Central Library in Taipei. The Yang shi Sizhi guan edition was formerly in the Usui Yukikaku collection and is described in Nagasawa Kikuya, *Min Shin sōzu hon zuroku*, reprinted in *Nagasawa Kikuya chosaku shū*, 3: 432 and pl. 65. The Yan Shaoxuan edition is in the Naikaku bunko.

57. I have counted at least nineteen works for which Liu Suming was an engraver and/or illustrator. (For a list of ten such works, see Fang Yanshou, "Jianyang Liu shi keshu kao" pt. 2, pp. 220–21.) Usually, the illustration notes "engraved by Suming" *Suming kan* 素明刊, or "executed" *zuo* 作, or "illustration engraved by" *ke xiang* 刻象, or sometimes "*xieke*" 寫刻. Sören Edgren has told me that he believes that *xieke* indicates that the blockcarver was also the calligrapher. At least five other Liu men from Minbei also worked as engravers during the late sixteenth and early seventeenth centuries. One of them, Liu Yuming 玉明, was a first cousin of Suming according to the *Jingzhao Liu shi Zhen fang zongpu*. Although the other four (Liu Ciquan 次泉, Liu Suwen 素文, Liu Fengzhou 鳳洲, and Liu Pinzhou 聘洲) do not appear in the genealogy, I believe that they were Minbei men based on the imprints they worked on, which were either Jianyang publications or had other Jianyang men credited as publisher, editor, and/or collator. The problem with determining which engravers named Liu came from the Jianyang area is rather tricky since there were

also Liu from Huizhou and the Jiangnan printing centers, and sometimes there were Liu carvers from Jianyang and other areas working on the same imprint. Thus, although Li Guoqing's *Ming dai kangong xingming suoyin* lists 99 engravers named Liu for the Ming, only six of them can definitely or very probably be said to be Minbei natives.

For the Huang blockcarvers from Anhui, see Zhang Xiumin, *Zhongguo yinshua shi*, pp. 747–49; and idem, "Mingdai Huipai banhua Huangxing kegong kaolüe," in *Zhang Xiumin yinshua shi lunwen ji*, pp. 171–79.

58. See Chapter 3 for the activities of the more prominent branch of the Xiong clan, the Eastern lineage (Dongzu 東族), to which the Southern Song scholar Xiong Ke and the Yuan scholar Xiong He belonged.

59. The name Zhonghe tang 中和堂, was also used, apparently interchangeably with Zhongde tang.

60. For *Furen daquan liangfang* and *Taiping huimin heji ju fang*, see Okanishi Tameto, *Song yiqian yiji kao*, pp. 1114–15 and 765–87, respectively; and *Quan guo Zhongyi tushu lianhe mulu*, entry 6607, pp. 428–29 and entry 2972, pp. 215–16.

61. The biographical note in the *shixi* of the genealogy, *Tanyang Xiong shi zongpu*. Much the same biographical note is found in all the extant Jianyang County gazetteers starting with the 1553 edition, 16.5a–b.

62. Although the name Xiong Damu does not appear in the genealogy, his *hao* Zhonggu 鍾谷 does; it belongs to a Fuzhen 福鎮 in the twenty-second generation (see Table 4). Fang Yanshou ("Mingdai xiaoshuojia Xiong Damu ji qi 'Bei Song zhizhuan,'" p. 55) has argued quite convincingly that Fuzhen and Damu are the same person. Fang's tentative dates for Damu, ca. 1506–79, seems less convincing.

The story in *Riji gushi*, 7.7a–b, gives the name of Zongli's grandson as Yiqing, which, according to the information in the *shixi* of the *Tanyang Xiong shi zongpu*, is the *zi* of Tianxuan (21st generation in the Xiong genealogy shown in Table 4).

63. Because there is so little information on Ming novelists like Xiong Damu (in contrast to much better known men like Feng Menglong), what can be learned comes mainly from the prefaces they might have written for their own works. For Xiong Damu, see Shelley Chang, *History and Legend*, pp. 10–11, 24–25; and Idema, "Novels About the Founding of the Sung Dynasty," pp. 2–9.

64. For his four extant historical novels, see Sun Kaidi, *Zhongguo tongsu xiaoshu shumu: Quan Han zhizhuan* 全漢志傳 (p. 32), *Tangshu zhizhuan tongsu yanyi* 唐書志傳通俗演義 (pp. 48–49), *Nan-Bei liang Song zhizhuan* 南北兩宋志傳 (pp. 55–57), and *Da Song zhongxing tongsu yanyi* 大宋中興通俗演義 (p. 60). The last work was apparently first published by the Yang family's Qingbai tang 楊氏清白堂 in Jianyang, and the publisher was probably Yang Yongquan 楊湧泉. According to Xiong's preface of 1552, his relative Yongquan had persuaded him to rework the official histories' accounts of the Northern–Southern Song transition to render it more accessible to "ignorant men and women." As for the *Riji gushi* 日記故事, there is a photofacsimile reprint of the 1542 Jianyang edition, with a preface by Xiong Damu in Zheng Zhenduo, *Zhongguo gudai banhua congkan*, vol. 2.

65. The book was the collected works of the Yuan scholar Xiong He, who retired from office when the Southern Song fell. It was actually printed by a Xiong Zhizhang 之璋, a member of the Eastern lineage and a direct descendant of Xiong He. The

active supporter of the Longwu Emperor was Xiong Zhixue 志學, a descendant of Xiong Zongli (Table 4, twenty-fifth generation), and the only other member of the Western line to have rated a biographical note in the local gazetteer. The *JYXZ* (1832 ed.), 13:491, omits mention of his Southern Ming loyalism, which *is* mentioned in the genealogy.

66. The tomb tablet is now at the Jianyang County Museum. The discussion in Fang Yanshou, "Minbei shiba wei keshujia shengping kaolüe" (1996), pp., 211–14, talks about Zheng Shikui, his younger brother Zheng Shirong 世容 (ca. 1547–1638) and the latter's two sons, Zheng Yiqi 以祺 and Zheng Yizhen 以禎, all of whom were publishers in the late sixteenth and early seventeenth centuries. According to the tomb epitaph, the ancestor who came to Minbei to escape the turmoil between the Northern and Southern Song was Zheng Qingzhi 清之 (1176–1251), a native of the Ningbo area and a high-level official (biography in *SS* 414:12419–23). There is no other information about any of the later Zheng men until the biography of Zheng Zhongyi 仲佾, the father of Shikui and Shirong, which appears in *JYXZ* (1832 ed.), p. 432. The paucity of information on the Zheng men in Minbei after Qingzhi suggests that none of them attained the official prominence of their ancestor, but did retain some distinction as members of the local elite, both through their activities as publishers and as community leaders, involved in the local militia (like Zhongyi).

67. These include the *Shuyan gushi* 書言故事, *Gushi baimei* 故事白眉, *Gushi huangmei* 故事黃眉, and the *Jinbi gushi* 金璧故事. Such collections are discussed in Chapter 6 in the section surveying Jianyang imprints.

68. Actually, the 1601 edition is a reprint of an earlier edition from the Jiajing period. Both are in the Naikaku bunko. That Li Mo was a Minbei (Jian'an) native may have spurred the Zheng publisher to reprint his work.

69. There is no evidence suggesting connections with the other well-known Zheng publishers in Nanjing known to be natives of Huizhou in Anhui. Zhou Wu, *Zhongguo banhua shi tulu*, entry 294, credits the picture of a 1593 imprint to a Zheng Shaozhai of Zongwen shuyuan of Huizhou (徽州鄭少齋宗文書院), but Zheng Shaozhai may well belong the Jianyang family, which had two publishers named Shaocong 少聰 and Shaoyuan 少垣, who were active in the late Wanli period. The Zongwen shuyuan may have referred to the printshop that the Jianyang Zheng established in Nanjing.

70. See Xiong Renlin, "Shulin xiangyin bin Chen Yuwo muzhiming" 書林鄉飲賓陳玉我墓誌銘, in idem, *Hetai Xiansheng Xiong Shan wenxuan*, *juan* 13. It is unclear how well Xiong knew the subject of his epitaph; the style of the piece is more perfunctory than the epitaph he wrote for Yu Youlong (see note 35 to this chapter) and for some of the Jianyang Xiong men. I assume, however, that Xiong (or Chen Yuwo's relatives) would have had the important facts correct, such as the name of Yuwo's father (Chen Qiquan/Sun'an 奇泉/孫安), another publisher.

71. This information is given in the entry for Zhu Bingtie in the *Ziyang tang Zhu shi zongpu*; see Fang Yanshou, "Minbei shisi wei keshujia shengping kaolüe," p. 217.

72. It is possible that a printer named Chen Wohan 我含, of Jicheng 吉澄 (Haicheng 海澄) on the southern Fujian coast, who published a work on family rituals for popular use in 1607, was related to the Jianyang Chen men. Van der Loon, *The Classical Theatre and Art Song of Southern Fukien*, p. 11, fig. 4, shows the

printer's colophon with its lotus-leaf design for Chen Wohan's work, which could easily be mistaken for that in Jianyang imprints of the same period. See also note 16 to Chapter 6.

73. This work, the *Wanbao shi shan,* was republished (from different blocks) by the Guangqin tang in 1429. For references to this work, see note 118 of Chapter 4.

74. All the publishers surnamed Ye were most likely related. Based on printers' colophons and other internal evidence from the imprints, we know for certain that a few, such as Ye Huiting 會廷, were associated with both the Guangqin tang and the Zuode tang. Generally speaking, it is difficult to discern any hard-and-fast distinction among the various *tangming* used by the Ye publishers (see Table B.5).

75. Yu Yingkui does not appear in the Yu genealogy, which includes the other men involved in publishing, but given the date of the imprint and the "Ying" in his name, it is likely that he was the nephew of Yu Xiangdou and Yu Zhangde.

76. Van der Loon (*The Classical Theatre and Art Song of South Fukien,* p. 3) suggests that Ye Wenqiao may have transferred the blocks to the Zhu family, since Ye is listed as the publisher at the start of three of the four *juan,* whereas the Zhu family's Yugeng tang is identified in a colophon. Given such evidence, it *is* possible, though less likely, that Ye and Zhu together financed the carving of the blocks. This practice, however, was quite common among commercial publishers, as we have pointed out.

77. See Chia, "Of Three Mountains Street: The Commercial Publishers of Ming Nanjing."

78. Copies of both the Ye Gui and the Tang Liyue Wenlin ge 唐鯉躍文林閣 "editions" are held in various libraries in China; the Spencer Collection of the New York Public Library has a copy of the Ye Gui version. The Zhongguo guji shanben shumu bianji weiyuanhui, *Zhongguo guji shanben shumu: zi bu,* no. 4073, conflates the two, listing the publisher as "Ye Gui Wenlin ge."

79. More libraries (including the Harvard-Yenching and Library of Congress) seem to have the Ye Baoshan tang edition; I have seen only one copy with the Ye Jinshan colophon, at the Naikaku bunko (316 函 150 號) in Tokyo. The "Sanqu Ye Baoshan tang" is given in a colophon at the end of the table of contents (*mulu* 目錄), and the "Zhejiang Ye Baoshan tang" is given in the colophon at the end of the work. The date of 1553 is given in yet another colophon, at the end of the preface and before the table of contents and reads "Jiajing guichou Shulin Ye shi Wujin zixing" 嘉靖癸丑 書林葉氏武進梓行 (printed in 1553 by Ye Wujin of Shulin).

80. This is the collection of examination essays *Tang Huiyuan jing xuan pidian Tang-Song ming xian ce lunwen cui* 唐會元精選批點唐宋名賢策論文粹 at the Princeton Gest Library (TC318/1152).

81. According to the Zhongguo guji shanben shumu bianji weiyuanhui, *Zhongguo shanben guji shumu: jingbu,* no. 467, the Nanjing Library has a copy of the *Yijing shaojie* 易經勺解 dated 1699 and printed by Shijian tang.

82. Xiao Mingsheng's style or *hao* was Jingwei, and Xiao Zhiwei 徵韋, who published one drama, *Ming zhu ji* 明珠記, in the Wanli period was probably either Mingsheng's brother or cousin of the same generation.

83. Xie Shuishun and Li Ting (*Fujian gudai keshu,* pp. 321–22) make the same observation but tend to overstate the differences between Xiao Shixi and Xiao Tenghong's publications. At least two imprints with Shixi's colophon resemble the

Nanjing works published by his brother and are noticeably different from his other books, but we lack the evidence to determine where the two works were actually produced.

84. In addition to Liu Suming, Liu Ciquan, a Jianyang native and possibly Suming's relative, drew and carved several other illustrations in this imprint (see note 57 to this chapter). Finally, some of his other collaborators, as well as Xiao Tenghong himself (signed "Qingyun" 慶雲), wrote the inscriptions on a number of illustrations. All men listed in the *Xiuru ji* (including Chen Jiru) are similarly credited in Xiao Tenghong's other illustrated plays.

85. It is possible that the commentaries were falsely attributed to Chen Jiru, whose name was often attached to works he did not work on.

86. National Library of China Rare Book Collection, no. 596.

87. 1390: *Taizu shilu, juan* 206; 1391: ibid., *juan* 214; 1404: *Taizong shilu, juan* 26. The work published in 1398 by Rui Lin 芮麟, the Jianning prefect, together with his friend, who was the Fujian salt controller, is *Wenguo zhai lu* 聞過齋錄, by the early Ming scholar-official (and Fujian native), Wu Hai 吳海. See *Siku quanshu zongmu*, entry 07517.

88. *Xuanzong shilu, juan* 50.

89. Gu Yanwu, in "Chaoshu zixu" 抄書自序, in idem, *Gu Tinglin shi-wenji*, p. 29. The dearth of imprints in the first century or so of the dynasty was noted by a number of Ming writers and later scholars. See below for further discussion.

90. Zhang was a native of Jianchang 建昌 across the Wuyi Mountains in Jiangxi. There is little information about him, except for bland, conventional one- and two-line biographical notes in various local histories, such as the *JYXZ* (1553 ed.), 13.6a–b.

91. A modern photofacsimile reprint of this work is included in the collection *Guben xiaoshuo congkan* 古本小說叢刊, set no. 5 (Beijing: Zhonghua shuju, 1990). As the notes in this reprint point out, the numbering of the *juan* is rather puzzling, and the entire 1433 publication may also have included the earlier *Jian deng xin hua* of Qu You, although it has not survived. For a discussion on the circulation and readership of the *New Tales* and *More Tales*, see McLaren, "Paratextual Discourse in Chinese Texts."

92. Original statement quoted by Gu Yanwu in *Rizhilu (zhi yu)*, 4: 1255; partially quoted in Zhang Xiumin, *Zhongguo yinshua shi*, p. 468.

93. Another serious fire in the same year (Hongzhi 12) at the Wenyuan ge 文淵閣 in Nanjing, which destroyed many Song and Yuan works stored there, might have added urgency to the mission to Shufang. For the Wenyuan ge fire, see Shen Defu, *Wanli yehuo bian*, 1:4.

94. Translation slightly modified from that in K. T. Wu, "Ming Printing and Printers," pp. 229–30. The *keshu jiang hu* 刻書匠戶 (blockcarver households) and the *ke jiang hu* in the tenth and twelfth columns of the original text (Fig. 3), respectively, are almost certainly the same as the *shu hu* 書戶 by which a few Jianyang publishers, such as Liu Hongyi, designated themselves. See notes 46 and 47 to this chapter.

95. Clarifying the circumstances of the printing of the Ji Cheng set and the reprinting by Yang Yi'e continue to pose a particular headache to rare book scholars. From my own examination of the works, including tabulations of the blockcarvers'

names, I tentatively suggest that the blocks for at least some of the imprints were carved by Jianyang blockcarvers, although where they worked is uncertain. Based on her lists of blockcarver names for the mid-Ming, Ji Shuying ("Tan tan Ming keben ji kegong," p. 216) suggests that the Ji Cheng editions were carved by engravers known to work in both Fujian and/or Suzhou.

96. It is interesting that Li Yuanyang 李元陽 (1497–1580), also a Fujian regional inspector, was embarking on his ambitious publication project of the Thirteen Classics with annotations and commentaries in Fuzhou around the same time. See also Brook, "Edifying Knowledge: The Building of School Libraries in Ming China." The Jiajing period is somewhat later than the dates of the majority of the school buildings and restorations listed in Brook's Table 1, but given the tendency of such schools and their libraries to fall into decay (judging from my examination of Fujian local histories, anyway), there may have been good reason for the continual publication of the Classics and other scholarly works.

97. See, e.g., the conventional two-line notice about him in *JYXZ* (1832), p. 347.

98. *JYXZ* (1504 supplement to the 1453 edition).

99. See also note 57 in Chapter 2 about women blockcarvers working on the imprint.

100. Santai guan is one of several names used by Yu Xiangdou for his publishing operation. This copy is held in the Special Collection of the library of Fujian Normal College in Fuzhou, No. 885.3 Cw 61/552223–246.

101. The note in the various works of the complete compendia merely states "Yu family of Shulin" (書林余氏).

102. The work is *Tanhuo zhuanmen* 痰火顓門. The title page of the Yu Siquan edition has *Tanhuo huichun* 痰火回春, but it is nearly identical in content to Ye Dashou's imprint, including the prefaces. Because the preface of the *Tanhuo huichun* is dated 1610, several libraries' catalogues give the publication date as 1610. Although this is uncertain, Yu Siquan's edition was probably published around that date.

103. The fourteen known imprints from the Qing have not been included, not only because we can say little that is conclusive about them, but also because at least five of them were very likely reprints from Ming blocks.

104. See, e.g., Rawski, "Economic and Social Foundations of Late Imperial Culture," p. 22; Ōki Yasushi, *Minmatsu Kōnan ni okeru shuppan bunka no kenkyū*, chap. 2; and Ko, *Teachers of the Inner Chambers*, esp. chap. 1.

105. For example, the holdings of Chinese rare books in Japanese and European libraries include a number of popular (i.e., nonscholarly) works, such as household encyclopedias, cheap writing manuals, and illustrated fiction and drama, which are not extant in China. Not surprisingly, some of these works, which have been the subject of recent studies and facsimile reprints, are Jianyang imprints. See, e.g., Li Fuqing and Li Ping, *Haiwai guben wan Ming xiju xuanji san zhong*; James J. Y. Liu, "The *Fêng-yüeh chin-nang* 風月錦襄"; and Walravens, *Two Recently Discovered Fragments of the Chinese Novels* San-kuo-chih yen-i *and* Shui-hu chuan. Such imprints have survived in part because of the broader or more tolerant interests of Japanese and European collectors, who acquired imprints that Chinese bibliophiles of the time would have disdained to buy either because of their perceived shoddiness or because of their frivolous contents. Most of the earlier European buyers were probably quite ignorant

of Chinese culture and bought a work for its pictures or for its exotic value in general. When such books reached Europe, some were split up, with different volumes of a single work going to different collectors. See, e.g., the discussion on the possible customers for the Chinese works offered by a leading Dutch bookseller in the early seventeenth century in van Selm, "Cornelis Claesz's 1605 Stock Catalogue." Thus today, different libraries may own portions of the same imprint, a minor inconvenience compared to the good fortune of the work's survival.

106. This near-total disappearance of certain kinds of printing materials occurs even in countries where an abundance of imprints survive. For example, Henri-Jean Martin could devote only three pages (largely speculative) to the reading materials of "the humblest readers" in his 640-page work on the book trade in seventeenth-century Paris (see *Print, Power, and People in 17th-Century France*, pp. 368–70). Rudolf Hirsch (*Printing, Selling and Reading 1450–1550*, p. 11), in talking about the first century of European imprints, lists twelve kinds of books "more likely to have disappeared than others." Most of the items on his list would be found on an equivalent list for Chinese books: cheap books, small books, household books (cookbooks, etc.), books classified as pseudo-scientific (prescriptions, almanacs, prognostications, dream books), school primers, vernacular popular literature, proscribed books, and aids in conducting business (e.g., books on commercial arithmetic, samples of letters with proper salutations). Although in imperial China much of this information has survived in the type of *leishu* known as household encyclopedias, small works devoted to just one of these topics were probably printed in abundance, sold well, and were read until they fell apart. Since the paper was more than likely recycled for other uses, almost none are extant.

107. See, e.g., Inoue Susumu, "Zōsho to dokusho," pp. 415–40; and McDermott, "The Ascendance of the Imprint."

108. I write *Chinese* libraries (including the National Central Library and the Palace Museum Library in Taipei) since rare book collections in other countries tend to focus on a particular period because of their acquisition histories and do not therefore give a "representative" sample of Chinese imprints throughout history. For example, most of the collections in Western libraries are strongest in works from the Ming and later. In Japan, the collections that are strongest in Ming, Qing, and Republican works, such as the Naikaku bunko and the National Diet Library, have far fewer Song and Yuan imprints, whereas the Song and Yuan holdings of the Seikadō bunko and the Sonkeikaku are especially strong. Therefore, in counting Ming imprints, I have used bibliographies compiled based on holdings in libraries in China.

109. Dividing the dynasty in half is admittedly arbitrary, but the second half does happen to start with the Zhengde period, when Jianyang publishing began to revive, partly with the contributions of government officials, as described above in this chapter.

110. The figures come from my compilation of Jianyang imprints (see Appendix C for details). For characterizations of commercial and private publishers, see Chapter 1. I have included both in the discussion because in many cases it is difficult to distinguish between the two, and in any case, those likely to be private individual publishers constitute a small fraction of the total.

111. Although it is difficult to determine the exact publication date of some 300 imprints, it is possible to make a reasonable guess whether each of these was published in the first or second half of the Ming.

112. See Chia, "Commercial Publishing in Jianyang from the Late Song to the Late Ming."

113. Little is known about Zhou Hongzhu (*js* 1559); since his biography in the *Ming shi* (215: 5676–77) states that he served as an assistant education-intendant censor (*tixue fushi* 提學副使) in Fujian, he may well have had some personal knowledge of Jianyang publishing. I assume a date of 1570 for his bibliography because of the titles listed in the "Jianyang shufang" section. In any case, it seems likely that Zhou's lists are pre-Wanli.

114. *JYXZ* (1553 ed.), 5.20b–30a. Comparison with my own bibliography of Jianyang imprints reveals that only 123 of the 384, or 32 percent, from the gazetteer list are known today, essentially the same as the 33 percent for the *Gujin shuke* list. It is unclear whether the 384 titles in the *JYXZ* include ones printed in the Song and Yuan, but even if the fourteen from these earlier periods are included, the survival rate increases to only about 36 percent. I did not use the bibliography in the 1601 edition of the *JYXZ*, 7.9b–13b, since it contains only 131 titles and seems like a sloppily compiled list. Not only are most of these works also in the earlier gazetteer, but given the dramatic increase in Jianyang imprints during the late sixteenth century, the 1601 list should have been far larger.

It is also worth noting that both the 1553 *JYXZ* and the Zhou bibliographies are incomplete in two ways. First, both fall short of a complete list of Jianyang imprints up to the date of compilation, even for the categories included. For example, whereas I count about 106 medical works published in Jianyang before the start of the Wanli period in 1573, Zhou only lists 48. Similarly, I count 85 literary works of individuals (*bieji*) published prior to 1573, whereas Zhou lists only 35. The tallies in the 1553 *JYXZ* similarly fall short. Second, neither works of fiction (novels and many story collections) nor plays (including drama miscellanies) are included in the *JYXZ* and Zhou bibliographies, an especially disappointing omission since the information would help test the belief of many modern scholars that the printing of such works grew tremendously in the late Ming.

115. *JYXZ* (1601 ed.), 7.2a–8b (leaves 7.5–6 are missing from the sole extant copy). This is a list of works by Minbei authors from the Song through the late sixteenth century. Of the 167 titles on the surviving pages, 117 are noted as "lacking blocks" (*wu ban* 無板), which implies that the blocks originally did exist in Jianyang. Although it is possible that the blocks for some of the works were taken away to be used elsewhere, it seems more likely that the blocks were destroyed or damaged beyond repair.

116. For more such statements, see McDermott, "The Ascendance of the Imprint."

117. Lu Rong, *Shuyuan zaji* (1494); quoted in Zhang Xiumin, *Zhongguo yinshua shi*, p. 337.

118. Hu Yinglin, *Jingji hui tong* 經籍會通, *juan* 4 in *Shaoshi shanfang bicong*, p. 68. Trace-copying by a "hired hand" obviously does not bestow on the reader the same benefits that he would gain by attentively copying the text himself.

119. For example, consider Zhu Xi's (*Zhuzi yulei*, 1: 171) complaint in the late twelfth century: "The reason why people today read books in a careless and superficial fashion is because there are so many printed volumes.... Because people of old lacked books, they could only acquire them by memorizing them from beginning to end."

120. Li Xu, "Shi yi fangke" 時藝坊刻, in *Jiean laoren manbi*, 8:334. Presumably, Li Xu was reminiscing about the early sixteenth century. But it still seems somewhat strange that as a native of Jiangyin 江陰 (in Jiangsu), which is quite close to Wuxi and Suzhou and not all that far from Nanjing, he could not find reliable commercial editions.

121. Shen Defu, "Lu jiu wen" 錄舊文, in idem, *Bizhou xuansheng yu*, pp. 42–43.

122. Although these bibliographic notes are subject to the same problem as the numerical distributions (i.e., a lower survival rate for early Ming imprints), there is a remarkably consistent preponderance of late over early Ming works in the dozen or so bibliographies I examined, including the various catalogues for the famous Tianyige 天一閣 collection, which was started in the late Jiajing period in the mid-sixteenth century.

123. Sun Congtian, "Jianbie" (Discrimination), in *Cangshu jiyao*, 2b–6b. See also the translation by Achilles Fang in "Bookman's Manual," p. 226. Sun's dates are not known, but Fang suggests mid-seventeenth to mid-eighteenth century.

124. Ye Dehui, *Shulin qinghua*, 5.5a–24b.

125. For the economic decline of certain Jiangnan areas in the early Ming, see von Glahn, "Towns and Temples: Market Town Growth and Decline in the Yangzi Delta, 1200–1500."

126. Xie Zhaozhe, *Wu za zu*, 13.21a–22a. Note the similarity between Xie's criticism of Fujian (i.e., Jianyang) printing and those of much earlier writers, such as Ye Mengde (see Chapter 3).

127. Obviously there are ways to present such information in a fuller fashion, such as plotting the number of imprints in each category (or subcategory) vs. the length of time into the dynasty. I have not shown every *siku* category because the number of imprints for several of them was extremely low. Furthermore, it would be useful to employ a classification scheme other than the *siku* system, whose categories encompass quite disparate types of works. Such refinements in presentation, however, would be more valuable when we apply them to more complete data.

128. I have included imprints of and about the Four Books in the Classics since books in both categories increased in the same proportions.

129. The publishing history (*chuban zhi* 出版志) that is part of the most recent edition of each provincial/regional gazetteer (*sheng zhi* 省志) represents the most accessible source of information on printing and publishing in different areas of China during the Qing and Republican periods. Although these works tend to devote most attention to post-1949 publishing activities, they also include a bit of information about publishers of earlier periods and their imprints. In addition, in a three-year research project funded by the Luce Foundation, several scholars from the United States and China have been interviewing local scholars, gathering relevant materials, and surveying the available imprints in a large number of Chinese libraries in order to identify printing centers in Qing and Republican China and determine what extant

sources are available for studying them. Some information in the present discussion comes from the work done in this project.

130. With the exception of the information about the Liu family's Rixin tang in Chapter 3.

131. Brief summaries of Mao Jin's publishing activities together with references to earlier sources are given in K. T. Wu, "Ming Printing and Printers," pp. 244–46; and Zhang Xiumin, *Zhongguo yinshua shi*, pp. 373–74. Mao Jin's son, Yi 扆, continued publishing through the early eighteenth century. It is interesting to note that although Mao Jin usually is classified as a private publisher, the scale of his printing operations, the wide distribution of his publications, especially throughout the Jiangnan area, and his far from impeccably proofed texts made him similar to the commercial publishers of the time.

132. These figures are given in a postface of 1710 by Mao Yi, quoted in Yang Shaohe's *Yingshu yulu*, 1.52a. It is unclear who precisely was included among the twenty *yin jiang* 印匠 mentioned, but I assume they refer to the carvers and printers (those who pulled impressions off the blocks), but not the book binders. The latter may also have been regular employees in the Mao establishment, given the scale of its operations.

133. Ji Shuying ("Tantan Ming keben ji kegong," pp. 217–26) has identified 645 blockcarvers working on Suzhou imprints in the mid-sixteenth century. This number is best taken as an approximation, for several reasons. First, as she admits, several of the imprints represented collaboration among carvers working in Suzhou, Nanjing, and Fujian. Second, at least 30 of the names in her table appear in Minbei imprints, suggesting that these blockcarvers might have traveled from one printing center to another in central and south China. Thus the number of blockcarvers in Suzhou at any given time in the mid-sixteenth century might not have been over 600 but closer to 300–400. In any case, Jianyang, as well as Nanjing, the other major printing center in Jiangnan, probably would have had about the same number.

134. See note 57 to Chapter 2.

135. Yu Yingke was probably a nephew of Yu Xiangdou. See the thirty-fifth generation in the Yu genealogy (Table 3).

136. It is always possible that at least a few of the listings were more honorary than actual, for example, Liu Kongjing, the elder son of the publisher, Liu Longtian (see the discussion on the Liu family in this chapter). On the other hand, apparently none of the Yu men listed were particularly exalted; yet all appear in a number of Jianyang imprints as publisher, editor, collator, or in some other capacity. Although no publisher is specifically identified in this work, it greatly resembles in its page layout and calligraphy other imprints from Yu Siquan's Cuiqing tang or one of the other Yu family printing establishments. There are copies of this work in the rare book collections of the National Diet Library, Call no. 160–65; and the Naikaku bunko, 277 函 95 號.

137. See the discussion on colophons in the section of the visual appearance of Ming Jianyang imprints in Chapter 6.

138. Song Pingsheng, the director of the Old Materials Research Institute at the library of the People's University and an expert on Beijing publishing, has told me about a number of instances in which several commercial publishers in that city collaborated to finance the carving of blocks for a particular work during the Qing. So

far, little systematic work has been published on commercial printing in premodern Beijing; for the Qing and Republican periods, see the brief treatment in *Beijing gongye zhi*, "Yinshua zhi," pp. 90–102. My own research in Ji'nan and Liaocheng, two of the chief printing centers in Shandong during the Qing and Republican eras, turned up evidence of the same practice. There is no reason to think that such ventures were unique to Beijing or Shandong publishers.

139. See note 4 in Chapter 2 about the Yu family's paper-making activities. The shop names of various publishers in Southern Song Hangzhou reveal they functioned as both stationery stores and printers of religious texts. For a list of these names, see Edgren, "Southern Song Printing at Hangzhou," p. 4, fig .1.

140. A number of stories in the Ming collection *Jianghu qiwen dupian xinshu* 江湖奇聞杜騙新書 (New book of exciting tales on avoiding scams and swindles) refer to traveling merchants in Minbei who sell goods brought from other areas of China and with their earnings buy local products to sell elsewhere. In one story, a man from the Nanjing area sells cloth in Jianning and then goes to Chongan intending to buy bamboo shoots, a well-known local specialty. But since bamboo shoots are scarce and expensive that year, he buys copperwares instead and arranges to transport them on a rapid "arrow boat" (*jian chuan* 箭船) to Shuikou 水口 (i.e., Hekou 河口) across the border in Jiangxi. The *Exciting Tales* survives in a Jianyang edition published by the Chen Huaixuan's Cunren tang 陳懷軒存仁堂, probably in the second or third decade of the seventeenth century. The Cunren tang may have added stories to the original collection, written by one Zhang Yingyu 張應俞 of Zhejiang; not only do 21 of the 84 tales describe some part of Minbei, but some of the descriptions are very detailed and give information about porters waiting on the riverbank at the Jianyang county seat or the false facade that looks like a house door on a lane off the main street of the same city. There are several extant copies of the Cunren tang edition, of which there is a photofacsimile reprint in the *Guben xiaoshuo jicheng* collection. There is also a modern annotated edition.

141. In late imperial China, this kind of hospitality apparently was commonly offered to traveling merchants (*xingshang* 行商 or *keshang* 客商) by brokers (*yaren* 牙人), who often doubled as wholesale distributors. As for printers playing the same role as the brokers, we have evidence of this from at least two large *nianhua* 年畫 production centers—Yang jia bu 楊家埠 in Shandong, and Zhuxian zhen 朱仙鎮 in Henan; see *Yang jiabu cunzhi*, pp. 214–16; and Guo Taiyun et al., "Zhu xian zhen nianhua yu minsu," p. 6.

A wealth of information for and on traveling merchants can be found in the various merchant route books and certain sections of the household encyclopedias published in late imperial China. A few of the Ming route books and even more of the encyclopedias were published in Jianyang. For example, Yu Xiangdou's 1599 *Wanyong zhengzong* 萬用正宗 has been mined by modern scholars for information about merchants and commerce of the time. Since much of this work was probably (re)written by Yu, his own business experience was probably quite extensive. Unfortunately, he did not discuss the details of the book trade specifically, an omission that may have signaled his desire to be identified as a literatus rather than a merchant.

142. In fact, as cumbersome as the process may seem, moving the printing blocks themselves from place to place was not exceptional. This is particularly true in areas

with easily accessible water transport. See Chapter 1 for a description of the geography of Minbei, including its waterways. The commerce of the area depended vitally on river transport. Nearly every single story in the *Dupian xinshu* that mentions merchants in Minbei refers to their hiring a boat to transport their goods, and apparently these river craft traveled quite rapidly. A day's journey could cover over a hundred *li*.

Similarly, the thriving printing industry in Liaocheng in Shandong during the Qing owed its existence in large part to the area's proximity to the Grand Canal. Books "published" in Liaocheng included not only those for which the woodblocks were carved locally (known as *fu shu* 府書) but also those whose blocks or whose loose, unbound leaves were shipped from somewhere in central or south China and were known as *nan shu* 南書; see *Liaocheng diqu zhi* (1997), pp. 781–89.

Finally, there were blockcarving centers in different areas in China that produced the blocks, unbound printed sheets, or even the bound imprints, which were transported to a more important urban center, which was then identified as the place of publication. We have more evidence of these production centers for the Qing and Republican periods, but they existed in earlier times. For very brief descriptions of a few of the later ones, see Brokaw et al., "Mapping the Book Trade," Year 1 (1999) and Year 2 (1999–2000).

143. Almost all these figures come from data collected by Shen Jin, who in the course of several decades of examining Chinese rare books has had the uncommon opportunity to find such information. See his article "Ming dai fangke zhi tushu liutong yu jiage." Shen Jin (pers. comm.) has argued that these prices stamped in the red seals were determined by the publishers, but I remain somewhat skeptical. In any case, the need for caution in interpreting any book price was borne out during a 1998 conference on books and printing in late imperial China, where Shen Jin presented a slightly revised version of his paper. In the discussion at the conference, it came out that many of the copies of works with prices recorded in them came from Japanese collections, so that it is possible that the prices were set with Japanese, rather than Chinese, customers in mind, and thus quite possibly steeper, and not generally meaningful for studying the book trade within China.

144. All the book prices are given in terms of silver taels (i.e., Chinese ounces of silver or *liang* 兩) and decimal subdivisions thereof (1 *liang* = 10 *qian* or *wen* 錢/文 = 100 *fen* 分 = 1,000 *li* 厘).

145. In the course of being rebound (often as part of repairing them) the leaves of a Chinese blockprinted book may be rearranged so that the number of bound fascicles or volumes may change. Thus I give the fascicle count simply to provide an approximate idea of the size of the entire work.

146. Shen Jin, "Ming dai fangke zhi tushu liutong yu jiage." Based on my direct comparison of the earlier 1505 Shendu zhai and the 1559 Guiren zhai editions of the *Da Ming yitong zhi* with the original *neifu* edition of 1461, the two Jianyang reprints are excellently produced works and among the best Ming commercial publications from Jianyang. Indeed, the Guiren tang edition actually adds information not contained in the original version.

147. Hu Yinglin, "Jingji huitong," 4: 56, in Jiabu of *Shaoshi shanfang bicong*. In the case of Fujian (i.e., Jianyang), Zhejiang, and Suzhou, it seems most likely that Hu

is referring to books printed in each of those places. But for Beijing, it is unclear whether he is talking about books printed there, or books sold there but printed elsewhere. This passage is quoted by nearly every scholar discussing Ming books and printing, partly because no other writer of the period addressed such issues in the same detail.

148. Hayes, "Specialists and Written Materials in the Village World," esp. pp. 107–11.

Chapter 6

1. In the National Central Library (Taipei) Rare Book Collection (no. 01065). The library's catalogue gives a date of 1519, which I believe is the date of the reprinting after some new blocks were carved. In fact, by 1519, the Zhan family publishers were probably using blocks originally carved in the Yuan or early Ming and then repaired for a previous 1492 printing. The newer calligraphy in this *Guangyun* is quite similar to the Yang family's Qingjiang tang edition of 1431 (no. 7988 of the Rare Book Collection of the National Library of China, Beijing) and clearly different from the Yuan editions shown in Figs. 22a–c.

2. One reason why the Shendu zhai's books were uniformly of high quality may have been the active interest and participation of local officials in producing them, as in Chapter 5.

3. See, e.g., Tsien, *Paper and Printing*, p. 153, fig. 1113.

4. It would be pointless to add to the huge amount of ink and paper already expended on the subject of movable-type printing in China. Not only does nearly every book on Chinese printing devote an inordinate amount of space to it, but there are also numerous articles in Chinese, Japanese, and Western languages. Too often, the discussions simply repeat each other in their insistence that movable type was indeed invented in China several centuries prior to the European invention. Some new work, however, is beginning to explore the technical and economic aspects of Chinese movable-type printing. See Heijdra, "Technology, Culture and Economics: Movable Type Versus Woodblock Printing in East Asia."

5. See, e.g., Tang Jin 唐錦 (*Longjiang meng yulu* 龍江夢餘錄, *juan* 3, in idem, *Longjiang ji*), who remarked on the efficiency of movable-type printing and the economy of type made from clay compared to bronze; and Lu Shen 陸深 (*Jintai ji wen* 金臺紀聞 [下], in idem, *Yanshan waiji*), who deemed the movable-type printing found in Piling 毘陵 (modern Changzhou in Jiangsu) more convenient than block printing.

6. The Jianning prefecture and the first commercial editions are definitely from the Jiajing period. My guess is that the second commercial edition postdates these other two, based on close examination of all three (in the Rare Book Collection of the National Central Library in Taipei). In turn, all three are probably based on a Song Jianyang edition.

7. During the Ming, the *shangtu xiawen* format was a Jianyang specialty, but not a monopoly. Examples of works in the *shangtu xiawen* format from other areas include chantefables (see below in the text), drama miscellanies published in southern Fujian, and a well-produced *Xixiang ji* from a commercial printer in Beijing in 1498.

For the chantefables, see the photofacsimile edition of *Xinbian quanxiang shuo-chang zuben Hua Guan Suo zhuan* 新編全相說唱足本花關索傳 in the collection *Guben xiaoshuo congkan*, pt. 23, vol. 3. For the drama miscellanies, see the illustrations in van der Loon, *The Classical Theatre and Art Song*. For the *Miaoqi quanxiang zhushi Xixiang ji* 妙奇全相注釋西相記 printed in Beijing, see figs. 382–83 in *ZBK*.

For a brief analysis of the pictorial elements commonly found in the Jianyang *shangtu xiawen* illustrations, see Farrer, "The *Shui-hu Chuan*: A Study in the Development of Late Ming Woodblock Illustration," pp. 102–24. I am grateful to Anne McLaren for bringing this study to my attention.

8. Hegel (*Reading Illustrated Fiction*, p. 172) makes much the same point in discussing the earlier *pinghua* historical narratives of the Yuan.

9. The full-folio *hua* spread across two facing pages was far more prevalent than one occupying the verso and recto sides of the same folio.

10. On illustration in works of fiction, see Hegel, *Reading Illustrated Fiction*.

11. Here we are focusing on the differences among the *tu* in these editions of the *Sanguo zhizhuan*. Later in this chapter I address differences in the texts in various versions of this work. For discussions of the distinction between the *zhizhuan* (chronicle) versions of the *Sanguo*, chiefly in the *shangtu xiawen* format, and the more textually sophisticated *yanyi* 演義 (comprehensively explicated) versions, see the two articles by McLaren, "Ming Audiences and Vernacular Hermeneutics: The Uses of *The Romance of the Three Kingdoms*" and "Popularizing *The Romance of the Three Kingdoms*: A Study of Two Early Editions."

12. Based on extant imprints, Yu Xiangdou apparently published at least three different *shangtu xiawen* versions of the *Sanguo*.

13. For a discussion of this work, see McLaren, *Chinese Popular Culture*, pp. 239–60.

14. Although it is useful to refer to the Huizhou school (*Huipai* 徽派) of illustrators/carvers, as represented by the Huang family, and possibly also a "Jianyang" look, my point is that many of the best-known carvers worked in various large printing centers. Thus many of the Huizhou Huang men worked as often in Nanjing as they did in Huizhou, and Jianyang natives like Liu Suming worked equally often in Minbei and Jiangnan.

15. In addition to the line crediting Yu Shiteng as the publisher at the beginning of several *juan*, Yu is also the author of a preface dated 1588. Based on the imprints that list Yu Shiteng as the publisher, it is quite likely that he is Yu Xiangdou. The Xiong Zhonggu listed as the editor in Fig. 45a is most likely Xiong Damu, the well-known author and editor from the Jianyang Xiong publisher family (see Chapter 5).

16. The lotus leaf design, however, was not exclusive to Jianyang. It was originally a motif that appears in Buddhist works, such as the Northern Song *Jing'an ban-ruo boluomi jing* (fig. 64 in *ZBK*). Figures 2 and 4 of van der Loon, *The Classical Theatre and Art Song*, p. 11, show colophons in two imprints from Haicheng in southern Fujian that are "dead-ringers" for the Jianyang lotus leaf design. Some commercial publishers in late Ming Nanjing also sported this lotus leaf colophon box, including the well-known Tang 唐 family's Shide tang 世德堂 (see the last page of their *Tongjian zuanyao chao hubai* 通鑑纂要抄狐白, Gest Rare Books TB137/3745).

Whether these publishers adopted it because it was familiar or because they had some connection with the Jianyang book trade is uncertain. Furthermore, the lotus leaf appeared not only in books—the potter's identification marks on many Jin dynasty Cizhou ceramic pillows have the same design (see the discussion in Chapter 4). I thank Piet van der Loon for bringing the Cizhou designs to my attention. Another Buddhist symbol, the flaming pearl, can be seen in the lower right corner of the colophon shown in Fig. 47a and was also occasionally carved on the last page of a work.

17. Apparently very few publishers inserted their own portraits into their imprints. For example, there is also a picture of a Mr. Yu of Shuanggui shutang 余氏雙桂書堂 above the publisher's colophon in his *Zhouyi chuanyi* 周易傳義. The colophon gives a date of 1496, but Wang Zhongmin (*Zhongguo shanbenshu tiyao*, 2b-3a) has suggested that this copy could be a Ming reprint of a Yuan edition. If so, then this is the earliest instance of a Jianyang publisher including his own picture in one of his books. In any case, there are eight extant imprints (either original or recut editions) from the Shuanggui shutang from the fourteenth century Yuan and the sixteenth-century Ming (but nothing in between). From a Nanjing imprint of 1615, the *Chu ci jijie* 楚辭集解 (*Chu ci* with collected commentaries), there is a portrait of the publisher, Tang Shaocun 唐少村 (or Shaoqiao 少橋). As for the portrait in the printer's colophon of the 1492 edition of the rhyming dictionary *Daguang yihui Yupian* 大廣益會玉篇, published by the Zhan family's Jinde tang (of Jianyang), 詹氏進德堂, it is uncertain whether the central figure does depict the publisher.

For Yu Xiangdou, we know of three different such portraits. Other than the one shown in Fig. 49b, there is another appearing in several imprints, in which he is seated at a table with books, attended by women of the household and two servant boys and contemplating the scene of domestic felicity around him, complete with a small duck pond. This picture is reproduced in several studies, including Ko, *Teachers of the Inner Chambers*, p. 42; and Brook, *The Confusions of Pleasure*, p. 214. A third, shown in Richard Wang, "Creating Artifacts," p. 87, shows Yu seated at a table reading the very work in which the portrait appears. See Wang, p. 86, for a listing of the imprints in which these portraits appear.

18. The term *jing* may also have meant Beijing, but Jinling was more likely since it was one of the largest markets for Jianyang imprints.

19. The exact title of this work is *Pian hai leibian* 篇海類編 (Sea of leaves, topically compiled) and speciously credits the early Ming scholar-official Song Lian 宋濂 with the arrangement and the late Ming author and critic Tu Long 屠隆 with the collation. No publisher is identified in the work, but it looks very much like a late Ming publication from Jianyang.

20. See Elman, *A Cultural History of Civil Examinations in Late Imperial China*, esp. pp. 488–99. Although the *gangmu* for the annalistic histories are classified as "Historical Criticism" (*shiping* 史評) by the editors of the *Siku quanshu zongmu*, I have included them together with the annalistic histories in Table C.2, since all these works should be discussed together.

21. Jin Lüxiang's chronicle-type history in the style of Sima Guang's original work provides a "prequel" for earlier periods, Chen Jing's work fills in the Song and Yuan, and Chen Jian's deals with the Ming through 1521. There were other supplements to Sima Guang's work, and *gangmu* for them as well.

22. Li Tingji was listed as the compiler or collator for about 25 Jianyang imprints, and Ye Xianggao for about ten. For Li Tingji, see *DMB*, esp. p. 329. For Yuan Huang, see Brokaw, *The Ledgers of Merit and Demerit*, esp. pp. 75–76, 86ff, and 110ff, and *DMB*, pp. 1632–35. For Ye Xianggao, see *DMB*, pp. 1567–70.

23. *JYZX* (1601 ed.), 7.9a. Although the lists of Jianyang imprints in the various editions of the county gazetteer give only a tiny fraction of the total output, books printed under official auspices are quite likely to be included.

24. See, e.g., Heijdra, Review of *Geographical Sources of Ming-Qing History* by Timothy Brook, pp. 66–68.

25. It is interesting to note that in this work, whereas violence is depicted without stint, there are no scenes showing sexual activities, which do appear in drama miscellanies, historical romances, and most of all in the court-case detective stories (*gongan*), discussed below. Possibly the publisher was exercising a bit of self-censorship and thus announcing that his intended audience was women, who should not be exposed to prurient pictures. For a study of the evolving styles of illustration in Ming editions of the *Lienü zhuan* and their range of readerships, see Carlitz, "The Social Uses of Female Virtue in Late Ming Editions of *Lienü Zhuan*."

26. In relation to total known output, medical works occupied the following proportions of the lists of these particular publishers: both extant imprints of the Puji tang, 14 of the 24 from the Mingde tang, 4 of 8 from the Xiyuan shutang, and 62 out of about 121 from the Zhongde tang.

27. For such distinctions, see Leung, "Transmission of Medical Knowledge from the Song to the Ming," pp. 19–25, 43–46.

28. Most likely, the illustrations and popularized explanations, along with Xiong's commentaries and annotations, were meant to aid doctors and others who already had some interest in and knowledge of the subject, rather than lay readers with no medical learning.

29. In traditional Chinese medicine, as Charlotte Furth (*A Flourishing Yin*, p. 180) points out, "Smallpox became more than an illness—it was a bodily passage through the polluted stages of neonatal and infant diseases to childhood health." As will be evident from my discussion on medical texts, I owe much to Furth's work and to Leung's paper just cited.

30. The title, which varies with the edition (*Furen liang fang, Furen liang fang daquan*, etc.) is deceptive, since in addition to prescriptions, it is also a treatise on both gynecology and obstetrics. Although the work was compiled in 1237 and revised in 1284, the earliest extant printed edition seems to be from Jianyang—that of Yu Zhi'an of Qinyou tang in the first half of the fourteenth century.

31. See Furth, *A Flourishing Yin*, pp. 143–45. The edition revised by Xue Ji was typically titled *Tai yiyuan jiaozhu furen liang fang* . . . 太醫院校注婦人良方 . . . (Effective prescriptions for women, collated and annotated by the Imperial Medical School).

32. See note 92 in Chapter 4. In addition to the references therein, see Sakai Tadao, "Mindai no nichiyō ruisho to shomin kyōiku"; and idem, "Confucian and Popular Educational Works," esp. pp. 332–34.

33. Despite the great influence of Li Han's 李瀚 work, it was supplanted by later compilations whose contents were selected to highlight approved Confucian moral

values and avoid Daoist and supernatural anecdotes. There are no Jianyang editions of the *Mengqiu* from any period. For a very brief discussion of this work, see Burton Watson's "Introduction" in his translation of Li Han and Hsü Tzu-kuang, *Meng Ch'iu: Famous Episodes from Chinese History and Legend.*

34. There seems to be no extant pre-Ming edition of the *Shuyan gushi*. Almost nothing is known about Hu Jizong 胡繼宗, the compiler of this work. Wang Zhongmin (*Zhongguo shanbenshu tiyao*, p. 363a), argues that Hu was probably a Southern Song native of Luling county in Jiangxi.

35. The nine-*juan* 1543 edition in a *shangtu xiawen* format was most likely a Jianyang publication, although the publisher is not identified in the colophon. Two later editions from Jianyang were printed by the Yu family's Xiyuan tang and a Liu publisher.

36. The 1618 Jianyang imprint was a truncated version based on a Nanjing edition that came out two years earlier. This collaboration between Deng and Yu was probably one of many, since Deng so frequently worked on publications from Cuiqing tang produced by Yu Yingqiu and his father, Yu Zhangde. Finally, Deng is also listed as the collator for several similar story collections for which there are only extant Nanjing editions.

37. In addition, Fig. 12a is from a Yuan edition of the *Shilin guangji*, an encyclopedia written in the late Song-early Yuan.

38. Indeed, in the array of information they offer, the late Ming household encyclopedias most closely resemble the works designated as *tongshu* today, which remain perennial best-sellers in the Chinese-speaking world outside the mainland.

39. For brief discussions of a number of these works, see Sakai Tadao, "Mindai no nichiyō ruisho to shomin kyōiku," especially pp. 79–93. Sakai's "nichiyō ruisho" 日用類書 (*leishu* for daily use) includes not only those I classify as household references but also some writing manuals and literary reference works.

40. Both this 43-*juan* edition of 1599 (at the Hōsa bunko) and the 35-*juan* edition of 1607 (with the slightly different title *Ding qin Chongwen ge huizuan shimin wanyong zhengzong bu qiu ren quanbian* 鼎鋟崇文閣彙纂士民萬用正宗不求人全編 (at several libraries) take much of their material from one or more earlier works published by Liu Longtian. For a number of works with similar titles and declarations in the prefaces, see Sakai, "Confucianism and Popular Educational Works," pp. 332–35.

41. See Chapter 4 for a brief discussion of this work.

42. Sakai, "Mindai no nichiyō ruisho to shomin kyōiku," pp. 62–74. Sakai also makes comparisons with some Song editions of similar *leishu*. Of the *Shilin guangji* he analyzes, at least one of the two Yuan editions and three of the six Ming editions were from Jianyang.

43. This is surprising given the likely overlap in audiences for *leishu* and morality books. Despite the popularity of these works in late imperial China, not a single one was produced by the Jianyang publishers. Brokaw suggest these books were most likely distributed through an entirely different network, including the religious associations devoted to the spread of these ideas (pers. comm.).

44. Yu Yingxue does not figure in the Yu genealogy. The *Sishu xun er su shuo* is in the Naikaku bunko (277 函71號). The medical work, *Yuan shi douzhen congshu*

袁氏痘疹叢書 (Collected works on smallpox treatment by Mr. Yuan) is by Yuan Hao 顥 (1414-94), Huang's great-grandfather and a professional physician, as well as a contemporary and possibly an acquaintance of Xiong Zongli. In addition to this 1607 edition, which has a preface by Yuan Huang, another late Ming / early Qing edition with a slightly different title (*Yuan shi douzhen quanshu* 全書) is the family product of three generations of Yuan physicians: written by Hao, supplemented by Hao's son Xiang 祥, and provided with digests by his grandson Ren 仁.

45. For consistency's sake, I have included all writing manuals under *leishu*, even though a number of libraries classify them in their catalogues under general collections.

46. This *Wanshou Tangren jueju* was not the one compiled by Hong Mai of the Song, but another work by a Jianyang man, Chen Jingxue 陳敬學, a member of the Chen family of printers, and the son-in-law of Zhu Bingtie 朱秉鐵, a direct descendant of Zhu Xi and an editor-printer for the Zhu family's printshop, Yugeng tang.

47. The Naikaku bunko catalogue of Chinese rare books lists twelve Ming editions, as well as Qing and Japanese editions.

48. Both the Library of Congress and the Naikaku bunko have the complete series. A sixth work in the series, *Chajiu zhengqi* 茶酒爭奇 (The contest of tea and wine), was printed by the Yang family's Qingbai tang of Jianyang.

49. Cf., e.g., the editions of dramas printed in the late Ming, such as the one in Fig. 26b.

50. I am indebted to Kathryn Lowry for providing me with her bibliographical notes on late Ming drama miscellanies.

51. See van der Loon, *The Classical Theatre and the Art Song*, pp. 2-3. The first work, printed in 1566 by the Yu family's Xin'an tang 新安堂 is *Chongkan wuse Chao-Quan chake zengru shici beiqu Goulan Lijing ji xiwen quanji* 重刊五色潮泉插科增入詩詞北曲勾欄荔鏡記戲文全集, consisting of arias from the *Lijing ji* and another Minnan play, as well as the *Xixiang ji* 西廂記 in the "standard" northern dialect. The second work is the *Xinke zengbu quanxiang xiangtan Lizhi ji* 新刻增補全像鄉談荔枝記, printed by the Zhu family's Yugeng tang in 1581. As stated in note 15 of this chapter, van der Loon shows printers' colophons for two other miscellanies, both printed in southern Fujian, with exactly the same lotus leaf design seen in Jianyang colophons. This may mean that there was some business and/or familial connections between the printers in northern and southern Fujian.

52. There are earlier examples of works in the dialect of one region being printed somewhere else. For example, the *shuochang cihua* 說唱詞話 texts found in the tomb of an official's family in the Jiading region of Suzhou prefecture not far from Shanghai have many southern Wu dialect expressions, but the works were reprints from a Beijing publisher (1471-78). These works may have been shipped to the Suzhou area for sale, but they could just as easily have been sold to Jiangsu natives in Beijing. See McLaren, *Chinese Popular Culture*, for an analysis of these works.

53. Although some library catalogues classify these *gongan* collections under "Anecdotists" (*xiaoshuo* 小說) of the *Zibu* category in the *siku* classification, it seems more useful to discuss them together with other works of fiction, given the similarity in format and the likely similarity of readership for such works in general.

54. In a number of collections, the magistrate is the legendary figure Judge Bao, who figures so prominently in all kinds of court-case literature, and is based on Bao Zheng 包拯 (992–1062), a Song official. In other collections, the magistrate could be either Judge Bao or another similarly courageous defender of the people, identified with some later real-life official.

55. In the Zongwen tang edition I examined at the Naikaku bunko (300 函61號), a written note stated that another copy has a preface (zixu 自序) by Yu Xiangdou, who was supposed to be the collator, although Yu's own collection by the same title is different.

56. See Y. W. Ma, "The Pao-kung Tradition in Chinese Popular Literature"; and idem, "The Textual Tradition of Ming *Kung-an* Fiction," for his examination of the interrelationship among the late Ming editions; and idem, "Themes and Characterization in the *Lung-t'u kung-an*" for a study of the one edition (*Longtu gongan* 龍圖公案, or Court cases of Academician Bao) that was reprinted in later times and used by Qing and Republican *gongan* collections.

57. This is the *Xinkan jingben tongsu yanyi quan xiang Bao Longtu pan bai jia gongan quan zhuan* 新刊京本通俗演義全像包龍圖判百家公案全傳 (Newly engraved capital edition of the complete stories of criminal cases of the hundred families judged by Academician Bao, with popular explanations, illustrated), published by the Yugeng tang of Zhu Renzhai 朱仁齋與耕堂. As Wolfgang Bauer ("The Tradition of the 'Criminal Cases of Master Pao,'" pp. 442–43) points out, this may not have been the first edition of this particular collection. There is at least one other edition, with a 1597 preface, published by the famous Nanjing establishment Wanjuan lou of Zhou Yuejiao 周曰校萬卷樓. In addition, Zhongguo guji shanben shumu bianji weiyuanhui, *Zhongguo guji shanben shumu: Zibu*, no. 8921, lists an incomplete copy of an imprint with the same title and same editor (n.d.), put out by one Yang Wen'gao 楊文高, who may have belonged to the Yang family of publishers in Jianyang. For a detailed examination of the stories in the Yugeng tang edition, see Hanan, "*Judge Bao's Hundred Cases* Reconstructed."

58. For plays, see Hayden, "The Courtroom Plays of the Yüan and Early Ming Periods." Hayden points out that these courtroom *zaju* apparently were no longer written, at least by known playwrights, after the early Ming, although such works continued to be included in late Ming collections of plays. None of these collections was published in Jianyang, although at least one was from a Nanjing commercial publisher, Chen Bangtai of Jizhi zhai 陳邦泰繼志齋. For the *chantefables* involving Judge Bao, see McLaren, *Chinese Popular Culture*, pp. 22, 115–18, and esp. 170–83.

59. Y. W. Ma, "The Textual Tradition of Ming *Kung-an* Fiction," p. 217.

60. Hanan, "*Judge Bao's Hundred Cases* Reconstructed," p. 302.

61. See McLaren, *Chinese Popular Culture*, p. 286, for the quote, and the back plates for reproductions of pages from the *chantefables*.

62. It is possible that at least some of the other Jianyang editions offered the same sort of information, but that it has disappeared from the extant copies. Indeed, analysis of the contents of the surviving *gongan* collections confirms that entire editions have most likely disappeared, as Y. W. Ma's work demonstrates.

63. Commercial publishers often recycled materials among works usually classified as popular encyclopedias (*tongsu leishu* 通俗類書) and story collections,

including the *gongan* works. For example, Y. W. Ma ("The Textual Tradition of Ming *Kung-an* Fiction," p. 207) points out that the part of the story of Judge Bao's childhood which appears in the 1594 Yugeng tang edition of *Baijia gongan* resurfaces in the encyclopedia *Guose tianxiang* 國色天香 published by Zhou Yuejiao's Wanjuan lou in Nanjing, which also put out an edition of the *Baijia gongan* (preface dated 1597, not 1587 as Ma states).

64. See note 140 to Chapter 5. The late Ming Jianyang reprint edition was published by Chen Huaixuan's Cunren tang, which also published a *gongan* collection around the same time. Sun Kaidi (*Riben Dongjing suo jian xiaoshuo shumu*, p. 129), who thinks that the latter was derived from another Jianyang edition, has scathing comments about its quality.

65. See Plaks, *The Four Masterworks of the Ming Novel*, for useful introductions to the modern scholarship on these works.

66. According to some scholars, editions belonging to the more literary recension often have *yanyi* 演義 in their titles, whereas those of the simpler recensions have *zhizhuan* 志傳. I find that the Jianyang imprints (nearly all of the latter type) have both terms in their titles. On these two textual traditions of the *Romance of the Three Kingdoms*, see McLaren, "Ming Audience and Vernacular Hermeneutics"; and idem, "Popularizing *The Romance of the Three Kingdoms*."

67. Three others, from my examination, also look very much like Jianyang productions, but nothing in the copies provides definite proof. For the total count of 32 Ming editions, see McLaren, "Popularizing *The Romance of the Three Kingdoms*," p. 170 and note 20. For a detailed comparison of the texts in five of the Ming *Sanguo* (all Jianyang editions), see Zhou Zhaoxin, *Sanguo yanyi kaoping*, pp. 200–306.

68. There is apparently only one incomplete copy of this work, the *Xinkan jingben jiaozheng yanyi quanxiang Sanguo zhizhuan pinglin* 新刊京本校正演義全像 三國志傳評林, consisting of six *juan* at the Waseda University Library in Japan.

69. Apparently, eight *juan* of this work from a single copy have been apportioned among four European libraries, and there may be more, lying uncatalogued somewhere. In addition to this and the other *shangtu xiawen* edition discussed above, which are definitely published by Yu Xiangdou, there is a third illustrated edition, *Xinke Tang Xueshi jiaozheng guben an Jian yanyi quanxiang tongsu Sanguo zhizhuan* 新刻湯學士校正古本按鑑演義全像通俗三國志傳 (in the National Library of China, Beijing); no publisher is identified, but it may be a third Yu Xiangdou publication. The attribution of the commentaries to Tang Binyin 湯賓尹 (*js* 1595), a chancellor of the Directorate of Education in Nanjing, may be spurious. In any case, Tang was also credited with the commentaries in two literary anthologies published by Yu Xiangdou and in three works on various histories that are examination literature published by Yu Liangmu's Zixin zhai 余良木自新齋. There are at least twelve Jianyang publications with commentaries attributed to Tang Binyin. Although I found no references, direct or indirect, to such commentaries in Tang's collected writings, it is difficult to determine whether the attributions were entirely false, since Ming literati did produce such commentaries and annotations, for money and for other motives. On Tang's involvement with commercial publishing, see also Kin Bunkyō's "Tō Hin'i to Minmatsu no shōgyō shuppan."

70. McLaren, "Ming Audiences and Vernacular Hermeneutics." Versions of the *Sanguo* continue to multiply today. Even without considering recasting the work into other media, including theater, film, and video games and only concentrating on printed narratives, we can point to the popularity of *Sanguo* in different East and Southeast Asian languages. Indeed, modern *Sam Kok* "versions" in Thai have allowed the real author cum commentator "to discuss just about anything," as Craig Reynolds describes in "Tycoons and Warlords: Modern Thai Social Formations and the Chinese Historical Romance." Just as Yu Xiangdou's edition allowed it to be read as "a manual for strategy and advice for everyday living" (McLaren, p. 27), modern versions continue to offer much to businessmen, politicians, and almost any other interested reader. Among the new rewritings in Thai, Reynolds (pp. 116–17) lists a "beggar's version," a "capitalist version," an "intimate version," and a "medical version," in which the new author "leaps from a seemingly innocent discussion of poison-tipped arrows for the crossbow—the weapon of choice in the ancient China of *Sam Kok*—to a chilling itemization of the toxins, pesticides, pollutants, food additives, and contaminants . . . that Bangkok residents now find in their diets."

71. Idema, *Chinese Vernacular Fiction*, p. 93. The works were printed by the Wuben tang of the Yú family of Jian'an and are collectively known as the *Xinkan quanxiang pinghua wuzhong* 新刊全像平話五種 (original in the Naikaku bunko in Tokyo, with several facsimile reprints). Idema argues that the customers were wealthy because the Yuan works are actually somewhat better produced than those of the Ming. For example, the illustrations spread over a full leaf, rather than just a page, as in the Ming works. See the discussion of these works in Chapter 4.

72. Kin Bunkyō, *Sangoku shi engi no seikai*, pp. 84–85.

73. It is telling that the higher-quality editions with which Jianyang men were involved were printed in Nanjing. Not only were the wealthier book buyers concentrated in the large cities, but it made financial sense not to print the books in Jianyang and then risk losing them in transit over the arduous mountain and river routes to Jiangnan.

74. There have always been scholars who objected to such a mixture of fact and fiction, but they were protesting against a situation over which they had no control. For example, on the *Sanguo zhi*, see Hu Yinglin, "Zhuang yu wei tan" 莊獄委談 (Xinbu 辛部) in idem, *Shaoshi shanfang bicong*, p. 571.

75. See Struve, "The Southern Ming, 1644–1662," pp. 673–76.

76. At least one other Yu man was also involved in this publication, in addition to Yu Yingqiu (who must have been quite old by 1645, since he published a book in 1598). This work is in the Naikaku bunko, 子18 函 4 號.

77. Two pages of this work are reproduced in *ZBK*, pls. 472–73.

78. See, e.g., the entry on Zhuang Tinglong (Chuang T'ing-lung) 莊廷鑨 in Hummel, *Eminent Chinese of the Ch'ing Period* (hereafter *ECCP*), pp. 205–6.

79. In addition, according to Zhu Weigan (*Fujian shigao*, 2: 411), the population of Jianning prefecture dropped by about 63 percent between the Ming Wanli period and 1694. Although the reliability of these numbers (extracted from the 1694 *JNFZ*) is somewhat questionable, historical events make this decrease plausible.

80. Zhou Lianggong, *Shuying*, 1: 8; quoted in Li Ruiliang, *Fujian chuban hua*, pp. 187–88. On Zhou, see *ECCP*, pp. 173–74.

81. See Pan Lei's "Yuan xu" 原序, dated 1695; in Gu Yanwu, *Rizhi lu (zhi yu)*, p. 1.

82. See note 23 in Chapter 5.

83. The Qing officials mistakenly associated Yu Renzhong with Qingyou tang instead of Wanjuan tang. See *Qing Gaozong shilu*, 9.3–5, in *Da Qing lichao shilu* 大清歷朝實錄; and Wang Xianqian, *Xu Donghua lu*, 81.2. A large portion of the official statement is quoted in Xiao Dongfa, "Jianyang Yu shi keshu kaolüe," pt. 1, p. 230.

84. Huang Peilie, *Shili ju cangshu tibaji, juan* 3, n.p.; quoted in Fang Yanshou, in "Jianyang Xiong shi keshu shulüe," p. 196. Zhu Xi, "Jianning fu Jianyang xianxue cangshuji" 建寧府建陽縣學藏書記, in *Zhuzi daquan*, vol. 9, *Wen: juan* 79, p. 16.

85. For an introduction to the publishing activities of the Ming principalities, see Zhang Xiumin, *Zhongguo yinshua shi*, pp. 402–45.

86. See the examples in McDermott, "The Ascendance of the Imprint."

87. The Jianyang edition of the *Tiangong kaiwu* was published in the late Ming (after 1637, which is the date of the original preface and the date assigned to the earliest extant edition) by Yang Suqing 楊素卿. A copy is in the National Library of China Rare Book Collection (no. 18064). The page layout (number of columns per page and number of characters per column) is the same as the 1637 edition, and the illustrations are very similar, but in general not as well executed.

88. For the history of printing during the Ming in general, see Zhang Xiumin, *Zhongguo yinshua shi*, pp. 334–543; K. T. Wu, "Ming Printing and Printers"; and Tsien, *Paper and Printing*, esp. pp. 172–84. All three authors agree on the sharp difference between early and late Ming printing, and that the history of printing and of the book in general is probably more usefully considered by grouping together the Yuan and early Ming separately from the late Ming, with the dividing line around 1500. Indeed, such a division is a useful one in general, given what we know of Ming history.

Chapter 7

1. This story, given in Poon, "Books and Printing in Sung China," pp. 37–38, is told in several sources, including Lang Ying, *Qiuxiu leigao*, pp. 171–72; and Ling Yangzao, *Li shao bian*, "Tui bei tu," 38: 619–20. Ling points out that the work had enjoyed a certain popularity ever since it had been written and was to be found in not a few book collections. Song Taizu's clever ploy even managed to induce many owners of the earlier editions to discard their copies.

2. "Large" in a comparative sense, meaning a small percentage of a population of one hundred million or more by the end of the eleventh century.

3. Similarly, Lyon in the late fifteenth century, which was one of the major publishing centers in Europe, was not a notable intellectual center, but it was one of the most important nexus on the main trade routes of the continent; see Martin, *The History and Power of Writing*, pp. 236–37.

4. On Nanjing publishing in the Ming, see Zhang Xiumin, *Zhongguo yinshua shi*, pp. 340–53; and Chia, "Of Three Mountains Street." Although my study addresses some of the issues described above, more can and should be done, given the wealth of materials on Ming Nanjing.

5. Ellen Widmer's "The Huanduzhai of Hangzhou and Suzhou" shows that it is possible to do a very rich and detailed study of certain publishers in the Jiangnan area during this period.

6. For a survey of academy publishing activities, Song–Qing, see Huang Qing-wen, "Zhongguo gudai shuyuan zhidu ji qi keshu tanjiu."

7. Actually, there were far fewer printshops in Huizhou than in Jianyang or in the large cities of Jiangnan, and many imprints in which Huizhou men are listed as publishers, editors, or blockcarvers were actually produced in Jiangnan. Nevertheless, there were a number of noted printers who did work in Huizhou. For a general introduction to Huizhou printing, see Jiang Yuanqing, "Huizhou diaoban yinshua shu de fazhan." See also Bussotti, *Gravures de Hui: Etudes du livre illustré chinois du XVIe siècle à la première moitié du XVIIe siècle.*

8. See, e.g., Zhang Xiumin, "Mingdai Huipai banhua Huang xing kegong kao-lüe," in idem, *Zhang Xiumin yinshua shi lunwen ji,* pp. 171–79.

9. Hayes, "Specialists and Written Materials in the Village World."

10. For Shaoyang in Hunan and for Shandong, see Brokaw et al., "Mapping the Book Trade," Reports for Year 1 (1999) and Year 2 (2000).

11. See Martin, *The History and Power of Writing,* p. 265.

Appendix C

1. The Research Libraries Information Network's (RLIN) Chinese Rare Books Project began in 1993 to catalogue on-line Chinese imprints published prior to 1796 that are in the collections of various libraries in North America, mainland China, and England. Although its usefulness is indisputable, it will be some time before the holdings even of the currently participating libraries are completely catalogued. A number of libraries in China (e.g., Liaoning Provincial Library, Shandong Provincial Library, and Nanjing Library) have now entered their rare books catalogues into computer databases, which allows for easier in-house searches. There has been no concerted effort, however, to standardize these computer catalogues in terms of bibliographic classifications (e.g., how to subdivide the *siku* system if used, what search parameters to be made available, or even rules on how to record book titles). Until such absolutely basic bibliographic standards are established, the uses of the on-line catalogues will continue to be limited.

2. The library catalogues, annotated bibliographies, and fascimile reproductions are listed in Part A of the Works Cited.

3. Although the situation is improving, readers using the Chinese rare book collections in a number of libraries all over the world generally feel fortunate if even a traditional card catalogue exists, despite omissions, errors, and wildly inconsistent cataloguing of similar works. Sometimes the card catalogue is considered "internal" and can be used only by the library staff. In certain libraries, the printed catalogues have not been updated for decades and in any case are highly uninformative, giving little information about the works other than title, author, and the dynasty in which it was published. Publication information, such as the name of the publisher and the place of publication, often is absent.

4. *Heikouben* refers to books with a black strip on the top and/or bottom of the center-fold of each leaf, a characteristic of Jianyang imprints (see Fig. 6). See Chapter 2 for a more detailed description of the visual appearance of the Chinese block-cut book.

5. Currently, I am using Microsoft Visual FoxPro. For someone interested in starting such a bibliographic database, however, I would recommend (for PC) Microsoft Access, which has somewhat more sophisticated sorting and searching capabilities and more options for printing out reports.

6. Because the bibliography is a relational data base, it is best presented on a computer disk for use with the appropriate software, rather than in just one arrangement (e.g., ordered by printer or by *siku* classification) on paper, and several arrangements would bloat this book to an impractical size.

7. See, e.g., the system devised by the Liaoning Provincial Library or the one currently being designed at the Nanjing Library.

Works Cited

Abbreviations

CSJC-CB   *Congshu jicheng chubian* 叢書集成初編. Reprinted—Beijing: Zhong-
           hua shuju, 1985.
CSJC-XB   *Congshu jicheng xinbian* 叢書集成新編. Taipei: Xin wenfeng, 1964.
SKQS   *Siku quanshu* 四庫全書. Taipei: Shangwu, 1986.

A. Catalogues and Bibliographies of Chinese Rare Books

NOTE: This is a select list of the most important works used in compiling the bibliography of Jianyang imprints. As a rule, works dealing with library collections are listed under the library names.

Beijing daxue tushuguan cang Lishi shumu 北京大學圖書館藏李氏書目. Comp. Zhao Wanli 趙苑里 et al. Beijing: Beijing daxue chubanshe, 1956.

Beijing daxue tushuguan, comp. 北京大學圖書館編. [Beijing daxue tushuguan cang] Guji shanben shumu [北京大學圖書藏] 古籍善本書目. Beijing: Beijing daxue chubanshe, 1999.

Beijing tushuguan, ed. *Beijing tushuguan guji shanben shumu* 北京圖書館古籍善本書目. 5 vols. Beijing: Shumu wenxian chubanshe, 1989.

———. *Beijing tushuguan putong guji zongmu* 北京圖書館普通古籍總目. Beijing: Shumu wenxian chubanshe, 1990.

———. *Xidi shumu* 西諦書目, 5 *juan*; *Tiba* 題跋, 1 *juan*. Beijing: Wenwu chubanshe, 1963.

———. *Yingyin shanbenshu mulu 1911–1984* 影印善本書目錄1911–1984. Beijing: Zhonghua shuju, 1992.

————. *Zhongguo banke tulu* 中國版刻圖錄. 8 vols. Beijing: Wenwu chubanshe, 1961.

(Guoli) Beiping tushuguan shanben shumu 國立北平圖書館善本書目. Comp. Zhao Wanli 趙宛里. Beiping: Beiping tushuguan, 1933.

(Guoli) Beiping tushuguan shanben shumu yibian, xumu (國立)北平圖書館善本書目乙編, 續目. 2 vols. Comp. Zhao Luchuo 趙錄綽. Beiping: Beiping tushuguan, 1935.

Boshan shuying 盇山書影. Compiled by Jiangsu sheng li Guoxue tushuguan. 3 vols. Reprinted—Shumu sibian Series. Taipei: Guangwen shuju, 1970.

Chang Bide (Chang Pi-te) 昌彼得, ed. *Taiwan gongcang Song-Yuan ben lianhe shumu* 台灣公藏宋元本聯合書目. Taipei: Zhongyang tushuguan, 1955.

Chao Gongwu 晁公武, with revision notes by Sun Meng 孫猛. *Junzhai dushuzhi jiaozheng* 郡齋讀書志校證. Shanghai: Guji, 1990.

Chao Li 晁瑮. *Chao shi Baowen tang shumu* 晁氏寶文堂書目. Beiping: Beiping tushuguan, 1929.

Chen Zhensun 陳振孫. *Zhizhai shulu jieti* 直齋書錄解題. *CSJC-CB* ed., vols. 0044–48.

Ch'ü Wan-li. *A Catalogue of the Chinese Rare Books in the Gest Collection of Princeton University Library*. Taipei: Yiwen yinshuguan, 1975.

Ding Bing 丁丙. *Shanben shushi cangshu zhi* 善本書室藏書志. Reprint of 1908 edition in *Qingren shumu tiba congkan* 清人書目題跋叢刊 2. Beijing: Zhonghua shuju, 1990.

Diping xian chubanshe 地平線出版社, ed. *Shiji shulu* 史記書錄. Taipei: Diping xian chubanshe, 1972.

Du Xinfu, ed. 杜信孚. *Mingdai banke zongmu* 明代版刻總目. 8 string-bound vols. Yangzhou: Jiangsu Guangling guji keyinshe, 1983.

Fang Pinguang 方品光. *Fujian banben ziliao huibian* 福建版本資料匯編. Fuzhou: Fujian shifan daxue tushuguan, 1979.

Feng Huimin 馮惠民 and Li Wanjian 李萬健, eds. *Ming dai shumu tiba congkan* 明代書目題跋叢刊. Beijing: Shumu wenxian chubanshe, 1994.

Fu Zengxiang 傅增湘. *Cangyuan qunshu jingyan lu* 藏園群書經眼錄. 5 vols. Reprinted—Beijing: Zhonghua shuju, 1983.

Gao Ru 高儒. *Bai chuan shuzhi* 百川書志. Reprinted—Shanghai: Gudian wenxue, 1957.

Geng Wenguang 耿文光. *Wanjuan jinghua lou cangshu ji* 萬卷精華樓藏書記. 4 vols. Harbin: Heilongjiang renmin, 1992.

Gu Guangqi 顧廣圻. *Gu Guangqi shumu tiba* 顧廣圻書目題跋. Reprinted in Qingren shumu tiba congcan 清人書目題跋叢刊 6. Beijing: Zhonghua shuju, 1993.

(Guoli) Gugong bowuyuan (國立) 故宮博物院 (Taipei), ed. *(Guoli) Gugong bowuyuan shanben jiuji zongmu* (國立)故宮博物院善本舊籍總目. 2 vols. Taipei: Guoli gugong bowuyuan, 1983.

————. *(Guoli) Gugong bowuyuan shanben shumu* (國立)故宮博物院善本書目. Taipei: Guoli Gugong bowuyuan, 1968.

————. *Song ban shu tezhan mulu* 宋版書特展目錄. Taipei: Guoli Gugong bowuyuan, 1986.

————. *Song ben tulu* 宋本圖錄. Taipei: Guoli Gugong bowuyuan, 1977.

Han Xiduo 韓錫鐸 and Wang Qingyuan 王清原. *Xiaoshuo shufang lu* 小說書坊錄. Shenyang: Chunfeng wenyi chubanshe, 1987.

Hangzhou Daxue tushuguan shanben mulu 杭州大橋圖書館善本目錄. Hangzhou: Hangzhou Daxue tushuguan, 1965.

Huang Pilie 黃丕烈. *Huang Pilie shumu tiba* 黃丕烈書目題跋. Reprinted in Qingren shumu tiba congkan 清人書目題跋叢刊 6. Beijing: Zhonghua shuju, 1993.

————. *Shili ju cangshu tiba ji* 士禮居藏書題跋記. 1882 ed.

Huang Yuji 黃虞稷. *Qianqing tang shumu* 千頃堂書目. Reprinted—Shanghai: Shanghai guji, 1990.

Hunan sheng guji shanben shumu bianzuan weiyuanhui 湖南省古籍善本書目編纂委員會, ed. *Hunan sheng guji shanben shumu* 湖南省古籍善本書目. Changsha: Yuelu shushe, 1998.

Kyōto daigaku Jinbun kagaku kenkyūjō kanseki bunrui mokuroku 京都大學人文科學研究所漢籍分類目錄. Kyoto: Kyoto University, 1963.

(Kokuritsu) Kokkai toshokan (國立) 國會圖書館, ed. *(Kokuritsu) Kokkai toshokan kanseki mokuroku* (國立) 國會圖書館漢籍目錄. Tokyo: (Kokuritsu) Kokkai Toshokan, 1987.

Lai Xinxia 來新夏, ed. *Qingdai mulu tiyao* 清代目錄提要. Ji'nan: Qilu shushe, 1997.

Lei Mengchen 雷夢辰. *Qingdai gesheng jinshu huikao* 清代各省禁書彙考. Beijing: Shumu wenxian chubanshe, 1989.

Li Ciming 李慈銘. *Yueman tang dushu ji* 越縵堂讀書記. Rev. ed. Shanghai: Shanghai shudian, 2000.

Li Shengduo 李盛鐸, ed. *Muxi xuan cangshu tiji ji shulu* 木犀軒藏書題記及書錄. Arranged by Zhang Yufan 張玉范. Beijing: Beijing daxue chubanshe, 1985.

Liang Zihan 梁子涵. *Zhongguo lidai shumu zonglu* 中國曆代書目總錄. Taipei: Zhonghua wenhua chuban shiye weiyuanhui, 1953.

Liu Ts'un-yan 劉存仁. *Lundun suo jian Zhongguo xiaoshuo shumu tiyao* 倫敦所見中國小說書目提要 [*Chinese Popular Fiction in Two London Libraries*]. Hong Kong: Lungmen, 1967.

Long Bojian 龍伯堅. *Xiancun bencao shulu* 現存本草書錄. Beijing: Renmin weisheng chubanshe, 1957.

Lu Xinyuan 陸心源. *Bisong lou cangshu zhi, xuzhi* 皕宋樓藏書志, 續志. 2 vols. Reprinted in Qingren shumu tiba congkan 清人書目題跋叢刊 1. Beijing: Zhonghua shuju, 1990.

————. *Yigu tang tiba, xuba* 儀顧堂題跋 · 續跋. Reprinted in Qingren shumu tiba congkan 清人書目題跋叢刊 2. Beijing: Zhonghua shuju, 1990.

Luo Weiguo 羅偉國 and Hu Ping 胡平, eds. *Guji banben tiji suoyin* 古籍版本題記索引. Shanghai: Shanghai shudian, 1991.

Ma Jixing 馬繼興, Zhen Liucheng 眞柳誠, Zheng Jinsheng 鄭金生, and Wang Tiece 王鐵策. *Riben xiancun Zhongguo sanyi gu yiji de chuancheng shi yanjiu liyong he fabiao* 日本現存中國散逸古醫籍的傳承史研究利用和發表. 1st Report. Beijing: Riben guoji jiaoliu jijin Yazhou zhongxin 日本國際交流基金亞洲中心, 1997.

Miao Quansun 繆荃孫. *Yifeng cangshu ji* 藝風藏書記; *Xuji* 續記; *Zaixuji* 再續記. Reprinted in Qingren shumu tiba congkan 清人書目題跋叢刊 7. Beijing: Zhonghua shuju, 1993.

Miao Quansun 繆荃孫, Wu Changshou 吳昌綬, Dong Kang 董康. *Jiaye tang cangshu zhi* 嘉業堂藏書志. Rev. Wu Ge 吳格. Shanghai: Fudan daxue, 1997.

Nagasawa Kikuya 長澤規矩也, ed., *Ashikaga gakkō zenpon zuroku* 足利學校善本圖錄. Ashikaga gakkō, 1973.

————. *Zhongguo banben muluxue shuji jieti* 中國版本目錄學書籍解題. Trans. Mei Xianhua 梅憲華 and Guo Baolin 郭寶林. Beijing: Shumu wenxian chubanshe, 1990.

Naikaku bunko 内閣文庫, ed. *Kaitei Naikaku bunko kanseki bunrui mokuroku* 改訂内閣文庫漢籍分類目錄. Tokyo: Naikaku bunko, 1971.

Okanishi Tameto 岡西爲人. *Song yiqian yiji kao* 宋以前醫籍考. 4 vols. Taiwan: Guting shuwu, 1970.

Otsuka Hidetaka 大塚秀高, comp. *Zōho Chūgoku tsūzoku shōsetsu shomoku* 增補中國通俗小說書目. Tokyo: Kyūko shoin, 1987.

Pan Chengbi 潘承弼 and Gu Tinglong 顧廷龍, eds. *Mingdai banben tulu chubian* 明代版本圖錄初編. Ji'nan: Qilu Daxue, 1941?.

Qian Qianyi 錢謙益. *Jiangyun lou tiba* 絳雲樓題跋. Reprinted in Qingren shumu tiba congkan 清人書目題跋叢刊 10. Beijing: Zhonghua shuju, 1995.

Qu Yong 瞿鏞. *Tieqin tongjian lou cangshu mulu* 鐵琴銅劍樓藏書目錄. Reprinted in Qingren shumu tiba congkan 清人書目題跋叢刊 3. Beijing: Zhonghua shuju, 1990.

Seikadō bunko 靜嘉堂文庫, ed. *Seikadō bunko kanseki bunrui mokuroku* 靜嘉堂文庫漢籍分類目錄. Tokyo: Seikadō bunko, 1930.

————. *Seikadō bunko Sō-Gen pan zuroku* 靜嘉堂文庫宋元版圖錄. 2 vols. Tokyo: Kyūko shoin, 1992.

Shandong sheng tushuguan 山東省圖書館, comp. [*Shandong sheng tushuguan cang*] *Haiyuan ge shumu* [山東省圖書館藏] 海源閣書目. Ji'nan: Qilu shushe, 1999.

Shanghai tushuguan 上海圖書館, ed. *Shanghai tushuguan shanben shumu* 上海圖書館善本書目. Shanghai, 1957.

————. *Zhongguo congshu zonglu* 中國叢書綜錄. 3 vols. Shanghai: Zhonghua shuju, 1959–62.

Shen Deshou 沈德壽. *Baojing lou cangshu zhi* 抱經樓藏書志. Reprinted in Qingren shumu tiba congcan 清人書目題跋叢刊 5. Beijing: Zhonghua shuju, 1990.

Shen Jin 沈津. *Meiguo Hafu daxue Hafu-Yanjing tushuguan zhongwen shanben shuzhi* 美國哈佛大學哈佛燕京圖書館中文善本書志. Shanghai: Shanghai Cishu chubanshe, 1999.

Shimada Fumi 島田翰. *Guwen jiushu kao* 古文舊書考. 5 vols. Beijing: Beijing Zaoyu tang 北京藻玉堂, 1927.

Siku quanshu zongmu 四庫全書總目. Compiled under imperial auspices by Ji Yun et al. 紀昀等. 10 vols. Reprinted—Shanghai: Dadong shuju, 1930.

Sun Dianqi 孫殿起, comp. *Fanshu ouji* 販書偶記. Beijing: Zhonghua shuju, 1959.

———. *Qingdai jinshu zhijianlu* 清代禁書知見錄. Shanghai: Commercial Press, 1957.

Sun Kaidi 孫楷第. *Riben Dongjing suo jian xiaoshuo shumu* 日本東京所見小說書目. Reprinted—Beijing: Renmin wenxue chubanshe, 1981.

———. *Zhongguo tongsu xiaoshuo shumu* 中國通俗小說書目. Reprinted—Beijing: Renmin wenxue chubanshe, 1991.

Tamba Mototane 丹波元胤. *Zhongguo yiji kao* 中國醫籍考. Beijing: Renmin weisheng chubanshe, 1956.

Tan Zekai 譚澤闓. *Wenlu tang fangshu ji* 文祿堂訪書記. Photolithographic reprint. Yangzhou: Jiangsu Guangling guji keyin she, 1985.

Tenri toshokan 天理圖書館, ed. *Tenri toshokan kisho mokuroku: Wa-Kan sho no bu daisan* 天理圖書館稀書目錄: 和漢書之部第三. Tenri: Tenri daigaku shuppansha, 1960.

Tianlu linlang shumu 天祿琳琅書目. Compiled under imperial auspices in 1744 and revised in 1775 by Yu Minzhong et al. 于敏中等. Beijing: Gugong bowuyuan tushuguan, 1932.

Tianlu linlang shumu houbian 天祿琳琅書目後編. Compiled under imperial auspices by Peng Yuanrui et al. 彭元瑞等, completed in 1798. Taipei: Guangwen shuju, 1968.

Tianyige shumu 天一閣書目. Compiled by Ruan Yuan 阮元. 10 vols. Woodblock ed. Yangzhou: Yangzhou Ruan Yuan Wenxuan lou, 1808.

Tiangyige shumu neibian 天一閣書目內編. Rev. ed. Ningbo: Tianyige Committee, 1940.

Tianyige xiancun shumu 天一閣現存書目. 4 vols. Wuxi: Xue shi woodblock ed., 1889.

Tieqin tongjian lou 鐵琴銅劍樓, ed. *Song-Jin-Yuan ben shuying* 宋金元本書影. 4 vols. Taipei: Guangwen shuju, 1970.

Tōkyō daigaku Bungakubu Chūgoku tetsugaku Chūgoku bunkaku kenkyūshitsu zōsho mokuroku 東京大學文學部中國哲學中國文學研究室藏書目錄. Tokyo: Tokyo University, 1964.

Wang Zhongmin 王重民. *Zhongguo shanbenshu tiyao* 中國善本書提要. Shanghai: Guji chubanshe, 1983.

———. *Zhongguo shanbenshu tiyao bubian* 中國善本書提要補編. Beijing: Shumu wenxian chubanshe, 1991.

Wang Zhongmin 王重民, comp., and T. L. Yuan, ed. *Guohui tushuguan cang Zhongguo shanben shulu* 國會圖書館藏中國善本書錄. 2 vols. Washington, D.C.: Library of Congress, 1957.

Wu Shouyang 吳壽暘. *Baijing lou cangshu tiba ji* 拜經樓藏書題跋記. Reprinted in Qingren shumu tiba congkan 清人書目題跋叢刊 10. Beijing: Zhonghua shuju, 1995.

Wu Zhuo 吳焯. *Xiugu ting xunxi lu* 繡谷亭薰習錄. Reprinted in Qingren shumu tiba congkan 清人書目題跋叢刊 10. Beijing: Zhonghua shuju, 1995.

Xiao Zhang 蕭章, ed. *Guoli Beiping tushuguan shumu: mululei* 國立北平圖書館書目: 目錄類, 2 vols. Beiping: Guoli Beiping tushuguan, 1934. Reprinted—Taiwan: n.p., n.d.

Yang Shaohe 楊紹和. *Yingshu yulu* 楹書隅錄. Reprinted in Qingren shumu tiba congkan 清人書目題跋叢刊 3. Beijing: Zhonghua shuju, 1990.

Yang Shengxin 楊繩信, ed. *Zhongguo banke zonglu* 中國版刻綜錄. Xianyang: Shaanxi renmin, 1989.

Yang Shoujing 楊守敬. *Riben fangshu zhi* 日本訪書志. Reprinted—Yangzhou: Jiangsu Guangling guji keyinshe, n.d.

Ye Changchi 葉昌熾 and Pan Zuyin 潘祖蔭. *Pangxi zhai cangshu ji* 滂喜齋書記. Photofacsimile reprint. Yangzhou: Jiangsu Guangling guji keyinshe, 1985.

Ye Dehui 葉德輝. *Guangu tang shumu congke* 觀古堂書目叢刻. Reprint in Series *Shumu wubian* 書目五編. 8 vols. Taipei: Guangwen shuju, 1972.

Zhang Jinwu 張金吾. *Airi jinglu cangshu zhi* 愛日精盧藏書志. Jiangsu, 1887.

Zhang Xincheng 張心澂. *Weishu tongkao* 偽書通考. 2 vols. Rev. ed. Shanghai: Commercial Press, 1959.

Zhongguo fensheng yiji kao 中國分省醫籍考. 2 vols. Ed. Guo Aichun 郭靄春 et al. Tianjin: Tianjin kexue jishu chubanshe, 1987.

Zhongguo guji shanben shumu bianji weiyuanhui 中國古籍善本書目編輯委員會, comp. *Zhongguo guji shanben shumu* 中國古籍善本書目. 9 vols. Shanghai: Shanghai guji, 1985–96.

Zhongguo kexue yuan tushuguan 中國科學院圖書館, ed. *Zhongguo kexue yuan tushuguan cang Zhongwen guji shanben shumu* 中國科學院圖書館藏中文古籍善本書目. Beijing: Kexue yuan chubanshe, 1994.

Zhongguo Renmin daxue tushuguan guji zhengli yanjiusuo 中國人民大學圖書館古籍整理研究所, comp. [Zhongguo Renmin daxue tushuguan] *Guji shanben shumu* [中國人民大學圖書館]古籍善本書目. Beijing: Renmin daxue chubanshe, 1991.

Zhongguo Zhongyi yanjiuyuan tushuguan, ed. *Quanguo Zhongyi tushu lianhe mulu* 全國中醫圖書聯合目錄. Beijing: Zhongyi guji chubanshe, 1989.

(Guoli) Zhongyang tushuguan (國立)中央圖書館, ed. *(Guoli) Beiping tushuguan shanben shumu* (國立)北平圖書館善本書目. Taipei: Guoli zhongyang tushuguan, 1969.

———. *(Guoli) Zhongyang tushuguan Jin-Yuan ben tulu* (國立)中央圖書館金元本圖錄. Taipei: Guoli zhongyang tushuguan, 1958.

———. *(Guoli) Zhongyang tushuguan shanben shumu* 國立中央圖書館善本書目. 4 vols. 2d rev. ed. Taipei: Guoli zhongyang tushuguan, 1986.

———. *(Guoli) Zhongyang tushuguan Songben tulu* (國立)中央圖書館宋本圖錄. Taipei: Guoli zhongyang tushuguan, 1958.

———. *(Guoli) Zhongyang tushuguan tecang xuanlu* (國立)中央圖書館特藏選錄. Taipei: Guoli zhongyang tushuguan, 1987.

———. *Manmu linlang Guoli Zhongyang tushuguan shanben tecang* 滿目琳瑯國立中央圖書館善本特藏. Taipei: Guoli zhongyang tushuguan, 1993.

———. *Taiwan gongcang shanben shumu renming suoyin* 台灣公藏善本書目人名索引. Taipei: Guoli zhongyang tushuguan, 1972.

———. *Taiwan gongcang shanben shumu shuming suoyin* 台灣公藏書目書名索引. 2 vols. Taipei: Guoli zhongyang tushuguan, 1971.

———. *Xiancun Song ren zhushu mulüe* 現存宋人著述目略. Taipei: Zhonghua congshu bianshen weiyuanhui, 1971.

(Guoli) Zhongyang yanjiuyuan lishi yuyan yanjiusuo shanben shumu (國立)中央研究院曆史語言研究所善本書目. Taipei: Guoli Zhongyang tushuguan, 1968.

Zhou Hongzu 周弘祖. *Gujin shuke* 古今書刻. Reprinted—Shanghai: Gudian wenxue, 1957.

Zhou Zhongfu 周中孚. *Zheng tang dushu ji* 鄭堂讀書記. Reprinted in Qingren shumu tiba congkan 清人書目題跋叢刊 8. Beijing: Zhonghua shuju, 1993.

Zhu Xuzeng 朱緒曾. *Kaiyouyi zhai dushu zhi* 開有益讀書志. Reprinted in Qingren shumu tiba congkan 清人書目題跋叢刊 7. Beijing: Zhonghua shuju, 1993.

B. Genealogies

Cai 蔡
———. *Lufeng Cai shi zupu* 廬峰蔡氏族譜, n.d. Jianyang County Library.

Chen 陳
———. *Chen shi zongpu* 陳氏宗譜. 9 vols., damaged and incomplete, last preface dated Tongzhi 13 (1874). Jianyang County Library.

Fu 傅
———. *Fu shi zongpu* 傅氏宗譜, n.d. Jianyang County Library.

Huang 黃
———. *Lai Jianxi shuyuan Huang shi zongpu* 敕建溪書院黃氏宗譜 (AKA *Jiangxia Huang shi zongpu* 江夏黃氏宗譜), n.d. Jianyang County Library.

Liao 廖
———. *Liao shi zupu* 廖氏族譜, n.d. In possession of family in Jianyang Masha Jiangfang cun 建陽麻沙江坊村.

Liu 劉
———. *Jingzhao Liu shi Zhen fang zongpu* 京兆劉氏貞房宗譜. 1920. In possession of Liu Xingrong 劉興榮 in Shufang xiang 書坊鄉.
———. *Liu shi zupu* 劉氏族譜. *Masha Yuan, Li er fang he xiu* 麻沙元, 利二房合修. 1880. 12 vols.; first ten consist of genealogical tables, last two vols., entitled "Jianzhou Liu shi zhongxian zhuan" 建州劉氏忠賢傳. Fujian Normal University.

Wang 王
———. *Langya Wang shi zongpu* 瑯琊王氏宗譜, n.d. Jianyang County Library.

Wei 魏
———. *Julu Weishi zongpu* 鉅鏕魏氏宗譜. Qing Guangxu (1875–1907) rev. ed. Jianyang County Library.

Xiao 蕭
———. *Xiao shi zupu* 蕭氏族譜. 1875 rev. ed. Fujian Provincial Library.

Xiong 熊
———. *Tanyang Xiong shi zongpu* 潭陽熊氏宗譜. 7 vols. 1875 rev. ed. Fujian Provincial Library.

Yang(1) 楊
———. *Jian'ou Xincun Yang shi zupu* 建甌新村楊氏族譜. After 1962. Jianyang County Library.

Yang(2) 楊
———. *Yang shi zupu* 楊氏族譜, n.d. Jianyang County Library.

Ye 葉
———. *Chongxiu Xishan Ye shi zongpu* 重修溪山葉氏宗譜. 19 vols. 1883. Jian-yang County Library.

You 游
———. *Guangping You shi zongpu* 廣平游氏宗譜. 12 vols. 1868. Jianyang County Library.

Yu 余
———. *Shulin Yushi zongpu* 書林余氏宗譜. One part printed by Yu Xianqing 余咸清 family's Xin'an tang 新安堂, Tongzhi Period, 1862–74; another two parts copied from 1896 edition revised by Yu Zhenhao 余振豪. Fujian Normal University.
———. *Tanxi Shulin Yushi zupu* 潭西書林余氏族譜. 7 vols. 1871. In possession of family of Yu Shitai 余世泰 of Shufang xiang 書坊鄉. (This is essentially the same edition as the preceding.)

Zhan 詹
———. *Jianfeng Zhan shi zongpu* 建峰詹氏宗譜. 1772 rev. ed. Jianyang County Library.

Zhou 周
———. *Zhou shi zongpu* 周氏宗譜, n.d. Jianyang County Library.

Zhu 朱
———. *Ziyang tang Zhu shi zongpu* 紫陽堂朱氏宗. 1895. Jianyang County Library.
———. *Ziyang Zhu shi Jian'an pu* 紫陽朱氏建安譜 (Jian'an pai 建安派 starting with Zhu Xi's eldest son, Zhu Shu), n.d. Jianyang County Library.

C. Other Works

Abe Ryūchi 阿部隆一. *Abe Ryūichi ikō-shū* 阿部隆一遺稿集. Vol. 1. Tokyo: Kyūko shoin, 1993.
———. *Chūgoku hōsho shi* 中國訪書志. Tokyo: Kyūko shoin, 1983.
Ashida Takaaki 蘆田孝昭. "Min Kampon ni okeru Binbon no ichi" 明刊本における閩本の位置. *Biblia* 95 (Oct. 1990): 91–117.
Bamin tongzhi 八閩通志. 1490. 87 *juan*. Comp. Huang Zhongzhao 黃仲昭 et al. 2 vols. Reprinted—Fuzhou: Fujian Renmin, 1989.
Barrett, Timothy H. "The *Feng-tao k'o* and Printing on Paper in 7th-century China." *Bulletin of the School of Oriental and African Studies* 60 (1997): 538–40.
———. "The Rise and Spread of Printing: A New Account of Religious Factors." *SOAS Working Papers in the Study of Religions*. London: School of Oriental and African Studies, 2001.
Bauer, Wolfgang. "The Tradition of the 'Criminal Cases of Master Pao' *Pao-Kung-An* (*Lung-t'u kung-an*)." *Oriens* 23–24 (1970–1971): 433–49.
Beard, Willard L. "The Foochow-Kienning Twentieth Century Limited." *Foochow Messenger* 9, no. 1 (Feb. 1930): 14–20.

Beijing gongye zhi: Yinshua zhi 北京工業志・印刷志. Comp. Beijing gongye zhi bian weiyuanhui. Beijing: Zhongguo kexue jishu chubanshe, 2001.

Bi Yuan et al. 畢沅等. *Xu Zizhi tongjian* 續資治通鑑. Beijing: Zhonghua shuju, 1957.

Bielenstein, Hans. "The Chinese Colonization of Fukien until the End of the T'ang." In *Studia Serica Bernhard Karlgren Dedicata*, ed. Sören Egerod and Elsa Glahn, pp. 98–122. Copenhagen: Ejnaar Munksgaard, 1959.

Bland, David. *The Illustration of Books*. London: Faber & Faber, 1962.

Bliss, Edward, Jr. *Beyond the Stone Arches; An American Missionary Doctor in China, 1892–1932*. New York: John Wiley & Sons, 2001.

Brokaw, Cynthia J. "Commercial Publishing in Late Imperial China: The Zou and Ma Family Businesses." *Late Imperial China* 17, no. 1 (June 1996): 49–92.

——. *The Ledgers of Merit and Demerit: Social Change and Moral Order in Late Imperial China*. Princeton: Princeton University Press, 1991.

——. "On the History of the Book in China." In *Printing and Book Culture in Late Imperial China*, ed. idem and Kai-wing Chow. Berkeley: University of California Press. Forthcoming.

——. "Reading the Bestsellers of the Nineteenth Century: Commercial Publishing in Sibao, Fujian." In *Printing and Book Culture in Late Imperial China*, ed. idem and Kai-wing Chow. Berkeley: University of California Press. Forthcoming.

Brokaw, Cynthia J., Lucille Chia, and Hou Zhenping. "Mapping the Book Trade: The Expansion of Print Culture in Late Imperial China." Reports for Year 1 (1999) and Year 2 (1999–2000). Unpublished.

Brook, Timothy. "Censorship in Eighteenth-Century China: A View from the Book Trade." *Canadian Journal of History* 22 (Aug. 1988): 177–96.

——. *The Confusions of Pleasure; Commerce and Culture in Ming China*. Berkeley: University of California Press, 1998.

——. "Edifying Knowledge: The Building of School Libraries in Ming China." *Late Imperial China* 17, no. 1 (June 1996): 93–119.

Bussotti, Michela. *Gravures de Hui: Étude du livre illustré chinois du XVIe siècle à la première moitié du XVIIe siècle*. Paris: École française d'Extrême-Orient, 2001.

Cai Xiang 蔡襄. *Cai Xiang ji* 蔡襄集 (*Cai Zhonghui ji* 蔡忠惠集). Shanghai: Shanghai guji, 1996.

Camille, Michael. "Reading the Printed Image: Illuminations and Woodcuts of the *Pèlerinage de la vie humaine* in the Fifteenth Century." In *Printing the Written Word*, ed. Sandra L. Hindman, pp. 259–91. Ithaca: Cornell University Press, 1991.

Cao Zhi 曹之. *Zhongguo guji banben xue* 中國古籍版本學. Wuhan: Wuhan University Press, 1992.

Carlitz, Katherine. "The Social Uses of Female Virtue in Late Ming Editions of *Lienü Zhuan*." *Late Imperial China* 12, no. 2 (Dec. 1991): 117–48.

Carter, T. F. *The Invention of Printing in China and Its Spread Westward*. 2d ed., rev. L. C. Goodrich. New York: Ronald Press, 1955.

Cavallo, Guglielmo, and Roger Chartier, eds. *A History of Reading in the West*. Trans. Lydia G. Cochrane. Amherst: University of Massachusetts Press, 1999.

Cedzich, Ursula-Angelika. "The Cult of the Wu-t'ung/Wu-hsien in History and Fiction: The Religious Roots of the *Journey to the South*." In *Ritual and Scripture in Chinese Popular Religion: Five Studies*, ed. David Johnson, pp. 137–218. Berkeley: Chinese Popular Culture Project, 1995.

Chaffee, John W. *The Thorny Gates of Learning in Sung China: A Social History of Examinations*. 2d ed. Albany: State University of New York Press, 1995.

Chan Hok-lam. "Sung Laws and Regulations on Publications and Circulation." Unpublished paper from ACLS/Rockefeller Research Conference on "The Transformation of Chinese Law, T'ang through Ming." Bellagio, 1981.

Chan Wing-Tsit. *Chu-Hsi: New Studies*. Honolulu: University of Hawai'i Press, 1989.

Chang Bide 昌彼德, Wang Deyi 王德毅, Cheng Yuanmin 程元敏, and Hou Junde 侯俊德, comp. *Song ren zhuanji ziliao suoyin* 宋人傳記資料索引. 6 vols. Taipei: Dingwen, 1974–76.

Chang Pin-tsun. "Chinese Maritime Trade: The Case of 16th Century Fu-chien." Ph.D. dissertation, Princeton University, 1983.

Chang, Shelley Hsueh-lun. *History and Legend: Ideas and Images in the Ming Historical Novels*. Ann Arbor: University of Michigan Press, 1990.

Chartier, Roger. ed. *The Culture of Print: Power and the Uses of Print in Early Modern Europe*. Trans. Lydia G. Cochrane. Princeton: Princeton University Press, 1989.

Chen Qingguang 陳擎光. "Yuan dai Fujian beibu ji qi linjin diqu suo shuchu de taoci qi" 元代福建北部及其鄰近地區所輸出的陶瓷器. *Gugong xueshu jikan* 故宮學術季刊 6.3 (Spring 1989): 1–38 + figures.

Chen Yuanjing 陳元靚. *Shilin guangji* 事林廣記. Reprint of 建安椿莊書院 (1330–32) ed. Tokyo: Chūbun, 1988.

Chen Zhaozhen 陳昭珍. "Mingdai shufang zhi yanjiu" 明代書坊之研究. M.A. thesis, Taiwan University, 1984.

Cherniack, Susan. "Book Culture and Textual Transmission in Sung China." *Harvard Journal of Asiatic Studies* 54, no.1 (1994): 5–125.

Chia, Lucille. "Commercial Publishing in Jianyang from the Late Song to the Late Ming." In Paul Jakov Smith and Richard von Glahn, eds., *The Song-Yuan-Ming Transition in Chinese History*. Cambridge, Mass.: Harvard University Asia Center, in press.

———. "Debatable Land: The Fujian-Jiangxi-Zhejiang Border Region during the Song." *Studies in Chinese History* 8 (Dec. 1998): 1–28.

———. "The Development of the Jianyang Book Trade, Song-Yuan." *Late Imperial China* 17, no. 1 (June 1996): 10–48.

———. "Of Three Mountains Street: The Commercial Publishers of Ming Nanjing." In *Printing and Book Culture in Late Imperial China*, ed. Cynthia J. Brokaw and Kai-wing Chow. Berkeley: University of California Press. Forthcoming.

———. "Printing for Profit: The Commercial Printers of Jianyang, Fujian (Song-Ming)." Ph.D. diss., Columbia University, 1996.

Chongan xianzhi 崇安縣志.

———. 1670. 8 *juan*. Comp. Guan Shengjun 管聲駿 et al.

———. 1733. 8 *juan*. Comp. Liu Yu 劉埼 et al.

———. 1808. 10 *juan*. Comp. Wei Daming 魏大名 et al.

———. 1924. 38 *juan*. Comp. Zheng Fengren 鄭豐稔 et al.

Chrisman, Miriam U. *Lay Culture, Learned Culture, Books and Social Change in Strasbourg, 1480–1599.* New Haven: Yale University Press, 1982.

Clark, Hugh R. *Community, Trade, and Networks: Southern Fujian Province from the Third to the Thirteenth Century.* Cambridge, Eng.: Cambridge University Press, 1991.

———. "The Consolidation of the South China Frontier: The Development of Ch'üan-Chou, 699–1126." Ph.D. diss., University of Pennsylvania, 1981.

Clunas, Craig. "The Book Trade, Book Collection and the Dissemination of Knowledge in Late Imperial China." Paper presented at the Annual Meeting of the Association for Asian Studies, Boston, Mar. 24–27, 1994.

———. *Pictures and Visuality in Early Modern China.* Princeton: Princeton University Press, 1997.

———. *Superfluous Things: Material Culture and Social Status in Early Modern China.* London: Polity Press, 1991.

———. "The West Chamber: A Literary Theme in Chinese Porcelain Decoration." *Transactions of the Oriental Ceramic Society* 46 (1981–82): 69–86.

Corsi, Elisabetta. "Scholars and Paper-Makers: Paper and Paper-Manufacture According to Tu Long's Notes on Paper." *Revista degli studi Orientali* 65 (1991): 69–107.

Dai Keyu 戴克瑜 and Tang Jianhua 唐建華, eds. *Leishu de yange* 類書的沿革. Chengdu?: Sichuan sheng zhongxin tushuguan xuehui, 1981.

Daniels, Christian. "Jūroku~jūshichi seiki Fukken no takegama seizō gijutsu [Tenkō kaibutsu] ni shōjutsu sareta—seizō no jidai kōshō" 16~17世紀福建の竹紙裝造技術「天工開物」に詳述された―裝紙技術の時代考証. *Journal of Asian-African Studies*, 30th Anniversary Commemorative Issue II, No. 48–49 (1995): 243–94.

Darnton, Robert. "The Printed Word." In idem, *The Kiss of Lamourette*, pp. 107–87. New York: Norton, 1990.

de Pee, Christian. "Negotiating Marriage: Weddings, Text, and Ritual in Song-Yuan China (10th Through 14th Centuries)." Ph.D. diss., Columbia University, 1997.

de Weerdt, Hilde. "Aspects of Song Intellectual Life: A Preliminary Inquiry into Some Southern Song Encyclopedias." *Papers on Chinese History* 3 (Spring 1994): 1–27.

———. "The Composition of Examination Standards: *Daoxue* and Southern Song Dynasty Examination Culture." Ph.D. diss., Harvard University, 1998.

Dolby, William. "Chung-yüan yin-yün" In *The Indiana Companion to Traditional Chinese Literature*, vol. 1, ed. and comp. William Nienhauser, Jr., pp. 370–71. Bloomington: Indiana University Press, 1986.

Drège, Jean-Pierre. *Les Bibliothèques en Chine au temps des manuscrits.* Paris: Ecole Française d'Extrême-Orient, 1991.

———. "Des effets de l'imprimérie en Chine sous la dynastie des Song." *Journal Asiatique* 282, no. 2 (1994): 409–42.

du Halde, Jean Baptiste. *The General History of China.* 4 vols. Trans. R. Brookes. London: John Watts, 1736.

Duan Xuanwu 段炫武, ed. *Song dai banke fazhi yanjiu* 宋代版刻法制研究. Taipei: Shishi chuban gongsi, 1975.

Edgren, Sören. "The Chinese Book as a Source for the History of the Book in China." Paper presented at the conference Printing and Book Culture in Late Imperial China, Timberline Lodge, Ore., June 1998.

———. "Southern Song Printing at Hangzhou." *Bulletin of the Museum of Far Eastern Antiquities* 62 (1989): 1–212.

Edgren, Sören, Tsien Tsuen-hsuin, Wang Fang-Yu, and Wan-go H.C. Weng. *Chinese Rare Books in American Collections*. New York: China Institute in America, 1984.

Eisenstein, Elizabeth L. *The Printing Press as An Agent of Change*. 2 vols. Cambridge, Eng.: Cambridge University Press, 1979.

———. *The Printing Revolution in Early Modern Europe*. Cambridge, Eng.: Cambridge University Press, 1983.

Elman, Benjamin A. *A Cultural History of Civil Examinations in Late Imperial China*. Berkeley: University of California Press, 2000.

Fang, Achilles. "Bookman's Manual." *Harvard Journal of Asiatic Studies* 14 (1951): 215–60.

Fang Yanshou 方彦壽. "Jianyang Liu shi keshu kao" 建陽劉氏刻書考. *Wenxian* 36 (1988, no. 2): 196–228; 37 (1988, no. 3): 217–29.

———. "Jianyang xian zhi keshu shulüe" 建陽縣治刻書述略. *Fujian tushuguan xuekan* 34 (1988, no. 2): 40–42.

———. "Jianyang Xiong shi keshu shulüe" 建陽熊氏刻書述略. *Guji zhengli yu yanjiu* 6 (1991): 193–208.

———. "Minbei Liu shi deng shisi wei keshujia shengping kaolüe" 閩北劉氏等十四位刻書家生平考略. *Wenxian* 47 (1991, no. 1): 222–30.

———. "Minbei shiba wei keshujia shengping kaolüe" 閩北十八位刻書家生平考略. *Wenxian* 59 (1994, no. 1): 224–33.

———. "Minbei shiba wei keshujia shengping kaolüe" 閩北十八位刻書家生平考略. *Chuban shi yanjiu* 4 (1996): 200–16.

———. "Minbei shisi wei keshujia shengping kaolüe" 閩北十四位刻書家生平考略. *Wenxian* (1993, no. 1): 210–19.

———. "Minbei Zhan Yu Xiong Cai Huang wu xing shisan wei keshujia shengping kaolüe" 閩北詹余熊蔡黃五姓十三位刻書家生平考略. *Wenxian* 41 (1989, no. 3): 233–42.

———. "Mingdai keshujia Xiong Zongli shukao" 明代刻書家熊宗立述考. *Wenxian* 31 (1987, no. 1): 228–43.

———. "Mingdai xiaoshuojia Xiong Damu ji qi 'Bei Song zhizhuan'" 明代小說家熊大木及其'北宋志傳.' *Fujian shizhi* 2 (1988): 54–56.

———. "Xiao Tenghong Shijiantang de keshu didian" 簫騰鴻師儉堂的刻書地點. *Wenxian* (1989, no. 1): 210.

———. "Xiong Yunbin yu Shidetang ben 'Xiyu ji'" 熊云濱與世德堂本'西遊記'. *Wenxian* (1988, no. 4): 285–88.

Farrer, Anne S. "The *Shui-hu Chuan*: A Study in the Development of Late Ming Woodblock Illustration." Ph.D. diss., School of Oriental and African Studies, University of London, 1984.

Febvre, Lucien and Henri-Jean Martin. *L'Apparition du Livre*. Paris: Editions Albin Michel, 1958. Trans. David Gerard as *The Coming of the Book: The Impact of Printing 1450–1800*. London: NLB, 1976.

Feng Menglong 馮夢龍. *Xin Lieguo zhi* 新列國志. 2 vols. Facsimile ed. Taipei: Lianjing chuban shiye, 1981.

Fortune, Robert. *Two Visits to the Tea Countries of China*. 2 vols. London: John Murray, 1853.

Fosdick, Sydney O. "Chinese Book Publishing during the Sung Dynasty (A. D. 960–1279); a Partial Translation of *Istoriia Kitaiskoi Pechatnoi Knigi Sunskoi Epokhi* by Konstantine Konstantinovich Flug with Added Notes and an Introduction." M. A. thesis, University of Chicago, 1968.

Franck, Harry A. *Roving Through Southern China*. New York & London: Century, 1925.

Fu Yiling 傅衣凌. *Ming-Qing nongcun shehui jingji* 明清農村社會經濟. Beijing: Sanlian shudian, 1961.

Fujian Tongji 福建通紀. 1922. Comp. Fujian Tongji ju 福建通紀局. Reprinted—Taipei: Datong Shuju, 1968.

Furth, Charlotte. *A Flourishing Yin: Gender in China's Medical History, 960–1665*. Berkeley: University of California Press, 1999.

Gardella, Robert P. "Fukien's Tea Industry and Trade in Ch'ing and Republican China: The Developmental Consequences of A Traditional Commodity Export." Ph.D. diss., University of Washington, 1976.

———. *Harvesting Mountains: Fujian and the China Tea Trade, 1757–1937*. Berkeley: University of California Press, 1994.

———. "The Min-Pei Tea Trade During the Late Ch'ien-Lung and Chia-Ch'ing Eras: Foreign Commerce and the Mid-Ch'ing Fu-chien Highlands." In *Development and Decline of Fukien Province in the 17th and 18th Centuries*, ed. E. B. Vermeer, pp. 317–47. Sinica Leidensia, vol. 22. Leiden: E. J. Brill, 1990.

Genette, Gerard. *Paratexts: Thresholds of Interpretation*. Trans. Jane E. Lewin. Cambridge, Eng.: Cambridge University Press, 1997.

Goodrich, L. Carrington, and Chaoying Fang, eds. *Dictionary of Ming Biography 1368–1644*. 2 vols. New York: Columbia University Press, 1976.

Griffin, Clive. *The Crombergers of Seville: The History of a Printing and Merchant Dynasty*. Oxford: Oxford University Press, 1988.

Gu Yanwu 顧炎武. *Gu Tinglin shiwen ji* 顧亭林詩文集. Reprinted—Beijing: Zhonghua shuju, 1983

———. *Rizhilu jishi* 日知錄集釋. Annot. Huang Rucheng 黃汝成. Changsha: Yuelu shushe, 1994.

Gu Zhixing 顧志興. *Zhejiang cangshujia shulou* 浙江藏書家書樓. Hangzhou: Zhejiang renmin, 1987.

———. *Zhejiang chuban shi yanjiu—Yuan Ming Qing shiqi* 浙江出版史研究—元明清時期. Hangzhou: Zhejiang guji, 1993.

———. *Zhejiang chuban shi yanjiu—Zhong-Tang Wudai Liang-Song shiqi* 浙江出版史研究—中唐五代兩宋時期. Hangzhou: Zhejiang Renmin, 1991.

Guan Guiquan 官桂銓. "Ming xiaoshuo jia Yu Xiangdou ji Yushi ke xiaoshuo xiqu"
明小說家余象斗及余氏刻小說戲曲. *Wenxue yichang zengkan* 15 (1983):
125–30.

Guben xiaoshuo congkan 古本小說叢刊. Beijing: Xinhua shudian, 1987–91.

Guo Bocang 郭伯蒼. *Min chan lu yi* 閩產錄異. Original 1886 ed.

Guo Taiyun 郭太運, oral account; Deng Ling 鄧岭 and Ren Helin 任鶴林,
comps. "Zhuxian zhen nianhua yu minsu" 朱仙鎮年畫與民俗. *Zhongzhou
minsu* 10 (Dec. 1989): 3–12.

Han Yuanji 韓元吉. *Nanjian jiayi gao* 南澗甲乙稿. *CSJC-CB* ed., vol. 1982.

Hanan, Patrick. "*Judge Bao's Hundred Cases* Reconstructed." *Harvard Journal of Asiatic Studies* 40, no.2 (1980): 301–23.

Hansen, Valerie. *Changing Gods in Medieval China, 1127–1276*. Princeton: Princeton
University Press, 1990.

Hartmann, Alfred and Beat Rudolf Jenny, eds. *Die Amerbachkorrespondenz*. 8 vols.
Basle: Verlag der Universitätsbibliothek, 1942–74.

Hayden, George A. "The Courtroom Plays of the Yüan and Early Ming Periods."
Harvard Journal of Asiatic Studies 34 (1974): 192–220.

Hayes, James. "Specialists and Written Materials in the Village World." In *Popular
Culture in Late Imperial China*, ed. David Johnson, Andrew J. Nathan, and
Evelyn S. Rawski, pp. 75–111. Berkeley: University of California Press, 1985.

He Changjiang 何長江. "*Yanju biji* bianzhe Yu Gongren xiaokao" 《燕居筆記》
編者余公仁小考. *Ming-Qing xiaoshuo yanjiu* 3 (1993): 105–8.

He Mengchun 何孟春. *Yudong xulu* 餘冬序錄. Original 1528 ed.

Hegel, Robert E. *Reading Illustrated Fiction in Late Imperial China*. Stanford: Stanford University Press, 1998.

Heijdra, Martin. Review of *Geographical Sources of Ming-Qing History* by Timothy
Brook. *Ming Studies* 29 (Spring 1990): 66–68.

———. "Technology, Culture and Economics: Movable Type versus Woodblock
Printing in East Asia." Paper presented at the First International Scientific Conference on Publishing Culture in East Asia, Tokyo, December 8–10, 2001.

Hennessey, William O. "The Song Emperor Huizong in Popular History and Romance: The Early Chinese Vernacular Novel *Xuanhe yishi*." Ph.D. diss., University of Michigan, 1980.

Hennessey, William O., trans. *Proclaiming Harmony*. Ann Arbor: University of
Michigan, Center for Chinese Studies, 1981.

Hervouet, Yves, ed. *A Sung Bibliography*. Hong Kong: Chinese University Press,
1978.

Hindman, Sandra L., ed. *Printing the Written Word: The Social History of Books, circa
1450–1520*. Ithaca: Cornell University Press, 1991.

Hirsch, Rudolf. *Printing, Selling and Reading 1450–1550*. Rev. ed. Wiesbaden: Otto
Harrossowitz, 1974.

Ho Ping-ti. "Early Ripening Rice in Chinese History." *Journal of Economic History*,
2d ser., 9, no. 2 (1956): 200–18.

Hong Mai 洪邁. *Rongzhai suibi* 容齋隨筆. Shanghai: Shanghai guji, 1993.

———. *Yi Jian zhi* 夷堅志. Reprint of Hanfen lou ed. Tokyo: Chūbun, 1980.

Hu Daojing 胡道靜. *Zhongguo gudai de leishu* 中國古代的類書. Beijing: Zhonghua shuju, 1982.

Hu Yin 胡寅. *Peiran ji* 斐然集. *SKQS* ed.

Hu Yinglin 胡應麟. *Shaoshi shanfang bicong* 少室山房筆叢. Shanghai: Zhonghua, 1958.

――――. *Shaoshi shanfang ji* 少室山房集. *Siku quanshu zhenben*, 12th collection.

Huang Lin 黃霖 and Han Tongwen 韓同文. *Zhongguo lidai xiaoshuo lunzhu xuan* 中國歷代小說論著選. Jiangxi: Renmin, 1982.

Huang Qingwen 黃晴文. "Zhongguo gudai shuyuan zhidu ji qi keshu tanjiu" 中國古代書院制度及其刻書探研. M.A. thesis, Zhongguo wenhua daxue (Taipei), 1984.

Hummel, Arthur W. "Division of Orientalia." In *Annual Report of the Librarian of Congress, 1940*, pp. 165–67. Washington, D.C.: United States Government Printing Office, 1941.

Hummel, Arthur W., ed. *Eminent Chinese of the Ch'ing Period*. Washington, D.C.: U.S. Government Printing Office, 1943.

Hunter, Dard. *Old Papermaking in China and Japan*. Chillicothe, Ohio: Mountain House Press, 1932.

――――. *Papermaking: The History and Technique of An Ancient Craft*. 2d ed. New York: Knopf, 1947. Reprinted—New York: Dover Press, 1978.

Hurlbut, Floy. "*The Fukienese: A Study of Human Geography*." Ph.D. diss., University of Nebraska. Published by the author, 1930.

Hymes, Robert P. "Not Quite Gentlemen? Doctors in Sung and Yuan." *Chinese Science* 8 (1987): 9–76.

――――. *Statesmen and Gentlemen: the Elite in Fu-chou, Chiang-hsi in the Northern and Southern Sung*. Cambridge, Eng.: Cambridge University Press, 1986.

Ichinose Yūichi 一の瀬雄一. "Nan-Sō Rinan no shoho ni kansuru ichi kōsatsu" 南宋臨安の書鋪に關する一考察. *Shisen* 63 (Feb. 1986): 1–22.

Idema, Wilt L. *Chinese Vernacular Fiction: The Formative Period*. Sinica Leidensia, vol. 13. Leiden: E. J. Brill, 1974.

――――. "Novels about the Founding of the Sung Dynasty." *Sung Studies Newsletter* 9 (June 1974): 2–9.

――――. "Ping-hua." In *The Indiana Companion to Traditional Chinese Literature*, vol. 1, ed. and comp. William Nienhauser, Jr., pp. 660–62. Bloomington: Indiana University Press, 1986.

――――. "Some Remarks and Speculations Concerning *P'ing-Hua*." *T'oung Pao* 60 (1974): 121–72.

Inoue Susumu 井上進. "Zōsho to dokusho" 藏書と讀書. *Tōhō gakuho* 62 (1990): 409–445.

――――. "Shoshi・shoko・bunjin" 書肆・書賈・文人. In *Chūka bunjin no seikatsu* 中華文人の生活, ed. Arai Ken 荒井健, pp. 304–38. Tokyo: Heibonsha, 1994.

――――. "Shuppan bunka to gakujutsu" 出版文化と學術. In *Min-Shin jidai no kihon mondai* 明清時代史の基本問題, ed. Mori Masao 森正夫, pp. 531–37. Tokyo: Kyūko shoin, 1997.

Ivins, William, Jr. *Prints and Visual Communication*. Cambridge, Mass.: Harvard University Press, 1953. Reprinted—Cambridge, Mass.: MIT Press, 1992.

Ji Shuying 冀叔英. "Tantan Ming keben ji kegong—fu Ming dai zhongqi Suzhou diqu kegong biao" 談談明刻本及刻工—附明代中期蘇州地區刻工表. *Wenxian* 7 (March 1981): 211–31.

Jiang Shaoyu 江少虞. *Song chao shishi leiyuan* 宋朝事實類苑. 2 vols. Shanghai: Shanghai guji, 1981.

Jiang Yuanqing 蔣元卿. "Huizhou diaoban yinshua shu de fazhan" 徽州雕版印刷術的發展. Reprinted in *Lidai keshu gaikuang* 歷代刻書概況, ed. Shanghai Xin Siku lishi yanjiu hui and the Yinshua yinchao fenhui, pp. 363–75. Beijing: Yinshu gongye, 1991.

Jianning fuzhi 建寧府志.

———. 1493. 60 *juan*. Comp. Liu Yu 劉瑛 et al.

———. 1541. 22 *juan*. Comp. Wang Dian 汪佃 et al. Reprinted as vols. 27–28 of *Tianyige Mingdai fangzhi xuankanben* 天一閣明代方志選刊本. Shanghai: Guji, 1964.

———. Ming Wanli era. 52 *juan*. Comp. Chen Ru 陳儒 et al.

———. 1694. 48 *juan*. Comp. Zhang Qi 張琦 et al.

Jianyang xianzhi 建陽縣志.

———. 1453 with 1504 supplement. 4 *juan*. Comp. Zhao Wen 趙文 et al.

———. 1553. 16 *juan*. Comp. Feng Jike 馮繼科 et al. Reprinted as vol. 31 of *Tianyige Mingdai fangzhi xuankanben* 天一閣明代方志選刊本. Shanghai: Guji, 1964.

———. 1601. 10 *juan*. Comp. Yang Dezheng 陽德政 et al. Reprinted in the Series *Riben cang Zhongguo hanjian difangzhi congkan* 日本藏中國罕見地方志叢刊. Beijing: Shumu wenxian chubanshe: 1991.

———. 1703. 9 *juan*. Comp. Liu Zhengfang 劉正芳 et al.

———. 1832. 21 *juan*. Comp. Jiang Yuanqing 江遠青 et al. Reprinted—Jianyang, Fujian: Jianyang xian difangzhi bianzuan weiyuanhui, 1986.

———. 1929, 1931. 13 *juan*. Reprinted in *Zhongguo fangzhi congshu* 中國方志叢書 series. Taipei: Chengwen, 1967.

———. 1994. 32 *juan* plus supplement. Comp. Li Jiaqin 李家欽 et al. Jianyang, Fujian: Jianyang xian difangzhi bianzuan weiyuanhui, 1994.

Jin Jian 金簡. *Wuying dian qu zhen ban chengshi* 武英殿聚珍版程式. *CSJC-XB*, vol. 48. Trans. Richard C. Rudolph as *A Chinese Printing Manual*. Los Angeles: Ward Ritchie Press: 1954.

Johnson, David, Andrew J. Nathan, and Evelyn S. Rawski, eds. *Popular Culture in Late Imperial China*. Berkeley: University of California Press, 1985.

Kin Bunkyō 金文京. "'Sangoku engi' hampon shitan—Kenan shobun o chūshin ni" '三國演義'版本試探—建安諸本を中心に. *Shūkan Tōyōgaku* 61 (May 1989): 43–64.

———. *Sangoku shi engi no seikai* 三國志演義の世界. Tokyo: Tōhō shoten, 1993.

———. "Tō Hin'i to Minmatsu no shōgyō shuppan" 湯賓尹と明末の商業出版. In *Chūka bunjin no seikatsu*, ed. Arai Ken 荒井健, pp. 339–83. Tokyo: Heibonsha, 1994.

Ko, Dorothy. *Teachers of the Inner Chambers: Women and Culture in Seventeenth-Century China*. Stanford: Stanford University Press, 1994.

Kornicki, Peter F. *The Book in Japan: A Cultural History from the Beginning to the Nineteenth Century*. Leiden: E. J. Brill, 1997.

(Jiatai) Kuiji zhi (嘉泰) 會稽志. 1201. Comp. Shi Su 施宿. 1510 ed.

Lang Ying 郎英. *Qixiu leigao* 七修類稿. 2 vols. Beijing: Wenhua yishu, 1998.

Lao Yan-shuan. "Southern Chinese Scholars and Educational Institutions in Early Yüan: Some Preliminary Remarks." In *China under Mongol Rule*, ed. John Langlois, Jr., pp. 107–33. Princeton: Princeton University Press, 1981.

Laufer, R. "Les Espaces du Livre." In *Histoire de l'Edition française*, ed. R. Chartier and H.-J. Martin, 2: 128–39. Paris: Promodis, 1984.

———. "L'Espace Visuel du Livre Ancien." In *Histoire de l'Edition française*, ed. R. Chartier and H.-J. Martin, 1: 579–601. Paris: Promodis, 1984.

Lee, Thomas H. C. "Books and Bookworms in Song China: Book Collection and the Appreciation of Books." *Journal of Sung-Yuan Studies* 25 (1995): 193–218.

———. *Government Education and Examinations in Sung China*. Hong Kong: Chinese University Press, 1985.

———. [Li Hongqi 李弘祺]. "Jingshe yu shuyuan" 精舍與書院. *Hanxue yanjiu* 10, no. 2 (Dec. 1992): 307–32.

———. "Life in the Schools of Sung China." *Journal of Asian Studies* 37, no. 1 (Nov. 1977): 45–60.

———. "Neo-Confucian Education in Chien-yang, Fu-chien, 1000–1400: Academies, Society and the Development of Local Culture." *Guoji Zhuzi xuehui yilun wenji*, pp. 945–96. Taipei: Academia Sinica Chinese Philosophy Research Institute, 1993.

Leung, Angela Ki Che. "Transmission of Medical Knowledge from the Sung to the Ming." Paper presented at the conference The Sung-Yuan-Ming Transition: A Turning Point in Chinese History, Lake Arrowhead, Calif., June 5–11, 1997.

Li Fuqing 李福清 (Boris Riftin) and Li Ping 李平, comps. *Haiwai guben wan Ming xiju xuanji san zhong* 海外孤本晚明戲劇選集三種. Shanghai: Shanghai guji, 1993.

Li Guoqing 李國慶, ed. *Ming dai kangong xingming suoyin* 明代刊工姓名索引. Shanghai: Shanghai guji, 1998.

Li Han and Hsü Tzu-kuang. *Meng ch'iu; Famous Episodes from Chinese History and Legend*. Trans. Burton Watson. Tokyo: Kodansha International, 1979.

Li Hongqi 李弘祺—see Lee, Thomas H. C.

Li Longqian 李龍潛. "Ming Zhengtong nianjian Ye Zongliu Deng Maoqi qiyi jingguo ji tedian" 明正統年間葉宗留鄧茂七起義之經過及特點. In *Zhongguo nongmin qiyi lunji* 中國農民起義論集, pp. 227–51. Beijing: Sanlian shudian, 1958.

Li Qingzhi 李清志. *Gushu banben jianding yanjiu* 古書版本鑒定研究. Taipei: Wenshizhe, 1986.

Li Ruiliang 李瑞良. *Fujian chuban hua* 福建出版話. Xiamen: Lujiang chubanshe, 1997.

———. *Zhongguo gudai tushu liutong shi* 中國古代圖書流通史. Shanghai: Shanghai renmin, 2000.

Li Tao 李燾. *Xu Zizhi tongjian changbian* 續資治通鑑長編. Taipei: Shijie shuju, 1967.

Li Xinchuan 李心傳. *Jianyan yilai chao ye zaji* 建炎以來朝野雜記. *CSJC-CB* ed., vols. 0836–41.

———. *Jianyan yilai xi nian yaolu* 建炎以來繫年要錄. *CSJC-CB* ed., vols. 3861–78.

Li Xu 李詡. *Jiean laoren manbi* 戒庵老人漫筆. Beijing: Zhonghua, 1982.

Li Zhitan 李之檀. "Fujian Jian'an pai muke banhua" 福建建安派木刻版畫. *Zhongguo lishi bowuguan guankan* (1986.8): 97–110.

Liang Fangzhong 梁方仲. *Zhongguo lidai hukou tiandi tianfu tongji* 中國歷代戶口田地田賦統計. Shanghai: Renmin, 1980.

Liaocheng diqu zhi 聊城地區志. Comp. Liaocheng diqu difang shizhi bianyuan weiyuanhui. Ji'nan: Qilu shushe, 1997.

Ling Yangzao 凌揚澡. *Li shao bian* 蠡勺編. *CSJC-CB* ed., vols. 0225–30.

Liu Hsiang-kwang. "Education and Society: The Development of Public and Private Institutions in Hui-chou, 960–1800." Ph.D. diss., Columbia University, 1996.

Liu, James J. Y. "The *Fêng-Yüeh Chin-Nang* 風月錦囊: A Ming collection of Yüan and Ming plays and lyrics preserved in the Royal Library of San Lorenzo, Escorial, Spain." *Journal of Oriental Studies* 4, nos. 1–2 (1957–8): 79–107.

Liu Renqing 劉仁慶, ed. *Xuanzhi yu shufa* 宣紙與書法. Beijing: Xinhua, 1989.

Liu Yeqiu 劉葉秋. *Zhongguo zidian shilüe* 中國字典史略. Beijing: Zhonghua shuju, 1992.

Loewe, M. A. N. "Some Recent Editions of the Ch'ien-Han-shu." *Asia Major*, n.s., 10, no. 2 (1964): 162–72.

Lou Yue 樓鑰. *Gongkui ji* 攻媿集. *CSJC-CB* ed., vols. 2003–22.

Lowry, Martin. *The World of Aldus Manutius*. Ithaca: Cornell University Press, 1979.

Lu Qian 盧前. *Shulin biehua* 書林別話. Reprinted in *Minguo Congshu* 民國叢書, 2d Ser., no. 50. Shanghai: Shanghai Shudian, 1990.

Lu Rong 陸容. *Shuyuan zaji* 菽園雜記. *CSJC-CB* ed., vols. 0329–30.

Lu Shen 陸深. *Yanshan waiji* 儼山外集. Ming Jiajing ed.

Lu You 陸游. *Laoxuean biji* 老學庵筆記. *CSJC-CB* ed., vol. 2766.

Lu Yü 陸羽. *Cha jing* 茶經. *SKQS* ed.

Ma Duanlin 馬端臨. *Wenxian tongkao* 文獻通考. Taipei: Xinxing shuju, 1964.

Ma, Y. W. "The Pao-kung Tradition in Chinese Popular Literature." Ph.D. diss., Yale University, 1971.

———. "The Textual Tradition of Ming *Kung-an* Fiction: A Study of the *Lung-t'u Kung-an*." *Harvard Journal of Asiatic Studies* 35 (1975): 190–220.

———. "Themes and Characterization in the *Lung-t'u kung-an*." *T'oung Pao* 59 (1973): 179–202.

Mair, Victor H. *T'ang Transformation Texts: A Study of the Buddhist Contribution to the Rise of Vernacular Fiction and Drama in China*. Cambridge, Mass.: Harvard University, Council on East Asian Studies, 1989.

Martin, Henri-Jean. *The History and Power of Writing*. Trans. Lydia G. Cochrane. Chicago: University of Chicago Press, 1994.

———. *Print, Power, and People in 17th-Century France*. Trans. David Gerard. Metuchen, N.J.: Scarecrow Press, 1993.

Martinique, Edward. *Chinese Traditional Bookbinding: A Study of Its Evolution and Techniques*. Asian Library Series no. 19. San Francisco: Chinese Materials Center, 1983.

Maruyama Hiroaki 丸山浩明. "Yo Shōto-bon kōryaku" 余象斗本考略. *Nishō Gakusha Daigaku jimbun ronsō* 50 (1993): 121–44.

McClure, Floyd A. *Chinese Handmade Paper*. Newtown, Penn.: Bird and Bull Press, 1986.

McDermott, Joseph. "The Ascendance of the Imprint in Late Imperial Chinese Culture." In *Printing and Book Culture in Late Imperial China*, ed. Cynthia J. Brokaw and Kai-wing Chow. Berkeley: University of California Press. Forthcoming.

McKenzie, D. F. "Bibliography and the Sociology of Texts." The Panizzi Lectures, 1985. London: The British Library, 1986.

———. "Typography and Meaning: The Case of William Congreve." In *Buch und Buchhandel in Europa im achtzehnten Jahrhundert*, ed. Giles Barber and Bernhard Fabian, pp. 81–125. Hamburg: Hauswedell, 1981.

McLaren, Anne E. "Chantefables and the Textual Evolution of the *San-kuo-chih yen-i*." *T'oung Pao* 71 (1985): 159–227.

———. *Chinese Popular Culture and Ming Chantefables*. Leiden: E. J. Brill, 1998.

———. "Constructing New Reading Publics in Late Ming China." In *Printing and Book Culture in Late Imperial China*, ed. Cynthia J. Brokaw and Kai-wing Chow. Berkeley: University of California Press. Forthcoming.

———. "The Discovery of Chinese Chantefable Narratives from the Fifteenth Century: A Reassessment of Their Likely Audience." *Ming Studies* 29 (Spring 1990): 1–29.

———. "Ming Audiences and Vernacular Hermeneutics: The Uses of *The Romance of the Three Kingdoms*." *T'oung Pao* 61 (1995): 51–80.

———. "Paratextual Discourse in Chinese Texts from the Twelfth to the Sixteenth Centuries—the Emergence of the Common Reader." Paper presented at The First Scientific Conference on Publishing Culture in East Asia, Tokyo, December 8–10, 2001.

———. "Popularizing *The Romance of the Three Kingdoms*: A Study of Two Early Editions." *Journal of Oriental Studies* 33, no. 2 (1995): 165–85.

McLuhan, Marshall. *The Gutenberg Galaxy*. Toronto: University of Toronto Press, 1962.

Mi Fu 米芾. *Shu shi* 書史. *CSJC-CB* ed., vol. 1593.

Ming shi 明史. 28 vols. Beijing: Zhonghua, 1974.

Ming Taizu Gao Huangdi shilu 明太祖高黃帝實錄. Taipei: Academia Sinica, 1962.

Mino Yutaka. *Freedom of Clay and Brush through Seven Centuries in North China: Tz'u-chou type ware, 960–1600*. Exhibition catalogue. Indianapolis: Indianapolis Museum of Art, 1980.

Minshu 閩書. 1630. 154 *juan*. Comp. He Qiaoyuan 何喬遠 et al. 5 vols. Reprinted—Fuzhou: Fujian renmin, 1995.

Morita Kenji 森田憲司. "Guanyu zai Riben de 'Shilin guangji' zhuben" 關于在日本的《事林廣記》諸本. In *Guoji Song shi yan tao hui lunwen xuan ji* 國際宋史研討會論文選集, edited by Deng Guangming 鄧廣銘 and Qi Sha 漆俠, pp. 266–80. Baoding, Hebei: Hebei daxue, 1992.

Mote, Frederick W. and Hung-lam Chu. *Calligraphy and the East Asian Book.* Gest Library Journal 2, no. 2 (Spring 1988).

Moxon, Joseph. *Mechanick Exercises on the Whole Art of Printing.* London: printed for J. Moxon, 1683–84. Facsimile reprint, ed. Herbert Davis and Harry Carter, 2nd ed.—London: Oxford University Press, 1962.

Nagasawa Kikuya 長澤規矩也. *Nagasawa Kikuya chosaku shū* 長澤規矩也 著作集. 11 vols. Tokyo: Kyūko Shoin, 1982–87.

Nienhauser, William, Jr., ed. *The Indiana Companion to Traditional Chinese Literature.* Vol. 1. Bloomington: Indiana University Press, 1986.

Niida Noboru 仁井田陞. *Chūgoku hōsei shi kenkyū* 中國法制史缸究. Vol. 2: *Tochi-hō torihiki-hō* 土地法取引法; vol. 4. *Hō to kanshū, hō to dōtoku* 法と 慣習,法と道德. Tokyo: Tokyo University Press, 1980.

Norman, Jerry. *Chinese.* Cambridge, Eng.: Cambridge University Press, 1988.

———. "The Kienyang Dialect of Fukien." Ph.D. diss., University of California, Berkeley, 1969.

Ogawa Yōichi 小川陽一. *Nichiyō ruisho ni yoru Min-Shin shōsetsu no kenkyū* 日用 類書による明清小說の研究. Tokyo: Kenbun shuppansha, 1995.

Ōki Yasushi 大木康. *Minmatsu Konan ni okeru shuppan bunka no kenkyū* 明末江南における出版文化の研究. *Hiroshima daigaku bungakubu kiyō* 50 (1992): 1–153.

Ong, Walter J. *Orality and Literacy: The Technologizing of the World.* Reprinted— London and New York: Routledge, 1982.

Ouyang Xiu 歐陽修. *Ouyang Xiu quanji* 歐陽修全集. 2 vols. Taipei: Shijie shuju, 1961.

Ozaki Yasushi 尾崎康. *Seishi Sō-Genpan no kenkyū* 正史宋元版の研究. Tokyo: Kyūko shoin, 1989.

Pan Jixing 潘吉星. *Zhongguo zaozhi jishu shigao* 中國造紙技術史稿. Beijing: Wenwu chubanshe, 1979.

Pan Mingxin 潘銘燊—see Poon Ming-sun

Parker, E. H. "A Journey from Foochow to Wenchow through Central Fukien." *Journal of the North China Branch, Royal Asiatic Society* 19 (1883): 1–19.

Peng Baichuan 彭百川. *Taiping zhi ji tong lei* 太平治蹟統類. Taipei: Chengwen, 1966.

Peng Guinian 彭龜年. *Zhitang ji* 止堂集. *CSJC-CB* ed., vols. 2023–25.

Plaks, Andrew H. *The Four Masterworks of the Ming Novel:* Ssu ta ch'i-shu. Princeton: Princeton University Press, 1987.

Poon Ming-sun. "Books and Printing in Sung China (960–1279)." Ph.D. diss., University of Chicago, 1979.

———. "The Printer's Colophon in Sung China, 960–1279." *Library Quarterly* 43 (1973): 39–52.

———. [Pan Mingxin 潘銘燊]. "Song dai si jia cang shu kao" 宋代私家藏書考. *Hua guo xuebao* 6 (July 1971): 201–62.

Da Qing lichao shilu 大清歷朝實錄. Taipei: Hualian, 1964.

Qingyuan tiaofa shilei 慶元條法事類. Comp. Xie Shenfu 謝深甫 et al. Reprint of Yenching University Library woodcut ed. Beijing: Zhongguo shudian, 1984?

Qu Mianliang 瞿冕良. *Zhongguo guji banke cidian* 中國古籍版刻辭典. Ji'nan: Qilu shushe, 1999.

Rawski, Evelyn S. *Agricultural Change and the Peasant Economy of South China.* Cambridge, Mass.: Harvard University Press, 1972.

———. "Economic and Social Foundations of Late Imperial Culture." In *Popular Culture in Late Imperial China*, ed. David Johnson, Andrew J. Nathan, and Evelyn S. Rawski, pp. 3–33. Berkeley: University of California Press, 1985.

———. *Education and Popular Literacy in Ch'ing China.* Ann Arbor: University of Michigan Press, 1979.

Reed, Christopher A. "Gutenberg in Shanghai: Mechanized Printing, Modern Publishing, and Their Effects on the City, 1876–1937." Ph.D. diss., University of California, Berkeley, 1996.

Reynolds, Craig. "Tycoons and Warlords: Modern Thai Social Formations and Chinese Historical Romance." In *Sojourners and Settlers: History of Southeast Asia and the Chinese: In Honour of Jennifer Cushman*, ed. Anthony Reid, pp. 115–47. St Leonards, NSW: Allen & Unwin, 1996.

Richardson, S. D. *Forestry in Communist China.* Baltimore: Johns Hopkins University Press, 1966.

Robbins, Michael. "The Inland Fukien Tea Industry: Five Dynasties to the Opium War." *Transactions of the International Conference of Orientalists in Japan*, no. 19 (1974): 121–42.

Rolston, David. *Traditional Chinese Fiction and Fiction Commentary.* Stanford: Stanford University Press, 1997.

Rolston, David, ed. *How to Read the Chinese Novel.* Princeton: Princeton University Press, 1990.

Rose, Jonathan. "The History of Books: Revised and Enlarged." In *The Darnton Debate: Books and Revolution in the Eighteenth Century*, ed. Haydn T. Mason, pp. 83–104. Oxford: The Voltaire Foundation, 1998.

———. "Rereading the *English Common Reader*: A Preface to the History of Audiences." *Journal of the History of Ideas* 53 (1992): 47–70.

Ruitenbeek, Klaas. "The *Lu Ban jing*: A Fifteenth-Century Chinese Carpenter's Manual." Ph.D. diss., Leiden University, 1989.

Saenger, Paul and Michael Heinlein. "Incunable Description and Its Implication for the Analysis of Fifteenth-Century Reading Habits." In *Printing the Written Word*, ed. Sandra L. Hindman, pp. 225–58. Ithaca: Cornell University Press, 1991.

Sakai, Tadao 酒井忠夫. "Chūgoku shijō no shomin kyōiku to zensho undō" 中國史上の庶民教育と善書運動. In *Chūsei Ajia kyōiku kenkyū* 中世アジア教育史研究, ed. Taga Akigoro 多賀秋五郎, pp. 294–323. Tokyo: Kokusho kankōkai, 1980.

———. "Confucianism and Popular Educational Works." In *Self and Society in Ming Thought*, ed. William T. deBary, pp. 331–66. New York: Columbia University Press, 1970.

———. "Mindai no nichiyō ruisho to shomin kyōiku" 明代の日用類書と庶民教育. In *Kinsei Chūgoku kyōikushi kenkyū* 近世中國教育史研究, ed. Hayashi Tomoharu 林友春, pp. 25–154. Tokyo: Kokudosha, 1958.

———. "Minmatsu no shinbunka to dokushojinsō" 明末の新文化と讀書人層. In *Shukyō shakaishi kenkyū* 宗教社會史研究, ed. Risshō daigaku shigakkai sōritsu gojūshūnen kinen jigyō jikkō iinkai, 立正大學史學會創立五十週年記念事業實行委員會, pp. 631–56. Tokyo: Yūzankaku, 1977.

———. "Minmatsu Shincho no shakai ni okeru taishūteki dokushojin to zensho seigen" 明末清初の社會における大衆的讀書人と善書・清言. In *Dōkyō no sōgōteki kenkyū* 道教の總合的研究, ed. idem, pp. 370–93. Tokyo: Kokusho kankōkai, 1977.

Sakai, Tadao 酒井忠夫 et al., eds. *Chūgoku nichiyō ruisho shūsei* 中國日用類書集成. Tokyo: Kyūko shoin, 1998.

Sanshan zhi 三山志. Early 12th c. 42 *juan*. Comp. Liang Kejia 梁克家 et al. In *Song-Yuan difang zhi congshu* 宋元地方志叢書, vol. 12. Taipei: Dahua shuju, 1987.

Schafer, Edward H. *The Empire of Min*. Rutland: Charles E. Tuttle, 1954.

Schlieder, Wolfgang, Pan Jixing, and Sybille Girmond, comms.; Maria Scholz, org. *Chinesische Bambuspapier Herstellung: Ein Bilderalbum aus dem 18. Jahrhundert*. Berlin: Akademie Verlag, 1993.

Shangdong sheng zhi: chuban zhi 山東省志・出版志. Ji'nan: Shandong renmin, 1993.

Shaowu fuzhi 邵武府志

———. 1543. 15 *juan*. Comp. Chen Rang 陳讓 et al. Reprinted in vol. 10 of *Tianyige Mingdai fangzhi xuankan* 天一閣明代方志選刊. Taipei: Xinwenfeng, 1985.

———. 1898. 31 *juan*. Comp. Xu Zhaofeng 徐兆豐 et al.

Shen Defu 沈德符. *Bizhou xuansheng yu (buyi)* 幣帚軒剩語（補遺）. *CSJC-CB* ed., vol. 2943.

———. *Wanli yehuo bian* 萬曆野獲編. 3 vols. Reprinted—Beijing: Zhonghua shuju, 1959.

Shen Jin 沈津. "Ming dai fangke tushu zhi liutong yu jiage" 明代坊刻圖書之流通與價格. *Guoli Gugong bowu guan guankan* no. 1 (June 1996): 101–18.

Shen Kua 沈括. (*Xin jiaozheng*) *Mengxi bitan* (新校正) 夢溪筆談. Ed. and annot. Hu Daojing 胡道靜. Hong Kong: Zhonghua shuju, 1975.

Shōji Kakuitsu 莊司格一. *Chūgoku no kōan shōsetsu* 中國の公案小說. Tokyo: Kenbun, 1994.

Sima Guang 司馬光. *Zizhi tongjian* 資治通鑑. Annot. Hu Sanxing 胡三省. *Sibu beiyao* ed.

So, Billy Kee-long. "Economic Developments in South Fukien, 946–1276." Ph.D. diss., Australian National University, 1982.

———. [Su Jilang 蘇基朗]. "Songdai Quanzhou ji qi nei lu jiaotong zhi yanjiu" 宋代泉州及其內陸交通之研究. M. Phil. thesis, Chinese University of Hong Kong, 1978.

Song Ci 宋慈. *The Washing Away of Wrongs*. Trans. Brian McKnight. Ann Arbor: Center for Chinese Studies, University of Michigan, 1981.

Song huiyao jigao 宋會要輯稿. Comp. Xu Song 徐松. 8 vols. Beijing: Zhonghua shuju, 1957.

Song shi 宋史. 40 vols. Beijing: Zhonghua shuju, 1985.

Song Yingxing 宋應星. *Tiangong kaiwu* 天工開物. 1637 ed. Facsimile reprint in Vol. 3 of *Zhongguo Gudai banhua congkan* 中國古代版畫叢刊, ed. Zheng

Zhenduo 鄭振鐸. Shanghai: Guji, 1988. Trans. E-Tu Zen Sun and Shiou-Chuan Sun as *T'ien-kung k'ai-wu: Chinese Technology in the Seventeenth Century*. University Park: Pennsylvania State University Press, 1966.

Spufford, Margaret. *Small Books and Pleasant Histories; Popular Fiction and Its Readership in Seventeenth-Century England*. Athens: University of Georgia Press, 1981.

Strickmann, Michel. "The Seal of the Law: A Ritual Implement and The Origins of Printing." *Asia Major* 3d ser., 6, no. 2 (1993): 1–81.

Struve, Lynn A. "The Southern Ming, 1644–1662." In *The Cambridge History of China*, vol. 7, *The Ming Dynasty, 1368–1644*, pt. 1, ed. Frederick W. Mote and Denis Twitchett, chap. 11. Cambridge, Eng.: Cambridge University Press, 1988.

Su Jilang 蘇基朗—see So, Billy Kee-long.

Su Shi 蘇軾. *Dongpo zhilin* 東坡志林. *CSJC-CB* ed., vol. 2850.

Su Yijian 蘇易簡. *Wenfang si pu* 文房四譜. *SKQS* ed.

Sun Congtian 孫從添. *Cangshu jiyao* 藏書記要. Lithographic ed. Shanghai: Shaoye shanfang, 1914.

Tan Zhengbi 譚正璧 (Tan Jiading 譚嘉定). *Zhongguo wenxue jia da cidian* 中國文學家大辭典. Reprinted—Hong Kong: Tiandi tushu, 1980.

Tanaka Seiji 田中贇治. "Goetsu to Binkoku to no kankei—Binkoku no nairan o chūshin to shite" 吳越と閩國との關系—閩國の內亂を中心として. *Tōyōshi kenkyū* 28 (1969): 28–51.

Tang Jin 唐錦. *Longjiang ji* 龍江集. 1569 ed.

Tao Chengqing 陶承慶, ed. (*Xinke jingben huayi feng wu*) *shang cheng yi lan* (新刻京本華夷風物) 商程一覽. Jianyang: Liu Longtian Qiaoshan jingshe 劉龍田喬山精舍, Ming Wanli Period (1573–1619).

Teng Ssu-yü and Knight Biggerstaff, eds. *An Annotated Bibliography of Selected Chinese Reference Works*. 3d ed. Cambridge, Mass.: Harvard University Press, 1971.

Tillman, Hoyt C. "Encyclopedias, Polymaths, and Tao-hsüeh Confucians: Preliminary Reflections With Special Reference to Chang Ju-yü." *Journal of Song-Yuan Studies* 22 (1990–92): 89–108.

Tsien Tsuen-hsuin 錢存訓. *Paper and Printing*. Vol. 5, pt. 1 of *Science and Civilisation in China*, ed. Joseph Needham. Cambridge, Eng.: Cambridge University Press, 1985.

———. "Zhongguo yinshua shi jianmu" 中國印刷史簡目. *Guoli Zhongyang tushuguan guan kan*, n.s. 23, no. 1 (June 1990): 179–199.

Twitchett, Denis C. *Printing and Publishing in Medieval China*. New York: Frederic C. Beil, 1983.

Unschuld, Paul U. *Medicine in China: A History of Pharmaceutics*. Berkeley: University of California Press, 1986.

Valenstein, Suzanne G. *A Handbook of Chinese Ceramics*. 2d ed., rev. and enl. New York: Metropolitan Museum of Art, 1989.

van der Loon, Piet. *The Classical Theatre and Art Song of South Fukien: A Study of Three Ming Anthologies*. Taipei: SMC, 1992.

van Selm, Bert. "Cornelis Claesz's 1605 Stock Catalogue of Chinese Books." *Quærendo* 13 (1983): 247–59.

Vöet, Leon. *The Golden Compasses: A History and Evaluation of the Printing and Publishing Activities of the Officina Plantiniana at Antwerp*. 2 vols. Amsterdam: Van Gend, 1969, 1972.

von Glahn, Richard. "Community and Welfare: Chu Hsi's Community Granary in Theory and Practice." In *Ordering the World: Approaches to State and Society in Sung Dynasty China*, ed. Robert Hymes and Conrad Schirokauer, pp. 221–54. Berkeley: University of California Press, 1993.

———. "Towns and Temples: Market Town Growth and Decline in the Yangzi Delta, 1200–1500." In *The Song-Yuan-Ming Transition in Chinese History*, ed. Paul Jakov Smith and Richard von Glahn. Cambridge, Mass.: Harvard University Asia Center, in press.

Walravens, Hartmut, ed. *Two Recently Discovered Fragments of the Chinese Novels San-kuo-chih yen-i and Shui-hu chuan*. With an Introduction by Y. W. Ma. Facsimile reprint of Ming editions. Hamburg: C. Bell Verlag, 1982.

Walton, Linda. *Academies and Society in Southern Sung China*. Honolulu: University of Hawai'i Press, 1999.

Wang Guowei 王國維. *Liang-Zhe gu kanben kao* 兩浙古刊本考. In vol. 7 of *Wang Guowei yi shu* 王國維遺書. Shanghai: Shanghai shudian, 1983.

Wang Hsiu-huei 王秀惠. "Un outil informatique sur le *Yijian zhi* de Hong Mai et ses applications à l'étude de la société des Song." Thesis, University of Paris VII, Etudes de l'Extrême-Orient, 1989.

Wang Liqi 王利器, ed. *Yuan-Ming-Qing san dai jinhui xiaoshuo xiju shiliao* 元明清三代禁毀小說戲劇史料. Rev. ed. Shanghai: Guji, 1981.

Wang Qinruo 王欽若 et al., eds. *Cefu yuangui* 册府元龜. Photofacsimile reprint of 1642 ed. Beijing: Zhonghua shuju, 1960.

Wang, Richard G. "Creating Artifacts: The Ming Erotic Novella in Cultural Practice." Ph.D. diss., University of Chicago, 1999.

Wang Shimao 王世懋. *Minbu shu* 閩部疏. *CSJC-XB* ed., vol. 95.

Wang Yeh-chien. "Food Supply in Eighteenth-Century Fukien." *Late Imperial China* 7, no. 2 (Dec. 1986): 80–117.

Wang Yun 王惲. *Yutang jiahua* 玉堂嘉話. *CSJC-CB* ed., vol. 0326.

Wang Yuquan. "Some Salient Features of the Ming Labor Service System." *Ming Studies* (Spring 1986): 1–44.

Wang Zhaowen 王肇文. *Guji Song-Yuan kangong xingming suoyin* 古籍宋元刊工姓名索引. Shanghai: Shanghai Guji chubanshe, 1990.

Wang Zhongluo 王仲犖. "Cong chaye jingji fazhan lishi kan Zhongguo fengjian shehui de yi ge tezheng" 從茶葉經濟發展歷史看中國封建社會的一個特徵. *Wenshizhe* 53, no. 2 (Mar. 1953): 33–42.

———. *Jin ni yu xie congkao* 金泥玉屑叢考. Beijing: Zhonghua shuju, 1998.

Wei Su 危素. *Wei Taipu ji* 危太僕集. Reprint. Taipei: Xin wenfeng, 1985.

Wei Yinru 魏隱儒 and Wang Jinyu 王金雨. *Guji banben jianding congtan* 古籍版本鑑定叢談. Beijing: Yinshua gongye chubanshe, 1984.

Whitfield, Roderick. "Tz'u-chou Pillows with Painted Decoration." In *Chinese Painting and the Decorative Style*, ed. Margaret Medley, pp. 74–94. A colloquy held June 23–25, 1975. Colloquies on art & archaeology in Asia 5. London: University of London School of Oriental and African Studies, Percival David Foundation of Chinese Art, 1976.

Widmer, Ellen. "The Huanduzhai of Hangzhou and Suzhou: A Study in Seventeenth-Century Publishing." *Harvard Journal of Asiatic Studies* 56, no. 1 (June 1996): 77–122.

Wilkinson, Endymion. *Chinese History: A Manual*. Rev. ed. Cambridge, Mass.: Harvard University Asia Center, 2000.

Winkelman, John. "The Imperial Library in Southern Sung China, 1127–1279: A Study of the Organization and Operation of the Scholarly Agencies of the Central Government." *Transactions of the American Philosophical Society*, n.s. 64, no. 8 (1974).

Wu Cheng'en. *The Journey to the West*. Trans. Anthony C. Yu. 4 vols. Chicago: University of Chicago Press, 1983.

Wu, K. T. "Chinese Printing Under Four Alien Dynasties." *Harvard Journal of Asiatic Studies* 13 (1950): 447–523.

———. "Ming Printing and Printers." *Harvard Journal of Asiatic Studies* 7 (1942): 203–60.

Xiao Dongfa 簫東發 "Jianyang Yu shi keshu kaolüe" 建陽余氏刻書考略. 3 pts. *Wenxian* 1984, no. 3: 230–247; 1984, no. 4: 195–219; 1985, no. 1: 236–250.

———. "Ming dai xiaoshuojia, keshujia Yu Xiangdou" 明代小說家、刻書家余象斗. In *Ming-Qing xiaoshuo biancong* 明清小說編叢 (4), 195–212. Shenyang: Chunfeng wenyi, 1986.

———. "Xiaoyi Minke 'Jingben'" 小議閩刻 '京本.' [Shanghai] *Tushuguan zazhi* 1984, no. 3: 67–68.

Xie Shuishun 謝水順 and Li Ting 李珽. *Fujian gudai keshu* 福建古代刻書. Fuzhou: Fujian Renmin, 1997.

Xie Zhaoshen 謝兆申. *Xie Erbo xiansheng quanqi* 謝耳伯先生全集 (preface 1640). Photographic reprint of original in Naikaku bunko. Tokyo: Takeo Hiraoka, 1976.

Xie Zhaozhe 謝肇淛. *Wu za zu* 五雜組. No. 1 in *Wakakuhon kanseki zuihitsu shū* 和刻本漢籍隨筆集. Tokyo: Kyūko shoin, 1982.

Xiong He 熊禾. *Xiong Wuxuan xiansheng wenji, fulu* 熊勿軒先生文集附錄. *CSJC-CB* ed., vol. 2407.

Xiong Ke 熊克. *Zhongxing xiaoji* 中興小記. Fuzhou: Fujian renmin, 1984.

Xiong Renlin 熊仁霖. *Hetai Xiansheng Xiong Shan wenxuan* 鶴臺先生熊山文選. Qing ed.

Xu Bo 徐𤊻. *Aofeng ji* 鰲峰集. 1625 ed.

———. *Xu shi bijing* 徐氏筆精. Taipei: Xuesheng shuju, 1970.

Xu Kang 徐康. *Qianchen mengying lu* 前塵夢影錄. Reprinted—Baibu congshu jicheng 百部叢書集成, 第六函, ser. 79, vol. 54. Yiwen yinshu guan.

Yamane Yukio 山根辛夫. *Mindai shi kenkyū bunken mokuroku* 明代史研究文獻目錄. Tokyo: Tōyō bunko Mindai shi kenkyūshi, 1960.

Yang Lien-sheng. "The Form of the Paper Note *Hui-tzu* of the Southern Sung Dynasty." *Harvard Journal of Asiatic Studies* 16 (1953): 365–73.

Yang Shengxin 楊繩信. "Cong *Qishazang* keyin kan Song-Yuan yinshua gongren de ji ge wenti" 從磧砂藏刻印看宋元印刷工人的幾個問題. *Zhonghua wenshi* 1 (1984): 41–58.

Yang Shuixin 楊水心 and Huang Shou'en 黃壽恩. "Jianyang zaozhi gujin tan" 建陽造紙古今談. *Fujian zaozhi* 10 (1986, no. 3): 13–17.

Yang Zhongxi 楊鍾羲. *Xueqiao shihua xuji* 雪橋詩話續集. Reprinted—Beijing: Guji, 1991.

Yangjiabu cunzhi 楊家埠村志. Comp. Yangjia bu cunzhi bianyuan weiyuanhui. Ji'nan: Qilu shushe, 1993.

Ye Changchi 葉昌熾. *Cangshu jishi shi, fu buzheng* 藏書紀事詩，附補正. Shanghai: Shanghai guji, 1999.

Ye Dehui 葉德輝. *Shulin qinghua* 書林清話. Reprint. Taipei: Wenshizhe, 1988.

Ye Mengde 葉夢得. *Shilin yanyu* 石林燕語. *SKQS* ed.

Yu Feiyin 于非闇. *Chinese Painting Colors: Studies of Their Preparation and Application in Traditional and Modern Times*. Trans. Jerome Silbergeld and Amy McNair. Seattle: University of Washington Press, 1988.

Yuan Cai. *Family and Property in Sung China: Yüan Ts'ai's Precepts for Social Life*. Trans. and annot. Patricia B. Ebrey. Princeton: Princeton University Press, 1984.

Yue Ke 岳珂. *Kuitan lu* 愧郯錄. *CSJC-CB* ed., vols. 0841–42.

———. *Ting shi* 桯史. *CSJC-CB* ed., vols. 2869–70.

Zai Zhi 載埴. *Shupu* 鼠璞. *CSJC-CB* ed., vol. 0319.

Zhang Dihua 張滌華. *Leishu liubie* 類書流別. Rev. ed. Beijing: Shangwu, 1985.

Zhang Xiumin 張秀民. *Zhang Xiumin yinshua shi lunwen ji* 張秀民印刷史論文集. Beijing: Yinshua gongye, 1988.

———. *Zhongguo yinshua shi* 中國印刷史. Shanghai: Renmin, 1989.

Zhang Yingyu 張應俞. *Du pian xin shu* 杜騙新書. Late Ming ed. Jianyang: Chen Huaixuan Cunren tang 陳懷軒存仁堂. Facsimile reprint—*Guben xiaoshuo jicheng* 古本小說集成. Shanghai: Shanghai guji, 1990. Modern annotated reprint—Zhengzhou: Zhongzhou guji, 1994.

Zhao Cheng 趙誠. *Zhongguo gudai yunshu* 中國古代韻書. Beijing: Zhonghua shuju, 1991.

Zhen Dexiu 眞德秀. *Xishan xiansheng Zhen Wenzhong gong wenji* 西山先生眞文忠文集. *Sibu congkan* ed.

Zheng Weizhang 鄭偉章 and Li Wanjian 李萬健. *Zhongguo zhuming cangshu jia zhuanlüe* 中國著名藏書家傳略. Beijing: Shumu wenxian, 1986.

Zheng Zhenduo 鄭振鐸, ed. *Zhongguo gudai banhua congkan* 中國古代版畫叢刊. 4 vols. Shanghai: Guji, 1988.

Zhou Lianggong 周亮工. *Min xiaoji* 閩小記. *CSJC-XB* ed., vol. 95.

———. *Shuying* 書影. Shanghai: Zhonghua shuju, 1958.

Zhou Mi 周密. *Qidong yeyu* 齊東野語. *CSJC-CB* ed., vols. 2779–82.

Zhou Wu 周蕪, ed. *Zhongguo banhua shi tulu* 中國版畫史圖錄. 2 vols. Shanghai: Shanghai Renmin meishu, 1988.

Zhou Xinhui 周心慧, ed. *Mingdai banke tushi* 明代版刻圖釋. 4 vols. Beijing: Xueyuan chubanshe, 1998.

Zhou Zhaoxin 周兆新. *Sanguo yanyi kaoping* 三國演義考評. Beijing: Beijing daxue chubanshe, 1990.

Zhu Chuanyu 朱傳譽. *Songdai xinwen shi* 宋代新聞史. Shanghai, 1934. Reprinted—Taipei: 1978.

Zhu Guozhen 朱國禎. *Yongzhuang xiaopin* 湧幢小品. Beijing: Zhonghua shuju, 1959.

Zhu Weigan 朱維幹. *Fujian shigao* 福建史稿. 2 vols. Fuzhou: Fujian Renmin, 1984.

Zhu Xi 朱熹. *Hui'an xiansheng Zhu Wengong wenji* 晦庵先生文公文集. Taipei: Shangwu, 1980.

———. *Zhu zi daquan* 朱子大全. *Sibu beiyao* ed. Taipei: Zhonghua, 1964.

———. *Zhu zi yulei* 朱子語類. 8 vols. Ed. Li Jingde 黎靖德. Beijing: Zhonghua shuju, 1994.

Zhu Yu 朱彧. *Pingzhou ke tan* 萍洲可談. *CSJC-CB* ed., vol. 2754.

Zhuang Yifu 莊一拂. *Gudian xiqu cunmu huikao* 古典戲曲存目彙考. 3 vols. Shanghai: Shanghai guji, 1982.

Glossary-Index

Most works are listed by their basic title in Chinese in *pinyin*, since different editions may have been discussed, and it is useful to see the references to all of them. For example, *Xinke an Jian quanxiang piping Sanguo zhizhuan* 新刻按鑑全像批評三國志傳 is listed under *Sanguo zhizhuan*, as are other editions of the *Sanguo zhizhuan*. Only publishers/printers mentioned in the main text or notes are included in this index; for comprehensive lists of commercial printers in the Jianyang area during the Song, Yuan, and Ming dynasties, see Appendix B. The entries are alphabetized letter-by-letter, ignoring word and syllable breaks, with the exception of personal names, which are grouped under the surname and then ordered alphabetically by the given name.

Harvard-Yenching Institute Monograph Series
(titles now in print)

11. *Han Shi Wai Chuan: Han Ying's Illustrations of the Didactic Application of the Classic of Songs*, translated and annotated by James Robert Hightower

21. *The Chinese Short Story: Studies in Dating, Authorship, and Composition*, by Patrick Hanan

22. *Songs of Flying Dragons: A Critical Reading*, by Peter H. Lee

23. *Early Chinese Civilization: Anthropological Perspectives*, by K. C. Chang

24. *Population, Disease, and Land in Early Japan, 645–900*, by William Wayne Farris

25. *Shikitei Sanba and the Comic Tradition in Edo Fiction*, by Robert W. Leutner

26. *Washing Silk: The Life and Selected Poetry of Wei Chuang (834?–910)*, by Robin D. S. Yates

27. *National Polity and Local Power: The Transformation of Late Imperial China*, by Min Tu-ki

28. *Tang Transformation Texts: A Study of the Buddhist Contribution to the Rise of Vernacular Fiction and Drama in China*, by Victor H. Mair

29. *Mongolian Rule in China: Local Administration in the Yuan Dynasty*, by Elizabeth Endicott-West

30. *Readings in Chinese Literary Thought*, by Stephen Owen

31. *Remembering Paradise: Nativism and Nostalgia in Eighteenth-Century Japan*, by Peter Nosco

32. *Taxing Heaven's Storehouse: Horses, Bureaucrats, and the Destruction of the Sichuan Tea Industry, 1074–1224*, by Paul J. Smith

33. *Escape from the Wasteland: Romanticism and Realism in the Fiction of Mishima Yukio and Oe Kenzaburo*, by Susan Jolliffe Napier

34. *Inside a Service Trade: Studies in Contemporary Chinese Prose*, by Rudolf G. Wagner

35. *The Willow in Autumn: Ryutei Tanehiko, 1783–1842*, by Andrew Lawrence Markus

36. *The Confucian Transformation of Korea: A Study of Society and Ideology*, by Martina Deuchler

37. *The Korean Singer of Tales*, by Marshall R. Pihl

38. *Praying for Power: Buddhism and the Formation of Gentry Society in Late-Ming China*, by Timothy Brook